UNDERSTANDING CIVIL PROCEDURE

THIRD EDITION

By

Gene R. Shreve
Richard S. Melvin Professor of Law
Indiana University School of Law, Bloomington

Peter Raven-Hansen
Glen Earl Weston Research Professor of Law
George Washington University Law School

LexisNexis™

Library of Congress Cataloging-in-Publication Data

Shreve, Gene R.
    Understanding civil procedure / Gene R. Shreve
    Peter Raven–Hansen.–[3rd ed]
        p. cm. – (Understanding series)
    Includes Bibliographical references and index.
    ISBN 0–8205–5368–9
        1. Civil Procedure–United States. I.Raven–Hansen,
    Peter, 1946– II Title
    KF8840 .S484 2002
    347.73'5–dc21   2001050731

LexisNexis, the knowledge burst logo, and Michie are trademarks of Reed Elsevier Properties Inc, used under license. Matthew Bender is a registered trademark of Matthew Bender Properties Inc.

Editorial Offices
744 Broad Street, Newark, NJ 07102 (973) 820-2000
201 Mission St., San Francisco, CA 94105-1831 (415) 908-3200
701 East Water Street, Charlottesville, VA 22902-7587 (804) 972-7600
www.lexis.com

PREFACE TO THIRD EDITION

When we wrote the last edition, the verdict was still out on supplemental jurisdiction, required disclosures, related discovery reforms, and changes to Rule 11. In this edition, we provide progress reports on these reforms and offer some less preliminary assessments of their effectiveness. We also address the December 1, 2000, tinkering with the discovery rules. In the meantime, the Internet revolution has not passed Civil Procedure by. We have therefore included a new discussion of personal jurisdiction in cyberspace, raising the question whether this is just old wine in a new bottle or new and evolving law, and a brief discussion of cyber-discovery problems. And, of course, we have updated all sections of the book to reflect significant new developments and re-organized several to make them more comprehensible and useful to the reader.

We continue to be grateful for comments and corrections from our adopters and readers. Gene Shreve also thanks Indiana University law students Sara Eastman and Philip Davis, and Peter Raven-Hansen thanks George Washington University law students Kristine Kassekert, Jennifer Riddle, Kevin Stack, and Richard Sugarman, for their assistance in preparing this third edition.

Bloomington, Indiana
Washington, D.C.
January, 2002

PREFACE TO SECOND EDITION

We wrote the first edition in the same way that we and most of our colleagues teach civil procedure: around a uniform set of federal rules of civil procedure. Since then, experimentation under the Civil Justice Reform Act of 1990 and local op-out options in the controversial December 1993 rule changes have partly destroyed that uniformity. It is even possible now to speak of "balkanized" civil procedure in federal courts.

We have treated this phenomenon in the second edition by noting it for our readers and re-emphasizing the multiple sources of civil procedure rules. But we have also explained and analyzed as fully as we could the "default" rules that went into effect December 1, 1993, unless district courts opted out. Because it is likely that most district courts (and, in time, many state courts) will adopt variants on these rules — including at least watered-down versions of the controversial provisions for required disclosure — after a period of experimentation, we felt that a full treatment of these rules was warranted. By surveying the critical literature, we also tried to identify the issues raised by the rules and, therefore, the points at which modification of the rules was most likely.

We extend our thanks to those of our readers who have brought errors and omissions in the first edition to our attention. We have tried to correct them. Thanks, too, to our colleagues in civil procedure for comments on the book and on the subject, many of which bore fruit in our revisions. We would also like to thank Joe Cecil and Thomas E. Willging of the Federal Judicial Center for their assistance with some of the data.

Gene Shreve thanks Indiana University law student Peter Song for his assistance and thanks Indiana University and the School of Law for research and faculty development grants supporting in part work on the second edition. Peter Raven-Hansen thanks George Washington University law students Todd Sinkins and Walt Williams for their assistance in preparing the second edition.

Bloomington, Indiana
Washington, D.C.
March, 1994

PREFACE TO FIRST EDITION

This text treats the entire subject of civil procedure. It is primarily intended as a reference for law school civil procedure students. However, its treatment of recent developments in areas like Federal Rules of Civil Procedure 11,16 and 26, personal jurisdiction and res judicata may make it useful to some practitioners as well.

If the law of contracts, torts or property reflects the substantive values of our society, civil procedure is the process for making those values real. The law of civil procedure governs the manner in which cases enter, transit and leave the judicial process. It establishes the authority of courts to hear cases, opportunities for litigants to create and use a record of decision, and the force and effect of judgments.

We believe that the key to understanding the principles of civil procedure is knowing why: why they were created and why they are invoked. To these ends we have used a variety of means. History is the key to personal jurisdiction and the Erie doctrine, and we have explained them accordingly by tracing their historical evolution. Pragmatic concerns chiefly shape the civil procedure of pretrial discovery and motion practice, as well as trial practice, and we start discussion of these subjects by assessing why a lawyer is interested in them. Federal Rule 11, discovery controls under Federal Rules 26(b)(1), 26(f), and 26(g), and expanded pretrial management under Federal Rule 16, are subjects so new that neither history nor pragmatic considerations are sufficient to anticipate their development. Using theory as well as both reported and unreported opinions available through early 1988, we have compensated by giving more prominence to these subjects than they presently enjoy in the typical civil procedure curriculum. This reflects our conviction that the subjects will grow in importance over the next few years. Finally, throughout the book we identify the latest sources which will enable readers with specialized needs to supplement the information we provide.

We have followed the practice of almost all civil procedure courses in using the Federal Rules of Civil Procedure as our model. However, we have also referred to different state rules and doctrines where appropriate, striving to use a representative cross-section of state models. We have also referred frequently to major civil procedure treatises, using a short form for citations explained in § 5.

We wish to thank professors Robert Casad and Daniel Conkle and Dean Bryant Garth for their helpful comments on parts of the manuscript.

From our experiences in practice and later as civil procedure teachers, we have found the subject rich and fascinating. Writing this book has given us the opportunity to share our fascination with a wider audience. It has also given us the opportunity to work with some fine law students. We gratefully acknowledge the invaluable assistance of George Washington University law students Tara L. Vautin, Anne Margaret Connolly and last in time, Andrew G. Mergen, who suffered the brunt of the production work, New York Law School students John Howley and Randolph Innacone and Indiana University Law School students William O'Connor, Jeff Pankranz and Brian Williams. Peter Raven-Hansen also thanks Winnie for her patience and support. Gene Shreve acknowledges with thanks a reseach grant from New York Law School which supported some of the preliminary work on this book.

Bloomington, Indiana
Washington, D.C.
May, 1988

SUMMARY TABLE OF CONTENTS

TABLE OF CONTENTS

Page

PART A

Received Traditions

PART B

Personal Jurisdiction Over Nonresident Defendants — *Pennoyer* and the Liberating Effects of *International Shoe*

Page

Page

CHAPTER 4

NOTICE AND OPPORTUNITY TO BE HEARD

CHAPTER 6

A CONVENIENT COURT

CHAPTER 7

ASCERTAINING THE APPLICABLE LAW

CHAPTER 8

SIMPLE PLEADING AND PRACTICE

Page

CHAPTER 9

COMPLEX PLEADING AND PRACTICE

CHAPTER 10

DISCOVERY

PART A

Scope of Discovery

Page

PART C

Control of Discovery

CHAPTER 11

DISPOSITION WITHOUT TRIAL

CHAPTER 12
TRIAL AND POST-TRIAL MOTIONS

PART A
Narrowing Issues and Allocating Burdens

CHAPTER 13

APPEAL

PART C

PART A

When? Appealability

PART D

Beyond Preclusion: Additional Doctrines of Repose

Chapter 1

INTRODUCTION

§ 1.01 What is Civil Procedure?

[1] Approaching the Subject

Like all law, the law of civil procedure can be seen as a series of expedients to influence, punish, reward and authoritatively explain human behavior. Perhaps the reason that beginning students sometimes find civil procedure especially difficult is that it is preoccupied with *litigation* behavior, and students come to the course with little sense of what litigation is.

Litigation is often described as a game. Litigants are like players and judges like umpires. The litigation game is remorselessly competitive and is often thought to have winners and losers. Its rules, like those of many other games, are difficult to understand in the abstract. They are given life and meaning by the experience of the game itself. Thus, the more we understand the phenomenon of civil litigation, the easier it will be to understand civil procedure.

Litigation differs from most games, however, in at least two important respects.

First, most games exist for the pleasure they give to participants or spectators. So long as they are relatively harmless, they are not difficult to justify. In contrast, the litigation game carries a heavy burden of justification. The game may impose onerous costs upon the parties, the court and the public, and frequently has only one enthusiastic player — the plaintiff.

Civil procedure cases and problems can therefore appropriately be considered from the perspective of cost control or resource allocation. Could the factual dispute between the parties have been resolved by any means that would have eliminated the need for litigation? Should particular tactics employed by litigants be viewed as legitimate procedural means to substantive ends, or unreasonably burdensome means that are disproportionate to the ends? What should the balance be between litigant autonomy and judicial control?

Inquiry about the most appropriate use of judicial resources also requires a developing appreciation of the different roles trial and appellate courts play. The law of civil procedure recognizes that some issues resolved by trial judges should rarely, if ever, be reviewed,[1] because appellate courts have an inferior vantage point or because redecision does not seem to justify expenditure of scarce appellate resources. Where and how the line should be drawn between matters freely reviewable and matters committed to the trial court's discretion (hence, largely unreviewable) is a recurring question in the civil procedure course.

A second difference between litigation and most games is that games are usually not of central importance to (at least amateur) participants or to society. In contrast, the plaintiff may be forced to play the litigation game in order to avert or recover from a crushing setback in life. To deny claimants opportunities to become effective players in the litigation game might make meaningless the rights secured by substantive law (*e.g.*, torts, contracts, civil rights).

Readers of Dickens' *Bleak House* will recall how the redundant and prolonged Chancery procedure consumed the merits of the case. And, as Kafka's *The Trial* suggests, too little procedure can be just as bad. At its worst, procedure displaces or blocks substance. This can happen either when the expense and delay of too much procedure makes it impossible for a player to stay in the game long enough to reach the merits, or when potential players are shut out of the game because there is too little procedure. We must also be sensitive to possible differences between rules in theory and in application. As Anatole France observed, "the law in its majestic equality forbids the rich as well as the poor to sleep under bridges, to beg in the streets and to steal bread."

Ultimately, then, the game analogy must be used cautiously because it risks trivializing both the costs and stakes of litigation. Unlike a game, civil litigation does not exist for its own sake. Civil Procedure works best when it validates substantive law (the merits) in the most expeditious, accessible and unobtrusive way possible.[2]

[2] Substance and Procedure

The study of the formation and content of substantive rules of decision — the standards by which society controls and affects "primary decisions respecting human conduct"[3] — is the subject of the traditional first year law courses of contracts, torts, property, and substantive criminal law. Civil procedure concerns itself with enforcing substantive rules by civil lawsuits.

---

[1] When the losing party can appeal a trial judge's procedural order and does so, the appellate court must decide whether the order under review should be upheld. Whatever it decides, the appellate court acts by issuing an order of its own, *e.g.*, to affirm, to reverse, to vacate and remand for further proceedings. It often explains its order in an accompanying opinion. Most of the edited opinions civil procedure students read are appellate rather than trial court opinions.

[2] *See, e.g.*, Fed. R. Civ. P. 1, which provides that the federal rules of civil procedure "shall be construed and administered to secure the just, speedy, and inexpensive determination of every action." Hereinafter we will cite to a Federal Rule of Civil Procedure as "Rule—."

[3] *Hanna v. Plumer*, 380 U.S. 460, 475 (1965) (Harlan, J., concurring).

Roughly speaking, substantive rules of decision control conduct outside the courtroom, and procedural rules control conduct within.[4]

The latter determine in what courts lawyers file lawsuits, how they frame claims, denials and defenses, how the lawsuits progress from commencement to judgment, and the effect judgments have on subsequent lawsuits.

[3] Civil Procedure in the United States

Civil procedure in the United States has three distinctive features. First, it follows an adversarial model of dispute resolution. Parties initiate and propel litigation in this model, and the judge, historically and at least in theory, plays the relatively passive role of umpire. The burden is on the parties to present their grievances and defenses. Unlike in so-called *inquisitorial* models of dispute resolution,[5] the judge rarely makes independent inquiries. The burden is also on the parties to prosecute their grievances and defenses; litigation stops unless the parties pursue it. Indeed, some scholars have argued that recent procedural rule changes have "undermined judicial evaluation of the merits of lawsuits and thereby vastly expanded attorneys' opportunities to twist procedure and substance on behalf of their clients."[6] These characteristics of our system of dispute resolution place on lawyers a heavy responsibility for assuring justice and mastering civil procedure.

Second, civil procedure in the United States is dominated by *positive law:* codified rules enacted by legislatures or their delegates. In contrast, the substantive rules of decision taught in the other traditional first year courses are more often doctrinal: declared by courts as part of the *common law.*

One difference between positive and common law lies in the materials containing the legal rules. The common-law materials are almost entirely judicial opinions, and the appropriate inquiry is: what rule best fits the case? In contrast, positive law materials are enacted laws or procedural rules and their legislative history. Emphasis in administering the latter is on legislative intent, in recognition of the superior lawmaking authority of legislatures and their delegates.

It is not always easy for the first year student to subordinate the comparatively freewheeling policy-oriented analysis of common law taught in many substantive courses to the plain language of positive law, principles of statutory construction and reading of legislative history. But mastery of the latter lays the groundwork not just for understanding much of civil procedure, but also for understanding upper level law courses. Significantly,

---

[4] For a detailed and illuminating discussion of distinctions between the two, *see* Cook, *"Substance" and "Procedure" in the Conflict of Laws,* 42 Yale L.J. 333 (1933).

[5] *See, e.g.,* Langbein, *The German Advantage in Civil Procedure,* 52 U. Chi. L. Rev. 823 (1985).

[6] Molot, *How Changes in the Legal Profession Reflect Changes in Civil Procedure,* 84 Va. L. Rev. 955, 958 (1998).

practicing lawyers rank "knowledge of statutory law" as the most important knowledge for practice, just ahead of "knowledge of procedural rules."[7]

Finally, the purpose of civil procedure is, as the Federal Rules of Civil Procedure state, "to secure the just, speedy, and inexpensive determination of every action."[8] Presumably, decisions are more likely to be just when they reach the merits. But the adversarial character of civil dispute resolution in the United States, the number of lawyers, and perhaps a national tendency to look too readily for judicial resolution of matters that other societies settle politically, administratively or privately,[9] have made the goals of "speedy and inexpensive" determinations increasingly difficult to attain.[10] As a result, there is constant pressure for more active judicial management of litigation and for judicial intervention to dispose of the litigation without trial, if possible. Thus, the 1993 amendment to Rule 1 requires the rules to be "administered" — as well as "construed" (the original term) — "to secure just, speedy, and inexpensive determination of every action." No one foresees the replacement of our adversarial model by the inquisitorial model of dispute resolution, yet the former is undergoing significant change in response to widespread criticisms of the cost and efficiency of civil litigation.

[4] Some Common Misperceptions of Civil Procedure

The study of civil procedure is often impeded by misperceptions formed before law school or by comparison of civil procedure with the substantive first year courses.

One is that civil procedure is, as scholars once labeled it, strictly *adjective* law that "exists for the sake of something else."[11] However, while it is true that civil procedure is not an end in itself,[12] it does not follow that

---

[7] Baird, *A Survey of the Relevance of Legal Training to Law School Graduates,* 29 J. Legal Educ. 264, 273 (1978) (explaining that knowledge of common law, constitutional law, ethics, and regulations were all ranked lower by practitioners).

[8] Rule 1.

[9] *See* W. Olson, *The Litigation Explosion: What Happened When America Unleashed the Lawsuit* (1991); M. Marks, *The Suing of America: Why and How We Take Each Other to Court* (1981); J. Lieberman, *The Litigious Society* (1983).

[10] *See, e.g.,* Trubek, *et al., The Costs of Ordinary Litigation,* 31 U.C.L.A. 72 (1983); Miller, *The Adversary System: Dinosaur or Phoenix,* 69 Minn. L. Rev. 1 (1984); Rand Inst., *The Costs of Asbestos Litigation* (1983), excerpted in *Legal Times of Washington,* Aug. 8, 1983, at 26, Table 6.2 (reporting that of every dollar expended per claim, 37 cents were attributable to defendant's litigation expenses, 26 cents attributable to plaintiff's litigation expenses, and 37 cents attributable to net compensation to plaintiffs). Litigation delays vary tremendously between courts. In federal trial courts, the median time between commencement of civil litigation and disposition at trial was 8.2 months, with 2% of the dispositions at trial taking more than 20 months. 2000 Admin. Office U.S. Courts Annual Report of the Dir., Table C-5, at 208.

[11] C. Hepburn, *The Historical Development of Code Pleading in America and England with Special Reference to the Codes of New York, Missouri, California, Kentucky, Iowa, Minnesota, Indiana, Ohio, Oregon, Washington, Nebraska, Wisconsin, Kansas, Nevada, North Dakota, South Dakota, Idaho, Montana, Arizona, North Carolina, South Carolina, Arkansas, Wyoming, Utah, Colorado, Connecticut, and Oklahoma* (1897).

[12] *See* § 1.01[1], *supra.*

procedural law is less significant than substantive law. At least one federal appellate court has suggested that procedures can have value independent of the merits, such that a lawyer's negligent waiver of the procedure may give rise to malpractice liability even when the procedure would not necessarily have improved the outcome.[13] The appellate cases (the chief vehicle by which substantive law is taught in law school) all reach courts by procedural initiatives, and the procedural posture in which the issues were presented to the appellate court often determines how much attention they will receive.[14] Moreover, courts sometimes rely on procedure to reach "just" results without changing inhospitable substantive law.[15] Procedure also interacts with substantive law outside the courtroom, as illustrated by the effect of the procedural device of class actions[16] on the substantive elements of securities fraud claims,[17] and the effect of the procedural requirement that plaintiffs pay for notice to class members on the effective enforcement of consumer laws.[18] Law has not escaped "the tendency of all modern scientific and philosophic thought . . . to emphasize the importance of method, process, or procedure."[19]

Another common misperception is that civil procedure is nothing more than the unimaginative and routine application of black-letter law to dry procedural issues. This may be a law student's initial reaction to the positive law materials from which civil procedure is primarily taught.[20] Yet positive law is more dynamic than the black letter of a rule or statute might indicate. Moreover, important parts of civil procedure, including personal jurisdiction (court's power to bind particular defendants) and *res judicata* (the effect of prior judgments on subsequent litigation), are based primarily on judicial doctrine.

It is important to understand that statutes or codified rules governing most procedural questions are not self-applying. Problems often elude solution by plain-language tests or application of simple canons of statutory

---

[13] *Jones Motor Co. v. Holtkamp, Liese, Beckmeier & Childress P.C.*, 197 F.3d 1190 (7th Cir. 1999) (asserting that failure to perfect jury demand may be such a procedure, but affirming judgement for malpractice defendant because plaintiffs had not proven resulting damages to a reasonable certainty).

[14] *See* §§ 13.08 & 13.09 (scope and intensity of review), *infra*.

[15] F. James *et al.*, *Civil Procedure* § 1.1 (4th ed. 1992) (quotation marks supplied). *See* Cover, *For James Wm. Moore: Some Reflections on a Reading of the Rules*, 84 Yale L.J. 718 (1975).

[16] Suits which may be brought by representative parties on behalf of a defined class of members who are not themselves participants in the litigation but may be bound by its outcome. *See* § 9.09 (class actions), *infra*.

[17] *See* Scott, *The Impact of Class Actions on Rule 10b-5*, 38 U. Chi. L. Rev. 337, 338 (1971) (arguing that class actions permit some class members to recover who would fail to satisfy reliance and materiality requirements in individual actions for securities fraud).

[18] *See* Scott, *Two Models of the Civil Process,* 27 Stan. L. Rev. 937, 944 (1975) (noting that the expense of such notice dooms most consumer actions because the expense of individual lawsuits exceeds the benefits that they could confer on individual plaintiffs).

[19] M. Cohen, "The Process of Judicial Legislation" in *Law and the Social Order: Essays in Legal Philosophy* (1994).

[20] *See* § 1.01[2], *supra*.

construction. Statutes over time acquire their own judicial gloss. The legislative product may be inarticulate, forcing courts to finish the lawmaking process. Or the legislature may deliberately create a rule that can never be completed in the abstract. Rules of the latter kind place courts at procedural crossroads, supplying general criteria for decision and leaving the result to courts' appreciation of the facts in particular cases.[21]

Furthermore, many, if not most, procedural questions are susceptible to more than one answer. Civil procedure, hence effective litigation, consists less of finding black-letter answers than of choices among tactical options. These choices turn not just on the rules and procedural posture of litigation, but also on the relative strengths and attitudes of the parties, the relationships between lawyers and judge, and all the other subtle factors that make lawyering an art as well as a profession.

A third misperception is that civil procedure is trial practice.[22] This may cause some law students who cannot picture themselves as trial lawyers to approach their civil procedure course with less enthusiasm. But even a brief glance at litigation statistics refutes this perception. For example, of all the federal civil actions terminated in the year ending Sept. 30, 2000, 72% ended before the pretrial conference that often precedes trial in federal court[23] (one in four of these ended without court action of any kind), 8% ended during or after pretrial, and only 2% lasted through trial.[24] More than half of those were tried to a judge rather than a jury,[25] calling upon far different lawyering skills than jury trial practice. State civil disposition statistics[26] send the same message: civil procedure is not about trial. Litigation in the United States is predominantly *pretrial* practice. In this phase of litigation, it is not theatrics, charisma or trial tactics that carry the day, but mastery of pretrial procedure, the ability to communicate effectively to the court, and a command of the details of the lawsuit.

§ 1.02 Sources of Civil Procedure

Constitutional law sets the outer limits of civil procedure. The United States Constitution limits the subject matter of the cases that federal courts may hear,[27] determines the effect courts of one state must give to the

---

[21] *See e.g.* § 9.05 (discussing Federal Rules 19 and 20 dealing with compulsory and permissive joinder) *infra.*

[22] For treatment of trial practice (jury selection, opening statements, presentation of evidence, closing argument, jury deliberation, and preservation of points for appeal), see Thomas A. Mauet, *Fundamentals of Trial Techniques* (3d ed. 1992); J. Jeans, *Trial Advocacy* (1975).

[23] *See* § 12.03 (pretrial conference), *infra.*

[24] 2000 *Admin. Office U.S. Courts Annual report of the Dir.*, note 9, *supra*, Table C-4A, at 205.

[25] *Id.*

[26] Only 2% of tort, contract, and real property cases in the nation's 75 largest counties were tried to a jury in 1992. Bureau of Justice statistics, U.S. Dept. of Justice (last modified Mar. 4, 1999) type = "http"address = "www.ojp.usdoj.gov/bjs/civil.htm">http://www.ojp.usdo j.gov/bjs/civil.htm

[27] U.S. Const. art. III. *See* Ch. 5 (subject matter jurisdiction), *infra.*

judgments of another,[28] and preserves the right to jury trial in certain categories of cases in federal court.[29] In addition, the Due Process Clause of the Fifth Amendment to the United States Constitution guarantees minimal due process to litigants in federal courts, and the Due Process Clause of the Fourteenth Amendment gives a comparable guarantee to litigants in state courts. Due process has helped shape procedural requirements for personal jurisdiction (judicial power to enter binding judgments with respect to particular defendants or property),[30] notice, and the opportunity to be heard in litigation.[31] Given their potential procedural reach, in fact, it is curious perhaps that the due process clauses have not been invoked more frequently as sources of procedure.[32]

Statutes are a second source of positive procedural law. In both the federal and state systems, they define the power of various courts to hear particular cases[33] and the convenient forums for litigation.[34] In all states, statutes also help define the personal jurisdiction of state courts.[35] In addition, a declining minority of states[36] have enacted statutory procedural codes.[37]

The most important sources of positive procedural law, however, are formally adopted rules of civil procedure. The federal courts and forty states have adopted them, usually by a judicial rulemaking process authorized by a statute.[38] Although these rules systems differ from state to state, as of 1986 twenty-three states had copied, with minor modifications, the Federal Rules of Civil Procedure.[39] As a result, almost all first year civil

---

[28] U.S. Const. art. IV. *See* §§ 15.10-15.11 (inter-system preclusion and full faith and credit), *infra.*

[29] U.S. Const. amend. VII. *See* § 12.07[1] (right to a jury), *infra.* Most state constitutions have analogous procedural provisions governing state courts.

[30] *See* Ch. 3 (personal jurisdiction), *infra.*

[31] *See* Ch. 4 (notice and opportunity to be heard) & § 9.09[2][b] (due process requirements in class actions), *infra.*

[32] *See* Leubsdorf, *Constitutional Civil Procedure,* 63 Tex. L. Rev. 579 (1984).

[33] *See* §§ 5.10[2] (citing federal statutes illustratively), 13.02-13.04 (federal appeals), *infra.*

[34] *See* Ch. 5 (venue), *infra.*

[35] *See* § 3.07[1] (long-arm statutes), *infra.*

[36] *See* Oakley & Coon, *The Federal Rules in State Courts: A Survey of State Court Systems of Civil Procedure,* 61 Wash. L. Rev. 1367, 1378 (1986) (listing California, Connecticut, Georgia, Illinois, Kansas, Louisiana, Nebraska, New York, North Carolina, and Oklahoma as the then remaining states with procedural codes).

[37] *See* § 8.03 (history and problems of code pleading), *infra.*

[38] *Oakley & Coon,* note 10, *supra,* at 1378.

[39] *Id.* at 1377 (listing Alabama, Alaska, Arizona, Colorado, District of Columbia, Hawaii, Indiana, Kentucky, Maine, Massachusetts, Minnesota, Montana, New Mexico, North Dakota, Ohio, Rhode Island, South Dakota, Tennessee, Utah, Vermont, Washington, West Virginia, and Wyoming). This statement tends to understate the influence of the federal rules, because four of the states with statutory procedural codes have codified versions of the federal rules (Georgia, Kansas, North Carolina, and Oklahoma), and three other states have rules that "show strong affinity to the content and organization of the Federal Rules. . . ." (Idaho, Michigan, and Nevada). *Id.* at 1377-1378. *See* Graham, *State Adaptation of the Federal Rules: The Pros and Cons,* 43 Okla. L. Rev. 293 (1990).

procedure courses and casebooks focus primarily on the federal rules, as we will here.

Some understanding of the federal rulemaking process[40] is essential to understanding the effect of the Federal Rules of Civil Procedure in federal courts. The Rules Enabling Act delegates lawmaking authority to the Supreme Court to make rules governing "general rules of practice and procedure" for cases in the federal courts.[41] The Judicial Conference of the United States, comprised of the Chief Justice of the Supreme Court and designated judges from other federal courts, oversees the rulemaking process. The Advisory Committee on Civil Rules to the Judicial Conference's Standing Committee on Rules of Practice and Procedure is charged with the actual work of drafting and recommending rules of civil procedure. The Advisory Committee is comprised of judges, practitioners and law professors. The Chief Justice appoints a Reporter who monitors developments in the field and aids the Advisory Committee.

Federal procedural rulemaking typically begins when the Advisory Committee notes a procedural need or problem. If the Committee so directs, the Reporter prepares a preliminary draft of responsive rule changes with "committee notes" explaining their purpose. The Committee meets and revises these materials and then reports them to the Standing Committee. If the Standing Committee approves the draft for publication, it is published in the *Federal Register* and the federal reporters for public comment. In addition, the Advisory Committee usually holds public hearings on the draft in diverse locations. After reviewing public comments, the Committee may make revisions and then submit the proposed rule changes and final comments[42] to the Standing Committee of the Judicial Conference. The latter reviews and ultimately forwards the proposal, revised if necessary, to the members of the Judicial Conference.

If the Conference approves the proposal, it sends the rule changes to the Supreme Court. In theory, the Supreme Court conducts a substantive review of the change. In fact, the Justices have differed about their true role. Justice Douglas, for example, described it as "merely perfunctory" and the Court as "a mere conduit" for transmittal of the rules to Congress.[43]

---

[40] *See generally* Walker, *A Comprehensive Reform for Federal Civil Rulemaking*, 61 Geo. Wash. L. Rev. 455 (1993); Baker, *An Introduction to Federal Court Rulemaking Procedure*, 22 Tex. Tech. L. Rev. 323 (1991); Brown, *Federal Rulemaking: Problems and Possibilities* (Federal Judicial Center 1981); Kaplan, *Amendments of the Federal Rules of Civil Procedure 1961-1963 (1),* 77 Harv. L. Rev. 601, 601–602 (1964).

[41] 28 U.S.C. §§ 2071-2074. *See generally* Burbank, *The Rules Enabling Act of 1934,* 130 U. Pa. L. Rev. 1015 (1982). The Act expressly mandates that such rules "shall not abridge, enlarge or modify any substantive right," thus reserving substantive lawmaking to the Congress and to the state legislatures within their proper spheres. *See generally* §§ 7.01-7.04 (the laws applied in federal courts and the applicability of federal procedural rules), *infra. See also* Carrington, *"Substance" and "Procedure" in the Rules Enabling Act,* 1989 Duke L.J. 281 (1989).

[42] When rule changes are adopted, the advisory committee's notes become an important source of legislative history for construing the changes. They are published in the Federal Rules Decisions, the principal civil procedure treatises, and in many rulebooks.

[43] See Statement of Douglas, 409 U.S. 1132 (1972) (Douglas, J., dissenting). More recently,

Individual justices may make statements concerning the rule changes. The Court then transmits the changes to Congress no later than May 1 of the year in which they are to become effective. The change becomes effective no earlier than December 1 of that year, unless Congress by statute modifies or rejects the rule.[44]

However, not all written rules governing federal practice are promulgated in this fashion. Rule 83 authorizes a majority of the judges of each district court to promulgate local rules "not inconsistent" with the formal federal rules of civil procedure. Many district courts have exercised this authority to issue housekeeping rules governing the length of briefs and the availability of oral hearings, attorney admissions, procedures for submitting requests for attorneys fees and other matters.[45]

The Civil Justice Reform Act of 1990 (CJRA) complicates matters further. There Congress authorized a nationwide rulemaking experiment to reduce expense and delay in the district courts.[46] The CJRA directed all district courts to appoint advisory groups to analyze their dockets and make cost- and delay-reducing recommendations. Selected courts put some of these recommendations into effect provisionally. Experimental recommendations under the CJRA need not be consistent with the Federal Rules of Civil Procedure.[47]

Individual judges may also establish rules governing procedures for scheduling and argument in their courtrooms. Rule 83 expressly provides that "[i]n all cases not provided for by rule, the district judges and magistrates may regulate their practice in any manner not inconsistent with these rules or those of the district in which they act."[48] Furthermore,

---

Justice White has said that the Court's role "is to transmit the Judicial Conference's recommendations without change and without careful study, as long as there is no suggestion that the committee system has not operated with integrity." Statement of J. White, 113 S. Ct. CCC, CCCIV (1993).

[44] Except for rules affecting an evidentiary privilege, Section 2074 contemplates (but does not require) a passive role for Congress; "[i]nertia means approval." Siegel, 28 U.S.C.A. § 2074 commentary (1988). Congress usually remains silent, but has shown a greater tendency to become active in recent years. *Cf.* Ely, *The Irrepressible Myth of Erie,* 87 Harv. L. Rev. 693, 693-694 (1974) (describing congressional resistance to the Court's proposed federal rules of evidence), and § 4.03[1] (describing congressional substitution of its own enactment for the Court's proposed amendment to Rule 4), *infra.* Congress's constitutional authority to change the rules is not undisputed. *Compare* Mullinex, *Judicial Power and the Rules Enabling Act,* 46 Mercer L. Rev. 733 (1995) (questioning such authority to supercede procedural rulemaking by the judiciary) *with* Redish, *Federal Judicial Independence: Constitutional and Political Perspectives,* 46 Mercer L. Rev. 697 (1995) (supporting such authority on majoritarian principles).

[45] *See* Wright & Miller, *Federal Practice and Procedure* § 3154 (giving examples). The scope of local rulemaking authority is a matter of continuing debate. *See, e.g.,* Levin, *Local Rules as Experiments: A Study in the Division of Power,* 139 U. Pa. L. Rev. 1567 (1991); Flanders, *Local Rules in Federal District Courts: Usurpation, Legislation, or Information?,* 14 Loy. L.A.L. Rev. 213 (1981). In 1988, Congress acted to subject such rulemaking to closer scrutiny. *See* 28 U.S.C. § 2071 and Siegel, 28 U.S.C.A. § 2071 commentary (1988).

[46] Codified at 28 U.S.C. §§ 471-482. *See generally* Tobias, *Judicial Oversight of Civil Justice Reform,* 140 F.R.D. 49 (1992).

[47] Some may not be. *See* Tobias, note 46, *supra,* at 51-52.

[48] *See, e.g.,* Schwarzer (J., N.D. Cal.), *Guidelines for Discovery, Motion Practice and Trial,*

judges always have what has been called "individual calendar" discretion over scheduling and hearing practice in a particular case.[49]

The parties themselves can also be an important source of procedural rules often overlooked by law students. A few federal rules expressly authorize parties themselves to stipulate to departures from the rules,[50] and parties can make other agreements that supplement and sometimes modify positive procedural law. They often agree by contract, for example, to the appropriate forum for litigation under the contract, the mode of service of the complaint and summons, or the applicable substantive law for such litigation, superseding the otherwise applicable law.[51] At a more mundane level, litigation counsel schedule many pretrial activities among themselves.

Finally, ethical rules bearing on civil litigation are promulgated as codes of professional responsibility or rules of the bar by courts acting in conjunction with bar associations. The American Bar Association's *Model Rules of Professional Conduct*,[52] substantially adopted by the majority of the states,[53] contain several rules concerning the zeal with which a lawyer may represent a client in litigation.[54] Although historically there have been serious doubts concerning the organized bar's capacity for self-enforcement of such rules,[55] it is probable that the majority of lawyers abide them. Moreover, several Federal Rules of Civil Procedure underscore professional responsibilities in federal courts and may become a vehicle for enforcement of some of the ethical rules adopted by the bar.[56]

§ 1.03 Briefing a Civil Procedure Case

The primary vehicles for class discussion in most civil procedure courses are assigned cases. These are judicial opinions, usually written by judges to accompany their orders (rulings) on civil procedure motions. An *order* may dispose of the lawsuit or simply resolve a skirmish between the litigants and leave the lawsuit to continue. Typically, the order simply says

---

117 F.R.D. 273 (1987). Judge Schwarzer's *Guidelines* admonish counsel to observe not only the Federal Rules of Civil Procedure and the District Court's Local Rules, but also "the rules and practices of the particular judge to whom the case is assigned." The latter are available "[b]y obtaining from the judge's courtroom deputy copies of the standing orders used by that judge; and [b]y inquiring of the deputy (not the law clerks) how the judge wants things done." *Id.* at 273.

[49] Siegel, 28 U.S.C.A. § 2077 commentary (1988).

[50] *See* Rules 15(a) (stipulation in lieu of court permission to amend pleadings), 26(f) (changes in discovery limitations), and Rule 29 (stipulation of discovery procedure).

[51] *See, e.g., National Equip. Rental v. Szukhent,* 375 U.S. 311 (1964) (enforcing contract that designated agent to receive service).

[52] American Bar Ass'n, *Model Rules of Professional Conduct and Code of Judicial Conduct* (1992).

[53] 56 U.S.L.W. 2466 (Feb. 23, 1988).

[54] *See, e.g.,* Model Rules 3.1-3.4, note 26, *supra.*

[55] American Bar Ass'n, Special Committee on Evaluation and Disciplinary Enforcement, *Problems and Recommendations on Disciplinary Enforcement* 1 (final draft, 1970).

[56] *See* Rule 11, *discussed in* § 8.05[2] *infra,* and Rule 26(g), *discussed in* § 10.13[1] *infra.*

who won — for example: "Plaintiff's motion for summary judgment is granted [denied]." The *opinion* is written by the judge to accompany the order and to explain why the judge decided to rule in favor of the prevailing party (or, in appellate opinions, why the ruling below was reversed or affirmed).

Virtually all the orders in cases we consider were on contested matters. That is to say, the parties urged upon the court opposing choices of judicial conduct before the court decided how to rule in the order. Not all orders are accompanied by opinions, and not all opinions are designated by the court for publication. Opinions are most likely to accompany orders which settle contested matters, because judges feel greater pressure to justify what they have done under such circumstances. In this sense, judges are advocates, too. The judicial opinions we will read are the judges' means of arguing that their orders reflect decisions most likely to advance the rule and logic of civil procedure and to do justice in the individual case.

The central purpose of case briefing is to enable students to get the most out of class. Briefing helps students prepare by giving structure to their consideration of cases before class begins. It also provides a working paper during class, making it easier for students to follow developments and to advance the discussion when called upon by the professor. On the other hand, briefs may not be terribly useful tools for course review. This is because they are made before class, before thoughts about the material have matured. Comments and addenda students make on their briefs during and after classroom discussion of the case are likely to be far more useful for exam study.

Casebooks and study aids suggest how to brief a case, and many students are taught briefing in first semester orientation lectures or legal methods classes. Our concern here is to explain how the generic briefing technique should be adapted for civil procedure cases.

Most briefs and many reported judicial opinions begin with a *recitation of the pre-litigation facts* which gave rise to the claims or defenses in the litigation. These are always important, if for no other reason than to remind the reader of the real world, flesh-and-blood implications of the legal issues put by the case. But they are often of less significance in civil procedure decisions than in those focusing on points of substantive law.

Instead, the crucial facts for us are *procedural facts:* what happened to the case after it was filed. The chronology of procedural steps taken by the litigants and the court is often important. For example, the pattern might be commencement of the litigation by the filing of a complaint, defendant's filing of a motion to dismiss the complaint for some reason, argument on the motion leading to its denial, fact-finding by the parties, trial, judgment for the plaintiff, and appeal by defendant (raising, among others, the same issue presented previously by motion). Retracing procedural steps is essential to understanding who's who, what has happened in the case, and how ripe procedural rulings are for review. It is also important to an appreciation of tactical aspects of litigation.[57] It facilitates reconstruction of the alternatives available to the parties as the litigation progresses.

Thus, while an elaborate general fact description may be unnecessary in briefing most civil procedure cases, students should include a full statement of facts setting the *procedural posture* of the case. This statement should ordinarily indicate who is suing whom, facts which may be easier to diagram in the margin of the brief or the casebook itself. The student might use arrows to represent claims (and sometimes defenses) instead of describing the process narratively. Here is an illustration.

Figure 1-1

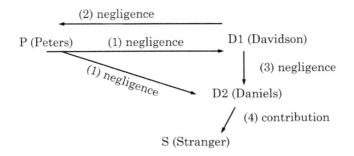

(Diagram shows that (1) Peters sued Davidson and Daniels for negligence, whereupon (2) Davidson counterclaimed against Peters and (3) cross-claimed against Daniels for negligence, and (4) Daniels impleaded Stranger on a theory of contribution.)

The chronology of procedural facts can be suggested by numbering the facts in the brief (as illustrated above) or in the case excerpt itself.

Next, it is useful to *identify the statutes or rules involved in the case.* Many study aids omit this step in briefing because they are geared primarily to briefing cases applying common law, not positive law (statutes or codified rules of procedure).[58]

For example, when you encounter positive federal law, consider the following approach. Read the cited statute or rule carefully, going to your rulebook if the text is not reproduced in the case itself. Is it clear from a reading of the provision how Congress intended to apply it to the case at hand? If so, has the court's decision given it that application? If it is not

---

[57] *See* § 1.01[3], *supra.*

[58] Since procedural decisions often turn on rules of positive law, a routine search for this material is a good briefing step. Note, on the other hand, that it is not useful and may even be harmful to attempt to paraphrase applicable positive law. Here there simply is no substitute for the actual language of the statute or rule. Nor is it enough to consider this kind of material in the abstract or in bulk at sporadic intervals during the semester. Students can best learn and understand statutes and rules of procedure in the context of particular case applications. It goes without saying that cases must be read with the rulebook close at hand.

clear from a reading of the provision how Congress intended it to apply to the case at hand, has the court resolved the provision's ambiguity in a satisfactory way?

Third, the brief should *frame the issues presented by the case*. Many opinions do this expressly, but when the opinion is unclear, framing the issue is often the crucial step towards understanding the court's decision and its reasoning.

Fourth, the brief should *describe the court's decision on the issue at two levels*. The court will both supply an *answer* to the issue put by the case and make a formal *disposition* of the case, as noted often in the final paragraph. For example, when the issue is whether the plaintiff's complaint has stated a claim upon which relief can be granted, the court may decide that it does not and then grant the motion to dismiss and enter an order of dismissal. But this latter disposition — an order of dismissal — need not go hand-in-hand with the decision of the issue. The court might instead grant the motion to dismiss with leave to plaintiff to amend his complaint.

Fifth, the brief should *describe and critique the reasoning articulated for the decision*. In describing the reasoning, the student should take full advantage of dissenting and concurring opinions, sometimes expressly written to limit the applicability of the court's reasoning. Presumptuous as it might seem at first, you must also evaluate the court's reasoning. This may take some effort, since students often arrive at law school believing that the laws they will study exist as part of a static natural order — like laws of physics. Unfortunately, this attitude permits no more than a superficial grasp of the law in civil procedure or other courses. It makes the student easy prey for the rhetoric in many judicial opinions that the result reached by the court is obvious. On the contrary, many cases — particularly those selected for casebook treatment — pose close and difficult questions. Great jurists may produce illuminating opinions, but they cannot make hard cases easy. What one often finds is "not a matter of right against wrong, but of right against right."[59]

This critical side of analysis and discussion is a good deal of what makes the course (and the professor) tick. Civil procedure professors strive to illustrate and teach the proposition that civil procedure involves hard choices. In turn, answers to examination questions must reflect judgment seasoned by an appreciation of both sides of the issue.[60] To respond, students cannot afford a passive approach to assigned materials.

The critique of the court's reasoning will be the most ambitious portion of your brief, the part most likely to require revision during and after civil

---

[59] Rosenberg, *Devising Procedures That Are Civil to Promote Justice That Is Civilized,* 69 Mich. L. Rev. 797 (1971).

[60] Contrary to what beginning students might assume, outright mistakes by students are fairly uncommon, at least in essay examinations. The difference between an "A" and a "C" examination more often lies in the imagination and agility demonstrated in applying course rules and concepts in a new setting, rather than in differences in bottom line conclusions. This demonstration is possible only with an approach to civil procedure that is both descriptive *and* critical.

procedure class. Don't worry. As noted earlier, unrevised case briefs are ultimately unreliable, anyway. The purpose of briefing is to enable you to get the most out of class and to stimulate (and ultimately reward) your critical thought. A marked up brief is evidence that the purpose was accomplished.

§ 1.04 Research and Drafting in Civil Procedure

The starting point for research on any legal problem is to frame the issue tentatively, something that students rehearse in their preparation of case briefs.[61] For law students and beginning lawyers, even this step will sometimes prove difficult. When it does, it may be helpful to consult a civil procedure treatise like this one to frame the issue correctly and to identify relevant statutes or rules.

The second step is to read carefully any statutes or rules of procedure involved in your problem, noting when necessary any time frame for acting under them. It is difficult to overstate the importance of rereading the text of a rule or statute with each succeeding problem. This is because these provisions are drafted to cover a variety of situations arising in cases. A subsequent case thus may be governed by the same rule of procedure, yet the demands of the new controversy may illuminate a different portion of the text. As a result, even experienced lawyers take the trouble to reread carefully rules and statutes.

For federal civil procedure problems, the third step is to consult the two federal practice treatises: *Moore's Federal Practice* (Matthew Bender) and C. Wright & A. Miller, *et al., Federal Practice and Procedure* (West). Both are organized primarily by federal rule number, providing easy access when the problem involves the federal rules.[62] Both also reproduce the Advisory Committee's notes that accompanied the rule and represent most of its legislative history. Federal courts often cite analyses and conclusions from these treatises, in recognition of their thoroughness and quality. Finally, both supply voluminous case citations, updated in pocket parts or inserts. Coverage overlaps considerably; yet style, analysis and case coverage in the two are sufficiently distinct to justify examination of both in researching the typical problem of federal civil procedure.

Treatises on state procedural law also exist, although they tend to be less thorough and to be updated less frequently. When state statutes bear on the issue, one can review annotations to the relevant statutory code.[63] These steps will help reframe the problem, suggest a more or less detailed analysis, and generate lists of possibly relevant cases for further research.[64]

---

[61] *See* § 1.03, *supra.*

[62] These treatises also cover some statutory issues of federal procedure, including, notably, jurisdiction.

[63] Annotations for federal rules of procedure and federal procedural statutes may also be helpful. Most can be found in Title 28 of the *United States Code Annotated.*

[64] For the typical federal procedural issue, it is rarely wise to go to the cases directly without reading the relevant sections of the treatises. Their unusual thoroughness and authority sometimes supplies an answer without need of additional case research, and they will at least focus the case search and thus ultimately save time for the issues that they address.

Another method of locating recent case authority for federal civil procedural rules is to use the *Federal Rules Service* (Callaghan), which digests cases by rule number.

With the development of computerized law research, however, the best way to generate a current case list and to review it is to use *Lexis* or *Westlaw.* Civil procedure problems that turn on statutes or rules are particularly well-suited to computer research, because it is easy to frame a search request around the statute or rule number. Students are cautioned, however, that there is no uniformity in judicial citation to such procedural law, and a complete search request must include in the alternative all of the likely variants. With regard to the Federal Rules of Civil Procedure, for example, these variants include at least "FRCP," "F. R. C. P.," "Fed. R. Civ. P.," "Rule," and "R." with the relevant number, and, ideally, some generic phrase to help exclude like-numbered federal rules of appellate or criminal procedure from the search.

For drafting problems involving the Federal Rules of Civil Procedure, students should consult the official appendix of forms immediately following the rules. These forms have been declared sufficient in federal practice by Rule 84. Students may also wish to examine unofficial forms. These may offer guidance in both state and federal practice.[65] They are collections of prior pleadings, motions or discovery requests. Most have passed muster at some time in a relevant court and may therefore serve as a form for current papers of the same kind.

For several reasons, such form books must be used with extreme caution and a heavy dose of common sense. First, unlike those in the official appendix to the federal rules, most published forms do not carry the imprimatur of any court system. All that stands behind many items memorialized as forms is that they worked once in a case. Close perusal of the fine print in the form books that give citations may reveal that the most recent approval of a particular form came in the nineteenth century. Arcane and dated wording in forms provides another danger signal. Second, because forms were originally created to meet the facts and demands of a different case, substantial adaptation is often necessary to make forms usable. Finally, a form may not have been selected for its brilliance, but for its (one-time) sufficiency. It may represent no more than the lowest common denominator. Yet form books (and, particularly in large law firms today, internally-generated forms and prior papers) are often a helpful starting point for procedural drafting.

---

[65] *See, e.g., American Jurisprudence Pleading and Practice Forms Annotated* (Lawyers Co-op.); L. Frumer & I. Hill, *et al. Bender's Federal Practice Forms* (Matthew Bender); *Bender's Forms of Discovery* (Matthew Bender); *Nichols Cyclopedia of Federal Procedure Forms* (Callaghan); *Federal Procedural Forms Lawyers Edition* (Lawyers Co-op); *West's Federal Forms* (West).

§ 1.05　Civil Procedure Bibliography and Short Form Citations

We cite in footnotes to the textbooks and articles on civil procedure that are useful sources for further reading. Several are cited often enough to warrant use of a short form citation. The following list gives the full citation for each such work, followed by the manner in which we cite it. We supply only the section numbers for these sources because the page numbers vary with succeeding editions.

I. *Hornbooks*

J. Friedenthal, M. Kane & A. Miller, *Civil Procedure* (West 3d ed. 1999) (*Friedenthal, Kane & Miller*).

F. James, J. Leubsdorf, & G. Hazard, *Civil Procedure* (Little Brown 4th ed. 1992) (*James, Hazard & Leubsdorf*).

L. Teply & R. Whitten, *Civil Procedure* (Foundation Press 2000) (*Teply & Whitten*).

C. Wright, *Hornbook on Federal Courts* (West 5th ed. 1994) (*Wright*).

II. *Treatises*

C. Wright & A. Miller, *Federal Practice and Procedure* (West) (*Wright & Miller;* volume number omitted because section numbers are unique).

J. Moore, *Moore's Federal Practice* (Matthew Bender 3d ed. 2000) (*Moore;* volume number omitted where section number is keyed to a Federal Rule of Civil Procedure). In rare cases where quoted material is taken from the second edition of *Moore*, we have left a full citation.

Chapter 2

SELECTING A COURT—IN GENERAL

§ 2.01 The Choices: State and Federal Judicial Systems

After a lawyer has agreed to represent a prospective plaintiff and tentatively determined one or more legal theories of recovery, she must select the court in which to sue. The choice of courts is enriched and complicated in the United States by the existence not only of fifty-one separate state judicial systems,[1] but also of the federal judicial system. Before we can introduce the factors that affect the choice, we need to describe these alternatives.

It is easiest to start with the federal system, because it is simplest. There are three layers of federal courts. At the bottom lie the federal district courts. These are courts of *original jurisdiction,* so called because they are where judicial cases originate — where they are filed and initially tried.[2] The district courts, like all federal courts, are also courts of *limited subject matter jurisdiction,* in that statutes authorize them to hear only certain kinds of cases.[3] The most important are those involving questions of federal law ("federal question cases") and those involving state law claims valued at more than $75,000 between citizens of different states ("diversity cases").[4] The district courts are assigned to districts whose boundaries correspond with those of the smallest states or with parts of the larger states.[5] For example, the federal trial courts for New York are the United States District Courts for the Southern, Eastern, Western and Northern Districts of New York.

United States Courts of Appeals make up the middle layer.[6] They are courts of *appellate jurisdiction,* so called because they are authorized only to review decisions which come to them on appeal from district courts,[7] certain specialized federal courts or federal administrative agencies. The country is divided into twelve geographic circuits,[8] and appeals from the

---

[1] The District of Columbia was given its own judicial system by District of Columbia Court Reform and Criminal Procedure Act of 1970, Pub. L.. 91-358, 84 Stat. 570 (codified in scattered sections of 28 U.S.C.).

[2] Cases may also originate in administrative agencies or in certain specialized courts created by Congress. *E.g.,* 28 U.S.C. §§ 171-180 (Court of Federal Claims); 28 U.S.C. §§ 1581-1585 (Court of International Trade).

[3] *See* § 5.01 (subject matter jurisdiction), *infra.*

[4] *See* §§ 5.01[1](federal jurisdiction in general); §§ 5.02-5.06 (particulars of federal question and diversity jurisdiction), *infra.*

[5] *See* 28 U.S.C. § 133.

[6] On appellate systems generally, see § 13.06, *infra.*

[7] *See* 28 U.S.C. §§ 1291-1292.

[8] *See* 28 U.S.C. § 41.

district courts in each circuit are taken to the court of appeals for that circuit. Appeals from many of the administrative agencies go to the Court of Appeals for the D.C. Circuit, while appeals from various specialized federal courts[9] are taken to a thirteenth circuit called the Court of Appeals for the Federal Circuit.[10]

The United States Supreme Court sits atop the federal system. It has original jurisdiction over cases affecting ambassadors and in which states are parties, and appellate jurisdiction in all others.[11] While most appellate jurisdiction exercised by federal courts of appeal is mandatory, the Supreme Court is largely free to choose the cases it wishes to hear.[12]

State judicial systems have three or four layers. At the bottom are usually a variety of courts of *limited* or *special subject matter jurisdiction,* authorized, for example, to hear only traffic, landlord-tenant, small claims or probate cases. All states also have one court of original and *general jurisdiction* that hears all claims not exclusively vested in courts of limited jurisdiction. These claims may include state claims and nonexclusive federal question claims that also could have been brought in federal district courts. State courts of general jurisdiction often exist at the county level, but their designations differ widely. In the District of Columbia, for example, they are called the superior courts, in Virginia circuit courts, and in New York (somewhat perversely) supreme courts. To add to the confusion, in some states these courts also enjoy some form of appellate jurisdiction over cases originally brought in state courts of limited jurisdiction.

State systems have at least one more layer, a court of exclusively or predominantly appellate jurisdiction at the top of their judicial systems, variously called the supreme court, the court of appeals, or, in Massachusetts, the Supreme Judicial Court. Many more populous states also have an intermediate appellate layer, roughly corresponding to courts of appeals in the federal system. Most of these intermediate state appellate courts are relatively recent inventions created to relieve the caseload burden on the highest state courts. Jurisdiction in inferior state appellate courts is usually mandatory, leaving the highest state court in the system to exercise considerable discretion in selecting cases for further review.[13]

On matters of state law, the highest state court has the last word. However, the United States Supreme Court has the authority to review state court rulings on the meaning and application of federal law. This creates the possibility of a level above state high courts in federal question adjudications. In practice, the possibility is remote because the Supreme Court usually denies review.[14] This means that the highest state courts,

---

[9] *See* note 2, *supra.*

[10] *See* 28 U.S.C §§ 1292(c), 1295.

[11] U.S. Const. art. III, § 2.

[12] *See* § 13.06 (appellate systems) *infra.*

[13] On appellate systems in general, *see* § 13.06 *infra.*

[14] The Supreme Court has traditionally kept abreast of its workload. Yet the Court has managed this in recent years only by refusing to review a large number of cases properly within its appellate jurisdiction. *See generally* Griswold, *Rationing Justice — The Supreme Court's Caseload and What the Court Does Not Do,* 60 Cornell L. Rev. 335 (1975).

as well as the federal courts of appeal, are in a real sense courts of last resort in many federal question cases. [15]

The coexistence of state and federal judicial systems may present the claimant with a choice of forums. A federal court option exists if the claim is for more than $75,000 and the prospective plaintiff and defendants are from different states, [16] or if the claim involves certain questions of federal law. [17] The option of trial in state court is less restricted, available except in the relatively few situations where federal courts enjoy exclusive subject matter jurisdiction. [18] And, as we shall examine in the next section, geographic affiliations of the parties or claims may offer claimant the choice of state and federal courts in more than one state.

§ 2.02   Factors Influencing the Selection of a Court

Every first year law student intuitively senses that it would be unfair to require a Vermonter who has never been to or had contact with Alaska to defend a lawsuit brought there. The law acknowledges that unfairness by limiting a court's *personal jurisdiction* (the power to issue a judgment binding a person or affecting his property), requiring some voluntary contact or political affiliation between the defendant and the *forum state* in which the action is brought. Historically, the principal basis for and limitation upon personal jurisdiction was territorial, hence our adoption of the term *territorial jurisdiction* as a generic description for this requirement. Chapter 3 discusses this essential factor in selecting a court.

We considered in the last section how the coexistence of state and federal judicial systems creates the possibility of choice within the same geographical area, choice limited by the constraints of *subject matter* jurisdiction. Chapter 5 discusses this factor. Of obvious interest to the plaintiff's lawyer, it also controls opportunities for the defendant to *remove* the action against his client from state to federal court, as discussed in § 5.07.

---

[15] According to one prominent study:

> Supreme Court review has become an exceedingly unlikely event in most federal litigation. Of about 8,000 cases decided after hearing and submission in the courts of appeals, only about one in a 100 will be given full consideration by the Supreme Court. Of the cases tried in the district courts, about one in 300 reaches the Supreme Court.

P. Carrington, D. Meador & M. Rosenberg, *Justice on Appeal* 209 (1976) (citations omitted). This has placed federal courts of appeal in a position "to create and to balkanize national law." Betten, *Institutional Reform in the Federal Courts,* 52 Ind. L.J. 63, 68 (1976). Less data exist on Supreme Court supervision of federal question decisions in state courts, but the lack of effective supervision there appears to be at least as pronounced. *See generally* Stolz, *Federal Review of State Court Decisions of Federal Questions: The Need for Additional Appellate Capacity,* 64 Calif. L. Rev. 943 (1976).

[16] *See* §§ 5.04-5.06 (diversity jurisdiction), *infra.*

[17] *See* § 5.03 *infra.*

[18] Plaintiffs can bring certain cases (federal antitrust, patent and copyright, bankruptcy, etc.) only in federal court. For discussion of the scope and intended purposes of exclusive federal jurisdiction, see M. Redish, *Federal Jurisdiction: Tensions in the Allocation of Judicial Power* 149-156 (2d ed. 1990); ALI, *Study of the Division of Jurisdiction Between State and Federal Courts* 182–186 (1969).

The defendant's concerns over the convenience of the forum selected by plaintiff are entitled to recognition. Beyond that, the judicial system as a whole has an efficiency interest in shifting litigation to the most generally convenient locations. These interests are served by the law of *venue,* discussed in Chapter 6.

Lawyers take these legal constraints into account in deciding where to file suit. They also consider a variety of tactical factors.[19] When legal constraints permit a choice, tactical factors should control the decision where to file.

One obvious tactical factor is the identity of the judge who will preside over the litigation. The manner in which cases are assigned to particular judges is often too random to permit accurate prediction. Yet lawyers frequently can make useful comparisons about the quality of judges in different kinds of courts. Some have argued, for example, that the appointment process, life tenure, prestige, salary and research resources of federal judges, and the quality of the federal caseload, attracts persons to the federal bench who are more capable and less susceptible to majoritarian pressures than those attracted to the state bench.[20] Lawyers given a choice thus tend to file civil rights actions in federal rather than state courts.[21]

The court's calendar can also be a tactical concern. In 2000, for example, the median time from commencement of a civil action to disposition at trial in federal district courts ranged from three and a half months in the fastest district to twenty-four and one-third months in the slowest.[22] A plaintiff's lawyer anxious to move the case through trial might file it in one of the faster federal district courts or opt instead for a state court with a better trial calendar.

Sundry procedural differences between courts may also influence court selection.[23] Extensive provision in the federal rules for discovery — court-supported fact-gathering by the parties — may attract some lawyers who need discovery to develop their cases and discourage others who already command the facts or whose clients are adverse to discovery of *their* facts. Many other procedural factors, including the availability of jury trial, the

---

[19] *See generally* R. McCullough & J. Underwood, *Civil Trial Manual* 89-140 (2d ed. 1987); Dooley, *Selecting the Forum —Plaintiff's Position,* 3 Am. Jur. Trials 553 (1963); Groce, *Selecting the Forum —Defendant's Position,* 3 Am. Jur. Trials 611 (1963); Flango, *Attorneys' Perspectives on Choice of Forum in Diversity Cases,* 25 Akron L. Rev. 41 (1991); Note, *Forum Shopping Reconsidered,* 103 Harv. L. Rev. 1677 (1990); Summers, *Analysis of Factors That Influence Choice of Forum in Diversity Cases,* 47 Iowa L. Rev. 933 (1962).

[20] *Compare, e.g.,* Neuborne, *The Myth of Parity,* 90 Harv. L. Rev. 1105 (1977) (federal courts are superior to state courts in protecting federal rights), and Marvell, *The Rationales for Federal Question Jurisdiction: An Empirical Examination of Student Rights Litigation,* 1984 Wis. L. Rev. 1315 (lawyers representing students select federal courts because they are more protective of student rights), *with* Solimine & Walker, *Constitutional Litigation in Federal and State Courts: An Empirical Analysis of Judicial Parity,* 10 Hastings Const. L.Q. 213 (1983) (state courts are no more hostile to vindication of federal rights than federal courts).

[21] *See, e.g., Neuborne,* note 20, *supra.*

[22] 2000 Admin. Off. U.S. Courts Annual Report of the Dir. Table C-5.

[23] *See generally Dooley,* note 19, *supra,* §§ 19-39; *Groce,* note 19, *supra,* §§ 9-15.

composition of jury panels, the required level of agreement for verdicts, the applicable rules of evidence, and the availability of appellate review can influence court selection. Of course, the lawyers' familiarity with procedures of particular courts also influences the choice of court.

Client characteristics may also be an important consideration in choice of court. Some lawyers prefer federal courts when their client is from outside the state.[24] One recent study suggests that client characteristics along with quality of judges and convenience, in fact, are the most important reasons lawyers choose one forum over another, outweighing procedural considerations.[25]

Finally, the substantive law that courts will apply can be a crucial factor in forum choice. Although there is much support in modern choice-of-law theory for the idea that the law chosen in a case should not vary according to where the case is tried, local choice-of-law ("conflicts") rules and the manner in which they are applied do not always reflect this idea. This can create enormous incentive for interstate forum–shopping in search for favorable substantive law.[26] Chapter 7 discusses the choice of applicable law in federal court, while the conflict of laws in general is treated in a companion to this volume.[27]

Although every plaintiff shops for a forum in selecting a court in which to sue (given a choice), courts sometimes decry "forum-shopping," flavoring it with a vague scent of impropriety. But as long as the intersection of jurisdictional rules and venue results in forum choices, parties will necessarily have to make them. Indeed, the *Model Rules of Professional Conduct* comment that a lawyer has a "duty to use legal procedure for the fullest benefit of the client's cause,"[28] leading one scholar to assert that this duty "may include selecting a forum with little connection to the events giving rise to a cause of action if that forum is an acceptable forum under the law, despite the fact that the attorney may be accused of taking advantage of 'loopholes' or 'technicalities.' "[29] These rules themselves guard against any resulting unfairness, as we shall see. If they waste resources by providing too many choices, the best solution is probably to go after the rules, not the lawyers who use them.

---

[24] *See Flango*, note 19, *supra*, at 105. *See* § 5.04, *infra*.

[25] Flango, note 19, *supra*, at 105.

[26] For a survey of recent developments, see Shreve, *Choice of Law and the Forgiving Constitution*, 71 Ind. L.J. 271 (1996).

[27] *See generally* W. Richman & W. Reynolds, *Understanding Conflict of Laws* Ch. 4 (2d ed. 1993).

[28] American Bar Ass'n, *Model Rules of Professional Conduct and Code of Judicial Conduct* Rule 3.1 cmt. 1 (1983).

[29] Algero, *In Defense of Forum Shopping: A Realistic Look at Selecting a Venue*, 78 Neb. L. Rev. 79, 106 (1999).

Chapter 3

A COURT WITH JURISDICTION OVER PERSONS AND THINGS

§ 3.01 Preliminary Observations

[1] How and Why Problems of Territorial Jurisdiction Arise

The function of civil litigation is to dispose of controversies by subjecting them to a formal, authoritative process. The process works by ultimately producing binding judgments.[1] For reasons that shall become clear, however, courts cannot be free to issue binding judgments in *any* civil action filed — no matter where the cause of action arose and no matter where the defendant resides. They are restrained by limitations on *territorial jurisdiction*[2] (courts' jurisdiction over persons and things). We will frequently substitute for territorial jurisdiction a narrower term, *personal jurisdiction* (jurisdiction over persons only).[3]

Consider the following example. A, a citizen of Hawaii, travels to New York City on business. A steps off of a curb into the path of an automobile

---

[1] *See generally* Chapter 15, *infra.* This is true unless the case settles or is dismissed without prejudice prior to final judgment.

[2] "Other names for this or similar concepts include judicial jurisdiction, adjudicatory jurisdiction, adjudicatory authority, amenability, nexus, and substantive due process." Clermont, *Restating Territorial Jurisdiction and Venue for State and Federal Courts,* 66 Cornell L. Rev. 411, 412 n.5 (1981). Many courts also use amenability to service of process or "subject to service" as a synonym for territorial jurisdiction, and Congress has sometimes used the terminology of "process" to confer nationwide territorial jurisdiction on federal courts for certain claims. *See, e.g.,* 28 U.S.C. § 2361 (interpleader); 15 U.S.C. § 77V(a) (Securities Act of 1933). The latter terminology can be confusing because service can often technically be accomplished (by certified mail, special process server or conformity with foreign service procedures) even in the absence of territorial jurisdiction. Fed.R.Civ.P. 12(b) reflects this possibility by separately listing the defenses of lack of personal jurisdiction and improper service.

On differences between the American law of personal jurisdiction and equivalent rules abroad, see Brochers, *Comparing Personal Jurisdiction in the United States and the European Community: Lessons for American Reform,* 40 Am. J. Comp. L. 121 (1992).

[3] The term "personal jurisdiction" derives from *in personam* jurisdiction, one of three traditional categories of territorial jurisdiction. The other two are *in rem* and *quasi in rem* jurisdiction. *See* § 3.02, *infra.* By far the largest number of cases entertained by courts are founded on personal jurisdiction. The Supreme Court's decisions setting limits on personal jurisdiction have added importance because it has extended them to all forms of territorial jurisdiction. *See* § 3.08, *infra.* These developments have encouraged interchangeable use of the terms territorial jurisdiction and personal jurisdiction. We will follow this approach in the text when the context permits.

driven by B. A receives medical treatment in New York, returns to Hawaii and files suit there for medical expenses incurred in New York resulting from the accident. Service of process in the Hawaii case reaches B in New York by mail. B is a lifetime citizen of New York state. He does no business in Hawaii, owns no property there, and has never visited the state.

Can a Hawaii court entertain this case? No. The Hawaii court would clearly lack personal jurisdiction. Even without benefit of details of the law of personal jurisdiction which follow, we can see why a Hawaii court should not have the power to hear the case. It would add substantially to B's burden of being a defendant for him to have to defend against A's claim in far-away Hawaii. Neither B nor the facts of the controversy have any connection with Hawaii which would suggest that imposition of Hawaii jurisdiction would be justified. B could go to Hawaii and question the Hawaii court's personal jurisdiction there, but even this would unfairly burden him. The law of personal jurisdiction should and does permit B to sit tight in New York, take no part in the Hawaii proceeding, and success- fully resist a Hawaii default judgment if A ever presents it for enforcement in New York.[4]

But what if we change the facts of the example? Suppose that B (not A) was the traveller, that B struck A while B was driving a rented car in Hawaii. Now the Hawaii court clearly has personal jurisdiction. Can you see why?[5] Or suppose we leave the accident in New York, but give B a condominium in Hawaii. Could B as safely assume that the Hawaii court lacked jurisdiction?[6] Even if B had a substantial personal jurisdiction argument to make, would it still be wise for him to refuse to appear and raise it in the Hawaii case?[7]

[2] Law Which Limits the Reach of Courts' Territorial Jurisdiction

[a] State Courts

The primary restraint on the territorial jurisdiction of state courts is the Due Process Clause of the Fourteenth Amendment to the United States Constitution. The Clause provides that "[n]o State shall . . . deprive any person of life, liberty, or property, without due process of law. . . ." A claim is "property" within the meaning of the Clause, which cannot be forfeited through state proceedings lacking due process.[8] The protections of due process are similarly available to those against whom claims are made.[9]

---

[4] See § 3.04 (the jurisdictional challenge), infra.

[5] Hawaii's authority to impose jurisdiction on B derives from a regulatory concern over acts committed in the forum state. See § 3.10 (specific jurisdiction), infra.

[6] Maybe not. See § 3.02 ((quasi in rem jurisdiction), infra.

[7] No. See § 3.04[3][a] (tactical considerations in collateral attack), infra.

[8] Logan v. Zimmerman Brush Co., 455 U.S. 422, 428-429 (1982).

[9] "Any claim asserted by a plaintiff is simply the reverse side of what is at stake to the defendant; the same property is at stake for both." Pielemeier, Due Process Limitations on the Application of Collateral Estoppel Against Nonparties to Prior Litigation, 63 B.U.L. Rev. 383, 398 (1983).

The Due Process Clause also affords litigants rights to notice and the opportunity to be heard in state court. [10] These rights, however, are secured by a branch of due process doctrine separate and distinct from that which governs territorial jurisdiction. [11]

The concerns which give the Due Process Clause life in the territorial jurisdiction setting are more elusive and less agreed upon by courts and commentators. There is agreement, however, that the Due Process Clause should protect the nonresident [12] defendant from suffering unreasonably from plaintiff's choice of forum. To uphold jurisdiction in the state forum selected by plaintiff at the very least forces the defendant to go there and move for a *forum non conveniens* dismissal — a dismissal on the ground that there is a more convenient place for the litigation. [13] When a court exercises its considerable discretion to deny the motion, defendant is forced to litigate the merits in the courts of that state.

State law may set additional limits on the reach of state courts' territorial jurisdiction. [14] Most state courts enjoy only as much territorial jurisdiction over nonresident defendants as their legislatures have chosen to confer by statute. It is therefore possible that the statutory scheme could leave the courts of a state short of the full scope of authority over nonresident defendants permitted under federal constitutional law. In practice, however, this does not seem to be much of a problem. All states now have so-called *long-arm statutes* which endow their courts with all or nearly all the jurisdictional authority permitted by due process. [15]

[b] Federal Courts

The Fourteenth Amendment does not apply to federal courts. However, the authority of federal courts is limited by the same Due Process Clause appearing in the Fifth Amendment to the Constitution. The Constitution does not, however, limit federal courts to the same degree. It is at least arguable that the Fifth Amendment permits federal courts to exercise

---

[10] *See* Chapter 4, *infra.*

[11] The Supreme Court explained and compared the two branches of due process doctrine in *Phillips Petroleum Co. v. Shutts,* 472 U.S. 797 (1985), concluding that the passive members of plaintiffs' nationwide class were entitled to due process protections of notice and the opportunity to be heard, but that the minimum contacts constraint imposed by due process on personal jurisdiction did not apply to their claims. For discussions of the case, see Miller & Crump, *Jurisdiction and Choice of Law in Multistate Class Actions,* 96 Yale L.J. 1 (1986); Kennedy, *The Supreme Court Meets the Bride of Frankenstein: Phillips Petroleum Co. v. Shutts and the Multistate State Class Action,* 34 Kan. L. Rev. 255 (1985); § 9.09[2][b], *infra.*

[12] Most significant territorial jurisdiction cases involve defendants who do not reside in the forum state. The distinction between the concepts of *residence* and *citizenship* is unclear. *See* § 3.03[1] (suit in defendant's home state), *infra.* However, it is at least true that the Due Process Clause poses no significant obstacle to the forum state's exercise of territorial jurisdiction over its own citizens.

[13] *See* § 6.02[1], *infra.*

[14] For a discussion of state law regulation of personal jurisdiction, see § 3.07[1] (state long-arm statutes), *infra.*

[15] *Id.*

territorial jurisdiction over all United States citizens,[16] permitting greater geographical reach than the Fourteenth Amendment permits state courts.[17]

The current difference in the reach of process, however, is not great. This is because federal courts are as dependent as their state counterparts on the legislative branch to delegate their powers by statute,[18] and Congress has created nationwide territorial jurisdiction for federal courts in only a few special circumstances.[19] Absent such a statute, federal courts will in most cases be limited to the jurisdictional reach of a local state court. This limitation results from Rule 4's provision that service or waiver of service will establish jurisdiction over any defendant "who could be subjected to the [territorial] jurisdiction of a court of general [subject matter] jurisdiction in the state in which the district court is located. . . ."[20] This provision effectively incorporates the forum state's law of personal jurisdiction, as well as the constitutional limitations upon it. By this indirect route, federal judges usually find themselves laboring under the same Fourteenth Amendment due process and state law limitations as their state court counterparts.[21] This means that federal courts often do not direct their concerns

---

[16] The principle that defendants submit to territorial jurisdiction in exchange for the benefits of forum citizenship is most fully developed in the law of state court jurisdiction. *See* § 3.03[1] (suit in defendant's home state), *infra*. But the Supreme Court has also applied the principle to uphold a federal court's territorial jurisdiction over a United States citizen. *Blackmer v. United States*, 284 U.S. 421 (1932).

[17] For differing views, compare Abrams, *Power, Convenience, and the Elimination of Personal Jurisdiction in the Federal Courts*, 58 Ind. L.J. 1 (1982) (supporting the point), *James, Hazard, & Leubsdorf* § 2.34 (same) with Fullerton, *Constitutional Limits on Nationwide Personal Jurisdiction in the Federal Courts*, 79 Nw. U.L. Rev. 1 (1984) (questioning whether the Fifth Amendment should permit a federal court to exercise territorial jurisdiction if the Fourteenth Amendment would prevent exercise of territorial jurisdiction by a state court in the same locale), and Brilmayer & Norchi, *Federal Extraterritoriality and Fifth Amendment Due Process*, 105 Harv. L. Rev. 1217, 1262 (1992) (arguing that Fifth Amendment constraints should in significant part be "parallel to those of the Fourteenth Amendment").

[18] Foster, *Long-Arm Jurisdiction in Federal Courts*, 1969 Wis. L. Rev. 9, 11. *Cf.* Note, *Alien Corporations and Aggregate Contacts: A Genuinely Federal Jurisdictional Standard*, 95 Harv. L. Rev. 470, 470 (1981) ("[I]n federal cases it is for Congress to determine whether a defendant is amenable to service and to establish the manner in which process may be served."). *Accord, Omni Capital Int. v. Rudolf Wolff & Co., Ltd.*, 484 U.S. 97 (1987).

[19] Thus, 28 U.S.C. § 2361 permits nationwide service of process in federal statutory interpleader proceedings. For a list of additional federal statutes authorizing nationwide service of process, see Note, *Pendent Personal Jurisdiction and Nationwide Service of Process*, 64 N.Y.U. L. Rev. 113 (1989).

[20] Rule 4(k)(1)(A). In limited circumstances involving impleader or compulsory joinder, Rule 4(k)(1)(B) permits service of process up to 100 miles from the federal court — whether or not the same service would have been possible in a local state case.

[21] *See generally* Casad, *Personal Jurisdiction in Federal Question Cases*, 70 Tex. L. Rev. 1589 (1992). With a limited exception discussed *infra*, Rule 4 makes no distinction between federal diversity and federal question cases. While incorporation of state court jurisdictional limitations has been applauded in the former, von Mehren & Trautman, *Jurisdiction to Adjudicate: A Suggested Analysis*, 79 Harv. L. Rev. 1121, 1123-1125 n.6 (1966), it has been criticized as too confining in federal question cases, particularly those involving alien defendants. *Alien Corporations*, note 18, *supra*; Degnan & Kane, *The Exercise of Jurisdiction Over and Enforcement of Judgments Against Alien Defendants*, 39 Hastings L. J. 799 (1988); Comment, *National Contacts As a Basis for In Personam Jurisdiction Over Aliens in Federal Question Suits*, 70 Calif. L. Rev. 686 (1982).

over territorial jurisdiction to a body of distinctly federal law.[22] This is in marked contrast to the preeminent role federal law plays in resolving questions of federal subject matter jurisdiction.[23]

The situation described above changed to a slight degree with the 1993 amendment of Rule 4 authorizing nationwide service of process in some cases brought under federal courts' federal question jurisdiction.[24] Relatively few cases, however, are likely to be affected by the amendment. It represents a "narrow extension of the federal reach. . . ."[25]

PART A
Received Traditions

The most significant modern developments in the law of territorial jurisdiction are those advancing (or limiting) the idea that nonresident defendants who cannot be found and served within the forum can nonetheless be subject to the court's authority. We will treat Supreme Court cases that bear on this in parts B and C of this chapter. Important as these cases are, alone they are inadequate to explain the law of territorial jurisdiction. The Court has rested its major decisions in part on principles which it appears to assume the reader will grasp without much explanation. It is essential to understand this material, surveyed in Part A, both to learn about important aspects of current law untreated by the Court's recent decisions and to better understand the decisions themselves. We begin in § 3.02 with an introduction to the three categories of territorial jurisdiction that evolved by the beginning of this century. Section 3.03 focuses on the most significant of the three, personal jurisdiction, examining current means of obtaining personal jurisdiction that antedate modern theory. In § 3.04 we consider the timing of jurisdictional challenges, an important

---

[22] *See, e.g., Burger King v. Rudzewicz,* 471 U.S. 462 (1985) (sufficiency of a federal court's territorial jurisdiction measured under Florida's long-arm statute); *Keeton v. Hustler Magazine,* 465 U.S. 770 (1984) (the same under New Hampshire's long-arm statute).

[23] For a particularly helpful discussion of the differences between territorial jurisdiction and subject matter jurisdiction in the federal courts, see *Insurance Corp. of Ireland, Ltd. v. Compagnie des Bauxites de Guinee,* 456 U.S. 694 (1982).

[24] Rule 4(k)(2) now states:

　If the exercise of jurisdiction is consistent with the Constitution and laws of the United States, serving a summons or filing a waiver of service is also effective, with respect to claims arising under federal law, to establish personal jurisdiction over the person of any defendant who is not subject to the jurisdiction of the courts of jurisdiction of any state.

[25] Rule 4 Advisory Committee notes (1993). The relative unimportance of the change can be explained as follows. Since defendants incorporated in or citizens of a state are subject to jurisdiction in that state, *see* § 3.03[1], *infra,* only aliens appear to fit within the category created in Rule 4(k)(2). Moreover, aliens would be subject to the new subsection only when minimum contacts existed between them and the United States *but* did not exist between them and any state. Richman, *Carnival Cruise Lines: Forum Selection Clauses in Adhesion Contracts,* 40 Am. J. of Comp. L. 977, 977 n.1 (1992). For a survey of lower federal court decisions under Rule 4(k)(2), *see* Corby, *Putting Personal Jurisdiction Within Reach: Just What Has Rule 4(k)(2) Done for the Personal Jurisdiction of Federal Courts?* 30 McGeorge L. Rev. 167 (1998).

aspect of modern practice, which supplies additional context for the subjects presented in parts B and C.

§ 3.02 Three Categories Of Territorial Jurisdiction

Historically, American courts have enjoyed three types of territorial jurisdiction: *in personam*,[26] *in rem*,[27] and *quasi in rem*.[28] The United States Supreme Court once distinguished the three as follows:

> A judgment *in personam* imposes a personal liability or obligation on one person in favor of another. A judgment *in rem* affects the interests of all persons in designated property. A judgment *quasi in rem* affects the interests of particular persons in designated property.[29]

The relative significance of these categories has changed since the Court's observation. But each has survived into contemporary law and the essential features of each remain unchanged.

[1] *In Personam* Jurisdiction

In personam jurisdiction, also called personal jurisdiction or jurisdiction over the person, provides courts with a basis for entirely determining controversies involving personal obligations (often tort or contract claims). Because the court's jurisdiction is over the person of the defendant, it can impose judgment indebtedness upon him to the full extent of the wrong done to the plaintiff. If an *in personam* judgment for damages cannot be fully satisfied where rendered,[30] plaintiff may collect the unsatisfied portion of the judgment in any other state or federal court.[31]

[2] *In Rem* Jurisdiction

In rem jurisdiction focuses not on the person of the defendant but on some property located within the forum. Courts use this form of jurisdiction to adjudicate questions concerning the ownership and control of such property — to settle questions, it is sometimes said, against the whole world.[32]

---

[26] *See* Kalo, *Jurisdiction as an Evolutionary Process: The Development of Quasi In Rem and In Personam Principles,* 1978 Duke L.J. 1147 (1978); Kurland, *The Supreme Court, the Due Process Clause and the In Personam Jurisdiction of State Courts—From Pennoyer to Denckla: A Review,* 25 U. Chi. L. Rev. 569 (1958).

[27] *See* Smit, *The Enduring Utility of In Rem Rules: A Lasting Legacy of Pennoyer v. Neff,* 43 Brooklyn L. Rev. 600 (1977).

[28] *See* Kalo, note 26, *supra;* Slomanson, *Real Property Unrelated to Claim: Due Process for Quasi In Rem Jurisdiction?,* 83 Dick. L. Rev. 51 (1978).

[29] *Hanson v. Denckla,* 357 U.S. 235, 246 n.12 (1958).

[30] For the manner in which judgments are enforced, *see* § 15.02, *infra.*

[31] "The Full Faith and Credit Clause makes the valid *in personam* judgment of one State enforceable in all other States." *Shaffer v. Heitner,* 433 U.S. 186, 210 (1977). Federal statutory law requires that the same respect be given to state judgments in federal court and to federal judgments in either state or other federal courts. *See* § 15.10, *infra.*

[32] "Examples of such actions include suits to quiet title to real estate that purport to conclude all adverse claims, and in rem libels in admiralty." R. Casad & R. Richman, *Jurisdiction in Civil Actions* § 1-1[3] (3rd ed. 1998).

Theoretically, the function of *in rem* jurisdiction is to act upon the thing, or *res,* itself, rather than to act directly upon rights of individuals. This is an artificial distinction, since both types affect the rights of others to the property.

[3] *Quasi In Rem* Jurisdiction

Like *in rem* jurisdiction, *quasi in rem* jurisdiction operates on property located within the forum and not directly against the person of individual defendants. Like an *in rem* judgment, a *quasi in rem* judgment binds the parties only with reference to their interests in the *res* upon which jurisdiction is based.[33] Thus, the value of a quasi in rem judgment cannot exceed the value of the res.

But, like *in personam* jurisdiction, *quasi in rem* jurisdiction can be used to adjudicate personal obligations.[34] *Harris v. Balk,*[35] perhaps the most famous *quasi in rem* case, provides an illustration. A Maryland plaintiff sued nonresident defendant Balk by serving one Harris to garnish[36] a debt owed by Harris to Balk. The *res* was the debt, deemed present wherever the debtor could be found. The plaintiff prevailed and recovered the *res* — Harris' debt. Thereafter, Balk sued Harris in North Carolina on the debt. Harris argued that he had discharged his obligation to Balk by paying the sum in the earlier case. Harris prevailed because the United States Supreme Court concluded that the Maryland court had properly exercised *quasi in rem* jurisdiction in the original case.[37]

Once the Supreme Court decided that exercises of *quasi in rem* jurisdiction must satisfy the same due process standards applicable to personal

---

[33] Thus, in contrast to *in personam* judgments, *see* note 6 and related text, *supra, in rem* and *quasi in rem* judgments usually have no effect elsewhere. A judgment *in rem* or *quasi in rem* only authorizes liquidation or alteration of the legal status of the *res* underpinning jurisdiction. In a few cases, courts limited to one of these two forms of jurisdiction have presumed to adjudicate the entire dollar amount of defendant's personal obligation to plaintiff. Courts elsewhere, however, are under no obligation to recognize such judgments. For example, in *Combs v. Combs,* 60 S.W.2d 368 (Ky. 1933), a Kentucky court refused to give effect to an Arkansas *in rem* judgment that not only adjudicated the status of Arkansas real estate, but also presumed to fix the entire sum defendant owed to plaintiff. *But see Harnischfeger Sales Corp. v. Sternberg Dredging Co.,* 191 So. 94 (Miss. 1940), where a Mississippi court noted that a prior Louisiana judgment was *in rem,* but gave it preclusive effect. However, "[t]here is scant judicial authority for this position." Bourne, *The Demise of Foreign Attachment,* 21 Creighton L. Rev. 141, 151 n.84 (1987).

[34] However, this use is now quite limited. *See* note 38 and related text, *infra.*

[35] 198 U.S. 215 (1905). For an illuminating discussion of this case, see W. Richman & W. Reynolds, *Understanding Conflict of Laws* § 41[b] (2d ed. 1993).

[36] *Garnishment* is the seizure of a debt by service of process on the debtor with a warning not to pay the debt pending litigation. *Attachment* is the actual or constructive seizure of real property using judicial process. Property may also be seized before judgment to provide security for an eventual judgment, rather than to confer territorial jurisdiction, or after judgment to execute upon the judgment. Pre-judgment seizures are subject to strict due process protection, *see* § 4.02[2], *infra,* while post-judgment seizures are typically subject to detailed local procedures, even in federal courts. *See generally* § 15.02 (enforcing money judgments), *infra.*

[37] For a further illustration of this form of *quasi in rem* jurisdiction, *see* the discussion of the *Seider* doctrine at § 3.08[2], *infra.*

jurisdiction, the form of *quasi in rem* jurisdiction exemplified by *Harris* lost its special appeal.[38] Plaintiffs no longer obtain any jurisdictional advantage by attaching nonresident defendants' property and proceeding under a *quasi in rem* theory; they may just as well proceed directly and assert personal jurisdiction. Other forms of *quasi in rem* jurisdiction, however, continue to have application.[39]

§ 3.03   Traditionally Accepted Forms Of Personal Jurisdiction

[1]   Suit in the Defendant's Home State

Courts of the defendant's home state traditionally have personal jurisdiction over the defendant in all cases.[40] The rule makes sense for several reasons.

Amenability to suit can be seen as a fair exchange for the benefits and protection which the defendant enjoys from state citizenship. The United States Supreme Court so held in the landmark case, *Milliken v. Meyer.*[41] The Court ruled that a Wyoming court had personal jurisdiction over a defendant then living in the forum state. "Domicile in the state is alone sufficient to bring an absent defendant within the reach of the state's jurisdiction," said the Court.[42] "The state which accords [the defendant] privileges and affords protection to him and his property by virtue of his domicile may also exact reciprocal duties."[43] The Court added that "[o]ne such incident of domicile is amenability to suit within the state."[44] As a separate matter, there is much to be said for having one place where the plaintiff can file suit and be certain that personal jurisdiction exists over the defendant. Moreover, defendants frequently suffer the least expense and inconvenience when defending at home.[45]

---

[38] For discussion of these developments, see §§ 3.08[1] & [2], *infra.*

[39] For example, an action against named defendants to remove a cloud on the title to real estate. Richman & Reynolds, note 35, *supra,* at § 40[b].

[40] "The notion that the plaintiff should sue the defendant at his home is of venerable age, and the rule permitting him to be sued there is universally accepted." Smit, *Common and Civil Law Rules of In Personam Adjudicatory Authority: An Analysis of Underlying Policies,* 21 Int'l & Comp. L.Q. 335, 336 (1972). "[A] state has control over its citizens and over all persons domiciled within the state even when they have gone outside the state." Scott, *Jurisdiction Over Nonresidents Doing Business Within A State,* 32 Harv. L. Rev. 871, 875 (1919).

[41] 311 U.S. 457 (1940).

[42] *Id.* at 462.

[43] *Id.* at 463.

[44] *Id.* at 464. *Cf.* Brilmayer, *How Contacts Count: Due Process Limitations on State Court Jurisdiction,* 1980 Sup. Ct. Rev. 77, 85 ("[T]here can be no sovereignty objections to a State requiring its own citizens to appear and defend a suit brought in its courts.").

[45] "The defendant's interest is to be sued at home, since this will cause him the least inconvenience and permit him to litigate before a court of his own environs." Smit, note 40, *supra,* at 350. *Accord,* Wasserman, *The Subpoena Power: Pennoyer's Last Vestige,* 74 Minn. L. Rev. 37, 62 (1989).

Which state is home for the defendant? The Supreme Court has never settled this, nor has it clearly identified the most appropriate terminology for resolving the question. In *Milliken* it used the terms *residence, citizenship* and *domicile* to describe a party's relationship to the forum, without distinguishing among them. Courts often appear to use the terms more or less interchangeably.

For defendants who are individuals (natural persons), *domicile* might seem to provide the best standard. Domicile has a more consistent meaning than residence[46] and generally connotes a stronger nexus between an individual and the state.[47] A legally competent person acquires a domicile by being present there with the intention of making the place his home. Every person has a domicile, but never more than one.[48]

Yet domicile may not always provide the most helpful guide. An individual retains his old domicile until his actions and intentions coalesce to form a new one. He may be absent from his domicile for years before this occurs. In the interim, the different place where he resides may carry indicia more significant to personal jurisdiction. It may be where he receives the most protection and benefits and where he could most conveniently defend. In such cases the more casual concept of residence would provide a better standard than domicile.[49]

Corporate defendants also may be sued at home. However, since corporations are legal creations rather than real persons, a different approach is necessary to determine what place or places serve as home for the corporation. Corporations have always been amenable to the jurisdiction of courts in the state in which they are incorporated.[50] Sometimes this will also be the state in which the corporation conducts its principal operations.[51] But when its principal operations are in a different state, it is likely that both will have personal jurisdiction over the corporation.[52] The matter becomes

---

[46] *See* Reese & Green, *That Elusive Word, "Residence"*, 6 Vand. L. Rev. 561 (1953).

[47] *See* Cavers, *"Habitual Residence": A Useful Concept?*, 21 Am. U.L. Rev. 475, 480 (1972).

[48] For an elaboration of these prerequisites, see *Restatement (Second) of Conflicts* Ch. 2 (1971). *See also* § 5.05 (diversity of citizenship), *infra*.

[49] *See* Lewis, *A Brave New World for Personal Jurisdiction: Flexible Tests Under Uniform Standards*, 37 Vand. L. Rev. 1, 48-49 (1984). *See also* § 6.01[2] (discussing residence as a basis for venue), *infra*.

[50] Kalo, *Jurisdiction as an Evolutionary Process: The Development of Quasi In Rem and In Personam Principles*, 1978 Duke L.J. 1147, 1166 (1978). *See also* Note, *Developments in the Law —State-Court Jurisdiction*, 73 Harv. L. Rev. 909, 919 (1960) ("To the extent that jurisdiction was based upon power over the defendant, a charter state had power over the corporations it created and allowed to continue in existence."). Matters become more complicated, however, when the question becomes whether personal jurisdiction extends to the parent as well as the subsidiary corporation. For a study, see Comment, *Jurisdiction Over a Parent Corporation in Its Subsidiary's State of Incorporation*, 141 U. Pa. L. Rev. 327 (1992).

[51] This creates something of a parallel between corporate and individual defendants: "The community that chartered the corporation and in which it has its head office occupies a position somewhat analogous to that of the community of a natural person's domicile and habitual residence." Von Mehren & Trautman, *Jurisdiction to Adjudicate: A Suggested Analysis*, 79 Harv. L. Rev. 1121, 1141-1142 (1966).

[52] *Id.*

more complicated when the corporation has substantial white-collar and blue-collar resources and they are located in different states, or when the corporation's major activities of the same kind are divided between two or more such states. Federal courts have addressed the same factual problems in determining corporate citizenship for purposes of diversity subject matter jurisdiction.[53] It would be tempting to resolve personal jurisdiction issues by reference to this case law, but this is probably unwise. The due process law of personal jurisdiction and the law of federal subject matter jurisdiction are grounded on fundamentally different policies.[54] It may be best to apply the home-state principle of personal jurisdiction to corporations only where the forum is the place of incorporation or where the activities of the corporation are clearly concentrated.[55] Clear concentration of defendant's corporate activities in one state suggests that it is receiving extensive benefits there and that suit in that state would not be particularly inconvenient. It seems reasonable to require the corporation to defend against all suits filed there. Absent a clear concentration of corporate activity in the forum, it is better to examine each case carefully to determine whether the corporation should be subject to the court's personal jurisdiction.[56]

[2] Personal Jurisdiction Over Nonresidents Through Waiver or Express Consent

[a] How Waiver Operates

State courts do not have the same authority to impose personal jurisdiction over nonresident defendants as they have over defendants who make their home in the forum state. But when the former have due process objections, they must take care to preserve them. The Supreme Court has observed that "[b]ecause the requirement of personal jurisdiction represents first of all an individual right, it can, like other such rights, be waived."[57]

Waiver need not be express. It is enough that a party act in a way which is incompatible with his argument that the forum lacks a basis for asserting personal jurisdiction over him. This is why nonresident plaintiffs waive due process objections to the court's jurisdiction by filing suit.[58] Note how the nonresident plaintiff's act of filing makes his relationship to the forum more intimate. He has now availed himself of the protection and benefits of the forum's judicial process. By setting up legal shop in the forum, plaintiff

---

[53] See, e.g., § 5.05, infra.

[54] The Supreme Court emphasized this point in *Insurance Corp. of Ireland, Ltd. v. Compagnie des Bauxites de Guinee*, 456 U.S. 694 (1982).

[55] But see von Mehren & Trautman, note 51, supra, suggesting that, when corporate white-collar activity is distributed evenly over two or more states, each should have jurisdiction.

[56] For example, the question how extensive defendant's contacts with the forum must be when the facts of the controversy arose elsewhere is serious and unsettled under current law. See § 311 (general jurisdiction), infra.

[57] Insurance Corp. of Ireland, Ltd. v. Compagnie des Bauxites de Guinee, 456 U.S. 694, 703 (1982).

[58] See Restatement (Second) of Conflicts Ch. 2, note 48, supra.

makes the forum a more convenient place not only to litigate his claim but to defend against such cross-claims or counterclaims as the forum might permit against him.[59]

Waiver of the right to challenge personal jurisdiction does not work quite so simply for nonresident *defendants*. Since it is unlikely that a court will respond to a defect in personal jurisdiction on its own initiative, defendant must move for dismissal. To say that the defendant waives his due process objection to personal jurisdiction by appearing in the case to press that objection as a ground for dismissal would create a *Catch-22* situation. Instead, procedural systems provide mechanisms for the defendant to appear and question the court's personal jurisdiction without curing plaintiff's problem in the process.

[b] Special and Limited Appearances

Once, the standard way for defendant to protect himself was to file a *special appearance*. The special appearance permitted defendant to participate in the case without submitting to the court's personal jurisdiction. It was crucial, however, that defendant styled his entry into the suit as a special appearance and that he was careful not to raise any other objections to plaintiff's case. If the defendant used this opportunity to urge any other reason why the case should be dismissed or to dispute the merits of plaintiff's case, his entry took on the character of a *general appearance*,[60] which functioned as a submission to the court's jurisdiction.[61]

Today most state courts have followed the lead of federal courts and dispensed with special appearances.[62] This means that the defendant will not prejudice his motion to dismiss by joining with it other grounds for dismissal.[63] However, care must be taken even in courts that follow the federal model. Defendant will waive his challenge to personal jurisdiction if he either fails to include it in a motion to dismiss made on other grounds, or fails to raise the matter by motion or pleading.[64] Moreover, the Supreme

---

[59] *Id.* The Court upheld personal jurisdiction under such circumstances in *Adam v. Saenger*, 303 U.S. 59 (1938).

[60] A general appearance is one where the defendant either enters an appearance in an action without limiting the purpose for which he appears or where he asks for relief which the court may give only if it has jurisdiction over him. An appearance which falls into either of these two categories is a general appearance even though the defendant protests at the same time that he does not submit himself to the jurisdiction of the court.

Restatement (Second) of Conflicts, note 48, *supra*, § 33 comment d. For discussion of the device in one jurisdiction, see L'Enfant, *In Personam Jurisdiction—General Appearance*, 52 La. L. Rev. 519 (1992).

[61] R. Casad & R. Richman, *Jurisdiction in Civil Actions* § 3-1[5][a] (3rd ed. 1998).

[62] *Id.* at ¶ 3.01[5][b]. For one example of special appearance practice, *see* Newton & Wicker, *Personal Jurisdiction and the Appearance to Challenge Jurisdiction in Texas*, 38 Baylor L. Rev. 491 (1986).

[63] *See* Rule 12(g). A majority of states have adopted Rule 12. *See generally* Oakley & Coon, *The Federal Rules in State Courts: A Survey of State Court Systems of Civil Procedure*, 61 Wash. L. Rev. 1367 (1986).

[64] Rule 12(h)(1). *See generally* § 8.07[2][b] (waivable defenses), *infra*.

Court held that defendant may also lose his personal jurisdiction challenge as a penalty for failure to comply with an order compelling discovery.[65]

Students sometimes confuse special appearances with *limited appearances*. Many jurisdictions permitted a defendant whose property was attached through *quasi in rem* jurisdiction to appear and resist a judgment on the merits against the property without, by so doing, submitting to the court's *in personam* jurisdiction. This was called a limited appearance. Recall that a *quasi in rem* judgment bound the defendant only with reference to his interest in the *res* upon which jurisdiction was based.[66] In contrast, an *in personam* judgment bound the defendant to the full measure of damages for his wrong to the plaintiff.[67] Limited appearances thus differed from special appearances in that the former were not a means of raising the personal jurisdiction issue but were instead designed to permit the defendant a full opportunity to litigate the case, while minimizing the effects of an adverse judgment.

Limited appearances have lost much of their importance. As soon as the Supreme Court required that *quasi in rem* cases satisfy more rigorous standards previously associated only with *in personam* jurisdiction,[68] the popularity of *quasi in rem* jurisdiction (and, hence, the necessity for limited appearances) declined dramatically.

[c] Preserving the Jurisdictional Challenge in the Face of an Initial Adverse Ruling

If defendant's jurisdictional challenge succeeds, the court will order plaintiff's case dismissed. Absent a successful appeal, plaintiff will have to refile against defendant[69] in a forum where the jurisdictional climate may be more favorable. But what if the trial court rules against the defendant?

Many systems do not permit defendant to appeal immediately because denial of a motion to dismiss for lack of personal jurisdiction is an interlocutory (nonfinal) order.[70]

This could place the defendant in a dilemma. If his further participation in the case constitutes a submission to jurisdiction, defendant will lose his jurisdictional challenge by pressing other reasons for dismissal or disputing the merits of plaintiff's case. To preserve the jurisdictional issue for appeal, he would have to stop participating at the trial level once the court rejects his jurisdictional challenge. This would draw a default judgment on the merits for plaintiff, and defendant could renew his jurisdictional challenge

---

[65] *Insurance Corp. of Ireland, Ltd. v. Compagnie des Bauxites de Guinee,* 456 U.S. 694 (1982). Plaintiff sought discovery of facts supporting personal jurisdiction.

[66] *See* § 3.02 and related text, *supra.*

[67] *See* § 3.02 and related text, *supra.*

[68] *See* § 3.08[1], *infra.*

[69] A dismissal for lack of personal jurisdiction has no preclusive effect on plaintiff's claim. *See* § 15.05, *infra.* It may, however, prejudice a subsequent attempt by plaintiff to refile the case in the same state. *See* § 15.06, *infra.*

[70] *See* § 13.04 (review of interlocutory orders), *infra.*

by appealing that final judgment. The risk in this option is that defendant will be bound on the merits, should he lose the jurisdictional argument.[71]

Fortunately, most systems do not pose this hard choice. They permit the defendant to renew his objection to the court's personal jurisdiction, even though he has fully contested the case during the interim.[72]

[d] Jurisdiction By Consent

Under a rule similar to waiver, it has long been true that defendants could consent to a court's personal jurisdiction in advance of suit. Such consent, if expressly made, still functions to cure any jurisdictional defects which might otherwise exist.[73]

A leading express consent case is *National Equipment Rental v. Szukhent.* The Supreme Court upheld New York jurisdiction over Michigan defendants in a federal breach of contract suit. It did so on the ground that one of the clauses of the contract signed by the defendants named an individual in New York to receive service there on their behalf. "[I]t is settled," said the Court, "that parties to a contract may agree in advance to submit to the jurisdiction of a given court. . . ."[74] Of course, the contract must be valid and enforceable. The only line of escape in such cases may be for defendant to argue that the provision is deceptive, unconscionable or a contract of adhesion.[75]

Two categories of express consent cases deserve special mention. The first concerns *forum-selection clauses* in contracts which both consent to jurisdiction in a particular court and bar litigation in any other court. Some courts were unwilling to enforce this second, anti-jurisdiction feature of forum-selection clauses. That is, they refused to dismiss cases filed in their courts in apparent violation of the agreement. The climate for forum-selection clauses improved, however, after the Supreme Court's decision in *Carnival Cruise Lines, Inc. v. Shute.* The Court upheld there a clause that had appeared on the back of an injured plaintiff's steamship ticket.[76]

---

[71] For further discussion of this dilemma, *see Casad & Richman,* note 23, *supra,* at § 3-1[5][a][i].

[72] Professor Casad offers representative cases from a number of states taking this view, and citations from three states (New Hampshire, Idaho and South Dakota) that do not. He observes that California also requires defendants to waive their jurisdictional challenge in order to contest the merits, but notes that defendants in California do have the option of interlocutory review of the jurisdictional question before they must proceed to the merits at trial. *Id.* Federal courts rarely permit interlocutory review but have long permitted defendants to renew their personal jurisdictional arguments on appeal, after fully litigating the case prior to final judgment. *Harkness v. Hyde,* 98 U.S. 476 (1879).

[73] *Friedenthal, Kane & Miller* § 3.5. On the other hand, it is doubtful whether the fictitious concept of implied consent continues to provide a sufficient basis for personal jurisdiction. *See* E. Scoles & P. Hay, *Conflict of Laws* § 9.5 (2nd ed. 1992).

[74] 375 U.S. 311, 315-316 (1964).

[75] Dissenting in *Szukhent,* Justice Black argued that the consent-to-jurisdiction portion of the contract was a "sham" and should be deemed unenforceable. *Id.* at 323-326.

[76] 499 U.S. 585 (1991). *Carnival Cruise* rested upon the interpretation of a federal statute, and Congress overturned the case in a narrow sense by subsequently amending the statute. Section 3006 of The Oceans Act of 1992 (P.L. 102-587).

A second category of important consent cases consists of those where foreign corporations have filed with state authorities a consent to jurisdiction as a condition for doing business in the forum. At the very least, such consent effectively confers personal jurisdiction over the corporation for the adjudication of all claims arising within the forum. Once it seemed equally clear that filing operated as consent to personal jurisdiction over claims arising elsewhere, if the sweep of the state consent statute was broad enough.[77] The position still seems to have wide acceptance,[78] but several courts have questioned whether this form of filing provides a basis for the adjudication of nonforum controversies against foreign corporations sufficient to satisfy due process.[79]

[3] Transient Jurisdiction

Transient jurisdiction is based on service within the forum of a nonresident defendant who happens to be passing through the state. In one well-known case, defendant was served while an aircraft was flying over the forum state.[80] Once questioned, the validity of transient jurisdiction now seems fairly secure.[81] We will return to the topics of statutory consent and transient jurisdiction when considering recent due process developments.[82]

§ 3.04 Timing the Jurisdictional Challenge

Two avenues have long been open to a defendant wishing to challenge the court's personal jurisdiction. First, defendant may use his challenge to keep the court from reaching the merits of the case. The defendant must participate in the lawsuit to use this option, called *direct attack*. Or the

---

However, interest in broader questions raised by *Carnival Cruise* is likely to continue. Mullenix, *Another Easy Case, Some More Bad Law: Carnival Cruise Lines and Contractional Personal Jurisdiction*, 27 Texas Int'l L. J. 323 (1992) (unfavorable;); Solimine, *Forum-Selection Clauses and the Privatization of Procedure*, 25 Cornell Int'l L. J. 51 (1992) (sympathetic). *See generally*, Fitzgerald, *A Comment on Forum Selection*, 30 Conn. L. Rev. 257 (1997) (discussing subsequent case developments).

[77] *Pennsylvania Fire Ins. Co. v. Gold Issue Mining & Milling Co.*, 243 U.S. 93 (1917) (opinion per Holmes, J.); *Smolik v. Philadelphia & Reading Coal & Iron Co.*, 222 F. 148 (1915) (opinion per L. Hand, J.). These decisions are criticized in Walker, *Foreign Corporation Laws: A Current Account*, 47 N.C.L. Rev. 733, 735–737 (1969).

[78] *Restatement (Second) of Conflicts*, note 48, *supra*, § 44 & comment (c); *Scoles & Hay*, note 73, *supra*, at 449. *But see* Hill, *Choice of Law and Jurisdiction in the Supreme Court*, 81 Colum. L. Rev. 960, 981-982 (1981).

[79] *In re Mid-Atlantic Toyota Antitrust Litig.*, 525 F. Supp. 1265 (D. Md. 1981); *Schreiber v. Allis-Chalmers Corp.*, 448 F. Supp. 1079 (D. Kan. 1978), *rev'd on other grounds*, 611 F.2d 790 (10th Cir. 1979); *Cedar Investment Co. v. Canal Ins. Co.*, 262 F. Supp. 337 (E.D. Mo. 1966). In *Bendix Autolite Corp. v. Midwestco Enterprises, Inc.*, 486 U.S. 888 (1988), the Supreme Court limited the authority of states to require foreign corporations to submit to jurisdiction in controversies arising outside the forum. However, the Court's constitutional ruling rested on commerce clause rather than due process grounds.

[80] *Grace v. MacArthur*, 170 F. Supp. 442 (E.D. Ark. 1959).

[81] *Burnham v. Superior Court*, 495 U.S. 604 (1990).

[82] *See* § 3.08[3][b], *infra*.

defendant may use his jurisdictional challenge later to argue that a judgment rendered against him is not entitled to enforcement. Defendant must avoid participating or making any kind of appearance in the case underlying judgment in order to use this option, called *collateral attack.*

[1] Direct Attack

Federal and state courts make ample opportunities available for a nonresident defendant to question personal jurisdiction prior to trial. Moreover, if the defendant is careful to observe the niceties of the local procedural system, he usually will be able to join with his jurisdictional attack other reasons why plaintiff's suit should be dismissed[83] and (if necessary) to resist the merits as well.[84] This is the great attraction of direct attack; it can be used with an array of other grounds for attacking plaintiff's case that are available in the initial forum.

The problem with direct attack is that it forces the defendant to give up part of the protection secured by due process.[85] He experiences the increased burden of defending in a distant and inconvenient forum as soon as he begins participating in the case. The difference in hardship between travelling to the forum in order to get the suit dismissed and remaining there to defend on the merits is one only of degree.

[2] Collateral Attack

Due process therefore requires that defendant have the second option of collateral attack. Collateral attack is founded on the principle that, if plaintiff's choice of forum is so unfair as to violate defendant's right to due process, defendant's complete refusal to participate there should not preclude him from later questioning personal jurisdiction.[86] The United States Supreme Court has noted that: "A defendant is always free to ignore the judicial proceedings, risk a default judgment, and then challenge that judgment on jurisdictional grounds in a collateral proceeding."[87]

For an illustration of jurisdictional challenge by collateral attack, recall the example presented at the beginning of this chapter.[88] New Yorker B takes no part in A's Hawaii lawsuit. A obtains a default judgment for $100,000 against B. Since B has no assets in Hawaii to satisfy the judgment, A must sue on the judgment in a court of B's home state of New York.[89]

---

[83] *See* § 3.03[2][b], *supra. See, e.g.,* Rule 12(b)(2).

[84] *See* § 3.03[2][c], *supra.*

[85] *See* § 3.01[2], *supra.*

[86] Under these circumstances, the "right to challenge jurisdiction makes" the defendant "an instrument for confining judicial authority to its prescribed limits." *Restatement (Second) of Judgments* § 65 comment (b) (1982).

[87] *Insurance Corp. of Ireland, Ltd. v. Compagnie des Bauxites de Guinee,* 456 U.S. 694, 706 (1982).

[88] § 3.01[1], *supra.*

[89] The process for suing on judgments is described in § 15.02, *infra.*

B defends against the judgment in New York court on the ground that the Hawaii court lacked personal jurisdiction. B wins, the court ruling (as it must on these facts) that the Hawaii judgment is not entitled to enforcement. If A wishes a judgment against B enforceable in New York, A will have to sue B all over again in New York.

The problems with the collateral attack are that it is often unavailable and, when available, often risky to use. Courts will usually entertain collateral attack for lack of personal jurisdiction only if the defendant took no part whatsoever in the initial proceeding. If the defendant participated in the first case without questioning the court's personal jurisdiction, he cured any defect by waiver.[90] If the defendant did challenge the court's personal jurisdiction in the first case, he is precluded from relitigating the question in the judgment-enforcement proceeding. The Supreme Court's decision in *Baldwin v. Iowa State Traveling Men's Association*[91] is a prominent example of the latter. Defendant appeared specially in the initial case and attacked the court's personal jurisdiction. When the trial court denied defendant's motion to dismiss, defendant withdrew from any further participation in the case and default judgment was thereafter entered against him. Defendant later attempted to renew his objection to personal jurisdiction by collaterally attacking the judgment. However, the Court refused to permit the challenge.

> The special appearance gives point to the fact that the respondent entered the Missouri court for the very purpose of litigating the question of jurisdiction over its person. It had the election not to appear at all. . . . It had also the right to appeal from the decision of the Missouri District Court. . . .[92]

The grounds upon which defendant can base a collateral attack are quite limited. Two which are clearly available — lack of notice[93] and the unenforceablity of the judgment where rendered[94] — require unusual supporting facts. Courts have occasionally permitted collateral attack on other grounds, but their availability in any given case is uncertain.[95] So,

---

[90] *See generally* § 3.03[2][a], *supra.*

[91] 283 U.S. 522 (1931).

[92] *Id.* at 525. *See also Underwriter's Nat'l Assurance Co. v. North Carolina Life & Accident & Health Ins. Guar. Ass'n,* 455 U.S. 691 (1982); *Stoll v. Gottleib,* 305 U.S. 165, 172 (1938).

[93] Defendants may assert denial of the notice and opportunity to be heard guaranteed by due process. *Restatement (Second) of Judgments,* note 86, *supra,* Chapter 2 at 18. *See generally* § 20, 4.01, *infra.*

[94] Defendants may invoke the sensible rule that a court need not enforce a foreign judgment if the rendering system would not. *See Ford v. Ford,* 371 U.S. 187 (1962) (full faith and credit does not obligate courts to give *greater* preclusive effect to a judgment than the rendering court). *See generally* § 15.11, *infra.*

[95] Cases like *Huntington v. Attrill,* 146 U.S. 657 (1892), raise the possibility that a judgment penal in character might be unenforceable, but "it is very possible that there is not much left of this penalty rule." Averill, *Choice-of-Law Problems Raised by Sister-State Judgments and the Full-Faith-and-Credit Mandate,* 64 Nw. U. L. Rev. 686, 694 (1970). Similarly, the modern trend is away from permitting collateral attacks on subject matter jurisdiction grounds. *See generally* Moore, *Collateral Attack on Subject Matter Jurisdiction: A Critique of the Restatement (Second) of Judgments,* 66 Cornell L. Rev. 534, 562 (1981).

if defendant's collateral attack for lack of personal jurisdiction fails, there will usually be nothing to shield him from an obligation to pay the default judgment.[96]

[3]   Considerations Influencing the Choice Between Direct and Collateral Attack

As the preceding discussion indicates, the moment of defendant's irrevocable decision whether to raise his personal jurisdiction challenge by direct or collateral attack usually comes when he decides whether to participate in the initial proceeding. The choice defendant should make turns on tactical considerations and will vary with the circumstances of each case. Here are some things to keep in mind.

[a]   The Relative Advantages of Direct Attack

While the defendant does not reside in the forum, he may have substantial assets there. Not only may this enhance plaintiff's case for personal jurisdiction,[97] it means that plaintiff can levy a default judgment against defendant's assets without ever leaving the forum state. It would be a tactical error for defendant to default under these circumstances. He would then be faced with the choice of travelling to the forum and collaterally attacking the judgment in the enforcement proceeding or remaining at home and losing his property. If defendant must eventually travel to the forum to make his jurisdictional challenge anyway, he is better off doing it earlier by direct attack. That way he can challenge other aspects of plaintiff's case, too.

Direct attack may be the more attractive option even when defendant has no assets in the forum state. The greater the recovery sought by plaintiff, the more defendant may put at risk by electing to default and raise his jurisdictional challenge through the collateral attack option. Similarly, the weaker plaintiff's case on the merits, the more problematical the collateral attack. Assume, for example, that the applicable statute of limitations has run on plaintiff's claim. For defendant to choose the option of collateral attack, his case against personal jurisdiction should be ironclad. Otherwise he should not imperil access to the statute of limitations defense by taking a default in the initial case.[98] Finally, if defendant's personal jurisdiction challenge is relatively weak, he should not hang a lot on it by opting for collateral attack.[99]

---

[96] Default judgments are judgments on the merits (*see* § 15.05, *infra*), and it is axiomatic that collateral attack may not be used to question the merits underlying a judgment. *E.g., Fauntleroy v. Lum*, 210 U.S. 230 (1908); *Milliken v. Meyer*, 311 U.S. 457 (1940). The only questions left for the judgment enforcement proceeding are: is defendant in fact the person named in the judgment, and how soon can defendant pay? *See* § 15.05, *infra*.

[97] *See* § 3.12[2] (aggregating defendant's contacts with the forum both related and unrelated to the controversy in order to satisfy due process), *infra*.

[98] Similarly, defendant may not wish to imperil grounds for pretrial dismissal (*e.g.,* improper joinder) which seem strong in a particular case, when he could join them to his jurisdictional challenge under the option of direct attack.

[99] *Cf.* § 3.06[2][a] (describing defendant's unfortunate choice of collateral attack in *McGee v. International Life Ins. Co.*, 355 U.S. 220 (1957)), *infra*.

[b] The Relative Advantages of Collateral Attack

Defendants often prefer to litigate at home.[100] There will be occasions when sound tactical considerations support this preference and defendant should opt for collateral rather than direct attack. One or more of the following may apply. Damages sought by plaintiff may be too inconsequential to justify the added expense and inconvenience of defending away from home. Plaintiff's case as to both liability and amount of damages may be clearcut and very strong, suggesting little advantage from an opportunity to contest the merits. Or defendant's case against personal jurisdiction may be so strong that it seems very likely that his collateral attack will succeed and that plaintiff will be forced to recommence suit in defendant's home state.[101]

Although it is not easy to quantify, there is a another factor which may favor the option of collateral attack: the home court advantage. Theoretically, there should be no advantage. The defendant's home forum is obliged to evaluate the sufficiency of the distant forum's personal jurisdiction under precisely the same legal criteria — due process sufficiency and compliance with the distant forum's local law[102] — which the distant forum would have used if defendant had elected the option of direct attack. The federal due process issue is, of course, the same for either court. And defendant's forum may not substitute for the jurisdictional framework of the judgment-rendering state a more limited jurisdictional law of its own.[103]

For all that, it may be reasonable to assume that judges are at times influenced by sympathetic impulses toward local litigants.[104] Given the complicated and fact-variable nature of current due process doctrine,[105] there are many personal jurisdiction cases over which reasonable judges might disagree. The uncertainty of United States Supreme Court review when state courts take liberties with federal law short of blatant error[106]

---

[100] Defendant's local attorney also might like to see the litigation unfold at home, since that is where the attorney can participate and collect a fee. It is, of course, unethical for the attorney to permit this factor to influence his advice to defendant concerning where to defend. *See, e.g.,* American Bar Ass'n, *Model Rules of Professional Conduct,* Rule 1.7 comment [5] (1983).

[101] On the other hand, the extreme case may work the other way. If plaintiff selects a forum clearly incapable of exercising personal jurisdiction over the defendant, and that forum is either a federal court or a state court using as its rule a recent version of Rule 11, defendant might be able to recover the costs of having the suit dismissed. On Rule 11, see generally § 8.05[2], *infra.* For a case imposing Rule 11 sanctions on plaintiff for selecting a forum clearly without personal jurisdiction, see *Phoenix Airway Inn Associates v. Essex Financial Serv., Inc.,* 741 F. Supp. 734 (N.D. Ill. 1990).

[102] *See* § 3.01[2][a], *supra.*

[103] *Adam v. Saenger,* 303 U.S. 59 (1938).

[104] Federal court diversity jurisdiction is built on this idea. Shreve, *Pragmatism Without Politics — A Half Measure of Authority for Jurisdictional Common Law,* 1991 BYU. L. Rev. 767, 787; Holt, *"To Establish Justice:" Politics, the Judiciary Act of 1789, and the Invention of Federal Courts,* 1989 Duke L.J. 1421, 1458. *See generally* § 5.04[1], *infra* (justification for diversity jurisdiction).

[105] *See* §§ 3.08-3.12, *infra.*

[106] *See* Stolz, *Federal Review of State Court Decisions of Federal Questions: The Need for Additional Appellate Capacity,* 64 Calif. L. Rev. 943 (1976).

creates a climate conducive to state court resolution of close questions in favor of local litigants.[107]

PART B
Personal Jurisdiction Over Nonresident Defendants — *Pennoyer* and the Liberating Effects of *International Shoe*

§ 3.05   Territorial Constraints On Personal Jurisdiction During the *Pennoyer* Era

[1]   Due Process Focussed on Forum State Boundaries

In 1877, the constitutional framework for regulating personal jurisdiction of state courts was uncertain.[108] Then, in *Pennoyer v. Neff*,[109] the United States Supreme Court laid the groundwork for a due process analysis restricting the effect of judgments. Perhaps the most enduring contribution of *Pennoyer* was the manner in which the case identified and resolved the tension between respect for judgments required under the Full Faith and Credit Clause of the Constitution and countervailing policies secured by the Due Process Clause.[110] It was clear after *Pennoyer* that, while the Full

---

[107] Conversely, plaintiff's home state court may be more inclined to resolve a close case in favor of personal jurisdiction — another reason for the defendant to litigate the question at his home, if possible.

[108] Ehrenzweig, *The Transient Rule of Personal Jurisdiction: The "Power" Myth and Forum Conveniens,* 65 Yale L. J. 289, 303, 308 (1956). See generally the historical studies by Professors Weinstein, Kogan and Trangsrud, note 110, *infra.*

[109] 95 U.S. 714 (1877). Overviews of *Pennoyer,* its precursors, and developments after the case, include Borchers, *Jurisdictional Pragmatism: International Shoe's Half-Buried Legacy,* 28 U. Cal. Davis L. Rev. 561 (1995); Oakley, *The Pitfalls of "Hint and Run" History: A Critique of Professor Borcher's "Limited View" of Pennoyer v. Neff,* 28 U. Cal. Davis L. Rev. 591 (1995); Borchers, *Pennoyer's Limited Legacy: A Reply to Professor Oakley,* 29 U. Cal. Davis L. Rev. 115 (1995); Hazard, *A General Theory of State-Court Jurisdiction,* 1965 Sup. Ct. Rev. 241; Kurland, *The Supreme Court, the Due Process Clause and the In Personam Jurisdiction of State Courts From Pennoyer to Denckla: A Review,* 25 U. Chi. L. Rev. 569 (1958). For an account of the principals in the case, see Perdue, *Sin, Scandal, and Substantive Due Process: Personal Jurisdiction and Pennoyer Reconsidered,* 62 Wash. L. Rev. 479 (1987).

[110] Since the adoption of the 14th Amendment to the Federal Constitution, the validity of such judgments may be directly questioned, and their enforcement in the State resisted, on the ground that proceedings in a court of justice to determine the personal rights and obligations of parties over whom the court has no jurisdiction, do not constitute due process of law.

95 U.S. at 733. Most see the *Pennoyer* case as a milestone, a view reflected in *Burnham v. Superior Court,* 495 U.S. 604 (1990).

There has been some interest in the legal history surrounding *Pennoyer.* Some contend that the requirement of in-state service on nonresident defendants existed well before *Pennoyer.* Weinstein, *The Early American Origins of Territoriality in Judicial Jurisdiction,* 37 St. Louis L. J. 1 (1992); Kogan, *A Neo-Federalist Tale of Personal Jurisdiction,* 63 S. Cal. L. Rev. 257 (1990). Another commentator has maintained that *Pennoyer* is best seen as a federal common law decision that later informed development of the due process test, accounting in large part for the persistence of territorial minimum contacts. Trangsrud, *The Federal Common Law of Jurisdiction,* 57 Geo. Wash. L. Rev. 849 (1989).

Faith and Credit Clause compelled interstate enforcement of state judgments, it did not purge those judgments of any problems they might have under the Due Process clause. Rather, the same federal due process grounds available to resist enforcement of a state judgment locally would also be available if enforcement was sought for that judgment in federal court or in the court of a sister state.

It remained for the Court to give content to its standard. The approach reflected in *Pennoyer* would dominate the law of personal jurisdiction for nearly seventy years. State courts could entertain suits against their citizens. They could also entertain suits against nonresidents so long as they consented or if they could be found and served within the forum state. But due process prevented suit against nonresident defendants who could only be found and served elsewhere.

Pennoyer involved two lawsuits. In the first, Mitchell obtained a default judgment in an Oregon state court against Neff for attorney's fees. Neff's Oregon property was seized and sold by the sheriff to Pennoyer in order to satisfy this judgment. In the second lawsuit, Neff sued Pennoyer in federal court for recovery of his property, and Pennoyer defended by claiming title under the sheriff's deed of sale.

Pennoyer's problem was that, when the Oregon court had entered a default judgment, Neff was neither a citizen of the forum nor had he been served there. Concluding that Oregon could not exercise personal jurisdiction over Neff, the United States Supreme Court invalidated the default judgment and resulting sheriff's sale. The Court held that if a state court attempts to exercise *in personam* jurisdiction over the defendant, that is, to adjudicate a case "that involves merely a determination of the personal liability of the defendant, he must be brought within its jurisdiction by service of process within the State, or his voluntary appearance."[111] The Court recognized that *quasi in rem* jurisdiction was an alternative when the defendant had property in the jurisdiction, but stressed that this form of territorial jurisdiction required a proper pre-judgment attachment of the property. Because Neff's property was first seized to enforce a judgment already obtained, *quasi in rem* jurisdiction was unavailable to save the Oregon judgment.

The boundaries of the forum state had transcendent importance in *Pennoyer*. "[E]very State possesses exclusive jurisdiction and sovereignty over persons and property within its territory,"[112] said the Court, but ". . . no State can exercise direct jurisdiction and authority over persons or property without its territory."[113] The Court drove the point home. "Process from the tribunals of one State cannot run into another State, and summon parties there domiciled to leave its territory and respond to proceedings against them."[114]

---

[111] 95 U.S. at 733.

[112] *Id.* at 722.

[113] *Id.*

[114] *Id.* at 727.

The Court's approach in *Pennoyer* was in tune with the times. Justice Holmes was to observe somewhat later that "[t]he foundation of jurisdiction is physical power. . . ."[115] He was speaking of a court's physical power over the defendant. While it was no longer necessary for the defendant to be under the court's physical control,[116] the power concept remained. Writing for the Court in *Pennoyer,* Justice Field was greatly influenced by the theories of Joseph Story.[117] Story urged a strong relationship between territory and legal authority. One of the ideas he advanced was that the geographical origin of case facts determined when or if legal authority materialized. This notion grew in appeal in the second half of the nineteenth century. However, belief in detached legal principles then began to lose ground in American legal thought to "a growing perception that legal principles were in fact nothing more than doctrines found in . . . local law. . . ."[118]

[2]　Restlessness Under *Pennoyer*

Pennoyer's power rationale became outmoded over time. It was a formalistic doctrine and as such reflected a view of the law as a "static and closed logical system."[119] Increasingly, *Pennoyer*'s analysis seemed inadequate either to explain the Court's rule or — perhaps more importantly — to accommodate the needs of an era of increasing interstate activity. Two developments put particular strain on the *Pennoyer* doctrine: the growth of national corporate activity and the advent of the motorcar.

Pennoyer made some provision for personal jurisdiction over foreign corporations and others who did business in the forum state but could not be found and served there. The Court made clear that states could require them to appoint an in-state agent to receive court process. Moreover, when

---

[115] *McDonald v. Mabee,* 243 U.S. 90, 91 (1917).

[116] In earlier times, "the power of a court to enter a judgment was dependent upon the actual physical presence of the defendant before the court." Kalo, *Jurisdiction As an Evolutionary Process: The Development of Quasi In Rem and In Personam Principles,* 1978 Duke L.J. 1147, 1148.

[117] *Hazard,* note 109, *supra,* at 262. *See generally* J. Story, *Commentaries on the Conflict of Laws* (1834).

[118] T. Freyer, *Harmony & Dissonance: The Swift & Erie Cases in American Federalism* 74 (1981). As Holmes said of the common law, it "is not a brooding omnipresence in the sky but the articulate voice of some sovereign. . . ." *Southern Pacific Co. v. Jensen,* 244 U.S. 205, 222 (1917) (Holmes, J., dissenting).

[119] Summers, *Pragmatic Instrumentalism in Twentieth Century American Legal Thought—A Synthesis and Critique of Our Dominant General Theory About Law and its Use,* 66 Cornell L. Rev. 861, 867 n.4 (1981). *Cf.* Vandevelde, *Ideology, Due Process and Civil Procedure,* 67 St. John's L. Rev. 265, 276 (1993) ("The law of personal jurisdiction articulated in *Pennoyer* . . . was consistent with the formalist ideology of the late nineteenth century conservatives.").

Restlessness under *Pennoyer* represented only part of a larger movement away from procedural formalism and toward a functional or instrumental understanding of civil procedure. The trend, which continues, is described in Shreve, *Pragmatism Without Politics — A Half Measure of Authority for Jurisdictional Common Law,* 1991 BYU L. Rev. 767, 793-96; Bone, *Mapping the Boundaries of a Dispute: Conceptions of Ideal Lawsuit Structure From the Field Code to the Federal Rules,* 89 Colum. L. Rev. 1 (1989).

these potential defendants refused to appoint someone, states appeared to have authority to designate a state official to accept service for them.[120]

Unfortunately, the Supreme Court was never able to develop an intelligible standard for determining when the forum involvement of the out-of-state defendant was sufficient to justify substituted service on a state officer. The Court invoked concepts of implied consent[121] and presence,[122] each leading to an inquiry about the amount of business done by the defendant in the forum state.[123] The results were arbitrary and unsatisfactory.[124] Ambiguity inherent in the nature of corporate identity compounded the problem. Legal confections, corporations did not literally exist anywhere. Thus, it was particularly difficult to subject them to *Pennoyer*'s legal metaphor based on geographical whereabouts and physical movement.[125]

Professor Hazard observed that *Pennoyer* "had a less secure place in particular application than it did in general theory."[126] The famous accident case, *Hess v. Pawloski,*[127] illustrates this point. Hess, a Pennsylvanian, struck and injured Pawloski while driving in Massachusetts. After Hess returned to Pennsylvania, Pawloski filed suit against him in a Massachusetts court. It was impossible to serve Hess personally in Massachusetts. Pawloski instead used a Massachusetts statute declaring that, by using Massachusetts highways, nonresident motorists constructively appointed a state officer to accept in-state service for them in Massachusetts accident cases. Hess challenged the appointment as fictitious, which, of course, it was. The Supreme Court nonetheless upheld personal jurisdiction.

The *Hess* Court acknowledged *Pennoyer*'s requirement that "actual service within the state" be made on the defendant "or upon someone authorized to accept service for him."[128] It also noted a previous case in which it had invalidated as fictitious an analogous use of the concept of

---

[120] *Pennoyer,* 95 U.S. at 735. "States that had no statutes of this sort soon enacted them." *Hazard,* note 109, *supra,* at 272. This arrangement honored, at least technically, *Pennoyer*'s limitation that service of process be completed within the forum state. *See* note 114 and related text, *supra.*

[121] *E.g., Simon v. Southern Ry.,* 236 U.S. 115 (1915).

[122] *E.g., International Harvester Co. v. Kentucky,* 234 U.S. 579 (1914).

[123] *E.g., St. Louis Southwestern Ry. v. Alexander,* 227 U.S. 218 (1913). *See Kurland,* note 109, *supra,* at 577-586; Scott, *Jurisdiction Over Nonresidents Doing Business Within a State,* 32 Harv. L. Rev. 871 (1919); Note, *Recent Interpretations of "Doing Business" Statutes,* 44 Iowa L. Rev. 345 (1959).

[124] *See Kurland,* note 109, *supra,* at 584-586; *Developments in the Law—State-Court Jurisdiction,* 73 Harv. L. Rev. 909, 919-923 (1960).

[125] *Developments,* note 124, *supra,* at 919. *See generally* Note, *"Doing Business": Defining State Control Over Foreign Corporations,* 32 Vand. L. Rev. 1105 (1979); Note, *Jurisdiction Over Foreign Corporations—An Analysis of Due Process,* 104 U. Pa. L. Rev. 381 (1955).

[126] *Hazard,* note 109, *supra,* at 272.

[127] 274 U.S. 352 (1927). *See generally* Scott, *Jurisdiction Over Nonresident Motorists,* 39 Harv. L. Rev. 563 (1926).

[128] 274 U.S. at 355.

implied consent.[129] However, it upheld jurisdiction under the statute because of the strong interest Massachusetts had in highway safety:

> Motor vehicles are dangerous machines; and, even when skillfully and carefully operated, their use is attended by serious dangers to persons and property. In the public interest the State may make and enforce regulations reasonably calculated to promote care on the part of all, residents and non-residents alike, who use its highways. The measure in question operates to require a non-resident to answer for his conduct in the State where arise causes of action alleged against him, as well as to provide for a claimant a convenient method by which he may sue to enforce his rights.[130]

Most commentators would agree that the Court reached the best result in *Hess* and, in the language above, offered the best of reasons. It is impossible, however, to square this rationale for personal jurisdiction with *Pennoyer*. However desirable it might be for Massachusetts courts to have an opportunity to adjudicate Pawloski's claim, this has nothing to do with whether Hess was served there, or whether he may be regarded as having consented to suit through appointment of an in-state agent.

This dichotomy reveals the legal climate in which *Hess* was decided. Lower courts and the United States Supreme Court were growing disenchanted with an interpretation of due process which denied states the opportunity to address by judicial proceedings conduct occurring within their borders. The language from *Hess* quoted above says as much.[131] But there was little room in the approach of *Pennoyer* for this kind of sentiment. *Hess* reveals the schizophrenia eventually created in the law of personal jurisdiction by *Pennoyer*'s territorial limitations.

The weight upon the old rule eventually became intolerable. As a result, the Court quietly overthrew the restraints of *Pennoyer* in *International Shoe Co. v. Washington*.[132]

---

[129] *Id.* (*citing Flexner v. Farson*, 248 U.S. 289 (1919)).

[130] *Id.* at 356.

[131] *Henry L. Doherty & Co. v. Goodman*, 294 U.S. 623 (1935), provides another example. The Court permitted personal jurisdiction over a nonresident individual who had operated a securities business in the forum state. Plaintiff had invoked an implied consent statute which was about as tenuous as the one in *Hess*. As in *Hess*, the Court cited but refused to follow *Flexner*. *See* note 129 and related text, *supra*. The real reason for the decision in *Doherty* seems to be the Court's observation that "Iowa treats the business of dealing in corporate securities as exceptional, and subjects it to special regulation." 294 U.S. at 627. *See* Reese & Galston, *Doing an Act or Causing Consequences as Bases of Judicial Jurisdiction*, 44 Iowa L. Rev. 249 (1959).

[132] 326 U.S. 310 (1945).

§ 3.06 *International Shoe* and the Beginning Of The Modern Era

[1] *International Shoe Co. v. Washington*[133]

[a] Due Process and the Reasonableness of Plaintiff's Forum Choice

The International Shoe Company was incorporated in Delaware and had its principal place of business in Missouri. International Shoe employed Washington residents to solicit orders there. They reported directly to the company's main office in St. Louis. Washington sued International Shoe to collect unemployment compensation tax upon salaries defendant had paid to its Washington employees. International Shoe challenged personal jurisdiction in Washington. The Washington Supreme Court ruled that personal jurisdiction existed over the defendant. It relied on United States Supreme Court doctrine[134] to conclude that International Shoe's Washington activities constituted a sufficient in-state presence to make it amenable to suit.

The United States Supreme Court affirmed, but on significantly broader grounds. Noting that "the corporate personality is a fiction," the Court proceeded to divest corporate "presence" of its special significance:

> To say that the corporation is so far "present" [in a state] as to satisfy due process requirements . . . is to beg the question to be decided. For the terms "present" or "presence" are used merely to symbolize those activities of the corporation's agent within the state which courts will deem to be sufficient to satisfy the demands of due process. . . . Those demands may be met by such contacts of the corporation with the state of the forum as make it reasonable, in the context of our federal system of government, to require the corporation to defend the particular suit which is brought there.[135]

This language from the Court's opinion is illuminating in several respects. First, it reminds the reader why due process protection is necessary. Without it, plaintiff can "require" the defendant "to defend the particular suit" wherever plaintiff chooses to bring it. The guaranty of due process permits defendant to minimize the ordeal created by plaintiff's forum choice by giving defendant a means of attacking it directly at the outset of suit.[136] Due process also provides defendant an alternative by tempering the effect of full faith and credit, permitting defendant to ignore plaintiff's case altogether and to collaterally attack the resulting default judgment if plaintiff tries to enforce it in defendant's home state.[137] Thus, plaintiff's

---

[133] 326 U.S. 310 (1945). *See generally, Symposium—Fifty Years of International Shoe: The Past and Future of Personal Jurisdiction,* 28 U. Cal. Davis L. Rev. 513 (1995).

[134] For discussion of the doctrine and illustrative cases, see § 3.05, *supra.*

[135] 326 U.S. at 316-317.

[136] For a discussion of the dynamics of direct attack, *see* § 3.04[1], *supra.*

[137] *E.g., Hanson v. Denckla,* 357 U.S. 235, 255 (1958) ("Delaware is under no obligation

power to require defendant to participate where plaintiff chooses is limited by the due process constraints on the scope of personal jurisdiction.[138]

Second, the above passage from *International Shoe* indicates that due process will limit plaintiff to "reasonable" choices and tells us that an important focus for determining jurisdiction will be on the "contacts" the corporate defendant has with the forum state. This is a pragmatic, fact-centered approach to setting limits on personal jurisdiction.[139] It differs from the formalistic approach of *Pennoyer* and lacks *Pennoyer*'s preoccupation with whether service of process has been completed within the territorial limits of the forum. Most important, the Supreme Court approved personal jurisdiction in *International Shoe* based upon service of process outside Washington's boundaries.[140]

For a nonresident defendant who cannot be found and served within the forum state, *Shoe* announced that good personal jurisdiction requires that the defendant "have certain *minimum contacts* with [the forum], such that the maintenance of the suit does not offend 'traditional notions of fair play and substantial justice.' "[141]

[b]　The Advent of Minimum Contacts

International Shoe's "minimum contacts" test has dominated the law of personal jurisdiction.[142] Absent consent, waiver, or suit in defendant's home state,[143] minimum contacts between the forum and the defendant are necessary to make plaintiff's choice a constitutional forum.[144] When plaintiff selects defendant's home forum, the reasonableness of the choice

---

to give full faith and credit to a Florida judgment invalid in Florida because offensive to the Due Process Clause of the Fourteenth Amendment"). For a discussion of collateral attack and of how direct and collateral attack options combine to secure due process protection, *see* § 3.04[2], *supra*.

[138] *See Ruhrgas AG v. Marathon Oil Co.,* 526 U.S. 574, 584 (1999).

[139] The Court notes this: "It is evident that the criteria by which we mark the boundary line between those activities which justify the subjection of a corporation to suit, and those which do not, cannot be simply mechanical or quantitative." *International Shoe,* 326 U.S. at 319.

[140] "In suggesting that service outside of the state without more would suffice, the opinion offered the states an opportunity to dispense with the cumbersome procedure of service on a state official plus extraterritorial notice, the method suggested in *Pennoyer* and utilized extensively by the states since." Kurland, *The Supreme Court, the Due Process Clause and the In Personam Jurisdiction of State Courts From Pennoyer to Denckla: A Review,* 25 U. Chi. L. Rev. 569, 590 (1958). *See also* Hay, *Refining Personal Jurisdiction in the United States,* 35 Int'l & Comp. L.Q. 32, 61 (1986) (observing that the case "freed American jurisdictional thinking from the territorial strait jacket of the historical requirement that the defendant be present in the forum at the time of service.").

[141] 326 U.S. at 316, *quoting Milliken v. Meyer,* 311 U.S. 457, 463 (1940) (emphasis added).

[142] *E.g., Burger King, Inc. v. Rudzewicz,* 471 U.S. 462, 474 (1985) ("[T]he constitutional touchstone remains whether the defendant purposefully established "minimum contacts' in the forum State" [*citing International Shoe*]). *International Shoe* also provides material for a due process hurdle beyond minimum contacts. *See* note 159 and accompanying text, *infra*.

[143] *See* § 3.03 (traditionally accepted forms of personal jurisdiction), *supra*.

[144] On how contacts function in the test, *see* § 3.09, *infra*.

will usually be so obvious as to gainsay the minimum contacts question.[145] But when and how is the minimum contacts test satisfied when plaintiff selects another forum?

For several reasons, *International Shoe* does not provide a complete answer to this question. To an extent, the problem is inherent in the approach announced by the case. Fairness is a vague concept. It is one thing to declare that due process permits jurisdiction over nonresident defendants when fair under the circumstances. It is another to sift the facts of cases in an effort to apply the standard.[146] Beyond that, the Court's analysis in *International Shoe* is blurred by reluctance to break sharply with prior decisions.[147] Finally, the facts of the case were not especially demanding. Washington state courts probably would have had personal jurisdiction over the case even under the Court's earlier, more restrictive case law.[148]

The broader jurisdictional implications of the minimum contacts test would become clear only in later cases. However, the Court's opinion did offer principles which were to provide much of the foundation for modern doctrine. To begin with, a geographical outlook concerning jurisdictional facts would be as important under *International Shoe* as it was under *Pennoyer*. The former simply attached clearer, more decisive importance to the location within the forum of facts about the controversy and about the defendant, and far less importance to whether service of process was completed there.[149]

International Shoe identified two types of contacts a nonresident defendant could have with the forum. Either, the case suggested, could support personal jurisdiction if sufficiently developed. The first type consisted of defendant's activity within the forum state related to the controversy. The second consisted of defendant's unrelated contacts.[150] The Court's recognition of the latter meant that, even when the facts of the controversy arose outside the forum, personal jurisdiction might be possible if a sufficient amount of the nonresident defendant's other activities occurred within the forum. "[T]here have been instances," observed the Court, "in which the continuous corporate operations within a state were thought so substantial

---

[145] *See* § 3.08[3][a] (a comparison of jurisdiction based on citizenship with jurisdiction over nonresident defendants supported by minimum contacts), *infra*.

[146] For discussion of how the fact-sensitive nature of the minimum contacts approach produces inherent uncertainties, see § 3.09[3], *infra*.

[147] "That the Supreme Court was cautious in developing the new approach and was unwilling to cut off precedent directly in *International Shoe* is not surprising. The history of jurisdiction has been one of gradual evolution, of new ideas growing out of old, until the new completely supplants the old." Kalo, *Jurisdiction as an Evolutionary Process: the Development of Quasi In Rem and In Personam Principles,* 1978 Duke L.J. 1147, 1184 n.234.

[148] *Kurland,* note 140, *supra,* at 592.

[149] While the case established the principle that personal jurisdiction would not necessarily require service of process to be completed within the forum, it was silent concerning the converse — whether service on the defendant within the forum would invariably create good personal jurisdiction. For recent developments on this issue, see § 3.08[3][b], *infra*.

[150] In the subsequent refinement of minimum contacts doctrine, these were to provide support for *specific* and *general jurisdiction,* respectively. *See* § 3.09[2], *infra*.

and of such a nature as to justify suit against it on causes of action arising from dealings entirely distinct from those activities."[151] The Court did not clearly indicate when either type alone would be sufficient to provide minimum contacts. Both types may have been present in *International Shoe*. The company's general activities in the forum had been "systematic and continuous."[152] At the same time, "[t]he obligation . . . sued upon arose out of [the] very activities" of the defendant.[153]

[c] Justifications for *Shoe*'s Extension of Personal Jurisdiction

The Supreme Court laid down three justifications for the Washington court's personal jurisdiction over International Shoe. Each provided a reason for attaching importance to defendant's contact with the forum; each would figure significantly in later cases.

First, the Court suggested that, given sufficient contacts, it would be unreasonable for the defendant to object to amenability to suit as less than a fair exchange for the advantages it received from the forum.

[T]o the extent that a corporation exercises the privilege of conducting activities within a state, it enjoys the benefits and protection of the laws of that state. The exercise of that privilege may give rise to obligations. . . .[154]

This suggests an analogy to forum citizenship as a basis for personal jurisdiction.[155] Granted, the nonresident defendant's enjoyment of forum benefits and protection is not likely to be as pervasive as that of a forum citizen, and thus the case for personal jurisdiction over the former may not be as easy to establish. However, the process of reasoning toward a conclusion of personal jurisdiction is much the same.[156] Under this

---

[151] 326 U.S. at 318.

[152] *Id.* at 320.

[153] *Id.*

[154] *Id.* at 319. This line of argument casts the nonresident defendant and the forum state into a relationship similar to that of contracting parties. Defendant thus bargains with the state by accepting benefits in return for consent to jurisdiction. "Consent is a seductive notion because it seems to explain obligations in terms of the obligated individual's voluntary choice." Brilmayer, *Consent, Contract and Territory*, 74 Minn. L. Rev. 1, 21 (1989). Note, however, that such jurisdiction does not require defendant's knowing and actual consent. The notion of consent or something like it continues to play a very important rule in *Shoe* doctrine. *See* § 3.10[2], *infra*. Yet consent has less descriptive power in this context than where plaintiff has expressly contracted for defendant's consent to jurisdiction. Brilmayer, *id.* at 24-30. This is why consent-to-jurisdiction clauses in contracts pose little analytic difficulty and are freely enforced. *See* § 3.03[2][d], *supra*.

[155] On forum citizenship as a basis for personal jurisdiction, *see* § 3.03[1], *supra*. It is significant that *International Shoe* describes its due process standard by quoting from *Milliken v. Meyer*, note 141 and related text, *supra*, an earlier case where the Supreme Court had confirmed a forum state's jurisdictional power over its own citizen.

[156] *Compare* the language from *International Shoe*, text accompanying note 154, *supra*, *with* the following from *Milliken v. Meyer*, 311 U.S. 457 (1940): "Domicile in the state is alone sufficient to bring an absent defendant within the reach of the state's jurisdiction. . . ." *Id.* at 462. "The state which accords him privileges and affords protection to him and his property by virtue of his domicile may also exact reciprocal duties." *Id.* at 463.

rationale, a nonresident defendant's contacts with the forum (understood as advantages conferred by the forum state) could be so extensive as to support personal jurisdiction for causes of action arising elsewhere.[157]

Second, personal jurisdiction will be possible even when advantages conferred on a nonresident defendant by the forum are so small as to strain the idea of amenability to suit as a fair exchange, so long as defendant acted within the forum to cause the controversy. The forum is entitled to exercise jurisdiction in such cases in furtherance of a regulatory interest. The passage from *International Shoe* quoted above continues:

> . . . so far as those obligations arise out of or are connected with the activities within the state, a procedure which requires the corporation to respond to a suit brought to enforce them can, in most instances, hardly be said to be undue.[158]

Finally, the Court suggested another way of evaluating defendant's relationship with the forum. The burden in having to defend away from home will vary depending, among other things, on how unfamiliar or inconvenient the forum really is to the defendant. The Court thus observed that "[a]n estimate of the inconveniences which would result to the corporation from a trial away from its home or principal place of business is relevant" to an examination of defendant's contacts with the forum.[159] It may again be useful to make an analogy between personal jurisdiction over nonresidents and the same over forum citizens. A further reason supporting near automatic jurisdiction over the latter is that citizens usually experience the least disorientation and inconvenience when defending at home.[160] Significant contacts between the nonresident defendant and the forum may suggest that the place for suit selected by plaintiff bears at least some resemblance to defendant's home turf. This may be true even if defendant's contacts with the forum are unrelated to the controversy.[161]

---

157 The Supreme Court confirmed this possibility in *Perkins v. Benguet Consol. Mining Co.,* 342 U.S. 437 (1952), *discussed in* § 3.06[2][b], *infra.*

158 326 U.S. at 319. The Court gave this regulatory rationale greater attention later in *McGee v. International Life Ins. Co.* , 355 U.S. 220 (1957), *discussed in* § 3.06[2][a], *infra.* The rationale is of major contemporary significance. *See* § 3.10[1], *infra.*

159 326 U.S. at 317, *citing Hutchinson v. Chase & Gilbert,* 45 F.2d 139, 141 (2nd Cir. 1930). This concern may now stand apart from the minimum contacts test. *Asahi Metal Ind. Co., Ltd. v. Superior Court,* 480 U.S. 102 (1987), indicates that a forum may have minimum contacts with a nonresident defendant yet be so inconvenient that due process prevents exercise of personal jurisdiction. Five justices in *Asahi* suggested minimum contacts between the forum and the defendant may have existed. But they joined three other members of the Court to conclude that forcing a Japanese litigant to defend in California against a Taiwanese claimant would (in language drawn from *International Shoe*) violate "traditional notions of fair play and substantial justice." *Id.* at 113. On *Asahi* see generally § 3.12[2], *infra.*

160 *See* § 3.03 *supra.*

161 "If the primary purpose of jurisdiction is to protect defendants from unfair litigation burdens, it is probably not oppressive for a defendant to be sued in a state where the defendant conducts highly regularized activities, even if those activities are unrelated to the plaintiff's particular claim." Waits, *Values, Intuitions, and Opinion Writing: The Judicial Process and State Court Jurisdiction,* 1983 Ill. L. Rev. 917, 940. *Accord,* R. Leflar, et al., *American Conflicts Law* § 22 (4th ed. 1986).

[2] Jurisdictional Sufficiency Elaborated — Two Significant Early Cases

Two succeeding decisions in which the Supreme Court attempted to sort out the implications of the *International Shoe* test contributed enough to current law to merit discussion.

[a] *McGee v. International Life Ins. Co.* [162]

The Court noted in *International Shoe* that a corporation's "single or isolated items of activities in a state . . . are not enough to subject it to suit on causes of action *unconnected* with the activities there."[163] At the same time, the case appeared to place a premium on the fact that there defendant's activities generating the controversy arose in the forum state.[164] What would happen if a foreign corporation's contacts with the forum state were "single or isolated," but the case arose out of those very contacts? The Supreme Court did not have to answer the question, because International Shoe's overall contacts with Washington were "systematic and continuous."[165] The Court subsequently answered the question in *McGee* and, in so doing, realized some of the more liberating implications of the minimum contacts approach.

McGee, as the beneficiary of her deceased son's life insurance policy, sued defendant International Life in California. Defendant was served by mail in Texas, its corporate home. International Life declined to appear in the case and plaintiff obtained a default judgment. Plaintiff took the California judgment to Texas and attempted to enforce it. International Life collaterally attacked the judgment, arguing that California did not have personal jurisdiction. Texas courts agreed. The United States Supreme Court did not question defendant's right to argue that the California court lacked jurisdiction in an effort to resist the California judgment,[166] but found the argument without merit and reversed.

The facts revealed that defendant conducted virtually no business in California. Decedent's policy had been the only one in force there. It would be hard to imagine a clearer example of "single or isolated" corporate activity in the forum state. The Court nonetheless held that California had validly exercised jurisdiction over International Life, demonstrating that

---

[162] 355 U.S. 220 (1957).

[163] 326 U.S. at 317 (emphasis added).

[164] *See* note 153 and related text, *supra.*

[165] *See* note 152 and related text, *supra.*

[166] Defendant was able to raise the personal jurisdiction issue only because it had not taken any part in the California proceeding. But, while defaulting in California preserved defendant's opportunity to litigate the personal jurisdiction question later in Texas, it also made everything turn on winning the issue. Because International Life lost, it was never able to present the substantial case it apparently had on the merits — that the policy was inapplicable because the insured died by suicide. 355 U.S. at 223. Such are the risks of favoring collateral over direct attack as a means of raising personal jurisdiction issues. For a discussion of direct and collateral attack on personal jurisdiction and considerations in choosing between the two, *see* § 3.04, *supra.*

minimum contacts can be minimal indeed — so long as they are sufficiently related to the lawsuit:

> [W]e think it apparent that the Due Process Clause did not preclude the California court from entering a judgment binding on respondent. It is sufficient for purposes of due process that the suit was based on a contract which had substantial connection with that State. . . . The contract was delivered in California, the premiums were mailed from there and the insured was a resident of that State when he died.[167]

The Court explained why it mattered that defendant's forum contacts were related to the controversy. "It cannot be denied that California has a manifest interest in providing effective means of redress for its residents when their insurers refuse to pay claims,"[168] it said. "These residents would be at a severe disadvantage if they were forced to follow the insurance company to a distant State in order to hold it legally accountable."[169] And the Court suggested that, on the whole, California might have been the most logical place to try the case.[170] There might have been some inconvenience for International Life, "but certainly nothing which amounts to a denial of due process."[171]

The most enduring aspect of *McGee* is that it established beyond question the forum's authority to exercise jurisdiction over nonresident defendants in lawsuits resulting from their forum-directed activities.[172] On the other

---

[167] 355 U.S. at 223.

[168] *Id.*

[169] *Id.*

[170] "Often the crucial witnesses — as here on the company's defense of suicide — will be found in the insured's locality." *Id.*

[171] *Id.* at 224. *Travelers Health Ass'n v. Virginia,* 339 U.S. 643 (1950), foreshadowed the Supreme Court's approach in *McGee.* Defendant Travelers sold insurance in Virginia without registering as required by state law. Virginia sued for an order forbidding Travelers from doing business in the state. Travelers was served by mail in its home state of Nebraska. The corporation appeared specially to challenge jurisdiction over it in Virginia. Virginia's highest court upheld personal jurisdiction over Travelers and the United States Supreme Court affirmed, holding the result to be "consistent with fair play and substantial justice," and . . . "not offensive to the Due Process Clause." 339 U.S. at 649. In *Travelers,* the Court gave a clearer indication than it had in *International Shoe* of a policy supporting longer jurisdictional reach of courts: the legitimate need of a forum to regulate through judicial proceedings activities occurring within its borders. The "state has a legitimate interest," said the Court, "in all insurance policies protecting its residents against risks," *id.* at 647, an interest sufficient to support personal jurisdiction even if the defendant cannot be found and served within the forum state. In addition, *Travelers* expanded upon *International Shoe*'s suggestion, note 159 and related text, *supra,* that courts address the actual degree of inconvenience to the defendant when evaluating minimum contacts in each case. The Court indicated that an examination of both sides of the convenience question might be in order, and that the inquiry might be expanded to take into account reasons why the present forum might be more convenient to plaintiff. *Id.* at 649.

[172] When, as in *McGee,* the cause of action arises entirely from activities of the defendant directed at the forum, it is universally accepted that due process does not prevent the forum from exercising jurisdiction. *Cf. Restatement (Second) of Conflicts* § 35 comment e (1971) ("It is always reasonable for a State to exercise judicial jurisdiction over an individual as to causes of action arising from business done by him within its territory."). *See, e.g., Burger King Corp. v. Rudzewicz,* 471 U.S. 462, 473 (1985) (applying the principle and citing *McGee*). *See generally* § 3.10[3] (discussing *Burger King*), *infra.*

hand, it is difficult to say how much reliance can safely be placed on some of the more freewheeling arguments made by the Court in support of its conclusion. The Supreme Court has neither questioned *McGee,* nor been reluctant to cite the case. Yet it may be true that Supreme Court decisions on personal jurisdiction represent more a spectrum of opinion than a single point of view. If this is so, then *McGee* exists at one end of the spectrum.[173] As Professor Weintraub observed, the case "was the high-water mark of personal jurisdiction."[174]

[b] *Perkins v. Benguet Consolidated Mining Co.*[175]

International Shoe noted the possibility that "continuous corporate operations within a state" could be "so substantial and of such a nature as to justify suit against it on causes of action arising from dealings entirely distinct from those activities."[176] *Perkins* furnished an example five years later.

Benguet was a Philippine corporation whose operations there were disrupted by World War II. Benguet's president moved to an office in Ohio and transacted "a continuous and systematic, but limited, part of its general business" in Ohio.[177] Perkins sued Benguet in Ohio over corporate obligations arising outside the forum. Believing that due process prevented personal jurisdiction over Benguet, the Ohio courts refused to hear the case. The United States Supreme Court reversed.

The Court considered whether Ohio was under an obligation to provide Perkins with a forum for suit against Benguet and concluded that it was not. It also considered

> whether as a matter of federal due process, the business done in Ohio by the respondent mining company was sufficiently substantial and of such a nature as to *permit* Ohio to entertain a cause of action against a foreign corporation, where the cause of action arose from activities entirely distinct from its activities in Ohio.[178]

Invoking *International Shoe,* the Supreme Court set out to answer the question by examining Benguet's unrelated contacts with the forum. Noting that the corporate president "carried on in Ohio a continuous and systematic supervision of the necessarily limited wartime activities of the

---

[173] *E.g.,* compare the *McGee* Court's recognition of the forum's interest in providing a means for its citizens to sue and of the significance of the forum as a generally convenient place for suit with the Court's rejection of the same concerns in *Hanson v. Denckla,* 357 U.S. 235 (1958). It may be possible to reconcile the results in the two cases, *see* § 3.07[2], *infra,* yet they do seem to reflect differences in attitude.

[174] Weintraub, *Due Process Limitations on the Personal Jurisdiction of State Courts: Time for Change,* 63 Or. L. Rev. 485, 489 (1984).

[175] 342 U.S. 437 (1952).

[176] 326 U.S. at 318.

[177] 342 U.S. at 438.

[178] *Id.* at 447 (emphasis in original).

company,"[179] the Court concluded that due process would permit Ohio courts to exercise personal jurisdiction over Perkins' claim.

Some commentators have read *Perkins* to suggest the possibility of personal jurisdiction wherever a corporation carries on activities capable of the "continuous and systematic" description.[180] Others argue a narrower reading of the case, pointing to exceptional circumstances which made Ohio the most feasible (perhaps the only) forum in which Perkins could have sued Benguet.[181] It is at least true that, like the facts of *International Shoe,* the facts of *Perkins* were so sympathetic to a finding of jurisdiction that the Court was not driven to explain what might satisfy due process in closer, more difficult cases.

At the same time, *Perkins* continues to figure importantly in the law of personal jurisdiction. It is one of only two cases in which the United States Supreme Court has applied *International Shoe* to chart the boundaries of personal jurisdiction when no contacts between the forum and the defendant could be funnelled through the controversy. In the second case,[182] the Court was careful not to disturb *Perkins'* authority.

§ 3.07 Personal Jurisdiction's Green-light Period — Developments Until 1977

Once state courts and legislatures were able to absorb the implications of *International Shoe* and succeeding cases, the results were dramatic. State legislatures greatly expanded the extraterritorial jurisdiction of their courts by equipping them with long-arm statutes.[183] Plaintiffs took advantage of the statutes to bring about a significant rise in interstate litigation.

Clearly, due process still imposed some limits on the extraterritorial jurisdiction of state courts. For over thirty years, however, the Supreme Court was relatively silent in declaring what those limits were. From the time of the Court's *International Shoe* decision until it decided *Shaffer v. Heitner*[184] in 1977, the Supreme Court handed down only one decision

---

[179] *Id.* at 448.

> He kept there office files . . . carried on there correspondence . . . drew and distributed there salary checks maintained in Clermont County, Ohio, two active bank accounts carrying substantial balances of company funds. . . . Several directors' meetings were held at his office or home in Clermont County. From that office he supervised policies dealing with the rehabilitation of the corporation's properties in the Philippines and he dispatched funds to cover purchases of machinery for such rehabilitation.

Id.

[180] *See* the authorities cited in note 161, *supra.*

[181] Von Mehren & Trautman, *Jurisdiction to Adjudicate: A Suggested Analysis,* 79 Harv. L. Rev. 1121, 1144 (1966); Note, *Developments in the Law—State Court Jurisdiction,* 73 Harv. L. Rev. 909, 932 (1960); *Restatement (Second) of Judgments* introduction at 25 (1982).

[182] *Helicopteros Nacionales de Columbia, S.A. v. Hall,* 466 U.S. 408 (1984), *discussed in* § 3.11[1], *infra.*

[183] *See* § 3.07[1], *infra.*

[184] 433 U.S. 186 (1977).

negating in general terms an attempted exercise of extraterritorial jurisdiction.

The case was *Hanson v. Denckla.* [185] *Hanson* was, however, a puzzling and rather unpopular decision. The Supreme Court all but abandoned it for twenty years. Meanwhile state and lower federal courts were left to grapple on their own with difficult questions in applying *International Shoe.* Some courts restrained themselves. Others did not. This was the great, freewheeling period of extraterritorial jurisdiction.

[1]   The Proliferation of State Long-Arm Statutes

International Shoe and succeeding cases [186] made clear that states could in appropriate cases exercise personal jurisdiction when service of process could not be completed in the forum state. But the Supreme Court's decisions alone did not give plaintiffs access to extraterritorial personal jurisdiction. States were under no obligation to endow their courts with such authority. [187] Even when they created extraterritorial jurisdiction, they were free to offer plaintiffs less than the full amount permitted by due process. [188]

Many rules of personal jurisdiction — for example, jurisdiction by domicile or actual consent [189] — had their origins in common law. [190] But personal jurisdiction in some types of cases was unknown under the common law. These were more likely to involve nonresident defendants, such as jurisdiction based on doing business in the forum [191] or on defendant's acts done or consequences caused in the forum. [192] Judicial authority in such cases traditionally derived from statutes. [193] Thus it was necessary for state legislatures to take the initiative if their courts were to capitalize on new opportunities for personal jurisdiction. [194]

---

[185] 357 U.S. 235 (1958). *See* § 3.07[2], *infra.*

[186] For a discussion of *International Shoe* and the Court's subsequent decisions in *McGee* and *Perkins,* see § 3.06, *supra.*

[187] *Perkins v. Consol. Benguet Mining Co.,* 342 U.S. 437, 440 (1952).

[188] E. Scoles & P. Hay, *Conflict of Laws* 313 (2d ed. 1992); *Restatement (Second) of Judgments* § 4 comment (c) (1982).

[189] For a discussion of these grounds for jurisdiction, *see* § 3.03, *supra.*

[190] Lilly, *Jurisdiction Over Domestic and Alien Defendants,* 69 Va. L. Rev. 85, 123 n.145 (1983).

[191] *See Restatement (Second) of Conflicts* § 35 comment (f) (1971).

[192] *See* Reese & Galston, *Doing an Act or Causing Consequences as Bases of Judicial Jurisdiction,* 44 Iowa L. Rev. 249, 265 (1959).

[193] *See Scoles & Hay,* note 188, *supra,* at 314.

[194] The response of state legislatures was rapid. Wasserman, *The Subpoena Power: Pennoyer's Last Vestige,* 74 Minn. L. Rev. 37, 54-56 (1989). Today, "[a]ll states have statutes dealing with the exercise of jurisdiction in transactions having out-of-state elements. . . . Their shape has evolved in response to evolving Supreme Court interpretations of the Constitutional limitations on state court jurisdiction." *Restatement (Second) of Judgments* § 4 reporter's note.

They responded by enacting what have come to be called *long-arm stat-utes*.[195] These provide personal jurisdiction over nonresident defendants who cannot be found and served in the forum state. They have generally taken one of two forms. The first attempts to categorize factual situations which seem likely to satisfy the minimum contacts test of *International Shoe* and authorizes the court to exercise jurisdiction over nonresidents in such cases.[196] The second takes a blanket approach, conferring all jurisdiction permitted by state and federal constitutional law.[197]

Neither approach is ideal. Implicit in the assumption of lawmaking authority by state legislatures is a judgment that they have a special function to perform in determining the appropriate reach of their court's personal jurisdiction.[198] They may be abdicating that responsibility when they enact blanket long-arm statutes. Moreover, in declining to be specific, the legislature withholds guidance from those wishing to learn in advance whether their instate activities will expose them to personal jurisdiction. On the other hand, legislatures enacting particularized long-arm statutes may unwittingly omit some legitimate factual category, impairing their courts' useful range of personal jurisdiction.[199]

Differences between the two approaches, however, have not turned out to be great in application. The state courts have tended to interpret their statutes to confer all of the jurisdiction permitted by due process, regardless of the statutes' language.[200]

[2] *Hanson v. Denckla* — The Court's Isolated Warning

The facts of *Hanson v. Denckla*[201] were quite complicated.[202] Two factions fought over distribution of a $400,000 estate. The Denckla group claimed that the money passed to them through decedent's will. The

---

[195] Typically, long-arm provisions have been directly enacted by legislatures, but they can also emerge as court rules promulgated under legislative authority. *Lilly,* note 190, *supra,* at 123.

[196] *E.g.,* Uniform Interstate and International Procedure Act § 1.03; New York Civ. Prac. Law and Rules § 302(a); Ill. Ann. Stat. Chapter 110, ¶ 2-209 (Smith-Hurd 1983).

[197] *E.g.,* California Code Civ. Proc. § 410.10 (Deering 1973); N.J. Civil Practice Rule 4:4-4(e); R.I. Gen. Laws Ann. § 9-5-33. For example, the California provision states: "A court of this state may exercise jurisdiction on any basis not inconsistent with the Constitution of this state or of the United States."

[198] *See* notes 193 and 194 and related text, *supra.*

[199] *See* R. Weintraub, *Commentary on the Conflict of Laws* 167 (3d ed. 1986).

[200] Abrams & Dimond, *Toward a Constitutional Framework for the Control of State Court Jurisdiction,* 69 Minn. L. Rev. 75, 84 n.43 (1984). For one such example, see Note, *Current Status of Personal and General Jurisdiction in Minnesota,* 16 William Mitchell L. Rev. 309, 334 (1990). But *cf.* M. Glannon, *Civil Procedure* 28 (4th ed. 2001) ("Unfortunately, courts have not always grasped [the] distinction between broad interpretation of . . . enumerated acts and absorbing the whole constitutional sphere.").

[201] 357 U.S. 235 (1958).

[202] For more detailed statements of the case, see Scott, *Hanson v. Denckla,* 72 Harv. L. Rev. 695 (1959); Kurland, *The Supreme Court, the Due Process Clause and the In Personam Jurisdiction of State Courts From Pennoyer to Denckla: A Review,* 25 U. Chi. L. Rev. 569, 610-623 (1958).

Hanson group claimed that the funds were not affected by the will because they were the subject of a trust (with the Hanson group as beneficiaries) created by the decedent before her death. The Denckla group brought suit in Florida to have the trust declared invalid. The Florida Supreme Court eventually ruled that it was. It also ruled that personal jurisdiction existed over two Delaware trust companies, defendants in the case who had been appointed trustees for the disputed trust. On review, a narrowly divided Supreme Court disagreed, finding that the Florida courts lacked personal jurisdiction over the trustees.

First reaching the somewhat surprising conclusion that defendants properly within the Florida courts' jurisdiction could question jurisdiction over the absent trustees,[203] the Court proceeded to the due process issue. Clearly, the case for personal jurisdiction was weaker in *Hanson* than in previous cases decided by the Court after *International Shoe*. Unlike the defendant in *Perkins v. Benguet Mining Co.*,[204] the Delaware trust companies did not conduct "continuous and systematic" operations in the forum. Indeed, they had no offices in Florida and transacted no business there.[205] The controversy centered on the validity of the trust, and the trust was created in Delaware. Therefore, unlike the defendant in *McGee*,[206] the trustees directed little if any of their activities at the forum state.[207]

What divided the Court was that two theories, which previously combined to support personal jurisdiction, seemed in *Hanson* to pull in opposite directions. The first of these, a power theory, was refined in *International Shoe*[208] from earlier cases. Under this theory, submission to suit is a fair

---

[203] Most of the Hanson-group defendants were Florida domiciliaries and were served there. However, the Delaware-trustee defendants were foreign corporations who maintained no office in Florida and had to be served out of state by mail. They refused to participate and ultimately defaulted. The challenge concerning Florida jurisdiction over the trustees was not raised by the trustees themselves, but by the Hanson group. Traditionally, the Court has been reluctant to permit litigants, whose own constitutional rights have not been injured, to object to the proceedings by raising the rights of others. The Court got around this in *Hanson* by reading Florida procedural law to make the Delaware trustees indispensable parties to the lawsuit. Thus, it reasoned, the case could not proceed if Florida was incapable of exercising jurisdiction over them. 357 U.S. at 254-255. *See* § 9.05[2] (compulsory joinder), *infra*. Dissenting, Justice Black questioned this interpretation of Florida law and argued that at the very least the case should be remanded to the Florida courts to give them an opportunity to pass on the indispensability question. *Id.* at 257-262. Professor Kurland called the Court's conclusion in *Hanson* that the due process issue was properly before it a "doubtful assumption." *Kurland, note 202, supra,* at 617.

[204] *See* § 3.06[2][b], *supra*.

[205] *Scott,* note 202, *supra,* at 702.

[206] *See* § 3.06[2][a], *supra*.

[207] On the other hand, Justice Black contended that the Delaware trustees were not altogether free of contact with Florida. The last time the decedent exercised her power under the trust instrument to redirect the remainder, she did so from Florida. 357 U.S. at 258 (Black, J. dissenting). Presumably, this required the assistance of at least one of the trustees. Also, at least one of the trustees transmitted trust income to the decedent while she was living in Florida. *Id.* at 257. The latter contact would have been more significant if the case concerned whether the trustee had breached its duty under the trust instrument, instead of whether the trust itself was valid.

[208] *See* § 3.06, *supra*.

exchange for the benefits and protection a nonresident defendant receives from the forum state. The second, which received more glancing treatment in *Shoe*,[209] focused on the logic or convenience of plaintiff's forum choice. The burden on defendant from litigating there is a factor. Other factors are the degree of difficulty for plaintiff in suing elsewhere and possible interest the forum state might have in making its courts available to hear the case. The Court had utilized both theories in intervening cases.[210] Never before *Hanson* had they seemed at odds.

Dissenting from the Court's refusal to permit personal jurisdiction, Justice Black argued the convenience theory: that Florida would be a logical and convenient place to adjudicate the lawsuit.[211] The question of the trust's validity bore not only on the trust itself but also on the scope and effect of decedent's will. And the will was probated in Florida. Thus, contended Justice Black, "Florida was seriously concerned with winding up Mrs. Donner's estate and with finally determining what property was to be distributed under her will."[212]

However, the *Hanson* majority adopted the power theory. In so doing, the majority did not really dispute the relative convenience of Florida as a place for suit or the interest of the plaintiffs and the State of Florida in a Florida adjudication. It simply concluded that, without minimum contacts between the nonresident defendants and the forum capable of supporting the power theory, these other considerations did not come into play.

First, the majority brushed aside the convenience of a Florida forum. The protections of due process, it said,

> are more than a guarantee of immunity from inconvenient or distant litigation. They are a consequence of territorial limitations on the power of the respective States. However minimal the burden of defending in a foreign tribunal, a defendant may not be called upon to do so unless he has had the "minimal contacts" with that State that are a prerequisite to its exercise of power over him.[213]

The *Hanson* majority similarly discounted the significance of contacts between the plaintiffs and the forum, stating that the "unilateral activity of those who claim some relationship with a nonresident defendant cannot satisfy the requirement of contact with the forum State."[214] The Court also

---

[209] *See* § 3.06, *supra*.

[210] The Court fleshed out the logic/convenience theory in *Traveler's Health Ass'n v. Virginia*, 339 U.S. 643 (1950) (*see* § 3.06[2][a], *supra*), and in *McGee v. International Life Ins. Co.*, 335 U.S. 220 (1957) (*see* § 3.06[2][a]*supra*). On the other hand, *Perkins v. Benguet Consol. Mining Co.*, 342 U.S. 437 (1952), *see* § 3.06[2][b], *supra*, seems to proceed on the power theory.

[211] "Florida, the home of the principal contenders for Mrs. Donner's largess, was a reasonably convenient forum for all." 357 U.S. at 259 (Black, J., dissenting).

[212] *Id.*

[213] 357 U.S. at 251 (citing *International Shoe*).

[214] *Id.* at 253.

refused to attach importance to Florida's interest in adjudicating this kind of lawsuit.[215]

The majority left no doubt that (1) focus on the relationship between the forum and *defendant* was both central and indispensable to its minimum contacts inquiry, and (2) contacts would achieve the minimum only if they were sufficient to support the power theory:

> The application of that rule will vary with the quality and nature of the defendant's activity, but it is essential in each case that there be some act by which the defendant purposefully avails itself of the privilege of conducting activities within the forum State, thus invoking the benefits and protections of its laws.[216]

Hanson's history as precedent reflects a reversal of the usual pattern. The contemporary force of the case is far greater than were its immediate effects.[217] For a long time, *Hanson*'s chief importance seemed to lie in confirming *International Shoe*'s admonition that due process "does not contemplate that a state may make binding a judgment *in personam* against an individual or corporate defendant with which the state has no contacts, ties, or relations."[218] Perhaps this was significant in itself, providing "a stopping place . . . on what had been the road toward nationwide in personam jurisdiction for state courts."[219]

But the case left unanswered important questions concerning how the "quality and nature of defendant's activity" should be measured in order to determine whether minimum forum contacts existed. The Court's failure to address these questions in *Hanson,* or to return to them until 1977, left considerable ambiguity in its due process doctrine. Isolated, the authority of the *Hanson* case also suffered from its complicated and somewhat bizarre facts and from the Court's questionable judgment that there was a due process issue in the case at all.[220] "In the ensuing years many

---

[215] The *Hanson* Court entertained the possibility that the facts of the controversy might so involve Florida state interests as to justify application of Florida substantive law, but stated flatly: "The issue is personal jurisdiction, not choice of law." *Id.* at 254. Granted, there are situations where a court constitutionally capable of applying its own substantive law to a controversy may lack contacts with the defendant necessary for personal jurisdiction. See the example provided in Shreve, *Interest Analysis as Constitutional Law,* 48 Ohio St. L.J. 51, 60 n.60 (1987). In *Hanson,* however, it might have been difficult for the Supreme Court to have upheld as constitutional the Florida court's rejection of Delaware trust law in favor of its own. Kirgis, *The Roles of Due Process and Full Faith and Credit in Choice of Law,* 62 Cornell L. Rev. 94, 144-146 (1976); Shreve, *In Search of a Choice-of-Law Reviewing Standard — Reflections on Allstate Insurance Co. v. Hague,* 66 Minn. L. Rev. 327, 334 (1982). Because of its ruling of no personal jurisdiction, it was unnecessary for the Court to reach the choice-of-law question.

[216] *Id.* at 253 (*citing International Shoe*).

[217] The case was to underpin modern decisions regulating extraterritorial jurisdiction more stringently. *E.g., Shaffer v. Heitner,* 433 U.S. 186, 215-216 (1977); *World-Wide Volkswagen Corp. v. Woodson,* 444 U.S. 286, 294-299 (1980). *See generally* § 3.10, *infra.*

[218] *International Shoe Co. v. Washington,* 326 U.S. 310, 319 (1945).

[219] *Kurland,* note 202, *supra,* at 622.

[220] *See* note 203, *supra.*

commentators and courts distinguished or effectively ignored it, while suggesting or taking a more expansive approach to jurisdiction. And there the Supreme Court let things lie for two decades."[221]

[3] Lower Courts Do (Or Do Not) Restrain Themselves

The Supreme Court's failure to give much guidance left state and lower federal courts with the task of sorting out the implications of *International Shoe*.[222] It is not surprising that some courts were more cautious in exercising personal jurisdiction than others. What most divided courts was determination of the point at which the quality and extent of the nonresident defendant's forum contacts satisfied the minimum required by due process.

Some courts read a good deal into the minimum contacts requirement. For example, in *Erlanger Mills, Inc. v. Cohoes Fibre Mills, Inc.*,[223] the court refused to hold a defendant New York corporation amenable to suit in North Carolina. Plaintiff's representative travelled to defendant's New York plant and contracted there for a shipment of synthetic yarn. Defendant shipped the yarn, FOB New York. The yarn arrived at plaintiff's North Carolina plant and plaintiff alleged it to be defective. Noting that the defendant had done no other business in North Carolina, the court found the transaction insufficient to provide minimum contacts between the defendant and the forum. The court feared grave consequences from finding personal jurisdiction in such cases: "It requires no flight of fancy to foresee the resulting maze of lawsuits adjudicating the interests of persons having only the faintest and most remote links with the State exercising authority."[224] Other decisions also reflect a relatively restrained view of the reach of personal jurisdiction permitted by the minimum contacts requirement.[225]

Some courts, however, were willing to entertain personal jurisdiction over nonresident defendants with less than extensive forum contacts. In the well-known case, *Gray v. American Radiator & Standard Sanitary Corp.*,[226] for example, one of the defendants challenged personal jurisdiction in an Illinois suit for injuries from a water heater which had exploded there. Defendant had manufactured the safety valve on the exploding heater, but it did no business in Illinois. It manufactured the valve in question in Ohio and sold it to another defendant who assembled the water heater in Pennsylvania. The Illinois Supreme Court conceded that any wrongful behavior attributable to the valve company occurred outside the

---

[221] Clermont, *Restating Territorial Jurisdiction and Venue for State and Federal Courts*, 66 Cornell L. Rev. 411, 419 (1981).

[222] For discussion of some of the decisions during this period see Cardozo, *The Reach of the Legislature and the Grasp of Jurisdiction*, 43 Cornell L.Q. 210 (1957); Currie, *The Growth of the Long Arm: Eight Years of Extended Jurisdiction in Illinois*, 1963 Ill. L. Rev. 533.

[223] 239 F.2d 502 (4th Cir. 1956).

[224] *Id.* at 509.

[225] *E.g., O'Brien v. Comstock Foods, Inc.*, 194 A.2d 568 (Vt. 1963); *Putnam v. Triangle Publications*, 96 S.E.2d 445 (N.C. 1957).

[226] 176 N.E.2d 761 (Ill. 1961).

forum state, but nonetheless concluded that its courts had personal jurisdiction. The defendant, said the court, could have contemplated that products containing its valves would be used in the forum. And, "it has undoubtedly benefited, to a degree, from the protection which our law has given to the marketing of hot water heaters containing its valves."[227]

Similarly in *Buckeye Boiler Co. v. Superior Court,*[228] plaintiff sued for injuries when a boiler manufactured by defendant Buckeye, an Ohio corporation, exploded in California. Buckeye had not sold the boiler for use in California. It had apparently been resold by the original purchaser, although how the boiler reached California was unclear. Buckeye's only known California contacts were limited sales there of a different boiler model. Nonetheless, the California Supreme Court ruled that California courts could exercise personal jurisdiction over Buckeye. It reasoned that the unrelated business Buckeye conducted in California met the threshold requirement of contacts between the defendant and the forum. The California Supreme Court then justified its decision —notwithstanding *Hanson v. Denckla*[229] —in part on plaintiff's interest in having a local forum and in California's interest in providing it.

The New York Court of Appeals used even less forum contact to justify personal jurisdiction over a nonresident defendant in *Bryant v. Finnish National Airline.*[230] Plaintiff alleged that her injuries at a Paris airport occurred as a consequence of defendant airline's negligent conduct there. She sued in New York state court. Defendant flew no aircraft in the United States. Finnair's only contact with the forum state was to employ a few persons in a small New York City office to take reservations for flights within Europe. Plaintiff had not used the office, nor was she a Finnair passenger when the accident occurred. Moreover, unlike *Buckeye* and *Gray,* no harm was inflicted upon plaintiff in the forum.[231] Nevertheless, the court found personal jurisdiction.

PART C
Territorial Jurisdiction in the Modern Era

§ 3.08 *International Shoe* Gives But Also Takes Away Jurisdiction — Spread of the Minimum Contacts Standard

International Shoe and the early cases following it were first and most easily seen as a force for expanding courts' personal jurisdiction. On another category of territorial jurisdiction, however, *Shoe* eventually exerted an

---

[227] 176 N.E.2d at 766.

[228] 458 P.2d 57 (Cal. 1969).

[229] 357 U.S. 235 (1958). *See* notes 214 and 215 and related text, *supra.*

[230] 208 N.E.2d 439 (N.Y. 1965).

[231] It is at least arguable that the United States Supreme Court's decision in *Helicopteros Nacionales de Columbia, S.A. v. Hall,* 466 U.S. 408 (1984), had the effect of overruling *Bryant.* For discussion of *Helicopteros,* see § 3.11[1] , *infra.*

opposite, restrictive effect. Supreme Court rulings in *Shaffer v. Heitner*[232] and *Rush v. Savchuk*[233] extended the minimum contacts standard to *quasi in rem* cases, stripping that jurisdictional category of much of its discrete significance and appeal to plaintiffs. These developments also make it useful to consider how remaining applications of territorial jurisdiction fare when subjected to *Shoe*'s minimum contacts test.

[1] Minimum Contacts and the Decline of *Quasi In Rem* Jurisdiction — *Shaffer v. Heitner*

Plaintiff brought a shareholder derivative suit[234] against officers and directors of the Greyhound Corp. and its subsidiary, Greyhound, Inc. Plaintiff filed the suit in Delaware, alleging that the individual defendants had caused Greyhound and its subsidiary to incur substantial expenses from civil antitrust damages and a fine for criminal contempt. The defendants neither resided in Delaware nor received service there. Moreover, the alleged wrongful acts occurred outside Delaware. Delaware may have lacked minimum contacts necessary to support personal jurisdiction over the defendants.[235] Plaintiff attempted to avoid the problem, however, by proceeding upon a *quasi in rem* (rather than *in personam*) theory of jurisdiction.[236] There seems little question that plaintiff's case met traditional *quasi in rem* standards.[237] Each of the defendants held stock in Greyhound. Greyhound was a Delaware corporation, and plaintiff relied on a Delaware statute which conferred *quasi in rem* jurisdiction over stock issued by corporations chartered there. The Delaware state courts rejected defendant's jurisdictional attack.

Reversing, the United States Supreme Court set out two propositions. First, exercises of *quasi in rem* jurisdiction would henceforth satisfy due process only if they met *International Shoe*'s minimum contacts test. Second, *Shaffer* failed that test. The first of the two propositions was *Shaffer*'s lasting contribution. In contrast, the Court's conclusion that Delaware lacked minimum contacts with the defendants and the controversy is open to question.[238]

---

[232] 433 U.S. 186 (1977).

[233] 444 U.S. 320 (1980).

[234] Shareholders bring this suit to assert rights of the corporation when its directors will not. *See* Rule 23.1. It is usually brought against the officers and directors of the corporation for fraud, breach of fiduciary duties and other mismanagement.

[235] However, that was by no means clear. *See* note 238, *infra*.

[236] For discussion of these two types of territorial jurisdiction and the third (*in rem*), see § 3.02 (classical categories of territorial jurisdiction), *supra*.

[237] *See* § 3.02[3], *supra*.

[238] Inasmuch as Greyhound was a Delaware corporation, the alleged dissipation of the worth of the corporation by the defendants was at least arguably forum-related. *See* Casad, *Shaffer v. Heitner: An End to Ambivalence in Jurisdictional Theory*, 26 Kan. L. Rev. 61, 74 (1977); Vernon, *Single-Factor Bases of In Personam Jurisdiction —A Speculation on the Impact of Shaffer v. Heitner*, 1978 Wash. U.L.Q. 273, 316. The Court's arguments to the contrary are somewhat clouded.

Concerning the first proposition, the Court flatly stated that "all assertions of state-court jurisdiction must be evaluated according to the standards set forth in *International Shoe* and its progeny."[239] This did not make *quasi in rem* jurisdiction unconstitutional per se. However, because the Court found defendant's in-state property to be "completely unrelated to the plaintiff's cause of action," it held that "the presence of the property alone would not support the State's jurisdiction."[240]

It is possible to overstate the impact of the Court's decision on prejudgment attachments. So long as minimum contacts exist, suits begun by attachment — whether called *in personam*[241] or *quasi in rem*[242] — survive *Shaffer*. In addition, the Court may have provided exceptions (albeit narrow) to its minimum contacts rule.[243]

The fact remains, however, that *Shaffer* divested *quasi in rem* jurisdiction of much of its special appeal. A great lure of *quasi in rem* for plaintiffs had been that it provided an end run around the minimum contacts requirements of personal jurisdiction. The availability of *quasi in rem* jurisdiction in courts incapable of exercising personal jurisdiction made them attract litigation, even though the scope of *quasi in rem* judgments cannot exceed the worth of forum property upon which jurisdiction is based.[244] Once the *Shaffer* principle was recognized,[245] however, it was evident that plaintiff had to make the same minimum contacts showing for *quasi in rem* (or *in rem*) jurisdiction that he did for personal jurisdiction. This means that plaintiff will usually have a case for personal jurisdiction if he has a jurisdictional case at all.[246] Given a choice, naturally plaintiff will invoke personal over *quasi in rem* jurisdiction in order to obtain a judgment compensating him for defendant's entire wrong.[247]

---

[239] 433 U.S. at 212. The Court's choice of words seemed calculated to make its rule as applicable to exercises of *in rem* jurisdiction as to the *quasi in rem* case at hand. Elsewhere in *Shaffer,* the Court made it clear that it was referring to "the minimum-contacts standard elucidated in *International Shoe.* " *Id.* at 207. In *Rush v. Savchuk,* 444 U.S. 320, 327 (1980), the Court reiterated that its purpose in invoking *International Shoe* in *Shaffer* was to give across-the-board application to the minimum contacts test.

[240] *Id.* at 209. For discussion of the effect of this ruling on subsequent cases, see Mushlin, *The New Quasi in Rem Jurisdiction: New York's Revival of a Doctrine Whose Time Has Passed,* 55 Brooklyn L. Rev. 1059 (1990).

[241] Courts exercising *in personam* jurisdiction may still under appropriate circumstances authorize security attachments to enhance the prospect of an enforceable judgment, should plaintiff prevail. *See* Silberman, *Shaffer v. Heitner: The End of an Era,* 53 NYU L. Rev. 33, 54 (1978).

[242] A case may be capable of satisfying the minimum contacts test yet be beyond the amount of personal jurisdiction over nonresident defendants conferred by the state's long-arm statute. If the same state has a *quasi in rem* statute or common law rule which does apply, the court may continue to use it in such cases. *See Vernon,* note 238, *supra,* at 280-281.

[243] *See* § 3.08[3][d], *infra.*

[244] This makes them less valuable than *in personam* judgments. *See* § 3.02, *supra.*

[245] *See* § 3.08[2], *infra.*

[246] In the event (now relatively rare) that minimum contacts are present but no personal jurisdiction statute reaches the case, plaintiff might have access only to *quasi in rem* jurisdiction. *See* note 242, *supra.*

[247] *See* § 3.02[1], *supra.*

The Court's decision in *Shaffer* was overdue. Insulation of *quasi in rem* jurisdiction from *Shoe's* minimum contacts test was indefensible. It was arbitrary to suggest that the concern for fairness to defendants explicit in *Shoe's* approach provided a basis for restricting only personal jurisdiction. To so confine due process protection under *Shoe* was to engage in a kind of formalism and artificiality at odds with the Court's modern cases.[248]

[2] Driving the Point Home — *Rush v. Savchuk*

Some of the most egregious exercises of *quasi in rem* jurisdiction prior to *Shaffer* occurred through application of the so-called *Seider* doctrine.[249] In *Harris v. Balk*,[250] the Court had earlier sanctioned *quasi in rem* jurisdiction based on the obligation of another to pay money to the defendant. A contemporary manifestation of this idea, the *Seider* doctrine permitted *quasi in rem* jurisdiction in accident cases where courts lacked minimum contacts with nonresident driver defendants. Courts reasoned that service within the forum on the nonresident driver's insurer[251] conferred *quasi in rem* jurisdiction. The property attached was the insurer's duty or "debt" under the policy to defend and indemnify the nonresident motorist.

Jurisdiction over nonresident drivers in these cases was unattainable under *International Shoe's* minimum contacts test. So it should have been obvious after *Shaffer* that continued reliance on the *Seider* doctrine would run afoul of due process. However, several of the jurisdictions which had used the device refused to give it up.[252] The Supreme Court responded by squarely rejecting the *Seider* doctrine in *Rush v. Savchuk*.[253]

Plaintiff in *Rush* was injured in an automobile accident in Indiana. Defendant was a resident of Indiana. Plaintiff was also an Indiana resident at the time of the accident, but later moved to Minnesota and sued the defendant there for his injuries. The Minnesota courts applied the *Seider* doctrine to reach the nonresident defendant through his insurer. Reversing, the Supreme Court held that jurisdiction over the defendant exceeded due process.

---

[248] Thus, reasoned the *Shaffer* Court, "if a direct assertion of personal jurisdiction over the defendant would violate the Constitution, it would seem that an indirect assertion of that jurisdiction should be equally impermissible." 433 U.S. at 209.

[249] The case giving name to the doctrine is *Seider v. Roth*, 216 N.E.2d 312 (N.Y. 1966). For other examples, *see Simpson v. Loehmann*, 234 N.E.2d 669 (N.Y. 1967); *Minichiello v. Rosenberg*, 410 F.2d 106 (2d Cir. 1968).

[250] 198 U.S. 215 (1905), *discussed in* § 3.02[3], *supra*.

[251] Usually the insurer did not issue the policy in question in the forum state, but was thought to have sufficient unrelated contacts by doing business there to support personal jurisdiction over the insurer. The sufficiency of personal jurisdiction under such circumstances may be more open to question today. *See* § 3.11 (developments in general jurisdiction), *infra*. With the demise of the *Seider* doctrine, however, the question became academic.

[252] *See Baden v. Staples*, 383 N.E.2d 110 (N.Y. 1978); *O'Connor v. Lee-Hy Paving Corp.*, 579 F.2d 1943, (2d Cir.), *cert. denied*, 439 U.S. 1034 (1978); *Savchuk v. Rush*, 272 N.W.2d 888 (Minn. 1978).

[253] 444 U.S. 320 (1980).

The Supreme Court applied the minimum contacts test. This meant that, "[i]n determining whether a particular exercise of state-court jurisdiction is consistent with due process, the inquiry must focus on the relationship among the defendant, the forum, and the litigation."[254] The Court concluded that defendant had no contact with the forum state, through the subject matter of the litigation or otherwise. The Court also rejected plaintiff's attempt to skirt the minimum contacts problem by arguing the existence of a "direct action" against the insurer.[255]

[3] The Effect of Increased Due Process Requirements on Other Assertions of Territorial Jurisdiction

If the Court's language in *Shaffer* is to be taken seriously, the minimum contacts requirement transcends jurisdictional categories. "[A]ll assertions of state-court jurisdiction," said the Court, "must be evaluated according to the standards set forth in *International Shoe* and its progeny."[256] It referred particularly to *Shoe*'s minimum contacts test.[257] Most applications of territorial jurisdiction not before the Court in *Shaffer* seem able to satisfy the test.

[a] Old Forms of Territorial Jurisdiction Likely to Survive

Personal jurisdiction based on citizenship[258] seems capable of satisfying *International Shoe*'s minimum contacts test. The same is true concerning *quasi in rem* and *in rem* suits to determine the status of property permanently located within the forum. Finally, jurisdiction based on waiver or consent appears unaffected by *Shaffer*.

Jurisdiction by citizenship would appear to pose no problem. Recall that a nonresident defendant's contacts with the forum state are significant under *Shoe* when they suggest (1) that defendant has received sufficient benefits to make amenability to suit a fair exchange, and (2) that it would not be particularly inconvenient for defendant to defend there.[259] Given

---

[254] *Id.* at 327 (*quoting from Shaffer*, 433 U.S. at 204).

[255] 444 U.S. at 330-331. *Seider* doctrine courts had frequently used direct action arguments to bolster their decisions. The argument proceeds from the assumption that governing substantive law makes the insurer directly liable for harm to the plaintiff caused by the insured. The court has good personal jurisdiction over the insurer, and, goes the argument, its jurisdiction over the nonresident driver is not a worry because the latter has nothing to lose. The *Rush* Court, however, felt that the insured would have something to lose, "if, for example, multiple plaintiffs sued in different States for an aggregate amount in excess of the policy limits, or if a successful claim would affect the policyholder's insurability." *Id.* at 331 n.20.

[256] 433 U.S. at 212. *See* note 239, *supra*. While *Shaffer* did not deal with an attempted exercise of *in rem* (as opposed to *quasi in rem*) jurisdiction, the categorical terms in which it extended *Shoe*'s reach clearly take in both *quasi in rem* and *in rem* jurisdiction.

[257] 433 U.S. at 207. On the present day significance of the minimum contacts test, see § 16[A], *infra*.

[258] *See generally* § 3.03[1], *supra*.

[259] *See* § 3.06[1][c], *supra*.

the pervasive relationship that usually exists between a citizen and his domicile, these justifications are likely to apply with at least as much force when a forum seeks to make its own citizens amenable to process.[260]

Prior to *Shaffer,* courts were free to adjudicate disputes over ownership of property (typically real estate) permanently located within the forum without worrying about *International Shoe's* minimum contacts test. This was because jurisdiction in such cases was *quasi in rem*[261] not *in personam.* Concurring in *Shaffer,* Justices Powell and Stevens expressed concern that states would be left without authority to hear this important category of cases. Responding, the Court suggested that *Shoe's* minimum contacts standard should not be difficult to satisfy in such cases:

> [W]hen claims to the property itself are the source of the underlying controversy between the plaintiff and the defendant, it would be unusual for the State where the property is located not to have jurisdiction. In such cases, the defendant's claim to property located in the State would normally indicate that he expected to benefit from the State's protection of his interest. The State's strong interests in assuring the marketability of property within its borders and in providing a procedure for peaceful resolution of disputes about the possession of that property would also support jurisdiction, as would the likelihood that important records and witnesses will be found in the State.[262]

Justices Powell and Stevens had confined their concerns to the future of *quasi in rem* jurisdiction in such cases. The Court's response was broad enough, however, to suggest that both *quasi in rem* and *in rem* cases settling interests in property permanently located within the forum would be likely to satisfy the minimum contacts test.[263]

Nonresident plaintiffs who voluntarily chose the forum to assert their claims would seem to provide the forum with minimum contacts. The same is true for nonresident defendants who fail to preserve objections to personal jurisdiction, or who consent in advance to suit in the forum. However, it is probably more useful to view these situations apart from the minimum contacts principle of *International Shoe.* Parties may waive their

---

[260] It is significant that *International Shoe* described its due process standard in part by quoting from *Milliken* v. *Meyer,* an earlier case where the Supreme Court upheld personal jurisdiction based on defendant's forum citizenship. *See* § 3.06, *supra. See also* § 3.03[1] (discussing *Milliken*), *supra.* Recognition of courts' authority to impose personal jurisdiction over forum citizens also promotes a measure of certainty. It "assures that there is one place in which defendant always may be sued." *Friedenthal, Kane & Miller* § 3.7.

[261] *See* § 3.02[3], *supra.*

[262] 433 U.S. at 207-208.

[263] *See* 433 U.S. at 207 n.24. The difference between *quasi in rem* and *in rem* cases is whether plaintiff's suit is against particular defendants (*quasi in rem*) or against "the whole world" (*in rem*). In actions involving real property, it seems clear that *Shaffer* preserves both. R. Weintraub, *Commentary on the Conflict of Laws* 201-202 (3d ed. 1986). *Shaffer* also suggested the continued viability of jurisdiction to adjudicate status, such as marital status. The majority stressed in a footnote that "[w]e do not suggest that jurisdictional doctrines other than those discussed in text, such as the particularized rules governing adjudications of status, are inconsistent with the standard of fairness." 433 U.S. at 208 n.30.

due process objections to personal jurisdiction, [264] and the three situations may best be understood as species of waiver. [265] There may be no need them for the Supreme Court ever to bring these situations within minimum contacts analysis. [266]

[b] The Triumph of Transient Jurisdiction —
Burnham v. Superior Court

When *Shaffer* subjected all assertions of personal jurisdiction to minimum contacts scrutiny, [267] it seemed to cast a shadow over transient jurisdiction, [268] a form of personal jurisdiction under fire even before *Shaffer*. Transient jurisdiction occurs when a nonresident defendant is actually found and served within the forum state, but when defendant's presence there is (1) only intended to be brief and (2) is unrelated to the controversy raised by plaintiff's claim. In the well-known case of *Grace v. McArthur*[269] transient jurisdiction was found to exist when defendant was served on an aircraft flying over the airspace of the forum state.

This means of bypassing minimum contacts was widely criticized, called by one commentator a "blot on American law." [270] Transient jurisdiction was valid prior to *International Shoe* because service was completed within the forum state. [271] So long as *Shoe* seemed only a means of adding to the jurisdictional reach of courts, transient jurisdiction was not in danger. Moreover, *Shoe* itself used language that implied that minimum contacts were required only if a defendant "be not present within the territory of the forum," [272] thereby suggesting the continuing viability of transient jurisdiction. *Shaffer* demonstrated unequivocally, however, that due process doctrine emerging from *Shoe* and later cases was also capable of shortening the reach of courts. Transient jurisdiction seemed vulnerable to some

---

[264] "Because the requirement of personal jurisdiction represents first of all an individual right, it can, like other such rights, be waived." *Insurance Corp. of Ireland Ltd. v. Compagnie Des Bauxites de Guinee,* 456 U.S. 694, 703 (1982).

[265] *See* § 3.03[2][a] (plaintiff's waiver through filing suit), *supra;* § 3.03[2][b] (defendant's waiver by acting other than to question personal jurisdiction), *supra;* § 3.03[2][d] (jurisdiction by consent, similar to waiver), *supra.*

[266] For another such situation, see *Phillips Petroleum Co. v. Shutts,* 472 U.S. 797 (1985) (Court refuses to use the minimum contacts test to measure the relationship between the forum and unnamed members of plaintiff's class).

[267] *See* note 239 and related text, *supra.* On the application of the minimum contacts test to assertions of personal jurisdiction generally, see § 3.08[3][a], *supra.*

[268] *See* § 3.03[3], *supra.*

[269] 170 F. Supp. 442 (E.D. Ark. 1959). For further examples, *see* E. Scoles & P. Hay, *Conflict of Laws* § 8.6 (2d ed. 1992)

[270] Ehrenzweig, *From State Jurisdiction to Interstate Venue,* 50 Or. L. Rev. 103, 108 (1971). In addition, *see Vernon,* note 7, *supra,* at 302-303; Kalo, *Jurisdiction as an Evolutionary Process: The Development of Quasi In Rem and In Personam Principles,* 1978 Duke L.J. 1147, 1191.

[271] Prior to *Shoe,* the Supreme Court was preoccupied with completion of service within the forum. *See* § 3.05[1] *supra.*

[272] *International Shoe Co. v. Washington,* 326 U.S. 310, 316 (1945).

commentators because defendant's contacts with the forum were typically slight and unrelated to the controversy.

Worry over the continuing validity of transient jurisdiction lessened considerably, however, after the Supreme Court's decision in *Burnham v. Superior Court*.[273] Burnham was served as defendant in a California action for separation, child support and spousal support during his brief visit there on business and to visit his children. The case seemed to present two basic questions. First, would applications of transient jurisdiction be subject to the standards of *International Shoe*? Second, if so, how would transient jurisdiction cases fare under *Shoe?*

All the Justices agreed in *Burnham* that California's attempt to exercise transient jurisdiction was permissible. They split, however, over the answer to the first question. Four Justices found it unnecessary to test the case under *International Shoe*. They were willing to uphold transient jurisdiction because it was satisfactory under the old *Pennoyer* doctrine.[274] Disagreeing, four other Justices applied *Shoe*. Yet the disagreement may not have been very significant. For the latter group posed a test under *Shoe* that should in most cases be quite easy to satisfy.[275] Overall, the effect of the opinions in *Burnham* was to give transient jurisdiction new life.

---

[273] 495 U.S. 604 (1990). The case prompted a good deal of commentary. *E.g.*, Borchers, *The Death of the Constitutional Law of Personal Jurisdiction: From Pennoyer to Burnham and Back Again*, 24 U.C. Davis L. Rev. 19 (1990); Hay, *Transient Jurisdiction, Especially Over International Defendants: Critical Comments on Burnham v. Superior Court*, 1990 U. Ill. L. Rev. 593; Symposium, *The Future of Personal Jurisdiction: A Symposium on Burnham v. Superior Court*, 22 Rutgers L. J. 559 (1991) (articles by Brilmayer, Silberman, Stein, Weintraub, Kogan, Twitchell, Redish, and Maltz); Cramer, *Constructing Alternative Avenues of Jurisdictional Protection: By Passing Burnham's Roadblock via Section 1404(a)*, 53 Vand. L. Rev. 311 (2000).

For a variety of reasons, many of these writers are troubled by the manner in which *Burnham* gives free play to transient jurisdiction. Professor Earl Maltz, on the other hand, views matters more favorably. Maltz, *Personal Jurisdiction and Constitutional Theory — A Comment on Burnham v. Superior Court*, 22 Rutgers L. Rev. 689 (1991); Maltz, *Sovereign Authority, Fairness, and Personal Jurisdiction: The Case for the Doctrine of Transient Jurisdiction*, 66 Wash. U. L.Q. 671 (1988).

[274] For discussion of the doctrine of *Pennoyer v. Neff, see* § 3.05[1], *supra*. Justice Scalia, in an opinion joined by the Chief Justice and Justice Kennedy, gave transient jurisdiction a ringing endorsement under the *Pennoyer* doctrine. Joining their opinion in part, Justice White left room for the theoretical possibility of an example of transient jurisdiction "so arbitrary and lacking in common sense" that a due process problem might arise. He added, however, that a due process problem is unlikely "where presence in the forum state is intentional." 495 U.S. at 638. He concluded: "Here, personal service in California, without more, is enough. . . ." *Id.*

[275] In an opinion joined by Justices Marshall, Blackmun and O'Connor, Justice Brennan found jurisdiction sufficient under *International Shoe* because Burnham had deliberately partaken (however briefly) of "significant benefits provided by the State." 495 U.S. at 637. Brennan left open the possibility of a different result under Shoe when defendant's "presence in a State" is "involuntary or unknowing." *Id.* at 637 n. 11. For a possible example of the latter situation, see *Grace v. McArthur*, discussed *supra*, at note 269 and accompanying text.

[c]　Jurisdiction by Coerced Consent

Another traditional basis for personal jurisdiction may not fare as well. Jurisdiction over nonresident defendants is at times based on defendant's compliance with the forum's consent-to-service statute, even though the controversy arose outside the forum.[276] It now seems clear that a nonresident defendant's contacts with the forum must be more extensive if none are related to the controversy. Slight contacts will not suffice.[277] This raises a due process question, at least for statutes where such broad-ranging consent seems coerced.[278] The Supreme Court seems to have taken notice of this problem, although its response has been through the Commerce Clause of the Constitution.[279]

[d]　Applications of Territorial Jurisdiction Exempt From the Minimum Contacts Test

Despite the sweep of its rule extending *Shoe's* minimum contacts test, the *Shaffer* Court may have exempted two situations from the test, and possibly a third.

First, the Court invoked another part of the Constitution to finesse the difficult question whether a court enforcing a judgment obtained in another state must have minimum contacts with a nonresident defendant. "The Full Faith and Credit Clause, after all, makes the valid *in personam* judgment of one State enforceable in all other States."[280] Second, the court went

---

[276] For a discussion of this practice, *see* § 3.03, *supra*.

[277] "[I]t remains true that more substantial contacts must be shown if general jurisdiction is sought." Brilmayer, *Related Contacts and Personal Jurisdiction*, 101 Harv. L. Rev. 1444 (1988). While precise lines are difficult to draw, it is clear that the amount of contact a nonresident defendant need have with the forum to satisfy minimum contacts is far less if the contact is related to the controversy. *Compare* defendant's limited but related contacts found sufficient in *McGee v. International Life Insurance Co.*, 355 U.S. 220 (1957) (an example of specific jurisdiction discussed at § 3.06[2][a], *supra*), with defendant's limited and unrelated contacts found insufficient in *Helicopteros Nacionales de Columbia, S.A. v. Hall*, 466 U.S. 408 (1984) (an attempt at general jurisdiction discussed at § 3.11[1], *infra*).

[278] This assumes, of course, that nonresident defendants in this category have not waived their due process objections by registering under the statutes. On how waiver functions to cut short minimum contacts inquiry, *see* note 265 and accompanying text, *supra*. When suit is wholly unrelated to defendant's forum activity, notions of waiver or consent to jurisdiction seem strained. The constitutionality after *International Shoe* of such coerced consent is open to question. *See* Brilmayer, Haverkamp, Logan, Lynch, Neuwirth & O'Brien, *A General Look at General Jurisdiction*, 66 Tex. L. Rev. 721, 759-760 (1988); Hill, *Choice of Law and Jurisdiction in the Supreme Court*, 81 Colum. L. Rev. 960, 981-982 (1981).

[279] The case, *Bendix Autolight Corp. v. Midwesco Enterprises*, 486 U.S. 888 (1988), found violative of the Commerce Clause Ohio law conditioning the availability of a favorable statute of limitations on consent to jurisdiction. For discussion of this case and criticism of the Court's failure frame a due process issue, see Perdue, *Personal Jurisdiction and the Beetle in the Box*, 32 B.C. L. Rev. 529, 557-560 (1991).

[280] 433 U.S. at 210. Given parallel obligations imposed by federal statutes on federal courts to recognize state judgments and on state and other federal courts to recognize federal judgments (*see* § 15.10, *infra*) the passage in the accompanying text probably means that relief from the minimum contacts standard exists across the board in inter-system enforcement of judgments.

further and approved attachment of defendant's property to secure payment of possible judgment in a case litigated in another forum (so-called "attachment for security"), so long as litigation in the latter could "be maintained consistently with *International Shoe.*"[281]

These exemptions are significant. Granted, many attachments described in the two situations above would have passed *Shoe's* minimum contacts test. Many of these cases undoubtedly are brought in defendant's home state, where defendant's citizenship provides the enforcement or attachment forum with sufficient material to satisfy the minimum contacts test.[282] In other cases, however, defendant may have property in, but only tangential contacts with, the forum. The latter were secure within the category of *quasi in rem* jurisdiction prior to *Shaffer,* and it seems the court did not wish to generate uncertainty about these cases by subjecting them to the rigors of *International Shoe.*

The Court entertained but stopped short of approving a third exemption for cases where the defendant has property in the forum and "no other forum is available to the plaintiff."[283] The scope of this exemption is unclear from *Shaffer,* and the Court has not really clarified it since.[284] It is reminiscent of the concept of "jurisdiction by necessity,"[285] which has largely failed to capture the imagination of the Court.[286]

§ 3.09 A Closer Look at the Minimum Contacts Test — When and How Contacts Count

[1] The Function of Contacts and the Special Importance of Defendant's Contacts With the Forum

In several later cases, the United States Supreme Court reaffirmed the requirement that assertions of personal jurisdiction over nonresident corporate and individual defendants[287] pass the minimum contacts test

---

[281] 433 U.S. at 210. The attachments are for security, and not for obtaining territorial jurisdiction in order to litigate a claim.

[282] *See* note 260 and related text, *supra.*

[283] 433 U.S. at 211 n.37.

[284] For commentary on this point in *Shaffer,* see Hay, *Refining Personal Jurisdiction in the United States,* 35 Int'l & Comp. L.Q. 32, 47-48 (1986).

[285] *See generally* Fraser, *Jurisdiction by Necessity — An Analysis of the Mullane Case,* 100 U. Pa. L. Rev. 305 (1951).

[286] *See Helicopteros Nacionales de Columbia, S.A. v. Hall,* 466 U.S. 408, 419 n.13 (1984) ("We decline to consider adoption of a doctrine of jurisdiction by necessity — a potentially far-reaching modification of existing law — in the absence of a more complete record."). *But cf.* Hazard, *Interstate Venue,* 74 Nw. U.L. Rev. 711, 718 (1979) (finding support in *Western Union Tel. Co. v. Pennsylvania,* 368 U.S. 71 (1961) and several state cases for "the idea that a reasonably convenient state court has jurisdiction over all persons whose joinder is necessary to do consistent justice a multiparty, multistate controversy.").

[287] Like *International Shoe,* many cases have involved nonresident corporate defendants. On the other hand, *Shoe* offered two cases involving individual defendants, *Milliken v. Meyer,* 311 U.S. 457 (1940), and *Hess v. Pawloski,* 274 U.S. 352 (1927), as background for its approach.

refined from *International Shoe.*[288] *Contacts* are geographical facts about the controversy or the parties — for example, where defendant allegedly committed the wrong. To understand the minimum contacts test, it is necessary to consider what types of contacts have significance and when forum contacts exist in sufficient quantity (when, in other words, sufficient geographical indicators point to the forum state) to satisfy the minimum requirements of due process. This section offers an overview of the process of ascertaining and weighing contacts which will be covered in greater detail in succeeding sections.

The relationship between the forum and the defendant is of overriding importance. Recall the context of the minimum contacts standard originally announced in *International Shoe.* Before forcing a nonresident defendant either to litigate (perhaps far from home) or accede to a default judgment,[289] it must be clear that the defendant has "certain minimum contacts" with the forum "such that the maintenance of the suit does not offend 'traditional notions of fair play and substantial justice.'"[290] So it follows that most due process inquiries about personal jurisdiction center on a minimum contacts test.[291]

There is some question whether due process protections afforded to nonresident individuals differ greatly, if at all, from those afforded to nonresident corporations. *See* Seidelson, *Jurisdiction Over Nonresident Defendants: Beyond "Minimum Contacts" and the Long-Arm Statutes,* 6 Duq. L. Rev. 221, 225 n.28 (1967-1968) (suggesting "the distinction between foreign corporations and nonresident natural persons for jurisdictional purposes probably has ceased to exist."). At the same time, jurisdictional issues can arise that are unique to the corporate defendant — e.g., the extent to which jurisdiction over a corporate subsidiary permits jurisdiction over the parent corporation. *See generally* Comment, *Jurisdiction Over a Parent Corporation in Its Subsidiary's State of Incorporation,* 141 U. Pa. L. Rev. 327 (1992).

[288] 326 U.S. 310 (1945). *E.g., World-Wide Volkswagen Corp. v. Woodson,* 444 U.S. 286, 291 (1980): "As has long been settled, and as we reaffirm today, a state court may exercise personal jurisdiction over a nonresident defendant only so long as there exist 'minimum contacts' between the defendant and the forum state." *International Shoe Co. v. Washington,* [326 U.S.] at 316. More recently, the Court observed, also quoting *Shoe,* "the constitutional touchstone remains whether the defendant purposefully established "minimum contacts" in the forum State." *Burger King Corp. v. Rudzewicz,* 471 U.S. 462, 474 (1985). The Supreme Court has never made entirely clear what "purposeful" conduct is. For a discussion of possible meanings, see Stewart, *A New Litany of Personal Jurisdiction,* 60 Colo. L. Rev. 5 (1989).

[289] *See* § 3.06[1][a], *supra.*

[290] *International Shoe,* 326 U.S. at 316, *quoting Milliken v. Meyer,* 311 U.S. 457, 463 (1940). For a recent assessment of the minimum contacts test, see McMunigal, *Desert, Utility, and Minimum Contacts: Toward a Mixed Theory of Personal Jurisdiction,* 108 Yale L.J. 189 (1998).

[291] But not all. The Court has demonstrated that satisfaction of the minimum contacts test may not be enough. *Asahi Metal Ind. Co., Ltd. v. Superior Court,* 480 U.S. 102 (1987). Using a due process test which stood apart from minimum contacts, the Court refused to permit a California state court to exercise personal jurisdiction over a Japanese third-party defendant. Five members of the Court suggested minimum contacts might have existed between the forum and the defendant. But they joined three other justices to conclude that forcing a Japanese litigant to defend in California against a Taiwanese claimant would (*quoting International Shoe*) violate "traditional notions of fair play and substantial justice." *Id.* at 113. The Court considered under this test the needs of other litigants for a California forum, California's interest in providing a forum, and the burden posed by a California forum on the party challenging jurisdiction.

How often will a court have minimum contacts with a nonresident defendant, yet lack

[2] Specific and General Jurisdiction

We have already seen that a nonresident defendant may have contacts with the forum sufficient to support personal jurisdiction when those contacts are either related[292] or unrelated[293] to the controversy. Personal jurisdiction based on the first type of contacts is sometimes called *specific* jurisdiction.[294] Personal jurisdiction based on the second is called *general* jurisdiction.[295] The Supreme Court has yet to indicate how extensive defendant's unrelated contacts need to be in order to support personal jurisdiction.[296] It is clear, however, that general jurisdiction requires far more extensive contact between the forum and the defendant than does specific jurisdiction.[297]

General jurisdiction proceeds from a relationship between the forum and defendant that is so extensive that defendant's submission to jurisdiction there is a fair exchange for the considerable privileges and protections that the forum state has extended to defendant. General jurisdiction is indifferent to where the controversy arose and its significance as a jurisdictional option comes in those cases where the controversy arose from outside the forum. Citizenship of defendant in the forum provides the strongest case for general jurisdiction, so strong that jurisdiction of the forum over its own citizens is unquestioned.

---

personal jurisdiction because of *Asahi*'s additional due process test? The Court indicated that minimum contacts will often indicate satisfaction of the latter: "When minimum contacts have been established, often the interests of the plaintiff and the forum in the exercise of jurisdiction will justify even the serious burdens placed on the alien defendant." *Id.* at 114. The facts of *Asahi* did not bear this out because "the interests of the plaintiff and the forum in California's assertion of jurisdiction over Asahi [a third-party defendant] are slight." *Id.* For further discussion of the *Asahi* case, see § 3.12[2], *infra.*

[292] *See* the discussion of *McGee v. International Life Ins. Co.* at § 3.06[2][a], *supra.*

[293] *See* the discussion of *Perkins v. Benguet Consol. Mining Co.* at § 3.06[2][b], *supra.*

[294] For a discussion of the Supreme Court's more recent specific jurisdiction decisions, see §§ 3.10 & 3.12, *infra.*

[295] The Supreme Court used these terms in *Helicopteros Nacionales de Columbia v. Hall,* 466 U.S. 408, 414 nn.8-9 (1984), describing specific jurisdiction as that "in a suit arising out of or related to the defendant's contacts with the forum" and general jurisdiction as that "in a suit not arising out of or related to the defendant's contacts with the forum." *See* Twitchell, *The Myth of General Jurisdiction,* 101 Harv. L. Rev. 610, 680 (1988): "The Supreme Court's recent use of the general/specific terminology suggests that this typology will continue to play a central role in personal jurisdiction decisions." *See generally* Note, *Specific and General Jurisdiction — The Reshuffling of Minimum Contacts Analysis,* 59 Tul. L. Rev. 826 (1985). To date, however, the Supreme Court has been far less informative about general jurisdiction. One writer has gone so far as to suggest: "The development of general jurisdiction analysis . . . seems to have atrophied at its 1945 level." George, *In Search of General Jurisdiction,* 64 Tul. L. Rev. 1097, 1141 (1990).

[296] For a discussion of developments in this area, see § 3.11, *supra.*

[297] Compare defendant's limited but related contact found sufficient in *McGee v. International Life Ins. Co.,* 355 U.S. 220 (1957) (discussed at § 3.06[2][a], *supra*), with defendant's limited and unrelated contact found insufficient in *Helicopteros Nacionales de Colombia, S.A. v. Hall,* 466 U.S. 408 (1984). For a recent discussion of the relation between general and specific jurisdiction, see Simard, *Hybrid Personal Jurisdiction: It's Not General Jurisdiction, or Specific Jurisdiction, But Is It Constitutional?,* 48 Case W. Res. L. Rev. 561 (1998).

The central question concerning general jurisdiction is: When a nonciti-zen defendant cannot be found and served within the forum, and when the cause of action arises entirely outside the forum, when do connections be-tween the defendant and the forum (from purposeful acts by defendant taken in the forum or directed into the forum) become so extensive that the forum can exercise the same general jurisdiction that it does over its own citizens? United States Supreme Court decisions to date do not provide a great deal of help in drawing that line.

Specific jurisdiction proceeds from a relationship between the forum and the noncitizen defendant funnelled through the facts of the controversy. When plaintiff alleges that defendant has purposefully acted in the forum (or has directed acts there) to harm plaintiff, the sovereign is entitled to investigate. This theory focuses on local judicial power as an appendage of state regulatory or police power. When the controversy centers in the forum state (*e.g.* an automobile accident there) applications of specific jurisdiction are as settled as are applications of general jurisdiction over the forum's own citizens.

Central questions concerning specific jurisdiction include: How related must defendant's forum acts be to the controversy? How purposeful must they be? Must they be such that defendant could forsee from his acts the possibility of being a defendant there? Again, the United States Supreme Court's decisions have not been terribly illuminating.

[3] The Fact-Sensitive Nature of Minimum Contacts Inquiries

The search for contacts requires courts to sift facts. Because facts register and combine differently from case to case, uncertainties inhere in the minimum contacts test. The Court acknowledged as much in *International Shoe:* "It is evident that the criteria by which we mark the boundary line between those activities which justify the subjection of a corporation to suit, and those which do not, cannot be simply mechanical or quantitative."[298] The fact-sensitive nature of the approach has made it unpopular with some critics.[299] No one, however, wishes to return to the law of territorial

---

[298] 326 U.S. at 319. For comments in a similar vein, see *Burger King Corp. v. Rudzewicz,* 471 U.S. 462, 485-86 & n.29 (1985); *Kulko v. Superior Court,* 436 U.S. 84, 92 (1978).

[299] *See, e.g.,* Hazard, *A General Theory of State-Court Jurisdiction,* 1965 Sup. Ct. Rev. 241, 283 ("the vagueness of the minimum-contacts general principle can make jurisdictional litigation uncertain at the trial level and frequent at the appellate level."). Weintraub, *A Map Out of the Personal Jurisdiction Labyrinth,* 28 U. Cal. Davis L. Rev. 531, 545 (1995) ("Courts cannot agree on how specific facts should influence the result.").

What has emerged recently as a due process test in addition to minimum contacts, see § 3.12[2], *infra,* seems in its way just as fact-sensitive. For a description of the new test, *see* Abramson, *Clarifying "Fair Play and Substantial Justice:" How the Courts Apply the Supreme Court Standard for Personal Jurisdiction,* 18 Hast. Const. L. Q. 441 (1991).

jurisdiction that *Shoe* replaced.[300] It remains to be seen whether a different modern test would achieve more satisfactory results.[301]

§ 3.10   Defendant's Forum Contacts Related to the Controversy (Specific Jurisdiction)[302] — Recent Developments

[1]   Jurisdiction in Cases Where Defendant Acts Elsewhere to Cause Harm in the Forum — An Introduction to the Problem

Specific jurisdiction exists when there is a connection between the forum and the acts of a nonresident defendant generating the controversy.[303] When defendant is alleged to have acted in the forum to wrong plaintiff, the court's authority to exercise personal jurisdiction is clear.[304] The same is usually true if defendant uses the mails or another mode of communication as a substitute for actually going to the forum,[305] or if the defendant sends another to the forum to act on his behalf.[306] The controversy may

---

[300] For discussion of the rigidity of the rule of *Pennoyer v. Neff* and the fictions and lapses in enforcement which accompanied the rule, *see* § 3.05, *supra*. Looking back at the rejection of *Pennoyer*, the Supreme Court recently observed: "We have abandoned more formalistic tests that focused on a defendant's presence within a State in favor of a more flexible inquiry into whether a defendant's contacts with the forum made it reasonable, in the context of our federal system of government, to require it to defend the suit in that State." *Quill Corp. v. North Dakota,* 504 U.S. 298, 307 (1992).

[301] Proposals for replacement of the minimum contacts test with something else have been varied and extensive. *See, e.g.,* the list of articles in R. Weintraub, *Commentary on the Conflict of Laws* 116 n.26 (3d ed. 1986), and the arguments for reworking the relationship between personal jurisdiction and venue noted at § 6.03, *infra.*

[302] On the distinction between specific and general jurisdiction, see § 3.09, *supra.*

[303] Even under settled law, the process of classifying jurisdictional facts as related or unrelated to the controversy would sometimes be difficult. In addition, the area is troubled by some legal uncertainty and considerable debate whether facts supporting specific jurisdiction must "arise out of" the claim — be necessary somehow to proof of the claim — or can be more distantly related to the controversy. Much recent debate centers on the refusal of the Court to take seriously the possibility of specific jurisdiction in *Helicopteros Nacionales de Columbia v. Hall,* 466 U.S. 408 (1984). For discussion of this point in *Helicopteros* and a critique of the debate, see § 3.11, *infra.*

[304] "[I]t is most obviously fair and reasonable to attribute a related contact to the defendant where the event is an act performed within the forum by the defendant." Brilmayer, *How Contacts Count: Due Process Limitations on State Court Jurisdiction,* 1980 Sup. Ct. Rev. 77, 90.

[305] "[I]f a foreign corporation purposefully avails itself of the benefits of an economic market in the forum State, it may subject itself to the State's in personam jurisdiction even if has no physical presence in the State." *Quill Corp. v. North Dakota,* 504 U.S. 298, 307 (1992). Additional applications of the principle appear in *Burger King Corp. v. Rudzewicz,* 471 U.S. 462, 476 (1985); *Travelers Health Ass'n v. Virginia,* 339 U.S. 643 (1950). *See generally* Reese & Galston, *Doing an Act or Causing Consequences as Bases of Judicial Jurisdiction,* 44 Iowa L. Rev. 249, 253 (1959).

[306] *Brilmayer,* note 304, *supra,* at 91.

grow out of defendant's continuous and systematic forum activity. [307] However, the court also has jurisdiction when the controversy arises from defendant's forum-connected acts which are but a random or isolated aspect of defendant's activity as a whole. [308]

To grasp why connecting the defendant's controversy-generating activity to the forum is so significant, recall the regulatory rationale supporting *International Shoe*'s expansion of personal jurisdiction beyond the limits set by *Pennoyer v. Neff.* [309] The forum has a legitimate interest in ascertaining through its judicial process whether wrongs have occurred there. "The most convincing justification" for imposition of jurisdiction over nonresident defendants "is the State's right to regulate activities occurring within the State." [310]

This principle explains why some cases involving random or isolated contacts definitely pass the minimum contacts test, [311] and why others definitely do not. [312] However, two important Supreme Court cases, addressed in this section, pose situations that seem closer to the line. In *World-Wide Volkswagen* defendants did not know where the ultimate effects of their acts would occur. When such acts caused injury in the forum and the defendant had no other contacts there, the Court was called upon to decide whether the minimum contacts test had been satisfied. In *Burger King,* another minimum contacts case, defendants directed more of their controversy-related activity elsewhere than at the forum and appeared to have no forum contacts unrelated to the controversy.

---

[307] *International Shoe* was such a case. 326 U.S. at 320. For discussion of this category and further case examples, see von Mehren & Trautman, *Jurisdiction to Adjudicate: A Suggested Analysis,* 79 Harv. L. Rev. 1121, 1147-1148 (1966).

[308] *McGee v. International Life Ins. Co.,* discussed in § 3.06[2][a], *supra,* and *Hess v. Pawloski,* a precursor to *International Shoe,* discussed in § 3.05[2], *supra,* are examples. For discussion of *McGee* and *Hess* in this context, see *von Mehren & Trautman,* note 307, *supra,* at 1149-1151.

[309] *See* § 3.06 *supra.*

[310] *Brilmayer,* note 304, *supra,* at 86. Addressing the field of tort law, the American Law Institute observed: "A state has an especial interest in exercising judicial jurisdiction over those who commit torts within its territory. This is because torts involve wrongful conduct which a state seeks to deter, and against which it attempts to afford protection, by providing that a tortfeasor shall be liable for damages which are the proximate result of his tort." *Restatement (Second) of Conflicts* § 36 comment (c) (1971). A state's interest in providing a judicial remedy may be most pronounced in tort cases, *see* Carrington & Martin, *Substantive Interests and the Jurisdiction of State Courts,* 66 Mich. L. Rev. 227, 232 (1967), but it can occur in other settings. For example, in *Burger King Corp. v. Rudzewicz,* 471 U.S. 462, 472-473 (1985), the Supreme Court offered a regulatory rationale for extraterritorial jurisdiction in a contracts case.

[311] *See* note 308, *supra.*

[312] "[I]f a State is relying upon a regulatory justification for jurisdiction by claiming a right to regulate substantive occurrences within the State, imposition of legal burdens on the defendant is reasonable only if the defendant was somehow responsible for those occurrences." *Brilmayer,* note 304, *supra,* at 89.

[2]   Forum Injury Is Not Enough — *World-Wide Volkswagen v. Woodson* [313]

Plaintiffs purchased an Audi automobile from defendant retailer Seaway Volkswagen in New York. Seaway had obtained the car from defendant World-Wide Volkswagen, a regional distributor. Plaintiffs thereafter moved from New York, travelling in their Audi toward a destination in Arizona. The gas tank ignited in an Oklahoma collision, seriously injuring several members of the family. Plaintiffs brought suit in an Oklahoma state court against manufacturer Audi, importer Volkswagen of America, World-Wide Volkswagen and Seaway.

Plaintiffs made a substantial case for personal jurisdiction. Since product failure and injuries were alleged to have occurred in the forum, it seemed a natural place for plaintiff to bring suit. Moreover, the fact of injury in the forum appeared to provide Oklahoma with a regulatory interest in adjudicating the case. Nonetheless, the Supreme Court upheld the challenges of retailer Seaway and regional distributor World-Wide Volkswagen. [314] Noting that these "defendants' only connection with Oklahoma is the fact that an automobile sold in New York to New York residents became involved in an accident in Oklahoma," [315] the Court held that Oklahoma courts were without minimum contacts necessary to assert personal jurisdiction. [316]

---

[313] 444 U.S. 286 (1980).

[314] Audi does not appear to have challenged jurisdiction. Volkswagen of America dropped its jurisdictional objection prior to Supreme Court review. 444 U.S. at 288 n.3.

[315] 444 U.S. at 287.

[316] The Oklahoma court lacked jurisdiction,

> [e]ven if the defendant would suffer minimal or no inconvenience from being forced to litigate before the tribunals of another State; even if the forum State has a strong interest in applying its law to the controversy; even if the forum State is the most convenient location for litigation

444 U.S. at 294.

The Court cited *Hanson v. Denckla*, 357 U.S. 235 (1958). Other modern cases, including *Shaffer v. Heitner*, 433 U.S. 186 (1977), discussed at § 3.08[1], *supra, Rush v. Savchuk*, 444 U.S. 320 (1980), discussed at § 3.08[2], *supra,* and *Kulko v. Superior Court*, 436 U.S. 84 (1978), also refurbished *Hanson's* authority. *Kulko* involved a California custody and child support proceeding. The Supreme Court held that the fact that the New York father provided his daughter with a one-way ticket to California did not establish requisite minimum contacts between the defendant-father and the forum. California's interest in adjudicating the case was real, deriving from the presence there of the mother and two children. To the Court, however, the lack of contacts between California and the defendant made California's interest academic. Quoting *Hanson,* the Court stated:

> The unilateral activity of those who claim some relationship with a nonresident defendant cannot satisfy the requirement of contact with the forum State. . . . [I]t is essential in each case that there be some act by which the defendant purposefully avails [him]self of the privilege of conducting activities within the forum State.

436 U.S at 93-94. For more on personal jurisdiction in the domestic relations setting, *see* Wasserman, *Parents, Partners, and Personal Jurisdiction*, 1995 U. Ill. L. Rev. 813.

The Supreme Court's refusal in *World-Wide Volkswagen* and *Kulko* to attach weight to forum convenience or forum interest in the absence of defendant's forum contacts is strongly reminiscent of the position it took in *Hanson.* For discussion of this and other aspects of *Hanson,* see § 3.07[2], *supra.*

The problem to the Court was the lack of contacts between the defendants and the Oklahoma forum.[317] Granted, defendants could have foreseen that so mobile a product might reach Oklahoma highways, but " 'foreseeability' alone has never been a sufficient benchmark for personal jurisdiction under the Due Process Clause."[318] The Court did not wish to discard the concept of foreseeability.

But the foreseeability that is critical to due process analysis is not the mere likelihood that a product will find its way into the forum State. Rather, it is that the defendant's conduct and connection with the forum State are such that he should reasonably anticipate being haled into court there.[319]

The Court reasoned that the conduct of the retailer and wholesaler in *World-Wide Volkswagen* was not such as to cause them to anticipate being haled into court in Oklahoma. Neither sold cars, advertised or carried on any other activity in the state.

World-Wide Volkswagen received a mixed reception.[320] Moreover, some lower court decisions continued to base personal jurisdiction over nonresidents on little more than the fact of injury in the forum.[321] The Court

---

[317] As it had in *Hanson*, the Court stressed that "the Due Process Clause does not contemplate that a state may make binding a judgment *in personam* against an individual or corporate defendant with which the state has no contacts, ties, or relations." 444 U.S. at 294 (*quoting* from *International Shoe Co. v. Washington*, 326 U.S. 310, 319 (1945)).

[318] 444 U.S. at 295. If it was, said the Court, failures to such products as tires, automobile jacks and soft drinks would expose local retailers to suit wherever plaintiff might transport the product. "Every seller of chattels would in effect appoint the chattel his agent for service of process. His amenability to suit would travel with the chattel." *Id.* at 296.

[319] 444 U.S. at 297. Then it is reasonable to impose personal jurisdiction because a corporation purposefully directing its activities at the forum

> has clear notice that it is subject to suit there, and can act to alleviate the risk of burdensome litigation by procuring insurance, passing the expected costs on to customers, or, if the risks are too great, severing its connection with the State.

Id.

[320] Professor Redish wrote of the case that "[t]he Court appeared to take a major step backward in its search for a viable, coherent theory of personal jurisdiction." *Due Process, Federalism, and Personal Jurisdiction: a Theoretical Evaluation*, 75 Nw. U.L. Rev. 1112 (1981). For further criticism, see Lewis, *A Brave New World for Personal Jurisdiction: Flexible Tests Under Uniform Standards*, 37 Vand. L. Rev. 1, 7-8 (1984). Some commentators generally approved of the case. *Brilmayer*, note 304, *supra*, at 92; Louis, *The Grasp of Long Arm Jurisdiction Finally Exceeds Its Reach: A Comment on World-Wide Volkswagen Corp. v. Woodson and Rush v. Savchuk*, 58 N.C. L. Rev. 407, 426-427 (1980). Others had mixed reactions. Seidelson, *Recasting World-Wide Volkswagen as a Source of Longer Jurisdictional Reach*, 19 Tulsa L.J. 1 (1983) (arguing that the rationale of the case could be reworked to expand rather than diminish jurisdiction); von Mehren, *Adjudicatory Jurisdiction: General Theories Compared and Evaluated*, 63 B.U. L. Rev. 279, 320 (1983) (approving the result in *World-Wide Volkswagen*, but suggesting that the Court should have written a different opinion).

[321] From his review of several such cases, Professor Weintraub observed: "When a court sees blood on the ground, it is very likely to find jurisdiction over a nonresident seller of the product that caused the injury." *Due Process Limitations on the Personal Jurisdiction of State Courts: Time for a Change*, 63 Or. L. Rev. 485, 516 (1984).

returned to the products liability area in *Asahi Metal Industry Co. v. Superior Court.*[322] Badly divided on the minimum contacts question, the *Asahi* Court used a different due process formula to restrain the personal jurisdiction of a California court.[323]

[3] All of Defendant's Contacts Related to the Controversy Need Not Be With the Forum — *Burger King Corp. v. Rudzewicz*[324]

World-Wide Volkswagen seemed to make clear that a nonresident defendant is not subject to specific personal jurisdiction unless he has directed acts toward the forum. However, a later case, *Burger King Corp. v. Rudzewicz,* demonstrated that not all of the defendant's contacts related to the controversy must be with the forum.

Through negotiation with Burger King's regional office in Michigan, Rudzewicz and another Michigan defendant obtained a franchise in that state. Defendants failed to make payments, and Burger King brought a federal diversity suit on the franchise agreement in Florida, its headquarters and place of incorporation. Rudzewicz appealed a judgment against him. Reversing, the Eleventh Circuit Court of Appeals held Rudzewicz to be beyond the constitutional reach of Florida's long-arm statute.[325] The Court of Appeals based its decision upon a determination that the bulk of the contacts giving rise to the controversy were with Michigan rather than Florida.[326]

Notwithstanding this, the United States Supreme Court concluded that personal jurisdiction over Rudzewicz was constitutional. Acknowledging the threshold importance of minimum contacts between defendant and the Florida forum, the Court held that there were enough Florida contacts related to the controversy to satisfy the test. Defendants at times dealt directly with Burger King's Miami headquarters; they contracted with Burger King to have Florida law govern the franchise agreement;[327] and they promised to send their franchise payments to Burger King's Florida address. Under the circumstances, the Court refused to attach importance to the fact that Rudzewicz had not been in the forum state.

---

[322] 480 U.S. 102 (1987).

[323] *See* § 3.12[2], *infra.*

[324] 471 U.S. 462 (1985).

[325] 724 F.2d 1505 (11th Cir. 1984).

[326] The two-judge majority stated that Rudzewicz had no office in Florida, nor did it appear that he had ever been there. Contract negotiations were conducted between Rudzewicz and Burger King's district representative entirely in Michigan. Anticipated profits from the franchise were to derive exclusively from Michigan food sales. Justice Stevens would later observe in his dissent: "Throughout the business relationship, appellee's principal contacts with appellant were with its Michigan office." 471 U.S. at 487.

[327] This is not to be confused with contractual consent to jurisdiction. Had Rudzewicz consented to Florida jurisdiction, his only basis for resistance presumably would have been to argue that the clause was unconscionable, or represented a contract of adhesion, and hence was unenforceable. For discussion of this point, see § 3.03[2][d], *supra.*

Although territorial presence frequently will enhance a potential defendant's affiliation with a State and reinforce the reasonable foreseeability of suit there, it is an inescapable fact of modern commercial life that a substantial amount of business is transacted solely by mail and wire communications across state lines, thus obviating the need for physical presence within a State in which business is conducted. So long as a commercial actor's efforts are "purposefully directed" toward residents of another State, we have consistently rejected the notion that an absence of physical contacts can defeat personal jurisdiction there.[328]

To save money and to place debtor-defendants at a financial and psychic disadvantage, a corporate creditor-plaintiff might prefer to file in its home state lawsuits arising from operations elsewhere. To read *Burger King* as a green light in such cases, so long as defendant directs some communications to the corporate home forum and accedes by contract to governance of the instrument by application of that forum's law, could lead to fundamentally unfair results.

Consider the following example. Maine consumer X reads a local advertisement placed by Y (a nationwide seller based in California) and orders a stereo by mail from Y. Y sends X an installment sales contract, which X signs and sends back to California. The stereo arrives and proves defective; therefore, X refuses to continue payments under the contract. Even with the contacts summarized in the preceding paragraph, California litigation by Y on the debt would be an unexpected and dislocating prospect for X — one seeming to lack fundamental fairness required by due process.[329] The *Burger King* Court may have anticipated this problem, stressing that Rudzewicz was commercially sophisticated and represented by an attorney throughout his negotiations with Burger King.[330]

On final analysis, *Burger King* may represent a realistic accommodation between the minimum contacts requirement of due process and the fact that controversy-related contacts are often spread over more than one state.[331]

---

[328] 471 U.S. at 476.

[329] *Cf. von Mehren,* note 320, *supra,* at 314 ("[A] party's economic and psychological ability to litigate in the other party's forum, as well as his expectations with respect to the possibility that he may have to do so, decrease as a direct function of the degree to which his normal activities are localized and have only local effects.").

[330] "We do not mean to suggest," the Court added, "that the jurisdictional outcome will always be the same in franchise cases. Some franchises may be primarily intrastate in character or involve different decision-making structures, such that a franchisee should not reasonably anticipate out-of-state litigation." 471 U.S. at 485 n.28.

[331] *See also Keeton v. Hustler Magazine,* 465 U.S. 770 (1984). The Court permitted jurisdiction under the New Hampshire long-arm statute in a defamation action, although only a small percentage of defendant's total circulation of the offending magazine issue occurred in the forum state. However, the facts of *Keeton* furnished added jurisdictional support not present in *Burger King.* Defendant had carried on continuous and systematic activity (albeit unrelated to the controversy) in New Hampshire. For discussion of *Keeton,* see § 3.12[1], *infra.* For further discussion of *Burger King,* see Perschbacher, *Minimum Contacts Reapplied: Mr. Justice Brennan Has It His Way in Burger King Corp. v. Rudzewicz,* 1986 Ariz. St. L. J. 585. Louis, *Jurisdiction Over Those Who Breach Their Contracts: The Lessons of Burger King,* 72 N.C. L. Rev. 55 (1993).

To recognize specific jurisdiction only in a place which is the exclusive or predominant source of related contacts would often deny forums the legitimate expression of their regulatory interests.[332]

§ 3.11 Defendant's Forum Contacts Unrelated to the Controversy (General Jurisdiction) — Recent Developments

General jurisdiction exists over a nonresident defendant when his contacts with the forum are so extensive that it is possible to overlook the fact the cause of action arose elsewhere — that no contacts related to the controversy exist between the forum and the defendant.[333] The Court raised the possibility in *International Shoe.*[334] Five years later it provided an example, *Perkins v. Benguet Consolidated Mining Company.*[335] The Supreme Court eventually returned to the subject of general jurisdiction and threw some additional light on matters. However (as with *Perkins*), it selected a relatively easy case.

[1] *Helicopteros Nacionales de Colombia v. Hall*[336]

Respondents brought this Texas state wrongful death action as the result of the Peruvian crash of a helicopter operated by Helicopteros, a Colombian corporation. In their claims against Helicopteros, respondents alleged that pilot error caused the crash. Appearing specially, Helicopteros moved to dismiss for lack of personal jurisdiction. The trial court denied the motion, and respondents obtained a jury award in excess of one million dollars. The Texas Supreme Court eventually decided that the Texas court had personal jurisdiction over Helicopteros.[337] The United States Supreme Court reversed.

Helicopteros sent a representative to Texas to contract with a Texas helicopter manufacturer for the purchase and transport of most of its helicopter fleet, and for the training of its pilots, management and maintenance personnel.[338] Helicopteros also received payments from a Texas bank

---

[332] On specific jurisdiction as an expression of the forum's regulatory interest, see § 3.10[1]. *supra.*

[333] In other words, when there is no material for specific jurisdiction. For further discussion of the distinction between specific and general jurisdiction, see § 3.09, *supra.*

[334] The Court speculated that "continuous corporate operations within a state" could be "so substantial and of such a nature as to justify suit against it on causes of action arising from dealings entirely distinct from those activities." *International Shoe Co. v. Washington,* 326 U.S. 310, 318 (1945).

[335] 342 U.S. 437 (1952), *discussed in* § 3.06[2][b], *supra.*

[336] 466 U.S. 408 (1984).

[337] 638 S.W.2d 870 (Tex. 1982). For a detailed account of the Texas decisions in the case, see Terez, *The Misguided Helicopteros Case: Confusion in the Courts Over Contacts,* 37 Baylor L. Rev. 913 (1985).

[338] The helicopter that crashed was manufactured in Texas and the pilot was trained there. 466 U.S. at 409-412.

account. The Supreme Court refused to consider whether these contacts provided a basis for specific jurisdiction because the plaintiffs apparently failed to argue this form of jurisdiction.[339] It framed the issue instead as one of general jurisdiction: whether contacts between Helicopteros and the Texas forum were sufficient when seen as unrelated to the controversy. Invoking *International Shoe* and *Perkins,* the Court concluded that the case failed the minimum contacts test. Helicopteros lacked "the kind of continuous and systematic general business contacts" with Texas necessary to satisfy due process.[340] Since Helicopteros flew no commercial routes in Texas and kept no personnel there, the conclusion that no general jurisdiction existed was not difficult to reach.

[2] The Future of General Jurisdiction

Clearly, minimum contacts necessary to support general jurisdiction are greater than those for specific jurisdiction.[341] But how much greater? *Helicopteros* may have the effect of overruling some of the most tenuous assertions of general jurisdiction among prior lower court decisions.[342] However, it left much unsettled. Particularly troublesome is the question when or whether a national concern that regularly conducts some business

---

[339] "All parties to the present case," said the Court, "concede that respondents' claims against [Helicopteros] did not 'arise out of,' and are not related to, [Helicopteros'] activities within Texas." 466 U.S. at 415. *See generally* §§ 13.08 *infra,* on the necessity of preserving and presenting a question for appeal. Dissenting, Justice Brennan would have found the case properly within Texas' specific jurisdiction. Several commentators have agreed. Weintraub, *Due Process Limitations on the Personal Jurisdiction of State Courts: Time for Change,* 63 Or. L. Rev. 485, 530 (1984); Weinberg, *The Helicopter Case and the Jurisprudence of Jurisdiction,* 58 S. Cal. L. Rev. 913, 915 (1985); Knudson, *Keeton, Calder, Helicopteros and Burger King — International Shoe's Most Recent Progeny,* 39 U. Miami L. Rev. 809, 832 (1985). For example, Professor Weintraub wrote: "The deaths in Peru 'arose out of' [Helicopteros'] Texas business contacts in the broadest 'but for' sense." Weintraub, *Due Process Limitations, supra.*

There may be problems, however, with so broad a conception of specific jurisdiction. Granted, Helicopteros' Texas contacts were not entirely isolated from the claims brought there. Yet a "but for" approach to specific jurisdiction seems capable of attaching significance to contacts which do not really provide the forum with regulatory concerns necessary to justify specific jurisdiction. *See* § 3.10[1], *supra.* In *Helicopteros,* "Texas probably has little interest in a wrongful death that occurred in Peru, especially when equipment manufactured and purchased in Texas was not at fault. . . ." *Terez,* note 337, *supra,* at 938. *See generally* Rose, *Related Contacts and Personal Jurisdiction: The "But For" Test,* 82 Calif. L. Rev. 1545 (1994).

[340] 466 U.S. at 416. Relying on an early case, *Rosenberg Bros. & Co. v. Curtis Brown Co.,* 260 U.S. 516 (1923), the Court added that the fact that the defendant purchased goods from the forum contributed little to respondent's case for jurisdiction. "[W]e hold that mere purchases, even if occurring at regular intervals, are not enough to warrant a State's assertion of *in personam* jurisdiction over a nonresident corporation in a cause of action not related to those purchase transactions." 466 U.S. at 418.

[341] *See* § 3.09[2], *supra;* Brilmayer, *Related Contacts and Personal Jurisdiction,* 101 Harv. L. Rev. 1444 (1988); Hill, *Choice of Law and Jurisdiction in the Supreme Court,* 81 Colum. L. Rev. 960, 980-981 (1981).

[342] *See, e.g., Bryant v. Finnish Nat'l Airline,* 208 N.E.2d 439 (N.Y. 1965), *discussed in* § 3.07[3], *supra,* and *criticized in* W. Reese et al., *Cases and Materials on Conflict of Laws* 124 (9th ed. 1990).

in the forum has by so doing made itself amenable to process on a theory of general jurisdiction. For example, is a car manufacturer or insurance company that routinely directs its product into many states within the general jurisdiction of the courts of each?

On one hand, it can be argued that all *International Shoe* and *Perkins* seem to require and all that should be required by the Due Process clause is that the business carried on by the nonresident defendant in each forum be continuous, systematic and substantial. By this view, it is reasonable for many state courts to exercise general jurisdiction over a defendant operating on a large scale.[343] On the other hand, it has been argued that doctrine shaping general jurisdiction is not as susceptible to refined analysis as doctrine associated with specific jurisdiction,[344] and that it would be preferable to confine *Perkins* to its unusual facts and permit jurisdiction for causes of action arising elsewhere only where the defendant is a citizen of or has its principal place of business in the forum.[345] Between these opposing views on how much significance to attach to defendant's forum contacts unrelated to the claim, there may be a useful middle ground.

First, it is easier to justify general jurisdiction in a place neither the home nor the principal place of business of the defendant when the claim presented is similar to one which *could* have arisen from defendant's forum dealings. This might be a sensible way of limiting the *Helicopteros* ruling. Because Helicopteros neither solicited passengers nor flew routes in Texas, it could not "reasonably anticipate being haled into court there"[346] to defend against a claim based on pilot error. However, general jurisdiction over claims arising elsewhere is defensible when the lawsuit is "precisely the

---

343

    If a corporation conducts a major, or even a substantial, portion of its activities in a particular state, it is as fair for it to be sued there on causes of action arising elsewhere as it is for a corporation (or an individual) to be sued at its domicile on such causes of action. The substantial character of corporate activities in the state indicates that the corporation is reasonably equipped to defend lawsuits there.

R. Leflar, *American Conflicts Law* 52 (3d ed. 1977). *Accord,* Waits, *Values, Intuitions, and Opinion Writing: The Judicial Process and State Court Jurisdiction,* 1983 U. Ill. L. Rev. 917, 940.

344 von Mehren & Trautman, *Jurisdiction to Adjudicate: A Suggested Analysis,* 79 Harv. L. Rev. 1121, 1144 (1966).

345 *Id.* at 1141-1142. *Accord, Developments in the Law — State-Court Jurisdiction,* 73 Harv. L. Rev. 909, 932 (1960).

346 *World-Wide Volkswagen v. Woodson,* 444 U.S. 286, 297 (1980). *World-Wide Volkswagen* dealt with attempted specific jurisdiction. But the point it made by the phrase quoted in the text — that it is reasonable to impose personal jurisdiction only if the defendant directed such activities toward the forum state to make the possibility of having to defend there reasonably foreseeable (*see* § 3.10[2][a], *supra*) — would also seem to bear on general jurisdiction. *Compare* Seidelson, *Recasting World-Wide Volkswagen as a Source of Longer Jurisdictional Reach,* 19 Tulsa L.J. 1, 17-19 (1983) (developing this point) *with* Twitchell, *The Myth of General Jurisdiction,* 101 Harv. L. Rev. 610, 680 (1988) (adopting a narrower view: "The court should exercise general jurisdiction only if it finds that the defendant's ties with the forum are so significant that the defendant should have expected to be answerable to most claims asserted against it within the forum.").

kind of action the defendant should have contemplated as a result of [forum] contacts."[347]

Second, in deciding whether the "continuous and systematic" standard is satisfied, the court should consider defendant's contacts as a whole for a reasonable period of time up until and including the date the suit was filed.[348] For example, in one case, the appellate court found that the district court had erred in limiting its jurisdictional inquiry to one year, and instead found the appropriate period to be six years in the circumstances of the case.[349]

Third, as we will examine in the following section, defendant's unrelated forum contacts may combine with some claim-related contacts between defendant and the forum to create jurisdiction when neither a theory of general nor specific jurisdiction alone would suffice.

§ 3.12 Further Developments

Two of the Supreme Court's more recent cases on the role of due process in regulating personal jurisdiction are discussed elsewhere.[350] We will review three more in this Section and discuss how each may have affected the shape of current law.

[1] Combining Defendant's Related and Unrelated Forum Contacts — *Keeton v. Hustler Magazine*[351]

It is clear that sufficient claim-related contacts between the forum and a nonresident defendant make the defendant amenable to suit on a theory of specific jurisdiction,[352] and that sufficient contacts between the two which are unrelated to the controversy will produce the same result on a theory of general jurisdiction.[353] There will be cases, however, where the forum

---

[347] *Seidelson,* note 346, *supra,* at 18-19; Simard, *Hybrid Personal Jurisdiction: Its Not General Jurisdiction, or Specific Jurisdiction, But Is It Constitutional?* 48 Case W. Res. L. Rev. 559, 590 (1998); George, *In Search of General Jurisdiction,* 64 Tul. L. Rev. 1097, 1134-1135 (1990). *See, e.g., Garfield v. Homowack Lodge, Inc.,* 378 A.2d 351 (Pa. Super. Ct. 1977) (upholding personal jurisdiction over a nonresident defendant regarding a tort claim arising outside the forum but comparable to claims which could have arisen from defendant's forum contacts).

[348] *See Metropolitan Life Ins. Co. v. Robertson-Ceco Corp.,* 84 F.3d 560, 569-571 (2d Cir. 1996).

[349] *Id.* at 570.

[350] In *Burger King Corp. v. Rudzewicz,* 471 U.S. 462 (1985), the Court permitted personal jurisdiction in Florida over a Michigan defendant — even though defendant had far more controversy-related contacts with Michigan than with Florida. The case is discussed at § 3.10[3], *supra.* In *Phillips Petroleum Co. v. Shutts,* 472 U.S. 797 (1985), the Court refused to invoke the minimum contacts test to measure the relationship between the forum and unnamed members of plaintiffs' class. The ruling permitted maintenance of nationwide, plaintiff class actions uncomplicated by *International Shoe. Shutts* is discussed at § 9.09[2][b], *infra.*

[351] 465 U.S. 770 (1984).

[352] *See* § 3.09[2] and the illustrations provided in § 3.10, *supra.*

[353] *See* § 3.06[2][b] and the illustrations provided in § 3.11, *supra.*

has both types of contacts with a nonresident defendant, but neither in sufficient quantity to alone support personal jurisdiction. May the forum satisfy due process in such cases by aggregating all of defendant's forum contacts?

The question once divided commentators[354] but now may be resolved in a way broadening opportunities for personal jurisdiction. Without endorsing general use of the technique, the Supreme Court appeared to combine related and unrelated contacts in holding that jurisdiction was proper in *Keeton v. Hustler Magazine.*

Plaintiff Keeton sued Hustler Magazine in New Hampshire federal court for libel. The First Circuit Court of Appeals upheld Hustler's objection to personal jurisdiction. It ruled that due process prevented New Hampshire's long-arm statute from reaching Hustler,[355] an Ohio corporation with its principal place of business in California. The Supreme Court reversed.

Hustler had some contacts with the New Hampshire forum both related and unrelated to the controversy. It had circulated in New Hampshire copies of the magazine alleged to have libeled plaintiff, and it had circulated other issues there in a continuous and systematic fashion. There is some indication, however, that neither defendant's related nor unrelated contacts would have alone been sufficient to support personal jurisdiction. The Court noted that the magnitude of the alleged libel was the total circulation of the offending issues and that "only a small portion" of that circulation occurred in New Hampshire.[356] Similarly, Hustler's activities in New Hampshire "may not" have been "so substantial as to support jurisdiction over a cause of action unrelated to those activities."[357] However, the combination of defendant's related and unrelated contacts with the forum proved enough. "[R]espondent is carrying on a 'part of its general business' in New Hampshire, and that is sufficient to support jurisdiction when the cause of action arises out of the very activity being conducted, in part, in New Hampshire."[358]

---

[354] *Compare, e.g.,* Lewis, *A Brave New World for Personal Jurisdiction: Flexible Tests Under Uniform Standards,* 37 Vand. L. Rev. 1, 34 (1984) (arguing the possibility of establishing personal jurisdiction through "partial satisfaction of both versions of the contacts tests."), *with* Brilmayer, *How Contacts Count: Due Process Limitations on State Court Jurisdiction,* 1980 Sup. Ct. Rev. 77, 88 ("These two bases are independent threshold tests, so that a greater quantum of unrelated activity does not compensate for attenuated related contacts."). For the latter view, see also Comment, *The Abuse of General Jurisdiction,* 66 Tul. L. Rev. 2085, 2093 (1992) (criticizing a recent Louisiana case for "merging the two doctrines").

[355] *Keeton v. Hustler Magazine,* 682 F.2d 33 (1st Cir. 1982). On the significance of state long-arm statutes to the personal jurisdiction of federal courts, *see* § 3.01[2][b], *supra.*

[356] 465 U.S. at 775.

[357] *Id.* at 779.

[358] *Id.* at 780 (*quoting Perkins v. Benguet Mining Co.,* 342 U.S. 437, 438 (1952)). The Court added that, "Where, as in this case, respondent has continuously and deliberately exploited the New Hampshire market, it must reasonably anticipate being haled into court there in a libel action based on the contents of its magazine." *Id.* at 781. The Supreme Court had given earlier indication that related and unrelated contacts might have combined effect. For example, in *World-Wide Volkswagen Corp. v. Woodson,* 444 U.S. 286 (1980), the court concluded that Oklahoma lacked jurisdiction only after finding that defendants' claim-related contacts with the forum were slight *and* that defendants had no contacts unrelated to the controversy. *Id.* at 295.

It may be that the Court is simply aggregating the contacts to reach a quantitative threshhold in a case like *Keeton*, but, if so, it has backtracked from its disavowal in *International Shoe* of any "simply mechanical or quantitative" test.[359] A more plausible theory for "hybrid" cases (combining related with unrelated contacts to uphold personal jurisdiction) rests on the suggestion that general and specific jurisdiction are simply opposite ends of a sliding scale, by which the quantity and quality of the defendant's contacts and the relatedness of the contacts to the claim are inversely related.[360] The availability of unrelated contacts can therefore compensate for the paucity of related contacts, even though the case is "a near-miss"[361] on both — it does not reach either end of the scale.

An alternative theory is that the causally unrelated contacts with the forum state (distributing magazines other than the offending issue) are so like the causally related, though slight contact (distributing the particular offending issue of the magazine) that the defendant could reasonably forsee having to defend some libel action based on its magazines distributed there and that the state has a regulatory interest in the content of magazines distributed there. As one commentator has put it, "if . . . the defendant could have forseen its forum contact resulting in factual circumstances similar to those that gave rise to the plaintiff's cause of action, then the defendant's contact should form the basis for asserting . . . jurisdiction in the forum."[362]

[2]   When Minimum Contacts Are Not Enough — *Asahi Metal Industry Co. v. Superior Court*[363]

Asahi was another product liability case.[364] Plaintiff sued in California over a serious accident there, allegedly caused by failure of the rear tire of plaintiff's motorcycle. Defendant Cheng Shin manufactured the tire in Taiwan. It attempted to bring Asahi, a Japanese concern and manufacturer of the tire's valve assembly, into the case on a theory of indemnification. Rejecting Asahi's jurisdictional challenge, the California Supreme Court

---

[359] *International Shoe*, 326 U.S. at 319. *See RAR, Inc. v. Turner Diesel Ltd.*, 107 F.3d 1272, 1277 (7th Cir. 1997):

> We cannot simply aggregate all of a defendant's contacts with a state — no matter how dissimilar in terms of geography, time, or substance . . . [W]hen doing business with a forum in one context, potential defendants should not have to wonder whether some aggregation of other past or future forum contacts will render them liable to suit there.

[360] *See* Richman, *A Sliding Scale to Supplement the Distinction Between General and Specific Jurisdiction*, 72 Cal. L. Rev. 1328 (1984).

[361] *Id.*

[362] Simard, *Hybrid Personal Jurisdiction: It's Not General Jurisdiction, or Specific Jurisdiction, but Is It Constitutional?*, 48 Case W. Res. L. Rev. 559, 590 (1998).

[363] 480 U.S. 102 (1987).

[364] In an earlier product liability case, *World-Wide Volkswagen v. Woodson*, 444 U.S. 286 (1980), the Court found contacts between an Oklahoma court and certain nonresident defendants insufficient to support personal jurisdiction. *See generally* § 3.10[2], *supra*.

held that it could exercise personal jurisdiction over Asahi without violating the Due Process Clause.[365] The United States Supreme Court reversed.

Seven justices joined in Justice O'Connor's conclusion that, whether or not minimum contacts existed between the forum and Asahi,[366] California's attempt to assert personal jurisdiction exceeded what the Court called a distinct "reasonableness" standard of due process. It drew the standard from language in *International Shoe* confining personal jurisdiction over nonresident defendants to "traditional notions of fair play and substantial justice."[367] The Court noted that

> the determination of the reasonableness of the exercise of jurisdiction in each case will depend on an evaluation of several factors. A court must consider the burden on the defendant, the interests of the forum state, and the plaintiff's interest in obtaining relief. It must also weigh in its determination "the interstate judicial system's interest in obtaining the most efficient resolution of controversies; and the shared interest of the several States in furthering fundamental substantive social policies."[368]

The Supreme Court found California's exercise of jurisdiction over Asahi to be unreasonable on balance. On one hand, "the interests of the plaintiff and the forum in California's assertion of jurisdiction over Asahi" were "slight." On the other hand, Asahi's burden from defending in California was "severe."[369]

---

[365] The California Supreme Court sought to neutralize *World-Wide Volkswagen* by finding in the case a "distinction between businesses that serve a local market and those that serve a broader market," deeming Asahi to be the latter. 39 Cal. 3d 35, 45, *rev'd*, 480 U.S. 102 (1987). In other words, while "a secondary distributor and retailer" was protected under *World-Wide Volkswagen*, "a manufacturer or primary distributor" was not. *Id.* at 46. The United States Supreme Court's decision in *Asahi* makes clear that this categorical distinction does not work.

[366] Only the Chief Justice and Justices Powell and Scalia joined the portion of Justice O'Connor's opinion concluding the California forum lacked minimum contacts. Justice Brennan (joined by Justices White, Marshall and Blackmun) argued in a concurring opinion that the record in the case indicated minimum contacts. Justice Stevens (joined by Justices White and Blackmun) suggested in another concurring opinion that California may have had minimum contacts, but it was unnecessary for the Court to rule on the issue. For a comparison of approaches taken by members of the Court prior to *Asahi*, see Leathers, *Supreme Court Voting Patterns Related to Jurisdictional Issues,* 62 Wash. L. Rev. 631 (1987).

[367] *International Shoe Co. v. Washington,* 326 U.S. 310, 316 (1945), quoted in *Asahi,* 480 U.S. at 105.

[368] 480 U.S. at 113 (*quoting World-Wide Volkswagen,* 444 U.S. at 292). The Court confuses matters, however, by relying directly on *World-Wide Volkswagen* for its reasonableness test. When the Court raised the same concerns in *World-Wide Volkswagen,* it was discussing "the concept of minimum contacts." 444 U.S. at 291. The *Asahi* Court shifted these concerns into a separate, free-standing due process test. *World-Wide Volkswagen* did not portend this development, but the intervening *Burger King* case did: "Once it has been decided that a defendant purposefully established minimum contacts within the forum State, these contacts may be considered in light of other factors to determine whether the assertion of personal jurisdiction would comport with fair play and substantial justice." *Burger King Corp. v. Rudzewicz,* 471 U.S. 462, 476 (1985) (*quoting International Shoe*). For an attempt to sort out the new test, see Abramham, *Clarifying "Fair Play and Substantial Justice:" How the Courts Apply the Supreme Court Standard for Personal Jurisdiction,* 18 Hast. Const. L.Q. 441 (1991).

[369] 480 U.S. at 114.

Asahi has been commanded not only to traverse the distance between Asahi's headquarters

Asahi's significance as a minimum contacts case is at best uncertain. No opinion on the issue commanded a majority, [370] and the suggestion of four justices that minimum contacts were lacking has been roundly criticized. [371] However, the Court invalidated jurisdiction in a due process holding divorced from minimum contacts analysis — and that is significant. The result in *Asahi* confirmed that minimum contacts between the forum and a nonresident defendant do not guarantee that assertion of personal jurisdiction comports with due process. In addition to minimum contacts, the plaintiff must still show reasonableness of personal jurisdiction under the criteria listed in *Asahi*. Furthermore, some courts have held that minimum contacts and reasonableness are inversely related, such that a borderline showing of minimum contacts will require "an especially strong showing of reasonableness" to support jurisdiction. [372]

Asahi's ultimate importance may depend in part on how frequently the situation posed there recurs. How often will courts have minimum contacts over a nonresident defendant yet be unable to exercise personal jurisdiction without offending notions of "fair play and substantial justice"? Perhaps not very often. [373] It still remains to be seen whether *Asahi* stiffened due process doctrine appreciably or merely distributed between two categories considerations once clustered around minimum contacts. [374] Yet, at the very

---

in Japan and the Superior Court of California but also to submit its dispute with Cheng Shin to a foreign nation's judicial system. The unique burdens placed upon one who must defend oneself in a foreign legal system should have significant weight in assessing the reasonableness of stretching the long arm of personal jurisdiction over national borders. *Id.*

[370] *See* note 366, *supra.*

[371] "The most ominous aspect of the *Asahi* opinion is that four Justices joined in the finding that Asahi did not have minimum contacts with California." Weintraub, *Asahi Sends Personal Jurisdiction Down the Tubes,* 23 Tex. Int'l L.J. 55, 66 (1988). *Cf.* Richman, *Understanding Personal Jurisdiction,* 25 Ariz. St. L. Rev. 599, 625 (1993) (the opinion poses an "ominous limitation" on the stream-of-commerce justification for personal jurisdiction); Wiseman, *Reconstructing the Citadel: The Advent of Jurisdictional Privity,* 54 Ohio St. L.J. 403, 405-406 (1993) (criticizing the plurality for applying a "narrowly-defined jurisdictional privity" test).

[372] *Ticketmaster-New York, Inc. v. Alioto,* 26 F.3d 201, 210 (1st Cir. 1994); *Ellicott Mach. Corp. v. John Holland Party, Ltd.,* 995 F.2d 474, 479 (4th Cir. 1993).

[373] The two tests — minimum contacts and reasonableness — may so overlap that usually to fail one will be to fail both. The *Asahi* Court seemed to suggest as much: "When minimum contacts have been established, often the interests of the plaintiff and the forum in the exercise of jurisdiction will justify even the serious burdens placed on the alien defendant." 480 U.S. at 114. To Justice Brennan, the fact that *Asahi* passed the minimum contacts test but failed the reasonableness test made it "one of those rare cases." 480 U.S. at 116. *Burger King,* where minimum contacts and reasonableness tests seem to provide the same answer, may be more indicative of future results under the two-test approach. On *Burger King* as a precursor for the Court's approach in *Asahi,* see note 368, *supra.*

[374] *See* note 368, *supra.* For further discussion of the case, see Silberman, *"Two Cheers" for International Shoe (and None for Asahi): An Essay on the Fiftieth Anniversary of International Shoe,* 28 U. Cal. Davis L. Rev. 755 (1995); Dessem, *Personal Jurisdiction After Asahi: The Other (International) Shoe Drops,* 55 Tenn. L. Rev. 41 (1987); Seidelson, *A Supreme Court Conclusion and Two Rationales that Defy Comprehension: Asahi Metal Indus. Co. Ltd. v. Superior Court of California,* 53 Brooklyn L. Rev. 563 (1987); Maltz, *Unraveling the Conundrum of the Law of Personal Jurisdiction: A Comment on Asahi Metal Industry Co, v. Superior Court of California,* 1987 Duke L.J. 669.

least, *Asahi* makes it necessary to frame some due process issues differently.

[3]   A Limited Role for Plaintiff's Forum Contacts — *Calder v. Jones*[375]

In *Calder,* a California plaintiff brought a libel suit there against a number of defendants concerning publication of a story about the plaintiff in a national tabloid. The defendant who wrote and the defendant who edited the story (both Floridians) attacked the California court's personal jurisdiction. The highest California court ruling on the matter concluded that jurisdiction over the defendants was valid, and the United States Supreme Court affirmed.

Keeton[376] made clear that due process does not require minimum contacts between the *plaintiff* and the forum.[377] However, could the existence of such contacts enhance plaintiff's case for personal jurisdiction?[378] The Supreme Court's minimum contacts inquiry prior to *Calder* often seemed preoccupied with "the relationship among the defendant, the forum, and the litigation,"[379] a formula slighting plaintiff's forum contacts.[380] For a

---

[375] 465 U.S. 783 (1984).

[376] *Keeton v. Hustler Magazine,* 465 U.S. 770 (1984).

[377] Plaintiff Keeton was a New Yorker. The Court found the fact that her contacts with New Hampshire were "extremely limited" to be no obstacle to jurisdiction.

> [W]e have not to date required a plaintiff to have "minimum contacts" with the forum State before permitting that State to assert personal jurisdiction over a nonresident defendant. On the contrary, we have upheld the assertion of jurisdiction where such contacts were entirely lacking.

465 U.S. at 779.

[378] Plaintiff's contacts most often derive from forum citizenship. Just as defendants usually prefer to litigate at home (*see* § 3.04[2], *supra*), so do plaintiffs. The interest in litigating at home is most compelling for plaintiffs lacking the mobility, resources or sophistication to sue nonresident defendants elsewhere. *See* von Mehren, *Adjudicatory Jurisdiction: General Theories Compared and Evaluated,* 63 B.U. L. Rev. 279, 311-314 (1983); von Mehren & Trautman, *Jurisdiction to Adjudicate: A Suggested Analysis,* 79 Harv. L. Rev. 1121, 1150 (1966); Note, *Jurisdiction Over Foreign Corporations — An Analysis of Due Process,* 104 U. Pa. L. Rev. 381, 383 (1955).

Plaintiff's interest in obtaining a local judicial remedy coincides with the forum's interest in providing one to its citizens. Von Mehren, *Adjudicatory Jurisdiction, supra*, at 308. However, the forum state also may have interests in providing a place to sue which are unrelated to plaintiff's citizenship.

> It may be interested in creating a local forum so that its laws can be properly applied. It may be interested in controlling the actions of its [citizens]. It may be interested in creating a forum that is convenient for resident witnesses. It may have an interest in efficient administration of justice. And it may be interested in creating a local forum for the adjudication of disputes that have an impact on the economic and social life of the State.

Smit, *Common and Civil Law Rules of In Personam Adjudicatory Authority: An Analysis of Underlying Policies,* 21 Int. & Comp. L.Q. 335, 351-352 (1972).

[379] *Shaffer v. Heitner,* 433 U.S. 186, 204 (1977); *Rush v. Savchuk,* 444 U.S. 320, 327 (1980). There are a few limited exceptions to this rule. *See* A. von Mehren & D. Trautman, *The Law of Multistate Problems* 703-706 (1965). "The law in the United States has long been that the

time at least, *Calder v. Jones* seemed to change that. The Court said there that plaintiff's contacts "may be so manifold as to permit jurisdiction when it would not exist in their absence."[381]

The Court needed to emphasize plaintiff's forum contacts to overcome added difficulties posed by personal jurisdiction over the individual defendants. *Keeton* suggested that jurisdiction over the tabloid itself would have been possible for plaintiff Jones in any state where the offending issue appeared as part of the tabloid's regular circulation.[382] However, jurisdiction over the tabloid would not necessarily mean jurisdiction over individual staff members.[383] The Court justified jurisdiction over the latter by noting how plaintiff's relationship with the forum intensified the importance of defendants' forum contacts.[384]

However, *Asahi*[385] may require a narrower reading of *Calder's* holding concerning plaintiff's forum contacts.[386] *Asahi* suggested that plaintiff must pass two separate due process tests: minimum contacts and reasonableness. Since plaintiff's forum contacts are now a focal point in the reasonableness test,[387] can they still tilt the balance in a minimum contacts test? The

---

plaintiff's domicile [supports] specific jurisdiction with respect to certain aspects of the marriage relation." *Id.* at 703.

[380] This is the accepted view. Von Mehren, *Adjudicatory Jurisdiction,* note 378, *supra,* at 310; Hay, *Refining Personal Jurisdiction in the United States,* 35 Int'l & Comp. L.Q. 32, 36 (1986). *Rush v. Savchuk,* 444 U.S. 320 (1980), leaves little room for doubt. There the Court rejected the argument that "plaintiff's contacts with the forum are decisive in determining whether the defendant's due process rights are violated," stating that "[s]uch an approach is forbidden by *International Shoe* and its progeny." *Id.* at 332. Whether this is fair to plaintiffs is a matter of debate. *Compare, e.g.,* Silberman, *Shaffer v. Heitner: The End of an Era,* 53 NYU L. Rev. 33, 87 (1978) (criticizing what she sees as "a depreciated role in jurisdictional questions" for the factor of plaintiff's interest in selecting the particular forum); *and* Lilly, *Jurisdiction Over Domestic and Alien Defendants,* 69 Va. L. Rev. 85, 108 (1983) ("The Court's fixation upon [defendant's forum contacts] has essentially destroyed the desirable balance among the interests of the plaintiff, the forum state, and the defendant.") *with Brilmayer,* note 354, *supra,* at 107 (questioning "why the legislative desire to provide a forum should be dispositive, or why residence of the plaintiff provides a basis for depriving this particular defendant of property.").

[381] 465 U.S. at 788. *Cf. Keeton v. Hustler Magazine,* 465 U.S. 770 (1984) ("plaintiff's residence in the forum may, because of defendant's relationship with the plaintiff, enhance defendant's contacts with the forum.").

[382] *See* § 3.12 and accompanying text, *supra.*

[383] "Petitioners are correct that their contacts with California are not to be judged according to their employer's activities there. Each defendant's contacts with the forum State must be assessed individually." *Calder,* 465 U.S. at 790.

[384]

The allegedly libelous story concerned the California activities of a California resident. It impugned the professionalism of an entertainer whose television career was centered in California. The article was drawn from California sources, and the brunt of the harm, in terms both of the respondent's emotional distress and the injury to her professional reputation, was suffered in California. In sum, California is the focal point both of the story and of the harm suffered.

Calder, 465 U.S. at 788-789.

[385] *Asahi Metal Indust. Co. v. Superior Court,* 480 U.S. 102 (1987).

[386] *See* note 381 and accompanying text, *supra.*

[387] For discussion of these and other points in the case, see § 3.12[2], *supra.*

Supreme Court has yet to confirm that, by creating a separate test for reasonableness concerns, it means to read the same concerns out of the minimum contacts test. [388] If that turns out to be true, however, *Calder's* significance as a plaintiff's-contacts case may be limited to the relatively few [389] cases surviving minimum contacts scrutiny where the outcome under the reasonableness test might be in doubt.

Of more lasting effect may be the holding in *Calder* that defendants could not as journalists use the First Amendment to the Constitution to bolster their case against California's personal jurisdiction. Prior to the decision, lower courts [390] and commentators [391] disagreed whether freedom-of-the-press concerns should make jurisdiction in libel cases more difficult to obtain. The response of the Court was simply to "reject the suggestion that First Amendment concerns enter into the jurisdictional analysis." [392]

[4] Jurisdiction in Cyberspace

Increasingly, personal jurisdiction issues arise in controversies based entirely, or in significant part, on internet activity. The question in such cases is whether or how the rules and reference points of personal jurisdiction law can be made to work concerning defendant's cyberspace activity. One of the authors of this book posed the problem in this way:

> {P}ersonal jurisdiction retains a strong geographical dimension, typically resting on physical acts that were purposefully directed at a forum state. But cyberspace is structurally indifferent to geography. Internet addresses are logical addresses on the network, rather than geographic addresses in real space. Neither party to a transaction in cyberspace (by E-mail, Usenet post, or Worldwide Website) may know or care where the other is geographically

---

[388] *Calder* itself is not of much help here. As it had in *World-Wide Volkswagen* (*see* note 368, *supra*) the *Calder* Court attempted to fit its entire due process analysis under the heading of minimum contacts. *Calder*, 465 U.S. at 788. *Asahi* discarded this approach, administering concerns other than defendant's relationship to the forum under a separate reasonableness test. *See* § 3.12[2], *supra*. It is arguable that by doing so the Court eliminated these concerns from its minimum contacts test. On the other hand, *Asahi* does not expressly confirm this. A majority of the Court *ruling* on a minimum contacts issue in *Burger King* seemed to take an opposite view. The Court said of factors now in *Asahi's* reasonableness test: "These considerations sometimes serve to establish the reasonableness of jurisdiction upon a lesser showing of minimum contacts than would otherwise be required." *Burger King Corp. v. Rudzewicz*, 471 U.S. 462, 477 (1985) (*citing, inter alia, Calder* and *Keeton*).

[389] *See* note 373 and accompanying text, *supra*.

[390] *See* the decisions cited in Comment, *Long-arm Jurisdiction Over Publishers: To Chill a Mocking Word*, 67 Colum. L. Rev. 342 (1967).

[391] *Compare* Clermont, *Restating Territorial Jurisdiction and Venue for State and Federal Courts*, 66 Cornell L. Rev. 411, 451-452 (1981), and Carrington & Martin, *Substantive Interests and the Jurisdiction of State Courts*, 66 Mich. L. Rev. 227, 240-241 (1967) (requirements for personal jurisdiction should be more demanding in libel cases), *with* Comment, *Long-Arm Jurisdiction Over Publishers*, note 36, *supra*, at 358, and Comment, *Constitutional Limitations to Long Arm Jurisdiction in Newspaper Libel Cases*, 34 U. Chi. L. Rev. 436 (1967) (requirements should be the same).

[392] *Calder*, 465 U.S. at 790.

located. If they transact in goods, their goods are likely to be digitized information products, not physical goods. And in many — if not most — cyberspace transactions, the remote party who is subsequently sued can hardly be said to have purposefully directed the information product or communication at a particular forum, except in the sense that she directed it at every forum.[393]

On the other hand, if cyberspace is indifferent to geography, "it does not and cannot change the fact that parties themselves exist in physical space."[394] This fact sounds a caution against any effort to jettison traditional personal jurisdiction law just because a suit arises out of a cyber transaction.

The subject of personal jurisdiction in cyberspace has already produced a great deal of academic commentary.[395] The United States Supreme Court has not yet ruled in a case presenting the problem. Lower courts, however, have begun to grapple with the problem, and their decisions may offer some guidance. Many of them have been influenced by the decision in *Zippo Manuf. Co. v. Zippo Dot Com, Inc.*,[396] categorizing cyber contacts by whether they were passive, commercially transactional, or interactive.

For example, it appears that due process does not permit exercise of personal jurisdiction based just on the fact that defendant's website is passive — merely accessible to internet users in the forum state.[397] Refusing personal jurisdiction in such circumstances, the Ninth Circuit observed:

> So far as we are aware, no court has ever held that an Internet advertisement alone is sufficient to subject the advertiser to jurisdiction in the plaintiff's home state. . . . Rather [in the internet cases permitting jurisdiction], there has been "something more" to indicate that the defendant purposefully (albeit electronically) directed his activity in a substantial way to the forum state.[398]

---

[393] P. Raven-Hansen, *Newsletter of the Section on Civil Procedure, Association of American Law Schools* at 2 (Fall, 1998). For a comprehensive study of commercial activity on the internet, see Rothchild, *Protecting the Digital Consumer: The Limits of Cyberspace Utopianism*, 74 Ind. L.J. 893 (1999).

[394] American Bar Association Jurisdiction in Cyberspace Project, *Achieving Legal and Business Order in Cyberspace: A Report on Global Jurisdiction Issues Created by the Internet* 8 (1999 draft) (hereinafter "ABA Cyberspace Report").

[395] *E.g.,* ABA Cyberspace Report, note 394, *supra*; Goldsmith, *Against Cyberanarchy*, 65 U. Chi. L. Rev. 1199, 1217-1220 (1998); Burk, *Federalism in Cyberspace*, 28 Conn. L. Rev. 1095 (1996); Kende, *Lost in Cyberspace: The Judiciary's Distracted Application of Free Speech and Personal Jurisdiction Doctrines to the Internet*, 77 Or. L. Rev. 1125 (1998); Mayewski, *The Presence of a Web Site as a Constitutionally Permissible Basis for Personal Jurisdiction*, 73 Ind. L.J. 297 (1997).

[396] 952 F. Supp 1119 (W.D. Pa. 1997).

[397] *See e.g., Bensusan Restaurant Corp. v. King*, 937 F. Supp. 295 (S.D.N.Y. 1996), *aff'd*, 126 F.3d 25 (2d Cir. 1997); *Cybersell, Inc. v. Cybersell*, Inc., 130 F.3d 414 (9th Cir. 1997); *Weber v. Jolly Hotels*, 977 F. Supp. 327 (D.N.J. 1997). *See also* ABA Cyberspace Report, note 395, *supra*, at 18 ("Personal or prescriptive jurisdiction should not be asserted based solely on the accessibility in the state of a passive web site that does not target the state").

[398] *Cybersell*, 130 F.3d at 418.

Any other rule would subject the sponsor of a passive website to personal jurisdiction the world over, because its website can be accessed by connected computers anywhere and it does not control the fora to which it connects by the site.[399]

But when, as in the case of *CompuServe Inc. v. Patterson*,[400] the defendant directs particular activity into the forum state that is related to the controversy, the forum acquires specific jurisdiction.[401] The Sixth Circuit in *CompuServe* ruled that defendant's contacts with the Ohio forum, while "almost entirely electronic in nature,"[402] were sufficient to support personal jurisdiction. The court noted that defendant

> was on notice that he had made contracts, to be governed by Ohio law, with an Ohio-based company. Then, he repeatedly sent his computer software, via electronic links, to the CompuServe system in Ohio, and he advertised that software on the CompuServe system. Moreover, he initiated the events that led to the filing of this suit by making demands of CompuServe via electronic and regular mail messages.[403]

The court was therefore able to conclude that defendant "purposefully availed himself of CompuServe's Ohio-based services."[404] This will generally be true of commercially transactional websites, through which the sponsor directs a product to a specified forum in exchange for payment by a purchaser in the forum.

The *Zippo* categorization is less helpful for the category in between these cases: the interactive website. How much interaction is required for jurisdiction and why? An Amercian Bar Association report on jurisdiction and cyberspace offers this explanation:

> Jurisdiction is about chosen contacts between the defendant and the forum. . . . [T]he sponsor of a passive web site has no way to control which fora she is "connected to" by the site. On the other hand, the site sponsor who does business electronically knows or can take reasonable steps to discover the location of the party with whom she is interacting. The provision of the interactive site, alone, may express the sponsor's willingness to become connected to all

---

[399] *ABA Cyberspace Report*, note 394, *supra*, at 59.

[400] 89 F.3d 1257 (6th Cir. 1996). The case is featured in Lenox, *Personal Jurisdiction in Cyberspace: Teaching the Stream of Commerce Dog New Internet Tricks: Compuserve, Inc. v. Patterson*, 22 U. Dayton L. Rev. 331 (1997); Logue, *If the International Shoe Fits, Wear It: Applying Traditional Personal Jurisdiction Analysis to Cyberspace in Compuserve, Inc. v. Patterson*, 42 Vill. L. Rev. 1213 (1997); VanderLaan, *Compuserve, Inc. v. Patterson: Civil Procedure Enters the Cyberage*, 41 St. Louis U.L.J. 1399 (1997); Tyler, *Personal Jurisdiction via E-mail: Has Personal Jurisdiction Changed in the Wake of Compuserve v. Patterson?*, 51 Ark. L. Rev. 429 (1998).

[401] For a discussion of specific jurisdiction as a subcategory of personal jurisdiction, see § 3.09[2]

[402] 89 F.3d at 1262

[403] *Id.* at 1264.

[404] *Id.* For a similar case, see *Panavision Int'l v. Toeppen*, 141 F.3d 1316 (9th Cir. 1998).

fora in which the site is accessible (assuming it does not contain any disclaimers, etc.) but it does not constitute that connection. Nor, of course, does the mere accessing of the site by forum residents. . . .

Reliance, then, on the nature of the web site alone is misplaced. If an interactive site is not targeted to a specific forum, courts should focus on how the site is actually used. Knowing and willing use of it by a nonpresent party to enter into dealings with persons or business in the forum demonstrates a chosen contact with the forum, provides the forum with an interest in the relationships thus created, and makes it less likely that multiple fora with different applicable laws will attempt to regulate the site and asset jurisdiction over its sponsor.[405]

This analysis suggests that *Zippo's* categorization is superficial, or, at least, just the beginning of the inquiry. The real inquiry ought to be how the website is used, whether it targets the forum, and the defendant's intent or willingness to contact forum users — in a word (or, more accurately, two words): "purposeful availment." It remains to be seen, however, whether the courts will probe beyond *Zippo's* categories or yet develop a new jurisdictional paradigm for new communications media like the internet.

---

[405] *ABA Cyberspace Report*, note 395, *supra*, at 60-61.

Chapter 4

NOTICE AND OPPORTUNITY TO BE HEARD

§ 4.01   The Due Process Guaranty of Notice and the Opportunity to be Heard

Federal and state adjudications are binding only when they satisfy the Due Process Clauses of the United States Constitution.[1] Having seen how the clauses impose limits on courts' territorial jurisdiction,[2] we will now consider how they deny effect to adjudications unless those to be bound were given prior notice and an opportunity to participate.[3]

Notice is tied to the procedure for service of process. The United States Supreme Court has reemphasized the importance of service of process, stating: "Service of process, under longstanding tradition in our system of justice, is fundamental to any procedural imposition on a named defendant."[4] As the Court observed in another case, "the core function of service is to supply notice of the pendency of a legal action, in a manner and at a time that affords the defendant a fair opportunity to answer the complaint and present defenses and objections."[5]

Process usually consists of a summons directing defendant to respond or appear in court on penalty of default and a copy of the complaint. *Service* is the formal means by which process is delivered to a defendant. Assurance of a quality of notice sufficient to satisfy due process is an important function of each system's service procedure. We shall see that actual notice is not an invariable due process requirement. That is, it is possible under the right circumstances for defendant to be bound by an adjudication although she neither participated in it nor made an informed decision to forego participation. At the same time, due process places a heavy burden of justification on attempts to bind those who have not received actual notice.

---

[1] Restricting federal and state courts respectively, the Fifth and Fourteenth amendments protect against deprivation of "life, liberty or property, without due process of law." A cause of action is "property" within the meaning of the amendments and cannot be forfeited through proceedings lacking in due process. Due process similarly protects litigants who are claimed against. For elaboration of these points, see § 3.01[2] (law limiting the court's reach), *supra*.

[2] Chapter 3, *supra*.

[3] These two branches of due process doctrine are explained and compared in *Phillips Petroleum Co. v. Shutts,* 472 U.S. 797 (1985). *See* § 3.01, *supra.* For restatement of the due process principle of notice and the opportunity to be heard, see *Nelson v. Adams USA, Inc.,* 529 U.S. 460, 466 (2000) (voiding a judgment without requisite prior notice). On the contemporary importance of the principle, see Wooley, *Rethinking the Adequacy of Adequate Representation,* 75 Tex. L. Rev. 571 (1997).

[4] *Murphy Bros. v. Michetti Pipe Stringing, Inc.,* 526 U.S. 344, 350 (1999).

[5] *Henderson v. United States,* 517 U.S. 654, 672 (1996).

The Court laid down the modern standard in *Mullane v. Central Hanover Bank & Trust Co.*[6]

An elementary and fundamental requirement of due process in any proceeding which is to be accorded finality is notice reasonably calculated, under all the circumstances, to apprise interested parties of the pendency of the action and afford them an opportunity to present their objections. . . . The notice must be of such nature as reasonably to convey the required information . . . , and it must afford a reasonable time for those interested to make their appearance. . . . But if with due regard for the practicalities and peculiarities of the case these conditions are reasonably met, the constitutional requirements are satisfied.[7]

Mullane involved adjudication by a New York state court of the interests of trust beneficiaries. The beneficiaries fell into three categories: (1) those whose names and addresses were known; (2) those who were unknowable; (3) and those whose names and addresses could be ascertained at considerable expense. The Court refused to permit notice by publication to the first category, "because under the circumstances it is not reasonably calculated to reach those who could easily be informed by other means at hand."[8] When addresses were known, "the reasons disappear for resort to means less likely than the mails to apprise them of [the] pendency [of the proceeding]."[9]

Since a substantial number of beneficiaries would thus have actual (individual) notice, the Court was willing to dispense with a requirement of individualized notice for beneficiaries in categories two and three.

This type of trust presupposes a large number of small interests. The individual interest does not stand alone but is identical with that of a class. The rights of each in the integrity of the fund and the fidelity of the trustee are shared by many other beneficiaries. Therefore notice reasonably certain to reach most of those interested in objecting is likely to safeguard the interest of all, since any objection sustained would inure to the benefit of all. We think that under such circumstances reasonable risks that notice might not actually reach every beneficiary are justifiable.[10]

Accordingly, the Court approved constructive notice by publication to the beneficiaries for whom individualized notice was impractical.

Mullane and its progeny "radically modified" the historical notice requirement.[11] *Mullane* curtailed notice by publication, holding that it could not substitute for individual notice when the latter was practicable.[12] On the

---

[6] 339 U.S. 306 (1950).

[7] *Id.* at 314-315.

[8] *Id.* at 319.

[9] *Id.* at 318.

[10] *Id* at 319.

[11] *Restatement (Second) of Judgments* 27 (introductory note to Ch. 2) (1982).

[12] 339 U.S. at 318.

other hand, *Mullane* authorized service by the best alternative means, possibly publication, [13] in some situations where individual notice was impracticable. The Court did not offer a comprehensive list of these situations and has not since. However, the manner in which the Court reacted to the circumstances in *Mullane* suggests that something less than individual notice is most likely to satisfy due process when proof of the impracticability of individual notice is accompanied by proof that (1) the suit is in the interest of the absentees, (2) they will be adequately represented by one before the court, and (3) the value of their individual interests is not too great.

The Supreme Court has subsequently adhered to the *Mullane* reasonableness-under-the-circumstances approach to notice. In *Greene v. Lindsey,* [14] it rejected a Kentucky state service of process scheme permitting notice of eviction proceedings to be left at the homes of defendants under circumstances where there was substantial possibility that passers-by would remove the notices before defendants knew of them. In *Greene* and in the subsequent case of *Mennonite Board of Missions v. Adams,* [15] the Court seemed to suggest that constitutional defects in service could have been cured through the additional step of mailing a copy of court process to the due process claimant. [16]

---

[13] "The rule in *Mullane* recognizes that persons can be bound even if they cannot be found through reasonably diligent search. Assuming that such a search has been made, the fiction is indulged that publication notifies the absentee." *Restatement (Second of Judgments)*, note 11, *supra,* § 2 comment g. "Publication of notice creates an additional possibility of bringing the proceeding to the absentee's attention. Perhaps more important, however, publication of notice is a ceremony whose performance assures that the termination of the absentee's rights is not done in secret." *Id.*

[14] 456 U.S. 444 (1982). For a discussion of *Greene*, see Greenbaum, *The Postman Never Rings Twice: The Constitutionality of Service of Process by Posting After Greene v. Lindsey,* 33 Am. U. L. Rev. 601-641 (1984).

[15] 462 U.S. 791 (1983). The case is examined in Note, *Mennonite Board of Missions v. Adams: Expansion of the Due Process Notice Requirements,* 46 La. L. Rev. 311 (1985). Later, in *Tulsa Prof. Col. Serv. v. Pope,* 485 U.S. 478 (1988), the Supreme Court again found circumstances requiring actual notice. Attention has turned to the constitutionality of internet service. *See* Cantor, *Internet Service of Process: A Constitutionally Adequate Alternative?* 66 U. Chi. L. Rev. 943 (1999).

[16] It seems desirable to permit the party initiating service to cure through informal mailing a constitutional insufficiency in the formal scheme. However, in *Wuchter v. Pizzutti,* 276 U.S. 13 (1928), the Court struck down a judgment on due process notice grounds because the statute failed to require service on the defendant, even though the defendant in the case had in fact received actual notice. The Supreme Court has not expressly overruled *Wuchter,* but the continuing authority of the case is in some doubt. *See* E. Scoles & P. Hay, *Conflict of Laws* § 8.32 (2nd ed. 1992). "It is difficult to see how one is denied due process by failure to receive the exact statutory formal notice if, in fact, constitutionally sufficient notice has otherwise been provided him." *Id.* "The more discerning cases have recognized that the requirement is adequate notice and that it is fulfilled by actual notice whose tenor indicates it ought to be taken seriously." *Restatement (Second) of Judgments,* note 11, *supra,* § 2 comment d.

§ 4.02   Special Due Process Concerns Arising from Class Actions and Prejudgment Attachments

[1]   Class Actions

While class actions and special due process considerations pertaining to them are discussed elsewhere,[17] it is useful to make a few observations here. The special contribution of the class action device is to conclude simultaneously the interests of a far greater number of persons than could actively participate in the case. Those who do not actively participate but are nonetheless bound by the adjudication of class issues are called *passive* members of the class.

Due process does not (and, for class actions to exist, could not) require the active participation of each person to be bound in a civil action. The Supreme Court's classic standard for applying the Due Process Clauses to class actions is "that there has been a failure of due process only in those cases where it cannot be said that the procedure adopted, fairly insures the protection of the interests of absent parties who are to be bound by it."[18] Read broadly, this might suggest that the due process touchstone for class actions is adequate representation, rather than actual notice. However, since class actions are fully subject to *Mullane*'s due process requirement of best notice practicable,[19] so broad a reading would probably be unwise. Actual notice is clearly the best notice, and due process requires it to be given to class members whenever practicable.[20]

[2]   Prejudgment Attachments

In theory, post-judgment attachment of the real or personal property of one against whom judgment is rendered (the judgment debtor) helps the judgment creditor to realize all or part of the value of the judgment.[21] The procedure is worthless, however, when the judgment debtor has little or nothing of value to attach. Pre-judgment attachment provides some hedge against this possibility because it "prevent[s] the defendant from disposing of or otherwise impairing the value of property that might be used to satisfy the judgment in an action."[22] Absent settlement, property remains frozen

---

[17] *See* § 9.09, *infra.*

[18] *Hansberry v. Lee,* 311 U.S. 32, 42 (1940) (citation omitted).

[19] For discussion of *Mullane*'s requirements, see § 4.01, *supra.* The Supreme Court has consistently applied *Mullane* to class actions. *E.g., Phillips Petroleum Co. v. Shutts,* 472 U.S. 797 (1985).

[20] In addition, federal class action Rule 23 and the rules of many states require actual notice to class members in some situations whether or not actual notice would be required by due process. *See* § 9.09[2][a], *infra.* Neither the rule, nor due process, requires notice in some class actions when it is impracticable. *See* § 9.09[2][c], *infra.*

[21] *See* § 15.02 (enforcement of judgments), *infra.*

[22] *Friedenthal, Kane & Miller* § 15.2. Garnishment, another so-called provisional remedy, functions the same way. Sometimes the latter term is favored to describe seizure of defendant's liquid assets, including wages and debts owed him by others. *See, e.g., Sniadach v. Family Finance Corp.,* 395 U.S. 337 (1969). For discussion of a different provisional remedy, the temporary injunction, see § 14.02[2], *infra.*

by prejudgment attachment until the plaintiff wins on the merits and is able to enforce his judgment against the property, or until defendant recaptures the property by having the attachment dissolved, posting surety, or winning on the merits.

At first glance, the due process law of notice[23] seems to restrain prejudgment attachments less than it does judicial proceedings generally. Current due process doctrine permits some decisions authorizing prejudgment attachments to be made after *ex parte* proceedings — proceedings conducted without notice to or participation by the defendant.[24] Defendant in such cases usually learns of the existence of suit only when prejudgment attachment separates him from his property. Earlier notice would make it possible for defendant to appear and contest plaintiff's application before the court decides to issue the attachment order. Since defendants in such cases typically are easy to find and notify prior to the attachment proceeding,[25] earlier notice might seem practicable in the *Mullane* sense and hence required by due process.[26]

Given the purpose of prejudgment attachments, however, requiring plaintiff to give notice to defendant before the fact of attachment might be impracticable in a different sense. Recall that prejudgment attachments exist to secure defendant's property to which plaintiff can look if he prevails on the merits. Alerting defendant to the attachment proceedings (or even to the existence of suit) may defeat this purpose. Defendant may transfer his interest in property to another, remove it from the jurisdiction, hide it, or otherwise diminish its value,[27] leaving little to attach.

It is unwise to ban *ex parte* attachments altogether for the reasons noted above. On the other hand, any use of the judicial process depriving one of notice and property in so calculated a fashion must be subjected to careful scrutiny. The Supreme Court has struggled in four decisions to find a middle ground. Whether these decisions, *North Georgia Finishing, Inc. v. Di-Chem, Inc.*,[28] *Mitchell v. W.T. Grant Co.*,[29] *Fuentes v. Shevin*,[30] and *Sniadach v. Family Finance Corp.*,[31] are entirely compatible is an open

---

[23] When prejudgment attachment cases proceed on a theory of *quasi in rem* jurisdiction, a second branch of due process doctrine (regulating the exercise of territorial jurisdiction over nonresident defendants) may also be a factor. *See* § 3.08[1], *supra.*

[24] The Court upheld such a procedure in *Mitchell v. W.T. Grant Co.*, 416 U.S. 600 (1974).

[25] Indeed, plaintiff will probably be required to notify defendant quite soon *after* the attachment.

[26] *See* § 4.01 (notice), *supra.*

[27] Not only is there a possibility of malicious waste of the property, but also decline in value through ordinary continued use by the defendant during the pendency of the case. This may be of special concern to plaintiff when it holds a security interest in the property, a factor noted in *Mitchell v. W.T. Grant Co.*, 416 U.S. 600, 608 (1974).

[28] 419 U.S. 601 (1975).

[29] 416 U.S. 600 (1974).

[30] 407 U.S. 67 (1972).

[31] 395 U.S. 337 (1969).

question.[32] The approach in each, however, centers on two common inquiries.

First, what is the nature of the *ex parte* proceeding? The Supreme Court has made clear that the fact that only the plaintiff participates should not decide the outcome. Rather, procedures for deciding an *ex parte* application for attachment should take into account the interests of the defendant *in absentia* and carry the possibility that the application would be refused in appropriate cases. When the Court struck down prejudgment attachment procedures in *Fuentes* and *Di-Chem,* therefore, it gave considerable weight to the fact that the applications required of plaintiffs were undemanding in form and content,[33] and that issuance of attachment was left to clerical employees. The Court noted that circumstances were different in *Grant.* A sworn and factually detailed showing was necessary under Louisiana law. Moreover, the decision to issue the writ was made by a judge — an official more used to saying "no" to attorneys. Overall, the Court was able to conclude in *Grant* that "[t]he system protects the debtor's interest in every conceivable way, except allowing him to have the property to start with. . . ."[34]

The second inquiry is: how long is defendant likely to be separated from custody or control of the property? Even systems invalidated in *Fuentes* and *Di-Chem* provided some procedure for defendant to recapture the property prior to the conclusion of the case. The problem was that the procedures were insufficiently prompt and accessible. *Grant* noted that the procedure available to defendants in *Fuentes* was too obscure, leaving them "in limbo to await a hearing that might or might not 'eventually' occur. . . ."[35] The scheme upheld in *Grant* did not suffer from this problem. "Louisiana law," stated the Court, "expressly provides for an immediate hearing and dissolution of the writ 'unless the plaintiff proves the grounds upon which the writ was issued.' "[36]

The Supreme Court's message continues to be that state legislatures must beef up defendant's side of the formal adversary process. In *Grant,* the quality of procedure before and after the attachment was clearly superior to that in *Sniadach, Fuentes,* and *Di-Chem.* Returning to the subject in 1991, the Court in *Connecticut v. Doehr* faulted a Connecticut statute for failing to reach the standard set in *Grant.* Instead, the statute permitted

---

[32] *See* Catz & Robinson, *Due Process and Creditor's Remedies: From Sniadach and Fuentes to Mitchell, North Georgia and Beyond,* 28 Rutgers L. Rev. 541 (1975); Comment, *A Confusing Course Made More Confusing: The Supreme Court, Due Process, and Summary Creditor Remedies,* 70 Nw. U. L. Rev. 331 (1975). In *Lugar v. Edmondson Oil Co., Inc.,* 457 U.S. 922, 927 (1982), the Court said that the four decisions could be read together as due process law governing prejudgment attachments.

[33] For example, Florida law in *Fuentes* required merely "the bare assertion of the party seeking the writ that he is entitled to one." 407 U.S. at 74.

[34] 416 U.S. at 618.

[35] 416 U.S. at 618. "Nor was it apparent in *Sniadach* with what speed the debtor could challenge the validity of the garnishment." *Id.* at 614.

[36] *Id.* at 618 (*quoting* state statute).

issuance of an *ex parte* attachment on "only a skeletal affidavit" constituting "one-sided, self-serving, and conclusory submissions." [37]

Yet, while the procedural scheme was best for the defendant in *Grant*, the question remains: was the defendant there treated fairly enough to satisfy what should be the requirements of due process? Greater protection before and after issuance of the *ex parte* order is a procedural advantage theoretically available to all defendants facing attachment. But will low-income debtors such as the defendant in *Grant* be as likely as other debtors to exploit the advantage? [38]

§ 4.03 Rules Regulating Service of Process

[1] The Interplay of Constitutional Law and Rules or Statutes; Diversity of Local Approaches

We have seen that the Constitution does no more than set a pragmatic general standard for the quality of service of process. [39] Important as due process doctrine is, it does not create the particular structure and detail necessary for service-of-process rules or statutes. Because constitutional notice can take different forms, and because nothing stops legislatures from creating service requirements more demanding than those required by due process, approaches to service vary. [40]

The legal consequences attached to service also vary. Some states use *service* to define commencement of civil suit for statute of limitations and other purposes. Other states use *filing* to define commencement, as do federal courts under Rule 3. When a state uses service to define commencement for limitations purposes, however, federal courts in diversity cases must follow the state law in determining whether state law claims are time-barred. [41]

---

[37] 501 U.S. 1, 14 (1991). Plaintiff in *Doehr* sought a real estate attachment against defendant pursuant to his claim for assault and battery. The fact that plaintiff wanted to attach real estate rather than movables of the defendant appeared to work against plaintiff. The Court noted that the "[p]laintiff had no existing interest in Doehr's real estate when he sought the attachment" and that "there was no allegation that Doehr was about to transfer or encumber his real estate. . . ." The Court concluded that "plaintiff's interest in attaching the property does not justify the burdening of Doehr's ownership rights without a hearing to determine the likelihood of recovery." *Id.* at 16.

[38] For an argument that the United States Supreme Court relies unduly on adversary formalities in its attempt to secure due process objectives, see Mashaw, *The Management Side of Due Process: Some Theoretical and Litigation Notes on the Assurance of Accuracy, Fairness, and Timeliness in the Adjudication of Social Welfare Claims,* 59 Cornell L. Rev. 772 (1974). In prejudgment attachment and other legal contexts, equality in theory may not be equality in fact.

[39] *See* § 4.01 (due process guaranty of notice), *supra.*

[40] *See, e.g.,* the comparison between Massachusetts law (requiring service in hand) and Rule 4(d)(1) (permitting process to be left at defendant's home under certain circumstances) as interpreted by the Supreme Court in *Hanna v. Plumer,* 380 U.S. 460 (1965).

[41] *Compare Walker v. Armco Steel Corp.,* 446 U.S. 740 (1980) (Rule 3 gave way to Oklahoma's service-based definition of commencement), *with Schiavone v. Fortune,* 477 U.S. 21 (1986) (Rule 3 followed when New Jersey law also used a filing-based definition of commencement). For more on the interplay of state law and the Federal Rules of Civil Procedure, see § 7.04, *infra.*

[2] The Federal Rule Model

Federal court service is said to have "changed drastically"[42] with the 1983 amendments to Rule 4. The process leading to this development was unusual in itself. A year earlier, the Supreme Court proposed to Congress extensive changes in Rule 4.[43] Congress did not follow its usual practice of remaining silent, thereby permitting the Court's recommendation to become law.[44] Instead, Congress first postponed the effective date of the Court's rule, then amended it by statute.[45]

The 1983 amendment to Rule 4 attempted to make two fundamental changes urged by the Supreme Court in its unsuccessful proposal.[46] The first was to give plaintiff (or plaintiff's attorney) control over service of process. The second was to permit service by mail as a form of federal service.

Prior to the 1983 amendment, federal marshals had usually been responsible for service of plaintiff's summons and complaint. "The principle purpose of the amendments adopted in 1983 was to end this."[47] Responsibility was placed "squarely on the plaintiff."[48]

The change made sense. Federal marshals and their deputies have always had many responsibilities involving both civil and criminal litigation. Even with provision in the prior rule for special appointment of process servers, backlogs in summons and complaint service were common prior to 1983. It is usually in plaintiff's best interest to move the case along.

---

[42] *Wright* § 64. *See generally* Sinclair, *Service of Process: Rethinking the Theory and Procedure of Serving Process Under Federal Rule 4(c)*, 73 Va. L. Rev. 1183 (1987).

[43] The Chief Justice's letter appears at 456 U.S. 1014 (1982). The Advisory Committee note intended to explain the Court's revision of Rule 4 appears at 93 F.R.D. 255, 262-263 (1982).

[44] The Rules Enabling Act, 28 U.S.C. § 2072, contemplates (but does not require) a passive role for Congress. Congress usually remains silent, but has shown a greater tendency to become actively involved in recent years. *Cf.* Ely, *The Irrepressible Myth of Erie,* 87 Harv. L. Rev. 693, 693-694 (1974) (describing congressional resistance to the Court's proposed Federal Rules of Evidence). For a general description of the federal procedural rule-making process, see § 1.02 (sources of civil procedure), *supra.*

[45] The Federal Rules of Civil Procedure Amendments Act of 1982, Public Law 97-462, 96 Stat. 2527 (Jan. 12, 1983). Since Congress discarded the work of the Advisory Committee, no Advisory Committee notes accompany this amendment to Rule 4. However, the legislative history for Public Law 97-462 offers some help in interpreting the amendment and is reprinted in Siegel, *Practice Commentary on Amendment of Federal Rule 4 (Eff. Feb. 26, 1983) With Special Statute of Limitations Precautions,* 96 F.R.D. 88, 116-130 (1983) [hereinafter *1983 Commentary*]. For discussion of subsequent practice under Rule 4, *see* Siegel, 28 U.S.C.A. Fed. R. Civ. P. 4, practice commentaries (1992) [hereinafter *1992 Commentary*].

[46] *See generally* Cantor, *Internet Service of Process: A Constitutionally Adequate Alternative?,* 66 U. Chi. L. Rev. 943 (1999); Mullenix, *The New Federal Express: Mail Service of Process Under Amended Rule 4,* 4 Rev. Litig. 299 (1985); Note, *Service of Process By First-Class Mail Under Rule 4 of the Federal Rules of Civil Procedure,* 15 Rutgers L.J. 993 (1984).

[47] *Wright* § 64.

[48] *Moore,* 1987 Rules Part 1, at 44. *Cf.* Siegel, *1983 Commentary,* note 45, *supra,* at 94 ("The main purpose of the 1983 revision was to take the marshals out of the summons serving business almost entirely."). In a limited number of situations stated in Rule 4, the marshal retains authority to make service of the summons and complaint when requested by the party wishing service.

Plaintiff's attorney can therefore be expected to handle responsibilities under Rule 4 quickly and correctly. To provide for cases which do not bear out this assumption, the rule gives the plaintiff 120 days from filing the complaint to serve the summons and complaint on defendant or (absent "good cause" for delay) suffer dismissal without prejudice.[49]

The 1983 provision for mail service was less successful than its proponents had hoped. The procedure for return of the acknowledgement form confused plaintiffs and defendants alike, and its applicability outside the forum state was unclear.[50] Moreover, defendants had little incentive to cooperate in the 1983 mail service because the only sanction for failure to return the acknowledgement form was the payment of usually insignificant costs of alternative service, and because the expense of collecting these costs discouraged enforcement of even this modest sanction.[51]

The 1993 rule amendment addressed all of these shortcomings. First, it substituted the language of waiver for acknowledgement, making its operation and effect clearer to all parties.[52] Plaintiff or plaintiff's attorney may now mail the complaint, a request for waiver of formal service, and a form explaining the consequences of waiver to the defendant by first class mail. Second, the new procedure was clearly made applicable to service outside the state.[53] Third, it imposed on the defendant "a duty to avoid unnecessary costs of serving the summons" and provided new incentives to defendant to discharge that duty. The defendant who returns a waiver of service form gets 60 days after the request for waiver was sent to answer the complaint instead of the usual 20. The defendant who does not is made liable not only for the costs of alternative service, but also for attorney's fees incurred in any motion to collect the costs of service.[54]

Professor Wright predicted after the 1983 amendment that the option of service of the summons and complaint by mail would "undoubtedly become the normal method of serving individuals and corporations."[55]

Changes in Rule 4 brought about by the 1993 amendment extend well beyond service by mail. The rule was almost completely rewritten. Much

---

[49] Rule 4(m).

[50] Rule 4 advisory committee's notes (1993).

[51] *Id. See generally* Welkowitz, *The Trouble with Service by Mail*, 67 Neb. L. Rev. 289 (1988); *Mullenix*, note 8, *supra*; Note, *Service of Process*, note 8, *supra*; *Report of the Committee on Federal Courts of the New York State Bar Association on Service of Process by Mail Pursuant to Rule 4(c)(2)(C)(ii) of the Federal Rules of Civil Procedure*, 116 F.R.D. 169 (1987).

[52] Rule 4(d)(2).

[53] Rule 4(k)(1) ("filing a waiver of service is effective to establish jurisdiction" over defendant who could be subjected to jurisdiction of forum state courts).

[54] Rule 4(d)(2), (3) & (5). Prior to the 1993 amendment to Rule 4, courts disagreed concerning the availability of attorney's fees necessitated by additional service arrangements. *E.g., compare Premier Bank v. Ward*, 129 F.R.D. 500 (D. La. 1990) (attorney's fees available) *with McCarthy v. Wolfeboro Restaurant Serv.*, 132 F.R.D. 613 (D. Mass. 1990) (attorney's fees unavailable). Much turned on this. "Without attorney's fees, costs awards will usually be paltry, depriving defendants of incentive to acknowledge mail service voluntarily." Siegel, *1992 Commentary*, note 45, *supra*.

[55] *Wright* § 64.

of the pre-1993 substance was preserved, but the amendment rearranged the sequence of matters discussed and worked a number of changes. These include authorization to use the service procedures of the state in which service is made as well as those of the forum state,[56] nationwide service of process in some cases founded on federal question jurisdiction,[57] and express reference to the Hague Convention.[58]

[3] Service Abroad; The Hague Convention

Rule 4(f)(2) offers means for effecting service of process in foreign countries. However, it does not in itself eliminate the risk that a federal court judgment might be denied enforcement abroad. This matters most in cases where assets sufficient to satisfy a judgment exist only in the foreign defendant's home country. Then it is essential that service on the defendant there comport with that foreign country's service requirements. Otherwise, the courts there may refuse for that reason to enforce the judgment.

For cases to which it applies, the Hague Convention[59] may offer a means of stabilizing international service of process from American courts. For example, each signatory to the Convention designates a "Central Authority" to process service in that country,[60] and the treaty makes some provision for service by mail.[61]

---

[56] Rule 4(e)(1).

[57] Rule 4(k)(2) states:

If the exercise of jurisdiction is consistent with the Constitution and laws of the United States, serving a summons or filing a waiver of service is also effective, with respect to claims arising under federal law, to establish personal jurisdiction over the person of any defendant who is not subject to the jurisdiction of the courts of jurisdiction of any state.

For discussion of the rather limited effect of this new subsection on the personal jurisdiction, see § 3.01[2][b], *supra.*

[58] Rule 4(f)(1).

[59] Hague Convention on Service Abroad of Judicial and Extrajudicial Documents in Civil and Commercial Matters, 20 U.S.T. 361; T.I.A.S. 6638. *See generally,* E. Scoles & P. Hay, *Conflict of Laws* § 12.7 (3d ed. 2000); Parmalee, *International Service of Process: A Guide to Serving Process Abroad Under the Hague Convention,* 39 Okla. L. Rev. 287 (1986); Hamilton, *An Interpretation of the Hague Convention on the Service of Process Abroad of Judicial and Extrajudicial Documents Concerning Personal Service in Japan,* 6 Loy. L.A. Int'l & Comp. L. J. 143 (1983).

The United States has also joined the Inter-American Convention on Letters Rogatory. 14 Int'l Leg. Mat. 339 (1975); 18 Int'l Leg. Mat. 1238 (1979). "[T]he Hague Service Convention and the Inter-American Convention adopt similar approaches to the service of process abroad." G. Born & D. Westin, *International Civil Litigation in the United States* 137 (1989). *See generally* Kim, *The Inter-American Convention and Additional Protocol on Letters Rogatory: The Hague Service Conventions "Country Cousins"?,* 36 Colum. J. Transnat'l L. 687 (1998); Low, *International Judicial Assistance Among the American States — The Inter-American Conventions,* 18 Int'l Law 705 (1984).

[60] Art. 2.

[61] Art. 10(a). Federal decisions are divided over whether 10(a) authorizes direct service abroad by mail without using the foreign country's central authority or diplomatic channels. *Compare Ackerman v. Levine,* 788 F.2d 830 (2d Cir. 1986) (yes); *Eli Lilly & Co. v. Roussel,* 23 F. Supp. 2d 460 (D.N.J. 1998) (yes) *with Bankston v. Toyota Motor Corp.,* 889 F.2d 172 (8th Cir. 1989) (no); *Knapp v. Yamaha Motor Corp.,* 60 F. Supp. 2d 566 (S.D.W.Va. 1999) (no).

At the same time, the treaty does not completely cure problems in international service of process. Not all countries are signatories to the Hague Convention. Moreover, those that have joined have often attached conditions to their participation.[62] It is useful, then, to note two alternatives to the Hague Convention. First, there may be means of effecting service abroad apart from that treaty.[63] Second, it will be possible in some cases to establish jurisdiction over foreign nationals without resorting to service of process abroad.

The availability of the second option was greatly enhanced by the Supreme Court's decision in *Volkswagenwerk v. Schlunk*.[64] The Court suggested the Hague Convention does not require jurisdiction to be established through service of process abroad when the facts of the case support a local theory of personal jurisdiction. That is, whenever the joint due process requirements of minimum contacts and of reasonableness are satisfied, jurisdiction exists in state (or federal) courts over foreign nationals — just as it does over Americans residing outside the forum in sister states. The Court held in *Schlunk* that service upon a German corporation was permissible under the Illinois long-arm statute. State law permitted substituted service on the defendant's subsidiary located in the United States. State law and federal due process provided the appropriate tests, and those tests were satisfied.[65]

---

[62] These reservations, called declarations, are used by countries to modify or negate obligations set out in the treaty. For examples, *see Born & Westin*, note 59, *supra*, pp. 655-669.

[63] "The Convention is not, as has occasionally been supposed, automatically preemptive of all methods that may be used for service abroad." *Siegel, 1992 Commentary*, note 7, *supra*. Professor Siegel adds: "As long as the nation concerned has not, in its ratification or in any other part of its law, imposed any limits on other methods, these others remain available and the Convention and its local implementing materials serve as supplements." *Id.*

[64] 486 U.S. 694 (1988). The decision is discussed in Note, *The Supreme Court Interprets the Hague Service Convention*, 23 Geo. Wash. J. Int'l L. & Econ. 769 (1990); Note, *Service of Process: Application of the Hague Service Convention in the United States*, 30 Harv. Int'l L. J. 277 (1989).

[65] "Where service on a domestic agent is valid and complete under both state law and the Due Process Clause, our inquiry ends and the Convention has no further implications." 486 U.S. at 707. *But see* Burbank, *The United States' Approach to International Civil Litigation: Recent Developments in Forum Selection*, 19 U. Pa. J. Int'l Econ. L. 1, 5-8 (endorsing recent lower court opinions requiring compliance with Hague Convention even after service was made in-state on foreign agent).

Chapter 5

A COURT WITH JURISDICTION OVER THE SUBJECT

§ 5.01   Introduction

[1]   Subject Matter Jurisdiction Generally

Subject matter jurisdiction refers to a court's power or "competence" to decide a particular kind of controversy. To render a binding decision, the court must be "competent by its constitution — that is, by the law of its creation — to pass upon the subject-matter of the suit."[1] Typically, that law will include the organic law (the constitution) of the sovereign, any implementing jurisdictional legislation and the common law gloss placed on such legislation by the courts. Because the constitutions and jurisdictional statutes of the states and the federal government differ, so does the subject matter jurisdiction of their respective courts.

Subject matter jurisdiction can, however, be described by certain generic terms. All states have courts of *limited, special or inferior jurisdiction,* which are vested only with the power to hear cases of a particular kind. Small claims courts or traffic courts are courts of limited jurisdiction, the former limited to cases of a particular amount in controversy and the latter obviously limited to traffic violation cases. Virtually every state has at least one court of *general jurisdiction,* which is vested with a comprehensive residual subject matter jurisdiction to hear all cases not exclusively allocated to courts of limited jurisdiction. Such general jurisdiction courts, frequently established at the county level, are the workhorses of the state judicial systems, hearing the majority of significant civil and criminal cases.

Another generic distinction is between *original* and *appellate jurisdiction.* Those courts in which suits are first filed have original jurisdiction; the cases originate there. Courts that review cases that originate elsewhere, either in lower courts or in administrative agencies, are vested with appellate jurisdiction, usually but not always requiring some degree of deference to the original decision and hence a limited intensity of review.[2]

Finally, subject matter jurisdiction can be *concurrent* — shared between several different kinds of courts — or *exclusive,* restricted to a particular kind of court. State courts of general jurisdiction and federal district courts, for example, have concurrent jurisdiction of most cases involving questions of federal constitutional or statutory law, but the latter are vested with

---

[1] *Pennoyer v. Neff,* 95 U.S. 714, 733 (1877).

[2] *See* § 13.09 (intensity of review on appeal), *infra.*

107

exclusive jurisdiction over *some* topics, including admiralty, maritime, patent, plant variety protection, copyright[3] and certain cases in which the United States is a defendant.[4]

It is more difficult to generalize about the timing and mode of challenging subject matter jurisdiction. These procedural incidents often differ depending upon whether the jurisdiction is general or limited. Strict rules for challenging subject matter jurisdiction have developed in federal courts because they are courts of limited jurisdiction. Subject matter jurisdiction implicates the distribution of federal judicial power and the separation of powers between the branches, rather than personal rights of the parties to a litigation. Consequently, the parties cannot enlarge a federal court's subject matter jurisdiction by consent or waiver.[5] Any other rule would effectively enable the parties by their acts to amend Article III of the Constitution or federal jurisdictional statutes. Parties may therefore challenge a federal court's subject matter jurisdiction at any point in the litigation,[6] including appeal.[7] Moreover, a federal court is required on its own motion (*sua sponte*) to consider whether it has subject matter jurisdiction when the litigants have not raised the question.[8] Finally, in courts of limited

---

[3] 28 U.S.C. §§ 1333, 1338.

[4] 28 U.S.C. § 1346(f).

[5] Nor may a federal rule, because Congress has not given the rulemakers authority to extend or restrict the subject matter jurisdiction conferred by statute. *See Willy v. Coastal Corp.*, 503 U.S. 131 (1992). Rule 82 acknowledges this fact expressly.

[6] However, a subject matter jurisdiction challenge does not necessarily take precedence over a challenge to personal jurisdiction; "there is no unyielding jurisdictional hierarchy." *Ruhrgas AG v. Marathon Oil Co.*, 526 U.S. 574, 578 (1999). In *Ruhrgas*, a unanimous Court held that a federal court has discretion to decide personal ahead of subject matter jurisdiction when the former question is more easily and readily resolved. This discretion helps the courts avoid unnecessary determination of complex and novel questions of subject matter jurisdiction. In contrast, the Court has emphasized that a court must decide subject matter jurisdiction before ruling on the merits. *Steel Co. v. Citizens for Better Environment*, 523 U.S. 83 (1998). *See generally* Friedenthal, *The Crack in the Steel Case*, 68 Geo. Wash. L. Rev. 258 (2000) (comparing *Steel* and *Ruhrgas*).

[7] In *Capron v. Van Noorden,* 6 U.S. (2 Cranch) 126 (1804), for example, the plaintiff lost at trial and then successfully appealed the judgment on the grounds that the court that he had selected lacked subject matter jurisdiction over his claim. However, collateral attacks on subject matter jurisdiction — challenges made not at trial or on direct appeal but in a separate litigation, such as one brought to enforce a prior judgment — are not allowed except in extraordinary circumstances, given the strong public interest in finality of judgments. *Des Moines Navigation & R.R. Co. v. Iowa Homestead Co.,* 123 U.S. 552 (1887). *See generally* Martineau, *Subject Matter Jurisdiction as a New Issue on Appeal: Reigning in an Unruly Horse,* 1988 B.Y.U. L. Rev. 1 (1988); Moore, *Collateral Attack on Subject Matter Jurisdiction: A Critique of the Restatement (Second) of Judgments,* 66 Cornell L. Rev. 534 (1981); Dobbs, *Beyond Bootstrap: Foreclosing the Issue of Subject Matter Jurisdiction Before Final Judgment,* 51 Minn. L. Rev. 491 (1967). *The Restatement (Second) of Judgments* would permit collateral attacks for lack of subject matter jurisdiction, just as they are permitted for lack of personal jurisdiction, but it acknowledges that few courts have agreed. *Compare Restatement (Second) of Judgments* § 65 (1982) *with id.* § 12 cmt. f.

[8] "Whenever it appears by suggestion of the parties or otherwise that the court lacks jurisdiction of the subject matter, the court shall dismiss the action." Rule 12(h)(3). The parties can assert the defense by a motion to dismiss for lack of jurisdiction over the subject matter. Rule 12(b)(1). *See* § 8.07[2][c] (challenging pleadings on the basis of non-waivable defenses), *infra.*

jurisdiction the burden of pleading and proving jurisdiction rests on the party who invokes jurisdiction.[9] Issues of jurisdictional fact are ordinarily for the judge to decide, looking to the pleadings, any record evidence, affidavits, deposition testimony and even live evidence.[10]

While some states apply similar rules, many have more relaxed attitudes towards subject matter jurisdiction. Some treat the objection to subject matter jurisdiction as waivable,[11] and most place the burden of raising the issue of subject matter jurisdiction on the party who challenges it.[12]

[2] Subject Matter Jurisdiction of the Federal Courts

The United States Constitution sets out the permissible scope of the judicial power of federal courts in Article III, § 2. It lists the following types of federal subject matter jurisdiction:

-cases "arising under this Constitution, the Laws of the United States, and Treaties made . . . under their Authority," popularly known as *federal question* jurisdiction;

-cases affecting ambassadors and other official representatives of foreign sovereigns;

-admiralty and maritime cases;

-controversies to which the United States is a party;

-controversies between states and between a state and citizens of another state;

-cases between citizens of different states, popularly known as *diversity* jurisdiction;

-cases between citizens of the same state claiming lands under grants of different states;

-and cases between a state or its citizens and foreign states and their citizens or subjects, sometimes known as *alienage* jurisdiction.[13]

Article III directly vests the Supreme Court with original jurisdiction of cases affecting ambassadors and other foreign officials and those to which a state is a party, and such appellate jurisdiction as Congress may create. In contrast, Article III vests no jurisdiction directly in lower federal courts. Instead, it authorizes Congress to create and endow them with subject matter jurisdiction.[14] Congress therefore has the constitutional authority

---

[9] Rule 8(a) & Form 2.

[10] *See 3 Moore* § 12.30.

[11] *See Dobbs,* note 7, *supra,* at 504.

[12] *See James, Hazard & Leubsdorf* § 2.22.

[13] U.S. Const. art. III, § 2.

[14] "The judicial power of the United States, shall be vested . . . in such inferior Courts as the Congress *may* from time to time ordain and establish." *Id.* § 1 (emphasis added).

to decide by legislation how much of the federal subject matter jurisdiction available under Article III shall be vested in the lower federal courts.[15]

While it established lower federal courts in the very first jurisdictional legislation, Congress has never vested them with as much subject matter jurisdiction as Article III permits. Except for the short-lived "Midnight Judges Act" in 1801,[16] the lower federal courts were not given general federal question jurisdiction until 1875.[17] They have never been given the whole of Article III diversity jurisdiction, as Congress has always limited this head of jurisdiction to cases that involve a specified amount in controversy.[18] Today, the main heads of federal jurisdiction are federal question jurisdiction and diversity jurisdiction, usually concurrent with state court jurisdiction.[19]

PART A
Federal Question Jurisdiction

§ 5.02 Constitutional Scope

The most important federal subject matter jurisdiction today is federal question jurisdiction. This head of jurisdiction is premised on the belief that federal courts should have the authority to expound and apply federal law because of their expertise in that law, their relative insulation from local and majoritarian pressures (and correspondingly more protective attitude toward federal rights), and their ability to give federal law more uniform application than state courts.[20] In *Osborn v. Bank of the United States*,[21]

---

[15] How little federal subject matter jurisdiction can be vested in the lower federal courts is a hotly debated question which arises in connection with proposed jurisdiction-stripping legislation. *See, e.g.,* Sager, *The Supreme Court 1980 Term, Foreword: Constitutional Limitations on Congress' Authority to Regulate the Jurisdiction of the Federal Courts,* 95 Harv. L. Rev. 17 (1981); Rotunda, *Congressional Power to Restrict the Jurisdiction of the Lower Federal Courts and the Problem of School Busing,* 64 Geo. L.J. 839, 842-843 (1976); Redish & Woods, *Congressional Power to Control the Jurisdiction of the Lower Federal Courts: A Critical Review and a New Synthesis,* 124 U. Pa. L. Rev. 45, 52-55 (1975); Eisenberg, *Congressional Authority to Restrict Lower Federal Court Jurisdiction,* 83 Yale L.J. 498 (1974).

[16] Act of Feb. 13, 1801, 2 Stat. 89, *repealed by* Act of March 8, 1802, 2 Stat. 132.

[17] Act of March 3, 1875, ch. 137, 18 Stat. 470. *See generally* F. Frankfurter & J. Landis, *The Business Of The Supreme Court* (1928) (history of federal judicial system).

[18] *See* 28 U.S.C. §§ 1332(a) (more than $75,000) & 1335(a) (disputed money or property of a value greater than $500 in interpleader actions). *See* § 9.07 (interpleader), *infra.*

[19] Federal diversity jurisdiction is always concurrent. Federal subject matter jurisdiction is presumptively concurrent unless it is expressly made exclusive by statute or impliedly "by incompatibility in its exercise arising from the nature of the particular case." *Claflin v. Houseman,* 93 U.S. 130, 136 (1876); *see also Tafflin v. Levitt,* 493 U.S. 455, 459 (1990); *Charles Dowd Box Co. v. Courtney,* 368 U.S. 502 (1962). For examples of exclusive federal jurisdiction, see 28 U.S.C. §§ 1333 (admiralty, maritime and prize cases), 1337 (antitrust; exclusive by implication), & 1338(a)(patent, plant variety protection, and copyright). *See generally* E. Chemerinsky, *Federal Jurisdiction* § 5.2 (3d ed. 1999); Solimine, *Rethinking Exclusive Federal Jurisdiction,* 52 U. Pitt. L. Rev. 383 (1991).

[20] *See* Neuborne, *The Myth of Parity,* 90 Harv. L. Rev. 1105 (1977). These premises have not gone unchallenged. *See, e.g.,* Bator, *The State Courts and Federal Constitutional Litigation,*

Chief Justice Marshall expounded in dicta upon the outer constitutional limits of that jurisdiction. He reasoned that the Article III federal question jurisdiction extends not only to the federal question in a lawsuit, but "to a whole case" and all the questions in it.[22]

> [W]hen a question to which the judicial power of the Union is extended by the constitution, forms an ingredient of the original cause, it is in the power of Congress to give the Circuit [trial] Courts jurisdiction of that cause, although other questions of fact or of law may be involved in it.[23]

Marshall did not define what he meant by "ingredient," but suggested that it is at least sufficient that the right or title asserted by a party may be defeated by one construction of federal law and sustained by the opposite.[24]

He went on to suggest it did not matter whether federal questions were actually put forth by the parties, as long as they were potentially available in the action.[25] Justice Frankfurter later explained that by this theory, federal question jurisdiction would be extended "whenever there exists in the background some federal proposition that might be challenged, despite the remoteness of the likelihood of actual presentation of such a federal question."[26]

Finally, Marshall extended his logic even to federal questions that had already been definitively answered by prior cases. Reasoning that the federal character of a legal question is not transformed by its having been answered, and that an answered federal question might well be renewed, he concluded that it is still an ingredient of the case sufficient to confer *constitutional* federal question jurisdiction.[27]

The Supreme Court has not again explored the reach of Article III's federal question jurisdiction as fully as Chief Justice Marshall did in *Osborn*. But as recently as 1983, it endorsed *Osborn* as "the controlling decision" on the scope of that jurisdiction.[28] The most frequently debated

---

22 Wm. & Mary L. Rev. 605 (1981) (noting practical inevitability of state court decision of federal law and resulting need to expand experience of state judges with federal law). For a general review of factors that are or should be considered in the allocation of business between federal and state courts, see Redish, *Reassessing the Allocation of Judicial Business Between State and Federal Courts: Federal Jurisdiction and "The Martian Chronicles,"* 78 Va. L. Rev. 1769 (1992).

[21] 22 U.S (9 Wheat.) 738, 821 (1824).

[22] By this reasoning, Marshall helped lay the groundwork for the subsequent development of the judicial doctrines of pendent and ancillary jurisdiction and the codification of supplemental jurisdiction over non-federal claims and parties in cases that also present federal questions. *See* § 5.08 (overview of supplemental jurisdiction and its antecedents), *infra*.

[23] *Osborn,* 22 U.S. at 823.

[24] *Id.*

[25] *Id.* at 825. *See The Pacific R.R. Removal Cases,* 115 U.S. 1 (1885) (federal question jurisdiction upheld over purely state law claims asserted by federally chartered railroads because federal questions concerning their charter could potentially arise).

[26] *Textile Workers Union of America v. Lincoln Mills,* 353 U.S. 448, 471 (1957) (Frankfurter, J., dissenting).

[27] *Osborn,* 22 U.S. at 825.

[28] *Verlinden B.V. v. Central Bank of Nigeria,* 461 U.S. 480, 492 (1983).

questions remaining involve less the theoretical scope of that jurisdiction than how much of it Congress has actually vested in the federal courts.

§ 5.03 Statutory Scope[29]

Although Congress approximated the language of Article III in vesting statutory federal question jurisdiction in the lower federal courts,[30] the courts have been reluctant, in light of the limited character of the federal judicial power in general, to construe their own authority expansively. They have therefore given a narrower scope to statutory federal question jurisdiction than Chief Justice Marshall gave constitutional federal question jurisdiction in *Osborn*. There is no "single, precise definition" of the statutory jurisdiction.[31] Most federal courts today cite Justice Cardozo's reformulation of Chief Justice Marshall's suggestion in *Osborn*:

> [A] right or immunity created by the Constitution or laws of the United States must be an element, and an essential one, of the plaintiff's cause of action. The right or immunity must be such that it will be supported if the Constitution or laws of the United States are given one construction or effect, and defeated if they receive another.[32]

This test requires [1] a pivotal and substantial, *i.e.,* not frivolous, federal element [2] to be part of the plaintiff's well-pleaded complaint.

[1] The Pivotal Federal Element

The vast majority of cases that come within the statutory federal question jurisdiction satisfy the "cause of action" or "creation" test embraced by Justice Holmes in *American Well Works Co. v. Layne & Bowler Co.*[33] There the Court was asked to decide whether federal jurisdiction was available for a claim that defendants had libeled and slandered plaintiff by falsely stating that plaintiff's pump infringed the defendants' federally granted

---

[29] *See generally* Hornstein, *Federalism, Judicial Power and the "Arising Under" Jurisdiction of the Federal Courts: A Hierarchical Analysis,* 56 Ind. L.J. 563 (1981); Cohen, *The Broken Compass: The Requirement That A Case Arise "Directly" Under Federal Law,* 115 U. Pa. L. Rev. 890 (1967); Mishkin, *The Federal "Question" In The District Courts,* 53 Colum. L. Rev. 157 (1953); Forrester, *The Nature Of A "Federal Question",* 16 Tul. L. Rev. 362 (1942).

[30] "The district courts shall have original jurisdiction of all civil actions arising under the Constitution, laws, or treaties of the United States." 28 U.S.C. § 1331. Similar language is also employed in 28 U.S.C. §§ 1337 and 1338(a) and they are usually given the same interpretation as § 1331. *See Carlson v. Coca-Cola Co.,* 483 F.2d 279 (9th Cir. 1973). *But see T. B. Harms Co. v. Eliscu,* 339 F.2d 823, 828 (2d Cir. 1964), *cert. denied,* 381 U.S. 915 (1965) (arguing that exclusivity of § 1338(a) jurisdiction justifies narrower construction). *See generally* Cohen, *"Arising Under" Jurisdiction and the Copyright Laws,* 44 Hastings L.J. 337 (1993). At least one commentator has argued that the drafters of the 1875 federal question statute intended to vest the full constitutional federal question jurisdiction in the lower federal courts. *See, e.g.,* Forrester, note 29, *supra,* 16 Tul. L. Rev. at 374-75.

[31] *Franchise Tax v. Constr. Laborers Vacation Trust,* 463 U.S. 1, 8 (1983).

[32] *Gully v. First Nat'l Bank,* 299 U.S. 109, 112 (1936) (citations omitted). Professor Mishkin's formulation is also popular: whether plaintiff asserts a "substantial claim founded 'directly' upon federal law." *Mishkin,* note 29, *supra,* at 168.

[33] 241 U.S. 257 (1916).

patent. Justice Holmes reasoned that "[a] suit arises under the law that creates the cause of action," and therefore found federal jurisdiction lacking, since libel and slander are state-created causes of action.[34] By this reasoning causes of action created expressly[35] or "impliedly" under federal statute[36] or under the Constitution[37] are within the statutory federal question jurisdiction of the federal courts. This is true whether or not the defendant challenges the existence of the cause of action. "The question whether a cause of action exists," the Court has said, "is not a question of jurisdiction, and therefore may be assumed without being decided."[38]

Just five years after *American Well Works,* the Court decided *Smith v. Kansas City Title & Trust Co.*[39] The plaintiff sought to enjoin the defendant trust company from investing its funds in federal farm loan bonds on the grounds that their issuance was unconstitutional. The cause of action clearly arose under state law, which prohibited the company's directors from making any investment not authorized by a valid law. Nevertheless, citing *Osborn,* the Court declared that "where it appears . . . that the right to relief depends upon the construction or application of [federal law] . . ., the District Court has jurisdiction."[40] Because the plaintiff shareholders would prevail if the federal law authorizing the bonds was found unconstitutional and lose on the opposite construction, the district court had jurisdiction of the case. The *pivotal federal question test* applied in the *Smith* case reached beyond Holmes' *creation test,* which has appropriately since been described as "more useful for inclusion than for the exclusion for which it was intended."[41]

At the same time, the Court has cautioned that the mere presence of a federal issue in a state-created cause of action does not automatically confer federal question jurisdiction.[42] Its availability depends in part on "an evaluation of the nature of the federal interest at stake":[43] whether it is sufficiently important to require a federal trial forum. In *Merrell Dow*

---

[34] *Id.* at 260.

[35] *E.g.,* 42 U.S.C. § 1983 (civil rights actions).

[36] *E.g., Cannon v. Univ. of Chicago,* 441 U.S. 677 (1979) (citing legislative intent to approve an implied cause of action for damages under federal statute).

[37] *E.g. , Bivens v. Six Unnamed Agents of Federal Bureau of Narcotics,* 403 U.S. 388 (1971) (approving an implied cause of action for damages as a necessary remedy for violation of plaintiff's Fourth Amendment rights).

[38] *Burks v. Lasker*, 441 U.S. 471, 476 n.5 (1979). *See also Bell v. Hood*, 327 U.S. 678 (1946). Rule 12 (identifying defenses that may be asserted by motion to dismiss) thus distinguishes between the defense of lack of subject matter jurisdiction (12(b)(1)) and the defense of failure to state a claim (12(b)(6)).

[39] 255 U.S. 180 (1921).

[40] *Id.* at 199. *See also Franchise Tax Bd.,* 463 U.S. at 13 (federal question jurisdiction appropriate when "it appears that some substantial, disputed question of federal law is a necessary element of one of the well-pleaded state claims").

[41] *T.B. Harms Co.* 339 F.2d at 827 (2d Cir. 1964), *cert. denied,* 381 U.S. 915 (1965).

[42] *Merrell Dow Pharmaceuticals, Inc. v. Thompson,* 478 U.S. 804, 809 (1986).

[43] *Id.* at 814-815 n.12 (endorsing this characterization by commentators of the Supreme Court's cases regarding federal question jurisdiction).

Pharmaceuticals, Inc. v. Thompson,[44] for example, the plaintiffs sued the defendant on a state claim of negligence, among others. They alleged also that the defendant had "misbranded" its products in violation of federal law, creating a rebuttable presumption of negligence under state law. The Supreme Court found that the federal issue thus incorporated into state law was "insufficiently substantial"[45] to confer federal question jurisdiction,[46] a conclusion suggested in part, if not compelled, according to the majority, by the fact that Congress had created no private cause of action for violations of the federal law at issue.[47] Insofar as such federal questions may eventually need federal appellate review, they are still subject to such review on appeal of the highest state court decision to the United States Supreme Court.[48]

The majority appears to conflate the question whether Congress intended to create a private right of action with the question of whether plaintiff's state law claim includes a pivotal federal question. Yet it hardly follows from Congress's intention to leave a statute's enforcement to public authorities that, when a federal statutory question arises as part of a state-created right of action, Congress also intended to leave the question to state court interpretation (subject only to the statistically remote possibility of Supreme Court review). On this score, the dissent may have the better argument; Congress's intent to rely on public enforcement "reflects congressional concern with obtaining more accurate implementation and more coordinated enforcement of a regulatory scheme," concerns which, if anything, strengthen the argument for federal jurisdiction over federal questions that are pivotal to state remedies.[49]

Although *Merrell Dow's* analysis led some lower courts to deny federal question jurisdiction absent a federally created right of action, the Supreme Court reaffirmed in 1997 that jurisdiction is available if a well-pleaded state

---

[44] 478 U.S. 804.

[45] *Id.* at 814. The Court's choice of the word "substantial" in *Merrell Dow* was unfortunate because the word is already used in the law of subject matter jurisdiction to mean not "wholly insubstantial and frivolous" or "patently without merit." *Bell v. Hood,* 327 U.S. 678, 682-683 (1946). The Supreme Court has so characterized questions when its "previous decisions . . . foreclose the subject and leave no room for the inference that the questions sought to be raised can be the subject of controversy." *Levering & Garriques Co. v. Morrin,* 289 U.S. 103, 105-106 (1933) (listing cases). *See Hagens v. Lavine,* 415 U.S. 528, 536-538 (1974) (listing cases). But in the context of the *Merrell* decision, the Supreme Court's use of "substantial" was clearly intended there to suggest significance or importance of the federal interest.

[46] *See also Moore v. Chesapeake & Ohio Ry.,* 291 U.S. 205 (1934). In fact, the Court has sometimes denied jurisdiction over even federally-created causes of action "because of an overwhelming predominance of state law issues." *Merrell Dow,* 478 U.S. at 814-815 n.12, *citing Shulthis v. McDougal,* 225 U.S. 561, 569-570 (1912); *Shoshone Mining Co. v. Rutter,* 177 U.S. 505, 507 (1900), both involving federally-created causes of action to vindicate property claims under state law.

[47] *Merrell Dow,* 478 U.S. at 810-812, 817.

[48] *Id.* at 816 n.14, *citing Moore,* 291 U.S. at 214-215.

[49] 478 U.S. at 832. *See generally* Alleva, *Prerogative Lost: The Trouble With Statutory Federal Question Doctrine After Merrell Dow,* 52 Ohio St. L.J. 1477 (1991); Note, *The Supreme Court, 1985 Term,* 100 Harv. L. Rev. 100, 230-240 (1986).

law claim requires decision of a substantial federal question.[50] How substantial, though, remains unclear. The federal courts which have invoked this branch of federal question law have weighed the importance of the federal question or interest without, unfortunately, casting much light on the scale they are using.[51]

[2] The Well-Pleaded Complaint Rule[52]

While the federal courts have at least partially embraced Chief Justice Marshall's suggested test in *Osborn* for the federal element in statutory federal question cases, they have squarely rejected his proposition[53] that the mere potentiality of a federal question will suffice. It is not enough that there is a *potential* federal question in a case; it must appear in plaintiff's well-pleaded complaint. A plaintiff cannot invoke the original jurisdiction of the federal courts either by anticipating a federal defense or otherwise importing a federal question into his complaint that is not essential to his case, and the federal court will examine only so much of the complaint as is well-pleaded — confined to the essential elements — to decide its federal question jurisdiction.[54]

The well-pleaded complaint rule is illustrated by *Louisville & Nashville R.R. v. Mottley.*[55] In 1871, the Mottleys settled a claim against the railroad in exchange for free lifetime passes. But in 1907, the railroad declined to renew the passes, citing a new federal statute allegedly prohibiting free passes. The Mottleys then sued in federal court for specific performance of the settlement agreement, alleging alternatively that the federal statute did not prohibit free passes or that, if it did, it offended the Fifth Amendment.

Neither party raised the issue of subject matter jurisdiction, but when the case reached the Supreme Court, the Court considered the issue on its own motion. Although the federal statute presented a potential and even likely defense by the railroad, "[i]t is not enough that the plaintiff alleges some anticipated defense to his cause of action and asserts that the defense is invalidated by . . . the Constitution."[56] Well-pleaded, *i.e.*, shorn of the anticipated federal defense, the Mottley complaint merely stated a state common law claim for specific performance of the settlement agreement and therefore presented no federal question.

---

[50] *Chicago v. International College of Surgeons*, 522 U.S. 156 (1997).

[51] *See Moore* § 1.03.31[5][a](discussing cases).

[52] *See generally* Miller, *Artful Pleading: A Doctrine in Search of Definition*, 76 Tex. L. Rev. 1781 (1998); Ragazzo, *Reconsidering the Artful Pleading Doctrine*, 44 Hastings L.J. 273, 317-27 (1993); Doernberg, *There's No Reason For It; Its Just Our Policy: Why The Well-Pleaded Complaint Rule Sabotages the Purposes of Federal Question Jurisdiction,* 38 Hastings L.J. 597 (1987).

[53] *See* § 5.02 (constitutional scope), *supra.*

[54] The Supreme court has endorsed this rule repeatedly. *See, e.g., Franchise Tax Bd. v. Const. Laborers Vacation Trust,* 463 U.S. 1 (1983).

[55] 211 U.S. 149 (1908).

[56] *Id.* at 152.

The well-pleaded complaint rule has its advantages. Because subject matter challenges go to the heart of federal judicial competence, they must be addressed promptly. The rule facilitates this, relieving the court of the burden of speculating what federal questions might later enter into the case. It also assures that a federal court will not waste its time and effort on a case that it is ultimately without jurisdiction to decide because the potential federal question fails to materialize. Consider, for example, the outcome if a federal court had taken jurisdiction of the Mottleys' complaint, only to find that the railroad never asserted the federal statute defense. The well-pleaded complaint rule also promotes federalism by leaving to state courts those cases that turn entirely or predominantly on state law. Finally, it reduces, if crudely, the federal question caseload burden on the federal courts by excluding cases in which the federal question is posed as a defense.

These advantages have been achieved at some cost, however. First, the rule substantially delays eventual federal decision of a federal defense or other post-complaint federal question. Such delay may seriously prejudice federal rights. In *Mottley,* for example, the railroad did assert the federal statute defense to the Mottleys' lawsuit in state court after the Supreme Court decision, and the case ultimately came to the Supreme Court for review,[57] resulting in a ruling for the railroad.[58] Application of the well-pleaded complaint rule thus only delayed for four years a federal court decision of the federal question.

Second, the rule can place a premium on pleading technicalities and distinctions between forms of action[59] that otherwise have no place in federal courts.[60] For example, it results in federal jurisdiction over an action to remove a specific cloud over title, but not over an action to quiet title, when defendant claims adversely under federal law. The difference is that in an action to remove a cloud, the plaintiff is required to plead facts showing the invalidity of the adverse claim which is dependent on federal law. But in an action to quiet title, the source and nature of the adverse claim is not an essential element of plaintiff's cause of action.[61]

These consequences of the well-pleaded complaint[62] rule could be mitigated by allowing removal to federal court of a state court action in which

---

[57] If the plaintiff is confined to state court, any resulting judgment may thereafter have preclusive effect in federal court. *See* § 15.10[2], *infra.* This limits the prospect of federal adjudication to United States Supreme Court review of the state decision — a possibility in some cases, but by no means a certainty. *See* Stoltz, *Federal Review of State Decisions of Federal Questions,* 64 Calif. L. Rev. 943 (1976).

[58] *Louisville & Nashville R.R. v. Mottley,* 219 U.S. 467 (1911).

[59] *See* § 8.02[1] (common law pleading), *infra.*

[60] *See* Rule 8(e)(1) ("No technical forms of pleadings or motions are required."); § 8.04 (modern notice pleading), *infra.*

[61] *See* 1 Moore § 2.03[1]. *See also Additive Controls & Measurements Systems, Inc. v. Flowdata, Inc.,* 986 F.2d 476, 478-479 (Fed. Cir. 1993) (deciding federal question jurisdiction by whether the state allocates burden of pleading truth or falsity of assertions of federal patent infringement to plaintiff or defendant in state-created business disparagement suit).

[62] *See Doernberg,* note 52, *supra,* for fuller discussion of negative consequences.

a federal defense or other post-complaint federal question is actually presented.[63] At present, however, the removal statute restricts removal just to those cases that could have been brought in federal court originally, *i.e.,* those presenting federal questions in the well-pleaded complaint.[64]

The undesirable consequences of the well-pleaded complaint rule can also be avoided by looking beyond a pleading in which the plaintiff has attempted to defeat removal to federal court by artfully leaving out a substantial federal question. The Supreme Court has used the "artful pleading doctrine" to look past such a pleading for a substantial federal question in two situations.[65] In the first, a substantial federal question is embedded in, but artfully omitted from, the pleaded state law claim. This is the converse of the well-pleaded pivotal federal question examined in the prior sub-section. The second "provides an exception when federal legislation reveals an intent by Congress to preempt a field completely, which means that regardless of what the plaintiffs plead, a federal claim—by definition raising a substantial federal question—has been raised."[66] In short, the formalism of the well-pleaded complaint rule is sometimes softened by the artful pleading doctrine to enable federal courts to take jurisdiction of substantial but not well-pleaded federal questions.

[63] In its study of federal jurisdiction, the American Law Institute (ALI) recommended that the law be changed to permit removal of these cases. Criticizing the well-pleaded complaint rule, the ALI observed that "[the] alignment of parties to a lawsuit is often quite fortuitous," and that "[t]he dangers against which jurisdiction guards are as likely to be met when federal law is relied on defensively as when it is relied on offensively." ALI, *Study of the Division of Jurisdiction Between State and Federal Courts* 189 (1969). *See also* Twitchell, *Characterizing Federal Claims: Preemption, Removal, and the Arising-Under Jurisdiction of the Federal Courts,* 54 Geo. Wash. L. Rev. 812 (1986); Collins, *The Unhappy History of Federal Question Removal,* 71 Iowa L. Rev. 717 (1986).

[64] *See* § 5.07[1](removal), *infra. See generally Ragazzo,* note 52, *supra*; Note, *Artful Pleading and Removal Jurisdiction: Ferreting Out the True Nature of a Claim,* 35 UCLA L. Rev. 315 (1987). The well-pleaded complaint rule has also substantially diminished the remedial scope of declaratory judgments. The federal Declaratory Judgment Act, 28 U.S.C. § 2201, was intended to help parties like the railroad in *Mottley,* which had no way to test its belief that federal law prohibited its renewal of the Mottleys' free pass other than to refuse renewal and invite suit by the Mottleys for breach of contract. Instead of waiting for that suit, under the Declaratory Judgment Act the railroad could have obtained a declaration of its rights from a federal court. In *Skelly Oil Co. v. Phillips Petroleum Co.,* 339 U.S. 667 (1950), however, the Supreme Court reasoned that because the Declaratory Judgment Act did not alter the federal courts' jurisdiction, it should not be construed to allow jurisdiction over a suit like the railroad's if, applying the well-pleaded complaint rule, there would be no jurisdiction over the coercive suit that would have been brought had declaratory relief been unavailable. The Court has since extended *Skelly* to state declaratory judgment complaints that defendants attempt to remove to federal court, explaining that at this late date it is for Congress, not the courts, to change the rule. *Franchise Tax Bd. v. Constr. Laborers Vacation Trust,* 463 U.S. 1 (1983). *See generally* Teply & Whitten Ch. 2, § C(5).

[65] *See Miller,* note 52, *supra,* at 1783-1784.

[66] *Id.* at 1818. The Court has explained that "Congress may so completely pre-empt a particular area that any civil complaint raising this select group of claims is necessarily federal in character." *Metropolitan Life Ins. Co. v. Tayloe,* 481 U.S. 58, 63-64 (1987). It reaffirmed the vitality of this branch of the artful pleading doctrine in *Rivet v. Regions Bank,* 522 U.S. 470, 476 (1998) (dictum).

PART B
Diversity Jurisdiction

§ 5.04 In General

[1] Rationale and the Modern Critique

The traditional justification for diversity jurisdiction[67] is that it protects out-of-state litigants from local bias.[68] With the passage of time and the decline in the intensity of state allegiances, many have criticized the continued availability of diversity jurisdiction.[69] First, they argue that local bias is no longer a serious concern in most cases. They add that even if it were, existing diversity jurisdiction is too broad in affording the choice of federal court even to a plaintiff who sues an out-of-state citizen in plaintiff's home state.[70] Advocates of diversity jurisdiction respond that some bias still exists, often exacerbated by the selection of state juries from a single county as opposed to district or state-wide jury pools. They add that, in any event, out-of-state litigants still need the protection of federal courts to avoid the prejudice inherent in their lack of familiarity with local judicial procedures.

Second, critics of diversity cite the caseload burden it imposes on the federal courts, interfering with their primary role in construing and protecting federal rights. Diversity cases consistently account for about 20% of the federal district court civil caseload. Moreover, they remain on the dockets longer, require more pretrial proceedings, go to trial more often, and require jury trials more frequently than other civil cases in the federal courts.[71] Diversity proponents respond that abolition of diversity

---

[67] 28 U.S.C. § 1332(a) confers jurisdiction *inter alia* over all civil actions between "citizens of different states" when the matter in controversy exceeds $75,000.

[68] Neither the records of the Constitutional Convention nor the records of the First Congress, which vested the federal courts with diversity jurisdiction of cases involving more than $400, describe this or any other justification in any detail. The historical reasons for the jurisdiction must therefore be gleaned from ratification debates and contemporary judicial opinions. *See, e.g.,* Friendly, *The Historic Basis of Diversity Jurisdiction,* 41 Harv. L. Rev. 483 (1928). Chief Justice Marshall explained that "the constitution itself either entertains apprehensions" about the impartiality of state courts towards non-resident litigants, "or views with . . . indulgence thei[r] possible fears and apprehensions." *Bank of the United States v. Deveaux,* 9 U.S. (5 Cranch) 61, 87 (1809). Subsequently the Court opined that the protection of diversity jurisdiction was intended principally to "give security to all contracts [and] stability to credit" by protecting out-of-state creditors from the bias of local courts. *Ogden v. Saunders,* 25 U.S. (12 Wheat.) 213, 237 (1827).

[69] The arguments for and against diversity jurisdiction have been rehearsed in a succession of congressional hearings and sundry articles. A typical collection of statements, from which the arguments in the text are drawn, may be found in *Diversity of Citizenship Jurisdiction 1982: Hearings on H.R. 6691 Before the Subcomm. on Courts, Civil Liberties and the Administration of Justice of the House Comm. on Judiciary,* 97th Cong., 2d Sess. (1982) (hereinafter cited as *1982 Diversity Hearings*).

[70] Even Chief Justice Rehnquist has urged abolition of at least this much of diversity jurisdiction. William H. Rehnquist, *Remarks of the Chief Justice,* 21 St. Mary's L.J. 5, 7-9 (1989).

[71] 1982 *Diversity Hearings* at 10 (statement of J. Rose, Assistant Attorney General). This

jurisdiction would only shift the burden to equally taxed state courts.[72] They contend that the solution to the federal caseload is instead to create more federal judges and magistrates and to reform federal pretrial process.

Third, critics of diversity jurisdiction emphasize the hopelessly complex procedural, jurisdictional and choice-of-law problems that it creates. Courts must now spend substantial time analyzing and applying elaborate, abstract and often quite arbitrary rules in determining citizenship, aggregating claims for purposes of computing amount in controversy, properly aligning parties, determining the effect of joinder and intervention in diversity cases, judging the propriety of separate and independent claim removal, and unmasking prohibited devices to manufacture diversity, all of which would be largely unnecessary were diversity to be eliminated.[73] Perhaps more significantly, the *Erie* doctrine requires federal courts sitting in diversity to apply state law as rules of decision, a task easier for their state court brethren to perform.[74] Diversity advocates respond that much of the complexity could be avoided by the elimination of the statutory requirement of complete diversity[75] in favor of minimal diversity,[76] and argue that the *Erie* problem is exaggerated. Moreover, they contend that diversity jurisdiction results in "cross-pollination" of state and federal courts to the lasting benefit of both.

At a time when federal caseloads are excessive and federal question cases must compete for scarce judicial resources with diversity cases, the critics of diversity appear to have the better of the arguments. It is both most efficient and most faithful to a federal scheme of dual judicial systems that the subject matter of litigation be allocated according to the systems' comparative advantages and the sovereigns' primary interests and responsibilities. Federal courts are best at and have a special protective interest in determining and applying federal law. The continuation of broad diversity jurisdiction diverts them from their primary mission to no better end, in most cases today, than assuring some litigants a tactical choice of forum. Yet, as long as more members of Congress come from the ranks of practicing

---

may be explained in part by the fact that nearly one-half of diversity cases are personal injury lawsuits in which the plaintiff expects to obtain a larger award from a jury than from the court. *Report of the Proceedings of the Judicial Conference of the United States* 136, Table C-2 (1999).

[72] Indeed, a statistical study conducted by the National Center for State Courts found that the abolition of just in-state plaintiff diversity jurisdiction, as urged by Chief Justice Rehnquist, *see* note 70, *supra,* "would have a surprisingly burdensome effect on state court caseloads . . . nearly as much . . . . as would . . . total abolition of diversity jurisdiction." Flango & Boersema, *Changes in Federal Diversity Jurisdiction: Effects on State Court Caseloads,* 15 U. Dayton L. Rev. 405, 455 (1990).

[73] *See* Rowe, *Abolishing Diversity Jurisdiction: Positive Side Effects and Potential for Further Reforms,* 92 Harv. L. Rev. 963, 980-981 (1979). For a discussion of some of these rules, *see* §§ 5.04[2]-[3], 5.05, 5.06, *infra.*

[74] *See* § 7.02[3](ascertaining the content of state law), *infra.*

[75] Complete diversity refers to the statutory requirement that every plaintiff be diverse from every defendant. *See* § 5.04[2], *infra.*

[76] Minimal diversity refers to the constitutional requirement that at least one plaintiff and one defendant be of diverse citizenship. *See* § 5.04[2], *infra.*

lawyers who value that choice[77] than from the academy or the bench, it appears unlikely that diversity will be abolished.[78]

[2] Diversity Between Whom?

While Congress has not yet acted to eliminate general diversity, the federal courts have often taken the matter into their own hands by construing diversity legislation narrowly.

> The policy of the [diversity] statute calls for its strict construction. The power reserved to the states, under the Constitution, to provide for the determination of controversies in their courts may be restricted only by the action of Congress in conformity to [Article III]. Due regard for the rightful independence of state governments, which should actuate federal courts, requires that they scrupulously confine their own jurisdiction to the precise limits which the statute has defined.[79]

This is most apparent in the requirement for complete diversity. Although the Supreme Court has held that Article III requires only *minimal diversity*[80] (that at least one party be a citizen of a different state from at least one opposing party), in *Strawbridge v. Curtiss*[81] it construed the general diversity statute to require complete diversity (that no party may share citizenship with any opposing party). In modern multi-party litigation, the statutory requirement for complete diversity is in theory quite restrictive; it defeats jurisdiction whenever there is a single plaintiff who is a citizen of the same state as any defendant.

The courts have further narrowed the availability of diversity jurisdiction by looking behind the pleadings in some disputes and "realigning" the parties according to their real interests. Assume, for example, that a mortgagee sues its mortgagor and a city with whom the mortgagor has a contract for specific performance of the contract. Since the mortgagee and mortgagor have the same interest in specific performance, they should be aligned together, which will destroy complete diversity if the mortgagor and the city are citizens of the same state.[82] Realignment is more difficult when

---

[77] *See* Flango, *Attorneys' Perspectives on Choice of Forum in Diversity Cases*, 25 Akron L. Rev. 41, 56, 105 (1991) (finding that fear of bias against non-resident clients was a significant factor in choice of forum for more than 60% of attorneys surveyed).

[78] Of course, it will never be wholly abolished. All agree that *alienage diversity,* jurisdiction over suits between citizens and foreign nationals, must remain in the federal courts. It is likely, too, that diversity jurisdiction will be continued over multi-party lawsuits that could otherwise not be brought in any single state court. *See* Report of the Federal Courts Study Comm. 38-42 (1990); *1982 Diversity Hearings,* note 3, *supra,* at 263 (multidistrict mass tort litigation consolidated under 28 U.S.C. § 1407); 28 U.S.C. § 1397 (interpleader).

[79] *Healy v. Ratta,* 292 U.S. 263, 270 (1934).

[80] *State Farm Fire & Casualty Co. v. Tashire,* 386 U.S. 523 (1967) (upholding constitutionality of federal interpleader statute, 28 U.S.C. § 1397, which requires only minimal diversity).

[81] 7 U.S. (3 Cranch) 266 (1806). *See* Fink, *Supplemental Jurisdiction — Take It to the Limit!,* 74 Ind. L.J. 161 (1998)(calling for elimination of rule of complete diversity); Currie, *The Federal Courts and the American Law Institute,* 36 U. Chi. L. Rev. 1, 18-21 (1968) (criticizing the rule of complete diversity).

[82] *See Dawson v. Columbia Trust Co.,* 197 U.S. 178 (1905).

interests are shared on some issues and divided on others, but the court will then look to the "principle purpose of the suit" and the "primary and controlling matter in dispute" for purposes of alignment.[83]

[3]　Further Limitations on Diversity Jurisdiction

Deferring to state courts, federal courts have traditionally declined to exercise jurisdiction in certain *in rem*[84] and probate cases and in domestic relations cases, even when the parties satisfy the requirements for diversity jurisdiction. In addition, they are also obliged by statute to deny jurisdiction which has been "improperly or collusively made."[85]

Considerations of comity owed state courts have motivated federal courts to decline jurisdiction over diversity suits in which, in order to give effect to their judgments, they must take control of property that is already in the custody of a state court of competent jurisdiction. Such suits may include "suits . . . brought to marshal assets, administer trusts, or liquidate estates."[86]

A time-honored but possibly erroneous construction of the diversity statute, as well as recognition that the "whole subject of husband and wife, parent and child, belongs to the laws of the states," account for the long-standing exclusion of domestic relations actions from diversity jurisdiction.[87] In *Ankenbrandt v. Richards*,[88] the Supreme Court traced the domestic relations exception to the historical assumption that alimony and divorce lay outside the jurisdiction of the chancery courts in England and therefore outside the diversity jurisdiction "in suits of a civil nature at common law or in equity" conferred by the Judiciary Act of 1789. Without confirming this assumption, the Court deferred to "Congress' apparent acceptance of this construction of the [early] diversity jurisdictional provisions" and its subsequent reenactment of diversity jurisdiction without substantive change.[89] This statutory conclusion has modern-day appeal. State

---

[83] *See, e.g., Indianapolis v. Chase Nat'l Bank,* 314 U.S. 63, 69 (1941) (*citing East Tennessee, V. & G. R. v. Grayson,* 119 U.S. 240, 244 (1886), and *Merchants' Cotton Press Co. v. Insurance Co.,* 151 U.S. 368, 385 (1894)). In *Chase Nat'l Bank* the Court dismissed several secondary issues on which the mortgagor and mortgagee were divided as mere "window-dressing designed to satisfy the requirements of diversity jurisdiction." 314 U.S. at 72. In a case which presents multiple issues of equal importance, it is arguable that a court should not realign parties who are truly divided on any one of the issues, but the case law is divided on this point. *See Wright* § 30.

[84] *See* § 3.02[2] (*in rem* jurisdiction), *supra.*

[85] 28 U.S.C. § 1359.

[86] *Princess Lida v. Thompson,* 305 U.S. 456, 466 (1939).

[87] *In re Burrus,* 136 U.S. 586, 593-594 (1890) (dictum). In a full account of the history of this exception, Judge Friendly has also traced it and the exception for probate actions to the belief that such cases were not "suits of a civil nature in law and equity" within the language of the first diversity jurisdiction statute because they were historically within the jurisdiction of ecclesiastical courts. *See Phillips, Nizer, Benjamin, Krim & Ballon v. Rosenstiel,* 490 F.2d 509, 513 (2d Cir. 1973).

[88] 504 U.S. 689 (1992).

[89] *Id.* at 701.

courts are more closely associated with state and local governmental units dedicated to monitoring compliance with domestic relations decrees, and federal judges understandably lack enthusiasm for burdensome, fact-bound and often protracted domestic relations disputes.[90]

On the other hand, the *Ankenbrandt* Court stressed the relatively narrow scope of the domestic relations exception. It divests the federal courts of the power to issue divorce, alimony, and child custody decrees. It does not encompass other intra-family legal claims, including ordinary tort or contract claims.[91]

Finally, the courts are barred by statute from asserting jurisdiction when a party contrives to create diversity. Assignments of claims between non-diverse parties to diverse parties for purposes of manufacturing diversity were outlawed in the very first Judiciary Act, but poor drafting invited evasion.[92] Today the statute prohibits this by denying jurisdiction when a party "by assignment or otherwise, has been improperly or collusively made or joined to invoke the jurisdiction of the court."[93] Appointment of out-of-state administrators to represent infants, incompetents, or the estates of decedents was also a popular device to create diversity. Since 1988, the diversity statute defeats this device by deeming the citizenship of a legal representative to be that of the infant, incompetent, or decedent.[94]

§ 5.05 Citizenship

In deciding diversity jurisdiction, the courts look to the citizenship of the parties at the commencement of the action. This measuring point provides precision, because actions in federal court commence on filing of the complaint with the court,[95] and certainty, because the existence of diversity jurisdiction is unaffected by the vicissitudes of the subsequent litigation. Post-commencement changes in citizenship of the parties can neither create jurisdiction where none existed at commencement, nor divest the court of jurisdiction which was proper at commencement. However, realignment of the parties during the litigation[96] may show that diversity was or was not

---

[90] *Id.* at 703 (noting sound policy considerations supporting the exception); *Rosentiel,* 490 F.2d at 516 n.8 (Friendly, J.) (candidly opining that taking jurisdiction would be a "waste" of scarce federal judicial resources).

[91] *See, e.g., Ankenbrandt,* 504 U.S. at 704 (finding that diversity jurisdiction exists over physical and sexual abuse claims by children against a parent).

[92] *See generally Wright* § 31.

[93] 28 U.S.C. § 1359. The statutory bar on collusive or improperly made diversity jurisdiction literally only applies to devices to "invoke" jurisdiction. The courts, however, are increasingly refusing to give effect to comparable devices to *defeat* diversity jurisdiction, typically arising in response to attempted removals of actions from state to federal court. *Wright.* § 31.

[94] 28 U.S.C. § 1332(c)(2).

[95] Rule 3.

[96] *See* § 5.04[2] (diversity between whom), *supra.*

present at commencement of the suit, and incomplete diversity can be cured by dropping the non-diverse parties during the litigation.[97]

Citizenship for diversity purposes requires a party to be a citizen of both the United States and of a state. United States citizenship ordinarily poses no analytic difficulties, since it is usually conferred by birth to citizen parents or on United States soil, but state citizenship can be more problematical. The courts have equated the state citizenship of natural persons with *domicile* in a state. Domicile itself, however, is a legal fiction imposed on persons in order to simplify legal determinations, unlike *residence,* which has a practical meaning outside the law. "The very meaning of domicile is the technically pre-eminent headquarters that every person is compelled to have in order that certain rights and duties that have been attached to it by the law may be determined."[98]

Domicile is created by the concurrent establishment of physical residence in a state and an intent to remain there indefinitely.[99] Although a person can have more than one residence at one time, he can by definition only form the requisite intent with respect to a single state at one time, and therefore can have only one domicile at a time.[100] Neither residence nor intent alone will suffice to establish domicile; both must be established concurrently. Accordingly, once established, domicile in one state continues until a person has changed both his residence and his intent concurrently. A mere change of residence without a concurrent formation of an intent to remain indefinitely in the state of new residence, or the mere formation of an intent to go elsewhere unaccompanied by a change in residence, will not alter a previously established domicile. Indeed, although the burden of pleading and proving citizenship is on the party invoking diversity jurisdiction, she enjoys a presumption in favor of her last-established domicile which must be rebutted by the party alleging a change in domicile.[101]

Because the requisite intent is a state of mind, it can only be shown circumstantially. Sundry affiliating circumstances may be offered in evidence of that intent: place of employment, voter or vehicle registration, driver's license, current residence, presence of other property or intangible interests, bank accounts, club memberships, mailing address, etc.[102] The

---

[97] Rule 21. *Cf. Newman-Green, Inc. v. Alejandro Alfonzo-Larrain,* 490 U.S. 826 (1989) (holding that courts of appeals also have authority under Rule 21 to dismiss dispensable nondiverse parties). Defective allegations of jurisdiction can also be amended during the litigation, provided that jurisdiction in fact existed at commencement. 28 U.S.C. § 1653.

[98] *Williamson v. Osenton,* 232 U.S. 619, 625 (1914) (Holmes, J.).

[99] The requisite intent has also been characterized as the intent to return to the residence when one is absent, *Wright* § 26, and the absence of any present intention to live elsewhere. *Williamson,* 232 U.S. at 623.

[100] *Id.* Thus, it is not usually sufficient for a plaintiff to allege mere residence of the parties in order to allege citizenship for diversity purposes. *See, e.g., Rosenquist v. Gustafson,* 803 F. Supp. 1325 (N.D. Ill. 1992).

[101] *Bank One, Texas, N.A. v. Montle,* 964 F.2d 48, 50 (1st Cir. 1992); *Janzen v. Goos,* 302 F.2d 421 (8th Cir. 1962).

[102] *See, e.g., Tanzymore v. Bethlehem Steel Corp.,* 457 F.2d 1320 (3d Cir. 1972) (affirming

courts originally shortcut such proof in some instances, however, by adopting the "now vanishing fiction of identity of person,"[103] by which the domicile of the husband was attributed to the wife and domicile of parent attributed to child. Modern courts have been increasingly willing to discard this fiction when appropriate and to determine the domicile of each of the parties on his or her individual facts.

This trend and many of the foregoing principles are well-illustrated by *Mas v. Perry.*[104] Mr. and Mrs. Mas, graduate students studying at Louisiana State University, sued their landlord, a Louisiana citizen, in federal court for damages resulting from his spying on their bedroom through a two-way mirror. The landlord challenged diversity jurisdiction. The challenge was clearly unsound as to Mr. Mas; he was a French national whose suit then fell within alienage jurisdiction.[105] By the fiction of identity of person, however, diversity was arguably lacking as to Mrs. Mas, as she would take the French domicile of her husband but, as a United States citizen, would not qualify for alienage jurisdiction.

Instead, the court discarded the fiction and traced her last established domicile to Mississippi, where she had lived with her parents before her marriage. Neither her establishment as a student of a Louisiana residence, nor her candid admission that she did not intend to return to Mississippi, changed her Mississippi domicile, because she had not yet formed an intent to remain indefinitely in Louisiana or any other location. Moreover, the Mas' change of residence to Illinois *after* commencement of the action was immaterial to jurisdiction. Not only had they formed no intent to remain indefinitely in Illinois, but Mrs. Mas' domicile at commencement of the action remained Mississippi. Thus, there was diversity at commencement of the action and the landlord's challenge failed.

Two legal fictions, domicile and the corporate entity, complicate the process of determining citizenship for corporations. But the amendment of the diversity statute to deem a corporation to be the citizen of "any State by which it has been incorporated and of the state where it has its principal place of business"[106] has simplified matters greatly. Because corporations often have dual citizenship under the statute, the party invoking diversity must plead not only its citizenship by incorporation, but also its citizenship by principal place of business.[107]

---

dismissal for lack of diversity, when deposition of plaintiff showed none of these affiliating circumstances); *Simmons v. Skyway of Ocala,* 592 F. Supp. 356, 360 (S.D. Ga. 1984) ("grab-bag of indicia having to do with everyday life" established Florida domicile).

[103] *Williamson,* 232 U.S. at 625.

[104] 489 F.2d 1396 (5th Cir. 1974).

[105] 28 U.S.C. § 1332(a)(2). However, a permanent resident alien is now deemed a citizen of the state where she is domiciled. *Id.* § 1332(a).

[106] 28 U.S.C. § 1332(c)(1). Some unnecessary ambiguity may have been perpetuated by the amendment's use of "any state" instead of "every state," but most courts and commentators are agreed that the latter is the intended meaning of the amendment. *See Wright* § 27.

[107] *Canton v. Angelina Casualty Co.,* 279 F.2d 553 (5th Cir. 1960). *See* Form 2 (plaintiff is a citizen of Connecticut and "defendant is a corporation incorporated under the laws of the State of New York and having its principal place of business in a State other than Connecticut").

Incorporation is a definite and ascertainable legal act, but determining the "principal place of business" can become difficult when a corporation conducts business in multiple states. The statute contemplates a single principal place of business; how should a pleader and the court choose among them? The test courts have used most looks to the locus of the bulk of the corporation's activities, measured by corporate assets, sales or other physical measures.[108] Alternatively, instead of this place-of-operations, bulk-of-the-assets, or "muscle" test, many courts apply the home office or "nerve center" test, looking to the locus of the corporation's operating headquarters.[109]

Lurie Co. v. Loew's San Francisco Hotel Corp.[110] illustrates the application and offers one possible reconciliation of the two tests. The corporation's officers and chief legal and financial advisers were located in New York, which was thus its nerve center where overall policy was formulated. The corporation's only asset, however, was located in California, the locus also of 95% of its employees, 93% of its operating expenses and all of its revenue. The court concluded that "these factors clearly establish California as the 'place of operations' or place of 'day-to-day activities,' " and therefore the principal place of business, reasoning that the nerve center test was only applicable when no single state could be identified as the locus of such activities because of the far-flung nature of a corporation's business.[111]

Finally, the federal courts have traditionally held that unincorporated associations, such as partnerships and labor unions, take the citizenship of each member.[112] This rule reflects the historical assumption that such organizations are not juridical persons and therefore must be disregarded for citizenship purposes. In 1990, the Court reaffirmed this view and distinguished an apparently contrary decision as going to the question whether parties who were natural persons were real parties to the controversy, not whether an artificial entity is a citizen.[113] However, the rule has not been applied to class actions; diversity is determined by the citizenship of the representative parties, without regard to the absent class members.[114]

---

[108] *See, e.g., Anniston Soil Pipe Co. v. Central Foundry Co.*, 329 F.2d 313 (5th Cir. 1964) (locus of plant and production facilities rather than of executive offices); *Kelly v. U.S. Steel Corp.*, 284 F.2d 850 (3d Cir. 1960) (locus of largest number of executive officers and corporate operating committee, as well as of largest percentage of employees and assets); *United States Fidelity & Guar. Co. v. DiMassa*, 561 F. Supp. 348 (D.C. Pa. 1983) (locus of corporate operations as well as main computer).

[109] *See, e.g., Scot Typewriter Co. v. Underwood Corp.*, 170 F. Supp. 862 (S.D.N.Y. 1959).

[110] 315 F. Supp. 405 (N.D. Cal. 1970).

[111] *Id.* at 416.

[112] *See, e.g., Carden v. Arkoma Assocs.*, 494 U.S. 185 (1990); *United Steelworkers v. Bouligny, Inc.*, 382 U.S. 145, 150-151 (1965).

[113] *Carden*, 494 U.S. 185 (distinguishing *Navarro Sav. Ass'n v. Lee*, 446 U.S. 458 (1980)).

[114] *Supreme Tribe of Ben-Hur v. Cauble*, 255 U.S. 356 (1921). Unincorporated associations or other entities that may be unable to satisfy diversity requirements due to the citizenship of their members may therefore be able to avoid diversity problems by suing through representative members in class actions. *See* Rule 23.2 (permitting such suits if representative parties will fairly and adequately protect the interests of the association and its members). *See generally* § 9.09 (class actions), *infra*.

§ 5.06   Amount in Controversy

[1]   The "Legal Certainty Test" and the Single Claim

Since the First Judiciary Act, Congress has imposed a monetary limitation on diversity jurisdiction.[115] The present amount in controversy is $75,000, exclusive of interest and costs.[116] The purpose of the limitation has always been to ration federal judicial resources by screening out penny-ante cases. The device has never really proven effective to this end, however, since litigants have often been able to adjust their pleadings as necessary to invoke jurisdiction. Moreover, the amount in controversy requirement has probably itself wasted federal judicial resources in uselessly complex disputes of the jurisdictional amount. Arguably then, little would be lost in terms of caseload control, and much gained in saved time and energy, were the jurisdictional amount in diversity cases eliminated.

Like citizenship, jurisdictional amount must be pled and (if challenged) proven by the plaintiff, and is determined as of the time of commencement of the action.[117] The Supreme Court stated the proper test for amount in controversy in the leading case of *St. Paul Mercury Indemnity Co. v. Red Cab Co.*:[118]

> [T]he sum claimed by the plaintiff controls if the claim is apparently made in good faith. It must appear to a legal certainty that the claim is really for less than the jurisdictional amount to justify dismissal. The inability of the plaintiff to recover an amount adequate to give the court jurisdiction does not show his bad faith or oust the jurisdiction. Nor does the fact that the complaint discloses the existence of a valid defense to the claim.[119]

Jurisdictional amount is thus ordinarily computed from the plaintiff's viewpoint without regard to possible defenses, and plaintiff's good faith pleading controls unless the court concludes to "a legal certainty" that he cannot recover the pleaded amount.

When plaintiff seeks only liquidated — arithmetically ascertainable — damages, the amount is easily determined. Suits seeking unliquidated

---

[115] Until 1980, Congress also imposed a monetary limitation on general federal question jurisdiction. However, dissatisfaction with its application to constitutional claims of incalculable monetary value and resulting relaxed applications of the requirement in many federal question cases led to the abandonment of the requirement. Act of Dec. 1, 1980, Pub.L. No. 96-486, 94 Stat. 2369. Nevertheless, many of the old federal question cases are still relevant authority for ascertaining amount in controversy in diversity cases.

[116] 28 U.S.C. § 1332(a).

[117] It is the direct effect of the immediate lawsuit that is relevant for ascertaining the jurisdictional amount, not its collateral effects or importance to strangers or society at large. *See, e.g., Healy v. Ratta*, 292 U.S. 263, 267 (1934) (collateral effect via *stare decisis* may not be considered). *See generally* 15 *Moore* §102.106.

[118] 303 U.S. 283 (1938).

[119] *Id.* at 288-289 (footnotes omitted). Plaintiff's eventual inability to recover the jurisdictional amount gives the court the discretion to reverse the usual award of costs. 28 U.S.C. § 1332(b).

damages, equitable relief or inherently unquantifiable relief have proven more difficult.

In suits seeking unliquidated damages, *legal certainty in law* [120] is established by the legal unavailability of relief necessary to reach the jurisdictional amount. For example, if the applicable law requires aggravating circumstances before punitive damages can be recovered in a contract action, and the plaintiff has not and cannot in good faith allege such circumstances, his prayer for punitive damages must be disregarded as a matter of law. [121] Similarly, the applicable law may place a statutory ceiling on the recovery [122] or may limit special damages to interest on property in a suit to recover personal property. [123] As the Supreme Court put it as early as 1798, [124] "where the law gives the rule, the legal cause of action, and not the plaintiff's demand, must be regarded."

Legal certainty in fact is much more difficult to find, because it requires a court to appraise the evidentiary basis for plaintiff's claim. The court must chart a course

> between a rule on the one hand that allows some cases involving inflated claims for relief to be brought in a federal forum in order to insure access to that forum for all those cases that properly may be brought there, and, on the other hand, a rule that closes the doors to the federal forum in the face of some claims that properly could be brought there in order to insure the denial of the forum to cases involving inflated claims. [125]

The cases divide between the two approaches.

Some courts give presumptive effect to plaintiff's claim of amount in controversy, no matter how unlikely it is that she will prevail on the facts at trial. [126] These courts reason that any other approach would run the risk of depriving the plaintiff of her right to a jury trial by converting the jurisdictional inquiry into a mini-trial of the merits.

Other courts test plaintiff's claim of amount in controversy for reasonableness in light of the evidence adduced in an evidentiary hearing on the motion to dismiss for lack of jurisdiction. [127] These courts assert that the focus on plaintiff's right to a jury trial begs the question, which is whether she *has* a right to come into the federal court room to try her claim. Since judges may, through their power to set aside excessive verdicts, [128] place upper limits on jury awards, they should not be timid in relating that upper

---

[120] *Kahal v. J.W. Wilson & Assocs. Inc.,* 673 F.2d 547, 548 (D.C. Cir. 1982) (distinguishing between legal certainty in law and in fact).

[121] *Id.* at 549 (dismissing contract claim in which compensatory damages were below the jurisdictional amount).

[122] *See, e.g., Ringsby Truck Lines, Inc. v. Beardsley,* 331 F.2d 14 (8th Cir. 1964).

[123] *See Vance v. Vandercook Co.,* 170 U.S. 468 (1898).

[124] *Wilson v. Daniel,* 3 U.S. (Dall.) 401, 408 (1798).

[125] *Deutsch v. Hewes St. Realty Corp.,* 359 F.2d 96, 100 (2d Cir. 1966).

[126] *See, e.g., id.*

[127] *See, e.g., Nelson v. Keefer,* 451 F.2d 289, 293 (3d Cir. 1971).

[128] *See* § 12.09[2][b] (new trials), *infra.*

limit to the jurisdictional floor for purposes of deciding diversity jurisdiction. [129]

Actions for equitable relief pose special problems. In *Mississippi & Missouri Railroad Co. v. Ward*, [130] a suit by a steamboat owner to abate the nuisance posed by a bridge over the Mississippi River, the Supreme Court declared that "[r]emoval of the obstruction is the matter of controversy, and the value of the object must govern." This rule focuses on the value of the object of the equitable relief, but value to whom? The value to plaintiff of having the obstruction removed will rarely be the same as the cost to defendant of having to remove it. A majority of courts have looked at the cost to the plaintiff if relief is not afforded, [131] while a minority have considered the greater of "the pecuniary result[s] to *either* party which the judgment would directly produce." [132] The minority rule seems preferable because otherwise a suit in which plaintiff seeks an injunction to remove a 50-story office building encroaching on a few inches of his land would fall outside the diversity jurisdiction of the federal courts despite the enormous expense, and therefore substantiality of the controversy, to the defendant. Since "[t]he purpose of an amount in controversy requirement is to ensure the substantiality of the suit itself, not solely the amount which the plaintiff stands to recover," a federal court should look to the largest effect on either party and take jurisdiction of such a suit, according to the minority view. [133]

Finally, the courts have found some claims involving inherently unquantifiable relief to fall outside monetarily limited jurisdiction grants. An early Supreme Court decision suggested that amount in controversy could be satisfied only "where the rights of property are concerned and where the matter in dispute has a known and certain value, which can be proved and calculated, in the ordinary mode of a business transaction." [134] While the Court has since rejected any distinction between personal and property rights for jurisdictional purposes, [135] some courts still insist on

---

[129] *Nelson*, 451 F.2d 289. *See also Jimenez Puig v. Avis Rent-A-Car Sys.*, 574 F.2d 37 (1st Cir. 1978) ("brief embarrassment" of having defendant's agent erroneously seize and destroy plaintiff's credit card for non-payment will not factually support punitive damages claim necessary to satisfy jurisdictional amount); *Sierra v. Lidchi*, 651 F. Supp. 1019 (D.P.R. 1986) (counterclaim for defamation based on hearsay allegation that plaintiff called defendant a thief will not support jurisdictional amount).

[130] 67 U.S. 485, 492 (1862).

[131] *See, e.g., City of Milwaukee v. Saxbe*, 546 F.2d 693, 702 (7th Cir. 1976); *cf. Glenwood Light & Water Co. v. Mutual Light, Heat & Power Co.*, 239 U.S. 121, 125 (1915) (measuring amount by harm to plaintiff's business rather than by defendant's cost of removal, without, however, expressly endorsing "plaintiff viewpoint" as the only test). The "plaintiff viewpoint" rule does not avail a defendant who seeks removal of a case brought in state court when the plaintiff's injury is below the jurisdictional amount. A few courts have therefore suggested that jurisdictional amount be measured from the viewpoint of the party who invokes federal jurisdiction. *See Moore* § 102.109[5].

[132] *Ronzio v. Denver & R.G.W.R. Co.*, 116 F.2d 604, 606 (10th Cir. 1940) (emphasis supplied). *See also McCarty v. Amoco Pipeline Co.*, 595 F.2d 389 (7th Cir. 1979) (discussing four tests for amounts in controversy in equitable actions); 1 *Moore* ¶ 0.91[1].

[133] *See Moore* § 1.02.109[4].

[134] *Barry v. Mercein*, 46 U.S. (5 How.) 103, 120 (1847).

[135] *Lynch v. Household Fin. Corp.*, 405 U.S. 538 (1972).

susceptibility of the claim to ready pecuniary appraisal. In a suit by the Senate Watergate Committee to compel President Nixon to give up the Watergate tapes, for example, the court refused to place any monetary value on the interference with the Committee's constitutional obligations and therefore denied jurisdiction.[136] Courts have reached the same result in suits to compel inspection of a corporation's books and records, to prohibit divulging of telephone intercepts, to adjudicate lunacy, and to declare marital status.[137]

[2] Aggregating Multiple Claims

The discussion of amount in controversy to this point has assumed that plaintiff asserts a single claim against a single defendant. But liberal modern joinder rules encourage multiple claims, posing the question whether the amounts in controversy on such claims can be aggregated to satisfy the jurisdictional amount.[138] Unfortunately, the judge-made aggregation rules do not track the joinder rules and do not follow transactional or any other apparent logic. Consequently, "it is not altogether easy to say what the law is in this area, and it is quite hard to say why it is as it seems to be."[139] Consider three joinder situations: the plaintiff joins multiple claims against a single defendant; multiple parties, whether plaintiffs or defendants or both, are joined on one or more claims; defendant counterclaims against plaintiff.

It is well-established that a plaintiff may aggregate all the claims he asserts against a single defendant, whether or not they are transactionally related and whether or not any of them alone satisfies the jurisdictional amount.[140] Thus, in this joinder situation, aggregation is co-extensive with joinder under Rule 18.[141]

The rule is different, however, when plaintiff joins several defendants to the same claim or several plaintiffs join in the same claim against one or more defendants pursuant to Rule 20.[142] Aggregation is possible if several parties have a common undivided interest or title, but not if they have separate and independent interests.[143] For example, when multiple

---

[136] *Senate Select Comm. on Presidential Campaign Activities v. Nixon,* 366 F. Supp. 51, 59 (D.D.C. 1973). The amount in controversy requirement has since been abolished in general federal question cases. *See* note 115, *supra.*

[137] *See* cases cited in J. Moore, *Moore's Federal Practice* ¶ 0.92[5] (2d. ed.).

[138] *See generally* Wright § 36; Note, *The Federal Jurisdictional Amount and Rule 20 Joinder of Parties: Aggregation of Claims,* 53 Minn. L. Rev. 94 (1968).

[139] Wright § 36. at 209. *But see* Rosenberger, *The Amount in Controversy: Understanding the Rules of Aggregation,* 26 Ariz. St. L.J. 925 (1994) (asserting that aggregation rules are more firmly rooted in policy than commentators have supposed).

[140] 15 *Moore* § 102.108[1].

[141] *See* § 9.02(claim joinder), *infra.*

[142] *See* § 9.05[1] (permissive party joinder), *infra.*

[143] Wright § 36; 15 *Moore* §§ 102.108[2][3]. The circuit courts are divided about whether punitive damages among plaintiff class members can be aggregated on the theory that they share a common and undivided interest in punishing the defendant and deterring the offending

plaintiffs sue on the basis of common title, or multiple defendants assert common title as a defense to a suit to recover land, the matter in controversy is the entire tract of land, not just its several parts. Aggregation is therefore permitted.[144] On the other hand, the necessary common and undivided interest is not established merely because claims derive from a single instrument or because multiple parties share a community of interest.[145] Nor will the fact that defendants are joint tortfeasors justify aggregation; plaintiff's claim against each is ordinarily still separate and distinct and must therefore stand alone for purposes of satisfying the jurisdictional amount. The aggregation rules are thus more restrictive than Rule 20, governing joinder of parties,[146] and are essentially artifacts of a bygone era before the liberalization of joinder in federal courts.

Finally, the logic of computing the amount in controversy from plaintiff's complaint and the separate and distinct nature of original claims and counterclaims suggest that their aggregation should not be permitted.[147] But in *Horton v. Liberty Mutual Insurance Co.*,[148] the Court held 5-4 that the then-$10,000 jurisdictional amount was satisfied when the plaintiff insurer alleged that defendant would counterclaim for $14,035, even though the insurer actually sued to set aside a workmen's compensation award of only $1050. Under Texas law, however, the insurer's suit reopened the entire compensation claim below regardless of the award and might therefore be viewed as an action for a judgment declaring the insurer's non-liability as to the entire $14,035 workmen's compensation claim. Most federal decisions have read the case as involving a quirk of Texas law and confined it to its facts.[149] But until the Supreme Court distinguishes or overrules *Horton* it leaves uncertain the question whether (and when)

---

conduct. *See* Willis, *Aggregation of Punitive Damages in Diversity Class Actions: Will the Real Amount in Controversy Please Stand Up*, 30 Loy. L.A.L. Rev. 775 (1997). The answer is important in consumer class actions where the class members' individualized compensatory damages fall below $75,000 and there is no federal question jurisdiction.

[144] *Cornell v. Mabe,* 206 F.2d 514, 516 (5th Cir. 1953).

[145] *Wright* § 36.

[146] Moreover, these rules apply to class actions as well and therefore required that each class member satisfy the jurisdictional amount when their claims are separate and distinct. *Snyder v. Harris,* 394 U.S. 332 (1969); *Zahn v. Int'l Paper Co.,* 414 U.S. 291 (1973). It is unclear whether this is still the law, however, because the supplemental jurisdiction statute, 28 U.S.C. § 1367(b), on its face now permits supplemental jurisdiction over insufficient class member claims as long as a representative party's claim is sufficient, contrary to the statute's reported legislative intent. *See* § 5.11, *infra.*

[147] On the other hand, a no-aggregation rule interacts with the removal provisions to permit a party with a small claim to force his adversary to litigate his much larger claim in state court, provided that the former wins the race to the courthouse. *Wright* § 37. It also risks a wasteful minuet whereby a plaintiff's complaint is dismissed in the face of a compulsory counterclaim that satisfies the jurisdictional amount, and then is reinstated as a compulsory counterclaim, within the court's supplemental jurisdiction, to the defendant's now independently standing claim. 1 J. Moore, *Moore's Federal Practice* ¶ 0.98[1] (2d ed.). This minuet, however, does serve to give the original defendant the choice whether to stay in the federal forum, which he would be denied by a rule of aggregation. *Id.*

[148] 367 U.S. 348 (1961).

[149] *See Wright* § 37.

claims and counterclaims can be aggregated to satisy the amount in controversy.

PART C
Removal and Supplemental Jurisdiction

§ 5.07   Removal Jurisdiction

[1]   In General

Removal jurisdiction is an exception to the usual rule that plaintiff chooses the court.[150] Although the Constitution makes no express provision for removal, it is now well-established that a defendant may, pursuant to statute,[151] remove a civil action from a state court with territorial jurisdiction[152] to federal court. The purpose of removal is to make the option of suit in federal court as available to defendants (except for resident defendants in a diversity-only case) as it is to plaintiffs.[153] This purpose has been given effect in several ways by the provisions of the general removal statute and by the judicial gloss upon them.

First, because removal is a protective option for defendants, only defendants may invoke it.[154] The courts have read this limitation strictly, prohibiting a plaintiff who is sued upon a federal counterclaim from removing on that account.[155] Moreover, they have added the gloss that all defendants must join in the petition to remove, save in cases of removal of "separate and independent" claims under 28 U.S.C. § 1441(c), in which case all defendants to such a claim must join in the petition.[156]

Second, because removal is intended just to make existing federal jurisdiction available to defendants, only civil actions "of which the district

---

[150] *See* Chapter 2, *supra*.

[151] The general removal statute is 28 U.S.C. § 1441, which is discussed in this section. Congress has also provided for removal of specific civil actions not discussed here. *See, e.g.,* 28 U.S.C. § 1442 (suits against federal officers); 28 U.S.C. § 1442a (suits against members of the armed forces); 28 U.S.C. § 1443 (suits in which civil rights are denied); 28 U.S.C. § 2679(d) (suits against federal employees arising out of motor vehicle accidents within the scope of employment). In addition, Congress has guaranteed plaintiffs their choice of forum by prohibiting removal in certain cases. *See, e.g.,* 28 U.S.C. § 1445(a) (Federal Employers' Liability Act suits); 28 U.S.C. § 1445(c) (workmen's compensation "suits); 46 U.S.C. § 688 (Jones Act suits).

[152] Removal jurisdiction presupposes that the state court had personal jurisdiction over the action. *See, e.g., Garden Homes, Inc. v. Mason,* 238 F.2d 651 (1st Cir. 1956) (removal improper when state court lacked personal jurisdiction due to insufficient service of process). State court subject matter jurisdiction is no longer a predicate for removal, however. 28 U.S.C. § 1441(e).

[153] *See* Miller, *An Empirical Study of Forum Choices in Removal Cases Under Diversity and Federal Question Jurisdiction,* 41 Am. U. L. Rev. 369 (1992) (finding that fear of local bias against out-of-state litigants is a significant factor in removal).

[154] 28 U.S.C. § 1441(a) (civil actions "may be removed by the defendant or the defendants").

[155] *See Shamrock Oil & Gas Corp. v. Sheets,* 313 U.S. 100 (1941). Realignment of the parties may affect designation of the "defendant." *See* § 5.04[2] (diversity between whom), *supra*.

[156] *See, e.g., Chicago, R.I. & P. Ry. v. Martin,* 178 U.S. 245 (1900); *Wright* § 40.

courts . . . have original jurisdiction . . . may be removed."[157] Removal jurisdiction is therefore keyed to original jurisdiction, and all the rules and principles previously discussed concerning federal question and diversity jurisdiction apply. That is, the court decides on the facts as they existed at the time the notice of removal was filed[158] whether the action would have satisfied the requirements for federal jurisdiction had it originally been filed in federal court. A court may consider post-removal evidence of what those facts were at the time of filing.[159] Furthermore, the plaintiff may cure problems in a case nonremovable when filed by amending to increase the amount in controversy or to add a removable claim or by dismissing a nondiverse defendant because removal jurisdiction is measured at the filing of the notice of removal, not the complaint.[160]

The application of the well-pleaded complaint rule[161] creates the anomaly that a defendant who asserts a federal defense or counterclaim to a non-diverse plaintiff's state claim cannot remove (unless federal law has completely preempted state law in this area), inasmuch as a federal court would not have had original jurisdiction over the plaintiff's claim.[162] On the other hand, the Court has repeatedly held that a plaintiff cannot defeat removal by artfully failing to plead potentially preemptive federal law.[163] "If the only remedy available to plaintiff is federal, because of preemption or otherwise, and the state court necessarily must look to federal law in passing on the claim, the case is removable regardless of what is in the pleading."[164]

Third, because the protective rationale for removal is inapplicable to a defendant sued upon state law claims in his own state court, diversity cases

---

[157] 28 U.S.C. § 1441(a).

[158] Ordinarily, therefore, the court does not have jurisdiction if it is only *after* removal that facts necessary to establish jurisdiction come into existence (for example, that the parties become diverse). In *Caterpillar Inc. v. Lewis*, 519 U.S. 61 (1996), however, the Supreme Court held that when incomplete diversity at filing was cured before final judgment, that judgment could stand. It explained that once a case has been tried, "considerations of finality, efficiency, and economy become overwhelming." *Id.* at 75. Setting aside a judgment entered when there was complete diversity would waste the federal resources expended in reaching the judgment and possibly impose the costs of retrying the case on state courts. Whether *Caterpillar* actually imposes greater costs by relaxing the usual requirement for a "front-end" jurisdictional inquiry remains to be seen.

[159] *See e.g., Sierminski v. Transouth Finan. Corp.*, 216 F.3d 945 (11th Cir. 2000).

[160] *Moore § 107.14[2][h].*

[161] *See § 5.03[2], supra.*

[162] *See, e.g., Oklahoma Tax Comm'n v. Graham*, 489 U.S. 838 (1989) (holding case not removable despite the federal defense of tribal immunity to state tax claims). The Supreme Court has acknowledged that a rational jurisdictional system might well discard the equation of original and removal jurisdiction in these circumstances, since "the defendant's petition for removal could furnish the necessary guarantee that the case necessarily presented a substantial question of federal law." But it has noted that removal is statutory and that reform must therefore come from the Congress. *Franchise Tax Bd. v. Construction Laborers Vacation Trust,* 463 U.S. 1, 11 n.9 (1983).

[163] *See, e.g. Avco Corp. v. Aero Lodge No. 735*, 390 U.S. 557 (1958). § 5.03[2], *supra.*

[164] *Wright & Miller § 3722. See generally* Miller, *Artful Pleading: A Doctrine in Search of Definition*, 76 Tex. L. Rev. 1781 (1998); Ragazzo, *Reconsidering the Artful Pleading Doctrine*, 44 Hastings L.J. 273 (1993).

are removable "only if none of the parties in interest properly joined and served as defendants is a citizen of the State in which such action is brought."[165] Thus, a citizen of Virginia sued in a Virginia state court by a citizen of Maryland may not remove the case to federal court. In this respect, removal jurisdiction is narrower than original jurisdiction.

The procedure for removal is clearly laid out by statute.[166] Within thirty days after receipt of the pleading or other paper affording grounds for removal,[167] defendant must file a bond and a notice of removal in the federal court for the district in which the state court action is pending, setting forth a short and plain statement of the grounds for removal, together with all filings from the state court action. Filing of a copy of the notice with the state court perfects removal and ousts that court of all further jurisdiction. The federal court thereafter proceeds under the Federal Rules of Civil Procedure[168] as if the case had been filed with it originally, without regard to the usual venue requirements.[169] Plaintiff may oppose the removal by a motion to remand, or the court will decide its jurisdiction *sua sponte*. If there is any doubt of removability, the court should remand in accord with the rule of strict construction of jurisdictional statutes.[170] A decision to remand on the grounds that "the case was removed improvidently and without jurisdiction" is unreviewable.[171] Denial of a motion to remand is, of course, reviewable on appeal of the final judgment by the federal court.

[2]　Removal of Separate and Independent Claims

Suppose that P, a citizen of Virginia, joins a state law claim to a federal question claim against D, also a citizen of Virginia. Should we allow D to remove the latter alone to federal court? This partial removal question is problematic. If partial removal is not allowed, plaintiffs will have an incentive to join non-removable claims to removable claims in state court in order to defeat removal of the case. On the other hand, if partial removal is allowed it could promote inefficiently duplicative litigation. Congress originally responded by authorizing removal of "the entire case" containing one or more "separate and independent claim[s] or cause[s] of action which would be removable if sued upon alone," vesting discretion in the federal judge to retain the entire case or to remand the independently non-removable claims. "Separate and independent" was originally given a

---

[165] 28 U.S.C. § 1441(b).

[166] 28 U.S.C. §§ 1446-50.

[167] 28 U.S.C. § 1446(b). In addition, actions removed on grounds of diversity must be removed no more than one year after they were commended in state court.

[168] *See* Rule 81(c).

[169] *See Wright & Miller* § 3726.

[170] *See Wright* § 41.

[171] 28 U.S.C. § 1447(d). A remand for other reasons may be reviewed for abuse of discretion. *Thermtron Products, Inc. v. Hermansdorfer*, 423 U.S. 336 (1976). Commentators have criticized the statutory bar on appeal as anachronistic and destructive of federal rights. *See* Wasserman, *Rethinking Review of Remands: Proposed Amendments to the Federal Statute*, 43 Emory L.J. 83 (1994).

restrictive interpretation by the Supreme Court in a diversity case,[172] and the lower court case law is complex and often inconsistent. Today it can perhaps best be generalized as construing the requirement to mean "factually unrelated."[173]

In 1990, Congress restricted separate and independent claim removal to cases in which the independently removable claim poses a federal question. Congress authorized the federal court, in the judge's discretion, to retain the whole removed case or to remand "all matters in which State law predominates."[174] However, Congress may have largely mooted this branch of removal jurisdiction by enacting supplemental jurisdiction at the same time.[175] If the otherwise non-removable state law claim is part of the same constitutional case or controversy as the federal question claim, then the state law claim falls within the supplemental jurisdiction of the court[176] and can be removed pursuant to section 1441(a) & (b) of the statute.

If the state law claim does not fall within the same constitutional case or controversy as the federal question claim, then the removal of the state law claim to federal court may present a serious constitutional question whether Article III permits jurisdiction absent diversity among the parties.[177] If this is true, it leaves only a small category of separate federal claims made unremovable by particular statutes, or separate state claims that satisfy minimal but not complete diversity requirements,[178] which a federal court could constitutionally hear by removal under § 1441(c). Presumably, most of the latter would then be remanded anyway because of the predominance of state law.[179] It may be hard, therefore, to escape the conclusion that "with the slim pickings [section 1441(c)] has in . . . [federal question cases], it may have to grope for some gainful employment."[180]

---

[172] *American Fire & Cas. Co. v. Finn*, 341 U.S. 6 (1951) (claims arising from a "single wrong" are not separate and independent).

[173] *See Moore* §§ 107.14[6][d] (discussing cases which appear to apply this interpretation) & 107.14[6][f].

[174] 28 U.S.C. § 1441(c).

[175] Siegel, 28 U.S.C.A. § 1441 commentary (1990).

[176] *See* § 5.11 *infra*.

[177] *See Teply & Whitten*, Chap. 2, § B(5); Cohen, *Problems in the Removal of a Separate and Independent Claim or Cause of Action*, 46 Minn. L. Rev. 1, 20-25 (1961). *But see* Steinman, *Supplemental Jurisdiction in § 1441 Removed Cases: An Unsurveyed Frontier of Congress' Handiwork*, 35 Ariz. L. Rev. 305 (1993). In *Twentieth Century-Fox Film Corp. v. Taylor*, 239 F. Supp. 913 (S.D.N.Y. 1965), the court suggested that the prior version § 1441(c) gave it removal jurisdiction over the independent claims and was a valid exercise of Congress' authority under the Necessary and Proper Clause. The Supreme Court has yet to rule on the question.

[178] *See* § 5.04[2], *supra*. *See* Hartnett, *A New Trick From an Old and Abused Dog: Section 1441(c) Lives and Now Permits the Remand of Federal Question Cases*, 63 Fordham L. Rev. 1099, 1150-1154 (1995).

[179] *Siegel*, note 175.

[180] *Id.*

§ 5.08 Overview of Supplemental Jurisdiction and Its Antecedents

All cases that fall within the subject matter jurisdiction of the federal courts must begin with the allegation of at least one claim capable of invoking a statutory grant of federal subject matter jurisdiction. Many federal cases are made up entirely of these claims. But sometimes a federal court will use its statutory subject matter jurisdiction over one such freestanding claim to anchor its adjudication of one or more related claims that would not independently satisfy subject matter jurisdictional requirements. Such extended jurisdiction[181] historically evolved under the separate labels of *pendent* and *ancillary* jurisdiction, although the courts' terminology was often inconsistent.[182] In 1990, Congress codified much of the prior law of pendent and ancillary jurisdiction as *supplemental jurisdiction*.[183] After introducing the terminology in this section, in succeeding sections we explore pendent, ancillary and supplemental jurisdiction in greater detail.

As used here, *pendent jurisdiction* refers to the courts' extension of jurisdiction from freestanding (usually federal question) claim[184] to an otherwise jurisdictionally insufficient *pendent* (usually state law) claim by a plaintiff or plaintiffs. It applied, for example, to a state claim for unauthorized use of a play which plaintiff joins with a freestanding federal claim for copyright violation against a non-diverse defendant. Commentators also coined the phrase *pendent party jurisdiction* to describe jurisdiction extended from the freestanding claim to a pendent claim against a new party which would not independently fall within the court's subject matter jurisdiction.

A rationale of convenience supported pendent jurisdiction.[185] It avoided piecemeal lawsuits and unnecessary decision of federal questions in federal

---

[181] *See, e.g.,* Freer, *A Principled Statutory Approach to Supplemental Jurisdiction,* 1987 Duke L.J. 34; Matasar, *Rediscovering "One Constitutional Case": Procedural Rules and the Rejection of the Gibbs Test for Supplemental Jurisdiction,* 71 Cal. L. Rev. 1399, 1402 n.3 (1983) ("supplemental jurisdiction . . . suggests an extension of power over claims normally outside federal jurisdiction in order to serve important federal interests that supplement the purposes underlying the decision of the original federal claims"); Note, *A Closer Look at Pendent and Ancillary Jurisdiction: Toward a Theory of Incidental Jurisdiction,* 95 Harv. L. Rev. 1935 (1982) [hereinafter cited as *Incidental Jurisdiction*].

[182] *See, e.g., County of Oakland v. City of Berkeley,* 742 F.2d 289, 296 (6th Cir. 1984) (court expresses uncertainty whether lower court exercised pendent or ancillary jurisdiction); *By-Prod Corp. v. Armen-berry Co.,* 668 F.2d 956, 962 (7th Cir. 1982) (discussing ancillary jurisdiction over defendant's counterclaim as "pendent jurisdiction").

[183] 28 U.S.C. § 1367.

[184] *See generally* § 25 (statutory scope), *supra.* Various federal jurisdictional grants will support the anchor claim, including admiralty jurisdiction. *See, e.g., Leathers Best, Inc. v. S.S. Mormaclynx,* 451 F.2d 800 (2d Cir. 1971) (admiralty). At least one court has held that even diversity jurisdiction will support the anchor. *See Seybold v. Francis P. Dean, Inc.,* 628 F. Supp. 912 (W.D. Pa. 1986) (diversity, where pendent claim was jurisdictionally insufficient federal claim).

[185] *See, e.g.,* Matasar, *A Pendent and Ancillary Jurisdiction Primer: The Scope and Limits of Supplemental Jurisdiction,* 17 U.C. Davis L. Rev. 103, 152 (1983); Note, *Unraveling the "Pendent Party" Controversy: A Revisionist Approach to Pendent and Ancillary Jurisdiction,* 64 B.U. L. Rev. 895, 900, 927 n.170 (1985) [hereinafter cited as *Revisionist Approach*].

courts by allowing them to hear and decide related state law questions, and it avoided duplicative litigation in state courts that might otherwise result from the plaintiff's splitting of related federal and state law claims between the two court systems. But convenience was not the sole rationale for pendent jurisdiction. It also promoted the protective purposes of federal jurisdiction by giving the plaintiff with related federal and state claims unimpeded access to the federal forum.[186]

In contrast, *ancillary jurisdiction* extended jurisdiction from the free-standing (often diversity) claim to an otherwise jurisdictionally insufficient claim by the defendant(s) or similarly situated parties such as intervenors as of right,[187] who, as a practical matter, did not choose the forum. In a diversity action, for example, ancillary jurisdiction supported a compulsory counterclaim or cross-claim for less than the jurisdictional amount or impleader of a non-diverse party. The rationale was one of fairness and necessity. It permitted the federal courts to give full and effective relief by hearing claims and deciding rights that might be lost or compromised if forced into another forum.[188] This is particularly necessary as a matter of fairness to parties who are involuntarily in the federal forum and who assert essentially defensive claims.[189]

Whether a court could exercise either pendent or ancillary jurisdiction was initially a question of constitutional power. Article III sets the constitutional boundaries on federal subject matter jurisdiction and appears to confine it to the nine listed heads of jurisdiction.[190] Yet Article III speaks to judicial power over "cases" arising under federal law and "controversies" between diverse citizens, not just over questions. Thus, provided that a civil action has within it at least one jurisdictionally sufficient anchor claim, a federal court arguably has the constitutional power to hear any otherwise jurisdictionally insufficient claims which are part of the same constitutional case.[191] The trick is to define the parameters of a constitutional case — to determine what relationship is required between the freestanding claim and the jurisdictionally dependent claims for them to be considered part of the same case. The focal point of analysis is therefore the particular

---

[186] *Matasar,* note 181, *supra,* 71 Cal. L. Rev. at 1402 n.3, 1404-1407 n.6; *Friedenthal, Kane & Miller* § 2.12. Absent pendent jurisdiction, plaintiff would have to (1) split her claims between federal and state courts, running the risk that a state court judgment would preclude her from relitigating common issues in the federal action; (2) forego one of her claims in favor of litigating just the other in one forum; or (3) pursue both claims in state court, when the federal claim is not within the exclusive jurisdiction of the federal court, thereby foregoing the protection of federal court jurisdiction. *Id.*

[187] *See* § 9.08[1], *infra.*

[188] *Revisionist Approach,* note 185, *supra,* at 900; *Matasar,* note 185, *supra,* 17 U.C. Davis L. Rev. at 151-152.

[189] *See, e.g., Incidental Jurisdiction,* note 181, *supra,* at 1937.

[190] *See* § 5.01[2] (federal subject matter jurisdiction), *supra.*

[191] *United Mine Workers v. Gibbs,* 383 U.S. 715, 725 (1966). *See also Osborn v. Bank of the United States,* 22 U.S. (9 Wheat) 738, 821 (1824), discussed *in* § 5.02, *supra.*

relationship between the freestanding claim,[192] which is statutorily self-sufficient, and the dependent claim, which is not.

Even if a court has constitutional power to extend its jurisdiction, it must still satisfy itself that it has statutory power and that it should exercise its power in the circumstances. If so, then it may hear and decide additional claims without regard to venue over them.[193] Personal jurisdiction over each of the parties is still required, but is often obtained for pendent or ancillary claims by plaintiff's reliance on the 100-mile bulge rule,[194] federal statutory provision for nationwide service of process on the federal claims,[195] or defendants' waiver of personal jurisdiction.

§ 5.09　Pendent Jurisdiction

[1]　Pendent Claim Jurisdiction

The leading case of pendent jurisdiction is *United Mine Workers v. Gibbs*.[196] Gibbs sued the non-diverse United Mine Workers in federal court for violations of the federal Labor Management Relations Act and of the common law of Tennessee as a result of its interference with his hauling contract during a labor dispute. After the jury decided for Gibbs on both claims, the trial court set aside the verdict on the federal claim, reasoning that the union interference was not cognizable under federal law, but entered judgment on the state law claim. The Court of Appeals affirmed, and the Supreme Court was presented the question whether the federal courts had jurisdiction over the state claim in the absence of diversity. The Court held that constitutional power exists to decide the nonfederal claim whenever it is so related to the federal claim that they comprise "but one constitutional 'case.'"[197] It suggested a three-part test for *constitutional case*.

First, to anchor such a case, plaintiff must assert a federal claim that has "substance sufficient to confer subject matter jurisdiction on the court."[198] Since Gibbs' freestanding claim was a federal law claim, it had to meet the statutory requirements for federal question jurisdiction.[199]

---

[192] The cases and commentators regularly refer to the anchor claim as a "federal" claim, and the dependent claim as the "nonfederal claim." *See, e.g., Owen Equipment & Erection Co. v. Kroger,* 437 U.S. 365, 372 n.11 (1978). Because the anchor claim can be an admiralty or a state claim within diversity jurisdiction, this usage is somewhat confusing and is therefore not followed here.

[193] *Wright* §§ 9 & 19.

[194] Rule 4(f) (allowing service within 100 miles of courthouse). *See generally* §§ 4.03[2] (service), *supra,* 9.05[2][b] (compulsory joinder) & 9.06 (impleader), *infra.*

[195] *Wright* § 9 (noting split of authority concerning whether availability of nationwide service confers ancillary jurisdiction over jurisdictionally insufficient claims).

[196] 383 U.S. 715 (1966).

[197] *Id.* at 725.

[198] *Id.*

[199] *See* § 5.03[2], *infra.*

Gibbs' claim met these requirements, asserting a right to relief created by the federal Labor Management Relations Act.

Second, the freestanding and pendent claims "must derive from a common nucleus of operative fact."[200] In so ruling, the Court discarded as "unnecessarily grudging" a "cause of action" test for constitutional case which confined *case* to alternative federal and nonfederal grounds for the same cause of action.[201] Since Gibbs' federal and pendent claims involved overlapping facts concerning the union's actions, the common nucleus requirement was satisfied. But it would also be consistent with an expansive exposition of Article III power over "cases" to find the requirement satisfied by less than substantial overlap, even just a common origin in the same-transaction-or-occurrence or simply a logical relationship between the claims, like that required for several forms of joinder under the federal rules of civil procedure.[202] Most courts have opted for this definition of common nucleus.[203]

Third, *Gibbs* seemed also to require that the federal and nonfederal claims be such that the plaintiff "would ordinarily be expected to try them all in one judicial proceeding."[204] This apparently referred to a plaintiff's anticipation of the possible claim-preclusive effects of a federal judgment on the freestanding claim in subsequent state court suits asserting the

---

[200] *Gibbs*, 383 U.S. at 725.

[201] The cause of action test was set forth in the pre-rules case of *Hurn v. Oursler*, 289 U.S. 238 (1933). But the concept of "cause of action" has presented serious ambiguities in all of its applications, *see, e.g.,* § 15.03 (res judicata), *infra,* causing the drafters of the rules to reject it in favor of "civil action." Rule 2. The *Gibbs* court noted this history in discarding *Hurn. Gibbs,* 383 U.S. at 722-725.

[202] Joinder under Rules 13(a) (compulsory counterclaims), 13(g) (cross-claims), and 20 (permissive joinder of parties) requires that the joined claim arise out of the same transaction or occurrence that is the subject matter of existing claims. Most modern courts have interpreted this transactional nexus to mean simply a "logical relationship" between the claims. *See, e.g., Great Lakes Rubber Corp. v. Herbert Cooper Co.,* 286 F.2d 631 (3d Cir. 1961). *See generally* §§ 9.02-9.05 (simple joinder), *infra.*

Professor Matasar illustrates the difference between factual overlap and logical relationship by positing an action by a welfare recipient from whom a social worker has gathered confidential information and then disclosed the same to third persons. *See* Matasar, *A Pendent and Ancillary Jurisdiction Primer: The Scope and Limits of Supplemental Jurisdiction,* 17 U.C. Davis L. Rev. 103, 129-132 (1983). If the federal claim is that the information was gathered in violation of federal regulations, and the state claim is that it was disclosed in violation of state privacy law, there is neither factual identity nor overlap between the claims. They arguably arise out of the same transaction and are logically related, however, which would permit pendent jurisdiction under the broadest interpretation of "common nucleus of operative fact." *Id.* at 132; *cf. Reyes v. Edmunds,* 416 F. Supp. 649 (D. Minn. 1976). *But cf. Mason v. Richmond Motor Co., Inc.,* 625 F. Supp. 883 (E.D. Va. 1986) (rejecting "mere commonality of facts" in favor of a stricter test).

[203] At least one court has suggested that the "common nucleus of operative fact" test is broader than the "transaction or occurrence" test of the federal rules. *See Ambromovage v. United Mine Workers,* 726 F.2d 972, 990 (3d Cir. 1984). The Supreme Court has also implied that the constitutional case may include factually unrelated claims whose resolution is necessary and proper to give full effect to a federal court's federal subject matter jurisdiction. *See* § 5.10 note 201, *infra.*

[204] *Gibbs,* 383 U.S. at 725.

jurisdictionally insufficient claims. Under the modern law of claim preclusion,[205] a plaintiff is expected to try all transactionally-related claims together, in that he is precluded by a final judgment on any of them from subsequently trying the others. The expected-to-try part of the *Gibbs* test for constitutional case was therefore perhaps best viewed as a restatement of the common nucleus requirement rather than an independent requirement, and that was the trend of the case law.[206]

Constitutional power to exercise pendent jurisdiction was decided on the pleadings. But *Gibbs* also held that the "power need not be exercised in every case in which it is found to exist."[207] "Needless decisions of state law should be avoided" to assure both comity and "surer-footed reading" of state law.[208] In addition, justification for pendent jurisdiction lay "in considerations of judicial economy, convenience and fairness to litigants," which differ from case to case and from one stage of a single case to another. Whether a court should exercise its power of pendent jurisdiction was therefore a question of discretion open throughout the case.

The factors that guided the exercise of discretion reflected these considerations and comity concerns. Timing of the disposition of the freestanding claim was a key factor. Ordinarily if the freestanding claim was resolved early in the litigation, refusing jurisdiction over pendent state claims would not result in wasteful duplication of effort, but could well yield a "surer-footed" decision of state law from the state court in which the refused claims would then have to be brought. In fact, dictum in *Gibbs* stated that state claims "[c]ertainly . . . should be dismissed" without prejudice if the federal claims were dismissed before trial.[209] The Court subsequently backed away from its dictum,[210] however, and most lower courts recognized that the timing of dismissal was only a surrogate for a more basic factor: the likelihood of wasteful duplication of effort should pendent jurisdiction be refused.[211]

---

[205] *See* §§ 15.02-15.05, *infra.* The older law of claim preclusion gave preclusive effect only to those claims which were part of the same "cause of action," *id.* § 108[B], *infra,* precisely the test that *Gibbs* expressly rejected in adopting the common nucleus test.

[206] *Matasar,* note 202, *supra,* at 138. *But see Wright & Miller* § 3567.1 (requirements are cumulative).

[207] 383 U.S. at 726.

[208] *Id.* Federal court decision of unsettled state law questions poses at least two serious federalism concerns. There is no mechanism by which federal errors of state law can be corrected on appeal by state courts, and state courts may be reluctant in later cases to reject even "lead-footed" federal decisions of state law because of intervening public reliance on the latter. *See Financial General Bankshares, Inc. v. Metzger,* 680 F.2d 768, 772-775 (D.C. Cir. 1982) (explaining why trial court abused its discretion in exercising jurisdiction over pendent claim involving unsettled state law after pretrial disposition of federal claims). On the difficulty of ascertaining the meaning of state law, see generally § 7.06, *infra.*

[209] 383 U.S. at 726.

[210] *See Rosado v. Wyman,* 397 U.S. 397 (1970) (approving pendent jurisdiction after federal claims became moot before trial, where substantial time and energy had been expended on case).

[211] *See, e.g., Financial General Bankshares, Inc. v. Metzger,* 680 F.2d 768, 773-774 (D.C. Cir. 1982) (and cases there cited).

Predominance of state claims, in terms of proof, scope or remedy, was also a factor weighing against pendent jurisdiction. Exercising it when the state claims predominate and the federal claims drop out of the case before trial "smacks of the tail wagging the dog."[212]

The possibility of jury confusion was another factor, since the possible cure of ordering separate trials on the anchor and pendent claims[213] could sacrifice the judicial economy that in part justified pendent jurisdiction.

On the other hand, these factors could be outweighed by a close connection between the state claims and federal policy. For example, in *Gibbs* itself there was a substantial question whether the state law claim was preempted by federal labor law, which "afforded a special reason for the exercise of pendent jurisdiction."[214]

[2] Pendent Party Jurisdiction[215]

Gibbs presented the classic case of pendent jurisdiction, in which the plaintiff appended state law claims to a freestanding federal law claim against the same defendant. But *Gibbs* also acknowledged that "[u]nder the [federal] rules, the impulse is toward entertaining the broadest possible scope of action consistent with fairness to the parties; joinder of claims, *parties* and remedies is strongly encouraged."[216] Accordingly, some plaintiffs invoked *pendent party jurisdiction* to assert claims against new parties over whom independent federal subject matter jurisdiction was unavailable.

Such jurisdiction, for example, was invoked in diversity cases to add a defendant on a claim for less than the jurisdictional amount in controversy.[217] This form of pendent party jurisdiction, however, offends the rule against aggregating claims for amount in controversy in diversity cases.[218] In *Zahn v. International Paper Co.*[219] the Court applied the rule forbidding aggregation of plaintiffs' claims against different defendants (absent suit upon a joint and undivided interest) to deny pendent party jurisdiction in a class action in which the parties did not all meet the amount in controversy requirement. *Zahn* thus suggested, though it did not decide, that pendent party jurisdiction generally cannot be used to avoid the rule against aggregation.[220]

Pendent party jurisdiction was also invoked in federal question cases to add non-diverse parties to state law claims. In *Aldinger v. Howard*,[221]

---

[212] *McFaddin Exp., Inc. v. Adley Corp.*, 346 F.2d 424, 427 (2d Cir. 1965), *cert. denied*, 382 U.S. 1026 (1966).

[213] *See* Rule 42(a) (separate trials).

[214] 383 U.S. at 729.

[215] *See generally* Currie, *Pendent Parties*, 45 U. Chi. L. Rev. 753 (1978).

[216] 383 U.S. at 724 (emphasis added).

[217] *See, e.g., F.C. Stiles Contracting Co. v. Home Ins. Co.*, 431 F.2d 917 (6th Cir. 1970).

[218] *See* § 5.06[2] (aggregating multiple claims), *supra*.

[219] 414 U.S. 291 (1973).

[220] *See* Bratton, *Pendent Jurisdiction in Diversity Cases — Some Doubts*, 11 San Diego L. Rev. 296, 322-323 (1974).

[221] 427 U.S. 1 (1976).

however, the Court cast doubt over this form of extended jurisdiction. Plaintiff had brought a civil rights action against the county treasurer and then appended a transactionally-related state law claim against the county and county commissioners. The Court refused jurisdiction over the state claim despite its factual overlap with the federal claims. It explained first that there is a difference between simply adding a state law claim against a defendant already in court on a jurisdictionally sufficient federal question and adding a new defendant on a pendent claim. Arguably the latter is a further, and often more burdensome, extension of jurisdiction than the former. The Court then noted that jurisdiction over the county was, in any event, expressly negated by a fair reading of the Civil Rights Act.[222]

At the same time, the Court in *Aldinger* was careful not to rule out pendent party jurisdiction altogether. "Other statutory grants and other alignments of parties and claims might call for a different result."[223] If, for example, the Court speculated,[224] a freestanding claim was within the exclusive jurisdiction of the federal courts, then *only* in federal court can all the claims be heard together. Allowing pendent party jurisdiction in this case would arguably effectuate the special protective purpose of exclusive federal jurisdiction. Consequently, *Aldinger* may still have held open the door of the federal court to pendent party jurisdiction when the freestanding and pendent claims share a common nucleus of operative fact, and when jurisdiction, given the alignment of the parties, was not expressly or impliedly negated by the anchoring jurisdictional statute.[225]

To the general surprise of commentators, however, the Court slammed that door shut in *Finley v. United States.*[226] *Finley* presented precisely the case about which the *Aldinger* Court had speculated: plaintiff asserted a freestanding claim within the exclusive jurisdiction of the federal courts[227] and sought to join transactionally-related state law claims against non-diverse defendants. Absent pendent party jurisdiction, plaintiff would be forced to forego her state law claims against the non-diverse parties or to

---

[222] *Id.* at 16. It later changed its mind about the Act. *Monell v. New York City Dept. of Social Serv.,* 436 U.S. 658 (1978). The Court also denied pendent party jurisdiction in a diversity case in which plaintiff tried to assert a state law claim against a non-diverse third party defendant. The statutory requirement of complete diversity negated the existence of pendent party jurisdiction in such circumstances. *Owen Equipment & Erection Co. v. Kroger,* 437 U.S. 365 (1978). *See* § 5.10, *infra,* for further discussion of *Kroger* as an ancillary jurisdiction case; § 9.06, *infra,* for further discussion of third-party practice.

[223] 427 U.S. at 18.

[224] 427 U.S. at 18.

[225] Every circuit but the Ninth upheld exercises of pendent party jurisdiction after *Aldinger*. *See Feigler v. Tidex, Inc.,* 826 F.2d 1435, 1438 (5th Cir. 1987) (so noting). *See generally* Note, *Unraveling the "Pendent Party" Controversy: A Revisionist Approach to Pendent and Ancillary Jurisdiction,* 64 B.U. L. Rev. 895, 938 (1985) (suggesting the test whether fairness in the circumstances compels a statutory interpretation that would allow jurisdiction); *Matasar,* note 202, *supra,* at 163-165 (expressing doubt that there is a practical difference between a claim and a party in light of possible net efficiency to judicial system of joining the latter).

[226] 490 U.S. 545 (1989).

[227] 28 U.S.C. § 1346(b) (conferring exclusive jurisdiction of "civil actions on claims against the United States").

bring separate actions in federal and state court. The Court acknowledged the inefficiency and inconvenience of this result, yet denied pendent party jurisdiction, because the underlying jurisdictional statute contained no "affirmative grant of pendent-party jurisdiction."[228] The Court thus turned the *Aldinger* search for implied congressional negation of pendent jurisdiction into a requirement for congressional affirmation of such jurisdiction.[229] Because Section 1331 (general federal question jurisdiction) and most other federal jurisdictional statutes are silent about pendent jurisdiction, the logic of *Aldinger* imperiled all pendent (and all ancillary) jurisdiction,[230] notwithstanding the Court's disclaimer of any "intent to limit or impair" the *Gibbs* line of cases.[231]

§ 5.10 Ancillary Jurisdiction

Ancillary jurisdiction originally developed independently of pendent jurisdiction. In *Freeman v. Howe*,[232] a United States marshal had seized certain railroad cars under a writ of attachment issued by a federal court sitting in diversity. The railroad's mortgagees sought replevin (return of property) against the marshal in state court, but were ultimately rebuffed when the Supreme Court held that the state court was powerless to interfere with property under federal judicial control. They were therefore left without a forum in which to pursue their claims to the property unless they could get into federal court. Despite their lack of diversity to the marshal and the absence of any federal question, the Court said that they could have asserted their claims in federal court on the theory that their claim was "ancillary and dependent, supplementary merely to the original suit, out of which it had arisen."[233] The justification for this extension of jurisdiction was clearly fairness — necessity from the perspective of the mortgagees — in that they were otherwise unable to assert their rights to the property in any forum.

Subsequently in *Moore v. New York Cotton Exchange*,[234] the Court extended ancillary jurisdiction in a federal antitrust action to a transactionally-related state law counterclaim, emphasizing the close, mirror-image relationship between the claims.[235] The necessity or fairness to defendant

---

[228] 490 U.S. at 553.

[229] *See, e.g.,* Freer, *Compounding Confusion and Hampering Diversity: Life After Finley and the Supplemental Jurisdiction Statute*, 40 Emory L.J. 445, 465-466 (1991) ("In *Finley*, the presumption [of congressional authorization for pendent jurisdiction] is turned 180 degrees.").

[230] Some courts read *Finley* "as sounding the death knell" for at least pendent party jurisdiction, *see, e.g., Sarmiento v. Texas Bd. of Veterinary Medical Examiners*, 939 F.2d 1242, 1247 (5th Cir. 1991), and the commentators went further. *See, e.g.,* Mengler, *The Demise of Pendent and Ancillary Jurisdiction*, 1990 BYU L. Rev. 247 (1990); Perdue, *Finley v. United States: Unstringing Pendent Jurisdiction*, 76 Va. L. Rev. 539 (1990).

[231] 490 U.S. at 556.

[232] 65 U.S. (24 How.) 450 (1860).

[233] *Id.* at 460.

[234] 270 U.S. 593 (1926).

[235] *Id.* at 610 ("It only needs the failure of the [antitrust claim] to establish a foundation for the [counterclaim].").

having such a counterclaim heard in federal court was not comparable to the necessity presented by the mortgagees in *Freeman.* Presumably the convenience of litigating the claims at the same time supported ancillary jurisdiction in this setting, although the Court did not elaborate or even characterize the jurisdiction as ancillary. But by premising the extension of jurisdiction on the close factual relationship between the claims, *Moore* led the eventual expansion of ancillary jurisdiction to transactionally-related joinders of claims and parties under the Federal Rules of Civil Procedure.

The expansion was summarized, and perhaps slowed, by the 1978 decision in *Owen Equipment & Erection Co. v. Kroger.*[236] There the Court found two broad requirements for ancillary jurisdiction in diversity cases.

First, ancillary jurisdiction, like pendent jurisdiction, required constitutional power to hear the jurisdictionally insufficient claims. The Court "assume[d] without deciding" that the *Gibbs* common nucleus requirement delineates the outer constitutional boundaries of federal diversity as well as federal question jurisdiction.[237]

Second, ancillary jurisdiction required a court to determine that Congress had neither expressly nor impliedly negated the exercise of jurisdiction, a determination based upon "the posture in which the nonfederal claim is asserted" and an examination of the anchoring jurisdictional statute.[238] In *Kroger,* the plaintiff was attempting to assert a state law claim against a non-diverse third-party defendant in a diversity case. Unlike the defendant who had brought the third-party defendant into the case, however, the plaintiff had voluntarily chosen the federal forum. "By contrast, ancillary jurisdiction involves claims by a defending party haled into court against his will, or by another person whose rights might be irretrievably lost unless he could assert them in an ongoing action in a federal court."[239] Thus, the posture in which the dependent claim was asserted did not suggest such unfairness to plaintiff from denying ancillary jurisdiction as to overcome the usual statutory requirement of complete diversity.[240] On the other

---

[236] 437 U.S. 365 (1978).

[237] The Court wisely declined to decide the question because its own prior cases suggest that a common nucleus of operative fact is only a sufficient and not a necessary predicate for constitutional power. *Freeman* itself allowed apparently unrelated claims to be asserted against the property under the court's ancillary jurisdiction, 65 U.S. (24 How.) 450, and the Court has approved ancillary jurisdiction over unrelated claims by a receiver to collect a debtor's assets and by and against trustees in bankruptcy. *See* cases cited in Matasar, *Rediscovering "One Constitutional Case": Procedural Rules and the Rejection of the Gibbs Test for Supplemental Jurisdiction,* 71 Cal. Law Rev. 1401, 1465-1474 (1983). If these claims fall within the concept of constitutional case, it must be because they are either necessary and proper to give full effect to a particular subject matter jurisdiction or, more doubtfully in light of Rule 82, because the constitutional case extends as far as the scope of permissible joinder under the rules. *Id.* at 1477-1490 (proposing the latter solution).

[238] *Kroger,* 437 U.S. at 373 (*citing Aldinger v. Howard,* 427 U.S. 1 (1976), discussed in § 5.09[2], *supra*).

[239] *Id.* at 364.

[240] *See* § 5.04[2] (diversity between whom), *supra*.

hand, the Court's analysis would presumably have supported a transaction-ally-related claim by the involuntary third-party defendant against the plaintiff, and, once such a claim is entertained, perhaps any claim by the plaintiff in the nature of a transactionally-related counterclaim, since such a claim would then be asserted defensively.[241]

The Court's analysis of ancillary jurisdiction explains the doctrine's extension to at least impleader under Rule 14,[242] presented by *Kroger* itself, cross-claims under Rule 13(g), compulsory counterclaims under Rule 13(a), parties added under Rule 13(h) to cross-claims and compulsory counter-claims, and sometimes intervention as of right under Rule 24(a).[243] Each of these kinds of joinder requires a transactional nexus under the rules between the joined and the freestanding claim (thus presumptively satisfy-ing the common nucleus requirement), and each is invoked defensively by a defendant or another party who has no practical choice of forum. Con-versely, ancillary jurisdiction was not extended to permissive counterclaims under Rule 13(b),[244] permissive joinder of parties under Rule 20 or permis-sive intervention under Rule 24(a). These kinds of joinder either involve transactionally-unrelated claims and/or are invoked by parties who volun-tarily chose the forum, and thus fail the *Kroger* test.

Once a court satisfied itself of constitutional power to assert ancillary jurisdiction, and that Congress had not negated such jurisdiction, there remained the question whether it *should* assert it as a matter of discretion. Some commentators and courts, stressing the historical roots of ancillary jurisdiction in "necessity," treated the doctrine as mandatory once power was found.[245] But as the rationale for ancillary jurisdiction evolved from strict necessity to a mixture of fairness and convenience, the better view was that a court had the discretion to decide whether to exercise ancillary jurisdiction.[246] The factors that the courts should consider were those

---

[241] *Friedenthal, Kane & Miller* § 2.12 (suggesting that a majority of courts have found ancillary jurisdiction for these claims and citing cases).

[242] For detailed analysis of joinder under Rule 14 and the other rules mentioned in the text, *see* §§ 9.02-9.08 (joinder), *infra*.

[243] *Kroger*, 437 U.S. at 375 n.18. The overlap between Rules 19 and Rule 24(a) led to an anomaly in ancillary jurisdiction. Because it is not available for necessary parties under Rule 19, *see* § 9.05[2], *infra*, the courts reasoned that it must also be unavailable when such a party tries to intervene as of right under Rule 24(a). *See generally Wright & Miller* § 1610; Kennedy, *Let's all Join In: Intervention Under Federal Rule 24,* 57 Ky. L.J. 329, 362-363 (1969).

[244] *But see Matasar,* note 237, *supra,* at 1474-1475 (noting that it has sometimes been extended to setoffs for liquidated claims). *See* § 9.03 note 253, *infra* (defining setoffs).

[245] *See, e.g.,* Note, note 225, *supra,* at 929. ("ancillary jurisdiction is an implied command to promote fairness"); Matasar, *A Pendent and Ancillary Jurisdiction Primer: The Scope and Limits of Supplemental Jurisdiction,* 17 U.C. Davis L. Rev. 103, 184 (1983) (it is unclear whether discretionary factors apply at all and few courts have considered the question); Miller, *Ancillary and Pendent Jurisdiction,* 26 S. Tex. L.J. 1, 7 (1985) (noting that the issue "has never been seriously adjudicated" and that there is an inconsistency between jurisdictional discretion and lack of discretion in the court in permitting compulsory counterclaims under Rule 13(a)).

[246] *See, e.g., Matasar,* note 245, *supra,* at 187-188; *Friedenthal, Kane & Miller* § 2.12; *Wright* § 76. Since the Court found no statutory power in *Kroger* it never reached the question of discretion. Justices White and Brennan, dissenting, assumed that the trial court had discretion, as it would in a case of pendent jurisdiction. *Kroger,* 437 U.S. at 382 n.4 (White, J., dissenting).

identified in *Gibbs*,[247] except that there was ordinarily no federal policy interest in a diversity case. "Necessity," or related considerations of fairness and convenience of involuntary parties, meant only that the discretionary part of the analysis should less often result in denial of ancillary jurisdiction, not that this jurisdiction was mandatory.

So the law stood when *Finley v. United States*[248] was decided. As we noted in the prior section, *Finley*'s insistence on affirmative evidence of congressional approval for pendent jurisdiction logically extended to ancillary jurisdiction as well. Some lower federal courts therefore began to restrict ancillary jurisdiction. Some even disallowed ancillary jurisdiction over third-party (impleader) claims[249] by defendants, despite the Supreme Court's endorsement of that application of ancillary jurisdiction in *Kroger*.[250] Other lower courts, however, confined *Finley* to its context — plaintiff's invocation of pendent party jurisdiction — and continued to uphold ancillary jurisdiction in other contexts. A few courts continued to uphold pendent party jurisdiction under different statutes.[251]

§ 5.11 Statutory Supplemental Jurisdiction[252]

The Court ended its opinion in *Finley* with the reminder that "[w]hatever we say regarding the scope of jurisdiction conferred by a particular statute can of course be changed by Congress."[253] Congress accepted the invitation in 1990 when it enacted the supplemental jurisdiction statute.[254] The House Report accompanying the statute explained that it "would authorize jurisdiction in a case like *Finley*, as well as essentially restore the pre-*Finley* understandings of the authorization for and limits on other forms of supplemental jurisdiction."[255] The law professors who helped write the bill added that the measure was intended "to repair *Finley*'s damage in a

---

[247] *See* § 5.09[1] (pendent claims), *supra.*

[248] 490 U.S. 545 (1989).

[249] See § 9.06 (impleader), *infra.*

[250] *See, e.g., Aetna Casualty & Sur. Co. v. Spartan Mechanical Corp.*, 738 F. Supp. 664, 675 (E.D.N.Y. 1990) (finding that a defendant's third-party claim against a non-diverse defendant "comes under the prohibition of *Finley*" because the diversity statute does not affirmatively grant jurisdiction).

[251] *See* Freer, *Compounding Confusion and Hampering Diversity: Life After Finley and the Supplemental Jurisdiction Statute*, 40 Emory L.J. 445, 467-469 (1991) (finding that most courts were reading *Finley* narrowly).

[252] For a thorough review of the initial commentary about and issues posed by statutory supplemental jurisdiction, see McLaughlin, *The Federal Supplemental Jurisdiction Statute — A Constitutional and Statutory Analysis*, 24 Ariz. St. L.J. 849 (1992). The statute engendered a heated debate between its first critics and the three law professors who helped to draft it, published in the articles cited by *McLaughlin, id.*, at 854 n.6. For a later reappraisal, see articles collected in *Symposium: A Reappraisal of the Supplemental Jurisdiction Statute: Title 28 U.S.C. § 1367*, 74 Ind. L.J. 1-250 (1998) (hereinafter "Reappraisal").

[253] 490 U.S. 545, 556 (1989).

[254] 28 U.S.C. § 1367.

[255] Federal Courts Study Committee Implementation Act of 1990, H.R. Rep. No. 101-734, 101st Cong., 2d Sess. 28 (1990) [hereinafter *H.R. Rep.*].

noncontroversial manner without expanding the scope of diversity jurisdiction" and "was therefore framed to restore and regularize jurisdiction, not to revamp it."[256] Whether Congress accomplished all it set out to do remains to be seen, but it has definitely not avoided controversy. Here we first consider what the supplemental jurisdiction statute has accomplished and how it works, and then consider several apparent problems it poses.

[1] The Three-Part Test for Supplemental Jurisdiction

Section 1367's subsections suggest three stages of inquiry in deciding the availability of supplemental jurisdiction over a claim for which there is no independent jurisdiction. The first is whether the claim qualifies for supplemental jurisdiction under section 1367(a) by falling within the same constitutional case or controversy as the freestanding claim which enjoys independent jurisdiction.[257] If § 1367(a) is satisfied, but the freestanding claim is based only on diversity, the second stage of inquiry is whether the supplemental claim is disqualified for supplemental jurisdiction by section 1367(b). If not, the third stage of inquiry is whether the court should nonetheless decline to exercise supplemental discretion for any of the reasons listed in section 1367(c).

[a] Qualifying Under Section 1367(a)

Subsection 1367(a) codifies the authority for the extension of jurisdiction that *Finley* found lacking. Authority for supplemental jurisdiction is extended to all claims satisfying this subsection unless it is withheld in diversity-only cases by subsection 1367(b) or expressly negated by another federal statute. Subsection 1367(a) overrules *Finley* by expressly providing that "supplemental jurisdiction shall include claims that involve joinder or intervention of parties," thereby authorizing jurisdiction over what were formerly called pendent party claims.

Moreover, the new statutory jurisdiction "go[es] the constitutional limit."[258] Despite legislative history suggesting that Congress intended to codify only the familiar transaction-or-occurrence test for extending jurisdiction,[259] subsection 1367[a] expressly extends federal jurisdiction from freestanding claims within the original jurisdiction of the federal court to supplemental claims that are "so related [to the freestanding claims . . .

---

[256] Mengler, *et al.*, *Congress Accepts Supreme Court's Invitation to Codify Supplemental Jurisdiction*, 74 Judicature 213, 214-215 (1991).

[257] A "freestanding" claim in federal litigation is a claim that would be jurisdictionally viable as the only claim in the case. *See* § 5.08, *supra*. Jurisdictional support for such a claim may come from one of several federal statutes. *E.g.*, 28 U.S.C. § 1331 (federal question jurisdiction). In contrast, a claim for which jurisdiction is sought under section 1367 is never viable alone. Rather, jurisdiction over such a claim depends upon whether it relates to an freestanding claim in a way that satisfies section 1367. We therefore call such a claim the "supplemental" claim.

[258] Siegel, 28 U.S.C.A. § 1367 practice commentary (1990).

[259] *See Teply & Whitten*, Chap. 2, § B(4)(d) (arguing for this intent by tracing § 1367(a) to Federal Courts Study Committee Report, but conceding that "Congress may have inadvertently exercised" the full Article III power).

that they form part of the same case or controversy under Article III of the United States Constitution." Whatever Congress's intent, its plain words refrain from creating yet another gap between statutory and constitutional jurisdiction. Assuming that the constitutional case is broader than same-transaction-or-occurrence, subsection 1367(a) apparently leaves scope for the exercise of supplemental jurisdiction over transactionally unrelated but logically related claims in the rare case where it may be appropriate.[260]

Despite Congress' adoption of the vague "same case or controversy" test for supplemental jurisdiction instead of the familiar "same transaction or occurrence" test which appeared in earlier legislative drafts of section 1367(a), the latter should still suffice for deciding to *include* a supplemental claim. Thus, most courts have found that claims which satisfy the same transaction or occurrence standard for joinder under Rules 13(a) (compulsory counterclaim)[261], 13(g) (crossclaim), or 20 (joinder of parties) also qualify for supplemental jurisdiction. As one court explained in deciding ancillary jurisdiction before section 1367 was enacted, "[t]he tests are the same because Rule 13(a) and . . . ancillary jurisdiction are designed to abolish the same evil, viz., piecemeal litigation in the federal courts."[262]

But a claim which does not meet the same transaction test is not necessarily *excluded* from supplemental jurisdiction. A court may properly take a narrower view of "transaction or occurrence" in the counterclaim context, because of the harsh result of finding that a previously unasserted claim was compulsory (it cannot be asserted later), than in the supplemental jurisdiction context, where the results are less draconian (the claim can still be heard in state court).[263] Thus, for example, one court has said that even if a supplemental counterclaim does not arise from the same transaction or occurrence as plaintiff's freestanding original claim (so that it is a permissive, not a compulsory counterclaim), it can still qualify for supplemental jurisdiction if it bears even a loose factual relationship to the freestanding claim.[264]

---

[260] *See* § 5.10 note 237, *supra* (citing cases); *Moore* §§ 106.24[1][2] (noting division in courts about logical-relation test for supplemental jurisdiction and rejection of mere "but for" relationship); *Teply & Whitten* Chap. 2, § B(4)(d) (asserting that the "better approach" to deciding the scope of a constitutional case would be "to examine every grant of authority over factually unrelated federal and nonfederal claims to determine whether Congress has sound reasons, grounded in the fair and efficient operation of federal subject-matter jurisdiction grants, for providing such authority"). Teply and Whitten, however, opt for a narrow transaction-or-occurrence construction of section 1367(a) to avoid " 'inconvenient' effects." *Id.*

[261] *See* § 9.03, *infra.*

[262] *Great Lakes Rubber Corp. v. Herbert Copper Co.*, 286 F.2d 631 (3d Cir. 1961).

[263] *See Moore* § 106.25 (arguing that different purposes of test for joinder and test for supplemental jurisdiction justify different applications, but acknowledging that "courts have generally continued to equate the factual identity for supplemental jurisdiction with that required for the presence of a compulsory counterclaim"); Kane, *Original Sin and the Transaction in Federal Civil Procedure*, 76 Tex. L. Rev. 1723, 1730-1733 (1998) (noting different policy purposes animating use of transaction test in different settings).

[264] *Polaris Pool Sys. v. Letro Prods., Inc.*, 161 F.R.D. 422, 425 (C.D. Cal. 1995). *See also Channell v. Citicorp Nat. Serv., Inc.*, 89 F.3d 379, 385-386 (7th Cir. 1996) (endorsing loose factual connection as sufficient for supplemental jurisdiction).

[b] Disqualifying Under § 1367 (b)

Subsection 1367(b) provides that in diversity-only cases the courts do not have supplemental jurisdiction over claims by plaintiffs against persons made parties by Rules 14, 19, 20 or 24, when exercising such jurisdiction "would be inconsistent with the jurisdictional requirements of subsection 1332." The House Report explains that the "net effect of subsection (b) is to implement the principal rationale of *Owen Equipment & Erection Co. v. Kroger.*"[265]

The subsection would thus deny supplemental jurisdiction for the claim that plaintiff Kroger asserted against the non-diverse third-party defendant, as well as other claims that a plaintiff might add to evade the complete diversity requirement of § 1332. As the House Report explains,

> [i]n diversity-only actions the district courts may not hear plaintiffs' supplemental claims when exercising supplemental jurisdiction would encourage plaintiffs to evade the jurisdictional requirement of 28 U.S.C. § 1332 by the simple expedient of naming initially only those defendants whose joinder satisfies § 1332's requirements and later adding claims not within original federal jurisdiction against other defendants who have intervened or been joined on a supplemental basis.[266]

A good case can be made for overruling *Kroger*, or, conversely, for mooting it by eliminating diversity altogether.[267] However, if it is to be left largely intact, the statute is generally faithful to the task,[268] although it suffers from several problems discussed below.[269]

[c] Discretion Under § 1367(c)

Subsection 1367 (c) codifies a discretionary step in what was pendent claim analysis. Although the subsection includes only some of the factors identified in the pendent claim cases, it invites courts, "in exceptional circumstances," to consider "other compelling reasons for declining jurisdiction."[270] Subsection 1367(c) thus serves as a counterweight to subsection

---

[265] *H.R. Rep.*, note 255, *supra*, at 29 n.16. For discusson of *Kroger*, see § 5.10, *supra*.

[266] *H.R. Rep.*, note 255, *supra*, at 29.

[267] *See* § 5.04[1] (reviewing the arguments for and against diversity jurisdiction), *supra*.

[268] Subsection 1367(b) makes what the House Report characterizes as "one small change" in *Kroger* and pre-*Finley* practice. *H.R. Rep.*, note 255, *supra*, at 29. *Kroger* noted that ancillary jurisdiction had been extended to interveners as of right, 437 U.S. at 375 n.18, subject to the anomaly that jurisdiction was denied interveners as of right who also qualified as necessary parties under Rule 19. *See* § 5.10 n.12. Subsection 1367(b) "cures" the anomaly by denying supplemental jurisdiction to all plaintiff-interveners. Critics have charged that this cure runs the wrong way and is worse than the anomaly, cutting off access to federal court for interveners whose interest forces them into the federal forum without any intent to evade complete diversity. *See, e.g., McLaughlin*, note 252, *supra*, at 960-970; Freer, *Compounding Confusion and Hampering Diversity: Life After Finley and the Supplemental Jurisdiction Statute*, 40 Emory L.J. 445, 476-478 (1991).

[269] *See* § 5.11[2], *infra*.

[270] *See McLaughlin*, note 252, *supra*, at 975-976.

1367(a). It gives courts discretion to refuse jurisdiction within the outer limits of their power, when dismissal of the freestanding claim on other than jurisdictional grounds,[271] the novelty or predominance of state law issues in federal question cases, or other good reasons suggest that the supplemental claims would more appropriately be decided by state courts. The Supreme Court has indicated that the statute reflects the understanding that a federal court " 'should consider and weigh in each case, and at every stage of the litigation, the values of judicial economy, convenience, fairness, and comity.' "[272]

On the other hand, the mandatory "shall" in § 1367(a) and § 1367(c)'s reference to "exceptional circumstances" and "compelling reasons" for declining supplemental jurisdiction has led some courts to conclude that § 1367(c) gives less discretion to decline than courts enjoyed under *Gibbs*. By this view, § 1367(a) effectively *requires* the court to exercise supplemental jurisdiction *unless* the court finds one of the listed grounds, or other *exceptional* circumstances, to be a *compelling* reason to decline.[273] A court could not therefore decline to exercise jurisdiction for an unlisted reason just because it promotes "economy, convenience, fairness, and comity," absent especially compelling circumstances. Another way of stating this view is that qualification for supplemental jurisdiction creates a presumption in favor of its exercise which can only be rebutted by one of the "compelling" reasons listed in § 1367(c).

[2] Problems With Subsection 1367(b)

It is chiefly what the statute did not say that has generated criticism. We identify only some of its alleged omissions here.

[a] Overinclusiveness?

We noted in § 5.10 that *Kroger*'s focus on the posture in which the supplemental claim is asserted did not necessarily foreclose the assertion in a diversity-only case of jurisdiction over a plaintiff's essentially defensive claims (*e.g.*, compulsory counterclaims or cross-claims against non-diverse parties), and some courts so held.[274] Does subsection 1367(b)'s restriction now prohibit even defensive claims by plaintiffs? That would require plaintiffs to bring separate state court actions for indemnification or contribution from non-diverse defendants, with the possibility that their transactionally-related federal claims could be precluded by state court judgments.[275]

---

[271] Dismissal of the putative freestanding claim for lack of subject matter jurisdiction deprives the court of supplemental jurisdiction because it eliminates the constitutional case or controversy. Dismissal of the freestanding claim for other reasons leaves the court the power to hear the supplemental claims at its discretion under subsection 1367(c)(3). *See McLaughlin*, note 252, *supra*, at 979. (citing cases).

[272] *City of Chicago v. International College of Surgeons*, 522 U.S. 156, 173 (1997) (quoting *Carnegie-Mellon Univ. v. Cohill*, 484 U.S. 343, 350 (1988)).

[273] *Moore* §§ 106.60-106.61.

[274] *See* note 241, *supra*; *Freer*, note 268, *supra*, at 463 & n.103 (citing cases).

[275] *See Freer*, note 268, *supra*, at 482-483.

One solution is to read subsection 1367(b) to reach only plaintiff's main claims, not counterclaims, cross-claims, or third-party claims.[276] This facile reading, however, is hard to square with subsection 1367(a)'s use of the generic "claims." Arguably, it is also unnecessary. Subsection 1367(b)'s restriction on claims by the plaintiff is not absolute. It applies only "when exercising supplemental jurisdiction over such claims would be inconsistent with the jurisdictional requirements of subsection 1332." The plaintiff who asserts a defensive claim against a non-diverse party is typically not attempting to evade the complete diversity requirement; therefore, exercising supplemental jurisdiction over that claim would not be inconsistent with the requirements of diversity as they were articulated in *Kroger*. So federal courts reasoned before enactment of supplemental jurisdiction, and the qualifying clause in subsection 1367(b) permits that precedent to continue undisturbed.[277]

[b] Underinclusiveness

A second troublesome omission in subsection 1367(b) concerns the joinder of claims by persons made parties by Rule 23, the class action rule.[278] We noted in subsection 5.09[2] that the Supreme Court had denied pendent party jurisdiction in plaintiffs' class actions over claims by class members that did not individually satisfy the amount in controversy.[279] Subsection 1367(b), however, omits joinder of such claims from its qualified restriction on supplemental jurisdiction. The inference is that supplemental jurisdiction is available pursuant to the general grant in subsection 1367(a). This inference contradicts the indications of congressional intent found in the statute's legislative history. Commentators and some courts have therefore favored the intent over the letter of the statute.[280] It is at least arguable that resort to the legislative history is warranted by subsection 1367(b)'s silence about Rule 23 joinder.

On the other hand, the principle of *expressio unius est exclusio alterius* (the expression of one thing is the exclusion of another) could be applied to uphold supplemental jurisdiction over supplemental plaintiffs' class action claims. Moreover, upholding such jurisdiction makes sense. In effect, the Supreme Court now allows supplemental jurisdiction over non-diverse

---

[276] *Freer, Reappraisal*, note 252, *supra*, at 12-15; *Siegel*, note 258, *supra*; *Mengler, et al.*, note 256, *supra*, at 215 n.17. A comparable solution is to read "plaintiff" in subsection 1367(b) to mean only a party who files an aggressive pleading rather than a defensive pleading. The rules themselves do not use "plaintiffs" this way, however. When they are intended to apply more generally, they use "parties claiming a right to relief" or "opposing parties." *Compare* Rule 20(a) *with* Rules 13 & 18.

[277] *See generally* Raven-Hansen, *Reappraisal*, note 252, *supra*, at 197.

[278] *See* § 63, *infra*.

[279] *Zahn v. International Paper Co.*, 414 U.S. 291 (1973) (denying aggregation of amounts to satisfy jurisdictional requirement).

[280] *See McLaughlin*, note 252, *supra*, 972-974 (citing *H.R. Rep.*, note 4, *supra*, at 29); *cf. Griffin v. Dana Point Condominium Ass'n*, 768 F. Supp. 1299, 1301-1302 (N.D. Ill. 1991) (refusing to exercise supplemental jurisdiction over co-plaintiffs' jurisdictionally insufficient claims).

class members in plaintiffs' class actions.[281] Reading subsection 1367(b) to allow supplemental jurisdiction over class members' monetarily insufficient claims would be perfectly consistent with the treatment of the diversity requirement in plaintiffs' class actions.[282]

This was how the Fifth Circuit read section 1367(b) in *In re Abbott Laboratories*.[283] Only the named plaintiffs in a class action there satisfied the amount in controversy; all of the absent class members had claims below the amount. Diversity jurisdiction would be unavailable for the entire class under *Zahn* because they could not aggregate their claims. The court, acknowledging that section 1367's legislative history indicated a congressional intent to preserve *Zahn*, reasoned that there was no occasion to consult it unless the statute was ambiguous. "[T]he statute is the sole repository of congressional intent where the statute is clear and does not demand an absurd result."[284] Because section 1367 was clear and abrogating the *Zahn* limitation would not be absurd, the court upheld supplemental jurisdiction over the below-amount claims. Unfortunately, when *Abbott* was appealed, the Supreme Court split 4-4 on this jurisdictional question,[285] which therefore remains open.

Other circuit courts are divided on the issue. The Tenth Circuit, for example, turns the "clear" language against supplemental jurisdiction by asserting that section 1367(a) "specifically addresses 'any civil action of which the courts have original jurisdiction,'" and then provides for "*supplemental* jurisdiction" over transactionally related claims.[286] Reasoning that "original" jurisdiction turns on the diversity statute, including the no-aggregation gloss which *Zahn* placed upon it, the court denied supplemental jurisdiction on facts similar to *Abbott*.

The omission of reference to Rule 20 joinder of plaintiffs presents a more difficult problem. The subsection does not restrict supplemental jurisdiction over joinder of non-diverse or below-amount plaintiffs' claims under Rule 20 in diversity-only cases. Some have argued that this is not really an omission, because "Rule 20 joinder by plaintiffs involves only original claims," and the statute "provides for supplemental jurisdiction *over additionally joined claims* 'in any civil action of which the district courts have original jurisdiction.'"[287] But nothing in Rule 20 suggests that its use is limited only to joinder in original claims. A better guide to interpretation is the admission by the statute's authors that the omission leaves a

---

[281] *See Supreme Tribe of Ben Hur v. Cauble*, 255 U.S. 356 (1921) (counting only the citizenship of the representative class action plaintiffs for purposes of diversity).

[282] *See* § 63[B][3] (discussing problems of federal class actions after *Zahn*), *infra*.

[283] 51 F.3d 524 (5th Cir. 1995).

[284] *Id.* at 529

[285] *Free v. Abbott Laboratories, Inc.*, 529 U.S. 333 (2000).

[286] *Leonhardt v. Western Sugar Co.*, 160 F.3d 631 (10th Cir. 1998). *See* Pfander, *Supplemental Jurisdiction and Section 1367: The Case for a Sympathetic Textualism*, 148 U. Pa. L. Rev. 109 (1999) (making similar argument as an answer to many of § 1367's problems).

[287] *Teply & Whitten*, Chap. 2, § B(4)(d) (emphasis added); Steinman, *Section 1367 — Another Party Heard From*, 41 Emory L.J. 85, 100-101 (1992). *See* note [c]; *supra*.

"potentially gaping hole."[288] This time, however, applying the principle of *expressio unius est exclusio alterius* to permit supplemental jurisdiction over non-diverse plaintiffs (or plaintiffs with claims below the jurisdictional amount in controversy) arguably *would* work an absurd result. It would create "blatant violations of § 1332's jurisdictional requirements" in settings in which courts have not previously allowed pendent party jurisdiction.[289] This is a gap that Congress should close. Whether courts may close it themselves in the interim, as at least one already has,[290] let alone whether they can close it and still allow supplemental jurisdiction in plaintiffs' class actions, is debatable.

[c] Solutions?

The various judicial solutions to section 1367's problems urged by commentators raise serious questions of judicial power and statutory interpretation. How, for example, can courts ignore the plain words of subsection 1367 to allow defensive claims by plaintiffs in diversity-only cases or unrestricted supplemental jurisdiction by alien plaintiffs, and at the same time rely upon the absence of plain words to allow the joinder of insufficient claims in class actions? Critics of the statute assert that "courts will be hard pressed to ignore section 1367(b)'s specifics in deciding such questions" and "will not feel free to use their discretion to reach what they see as 'sensible' results in the face of a statute which . . . clearly occupies the field."[291]

A partial answer to this critique is the one given above: that restrictions in subsection 1367(b) — the source of most of the statute's shortcomings — are qualified and conditional; they apply only if exercising supplemental jurisdiction would be inconsistent with judicial interpretations of the requirements of the diversity statute. Subsection 1367(a), in contrast, is qualified only by the constitutional case requirement.

> When the claim in question is not listed in § 1367(b), then under § 1367(a) the question is no longer whether an assertion of jurisdiction would be inconsistent with § 1332, but becomes whether the claim is "so related to claims in the action within such original jurisdiction that they form part of the same case or controversy under Article III of the Constitution."[292]

Perhaps, then, supplemental jurisdiction over plaintiff's defensive nondiversity claims is proper under subsection 1367(b), because it is not inconsistent

---

[288] Rowe, *et al.*, *Compounding or Creating Confusion About Supplemental Jurisdiction? A Reply to Professor Freer*, 40 Emory L.J. 943, 961 n.91 (1991).

[289] *McLaughlin*, note 252, *supra*, at 941.

[290] *See Griffin v. Dana Point Condominium Ass'n*, 768 F. Supp. 1299, 1301-1302 (N.D. Ill. 1991); *see generally McLaughlin*, note 1, *supra*, at 941-942 (arguing that until Congress amends the statute, "courts should interpret § 1367(b) as restricting supplemental claims by plaintiffs joined under Rule 20").

[291] Arthur & Freer, *Grasping at Burnt Straws: The Disaster of the Supplemental Jurisdiction Statute*, 40 Emory L.J. 963, 986 (1991).

[292] *Steinman*, note 287, *supra*, at 95 (footnote omitted).

with the requirements of diversity (and the policy of avoiding evasion of the complete diversity requirement). And supplemental jurisdiction over class members' insufficient claims is proper under subsection 1367(a) because such claims are within the constitutional case and subsection 1367(b) does not apply by its terms.

A cleaner solution may be to revise the statute. At this writing, in fact, the American Law Institute is developing a proposal intended to cure the foregoing and other problems with section 1367,[293] and one of its original drafters has weighed in with his own revision.[294] Still others have argued that supplemental jurisdiction "is a concept too complex to be captured by complicated statutory drafting."[295] The variety of contexts in which supplemental claims are asserted may be a factor counseling case-by-case judicial rather than categorical statutory treatment.

In any event, the flaws of section 1367 should not be allowed to obscure its virtues. The statute does *most* of what it set out to do and should be easy to apply to the majority of cases in which it is invoked. As for the rest, the Supreme Court and perhaps the Congress will have to resolve the statute's ambiguities after a period of percolation in the lower federal courts.

---

[293] Oakley, *Integrating Supplemental Jurisdiction and Diversity Jurisdiction: a Progress Report on the Work of the American Law Institute*, in *Reappraisal*, note 252, *supra*, at 25, 35-41.

[294] Rowe, *1367 and All That: Recodifying Federal Supplemental Jurisdiction*, in *Reappraisal*, note 252, *supra*, at 53, 70-73.

[295] Cooper, *An Alternative and Discretionary § 1367*, in *Reappraisal*, note 252, *supra*, at 153, 157.

Chapter 6

A CONVENIENT COURT

§ 6.01 Traditional Bases for Venue

[1] In General

The law of venue is founded on the realization that a court with subject matter and territorial jurisdiction can still be an inefficient, inconvenient location for litigation. Justice Scalia has observed that

> {v}enue is often a vitally important matter, as shown by the frequency with which parties contractually provide for and litigate the issue. Suit might well not be pursued, or might not be as successful, in a significantly less convenient forum. Transfer to such a less desirable forum is, therefore, of sufficient import that plaintiffs will base their decisions on the likelihood of that eventuality when they are choosing whether to sue in state or federal court. [1]

Rules of *venue* are rules of convenience for allocating cases territorially, usually among counties within a state and among judicial districts and their divisions within the federal judicial system.

Venue differs from subject matter jurisdiction in several ways. Objection to improper venue is waived if not promptly asserted. [2] Similarly, a court is not obliged to question venue on its own initiative, and parties can stipulate or contract to an otherwise improper venue. While courts typically entertain objections to subject matter jurisdiction throughout the lawsuit, venue questions are likely to be resolved at the outset usually. Jurisdictional defects usually require dismissal of a lawsuit, but improper venue can frequently be cured by transfer of the action to another court within the same judicial system. Finally, unlike some jurisdictional defects, improper venue does not subject a judgment to collateral attack.

Venue also differs from personal jurisdiction in several respects. Unlike personal jurisdiction, venue applies chiefly to original claims (the general federal venue statute speaks of where an "action . . . may . . . be brought"), [3] and not to added claims. [4] The original parties, already present

---

[1] *Stewart Organization, Inc. v. Ricoh Corp.*, 487 U.S. 22, 39-40 (1988) (Scalia, J., dissenting).

[2] *See, e.g.,* Rule 12(h)(1). Note, however, that Rule 12 only governs the defense of "improper venue." Motions to transfer venue from one proper venue to another that is better — more convenient — may be made at any time. *Wright* § 44.

[3] 28 U.S.C. §§ 1391(a) & (b).

[4] *Moore* § 110.06. However, if the plaintiff amends its complaint, the amended complaint is treated as a new action for venue purposes. The plaintiff could otherwise avoid venue requirements by artful pleading.

and litigating, are unlikely to be inconvenienced by litigating additional claims. Claims against additional parties enjoy what might be termed "ancillary venue" if those claims are sufficiently related to the original claims.[5] Finally, defendant must plead the defenses of improper venue and lack of personal jurisdiction alike. But improper venue is treated like an affirmative defense which the defendant must prove, while personal jurisdiction must be demonstrated by the party invoking it.

As statutory rules, venue requirements differ from judicial system to system, but similarities predominate. Subsection 2 describes the usual statutory bases for venue, using the general federal venue statute to illustrate some of them. Subsection 3 then discusses several judge-made exceptions to venue requirements.

[2] Bases for Venue

To promote party and forum convenience, most venue statutes are based on some logical relationship between the parties or subject matter of the lawsuit and the place of trial. A comprehensive survey of typical venue statutes identified the following kinds of relationships as typical:

(1)   the locus of the *res* (property) or event that is the subject of the lawsuit;

(2)   where the claim arose;

(3)   where the defendant resides, does business, or retains an agent;

(4)   where the plaintiff resides; or,

(5)   in suits by or against government parties, where the seat of government is located.[6]

"The most common provision," the survey concluded, "and the basic one, appears to be venue based upon the residence of the defendant."[7] But venue provisions are also based on other criteria, usually designed to facilitate suit, such as where the defendant is served or may be found.[8]

The general federal venue provision[9] illustrates some of the common criteria.[10] It provides two general alternatives for venue and a fallback provision keyed to the limits of personal jurisdiction.

---

[5] *Wright & Miller* § 3808.

[6] *See* Stevens, *Venue Statutes: Diagnosis and Proposed Cure,* 49 Mich. L. Rev. 307, 331-332 (1951).

[7] *Id.* at 315.

[8] *See id.* at 332.

[9] 28 U.S.C. § 1391. In addition to 28 U.S.C. § 1391, there are numerous special federal venue statutes. See 28 U.S.C. §§ 1394-1403, 1407-1410. For discussion of 28 U.S.C. § 1407, authorizing venue consolidation for multidistrict litigation, see § 9.10[2] (multidistrict litigation), *supra.*

[10] *See generally* Mammen, Note, *Here Today, Gone Tomorrow: The Timing of Contacts for Jurisdiction and Venue Under 28 U.S.C. § 1391,* 78 Cornell L. Rev. 707 (1993); Siegel, 28 U.S.C.A. § 1391 commentary on 1990 revision of subdivisions (a), (b), and (e).

First, it lays venue literally at the doorstep of a single defendants, or multiple defendants who reside in the same state, by allowing suit to be brought in the judicial district where any of them reside.[11] The courts are split on whether residence for venue purposes should be equated with domicile or citizenship as these terms are used for deciding diversity jurisdiction (probably the majority rule), or given an independent definition.[12] The practical difference lies in the number of proper venues; an individual can only have one domicile or state citizenship at a time,[13] while she may maintain several residences. An 1892 Supreme Court dictum is authority for equating residence and citizenship.[14] Most courts have equated residence with domicile for venue purposes.[15] But giving residence an independent and natural meaning may be more consistent with the convenience rationale of the general federal venue statute because it will often expand the number of possible venues.

Subsection 1391(c) was intended to resolve another interpretative issue by defining the residence of a defendant corporation to be "any judicial district in which it is subject to personal jurisdiction at the time the action is commenced." In using the general phrase "personal jurisdiction," the subsection appears to subsume both specific and general jurisdiction.[16] The courts have divided about whether to measure personal jurisdiction under § 1391(c) by the constitutional minimum contacts test alone, or by the state's long arm statute or other jurisdictional provisions as well. Because § 1391 venue is a question of federal law, the better view is that it is the former alone which controls.[17] In multi-district states in which the corporation is subject to personal jurisdiction, the corporation is deemed to reside in any district "within which its contacts would be sufficient to subject it to personal jurisdiction if that district were a separate state," or, if there is none, "in the district within which it has the most significant contacts."[18] This provision is designed to provide some additional venue protection to the corporation that does business only in one district of the state, although it is doubtful that the benefit it affords is worth the costs of re-targeting the contacts analysis.

Second, a plaintiff may lay venue in the judicial district "in which a substantial part of the events or omissions giving rise to the claim occurred, or a substantial part of the property that is the subject of the action is situated."[19] Under a prior version of the statute, this venue alternative depended, like many state venue statutes, on where "the claim arose."[20]

---

[11] 28 U.S.C. §§ 1391(a)(1) & 1391(b)(1).

[12] *Wright* § 42.

[13] *See* § 5.05 (citizenship), *supra*.

[14] *Shaw v. Quincy Mining Co. Ex Parte Shaw,* 145 U.S. 444, 447 (1892).

[15] *Moore* § 110.03[1].

[16] *See* § 3.09[2] (specific and general jurisdiction), *supra*.

[17] *Moore* § 110.03[4][c].

[18] 28 U.S.C. § 1391(c).

[19] 28 U.S.C. §§ 1391(a)(2) & (b)(2).

[20] Act of Nov. 2, 1966, Pub. L.. No. 89-714, 80 Stat. 1111, *amending* 28 U.S.C. §§ 1391(a) & (b) [emphasis added]. *See Wright & Miller* § 3806.

But identifying the single district in which the claim arose will be problematic for many cases in which the facts giving rise to the claim occur in two or more districts.[21] By substituting "a" for "the" district, and looking to "a substantial part" of the events or omissions giving rise to the claim, the new subsection eases the problem by enlarging the number of permissible venues. For example, in a civil racketeering suit against a California-based defendant who phoned a party in Kansas and sent mail there, the court held these contacts substantial enough under subsection 1391(b)(2) to make the District of Kansas a proper venue, even though defendant's activities in California "might have been more substantial, or the most substantial."[22]

Finally, if neither of these venue alternatives is available, the plaintiff has a fallback venue. In diversity-only cases, he may sue in "a judicial district in which any defendant is subject to personal jurisdiction at the time the action is commenced. . . ."[23] In other cases, he may sue in a judicial district "in which any defendant may be found."[24] The legislative history of section 1391 indicates that the purpose of the fallback provisions was to provide a venue "safety net" in cases "in which no substantial part of the events happened in the United States and in which all the defendants do not reside in the same state."[25] The fallback provisions in effect waive venue if there are defendants who do not reside in the same state and either the claim arose outside the United States or all of the defendants are not subject to personal jurisdiction where a substantial part of the claim-related events occurred.[26]

The difference between "subject to personal jurisdiction" in subsection 1391(a)(3) and "may be found" in subsection 1391(b)(3) is probably unintended. The may-be-found formula could literally refer only to jurisdiction based on presence at the time of service (transient jurisdiction),[27] to the exclusion of long-arm jurisdiction based on contacts.[28] Yet this reading may conflict with the legislative history, which seems to use the may-be-found formula interchangeably with "subject to personal jurisdiction."[29]

Instead of a statutory venue, parties may select a venue by including a forum selection clause in their contract. In *Bremen v. Zapata*,[30] the

---

[21] *See, e.g., Leroy v. Great Western United Corp.*, 443 U.S. 173 (1979) (involving claims arising out of public tender offer by Delaware-incorporated and Texas-based corporation trying to take over publicly-listed Washington-incorporated corporation with executive offices and assets in Idaho and business in New York and Maryland).

[22] *Merchants Nat'l Bank v. Safrabank*, 776 F. Supp. 538, 541 (D. Kan. 1991).

[23] 28 U.S.C. § 1391(a)(3).

[24] *Id.* § 1391(b)(3).

[25] H.R. Rep. No. 101-734, 101st Cong., 2d Sess. 23 (1990).

[26] *Mammen*, note 10, *supra*, at 739-40.

[27] *See* § 3.08[3][b], *supra*.

[28] Courts interpreting the same phrase in other venue statutes are divided on this issue. *See Wright & Miller* § 3802.1.

[29] Unfortunately, the legislative history is itself confused and marred by what may be typographical errors. *See Siegel*, note 10, *supra*.

[30] 407 U.S. 1 (1972).

Supreme Court held that federal courts sitting in admiralty should enforce such clauses absent a showing that doing so "would be unreasonable or unjust, and that the clause was invalid for such reasons as fraud or over-reaching."[31] It has since enforced even non-negotiable forum selection clauses.[32]

The applicability of this law to forum selection clauses in the Internet era is illustrated by *Caspi v. The Microsoft Network, L.L.C.*[33] There a state appellate court upheld enforcement of such a clause in an online subscriber agreement because it found that the plaintiffs had validly assented to it by mouse click. Notwithstanding disparity in size between the plaintiff class and Microsoft, the court found that the on-line computer service industry offered plaintiffs competitive choices, and that they were free to scroll through computer screens presenting the terms of the bargain before click-ing their assent. Finally, it dismissed the plaintiffs' lack-of-notice argument. It concluded that nothing in the content, size, or placement of the clause in the online subscriber agreement was unusual or obfuscatory. Since the vast majority of web surfers click assent indiscriminately without reading the terms of online subscriber agreements, the court's analysis makes it clear that it is the *opportunity* to notice, comprehend, and reject the agree-ment that counts.

[3] Judge-Made Exceptions

Courts have carved several exceptions out of the usual venue statutes. They have held that actions properly removed to federal courts need not satisfy federal venue requirements because the removal statute itself specifies the district to which the case must be removed.[34] As we noted above, courts usually have not applied federal venue requirements to supplemental claims when venue was proper on the freestanding claim, partly on the theory that convenience was already taken into account in the jurisdictional analysis in such cases.[35]

A broader exception, made by most state courts as well as federal courts, is for *local actions,* for which the only proper venue is the locus of the property which is the subject of the action. This exception is an artifact of history, tracing its origin to an era in which juries were selected for their knowledge of the case. When an action involved property, the only proper venue was necessarily where the property was located because only juries from that location knew enough about the property to decide the facts.[36]

---

[31] *Id.* at 15.

[32] *See Carnival Cruise Lines, Inc. v. Shute,* 499 U.S. 585 (1991). A more extended discussion of forum selection clauses appears in section 3.03[2][d], *supra.*

[33] 732 A.2d 528 (N.J. Super.), *cert. denied,* 743 A.2d 851 (N.J. 1999).

[34] *Wright & Miller* § 3804. On removal, *see generally* § 5.07, *supra.* Once the case has been removed, however, any party may seek a transfer of venue in accord with 28 U.S.C. § 1404. *See* § 6.02[2] (transfer), *infra.*

[35] *Moore's* § 110.06.

[36] *See, e.g., Wright* § 42. The local action exception was also historically based on judicial

In contrast, *transitory actions,* not tied to particular property, could be heard wherever they arose. Distinguishing local from transitory actions, however, was no easy task, since at English common law the former included not only *in rem* and real actions for possession, ejectment, partition, foreclosure and quieting title, but also certain actions for trespass.[37] Nevertheless, most courts continue to make this exception to the statutory venue requirements, and the federal statute, among others, makes passing reference to it,[38] which may help account for its continued vitality in the federal system.

§ 6.02 Change of Venue

[1] Dismissal and Forum Non Conveniens[39]

Objection to improper venue is ordinarily made by a preliminary motion to dismiss, and the indicated remedy is, therefore, dismissal of the action without prejudice. If, however, the statute of limitations has since expired,[40] a dismissal effectively extinguishes the plaintiff's right of action, irrespective of the merits. To avoid this harsh result, and otherwise to avoid the expense of starting over, the plaintiff will usually seek, and most jurisdictions today permit, as an alternative to dismissal, the transfer of the action to a proper venue within the same judicial system.

In the federal system, for example, a court in which venue has improperly been laid may dismiss, "or if it be in the interest of justice, transfer [the] case to any district or division in which it could have been brought."[41] As federal courts have interpreted this provision, a court with subject matter jurisdiction, whether or not it has personal jurisdiction over the parties,[42] may transfer a case laying improper venue to any federal forum which, without defendants' consent, would have had personal jurisdiction over

---

reluctance, for reasons of sovereignty and ability, to decide disputes concerning foreign property. *See Reasor-Hill Corp. v. Harrison,* 249 S.W.2d 994 (Ark. 1952) (questioning application of this reasoning to interstate disputes about property, in rejecting the "majority [local action] rule").

[37] *See, e.g., Livingston v. Jefferson,* 15 Fed. Cas. 660 (C.C.D. Va. 1811) (No. 8,411) (applying local action rule to dismiss suit in Virginia federal court against former President Jefferson for trespass to property in Louisiana Territory).

[38] *See* 28 U.S.C. §§ 1392 & 1393(a). *See generally* Note, *Local Actions in the Federal Courts,* 70 Harv. L. Rev. 708 (1957). Subsections 1391(a)(2) & (b)(2) may now supplant the local action rule in federal court rendering it unnecessary.

[39] *See generally* Robertson & Speck, *Access to State Courts in Transnational Personal Injury Cases: Forum Non Conveniens and Antisuit Injunctions,* 68 Tex. L. Rev. 937 (1990); Stein, *Forum Non Conveniens and the Redundancy of Court-Access Doctrine,* 133 U. Pa. L. Rev. 781 (1985); Stewart, *Forum Non Conveniens: A Doctrine in Search of a Role,* 74 Cal. L. Rev. 1259 (1986).

[40] Under some statutes, the pendency of the lawsuit — even in an improper venue — tolls the statute. *See generally* § 8.08[2][b] (limitations defense), *infra.*

[41] 28 U.S.C. § 1406(a).

[42] *Goldlawr, Inc. v. Heiman,* 369 U.S. 463 (1962).

defendants and would have been a proper venue initially.[43] Almost all states have similar or less restrictive provisions for transfer in lieu of dismissal, if there is a proper alternative venue within the state judicial system.

Suppose, however, that the alternative forum is outside the state's judicial system or even outside the United States. State courts have no power to transfer cases to the courts of other states, and neither state nor federal courts have the power to transfer cases to the courts of foreign countries.[44] In such cases, most judicial systems permit dismissal of suits under the doctrine of *forum non conveniens,* in anticipation that the plaintiff will recommence the suit in the alternative foreign venue. To obtain a *forum non conveniens* dismissal, defendant must satisfy two requirements.

First, he must show that an adequate alternative forum is available.[45] Since *forum non conveniens* presupposes a proper original venue, it would be unfair to plaintiff who correctly chose it and would frustrate the purposes of venue law to dismiss a case for which there was no adequate alternative forum. In *Piper Aircraft Co. v. Reyno,*[46] plaintiff argued that his case should not be dismissed from a proper federal venue under the doctrine of *forum non conveniens* when the alternative Scottish forum would apply less favorable substantive law. The Supreme Court held that the mere possibility of an unfavorable change in the applicable law does not bar a *forum non conveniens* dismissal, unless the change makes the remedy "so clearly inadequate or unsatisfactory that it is no remedy at all."[47] More recently, a federal district court ruled that alleged defects and disadvantages of the Indian legal system, including prohibitive filing fees of up to 5% of total damages sought, serious case backlogs occasioned in part by unlimited interlocutory appeals, and underdeveloped tort laws,[48] did not render an

---

[43] *Cf. Hoffman v. Blaski,* 363 U.S. 335 (1960) (rejecting argument under federal venue transfer provision, 28 U.S.C. § 1404, that a forum in which case "might have been brought" includes an otherwise improper venue to which defendants consent, and, by implication, rejecting same "consent" argument for a forum that otherwise lacks personal jurisdiction over defendants). *Hoffman*'s analysis should apply with even greater force to transfers in lieu of dismissal under 28 U.S.C. § 1406, since it speaks of districts where the action "could have been brought." *See generally* Wright § 44.

[44] Nor can federal courts transfer cases onto the dockets of state courts. However, there is less need for transfer in this setting. A state court in the state where the federal court is sitting usually will not be appreciably more convenient than the federal court there. The court of a second state might be more convenient, but so too would a federal court in the second state. The federal court where suit originated can affect intra-system transfer to the latter under 28 U.S.C. § 1404. *See* § 6.02[2] (transfer of venue), *infra.*

[45] *Gulf Oil Corp. v. Gilbert,* 330 U.S. 501, 506-507 (1947). *See generally* Annotation, *Forum Non Conveniens — Availability of Alternative Forum,* 57 A.L.R.4th 973 (1987); Note, *Forum Non Conveniens in the Absence of An Alternative Forum,* 86 Colum. L. Rev. 1000 (1986); Note, *Requirement of a Second Forum for Application of Forum Non Conveniens,* 43 Minn. L. Rev. 1199 (1959). A few courts have treated the availability of an adequate alternative forum as just one factor to weigh in a *forum non conveniens* decision, rather than a prerequisite to such a decision. *E.g., Islamic Republic of Iran v. Pahlavi,* 467 N.E.2d 245 (N.Y. 1984).

[46] 454 U.S. 235 (1981).

[47] *Id.* at 254.

[48] *See generally* Galanter, *Legal Torpor: Why So Little Has Happened in India After the Bhopal Tragedy,* 20 Tex. Int'l. L.J. 273 (1985); Stewart, *Why Suits for Damages Such as Bhopal Claims Are Very Rare in India,* Wall St. J., Jan. 23, 1985, at 1.

Indian forum inadequate in the litigation spawned by the catastrophic Bhopal pesticide leak.[49] On the other hand, a lack of jurisdiction in the alternative forum clearly renders it inadequate for *forum non conveniens* purposes.[50]

Second, the defendant must show that considerations of party and forum convenience override the plaintiff's choice of forum and justify dismissal. Typical party or private considerations include relative ease of access to proof, availability of compulsory process for attendance of witnesses, the cost of obtaining their attendance, the possibility of obtaining a jury view of the scene of the accident or property which is the subject of the action, and the enforceability of any eventual judgment in the original forum.[51] Ordinarily the plaintiff's choice of forum enjoys a presumption of convenience. When these factors indicate that the alternative forum would be more convenient for the parties, however, then the plaintiff's choice was presumably tactical, or even harassing, and may therefore be disturbed.

Forum or public considerations reflect chiefly the relative burdens and benefits of imposing the litigation on the contending forums, including effect on judicial calendars, imposition of jury duty on the forum community, local interest in the controversy, and the choice of law.[52] Clearly, forum convenience — the public interest — is best served by localizing the litigation and assigning it to the forum most familiar with the applicable law.

The *forum non conveniens* determination is committed to the sound discretion of the trial court,[53] and, as such, is largely immune from effective appellate review.[54] Included within that discretion is the power to condition dismissal on defendants' satisfaction of various conditions that will ensure the adequacy of the alternative forum (such as agreement to waive a

---

[49] *In re Union Carbide Corp. Gas Plant Disaster at Bhopal, India,* 634 F. Supp. 842 (S.D.N.Y. 1986) (hereinafter cited as *Bhopal Litigation*), *aff'd as modified,* 809 F.2d 195 (2d Cir. 1987). On the Bhopal Litigation generally, see Covell, *The Bhopal Disaster Litigation: It's Not Over Yet,* 16 N.C. J. Int'l L. & Com. Reg. 279 (1991); Darmody, *An Economic Approach to Forum Non Conveniens Dismissals Requested by U.S. Multinational Corporations — the Bhopal Case,* 22 Geo. Wash. J. Int'l L. & Econ. 215 (1988); Nanda, *For Whom the Bell Tolls in the Aftermath of the Bhopal Tragedy: Reflections on Forum Non Conveniens and Alternative Methods of Resolving the Bhopal Dispute,* 15 Denv. J. Int'l L. & Pol'y 235 (1987); Schwadron, Note, *The Bhopal Incident: How the Courts Have Faced Complex International Litigation,* 5 B.U. Int'l L.J. 445 (1987).

[50] *Piper Aircraft,* 454 U.S. at 254 n.22 (ordinarily amenability of defendants to suit in the alternative forum evidences its adequacy, while lack of subject matter jurisdiction in the alternative forum makes it inadequate).

[51] *See, e.g., Piper Aircraft,* 454 U.S. at 257-258; *Gulf Oil,* 330 U.S. at 508. In some states, a resident plaintiff's interest in having his case heard by his own courts trumps all other private and public considerations and bars dismissal. *See, e.g., Ferreira v. Ferreira,* 512 P.2d 304 (Cal. 1973); *Iacouzze v. Iacouzze,* 672 P.2d 949 (Ariz. Ct. App. 1983). *See generally* McAllen, *Deference to the Plaintiff in Forum Non Conveniens,* 13 S. Ill. U. L.J. 191 (1989).

[52] *Piper Aircraft,* 454 U.S. at 259-261; *Gulf Oil,* 330 U.S. at 508-509.

[53] *Piper Aircraft,* 451 U.S. at 257.

[54] *See Stein,* note 39, *supra,* at 831-832; Morin, Note, *Review and Appeal of Forum Non Conveniens and Venue Transfer Orders,* 59 Geo. Wash. L. Rev. 715 (1991); § 13.04[2] (noting unavailability of statutory interlocutory appeal under 28 U.S.C. § 1292(b) for review of venue transfer decisions), *infra.*

limitations defense to a refiled suit or to submit to the jurisdiction of the alternative forum)[55] or conditions that will enhance the party convenience of that forum (such as defendants' agreement to provide certain discovery).[56]

[2] Transfer of Venue

In section 2.02 we discussed factors influencing the choice of court. But defendants also forum shop by moving to transfer venue. Indeed, one commentator alleges that "the transfer motion has become a common, almost reflexive defendant response to a lawsuit."[57] Because courts lack the power to transfer cases outside their own judicial system, the doctrine of *forum non conveniens* is still used as a form of inter-system "transfer" from state or federal courts to state or foreign courts.[58] For intra-system transfers, however, relaxed versions of the doctrine have been codified in many jurisdictions.

The statutory provision for transfer of venue within the federal system[59] is probably typical. Unlike the common law *forum non conveniens* doctrine, the statute provides for transfer to a district where the case might have been brought,[60] instead of dismissal. Because the statute provides this milder remedy of transfer, it is available upon a lesser showing[61] than required for *forum non conveniens* dismissal. The relaxed showing is phrased generally and unhelpfully as "the convenience of parties and witnesses, [or] in the interest of justice."[62] The parties' contractual choice of forum is not dispositive in this showing, but only a factor to be considered.[63] Moreover, unlike *forum non conveniens* dismissals, transfers of

---

[55] *Bhopal Litigation,* 809 F.2d at 203, 204 (conditioning dismissal in part on defendant's consent to jurisdiction of Indian courts and waiver of limitations defenses).

[56] *See Piper Aircraft,* 454 U.S. at 257 n.25. *See generally* J. Bies, *Conditioning Forum Non Conveniens,* 67 U. Chi. L. Rev. 489 (2000).

[57] Kelner, Note, *"Adrift on an Unchartered Sea: A Survey of Section 1404(a) Transfer in the Federal System,* 67 N.Y.U. L. Rev. 612, 615 (1992).

[58] *See* note 44 and accompanying text, *supra.* It is not the only inter-system venue device, however. Some courts will stay proceedings before them until the plaintiff has refiled and defendant has submitted in a better foreign venue, and others will entertain actions by parties who are defendants in an inconvenient foreign venue to enjoin the plaintiff from prosecuting her action there. *See generally* Robertson & Speck, n.1, *supra;* Comment, *Forum non Conveniens, Injunctions Against Suit and Full Faith and Credit,* 29 U. Chi. L. Rev. 740, 741 (1962).

[59] 28 U.S.C. § 1404. *See generally* Corna, Note, *Confusion and Dissension Surrounding the Venue Transfer Statutes,* 53 Ohio St. L.J. 319 (1992); *Kelner,* note 57, *supra;* Steinberg, *The Motion to Transfer and the Interests of Justice,* 66 Notre Dame L. Rev. 443 (1990).

[60] *Id.* § 1404(a).

[61] *Piper Aircraft,* 454 U.S. at 253; *Norwood v. Kirkpatrick,* 349 U.S. 29, 29-33 (1955) (§ 1404 is not merely a codification of *forum non conveniens,* but adopts a more relaxed test for transfer in the federal system).

[62] 28 U.S.C § 1404(a).

[63] *See Stewart Organization, Inc. v. Ricoh Corp.,* 487 U.S. 22 (1988). *See generally* Lederman, Note, *Viva Zapata! Toward a Rational System of Forum-Selection Clause Enforcement in Diversity Cases,* 66 N.Y.U. L. Rev. 422, 450-464 (1991).

venue between federal courts are available to plaintiffs and defendants alike.[64]

The effect of a transfer is also different from the effect of a dismissal. Statutory transfer is intended only to change the place of trial, and not the applicable law or the availability of limitations defenses. Accordingly, the Supreme Court has held that a federal transferee court must apply the law that would have been applied in the transferor court, whether the movant was the plaintiff or the defendant.[65] Upon transfer, the transferee court takes up the litigation where the transferor court left it, and no recommencement of the action is necessary, which preserves to plaintiff any tolling benefits of the original commencement for the plaintiff.

The interaction of liberal federal venue, relaxed federal transfer standards, the uncertain effects of the parties' contractual choice of forum, and the general absence of effective appellate supervision of transfer decisions has bred substantial confusion in the caselaw and new opportunities to forum shop.[66] Whether a given court will transfer is unpredictable. The rule applying the law that the transferor court would apply lets plaintiffs forum-shop for the statute of limitations in some cases; less obviously, the willingness of at least some transferee courts to overrule the law of the case[67] lets defendants forum-shop for reconsideration of adverse interlocutory decisions.[68] Critics of the current system, however, are undecided whether closer appellate supervision or statutory reform is the better solution.

§ 6.03 Proposals Regarding the Relationship of Personal Jurisdiction and Venue

A careful reader of Chapters 3 and 6 cannot help but note the similarities between personal jurisdiction and venue. Both address in part the reasonableness of the forum from defendant's perspective and the forum interests in the locus of suit. More generally, these doctrines of court access share common historical roots and purposes and have similar analytic structures.[69]

---

[64] See Ferens v. John Deere Co., 494 U.S. 516 (1990) (discussing choice of law after plaintiff-initiated transfer).

[65] Id. at 516 (plaintiff's transfer under 28 U.S.C. § 1404); Van Dusen v. Barrack, 376 U.S. 612, 639 (1964) (defendant's transfer under 28 U.S.C. § 1404). See generally § 7.05[3] (Klaxon and § 1404(a)), infra. This rule is not applied to transfer made under 28 U.S.C. § 1406 as an alternative to dismissal for improper venue. See Moore § 111.38[1]. It is unclear whether it applies when a federal court transfers under circumstances in which a forum state court would have dismissed under the doctrine of forum non conveniens. See Wright § 44. Note, Choice of Law in Federal Court After Transfer of Venue, 63 Cornell L. Rev. 149 (1977).

[66] See, e.g., K. Norwood, Double Forum Shopping and the Extension of Ferens to Federal Claims that Borrow State Limitation Periods, 44 Emory L.J. 501 (1995); Corna, note 59, supra; Kelner, note 58, supra.

[67] See § 15.14 (law of the case), infra.

[68] See Kelner, note 58, supra, at 636-642; Steinman, Law of the Case: A Judicial Puzzle in Consolidated and Transferred Cases and in Multidistrict Litigation, 135 U. Pa. L. Rev. 595 (1987).

[69] See Clermont, Restating Territorial Jurisdiction and Venue for State and Federal Courts, 66 Cornell L. Rev. 411, 430-434 (1981).

Little wonder that students and lawyers alike occasionally have difficulty understanding how a court that may "reasonably" exercise personal jurisdiction over a defendant can be too inconvenient to the defendant to serve as an appropriate venue.

Critics have attempted to reformulate these court-access doctrines to eliminate or explain their overlap within a judicial system. One approach is capsulized in the prediction, "Jurisdiction must become venue."[70] Proponents of this reformulation urge a system of nationwide service of federal process, under which the venue rules alone carry the full burden of assuring a reasonably convenient forum.[71]

"Venue must become jurisdiction" summarizes another alternative. Its approach is to abolish federal venue requirements and look solely to a federal long-arm statute to ensure a reasonably convenient forum.[72] Long-arm jurisdiction would be available in any district where a substantial part of the events giving rise to suit occurred or where defendant resides. To a significant degree, the 1990 amendments to the general federal venue statute moved in this direction, by laying venue in the district in which significant contacts occur, or, for corporate defendants, where they are subject to personal jurisdiction, or, when these venues are unavailable, in the district in which the defendants are subject to personal jurisdiction.[73]

Alternatively, and more modestly, the *forum non conveniens* doctrine alone could be eliminated from venue law in favor of an expanded jurisdictional inquiry that expressly takes into account the private and public interests now canvassed under that doctrine.[74] Courts in Texas, for example, have taken this approach, finding themselves prohibited by statute from entertaining *forum non conveniens* motions and therefore importing *forum non conveniens* considerations into the law of personal jurisdiction.[75]

Another approach is to retain an assortment of access doctrines, but redefine their content to minimize overlap. This approach proposes a three-part inquiry: power (requiring only some contact with the forum), reasonableness (a constitutional due process requirement), and subconstitutional convenience (all other restrictions on geographic choice of forum, including the local action rule).[76] No system has yet adopted these approaches, and it remains to be seen whether any would respond more effectively to concerns treated by current law.

---

[70] Ehrenzweig, *From State Jurisdiction to Interstate Venue,* 50 Or. L. Rev. 103, 113 (1971).

[71] *See* Barrett, *Venue and Service of Process in the Federal Courts — Suggestions for Reform,* 7 Vand. L. Rev. 608, 627-635 (1954); Seidelson, *Jurisdiction of Federal Courts Hearing Federal Cases: An Examination of the Propriety of the Limitations Imposed by Venue Restrictions,* 37 Geo. Wash. L. Rev. 82, 84 (1968).

[72] *See* Currie, *The Federal Courts and the American Law Institute* (pt. 2), 36 U. Chi. L. Rev. 268, 299-311 (1969).

[73] *See* 28 U.S.C. § 1391, discussed in § 6.01, *supra.*

[74] Stein, *Forum Non Conveniens and the Redundancy of Court-Access Doctrine,* 133 U. Pa. L. Rev. 781, 845 (1985).

[75] *See generally* Albright, *In Personam Jurisdiction: A Confused and Inappropriate Substitute for Forum Non Conveniens,* 71 Texas L. Rev. 351 (1992).

[76] *Clermont,* note 39, *supra,* at 437-443.

Chapter 7

ASCERTAINING THE APPLICABLE LAW

§ 7.01   Overview

This chapter explores the duty of federal courts to ascertain and apply state law when deciding cases within their diversity jurisdiction.[1] The source of the obligation is the *Erie* doctrine,[2] which reads the federal Rules of Decision Act[3] to require use of state law when the difference between state and federal law might substantially affect the outcome of the case.

Section 7.02 of this chapter examines the origins of the *Erie* doctrine and the policies responsible for its creation that have contemporary significance. Section 7.03 examines subsequent developments in the doctrine and offers some suggestions for understanding and applying the various tests that have emerged from United States Supreme Court decisions. Section 7.04 looks at how federal courts have used the *Erie* doctrine to resolve tensions between the federal rules of procedure and state law.

To decide that *Erie* requires a federal diversity court to look to state rather than federal law may be only the first step toward decision. Difficult questions can also arise concerning which of the conflicting laws of two or more states should govern the case, and concerning the content of state law. These questions are discussed in Sections 7.05 and 7.06, respectively.

Erie eliminated general federal common law, but left specific federal common law undisturbed in federal question cases. Section 7.07 examines when that law applies and how it is determined.

§ 7.02   The Evolution from *Swift* to *Erie*[4]

[1]   *Swift v. Tyson*

The Supreme Court held in *Swift v. Tyson*,[5] a federal diversity case, that the Rules of Decision Act[6] did not require it to follow New York state

---

[1] General diversity jurisdiction exists for federal courts under 28 U.S.C. § 1332. For a discussion of federal diversity jurisdiction, see § 5.04, *supra*.

[2] *See Erie R. R. Co. v. Tompkins,* 304 U.S. 64 (1938), and its progeny, discussed *infra*.

[3] 28 U.S.C. § 1652:

> The laws of the several states, except where the Constitution or treaties of the United States or Acts of Congress otherwise require or provide, shall be regarded as rules of decision in civil actions in the courts of the United States, in cases where they apply.

[4] For an extended version of this Section, see Shreve, *From Swift to Erie: An Historical Perspective,* 82 Mich. L. Rev. 869 (1984).

[5] 41 U.S. (16 Pet.) 1 (1842).

[6] The statute was enacted as § 34 of the Judiciary Act of 1789. It has been amended in respects which do not bear on this discussion and now appears as 28 U.S.C. § 1652. Section 1652 is reproduced in § 7.01, *supra*.

judicial decisions concerning the law of negotiable instruments. Writing for the Court, Justice Story stated that, at least with regard to "contracts and other instruments of a commercial nature," federal diversity courts were free to follow their own best understanding of the "general principles and doctrines of commercial jurisprudence."[7] In such cases, said Justice Story, state judicial decisions to the contrary were not part of the "laws of the several states," as that term was used in the Rules of Decision Act. The Act's mandate that state laws be followed "as rules of decision" did not apply because the *Swift* Court regarded its application to be limited

> to state laws strictly *local,* that is to say, to the positive statutes of the state, and the construction thereof adopted by the local tribunals, and to rights and titles to things having a permanent locality. . . . It never has been supposed by us, that the section did apply, or was designed to apply, to questions of a more *general* nature.[8]

[2] The Controversial Reign of the *Swift* Doctrine

Swift and the succeeding cases that made up the *Swift* doctrine permitted federal judges to displace state with federal common law simply because the federal court's diversity jurisdiction had been invoked. Law federal judges made and applied under these circumstances came to be called *federal general common law.* At the time *Swift* was decided, assertion of this lawmaking authority does not seem to have been questioned.[9] During nearly a century when the *Swift* doctrine was in force, attitudes toward it changed and the doctrine became increasingly controversial. Two developments help explain this.

First, federal general common law expanded to rival state common law in a growing number of fields. The "general" and local categories created in *Swift* left many points of law unaccounted for, and usually it was the general law category into which the new problems were placed. Moreover, the Supreme Court increasingly tended to displace state law even within the sanctuary of "local" matters originally defined in *Swift.*[10]

Second, it became relatively easy for corporate litigants to gain access to a federal court by invoking its diversity jurisdiction. Corporations had grown enormously as a class of litigants since the time of *Swift.* They frequently found federal general common law more congenial than state common law.[11] Through tactical selection of the place of incorporation, a

---

[7] 41 U.S. at 19.

[8] 41 U.S. at 17-18 (emphasis added).

[9] *See* T. Freyer, *Harmony & Dissonance: The Swift and Erie Cases in American Federalism* 36 (1981); G. Gilmore, *The Ages of American Law* 33-34 (1977).

[10] The most significant example was the withdrawal of state cases interpreting state statutes or constitutions from the preserve of "local" law created by *Swift. See Rowan v. Runnels,* 46 U.S. (5 How.) 134 (1847); *Watson v. Tarpley,* 59 U.S. (18 How.) 517 (1855); *Gelpcke v. City of Dubuque,* 68 U.S. (1 Wall) 175 (1863); *Burgess v. Seligman,* 107 U.S. 20 (1882). These cases are discussed in Jackson, *The Rise and Fall of Swift v. Tyson,* 24 A.B.A.J. 609, 611-613 (1938).

[11] *See* J.W. Hurst, *The Growth of American Law — The Law Makers* 190 (1950); Teton, *The Story of Swift v. Tyson,* 35 Ill. L. Rev. 519, 529-530 (1941).

corporation was often able to forum shop — to insure that suits by or against it would be litigated in a federal diversity court — which gave it the benefit of federal general common law. This was especially true after Congress enlarged the scope of general diversity jurisdiction and removal in 1875.[12]

The *Swift* doctrine was never without its champions, who hoped it would promote uniformity among state and federal courts. By the twentieth century, however, it drew strong criticism from the legal community. Many saw federal diversity courts as protectors of the monied, corporate interests. But at the heart of the problem was the more basic issue of federalism. Which sovereign should have authority to create rules of decision to govern federal diversity cases? Forceful arguments were made in Supreme Court dissents that only states had such authority.[13]

[3] *Erie R.R. Co. v. Tompkins*

The reign of *Swift* was finally brought to an end in 1938 by the Supreme Court's decision in *Erie R.R. Co. v. Tompkins*.[14] Plaintiff there sought to recover for injuries he received when struck by an object protruding from defendant's passing train. Plaintiff was on a path adjacent to the tracks at the time of the accident. The defendant railroad argued that the common law of Pennsylvania regarded the plaintiff as a trespasser under such circumstances and therefore imposed upon the defendant railroad only the duty to refrain from acts of wanton negligence. Plaintiff countered that the federal diversity court was free under *Swift* to disregard Pennsylvania judicial precedents and to regard plaintiff as an invitee to whom defendant owed a duty of ordinary care under federal general common law.

When the case finally reached the United States Supreme Court, it ruled in favor of the defendant and, in so doing, overruled *Swift*'s interpretation of the Rules of Decision Act. Writing for the Court, Justice Brandeis stated:

> Except in matters governed by the Federal Constitution or by Acts of Congress, the law to be applied in any case is the law of the State. And whether the law of the State shall be declared by its Legislature in a statute or by its highest court in a decision is not a matter of federal concern. There is no federal general common law.[15]

---

[12] *Freyer*, note 9, *supra*, at 55-56.

[13] *See, e.g., Black & White Taxicab & Transfer Co. v. Brown & Yellow Taxicab & Transfer Co.*, 276 U.S. 518 (1928) (dissenting opinion of Justices Holmes, Brandeis and Stone). For a survey of other attacks on the *Swift* doctrine by Supreme Court dissenters, *see* Casto, *The Erie Doctrine and the Structure of Constitutional Revolutions*, 62 Tul. L. Rev. 907, 914-927 (1988); Shreve, note 4, *supra*, at 875 n.41.

[14] 304 U.S. 64. For an illuminating and entertaining discussion of the facts and procedural history of *Erie, see* Younger, *What Happened in Erie*, 56 Tex. L. Rev. 1011 (1978).

[15] 304 U.S. at 78. Of course, Justice Brandeis did not suggest that federal courts should entirely give up making common law. "[T]he same justice the same day in another case pointed out that there may be questions of 'federal common law' upon which state statutes and decisions cannot be conclusive, such as the apportionment between two states of the water of an interstate stream." Clark, *State Law in the Federal Courts: The Brooding Omnipresence*

Brandeis noted that the uniformity of law sought by the advocates of the *Swift* doctrine had not materialized. State courts continued to make and adhere to their own precedents, while federal diversity courts were free to disregard them. Moreover, Brandeis observed that *Swift* had actually produced three undesirable results. First, the inability of courts to draw a clear line between local and general law had led to considerable confusion. Second, *Swift* worked mischief by providing non-citizens the forum-shopping advantage of invoking diversity jurisdiction to evade state common law rules, when plaintiffs who shared the citizenship of their defendants could not.[16] Third and most important, *Swift* had eroded the states' legitimate authority to regulate their own affairs.[17]

Erie was a momentous decision for several reasons. *Erie* not only overruled *Swift* and the long line of Supreme Court decisions adhering to it, it also invalidated hundreds — perhaps thousands — of federal general common law precedents in torts, commercial law and many other fields. In so doing, *Erie* repudiated the Court's prior settled interpretation of an act of Congress — something the Court does only with great reluctance.[18] This may explain why, despite the strong policy arguments for the result in *Erie* previously discussed, the Court found it necessary to further justify its decision by suggesting that the *Swift* doctrine was constitutionally suspect.[19] Finally, *Erie* worked a lasting change in the judicial

---

of Erie v. Tompkins, 55 Yale L.J. 268, 273 (1946) (*citing Hinderlider v. La Plata River and Cherry Creek Ditch Co.,* 304 U.S. 92, 110 (1938)). Federal common law is discussed in § 7.07, *infra.*

[16] In overruling *Swift, Erie* deprived litigants of their greatest gain from manipulating federal diversity jurisdiction — access to federal general common law. But *Erie* did not actually restrict the manipulation itself. Congress has since addressed the problem by barring the exercise of diversity jurisdiction when a party "has been improperly or collusively made or joined to invoke the jurisdiction of such court," 28 U.S.C.§ 1359, and by rendering jurisdictional manipulation through incorporation, *see* note 12 and accompanying text *supra,* more difficult by extending the citizenship of a corporation to the additional state, if any, "where it has its principal place of business." 28 U.S.C. § 1332(c). On developments in federal diversity jurisdiction generally, *see* § 5.04, *supra. See also* § 5.05 (corporate citizenship), *supra.*

[17] Brandeis suggested that *Swift* was simply wrong in reading the Rules of Decision Act to permit federal diversity courts to disregard state common law. He based this part of his attack on *Swift* upon Professor Charles Warren's research and argument that Justice Story had misconstrued the original purpose of the Rules of Decision Act. Warren, *New Light on the History of the Federal Judiciary Act of 1789,* 37 Harv. L. Rev. 49, 51-52, 81-88, 108 (1923). Brandeis' reliance upon this article was to cast a slight shadow over *Erie,* since Warren's methods and conclusions were, in time, roundly attacked. *See* the authorities cited in *Wright* § 54; *Freyer,* note 9, *supra,* at 178 n.21. *Erie's* authority was undamaged, however, because the principle of state lawmaking autonomy it vindicated rested upon a foundation broader than Warren's work. The principle was extended in decisions beginning with *Guaranty Trust Co. v. York,* 326 U.S. 99 (1945).

[18] *See, e.g.,* E. Levi, *An Introduction to Legal Reasoning* 32 (1948).

[19] Writing of the *Swift* doctrine, Justice Brandeis stated: "If only a question of statutory construction were involved, we should not be prepared to abandon a doctrine so widely applied throughout nearly a century. But the unconstitutionality of the course pursued has now been made clear and compels us to do so." *Erie,* 304 U.S. at 77-78. Concurring separately, Justice Reed saw no need to raise a constitutional question in order to overrule *Swift.* 304 U.S. at 90-92. The Supreme Court has not chosen since to clarify or refine *Erie's* constitutional dimension beyond the cryptic observation that *Erie* "indicated that Congress does not have

arrangements of federalism. The case "announces no technical doctrine of procedure or jurisdiction but goes to the heart of the relations between the federal government and the states, and returns to the states a power that had for nearly a century been exercised by the federal government."[20]

Some of the implications of this power shift are still being worked out by the courts, and the resulting *Erie*-doctrine questions will be the subject of the sections that follow.

§ 7.03 Tests for Applying *Erie*

[1] The Substance-Versus-Procedure Test and Its Criticism in *York*

The choice between state and federal common law in *Erie* involved competing standards of duty in tort law — what was then and is now understood to be *substantive law*.[21] It was never doubted that substantive law was most directly and obviously contemplated by the term "rules of decision" in the Rules of Decision Act. Therefore, once the Supreme Court reached the conclusion that the Act extended to state common law, *Erie* was easy to decide.

Subsequent litigants, however, were not content to confine their state law arguments under *Erie* to matters of torts or contracts. They argued that conflicting federal law must give way to local state law not only to determine

---

the constitutional authority to make the law that is applicable to controversies in diversity of citizenship cases," *Bernhardt v. Polygraphic Co. of America, Inc.*, 350 U.S. 198, 202 (1956).

The matter has been much debated in the literature. A number of commentators have endorsed the suggestion in *Erie* that the Constitution required the result there. *See, e.g.,* Mishkin, *Further Last Words on Erie— The Thread,* 87 Harv. L. Rev. 1682 (1974); Friendly, *In Praise of Erie —and of the New Common Law* 39 N.Y.U. L. Rev. 383, 392-398 (1964); Hart, *The Relations Between State and Federal Law,* 54 Colum. L. Rev. 489, 509-510 (1954); Wechsler, *Federal Jurisdiction and the Revision of the Judicial Code,* 13 Law and Contemp. Probs. 216, 239 n.121 (1948); Note, *The Competence of Federal Courts to Formulate Rules of Decision,* 77 Harv. L. Rev. 1084, 1086 (1964). *But see, e.g.,* Clark, *State Law in the Federal Courts: The Brooding Omnipresence of Erie v. Tompkins,* 55 Yale L.J. 267, 278-279 (1946); Kurland, *Mr. Justice Frankfurter, The Supreme Court and the Erie Doctrine in Diversity Cases,* 67 Yale L.J. 187, 197 (1957); *cf.* Ely, *The Irrepressible Myth of Erie,* 87 Harv. L. Rev. 693 (1974) (suggesting a less restrictive role for the Constitution and a commensurately greater range of options for Congress); American Law Institute, *Study of the Division of Jurisdiction Between State and Federal Courts* 442 (1969) ("[I]t does not necessarily follow that the *Erie* holding was constitutionally compelled in the technical sense of being legally imposed by the fundamental instrument.").

[20] *Wright* § 55. Most commentators have supported this turn of events, but not all. *See, e.g.,* Corr, *Thoughts on the Vitality of Erie,* 41 Am. U. L. Rev. 1087 (1992) (suggesting that *Swift* was preferable to *Erie*). *cf.* Borchers, *The Origins of Diversity Jurisdiction, The Rise of Legal Positivism, and a Brave New World for Erie and Klaxon,* 72 Tex. L. Rev. 79 (1993) (questioning the continued desirability of *Erie*).

[21] *Swift* and virtually all intervening cases had, in the same sense, also involved substantive law. *See, e.g., Black & White Taxicab & Transfer Co. v. Brown & Yellow Taxicab & Transfer Co.,* 276 U.S. 518 (1928) (a federal diversity action in which a contract, unenforceable under Kentucky state common law, was enforced under federal general common law).

the content of rights, but also to decide how and under what circumstances rights would be vindicated. These questions, which concern the processes by which the claims of rights are examined, are resolved according to a body of law often regarded as *procedural* rather than substantive in character.[22]

Those wishing to check the expansion of *Erie* attempted to use the distinction between substance and procedure as a dividing line. Under a substance-versus-procedure test, matters characterized as substantive would be governed by state law, and those characterized as procedural would be governed by federal law.[23] With the Supreme Court's decision in *Guaranty Trust Co. v. York*,[24] however, it became clear that this test would not be adequate to resolve all issues arising under the Rules of Decision Act.

Plaintiff in *York* brought a class action alleging that defendant breached its fiduciary duty as trustee in a corporate financing transaction. *Erie* left no doubt that the scope of defendant's fiduciary duty to plaintiff was to be determined under New York state law. Defendant urged, however, that *Erie* also required application of the state statute of limitations, which barred the action.[25] Plaintiff countered that the limitations question was instead governed by federal law. The Court sided with the defendant and, in a majority opinion written by Justice Frankfurter, held *Erie* to be fully applicable.

Justice Frankfurter did not, however, adopt the defendant's argument that *Erie* was applicable because the limitations issue in *York* was substantive in character. He found the substance-versus-procedure test inadequate to explain the result in the case, observing that " 'substance' and 'procedure' are the same key-words to very different problems. . . . Each implies different variables depending upon the particular problem for which it is used."[26]

[2]   The Outcome-Determination Test

In *York* Justice Frankfurter read *Erie* to provide a different test. He wrote:

In essence, the intent of that decision was to insure that, in all cases where a federal court is exercising jurisdiction solely because of the

---

[22] *See* § 101[2] (substance and procedure), *supra.*

[23] Concurring in *Erie*, Justice Reed had said, "[n]o one doubts federal power over procedure." 304 U.S. at 92. The institution most obviously empowered to make federal procedural law is Congress. *Cf.* Note, *The Proper Scope of Pendent Appellate Jurisdiction in the Collateral Order Context*, 100 Yale L. J. 511, 522 (1990) ("Congress' Article III power to create the lower federal courts enables it to organize their operations as it sees fit."). When no statute interferes with their power to do so, federal courts too may make federal procedural law. For examples, see *Byrd v. Blue Ridge Rural Electric Cooperative, Inc.*, 356 U.S. 525 (1958); *Chambers v. NASCO, Inc.*, 501 U.S. 32 (1991).

[24] 326 U.S. 99 (1945). For extended discussion of *York*, see Kurland, *Mr. Justice Frankfurter, the Supreme Court and the Erie Doctrine in Diversity Cases,* 67 Yale L.J. 187 (1957).

[25] On statutes of limitation generally, *see* § 8.08[2][b], *infra.*

[26] 326 U.S. at 108.

diversity of citizenship of the parties, the outcome of the litigation in the federal court should be substantially the same, so far as legal rules determine the outcome of a litigation, as it would be if tried in a State court. [27]

This came to be regarded as the *outcome-determination* test. Under it, state rules controlled if the choice between state or federal law could be outcome-determinative in the case.

Clearly, the *York* decision carried the rule of *Erie* well beyond the facts of the *Erie* case. But just how far? One commentator observed that "to such a principle there is no apparent stopping place." [28] In three cases decided after *York*, the Supreme Court indeed seemed unable to find a stopping place in applying the outcome-determination test. These cases seemed to suggest that federal law could not be employed to decide questions of *procedure* [29] in diversity cases if state law conflicted and the choice could possibly affect the outcome. Some lower federal courts so applied the outcome-determination test during the nine years before the Supreme Court again addressed the subject. Then, in *Byrd v. Blue Ridge Rural Electric Cooperative, Inc.*, [30] the Supreme Court relaxed the test.

[3] *Byrd* and the Assessment of State and Federal Interests

The plaintiff in *Byrd* brought a federal diversity action for negligence, alleging injury while working on defendant's power line. The defendant argued that the work undertaken by plaintiff was the same as that done by defendant's own employees; therefore, plaintiff's only remedy was under the South Carolina worker's compensation act. Plaintiff contended that his work was not sufficiently like that of defendant's employees to satisfy the statute and sought a jury trial of this and other factual issues. Had plaintiff sued in South Carolina state court, a jury trial would not have been available on the statutory coverage issue. The defendant argued that the *Erie* doctrine operated to bar a federal jury trial as well.

The Supreme Court held that the plaintiff was entitled to a jury trial, notwithstanding the possibility "that in the instant personal-injury case the outcome would be substantially affected by whether the issue . . . is decided by a judge or a jury." [31] The Court did not repudiate the outcome-determination test, but made clear that outcome determination would not settle the *Erie* question in all cases.

---

[27] *Id.* at 109.

[28] *Wright* § 59.

[29] *Ragan v. Merchants Transfer & Warehouse Co.*, 337 U.S. 530 (1949) (time of commencement for purpose of tolling limitations); *Cohen v. Beneficial Industrial Loan Corp.*, 337 U.S. 541 (1949) (whether plaintiff must post security-for-expenses bond); *Woods v. Interstate Realty Co.*, 337 U.S. 535 (1949) (whether corporate plaintiff must meet state business qualification requirement in order to sue). *Ragan* and *Cohen* are discussed in § 7.04, *infra*.

[30] 356 U.S. 525 (1958).

[31] *Id.* at 537.

Byrd added a new mode of analysis: an assessment of governmental interests behind the rules contending for application. The Court concluded that the policies supporting the federal jury rule would be sacrificed if plaintiff could not claim a jury in *Byrd*, but that it was far from clear that policies accounting for the South Carolina rule would be offended if plaintiff got his jury trial. Thus, it might be said that only the federal government was demonstrably interested in the application of its rule.

Byrd is the most perplexing of the *Erie* doctrine cases, in part because of the innate difficulty of interest-balancing analysis[32] and in part because portions of the Court's opinion in *Byrd* are not altogether clear. To begin with, the Court did not say that plaintiff had a constitutional right to a federal jury trial under the Seventh Amendment.[33] Rather, it favored plaintiff because neither the outcome-determination implication of the case nor the policy force behind South Carolina's rule against jury trials was sufficient to displace "[a]n essential characteristic of the [federal court system:] . . . the manner in which . . . it distributes trial functions between judge and jury. . . ."[34] Given the Supreme Court's approach in *Byrd,* the result might have been different if the policy interests of the federal courts had been weaker, or those of South Carolina stronger.[35] *Byrd* shortened the reach of *York's* outcome-determination test. At least in close cases, *Erie* questions were to be answered by assessing the state and federal interests behind the laws vying for application.

[4] *Hanna* and the Modified Outcome-Determination Test

The Supreme Court completed its modification of the outcome-determination test in *Hanna v. Plumer.*[36] The plaintiff there suffered personal injuries in an automobile accident and brought a federal diversity action against the estate of the alleged wrongdoer. The administrator of the estate was served by leaving a copy of the papers at his home in compliance with federal Rule (4)(d)(1). The defendant-administrator argued, however, that the action could not be maintained because he had not been personally served as required by Massachusetts law. The Supreme Court rejected this argument and held service under Rule 4(d)(1) adequate.

The *Hanna* Court dismissed defendant's outcome-determination argument as too literal-minded. Granted, once the lawsuit was filed, plaintiff

---

[32] *See* Bauer, *The Erie Doctrine Revisited: How a Conflicts Perspective Can Aid the Analysis,* 74 Notre Dame L. Rev. 1235, 1281-1299 (1999) (suggesting refinements in interest balancing).

[33] "Our conclusion makes unnecessary the consideration of — and we intimate no view upon — the constitutional question whether the right of jury trial protected in federal courts by the Seventh Amendment embraces the factual issue . . . here. . . ."*Id.* at 537 n.10. If the Court had found that plaintiff had a Seventh Amendment right to a jury trial, the *Erie* issue would not have arisen because the Constitution would control. For a discussion of the Seventh Amendment right to jury trials in federal court, *see* § 12.07[1], *infra.*

[34] 356 U.S. at 537.

[35] The Court indicated in *Byrd* that no strong state policy would be sacrificed by refusal to follow the South Carolina rule in a federal diversity case. *Id.* at 535-536.

[36] 380 U.S. 460 (1965).

would lose if the state rule applied, while the litigation would continue if the federal rule applied. "[I]n this sense," observed the Court, "*every procedural variation is 'outcome determinative.'*"[37] The Court made clear, however, that such differences alone were insignificant. It was more important to ask

> whether application of the [state] rule would make so important a difference to the character or result of the litigation that failure to enforce it would unfairly discriminate against citizens of the forum state, or whether application of the rule would have so important an effect upon the fortunes of one or both of the litigants that failure to enforce it would be likely to cause a plaintiff to choose the federal court.[38]

Applying this more subdued version of the outcome determination test, the *Hanna* Court found the difference between the state and federal rules to be too insubstantial to raise the danger of inequitable administration of law posed in *Erie*.

[5] Later *Erie* Issues

A subsequent issue involving *Erie* has been whether federal diversity courts will enforce state statutory requirements that certain claims must be submitted in the first instance to state administrative tribunals. After some initial resistance,[39] several federal courts have concluded that *Erie* requires the enforcement of such provisions.

Typical of these cases is the First Circuit's decision in *Feinstein v. Massachusetts General Hospital.*[40] The plaintiff sued defendant hospital for medical malpractice, invoking the federal court's diversity jurisdiction. Defendant moved to refer plaintiff's claim to a medical malpractice panel appointed under a Massachusetts statute. The purpose of the panel was to screen malpractice claims, reviewing plaintiff's proof by a standard similar to that used for directed verdicts.[41] If the panel found for defendant, plaintiff was to post a bond payable to defendant in the event plaintiff did not prevail at trial. The plaintiff conceded that the statute would have

---

[37] *Id.* at 468 (emphasis in original).

[38] *Id.* at 468 n.9. The court reiterated these points in *Chambers v. NASCO, Inc.*, 501 U.S. 32, 52 (1991). Note, however, that the *Erie* doctrine will require choice of the state rule in some cases where plaintiff does not appear to have shopped for the federal rule. The Court subsequently held a federal diversity court to a state law definition of "commencement" of suit, even though there was "no indication that when petitioner filed his suit in federal court he had any reason to believe that he would be unable to comply with the service requirements of Oklahoma law or that he chose to sue in federal court in an attempt to avoid those service requirements." *Walker v. Armco Steel Corp.*, 446 U.S. 740, 753 n.15 (1980). *Walker* is discussed more fully in § 7.04, *infra*.

[39] *See Wheeler v. Shoemaker*, 78 F.R.D. 218 (D.R.I. 1978) (denying defendant's motion to refer plaintiff's claim to a state malpractice panel).

[40] 643 F.2d 880 (1st Cir. 1981). *See also DiAntonio v. Northampton-Accomack Memorial Hosp.*, 628 F.2d 287 (4th Cir. 1980); *Hines v. Elkhart General Hosp.*, 603 F.2d 646 (7th Cir. 1979).

[41] *See generally* § 12.09[1] (directed verdicts and judgments n.o.v.), *infra*.

applied had he filed his malpractice case in Massachusetts state court, but argued that it was without effect in federal proceedings.

The First Circuit, however, agreed with defendant that *Erie* required that the Massachusetts statute be followed. The Court observed that "[t]he statute's referral procedure and associated provisions were designed to serve . . . substantive policy objectives. . . ."[42]

The approach taken in *Feinstein* has been viewed sympathetically.[43] At least part of the motivation for state creation of administrative panel prerequisites is to reduce the size and incidence of recoveries obtained through either trial or settlement, and some plaintiffs may have shopped for a federal forum in order to avoid this consequence. State statutes establishing administrative prerequisites to suit are somewhat analogous to state "door-closing" rules which operate to prevent certain types of cases from being heard altogether. The *Feinstein* approach thus may draw support from the fact that the Supreme Court has interpreted the *Erie* doctrine to mean that state door-closing doctrine bars federal diversity litigation.[44]

At the same time, to graft administrative referrals (or other satellite procedures contemplated by state litigation) onto federal cases creates "significant burdens on the parties and on the federal courts" in diversity litigation "of a sort inconsistent with the concept of those courts as an independently functioning judicial system."[45] Until federal courts are

---

[42] *Feinstein,* 643 F.2d at 885. The Court described the objectives as "providing for a prompt determination of the likely merits of a claim and requiring that a plaintiff who is unsuccessful before the malpractice tribunal post a bond" if he wishes to continue suit. Therefore, stated the Court, "[i]n the absence of any overriding federal interest in not applying the statute . . . we conclude that the Rules of Decision Act requires that federal courts to apply the state rules at issue here." *Id.*

[43] Alexander, *State Medical Malpractice Screening Panels in Federal Diversity Actions,* 21 Ariz. L. Rev. 959 (1979).

[44] *Angel v. Bullington,* 330 U.S. 183 (1947). "[D]iversity jurisdiction must follow State law and policy. A federal court in North Carolina, when invoked on grounds of diversity of citizenship, cannot give that which North Carolina has withheld." *Id.* at 192. Despite the breadth of this language, the reach of *Angel* is limited in at least two respects. First, the constitutionality of a state closing its doors to particular litigation may be open to question. R. Weintraub, *Commentary on the Conflict of Laws* § 106B (3rd ed. 1986). Naturally, if a state court could not constitutionally close its doors to a lawsuit, *Erie* cannot require a federal diversity court to do so. Second, the door-closing rule must reflect state substantive rather than procedural policies. If, for example, the state door-closing rule rests on a concern of *forum non conveniens, see* § 6.02[1], *supra, Erie* should impose no obligation on a federal diversity court to follow it. *Id.* at 576. *Stewart Org., Inc. v. Ricoh Corp.,* 810 F.2d 1066 (11th Cir. 1987), *aff'd* 487 U.S. 22 (1988), presents the converse situation where Alabama law opens its courts to suit, notwithstanding an agreement between the parties to confine suit to New York. The Eleventh Circuit invokes a federal law principle to honor the agreement.

[45] P. Bator, P. Miskin, D. Shapiro, & H. Wechsler, *The Federal Courts and the Federal System* 171 (2d ed. 1981 supplement).

A similar issue is whether a federal diversity judge must defer to a state arbitration award when a state court would have been required to do so. *See Towey v. Catling,* 743 F. Supp. 738, 740 (D. Hawaii 1990) (following state law to enforce an arbitration award, because that law was "an integral, substantive part of state policy. . ."). *Towey* is featured in Note, *Enforcement of State Annexed-arbitration Rules in Federal Courts with Diversity Jurisdiction,* 1991 J. Disp. Resol. 397.

willing to view this concern as overriding, however, *Byrd*'s interest assessment test is unlikely to lead to a refusal to honor state administrative law in medical malpractice cases.

In *Gasperini v. Center for Humanities, Inc.*,[46] the United States Supreme Court invoked the Rules Decision Act to require use of a state-law standard to determine whether a verdict was excessive as to warrant a new federal trial under Rule 59(a)(1).[47] That provision authorizes a new trial "for any of the reasons for which new trials have heretofore been granted in actions at law in the courts of the United States." The Rule does not offer a test for determining when new trial orders (or conditional new trial orders[48]) are warranted in response to excessive jury verdicts, and federal courts have often applied a "shocks the conscience" test.[49] But defendant in *Gasperini* invoked the more favorable New York state law standard permitting court intervention whenever the verdict "deviates materially from what would be reasonable compensation."[50]

Once it ruled that Rule 59 did not govern the issue,[51] the Supreme Court was able to turn to the question whether application of the state court "deviates materially" standard was required by the Rules of Decision Act. The Court concluded that it was, because New York's "objective is manifestly substantive."[52] Apart from this observation, the majority's opinion in *Gasperini* is not terribly clear. One commentator has observed: "It is possible that *Gasperini* employs an overarching RDA [Rules of Decision Act] approach similar to that embraced in *Byrd*. But such an interpretation is more the result of the reader's speculation than the Court's explanation."[53]

[6] Analytical Summary: Three Contemporary Tests Under the *Erie* Doctrine

Byrd's interest-dominated inquiry is analytic labor of the most demanding sort. It requires a determination of the nature and force of state and federal policies that might be implicated in the case. Often, only the policy (or policies) supporting one of the two rules will actually be at stake in the outcome. Then only the source (federal or state) providing that rule is really interested in having its law applied. This level of interest analysis may be

---

[46] 518 U.S. 415 (1996).

[47] *See* § 12.09, *infra* (new trial motions).

[48] That is, when the trial judge grants the motion for new trial unless the opposing party agrees to a reduction (remittitur) of the verdict. *See* § 12.09(2)(b), *infra*.

[49] *E.g.*, *Abrams v. Lightolier*, 841 F.Supp. 584 (D.C.N.J. 1994). For additional cases, *see* Wright & Miller, § 2807 n.7.

[50] N.Y. Civ. Prac. L. & R. 5501(c).

[51] Had Rule 59 itself provided the federal-law standard, any conflicting state law would have given way as a result of Rules Enabling Act analysis. *See* § 7.04, *infra*.

[52] 518 U.S. at 429.

[53] Freer, *The State of Erie After Gasperini*, 76 Tex. L. Rev. 1637, 1641 (1998). Also, *see* Rowe, *Not Bad for Government Work: Does Anyone Else Think the Supreme Court is Doing a Halfway Decent Job in its Erie-Hanna Jurisprudence?*, 73 Notre Dame L. Rev. 963 (1998); Floyd, *Eries Awry: A Comment on Gasperini v. Center for Humanities, Inc*, 1997 BYU L. Rev. 267.

sufficient to account for most or all of the Court's actual work under the *Byrd* branch of the *Erie* doctrine.[54] There is, however, the specter of cases even more taxing, those where *both* a state and the federal government would be interested in having their conflicting rules applied.[55]

Yet it would exaggerate the difficulty of the *Erie* doctrine to assume that the *Byrd* test need be applied in every case. Actually, all three tests that we have considered — substance-versus-procedure, modified outcome-determination, and the assessment of state and federal interests — have some role in contemporary analysis. It is only those cases that cannot be decided by one of the first two tests that require resort to *Byrd*-type interest assessment.

The substance-versus-procedure test serves as a first-stage screening device in modern *Erie* analysis. It is true that the words of the test still carry a stigma from their unsympathetic reception in *York*.[56] It is also true that the closer the *Erie* question, the more unreliable the substance-versus-procedure distinction becomes. For all that, however, the difference between substance and procedure, between the body of "rules which define legal rights" and rules "structuring and regulating the judicial process"[57] retains

---

[54] The opposing results in two cases illustrate the point. The Supreme Court seemed to question in *Byrd* whether South Carolina was much if at all interested in application of its no-jury rule. Since the interests behind the federal jury rule were strongly implicated by the case (*see* § 7.03[3], note 13 and related text, *supra*), *Byrd* directed choice of the federal rule. In *Walker v. Armco Steel Corp.*, 446 U.S. 740 (1980), the situation was reversed and the Supreme Court therefore applied state law. Policies behind the Oklahoma state statute of limitations were at stake in the case and no federal interest supported a refusal to treat the action as time-barred. The Court concluded:

> There is simply no reason why . . . an action based on state law which concededly would be barred in the state courts by the state statute of limitations should proceed through litigation to judgment in federal court solely because of the fortuity that there is diversity of citizenship between litigants. The policies underlying diversity jurisdiction do not support such a distinction between state and federal plaintiffs, and *Erie* and its progeny do not permit it.

Id. at 753.

[55] Difficulties in determining whether law sources are interested and, if two or more are, which law to choose, are also at the center of modern choice-of-law analysis. Shreve, *Conflicts Law — State or Federal?*, 68 Ind. L.J. 907 (1993); E. Scoles & P. Hay, *Conflict of Laws* ch. 3 (3d ed. 2000); Shreve, *Teaching Conflicts, Improving the Odds*, 90 Mich. L. Rev. 1672, 1673-1675 (1992). The main difference between mainstream choice-of-law cases and those under the *Erie* doctrine is that sovereigns providing conflicting laws in the former are roughly co-equal, *e.g.*, a conflict between New York and Colorado. Yet the parallel is stronger than one might think. A federal diversity judge using *Byrd*'s interest analysis might give federal law the nod when both federal and state sources are interested; similarly, state judges are free under the Constitution to favor their own law over that of a sister state when both states are interested. *See* Weinberg, *Choice of Law and Minimal Scrutiny*, 49 U. Chi. L. Rev. 440 (1982); Shreve, *Interest Analysis as Constitutional Law*, 48 Ohio St. L.J. 51 (1987).

[56] *See* § 7.03[1], *supra*.

[57] Note, *The Law Applied in Diversity Cases: The Rules of Decision Act and the Erie Doctrine*, 85 Yale L.J. 678, 696 (1976).

importance under the Rules of Decision Act.[58] In many cases, application of the distinction is all that will be necessary to resolve the *Erie* issue.[59]

Some cases eluding treatment under a substance-versus-procedure test will be appropriate for decision under the modified outcome-determination test. This test will suffice for statute of limitations problems, as in *York,* where the state law is not grounded entirely on substantive or procedural policies but instead derives from both.[60] Absent compelling circumstances for applying the federal rule, the modified outcome-determination test should advance state law when that law serves substantive interests at least in part. The *Byrd* interest assessment test is available as a last resort, when state substantive policies become more difficult to discern, or when policies supporting federal law approach overriding importance.

Functionally, the three tests can be linked as follows. Substance-versus-procedure marked the initial boundaries of the *Erie* doctrine and remains an easy and useful means for demonstrating why law made possible through exercise of federal diversity jurisdiction cannot displace state law created to advance substantive interests. The modified outcome-determination test recognizes that a state law which is both substantive and procedural in purpose should be honored under *Erie* whenever possible, because of its substantive dimension. *Byrd*'s interest assessment test requires more precise calibration of the substantive state interests and the procedural federal interests underlying the competing rules. It can lead (as in *Byrd*) to nullification of the result of the outcome-determination test and application of federal law.

It is useful to remember that, for all their quirks, the cases making up the *Erie* doctrine have never strayed far from the notions of reason and justice central to *Erie* itself. When a federal diversity judge makes victory possible for a plaintiff who could not have won in state court, that judge must be saying to the defendant: "You lost because you and the plaintiff live in different states." That is an unacceptable reason for choosing winners and losers in our legal system. It is unacceptable because it is substantively grotesque to use the accident of diversity to shrink or swell rights, because it blocks the legitimate efforts of states to regulate local conduct through substantive laws, and because forum shopping would exacerbate these evils and hold federal courts up to ridicule.

---

[58] The substance-procedure distinction continues to command attention in commentary on the *Erie* doctrine. *E.g.,* Stein, *Erie and Court Access,* 100 Yale L. J. 1935, 1942-1946 (1991); Freer, *Erie's Mid-Life Crisis,* 63 Tul. L.R. 1087, 1131-1134 (1989); Gelfand & Abrams, *Putting Erie on the Right Track,* 49 U. Pitt. L. Rev. 937, 958-964 (1988).

[59] For example, in *Stineman v. Fontbonne College,* 664 F.2d 1082 (8th Cir. 1981), the Eighth Circuit held that a federal diversity judge was required to follow state law to decide whether damages in a tort action were excessive, but was not required to follow state law requiring that instructions be given to the jury in writing. The first issue was clearly substantive, and the second clearly procedural.

[60] *Cf. Walker v. Armco Steel Corp.,* 446 U.S. 740, 751 (1980) (referring to Oklahoma law defining its statute of limitation as "a statement of a substantive decision by that State").

§ 7.04 State Law Versus the Federal Rules of Civil Procedure — The Importance of the Rules Enabling Act

[1] Early Uncertainty

The Federal Rules of Civil Procedure were promulgated in 1938, the same year in which *Erie* was decided. The new rules promised sweeping reforms.[61] The emerging *Erie* doctrine, however, was to cast a shadow over their operation in diversity cases.

York and the outcome-determination cases which followed it appeared to suggest that state law controlled whenever the outcome of a diversity case might conceivably be affected by the choice of state, as opposed to federal law.[62] In two post-*York* cases, the Supreme Court invoked the outcome-determination test in refusing to apply a Federal Rule of Civil Procedure. In *Ragan v. Merchants Transfer & Warehouse Co.*,[63] the Court used the Kansas rule that suit commenced with service of process to conclude that plaintiff failed to sue within the time permitted by Kansas' statute of limitations. Plaintiff unsuccessfully argued that the definition of commencement contained in Federal Rule 3 should govern.[64] In *Cohen v. Beneficial Industrial Loan Corp.*,[65] the Supreme Court imposed a New Jersey requirement that plaintiff in a stockholder's derivative suit must post a bond. The Court rejected plaintiff's argument that federal Rule 23.1, which did not require a bond, should govern.

These cases led many observers to fear that the Federal Rules of Civil Procedure would be thwarted in diversity cases, unless they coincided with state law. The Supreme Court eventually put these fears to rest in *Hanna v. Plumer.*[66]

---

[61] On the effect of the Federal Rules of Civil Procedure on existing practice, see *Wright* § 62; Bone, *Mapping the Boundaries of a Dispute: Conceptions of Ideal Lawsuit Structure From the Field Code to the Federal Rules*, 89 Colum. L. Rev. 1 (1989); Subrin, *How Equity Conquered Common Law: The Federal Rules of Civil Procedure in Historical Perspective*, 135 U. Pa. L. Rev. 909 (1987). For contemporary assessments of the Rules, see *Symposium, The 50th Anniversary of the Federal Rules of Civil Procedure, 1938-1988*, 137 U. Pa. L. Rev. 1874 (1989); *Symposium, The Fiftieth Anniversary of the Federal Rules of Civil Procedure*, 63 Notre Dame L. Rev. 597 (1988).

[62] *See* § 7.03[2], *supra.*

[63] 337 U.S. 530 (1949).

[64] Rule 3 states that "[a] civil action is commenced by filing a complaint with the court." Plaintiff filed his action within the applicable limitations period, but served the complaint after it had run. Regarding statutes of limitations generally, see § 8.02[2][b], *infra.*

[65] 337 U.S. 541 (1949).

[66] 380 U.S. 460 (1965). *See generally* McCoid, *Hanna v. Plummer: The Erie Doctrine Changes Shape*, 51 Va. L. Rev. 884 (1965).

[2]   *Hanna, Walker* and *Woods*: The Resilience of Federal Rules of Procedure

Hanna seems to rest on alternative holdings. We have already seen how the first holding, that *Erie* did not require the application of state law, was notable because it softened the outcome-determination test.[67]

The second holding, that *Erie* did not even apply, bolstered the authority of the Federal Rules of Civil Procedure in diversity cases. The Supreme Court called "incorrect" the "assumption that the rule of *Erie* constitutes the appropriate test of the validity and therefore the applicability of a Federal Rule of Civil Procedure."[68] The *Hanna* Court found Rule 4(d)(1) valid because it "neither exceeded the congressional mandate embodied in the Rules Enabling Act[69] nor transgressed constitutional bounds."[70] Since the rule answered the service question in *Hanna,* Massachusetts state law had to give way.

The majority did not fully explain its reasoning, but the message conveyed by the Court's opinion in *Hanna* was clear. When challenged under *Erie,* federal rules of procedure were to receive different and more protective treatment than that given to other federal doctrine. The Court stated that the constitutional authority to make a federal court system, augmented by the Necessary and Proper Clause of the United States Constitution,

> carries with it congressional power to make rules governing the practice and pleading in those courts, which in turn includes a power to regulate matters which, though falling within the uncertain area between substance and procedure, are rationally capable of classification as either.[71]

Compared to the "relatively unguided *Erie* choice"[72] used when neither a federal statute nor rule of procedure is involved, the approach of the majority in *Hanna* seemed simple and direct. An applicable Federal Rule of Civil Procedure controls, so long as it is constitutional and complies with the Rules Enabling Act.[73]

In 1980, the Supreme Court again considered whether state law or a Federal Rule of Civil Procedure should apply in a diversity case, this time deciding in favor of state law. In *Walker v. Armco Steel Corp.,*[74] plaintiff sued for injuries he received while using defendant's product. Relying on the definition of commencement found in federal Rule 3, plaintiff argued

---

[67] *See* § 7.03[4], *supra.*

[68] 380 U.S. at 469-470.

[69] 28 U.S.C. § 2072. On the process of rule creation and revision under the Rules Enabling Act, see note 104, *infra,* and § 1.02, *supra.*

[70] 380 U.S. at 464.

[71] *Id.* at 472.

[72] *Id.* at 471.

[73] 28 U.S.C. § 2072. For extended discussion of developments under the Act, see Moore, *The Supreme Court's Role in Interpreting the Federal Rules of Civil Procedure,* 44 Hast. L. J. 1039, 1041-1053 (1993); Burbank, *The Rules Enabling Act of 1934,* 130 U. Pa. L. Rev. 1015 (1982).

[74] 446 U.S. 740 (1980).

that he had filed suit within the Oklahoma statute of limitations. The defendant argued that *Erie* required the court to follow the Oklahoma law defining commencement as service of process, and that service of process had not been made within the limitations period. The defendant relied on the Court's decision in *Ragan v. Merchant's Transfer & Warehouse Co.*[75] While *Ragan* appeared indistinguishable, plaintiff's argument proceeded on the assumption — shared by many observers — that *Ragan* had been weakened, if not overruled, by *Hanna v. Plumer.*

The Supreme Court did not agree. It refused to apply the Rules Enabling Act approach it announced in *Hanna* because it found "no direct conflict between the Federal Rule and the state law."[76] For there to be a conflict, refusal to apply Rule 3 would have to thwart some purpose the federal rule was intended to achieve. This did not happen in *Walker,* since "Rule 3 governs the date from which various timing requirements of the Federal Rules begin to run,[77] but does not affect state statutes of limitations."[78]

Walker is a useful reminder that favored treatment for federal procedural rules under the Rules Enabling Act is only appropriate *when the rules apply*. Because Rule 3 did not bear on the case, "the *Hanna* analysis does not apply. Instead, the policies behind *Erie* . . . control the issue. . . ."[79] This permitted the substantive purpose behind Oklahoma's definition of commencement to become more of a factor in the decision.[80] The choice of Oklahoma law became clear once *Erie* and the Rules of Decision Act came into play.[81]

> There is simply no reason why, in the absence of a controlling federal rule, an action based on state law which concededly would be barred in the state courts by the state statute of limitations should proceed through litigation to judgment in federal court solely because of the fortuity that there is diversity of citizenship between the litigants.[82]

The case settled the question whether Rule 3 has any effect on state statute of limitations questions.[83]

---

[75] *See* note 63 and accompanying text, *supra*.

[76] *Walker,* 446 U.S. at 752. But Rule 3 probably would be used to measure commencement within the running of the statute of limitations had the case rested on the court's federal question jurisdiction. *See Henderson v. United States,* 517 U.S. 654, 657 (1990).

[77] The Court presumably had in mind the use of Rule 3's definition of commencement for timing requirements contained in such rules as 13(a), 14(a), 30(a), 31(a) and 33(a).

[78] *Walker,* 446 U.S. at 751.

[79] *Id.* at 752.

[80] The Court noted that "the Oklahoma statute is a statement of a substantive decision by that State that actual service on, and accordingly actual notice by, the defendant is an integral part of the several policies served by the statute of limitations." *Id.* at 751. It read Oklahoma law to have substantially the same statute-of-imitations effect as Kansas law did in *Ragan;* therefore, *Walker* followed *Ragan* in holding plaintiff's claim to be time-barred.

[81] For more on the relationship between the Rules of Decision Act and the Rules Enabling Act, *see* § 7.04[3][b], *infra*.

[82] 446 U.S. at 753.

[83] *See, e.g., Cambridge Mutual Fire Ins. Co. v. City of Claxton,* 720 F.2d 1230 (11th Cir.

Although *Walker* applied state law, it accepted the principle announced in *Hanna* that validly enacted and properly applied Federal Rules of Civil Procedure control. This raises the possibility that, no matter how substantive applicable state law may be in such cases, the *Erie* doctrine offers it no protection.

The Supreme Court did nothing to negate this suggestion in a later decision, *Burlington Northern Ry. v. Woods.* [84] *Woods* presented the Court with a choice between Federal Rule of Appellate Procedure 38 (giving federal courts of appeal discretion to award damages for frivolous appeals) and Alabama state law (making damages in such cases mandatory). Unlike *Walker,* the Court found the federal rule applicable. Faced with a "direct collision" between the federal and state rules, the *Woods* Court returned to the two-part test it used in *Hanna.* Because the issue before the court was within the scope of Federal Rule 38, that rule "must . . . be applied if it represents a valid exercise of Congress' rule-making authority, which originates in the Constitution and has been bestowed on this Court by the Rules Enabling Act. . . ." [85]

Beginning with the constitutional phase of its test, the Court noted that "constitutional constraints on the exercise of this rulemaking authority define a test of reasonableness . . .," and that "[r]ules regulating matters indisputably procedural are *a priori* constitutional." [86] The Court seemed to see no constitutional problem in the fact that damage to state substantive interests might occur in the process. Quoting *Hanna,* it observed, "Rules regulating matters which, though falling within the uncertain area between substance and procedure, are rationally capable of classification as either, also satisfy this constitutional standard." [87]

Turning to the Rules Enabling Act, it interpreted the Act's limitation that federal rules "shall not abridge, enlarge or modify any substantive right. . . ."

> The cardinal purpose of Congress in authorizing the development of a uniform and consistent system of rules governing federal practice and procedure suggests that *rules which incidentally* affect litigants' substantive rights do not violate this provision if reasonably necessary to maintain the integrity of that system of rules. [88]

1983) (use of Rule 3 to enlarge the Georgia statute of limitations refused upon the authority of *Walker*). Applications of the *Walker* case are confined to exercises of federal diversity jurisdiction. When plaintiff's claim is based on federal law, "the action is not barred if it has been 'commenced' in compliance with Rule 3 within the . . . [limitations] period." *West v. Conrail,* 481 U.S. 35, 39 (1987).

[84] 480 U.S. 1 (1987). For discussions of the case, see Whitten, *Erie and the Federal Rules: A Review and Reappraisal After Burlington Northern Railroad v. Woods,* 21 Creighton L. Rev. (1987); Saunders, *Plying the Erie Waters: Choice of Law in the Deterrence of Frivolous Appeals,* 21 Ga. L. Rev. 653 (1987).

[85] 480 U.S. at 5.

[86] *Id.*

[87] *Id.*

[88] *Id.* (emphasis added). *Cf. Business Guides v. Chromatic Communications Ent.*, 498 U.S 533, 552 (1991) ("There is little doubt that Rule 11 is reasonably necessary to maintain the integrity of the system of federal practice and procedure, and that any effect on substantive rights is incidental.").

Note that the key word in this test is "incidental" — not "insignificant." This suggests that any impact upon state substantive interests (no matter how serious) is tolerable, so long it is a byproduct of (incidental to) advancement of a federal procedural policy. Thus, at both the constitutional and Rules Enabling Act levels, the *Woods* Court seems to accept disruption of state substantive interests, so long as application of federal law would advance clear procedural interests.

[3] Modern Analysis

[a] Matters "Procedural" Within the Meaning of the Rules Enabling Act

Rules validated as properly procedural in *Hanna* (service of process) and in *Woods* (regulation of frivolous appeals) are but some of those protected by the Rules Enabling Act.[89] Recall the Court's description in *Woods* of congressional intent in the Rules Enabling Act to create "a uniform and consistent system of rules governing federal practice and procedure." Consider the purpose of the Federal Rules of Civil Procedure "to secure the just, speedy, and inexpensive determination of every action."[90] The breadth of such mandates suggests that a rule regulating any aspect of judicial administration is probably procedural within the meaning of the Rules Enabling Act.

To illustrate, note that the Supreme Court's refusal to follow a federal rule in *Walker* was based on the conclusion that the particular federal rule had no application concerning statutes of limitation.[91] *Walker* did not say that a Federal Rule of Civil Procedure was incapable of nullifying a state statute of limitations in diversity cases. Rule 15(c) in fact does just that, allowing plaintiff under certain circumstances to amend her complaint by claiming against a new defendant, even though the statute of limitations[92] has run since the suit was originally filed.[93] This "relation-back" feature of Federal Rule 15[94] reflects a strong procedural policy favoring liberal pleading.[95] State law in direct collision with Rule 15(c) has thus given way in diversity cases.[96]

---

[89] The Supreme Court recently invoked *Woods* and *Hanna* to give broad application to Rule 11. *Business Guides v. Chromatic Communications Ent.*, 498 U.S. 533 (1991). In *Business Guides*, a diversity case, the Court read Rule 11 to impose a form of liability on represented parties that did not exist under state law.

[90] Rule 1.

[91] *See* § 7.04[2], *supra.*

[92] On statutes of limitations generally, see § 8.08[2][b], *infra.*

[93] *See generally* § 8.10[3][b] (relation back of amendments changing parties), *infra.*

[94] See § 8.10[3], *infra.*

[95] *Id.*

[96] "Application of Rule 15(c) will mean in some instances that the action can go forward against the new defendant even though in state court he would have a good defense of limitations. In this situation the courts have uniformly held . . . that Rule 15(c) can be applied and that to do so does not violate the substantive rights' proviso of the Enabling Act." *Wright* § 59.

[b] The Relationship Between the Rules Enabling Act and the Rules of Decision Act

Subsequent cases have confirmed Professor Ely's distinction:

[W]here there is no relevant Federal Rule of Civil Procedure or other Rule promulgated pursuant to the Enabling Act and the federal rule in issue is therefore wholly judge-made, whether state or federal law should be applied is controlled by the Rules of Decision Act, the statute construed in *Erie* and *York*. Where the matter in issue is covered by a Federal Rule, however, the Enabling Act — and not the Rules of Decision Act itself or the line of cases construing it — constitutes the relevant standard.[97]

This distinction can alter the choice between state and federal law. For example, consider what would happen if the relation-back principle was not embedded in Rule 15(c), as discussed above,[98] but instead derived from federal judicial doctrine. Because the Rules Enabling Act would then be inapplicable, it would not insulate federal law from scrutiny under the Rules of Decision Act. Enforcement of the Rules of Decision Act through the *Erie* doctrine would likely lead to the choice of state over federal law.[99]

State substantive interests clearly receive less respect under the Rules Enabling Act approach of *Hanna* and *Woods* than they would under the *Erie* doctrine and the Rules of Decision Act. Some have questioned this discrepancy, suggesting a role for *Erie* and the Rules of Decision Act even when federal diversity courts are presented with applicable and valid rules of procedure.[100] More basically, the language of the Rules Enabling Act simply fails to support the conclusion that federal rules of procedure fare better against state law than does judge-made federal law. On the contrary, the provision in the Act denying federal rules authority to "abridge . . . any substantive right. . . ." would seem to vindicate substantive state interests even at the sacrifice of federal procedural objectives.[101]

But cf. Douglas v. NCNB Texas Nat'l Bank, 979 F.2d 1128, 1130 (5th Cir. 1992). Invoking the substantive abridgement clause of § 2072, *Douglas* refused to give effect to the compulsory counterclaim requirement of Rule 13(a). Texas state law made clear that a secured lender's opportunity to recover could not be cut off through preclusion by rule. "Application of rule 13(a)", stated the court, "would abridge the lender's substantive rights and enlarge the debtor's substantive rights." While the case involves a different federal rule, the position on § 2072 taken in *Douglas* is difficult to reconcile with the Rule 15(c) cases surveyed by Professor Wright.

[97] Ely, *The Irrepressible Myth of Erie,* 87 Harv. L. Rev. 693, 698 (1974).

[98] *See* § 7.04[3][a], *supra* (state statutes of limitation yield to the relation-back principle in Rule 15(c)).

[99] Defendant need merely demonstrate that the state statute of limitations functions at least in part to secure substantive policies. The Court in *Walker* enforced a state statute of limitations upon such a showing, once it concluded that the federal rules did not require the result sought by plaintiff.

[100] *See, e.g.,* Justice Harlan's concurrence in *Hanna,* entertaining the possibility that "*Erie* and the Constitution" might "require that the state rule prevail, even in the face of a conflicting federal rule." 380 U.S. at 475; Redish & Phillips, *Erie and the Rules of Decision Act: In Search of the Appropriate Dilemma,* 91 Harv. L. Rev. 356 (1977) (advocating an interest-weighing approach for *Hanna*).

[101] Despite its apparent clarity, this passage of the Rules Enabling Act "has been a source

Nevertheless, the Supreme Court reads the Act differently, vindicating federal procedural objectives even at the sacrifice of state substantive interests.[102] The position taken by the Court is not altogether surprising. It is natural for the Court to be concerned about the resilience of procedural law governing federal litigation.[103] Moreover, the Rules Enabling Act assigns to the Supreme Court a major role in the creation of most rules. The Court must give serious thought — albeit in the abstract — to the constitutionality and Rules Enabling Act validity of rules before it transmits them to Congress for final approval.[104] All this may explain why the Supreme Court has never invoked the abridging-substance limitation of the Act to deny effect to a Federal Rule of Civil Procedure.[105]

§ 7.05 Which State's Law?

[1] The Conflict-of-Laws Problem

When the parties come from different states or when facts creating the controversy occur in more than one state, the source of governing law may

---

of substantial controversy in the courts and among commentators over the years." Moore, note 73, *supra*, at 1042. Thus, while there is much support in the literature for the view that "Congress' concern in formulating the procedure/substance dichotomy was the preservation of an enclave of state law in diversity cases," *Burbank,* note 73, *supra,* at 1110, Burbank himself disagrees. He argues that the purpose of the dichotomy was to protect laws made by Congress from abridgment through court-generated rulemaking. *Id.* at 1122-1123. For more on substantive-abridgement provision of the Rules Enabling Act, *see* Kelleher, *Taking "Substantial Rights" (in the Rules Enabling Act) More Seriously*, 74 Notre Dame L. Rev. 47 (1998); Carrington, *Substance and Procedure in the Rules Enabling Act*, 1989 Duke L. J. 281 (1989).

[102] *See* note 88 and related text, *supra.*

[103] To give as much play to state substantive interests as the language of the Act suggests would create considerable uncertainty over application of federal rules of procedure in diversity cases. *Cf. Ely,* note 98, *supra,* at 698 ("The Court has correctly sensed that [the Enabling Act] cannot be construed to protect state prerogatives as strenuously as the Rules of Decision Act protects them in the absence of a Federal Rule."). *But see Whitten,* note 84, *supra,* at 42 (criticizing the approach of Court and concluding: "the one constant in the Court's decisions dealing with Federal Rules-state law conflicts . . . has been its refusal to provide significant content to the Act's substantive rights restriction."); Kelleher, *Amenability to Jurisdiction as a "Substantive Right": The Invalidity of Rule 4(k) Under the Rules Enabling Act*, 75 Ind. L.J. 1191 (2000).

[104] "[T]he recommendations of the [Judicial] Conference pass to the Court; any rule changes finally adopted by the Court are laid on the tables of Congress in accordance with the Rules Enabling Act." Kaplan, *Amendments of the Federal Rules of Civil Procedure, 1961-63 (I)*, 77 Harv. L. Rev. 601, 602 (1964). *See generally* § 1.02 (the federal rulemaking process), *supra.*

[105] As the Court observed recently, one challenging a federal rule under the Rules Enabling Act "has a large hurdle to get over." *Business Guides v. Chromatic Communications Ent.*, 498 U.S. 533, 552 (1991). That hurdle has proven insurmountable in cases before the United States Supreme Court. Perhaps the closest a challenge came to succeeding was in *Sibbach v. Wilson & Co., Inc.,* 312 U.S. 1 (1941). The Court ruled 5 to 4 there that (notwithstanding the substantive-abridgement provision of the Rules Enabling Act) state law protecting litigants from physical examinations had to yield to federal discovery Rule 35. Three justices who dissented in *Business Guides* raised the substantive-abridgment provision to argue for a narrower interpretation of Rule 11, but they reserved opinion "[w]hether or not Rule 11 as construed by the majority exceeds our rule-making authority. . . ." 498 U.S. at 568.

become one of the issues in the case. This happens when laws of different states appear to produce contradictory results. For example, the same facts may make defendant liable to plaintiff under the law of New York but not under the law of California.

The variety of approaches courts use to resolve conflicts can lead to differences in the law chosen.[106] It thus becomes important to determine which body of choice-of-law rules apply to resolve a given conflict. State courts usually apply their own common law rules. Federal courts apply their own conflicts law in federal question cases.[107] Prior to *Erie*, federal conflicts doctrine governed in diversity cases as well. That changed with *Klaxon Co. v. Stentor Electric Mfg.*,[108] in which the Supreme Court extended the *Erie* principle to conflicts.

[2]　The *Klaxon* Rule

Klaxon ended brief uncertainty whether federal conflicts doctrine was still available to federal courts sitting in diversity or was part of the federal general common law that *Erie* invalidated.[109] Ruling it to be the latter, *Klaxon* required federal diversity courts to administer the conflicts law of the states in which they were sitting ("forum states"). Reasoning from *Erie*, *Klaxon* held that a plaintiff should not be permitted to use federal diversity jurisdiction to obtain a more favorable conflicts law.

The *Klaxon* rule has been both criticized and defended.[110] Critics note that it forces federal judges to use a kind of state law (conflicts doctrine) that is particularly difficult to fathom[111] and that it imported local state bias into federal court decision-making.[112] Nonetheless, conflicts rules do

---

[106] For surveys of approaches currently in use, *see* E. Scoles & P. Hay, *Conflict of Laws* §§ 2.18-2.25 (3d ed. 2000); Kay, *Theory into Practice: Choice of Law in the Courts*, 34 Mercer L. Rev. 521 (1983); Shreve, *In Search of a Choice-of-Law Reviewing Standard—Reflections on Allstate Insurance Co. v. Hague*, 66 Minn. L. Rev. 327, 341-344 (1982). *See also* § 7.03[6], *supra* (comparing the choice-of-law process with certain applications of the *Erie* doctrine).

[107] *E.g., United States v. Little Lake Misere Land Co.*, 412 U.S. 580 (1973); *Siegelman v. Cunard White Star, Ltd.*, 221 F.2d 189 (2nd Cir. 1955).

[108] 313 U.S. 487 (1941).

[109] *See* § 7.02[2], *supra*.

[110] *Compare* R. Bridwell & R. Whitten, *The Constitution and the Common Law: The Decline of the Doctrines of Separation of Powers and Federalism* 135 (1977), and the authorities appearing in *Wright* § 57 (attacking *Klaxon*), *with* Cavers, *The Changing Choice-of-Law Process and the Federal Courts*, 28 Law & Contemp. Probs. 732 (1963); American Law Institute, *Study of the Division of Jurisdiction of State and Federal Courts* 379 n.7 (1969) (defending *Klaxon*). *Cf.* Maltz, *Choice of Forum and Choice of Law in the Federal Courts: A Reconsideration of Erie Principles*, 79 Ky. L.J. 231 (1990-91) (*Klaxon* defensible when decided but incompatible with modern conflicts doctrine).

[111] Ascertaining state law when the same is "confused or nonexistent" is a chronic problem in administering the *Erie* doctrine. Clark, *State Law in the Federal Courts: The Brooding Omnipresence of Erie v. Tompkins*, 55 Yale L.J. 267, 290 (1946). *See generally* § 7.06, *infra*. The problem is especially great in ascertaining state conflicts law under *Klaxon*, due in part to the innate difficulty of conflicts doctrine. *Cf.* Rheinstein, *How to Review a Festschrift*, 11 Am. J. Comp. L. 632, 655 (1962) (calling conflicts the "most difficult and most confused of all branches of the law").

[112] "At bottom, the argument that federal courts should always apply their own conflict

determine the content of *substantive* law governing the case. It would therefore seem outcome-determinative [113] in the clearest, forum-shopping sense for federal diversity courts to be able to declare a different winner by choosing different law. The Supreme Court has since reaffirmed the *Klaxon* rule in *Day & Zimmerman, Inc. v. Challoner.* [114]

[3] *Klaxon* and § 1404(a)

We will consider the interplay of *Klaxon* and federal change-of-venue law with the aid of an example. A New York plaintiff files a federal diversity action in New York against a California defendant. The case is transferred under § 1404(a) [115] to a federal diversity court in California. Assume that applicable tort laws from New York and California conflict. Assume further that New York conflicts doctrine would require application of New York tort law, while California conflicts doctrine would require California tort law. Does the state conflicts law of the transferor forum (New York) or that of the transferee forum (California) govern? Current law reads *Erie, Klaxon,* and § 1404(a) to require the governing state conflicts doctrine to be that of the transferor forum (New York). As the Supreme Court stated in a leading case, *Van Dusen v. Barrack,*

> . . . the transferee district court must be obligated to apply the state law that would have been applied if there had been no change of venue. A change of venue under § 1404(a) generally should be, with respect to state law, but a change of courtrooms. [116]

Van Dusen left open the question whether the same rule applied to actions which, if originally filed in state court, would have been dismissed there [117] on *forum non conveniens* grounds. [118] Some lower federal courts have applied the rule in such cases. [119] Yet to do so may actually frustrate *Erie* by permitting plaintiffs to use federal diversity jurisdiction to shop for favorable substantive law. Two points explain this.

First, it is useful to understand why plaintiff might want to shop for conflicts doctrine. Return to the example. Assume that the New York

---

rules assumes that federal courts, being by nature less parochial than the courts of the state in which they are sitting, will be far more likely to evolve better choice-of-law rules. . . ." R. Weintraub, *Commentary on the Conflict of Laws* 592 (3d ed. 1986).

[113] On the contemporary use of the outcome-determination test, *see* § 7.03[6], *supra.*

[114] 423 U.S. 3 (1975).

[115] For a discussion of the federal change-of-venue statute, 28 U.S.C. § 1404(a), *see* § 6.02[2] *supra.* The focus here will be on § 1404(a) transfers in diversity cases, although the statute governs transfer of cases under other forms of federal subject matter jurisdiction.

[116] 376 U.S. 612, 639 (1964). The Court applied the rule to " 'ensure that the accident' of federal diversity jurisdiction does not enable a party to utilize a transfer to achieve a result in federal court which could not have been achieved in the courts of the State where the action was filed." *Id.* at 638 (quoting *York*). The Supreme Court reiterated the *Van Dusen* rule and rationale in *Ferens v. John Deere Co.,* 494 U.S. 516 (1990).

[117] *Id.* at 640.

[118] On the doctrine generally, *see* § 6.02[1], *supra.*

[119] *See, e.g., In re Korean Air Lines Disaster of September 1, 1983,* 664 F. Supp. 1478 (D.D.C. 1986); *In re Air Crash Disaster at Boston, Mass.,* 399 F. Supp. 1106 (D. Mass. 1975).

plaintiff wants New York tort law applied because it is easier to recover under that law. The plaintiff also wants New York's own state conflicts doctrine to be used because that doctrine happens to use litigant citizenship as a tool for choosing law and would permit plaintiff to use his New York citizenship to obtain application of New York tort law.[120]

Second, the *Erie* problem arises if our plaintiff is unable to obtain application of New York conflicts doctrine (and hence favorable New York substantive law) in any state court but is able to obtain New York conflicts doctrine in a federal diversity case originating in New York and transferred to California. To understand how state *forum non conveniens* doctrine can bring this about, note that our plaintiff can file his case in one of four courts: (1) a state or (2) federal diversity court in New York, or (3) a state or (4) federal diversity court in California.

Assume that plaintiff begins with option (1). New York state courts lack authority to transfer cases to the docket of another court system; therefore, if plaintiff runs afoul of New York state *forum non conveniens* doctrine, his New York state case would simply be dismissed without prejudice. Naturally, plaintiff in this situation would not last long enough in New York state court to benefit from favorable New York tort law.

If plaintiff files (or refiles) the same case in California state court, the suit would be governed by California conflicts law. California conflicts law will also govern if plaintiff files (or refiles) in California federal district court — this time under *Klaxon*'s directive.

Only through strategic use of the *Van Dusen* rule could our plaintiff sidestep the application of California conflicts doctrine. Plaintiff's route would be to begin with a federal diversity action in New York, and then either finesse defendant into seeking a § 1404(a) transfer or move for one himself.[121] In short, rigid application of *Van Dusen*'s requirement that conflicts law of the transferor forum governs would permit plaintiff to exploit the availability of diversity jurisdiction in New York to alter eventual decision on the merits in California.

Commentators have urged more sensitivity in determining whether transferor or transferee law should be applied regarding § 1404(a) transfers.[122] Federal courts should at least have flexibility to choose transferee

---

[120] For an illustrative New York case, *see Tooker v. Lopez*, 249 N.E.2d 394 (N.Y. 1969). The practice has been criticized, Ely, *Choice of Law and the State's Interest in Protecting Its Own*, 23 Wm. & Mary L. Rev. 173 (1981). But it is constitutional (and common) for a state to advance through its conflicts law the object that its citizens be compensated. For discussion how and why this controversial principle dominates modern conflicts doctrine, see Shreve, *Conflicts Law — State or Federal?*, 68 Ind. L.J. 907 (1993).

[121] In *Ferens v. John Deere Co.*, 494 U.S. 516 (1990), the Supreme Court required application of the conflicts law of the transferor forum even though plaintiff initiated the transfer. Thus, "the legal system allowed the plaintiffs to shop for Mississippi law. . . ." Brown, *The Ideologies of Forum Shopping —Why Doesn't A Conservative Court Protect Defendants?*, 71 N.C. L. Rev. 649, 655 (1993).

[122] Comment, *Is 28 U.S.C. § 1404(a) a Federal Forum-Shopping Statute?*, 66 Wash. L. Rev. 851 (1991); Comment, *The Plaintiff's Forum Shopping Gold Card: Choice of Law in Federal Courts After Transfer of Venue Under § 1404(a) — Ferens v. John Deere Co.*, 26 Wake Forest L. Rev. 809 (1991); *Scoles & Hay*, note 106, *supra*, at § 3.46; *Maltz*, note 110, *supra*.

over transferor law in situations where plaintiff uses federal diversity jurisdiction to orchestrate a choice-of-law result. The Supreme Court's decision in *Ferens v. John Deere Co.,*[123] however, does not support a flexible approach. Plaintiffs there filed in a federal forum (Mississippi) where apparently they never intended to litigate. Rather, plaintiffs moved successfully under § 1404(a) for transfer to a Pennsylvania federal court and sought to use Mississippi (transferor) law to maintain an action barred under Pennsylvania (transferee) law. The Supreme Court followed its *Van Dusen* rule and rewarded plaintiffs with Mississippi law. The dissent observed,

> one must be blind to reality to say that it is the *Mississippi* federal court in which these plaintiffs have chosen to sue. That was merely a way station in route to suit in the Pennsylvania federal court. The plaintiffs were seeking to achieve exactly what Klaxon was designed to prevent: the use of a Pennsylvania federal court instead of a Pennsylvania state court in order to obtain application of a different substantive law.[124]

§ 7.06 Ascertaining the Content of State Law

[1] The Elusive Model of the Highest State Court

State law controlling in federal court under *Erie*[125] must be determined and applied as it would have been if the case had, instead, been adjudicated by the highest state court whose law is being applied. This rule reflects the fact that the ultimate authority on the meaning of state law is the state's highest court,[126] just as the United States Supreme Court is the ultimate authority on the meaning of federal law.

The problem is that a federal diversity court may not know how a state high court would rule on the case at hand because it is often impossible or impracticable for federal judges to certify state law questions to state courts in order to find out.[127] This leaves federal courts in an awkward

---

[123] 494 U.S. 516 (1990).

[124] 494 U.S. at 535.

[125] The process for determining state law discussed in this section also applies in federal court searches for the meaning of state laws that are not required under *Erie*. For examples, *see* § 7.07, *infra*.

[126] The principle is well-established. *E.g., Exxon Corp. v. Eagerton,* 462 U.S. 176, 181 n.3 (1983); *Commissioner v. Estate of Bosch,* 387 U.S. 456, 465 (1967). *See generally* Caron, *The Role of State Court Decisions in Federal Tax Litigation: Bosch, Erie, and Beyond,* 71 Or. L. Rev. 781 (1992). *Cf. City of Chicago v. Morales,* 527 U.S. 41, 61 (1999) ("We have no authority to construe the language of a state statute more narrowly than the instruction given by that State's highest court.").

[127] "Except in those few jurisdictions permitting a federal court to certify an unsettled question of state law to the state's highest court, a federal court's decision on state law cannot be corrected, for the benefit of the litigants in the particular case, by the state's authoritative tribunal." *Factors Etc., Inc. v. Pro Arts, Inc.,* 652 F.2d 278, 282 (2d Cir.), *cert. denied,* 456 U.S. 927 (1982).

The Supreme Court gave guarded approval to the technique of certification in *Save Regina* position, particularly when state law is unsettled. No federal court can give genuinely authoritative meaning to state law.[128] Yet federal courts usually cannot avoid the ambiguities of state law by declining jurisdiction.[129] Instead, they must "vicariously"[130] create enough state law to decide the case at hand by attempting to "forecast" the state's law "as it would be expressed by its highest court."[131]

[2] Data to Be Used in Forecasting State Law

The most authoritative indication of how the state's high court would rule on the same case frequently will be found in that court's opinions. In keeping with the principle of *stare decisis,* a court usually can be expected to adhere to its own precedents.[132] If the precedent of the state's highest court is indistinguishable, a federal diversity court usually will have no choice but to follow it.[133] Since, however, all appellate courts overrule some of their own precedents over time, the requirement that federal diversity courts follow apposite state high court cases is not ironclad. Federal diversity courts have refused to follow state high court precedents when they are convinced that the state high court would not follow them either.[134] At least by negative implication, the Supreme Court lent support

---

College v. Russell, 499 U.S. 225, 237 (1991). For examples where certification was workable, see *Reyes-Cardona v. J.C. Penny Co.*, 694 F.2d 894 (1st Cir. 1982); *Strange v. Krebs*, 658 F.2d 268 (5th Cir. 1981). On certification generally, see Yonover, *A Kinder, Gentler Erie: Reigning in the Use of Certification*, 47 Ark. L. Rev. 305 (1994); Note, *A State Court's Refusal to Answer Certified Questions: Are Inferences Permitted?*, 66 St. John's L. Rev. 407 (1992); Corr & Robbins, *Interjurisdictional Certification and Choice of Law*, 41 Vand. L. Rev. 411 (1988); C. Seron, *Certifying Questions of State Law: Experience of Federal Judges* (Federal Judicial Center 1983).

[128] At times, a federal decision on the meaning of state law has been followed by a subsequent federal court. *E.g., Factor Etc., Inc. v. Pro Arts, Inc.*, 652 F.2d 278, 282 (2d Cir.), *cert. denied*, 456 U.S. 927 (1982). But it is clear that the courts of the state are free to disregard all federal court pronouncements — even those of the Supreme Court — concerning the meaning of state law. The Supreme Court has acknowledged on numerous occasions the need to look to state courts for "an authoritative construction" of state law. *See, e.g., Babbitt v. United Farm Workers Nat'l Union*, 442 U.S. 289, 308 (1979).

[129] *Meredith v. City of Winter Haven*, 320 U.S. 228 (1943). For instances where extraordinary circumstances required federal diversity courts to abstain from decision, see *Burford v. Sun Oil Co.*, 319 U.S. 315 (1943); *Louisiana Power & Light Co. v. City of Thibodaux*, 360 U.S. 25 (1959).

[130] The term is from *Wright & Miller* § 4507.

[131] *McKenna v. Ortho Pharmaceutical Corp.*, 622 F.2d 657, 662 (3d Cir.), *cert. denied*, 449 U.S. 976 (1980).

[132] On stare decisis generally, see § 15.13, *infra.*

[133] "[T]he duty rests upon federal courts to apply state law under the Rules of Decision statute in accordance with the then controlling decision of the highest state court." *Vandenbark v. Owens-Illinois Glass Co.*, 311 U.S. 538, 543 (1941). *Vandenbark* held that a federal circuit court was not free to disregard an apposite decision handed down by the Ohio Supreme Court while the federal case was on appeal.

[134] *See Rock Island Improvement Co. v. Helmerich & Payne, Inc.*, 698 F.2d 1075 (10th Cir.), *cert. denied*, 461 U.S. 944 (1983) (refusing to follow an Oklahoma Supreme Court case because of an intervening declaration of policy by the Oklahoma legislature); *Mason v. American Emery Wheel Works*, 241 F.2d 906 (1st Cir.), *cert. denied*, 355 U.S. 815 (1957) (refusing to follow a thirty-year-old Mississippi Supreme Court case, noting that the liability limitation imposed by the case had been discredited in other state jurisdictions and reasoning that the Mississippi Supreme Court would overrule it).

to this view in *Bernhardt v. Polygraphic Company of America.*[135] It was aided in part in reaching its decision to follow a 40-year old Vermont Supreme Court precedent by the fact that

> there appears to be no confusion in the Vermont decisions, no developing line of authorities that casts a shadow over the established ones, no dicta, doubts or ambiguities in the opinions of Vermont judges on the question, no legislative development that promises to undermine the judicial rule.[136]

When no decision of the highest state court is on point, federal courts must base their forecasts on other material. Decisions of intermediate state appellate courts carry considerable weight in such situations. The rule was once that federal diversity courts "must follow the decisions of intermediate state courts in the absence of convincing evidence that the highest court of the state would decide differently."[137] While some federal circuit courts have restated the rule,[138] the Supreme Court appeared to relax it in *Commissioner v. Estate of Bosch.*[139] The Court noted that "under some conditions, federal authority may not be bound by an intermediate state appellate court ruling."[140] An influential circuit court opinion has read *Bosch* to permit a wide-ranging examination of legal sources in order to forecast the Ohio Supreme Court's position when none of its decisions were on point:

> The primary source that must be analyzed, of course, is the decisional law of the Ohio Supreme Court. In the absence of authority directly on point, decisions by that court in analogous cases provide useful indications of the court's probable disposition of a particular question of law . . . . Considered dicta by the state's highest court may also provide a federal court with reliable indicia of how the state tribunal might rule on a particular question. . . . Of somewhat less importance to a prognostication of what the highest state court will do are decisions of lower state courts and other federal courts. Such decisions should be accorded "proper regard" of course, but not conclusive effect . . . . Additionally, federal courts may consider scholarly treatises, the Restatement of Law, and germane law review articles . . . .[141]

---

[135] 350 U.S. 198 (1956).

[136] *Id.* at 205.

[137] *Stoner v. New York Life Ins. Co.*, 311 U.S. 464, 467 (1940).

[138] *E.g., Silverberg v. Paine, Webber, Jackson & Curtis, Inc.,* 710 F.2d 678, 690 (11th Cir. 1983); *Delano v. Kitch,* 663 F.2d 990, 996 (10th Cir.), *cert. denied,* 456 U.S. 946 (1982).

[139] 387 U.S. 456 (1967).

[140] *Id.* at 465. Citing *Bernhardt,* the Court went on to observe, "If there be no decision by [the state's highest court] then federal authorities must apply what they find to be the state law after giving 'proper regard' to relevant rulings of other courts of the State." *Id.*

[141] *McKenna v. Ortho Pharmaceutical Corp.,* 622 F.2d 657, 662 (3d Cir.) (*quoting Bosch,* 387 U.S. at 471), *cert. denied,* 449 U.S. 976 (1980). For discussion of the uses and limitations of state high-court dicta in forecasting state law, see *Moore* § 124.22[3]. Federal diversity courts also may be influenced by broad trends in the development of a substantive field of law. *See, e.g., Michelin Tires Ltd. v. First Nat'l Bank of Boston,* 666 F.2d 673, 682 (1st Cir. 1981); *Mason v. American Emery Wheel Works,* 241 F.2d 906, 908 (1st Cir.), *cert. denied,* 355

[3] How Much Freedom Do Federal Judges Have in Handling State Law?

The inability of federal courts to make truly authoritative pronouncements of state law and the constraints of the *Erie* doctrine make it impossible to reduce the process of forecasting state law to a simple formula. Federal judges use state law in a way which is not comparable to how either trial or appellate judges use it within the state judicial system.

On one hand, federal judges — whether trial or appellate[142] — require greater freedom than state trial judges in handling state precedents. State trial judges are controlled by precedents created by their superiors in the state judicial hierarchy.[143] Federal courts similarly constrained would not really be applying state law as state courts would, since state adjudication carries the possibility of review by a state appellate court powerful enough to overrule the state precedent.

On the other hand, federal courts cannot have as much freedom to react to state precedents as the state appellate courts which created them. All courts have the power to repudiate their own precedents at any time, although the doctrine of *stare decisis* usually restrains them.[144] However, forecasts whether or when a state appellate court will overrule its own precedent are likely to be speculative.[145] Moreover, guesses by federal diversity judges that state precedents would be overruled are likely to be colored by their own convictions about what the law ought to be. This kind of forecasting is dangerously akin to the federal general common law approach banned by *Erie*.[146]

All this explains why, in discharging the obligation to apply state law, federal diversity judges do not function as exact equivalents of either state lower or high court judges. They exercise instead a degree of authority somewhere between the two. When required to forecast whether the highest

---

U.S. 815 (1957). On sources for determining state law, *see* Bergman, *Putting Precedent in Its Place: Stare Decisis and Federal Predictions of State Law*, 96 Colum. L. Rev. 969 (1996); Note, *Federal Interpretation of State Law — An Argument for Expanded Scope of Inquiry,* 53 Minn. L. Rev. 806 (1969).

[142] In *Salve Regina College v. Russell*, 499 U.S. 225 (1991), the Supreme Court ruled that determinations by federal trial judges of the meaning of state law are to receive no special weight. Rather, state law issues are reviewable *de novo* in federal courts of appeals.

Salve seems correctly decided. As we argued in the first edition of this book, the distinction between federal trial and federal appellate judges is unimportant in this context. Both address the same issue: how would the highest state court rule? *See* note 126 and accompanying text, *supra.* A federal appellate court may reverse because it disagrees with the federal district court's answer to this question, but both are alike in their inability to give authoritative meaning to state law. *See* note 128, *supra.*

[143] *See* § 15.13, *infra.*

[144] *Id.*

[145] The lines of the doctrine of *stare decisis* are indistinct and departures from it are episodic and frequently controversial. *See, e.g.,* Chief Justice Bell's vigorous dissent to the Pennsylvania Supreme Court's overruling of its decisions which had limited recovery for negligently inflicted emotional distress. *Niederman v. Brodsky,* 261 A.2d 84, 90 (Pa. 1970).

[146] *See* § 7.02, *supra.*

state court would overrule its own cases, federal courts should — and usually do —proceed with caution.[147] They have more latitude in resolving state law questions of first impression.[148] Even then, however, federal courts should weigh matters carefully before vicariously creating new state law. A noted circuit decision reflects this view.

> Like many other plaintiffs in diversity cases filed in federal courts, the appellant here is asking that we anticipate the birth of a state law doctrine in the womb of time, but whose birth is distant. We have been asked to deliver prematurely a new doctrine of Pennsylvania tort law, and as a federal court we are unwilling to do so.[149]

When particularly close questions arise over the content of state law, there is something to be said for resolving them against the litigant invoking federal diversity jurisdiction.[150] This seems fair since, by directing the case to federal rather than state court, that litigant has effectively avoided authoritative state court decision in favor of what will be at best an informed federal court guess how the highest state court would rule.[151] This approach is also in keeping with the *Erie* doctrine's objective of keeping litigants from obtaining a substantive law advantage simply because they are capable of invoking federal diversity jurisdiction.[152]

§ 7.07   Federal Common Law

The same day that Justice Brandeis declared in *Erie R.R. v. Tompkins*[154] that "[t]here is no federal general common law,"[155] he wrote that "whether the water of an interstate stream must be apportioned between the States is a question of 'federal common law' upon which neither the statutes nor the decisions of either State can be conclusive."[156] Justice Jackson subsequently explained this apparent inconsistency:

> The federal courts have no *general* common law, as in a sense they have no general or comprehensive jurisprudence of any kind, because many subjects of private law which bulk large in the traditional common law are ordinarily within the province of the states and not of the federal government. But this is not to say that wherever we have occasion to

---

[147] *See* § 7.06[2], *supra.*

[148] *Cf. Moore* § 124.22[3].

[149] *Vargus v. Pittman Mfg. Co.,* 675 F.2d 73, 76 (3d Cir. 1982).

[150] The litigant may be either a plaintiff who has invoked the federal court's original diversity jurisdiction under 28 U.S.C. § 1332, *see* §§ 5.04-5.06, *supra,* or a defendant who has removed the case on federal diversity grounds under 28 U.S.C. § 1441. *See* § 5.07, *supra.*

[151] There are some cases, however, where uncertainty over the meaning of state law will be as perplexing for state judges. In conflict-of-laws situations, a state court may be called upon to ascertain the meaning of the law of another state. *See* § 7.05[1], *supra.* In grappling with the law of another state, state judges face essentially the same analytic difficulties as federal judges do in administering the *Erie* doctrine. *See* Corr & Robbins, note 127, *supra.*

[152] *See* § 7.02 (evolution from *Swift* to *Erie*), *supra.*

[154] 304 U.S. 64 (1938), discussed in § 7.02[3], *supra.*

[155] *Id.* at 78.

[156] *Hinderlider v. La Plata River & Cherry Creek Ditch Co.,* 304 U.S. 92, 110 (1938).

decide a federal question which cannot be answered from federal statutes alone we may not resort to all of the source materials of the common law, or that when we have fashioned an answer it does not become a part of the federal non-statutory or common law.[157]

Whenever a federal court is free to decide for itself what rule of decision to apply, it is making or applying federal common law.[158] Federal common law has been applied to interstate water disputes,[159] as Justice Brandeis noted, other interstate disputes,[160] questions regarding the proprietary (commercial) interests of the United States,[161] foreign relations questions,[162] maritime and admiralty questions,[163] questions regarding the defenses available to federal officials sued in private actions,[164] statute of limitations questions when relevant federal statutes are silent,[165] and the question whether a plaintiff has an implied cause of action under a federal statute[166] or constitutional provision.[167] Despite this range of subjects, the Supreme Court has said that applications of federal common law are "few and restricted."[168] Once it applies, however, it is controlling under the Supremacy Clause of the Constitution,[169] whether the forum is state or federal,[170] and whether the federal jurisdiction is diversity or federal question,[171] until and unless Congress overrides it by legislation.[172]

---

[157] *D'Oench, Duhme & Co. v. FDIC,* 315 U.S. 447, 469 (1942) (Jackson, J., concurring) (emphasis in original).

[158] *Wright* § 60.

[159] Including questions of interstate pollution. *See Illinois v. City of Milwaukee,* 406 U.S. 91 (1972).

[160] *See, e.g., Texas v. New Jersey,* 379 U.S. 674 (1965).

[161] *See, e.g., United States v. Kimbell Foods, Inc.,* 440 U.S. 715 (1979) (priority of federal lien over private liens); *Clearfield Trust Co. v. United States,* 318 U.S. 363 (1943) (effect of late notice of forgery on U.S. rights as drawee to recover on guaranty of endorsements on check).

[162] *See, e.g., Banco Nacional de Cuba v. Sabbatino,* 376 U.S. 398 (1964) (effect of act of state doctrine on private litigation).

[163] *See, e.g., Edmonds v. Compagnie Generale Transatlantique,* 443 U.S. 256 (1979).

[164] *See, e.g., Howard v. Lyons,* 360 U.S. 593 (1959) (availability of privilege as defense to libel action).

[165] *See, e.g., Johnson v. Railway Express Agency, Inc.,* 421 U.S. 454, 462-466 (1975). *See generally* Note, *Limitation Borrowing in Federal Courts,* 77 Mich. L. Rev. 1127 (1979) [hereinafter called *Limitation Borrowing*]; § 8.08[2][b] (the affirmative defense of limitations), *infra.*

[166] *See Cort v. Ash,* 422 U.S. 66, 78 (1975); § 5.03[1] (creation test for federal question jurisdiction), *supra.*

[167] *See Bivens v. Six Unknown Named Agents of Federal Bureau of Narcotics,* 403 U.S. 388 (1971).

[168] *City of Milwaukee v. Illinois,* 451 U.S. 304, 313 (1981) *citing Wheeldin v. Wheeler,* 373 U.S. 647, 651 (1963). *See also Redish,* note 153, *supra,* at 80; *Field,* note 153, *supra,* at 885 (federal common law is usually said to be the exception, not the rule).

[169] U.S. Const. art. VI.

[170] *Field,* note 153, *supra,* at 897.

[171] *See, e.g., Banco Nacional de Cuba,* 376 U.S. at 421; *Howard,* 360 U.S. 593.

[172] *Redish,* note 153, *supra,* at 97. *See, e.g., City of Milwaukee,* 451 U.S. at 313 (acknowledging "paramount authority of Congress" to override federal common law announced just one year earlier).

Beyond these generalizations, there is little clarity. Federal common law can be viewed as posing three questions, although they are not distinct in practice: (1) whether a federal court may make common law, (2) when it should make such law, and (3) what law it should make?

The threshold problem is that there is no general authority for federal common lawmaking. The federal government, unlike the state governments, is a government of limited powers. Its limitations are reflected in the Rules of Decision Act, which provides that the laws of the states shall be regarded as rules of decision in cases where they apply, "except where the Constitution or treaties of the United States or Acts of Congress otherwise require or provide."[173] The most common rationale for federal common lawmaking is that it is interstitial; it "implements the federal Constitution and statutes, and is conditioned by them," by filling gaps in such law.[174] These positive laws can be read as "requiring" such common lawmaking in the sense of the Rules of Decision Act because the gaps must be filled to decide cases. Another rationale for federal common lawmaking is that Congress or the Constitution has delegated lawmaking for particular subjects to the courts.[175] The positive laws can be read as "providing" for delegated judicial lawmaking in the sense of the Rules of Decision Act.

Whether a bare jurisdictional grant can alone serve as a delegation of lawmaking authority is unclear. Article III's grant of original jurisdiction to the Supreme Court to decide interstate disputes, and its authorization of lower court jurisdiction over admiralty and maritime cases and over controversies to which the United States is a party are sometimes cited as authority for federal common lawmaking in these areas.[176] Yet the analogous theory of delegated authority under the grant of diversity jurisdiction was rejected in *Erie*.[177] Arguably something more than just the jurisdictional grant is required, whether it is a practical necessity created by the absence of any logically applicable state law (to decide, for example, foreign relations questions or interstate boundary disputes), or "a bit of legislative history" consistent with federal common lawmaking.[178]

---

[173] 28 U.S.C. § 1652.

[174] *D'Oench, Duhme,* 315 U.S. at 471-72 (Jackson, J., concurring). *See generally* Johnson, *Bridging the Gap: Some Thoughts About Interstitial Lawmaking and the Federal Securities Laws,* 48 Wash. & Lee L. Rev. 879 (1991). One commentator has characterized the process as "preemptive lawmaking," by which a court "finds that some federal policy specifically intended by an enacting body 'preempts' the application of state law to some collateral or subsidiary point about which the enacting body has been silent." *Merrill,* note 153, *supra,* at 36. *See generally* Hart, *The Relations Between State and Federal Law,* 54 Colum. L. Rev. 489 (1954).

[175] *See, e.g., Textile Workers Union of America v. Lincoln Mills,* 353 U.S. 448, 451 (1957) (§ 301(a) of the Labor Management Relations Act of 1947, 29 U.S.C. § 185, "authorizes federal courts to fashion a body of federal law for the enforcement of . . . collective bargaining agreements").

[176] *See Field,* note 153, *supra,* at 916, 953-54 n.309 (citing authorities); *Redish,* note 1, *supra,* at 81-82.

[177] *See* § 184, *supra; Field,* note 153, *supra,* at 916.

[178] Friendly, *In Praise of Erie — and of the New Federal Common Law,* 39 N.Y.U. L. Rev. 383, 413 (1964) (suggesting that for federal common lawmaking it is sufficient that there is a "grant of federal jurisdiction . . . adorned with a bit of legislative history").

When a court *should* make federal common law is also unclear. The predicate for making it appears to be a showing that the choice of the substantive legal rule will significantly affect an "identifiable federal policy or interest."[179] More recently, the Court has endorsed the description of the predicate or "precondition" for making federal common law as "a significant conflict between some federal policy or interest and the use of state law."[180] In the leading case of *Clearfield Trust Co. v. United States*,[181] for example, the issue was whether late notice by the United States of a forged signature on its check kept it from recovering against guarantor Clearfield Trust. Under state law, prejudice to Clearfield from the late notice was presumed and recovery by the United States barred, while under pre-*Erie* federal commercial law Clearfield had the burden of proving prejudice. A web of federal statutes and regulations governed the rights and duties of the United States on commercial paper, but none addressed the precise issue in the case. Citing these laws to demonstrate the federal interest in the subject, the Supreme Court held that in the absence of an applicable statute, "it is for the federal courts to fashion the governing rule of law according to their own standards."[182] Clearly, here the federal interest in recovering from the guarantor absent prejudice from late notice was in conflict with the state's presumption of prejudice.

In contrast, the Court held in *Bank of America National Trust & Savings Association v. Parnell*[183] that state law rather than federal common law set the burden of proof on the issue of good faith in the purchase of bearer bonds guaranteed by the United States. The suit involved only private parties and the Court saw no significant federal interest at stake. *Parnell* demonstrated that analysis of the federal interest must proceed on an issue-by-issue basis, for the Court upheld application of federal common law to the collateral issue of overdueness of the bonds.[184]

Finally, when the federal common lawmaking authority is exercised, the question of the content of the law remains. In fact, the phrase federal common law is somewhat misleading. It is more accurately called the "law

---

[179] *See Wallis v. Pan Am Petroleum Corp.*, 384 U.S. 63, 68 (1966). *See Redish*, note 153, *supra*, at 80. Some scholars have attempted to refine these interests in order to escape the "enclave approach" to federal common law, which simply lists subjects to which it applies. One such effort suggests that federal common law should only be made when the transactions to which it will apply fall beyond the legislative competence of the states, and when making federal law promotes a constitutional structure or relationship such as the separation of powers (e.g., the "exclusive" foreign relations authority of the political branches) or the constitutional equality of the states (e.g., interstate disputes). *See* Clark, *Federal Common Law*, 144 U. Pa. L. Rev. 1245, 1251-1252 (1996).

[180] *Atherton v. FDIC*, 519 U.S. 213 (1997) (*quoting O'Melveny &Myers v. FDIC*, 512 U.S. 79, 87 (1994)).

[181] 318 U.S. 363 (1943).

[182] *Id.* at 367. Whether the background federal statutes and regulations truly declared any identifiable policy or interest has been questioned. *See* Note, *Clearfield: Clouded Field of Federal Common Law*, 53 Colum. L. Rev. 991, 1002-1005 (1953).

[183] 352 U.S. 29 (1956).

[184] *Id.* at 34.

of independent federal judicial decision,"[185] because once a court is satisfied that it should exercise lawmaking power, it is free to choose state law, fashion distinct federal law, or create some hybrid of the two.[186] Because states do not make their laws with federal interests in mind, the choice of state law as the content of federal common law would sometimes frustrate federal policy. But if a court finds as a threshold matter that the choice of state law would not frustrate federal policy, it may then consider such additional factors as the need for uniformity, the strength of a state's interest in having its own rules govern, the availability of developed state law, and the feasibility of judicially fashioning a substitute.[187] For example, this analysis has generally led the federal courts to "borrow" state limitations periods in federal causes of action for which Congress has not expressly provided limitations, and at the same time caused them to fashion distinct federal equitable tolling rules[188] in order to give effect to federal interests in the underlying cause of action.[189] Similarly, the Court concluded there was no federal interest in a uniform rule for determining the res judicata effect of a federal diversity judgment and therefore chose, as the applicable federal common law, the res judicata rule that would be applied by the forum state's courts.[190] At the same time, it was careful to note "the federal reference to state law will not obtain, of course, in situations in which the state law is incompatible with federal interests," such as a state law which would deny res judicata effect to a federal court dismissal for wilful violation of discovery orders.[191]

Of course, state law borrowed to supply the content of federal common law does not apply of its own force or by force of the Rules of Decision Act. It applies only because the federal court chose it. By the same token, the authority of state law as such is unaffected by its adoption (or later displacement) as federal common law.[192]

---

[185] *United States v. Standard Oil Co.,* 332 U.S. 301, 308 (1947).

[186] *United States v. Kimbell Foods, Inc.,* 440 U.S. 715, 728 (1979). The Supreme Court has described federal common law "in the strictest sense" as a "rule of decision that amounts, not simply to an interpretation of a federal statute or a properly promulgated administrative rule, but, rather, to a judicial 'creation' of a specific federal rule of decision." *Atherton,* 519 U.S. at 670.

[187] *See Wallis,* 384 U.S. at 68-69. *See generally Field,* note 1, at 953-62, *supra.* The borrowing court applies federal law to decide which state's law it will borrow. *De Sylva v. Ballentine,* 351 U.S. 570 (1956).

[188] Equitable tolling rules stop the running of the statute limitations because of the defendant's conduct. *See* § 8.08[2][b] (the affirmative defense of limitations), *infra.*

[189] *See generally Limitation Borrowing,* note 165, *supra.*

[190] *Semtek Int'l Inc.v. Lockheed Martin Corp.,* 531 U.S. 497, 121 S. Ct. 1021, 1028 (2001).

[191] *Id.*

[192] *Field,* note 153, *supra,* at 887.

Chapter 8

SIMPLE PLEADING AND PRACTICE

§ 8.01 Overview: The Functions and History of Pleading

Pleading is the exchange of written allegations to ascertain the subject for decision in a civil action. The pleadings are usually only those documents containing statements (averments) or denials of facts: the complaint, the answer and, where permitted, the reply.[1] Legal objections to pleadings are made by *demurrer* (in some state courts) or a *motion to dismiss* the pleading — requests for action by the court against the pleading.[2] This chapter introduces the basics of pleading in the simple case of a single claim by a single plaintiff against a single defendant. Chapter 9 treats the more common and complex case in which multiple parties or claims are *joined* in the litigation.

To understand fully the requirements of pleading and their evolution, it is necessary to understand the functions of pleading. First, pleading can *give notice* to the parties of the nature of claims and defenses, helping them prepare their case. Second, pleading can help to *eliminate sham or insufficient claims or defenses*, conserving scarce judicial resources and protecting litigants against harassing litigation. Third, pleading can help to *narrow the issues*, streamlining a case for trial and efficiently focusing the attention of the decisionmakers. Fourth, pleading can *guide the parties and the court in the conduct of the case*, helping them to define the scope of pretrial factual preparation and of evidentiary relevance at trial. Finally, pleading can *supply a record* for judgment, permitting the eventual application of the law of *res judicata* to preclude relitigation of once-decided claims and issues.[3]

The priority assigned these systemic functions of pleading determines the rules of pleading. Historically in Anglo-American law, the most important function of pleading was issue identification and narrowing. *Common law pleading* and practice developed elaborate and arcane rules to this end, until it grew so technical and arbitrary that it was discarded by most states in favor of simplified pleading codes. The primary functions of *code pleading* were notice and guidance. To these ends, it emphasized the pleading of facts constituting a *cause of action*, but it eventually also bogged down in disputation about the required specificity of fact pleading and the meaning of the term "cause of action."

In 1938 the Federal Rules of Civil Procedure abolished fact pleading and the concept of cause of action in favor of *notice pleading*. As the term

---

[1] *See* Rule 7(a); §§ 8.06 & 8.08-8.09, *infra.*

[2] *See* Rule 7(b); § 8.07, *infra.*

[3] *See generally* Chapter 15, *infra.*

suggests, modern federal pleading — since copied in whole or part by a majority of states[4] — serves primarily the function of notice. Other procedural devices such as discovery (fact-gathering), summary judgment (pretrial disposition on the law when the material facts are undisputed), and pretrial conferences serve the remaining functions.

No American jurisdiction requires pure common law pleading today, and a declining number follow code pleading. Yet exposure to these systems of pleading aids the understanding of modern pleading for several reasons. Much of the terminology of modern pleading is inherited from common law or code pleading. Many of the rules of modern pleading are best understood as attempts to cure problems that dogged common law or code pleading. Moreover, the legal-theory orientation of common law and code pleading is still important. Finally, as the father of the federal rules observed, "by a kind of Gresham's Law, the bad or harsh procedural decisions drive out the good, so that in time a rule becomes entirely obscured by its interpretive barnacles."[5] To the extent that some of the barnacles on modern pleading are of ancient lineage, it is worth tracing that lineage at least in outline.

Accordingly, sections 8.02 and 8.03 sketch some of the essential elements of common law/equity and code pleading, respectively. Section 8.04 then introduces modern "notice pleading," and section 8.05 discusses the candor and care requirements of modern pleading. The remaining sections trace the course of modern pleading and practice chronologically from complaint to amendment.

§ 8.02 Pre-Code Pleading and Practice

[1] Common Law Issue Pleading and Practice[6]

Pleading in early English history consisted of oral exchanges before feudal and communal courts. The difficulty of remembering long oral presentations probably compelled pleaders to exchange short allegations until they had reduced the dispute to a specific issue that the decider and the pleaders could easily keep in mind.[7]

Two developments transpired over a period of centuries to mature this system. In the 14th century, written pleadings were introduced, permitting the elaboration of pleading allegations and the formalization of the oral practice of "pleading to the issue." The necessity for pleading to a single issue became the driving force of an increasingly formalistic common law pleading system.

---

[4] Oakley & Coon, *The Federal Rules in State Courts: A Survey of State Court Systems of Civil Procedure*, 61 Wash. L. Rev. 1367, 1369 (1986).

[5] Clark, *Special Problems in Drafting and Interpreting Procedural Codes and Rules*, 3 Vand. L. Rev. 493, 498 (1950).

[6] The outline of historical pleading requirements and practices given in this section is drawn largely from J. Koffler & A. Reppy, *Handbook of Common Law Pleading* (1969), and B. Shipman, *Handbook of Common-Law Pleading* (H. Ballantine 3d ed. 1923), except as otherwise noted.

[7] J. Stephen, *The Principles of Pleading in Civil Actions* 37, 147-150 (Tyler ed. 1882).

In addition, jurisdictional turf-building by the royal courts led to the development of entire modes or *forms of action*. A plaintiff in the royal courts began his action by obtaining a *writ* from the king's representative ordering a sheriff to compel the defendant to satisfy the plaintiff's claim or to appear in court to defend himself. As long as feudal and communal courts still heard the major share of the judicial business, such writs were limited to a small number of claims on which the king could give relief. The writ, in effect, conferred a limited jurisdiction on and between the several royal courts, and the plaintiff's claim had to fall within the writ — the particular royal court's jurisdiction — or it would fail. The royal courts gradually expanded their jurisdiction by issuing new writs or by stretching the limits of existing writs through legal fictions.

Eventually each permitted writ became associated with its own substantive legal theory and developed its own procedural incidents. As a result, a form of action[8] came to embrace not only the appropriate writ, court, and substantive law, but also the forms of pleas, modes of trial, and forms of judgment.[9] At the same time, the language of the plaintiff's pleading was increasingly divorced from reality, as it was used largely to justify a particular writ under the formulary system rather than to describe the actual case. "The primary question before the [common law] courts has not been the general one whether the plaintiff's statement of his case showed a right in him and a violation by the defendant; it has rather been whether the case presented facts which constituted a 'cause of action' in 'trespass,' 'assumpsit,' or other particular form attempted to be used."[10]

Once the writ was issued, the plaintiff would begin the pleading process by filing a *declaration*, describing his case in the formalistic and often fictitious language held necessary under the particular writ and associated with the attendant form of action. Consistent with the objective of reducing the case to a single issue, no hypothetical (if, then) or alternative (either/or) pleading was permitted. From the outset, the plaintiff had to elect a particular set of facts, and by virtue of the formulary system, a particular legal theory. Any deviation between the writ selected and the declaration, or between the declaration and eventual proof at trial, was termed a *variance* and forbidden.[11] Any pleading *departure* from the previously pleaded facts or legal theory was fatal to the pleading, because it was inconsistent with narrowing the issues.[12] Relief was limited to that sought in the declaration upon the facts and legal theory there asserted. The harshness of these principles is illustrated by a decision reversing a judgment

---

[8] The forms of action evolved gradually. They included, at different points in time, trespass, trespass on the case (encompassing various indirect injuries and non-physical torts), trover (for the return of property), ejectment, detinue (return of property and damages for its wrongful detention), replevin, debt, and special assumpsit. *See Koffler & Reppy*, note 6, *supra*, Chs. 7-13, 16.

[9] *See generally* F. Maitland, *Equity, Also the Forms of Action At Common Law* (1909); C. Fifoot, *History and Sources of the Common Law — Tort and Contract* (1949).

[10] *Shipman*, note 6, *supra*, § 27.

[11] *Koffler & Reppy*, note 6, *supra*, §§ 26-27; *Shipman*, note 1, *supra*, § 82.

[12] *Shipman*, note 6, *supra*, §§ 217-229.

for plaintiff because he had pleaded a debt of $2,979.57, but proved a debt of $2,979.57 1/2![13]

The drive toward a single issue was also reflected in the requirements for further pleading. There were three possible responses to a claim.

First, a party could *demur*, asserting that, even if true, the claimant's allegations state no legal claim. The demurrer had to attack a pleading on its face; so-called *speaking demurrers*, which relied on additional matter beyond the four corners of the pleading, were prohibited. At first, the demurrer did not specify the defect in the pleading that it attacked. This left the pleader in the dark as to whether his legal theory was deficient, he had omitted some necessary ritualistic language, or he had simply committed some other minor and easily corrected error of form. After a 16th century reform, however, defects of form had to be attacked by *special demurrer* specifying the defect or they were waived. The *general demurrer* was reserved for substantive legal defects.

Second, a party could respond with a *dilatory plea*, asserting some legal reason, incidental to the merits, why the court could not hear the case.[14] *Pleas to the court's jurisdiction* challenged the court's subject matter jurisdiction and, if sustained, required dismissal of the case. *Pleas in suspension* sought to suspend the action until some problem, such as the plaintiff's legal disability through outlawry, had been removed. *Pleas in abatement* challenged defects in the pleading itself, going to the capacity of the pleader, misjoinder of claims or parties, etc.

Third, the party could respond on the merits with a *plea in bar*, also called a *peremptory plea*, asserting a defense that could bar recovery. By asserting the plea in bar called the *traverse*, the pleader denied the allegations of the claim against him, creating a factual issue for trial. To assure singleness of issue, however, treacherous rules evolved concerning the precise form of denials in a traverse. The traps which these rules set for the unwary eventually made a different form of traverse popular — the *general issue*, essentially the civil version of a "not guilty" plea. By filing the general issue, a defendant could contest liability and even assert various affirmative defenses without having to specify which allegations of the complaint he denied or which of the affirmative defenses he would assert at trial.[15] The plea of the general issue neither gave notice nor helped to reduce the case to a single issue, but its "popularity with the common law pleaders may be in part explained on the theory that it was a practical method of simplifying a system of pleading which had grown too technical for success-ful application."[16] Finally, an alternative plea in bar was the *plea in confession and avoidance*. It required defendant to admit (confess) plaintiff's claim and to plead an excuse: new matter that avoided the claim.

---

[13] *Spangler v. Pugh*, 21 Ill. 85 (1859).

[14] Most such pleas asserted curable preliminary defects or problems and would only delay rather than permanently bar an action by a persistent plaintiff — hence the generic term, *dilatory pleas. Koffler & Reppy*, note 6, *supra*, § 203.

[15] *See Koffler & Reppy*, note 6, *supra*, § 224.

[16] Crum, *Scope of the General Denial*, 27 N.D. L. Rev. 11, 14 (1951).

Both the demurrer and the dilatory plea created legal issues, while the traverse created a factual issue. Additional pleading was necessary to raise an issue on the plea of confession and avoidance, since no issue was created by the confession of plaintiff's claim. To achieve singleness in pleading, the demurrer, traverse and plea in confession and avoidance were mutually exclusive; combining pleas or otherwise raising more than one issue in a pleading was prohibited as *duplicity*.[17]

Once the defendant had answered, it was the plaintiff's turn to respond by filing a *replication*, asserting one of the three possible analytic responses described above. If the issue was still not joined, the defendant then filed a *rejoinder*. Additional rounds of pleading by way of *surrejoinder*, *rebutter*, *surrebutter* and theoretically beyond were also possible until issues had been joined. At the conclusion of this usually protracted and procedurally land-mined pleading process, trial with fact-finding by a jury was often "something of an afterthought."[18]

Complicated as this outline sounds, it does not begin to portray the true technicality of the common law pleading system in its heyday, or to illustrate the extent of the legal fictions which permeated the forms of action. Professor Charles Alan Wright pronounced a just and fitting verdict on the system: "This system was wonderfully scientific. It was also wonderfully slow, expensive and unworkable. The system was better calculated to vindicate scientific rules of pleading than it was to dispense justice."[19]

[2] Equity Pleading and Practice[20]

For dispensation of justice frustrated by the scientific complexities of the common law system or by the unavailability of a suitable writ or of adequate law relief in the traditional form of damages,[21] plaintiffs petitioned the king directly. He sent them to his chief minister, the chancellor, and by the 16th century, a court of chancery had developed to hear such petitions or *bills of complaint*.[22] The predicate for seeking equity in the chancery court was a showing of inadequate remedy at law. The remedy at equity was a decree ordering the respondent personally and directly to do or not to do something, *i.e.*, an injunction or decree of specific performance.[23]

---

[17] *Koffler & Reppy*, note 6, *supra*, §§ 234-235.

[18] Marcus, *The Revival of Fact Pleading Under the Federal Rules of Civil Procedure*, 86 Colum. L. Rev. 433, 437 (1986) (citations omitted).

[19] *Wright* § 68.

[20] *See generally* F. Maitland, *Equity* (2d rev. ed. 1936); J. Pomeroy, *Code Remedies* (5th ed. 1929). The following outline is drawn primarily from these sources, except as otherwise noted.

[21] Actually the law courts granted relief by declaring a legal relationship between plaintiff and defendant, usually that plaintiff was entitled to a sum of money ("damages") from the defendant. *See generally* § 14.01 (damages remedies), *infra*.

[22] Some scholars date the development of equity as a separate system to the 14th century. *See, e.g.*, Hazeltine, "The Early History of English Equity," in *Essays in Legal History* 261-285 (P. Vinogradoff ed. 1913).

[23] *See generally* § 14.02 (equitable relief), *infra*.

As an alternative to the common law system, equity developed its own procedures. First, the bill of complaint consisted of a repetitive narrative of evidentiary facts culminating in *interrogatories* to respondent. The bill of complaint, framed partly to force disclosure of the defendant's case by his sworn answer and partly to serve as evidence in lieu of oral testimony at trial to the chancellor,[24] thus served as an early form of discovery of evidence from the adversary, unknown at common law. Eventually it gave rise to a *bill of discovery*, which could be brought in equity in aid of an action or defense at law.

Second, in order to do full justice, equity permitted the joinder of parties who could not be joined in a common law suit. *Cross-bills* in equity permitted claims between co-defendants, by defendant against the plaintiff, and against some third parties, while *interpleaders* and *derivative suits* permitted even more sophisticated forms of joinder. Equity procedures, then, were the forerunners of modern complex joinder devices.[25]

Third, equity did not ordinarily use the jury as a fact-finder. The trial was instead to the chancellor on the pleadings, answers to interrogatories, depositions (written examinations of witnesses under oath) and documentary evidence rather than on oral testimony. The role of the chancellor as fact-finder led eventually to a different degree of appellate deference to his findings than to jury findings, which is today reflected in the federal standards of appellate review.[26]

Despite equity's origins as a flexible alternative to the rigidities of common law practice and procedure, it became encrusted with its own procedural barnacles. One study of equity practice concluded that equity actions were frequently interminable and that even in those which came to a successful conclusion, "the honest suitor emerged from the ordeal victorious rather than triumphant, for too often he had been ruined by the way."[27]

§ 8.03   Code Fact Pleading and Procedure[28]

[1]   In General

Neither common law nor equity pleading was imported in all its technical glory to the colonies. But enough was adopted to prompt reform by the mid-19th century. New York led the way in 1848 with the adoption of the *Field Code of Civil Procedure*. It became a model for pleading reforms in more

---

[24] *Maitland*, note 20, *supra*, Lecture 1, at 5.

[25] *See generally* Chapter 9 (complex pleading and practice), *infra*.

[26] *See* § 13.09[2][b] (clearly erroneous standard of review), *infra*.

[27] C. Bowen, "Progress in the Administration of Justice During the Victorian Period," in 1 *Select Essays in Anglo-American Legal History* 516, 527 (E. Freund, et al. eds. 1907).

[28] *See generally* C. Clark, *Handbook of the Law of Code Pleading* (2d ed. 1947), by any measure the leading authority on the subject, from which the following outline is drawn, except as otherwise noted.

than half the states, and the code pleading which it introduced is still retained in a few.[29]

The *Field Code* abolished the forms of action and the distinction between law and equity actions in favor of "one form of action, denominated a civil action."[30] It also discarded all existing pleading rules that were inconsistent with its provisions. The hallmark of the code was *fact pleading*: the requirement that the complaint state "facts constituting a cause of action, in ordinary and concise language."[31] Issue-narrowing was no longer the primary function of pleading. Its objective, instead, was "three-fold: to present the facts on which the court is to pronounce the law; to present them in such a manner, as that the precise points in dispute shall be perceived, to which the proofs may be directed; and to preserve the record of the rights determined."[32] Since pleading no longer had to generate a single issue, pleadings were confined to a complaint, answer and reply, which were all to be liberally construed.[33]

The adoption of code pleading brought with it two major problems: what constituted a cause of action, and how specifically did plaintiff have to plead facts constituting a cause of action? These are explored in the discussion which follows.

[2] The Cause of Action and the Theory of the Pleadings

The code drafters agreed that "[i]n some manner, it is necessary to state the limits to which relief for a number of grievances or one severe and long-continued grievance may be accorded in a *single* suit."[34] The common law, of course, established narrow and seemingly precise limits through the forms of action and the attendant pleading niceties. But the abolition of the forms and old pleading rules made it unnecessary and arguably improper to plead the discarded common law allegations in order to set forth facts constituting a cause of action. On the other hand, conclusory pleading would not do either, in view of the code's emphasis on facts.

Between these extremes, at least two approaches to limiting the suit developed. The first equated a cause of action with a right of action or the legal or primary right suggested by the facts relied upon by the plaintiff.[35]

---

[29] For example, California, Oklahoma, South Carolina, and Virginia have retained fact pleading requirements among other code pleading rules at the same time that they have adapted discovery, amendment and sometimes summary judgment provisions from the Federal Rules of Civil Procedure. *Friendenthal, Kane & Miller*, § 5.1. *See, e.g.*, Va. Code Ann. §§ 8.01 (2000); *See generally* Wilson & Payne, Note, *The Specificity of Pleading in Modern Civil Practice*, 25 U. Rich. L. Rev. 135 (1990) (discussing Virginia fact pleading).

[30] N.Y. Code Civ. Proc. § 69 (1848) (hereinafter *Field Code*).

[31] *Id.* § 142(2).

[32] *First Report of the Commissioners on Practice and Pleadings*, 123-24, 137-38, 140-41, 144 (1848) (report which led to promulgation of the Field Code).

[33] *Field Code* §§ 156 & 159.

[34] *Clark*, note 28, *supra*, § 19, at 128 (emphasis in original). Because such limits are also necessary to define the scope of a final judgment for purposes of the law of claim preclusion, detailed discussion of them is deferred until Chapter 15. *See* § 15.03 (claim preclusion), *infra*.

[35] *See Clark*, note 28, *supra*, § 19; J. Pomeroy, 1 *Equity Jurisprudence* § 347 (5th ed. 1941).

The second looked to the "aggregate of operative facts, limited as a lay onlooker would to a single occurrence or affair, without particular reference to the resulting legal right or rights."[36] The latter pragmatically anticipated the unit of facts that would most naturally and conveniently be presented at trial. But it was ahead of its time. Its very flexibility appeared to threaten the objective of notice by leaving unclear which legal rights arose from the aggregate of operative facts and therefore what law applied.

Consequently, most observers "agreed on the need of some sort of legal right as the measuring stick of the cause."[37] The result was a *theory of pleadings* approach to defining a cause of action in many, though not all, code states, which unfortunately helped perpetuate much of the rigidity of formulary pleading and its corresponding rules against variance and departure. In *Jones v. Winsor*,[38] for example, the plaintiffs sued for return of money deposited with their attorney, alleging in part that his fee was unjust, unlawful and fraudulent. But the complaint failed to state a cause of action for conversion because of plaintiffs' omission of allegations of ownership or possession of the money entrusted to the attorney. On the other hand, if the cause of action was taken to be a contractual one for money had and received, the complaint was good and the allegations of fraudulent conversion were just surplusage. The court upheld a demurrer, reasoning that

> [a] complaint should be framed upon the theory that it is either a complaint in tort or one *ex contractu*, and the two theories cannot be combined in one action; neither can an action at law and an action in equity be combined in one count in the same action. . . . "On demurrer to a complaint, or any count thereof, the court must determine what cause of action such complaint or count is designed to state, and then whether it states facts sufficient to constitute such a cause of action; and, if not, the demurrer must be sustained, though facts may be stated sufficient to show that plaintiff has a cause of action of a different character."[39]

Similarly, other courts held that if a complaint stated a cause of action on one legal theory, the action would fail if that legal theory was not proven at trial, even though allegations in the complaint and proof at trial would have supported a cause of action on a different legal theory.[40] Plaintiff had, in effect, made a fatal departure or variance from the legal theory articulated by his complaint; he should have elected the successful legal theory before trial. Other courts rejected such harsh applications of the theory-of-the-pleadings approach by considering whether defendants were adequately apprised of the theory plaintiff ultimately argued at trial or whether they were surprised — considerations more in keeping with the objectives of fact pleading under the codes. Yet even these courts gave defendants the option of moving before trial to strike surplusage from the complaint and "to

---

[36] *Clark*, note 28, *supra*, § 19.

[37] *Id.*

[38] 118 N.W. 716 (S.D. 1908). *See also Mescall v. Tully*, 91 Ind. 96, 99 (1883).

[39] 118 N.W. at 718 (*quoting Supervisors of Kewaunee County v. Decker*, 30 Wis. 624 (1872)).

[40] *See Ross v. Mather*, 51 N.Y. 108 (1872).

compel the plaintiff to make it more definite, or to elect in regard to the *form of action.*"[41] As the language of this "progressive" ruling reveals, in many states the forms of action still ruled code pleading from the grave.

[3] The Specificity of Fact Pleading Under the Codes

In reaction to the often fictitious quality of common law pleading, the codes required the pleading of only "dry, naked actual facts,"[42] to which the court would apply the substantive law. Plaintiff was therefore obliged to avoid pleading a conclusory legal evaluation of his facts. At the same time, he was charged with pleading concisely. In short, he could plead neither too little nor too much, but just the so-called *ultimate facts* from which an appropriate cause of action could be inferred.

Pleading too little — bare conclusions of law — subjected the complaint to demurrer. But the dividing line between improper conclusions of law and proper ultimate facts proved evanescent. Typically nettlesome allegations included the following: plaintiff and defendant mutually agreed; plaintiff is the owner of property; defendant's servant was acting within the scope of his employment; defendant was in charge of the construction. Sometimes the allegations as a group were held conclusory. In *Gillespie v. Goodyear Service Stores,*[43] plaintiff alleged that

> [o]n or about May 5, 1959, and May 6, 1959, the defendants, *without cause or just excuse and maliciously* came upon and trespassed upon the premises occupied by the plaintiff as a residence, and by the use of harsh and threatening language and physical force directed against the plaintiff assaulted the plaintiff and placed her in great fear, and humiliated and embarrassed her by subjecting her to public scorn and ridicule, and caused her to be seized and exhibited to the public as a prisoner, and to be confined in a public jail.[44]

The appellate court affirmed dismissal of the complaint on a demurrer, reasoning that it stated no facts upon which the italicized "legal conclusions" could be predicated.[45] "Plaintiff's allegations do not disclose *what* occurred, *when* it occurred, *where* it occurred, *who* did *what*, the relationships between defendants and plaintiff or of defendants *inter se*, or any other factual data that might identify the occasion or describe the circumstances."[46]

The plaintiff who sought to avoid such a result by pleading detailed *evidentiary facts*, however, risked pleading too much. Although this vice was rarely fatal, because the court could usually still draw the necessary legal

---

[41] *Conaughty v. Nichols*, 42 N.Y. 83, 88 (1870) (emphasis supplied) (permitting plaintiff to amend his complaint after trial by striking language of conversion, in order to recover on a contractual theory). *Contra, Jones, supra*, 118 N.W. 716.

[42] *Wright*, § 68 (quoting Pomeroy, *Code Remedies* 640 (1929).

[43] 128 S.E. 2d 762 (N.C. 1963).

[44] *Id.* at 763 (emphasis supplied).

[45] *Id.* at 766.

[46] *Id.*

inferences from the collective evidentiary facts, the plaintiff could never be sure that the consequences would not be more serious. In *McGaughey v. Schuette*,[47] the appellate court actually reversed a judgment for plaintiff because his complaint seeking possession of property contained only "a statement of evidentiary facts, which, if proven at the trial, would authorize the court in finding the ultimate fact of ownership and right to possession in the plaintiff."[48]

The codes attempted to distinguish among legal conclusions, ultimate facts, and evidentiary facts, that was "one of degree only," not of kind.[49] Even frequent appellate treatments of the distinction furnished no guidance to the trial courts because they were inescapably ad hoc. When the issue was essentially whether the pleader had pleaded too little or too much, most precedents were distinguishable, most pleadings were fair game, and form was again elevated over substance as it had been under the common law.

§ 8.04 Modern Notice Pleading

The drafters of the Federal Rules of Civil Procedure attempted to adopt the successes and avoid the failures of code pleading. In prescribing the basic federal pleading requirement, they therefore rejected both the phrases "facts" and "cause of action" in favor of the rule that a pleading contain "a short and plain statement of the claim showing that the pleader is entitled to relief."[50] Under the federal rules, issue-narrowing, fact development and guidance, and screening of sham or insufficient claims or defenses are accomplished by devices other than pleading. The chief remaining function of modern *notice pleading* is to give notice of claims or defenses. "The real importance of the Rules dealing with pleadings is that they make pleadings, in and of themselves, relatively unimportant. Cases are to be decided on their merits."[51]

We will examine four questions surrounding "notice pleading." First, how specific must notice be? Second, has the theory-of-the-pleadings doctrine been finally abandoned? Third, what form must notice pleading take? Finally, what specific pleading rules have survived and why?

[1] The Specificity of Notice Pleading

The phrase "notice pleading" suggests more the spirit than the letter of a sufficient pleading and was disavowed by the federal rulemakers.[52] But Rule 8(a)(2)'s requirement of a "short and plain statement of claim showing that the pleader is entitled to relief" is hardly more helpful. On one hand, it could mean that a sufficient pleading could inform defendant of little

---

[47] 48 P. 1088 (Cal. 1897) *(per curiam)*.

[48] *Id.*

[49] *Clark*, note 28, *supra*, § 38.

[50] Rule 8(a)(2).

[51] J. Moore, *Moore's Federal Practice* ¶ 8.02 (2d ed.)

[52] *See* Clark, *Two Decades of the Federal Civil Rules*, 58 Colum. L. Rev. 435, 450-451 (1958).

more than that she has been sued. On the other hand, it could contemplate a detailed statement of facts making out each and every element of a claim. Both extremes find support in the case law, although most courts have charted a middle course.

The Supreme Court lent some support to the first view in *Conley v. Gibson* [53] by endorsing what it called "simplified notice pleading" and "the accepted rule that a complaint should not be dismissed for failure to state a claim unless it appears beyond doubt that the plaintiff can prove no set of facts in support of his claim which would entitle him to relief." While this *is* the most oft-quoted rule, it can hardly be taken literally, [54] or a pleading that alleged nothing but that defendant was liable to plaintiff would pass muster. The allegations in *Conley* itself went well beyond this, and the form complaints accompanying the federal rules and declared "sufficient" thereunder by Rule 84 also supply some specific factual matter in addition to the conclusory statements that "defendant owes plaintiff money" or that "defendant negligently drove a motor vehicle against plaintiff." [55]

Dioguardi v. Durning, [56] cited with approval in *Conley* and penned by the chief drafter of the federal rules, appeared to set a very modest standard for the statement of such matter. Plaintiff's "obviously home drawn" complaint against the Collector of Customs alleged cryptically that certain "medicinal extracts" imported by plaintiff had disappeared and that others had been given to a third party "with my betting [bidding?] price of $110; and not their price of $120." [57] Judge Clark reversed the dismissal of the action for failure to state a claim, concluding that the plaintiff had stated claims against the collector for conversion and improper public sale, "however inartistically." [58] Read together, *Conley* and *Dioguardi* appear to embrace a liberal view of notice pleading whereby no complaint will be held insufficient for failure to state a claim unless "the pleader makes allegations that show on the face of the complaint some insuperable bar to relief." [59] By this view, a plaintiff does not have to allege all the facts necessary to prove its claim. [60] This is consistent with a theory of pleading that emphasizes notice and notice alone as the essential function of pleadings.

Another view is that screening sham or legally insufficient complaints is still a proper secondary function. As Judge Posner has put it, the purpose

---

[53] 355 U.S. 41, 45-46, 48 (1957).

[54] *See Car Carriers, Inc. v. Ford Motor Co.*, 745 F.2d 1101, 1106 (7th Cir. 1984), *cert. denied*, 470 U.S. 1054 (1985); Marcus, *The Revival of Fact Pleading Under the Federal Rules of Civil Procedure*, 86 Colum. L. Rev. 433, 434 (1986) ("Taken literally, it might have precluded dismissal in any case where the plaintiff invoked a valid legal theory.").

[55] Forms 3-10.

[56] 139 F.2d 774 (2d Cir. 1944).

[57] *Id.* at 775 (bracketed material in original). The full amended complaint is reproduced in J. Cound, J. Friendenthal, A. Miller & J. Sexton, *Civil Procedure: Cases and Materials* 502-503 n.1 (7th ed. 1997).

[58] *Dioguardi*, 139 F.2d at 775.

[59] *Wright* § 68 (citations omitted).

[60] *See, e.g., Sparrow v. United Air Lines, Inc.*, 216 F.3d 1111 (D.C. Cir. 2000).

of the federal pleading rule under this view is less to give defendant information with which to prepare his defense "than to allow the court to determine at the outset . . . whether the plaintiff has any tenable theory or basis of suit, so that if he does not the case can be got rid of immediately without clogging the court's docket and imposing needless expense on the defendant."[61] By this view of modern pleading, "a complaint must contain either direct or inferential allegations respecting all material elements necessary to sustain a recovery under *some* viable legal theory."[62] Bare notice is insufficient; the pleader must at least allege sufficient factual detail to set out all the elements necessary to establish a claim — usually duty, breach, injury and causation.[63] Such a complaint is said to state a *prima facie* claim.

Until 1993, some circuits selectively used an especially demanding version of this approach to dispose of disfavored actions on the pleadings. Typically these actions were disfavored because of the heavy burden they placed on the courts relative to their apparent rate of success. The "heightened pleading standard" — essentially a revival of fact pleading[64] — was thus applied to prisoners' complaints, partly because incarcerated plaintiffs are uninhibited by the usual practical and ethical restraints on frivolous suits against governmental officials.[65] Some circuits also applied it to other civil rights actions,[66] citing the volume of such cases, the number that are frivolous, and a consequential "public policy to weed out the [latter] at an early stage in the litigation."[67] Less systematically, courts applied the heightened pleading standard to securities fraud and antitrust complaints[68] and complaints against government action.[69]

From the start, this trend raised problems that had been associated with fact pleading under the codes.[70] Imposing special fact pleading

---

[61] *Ryan v. Immaculate Queen Center*, 188 F.3d 857, 860 (7th Cir. 1999).

[62] *In re Plywood Antitrust Litigation*, 655 F.2d 627, 641 (5th Cir. 1981) (emphasis in original), *cert. denied*, 462 U.S. 1125 (1983); *Car Carriers, Inc. v. Ford Motor Co.*, 745 F.2d 1101 (7th Cir. 1984), *cert. denied*, 470 U.S. 1054 (1985). *See generally Marcus*, note 54, *supra*, at 459-465.

[63] *See* § 8.06[2], *infra*.

[64] *See Marcus*, note 54, *supra*, at 433.

[65] *See* Phillips, *Foreword*, 39 Wash. & Lee L. Rev. 425, 428 (1982).

[66] *See* Blaze, *Presumed Frivolous: Application of Stringent Pleading Requirements in Civil Rights Litigation*, 31 Wm. & Mary L. Rev. 935 (1990); Wingate, *A Special Pleading Rule for Civil Rights Complaints: A Step Forward or a Step Back?*, 49 Mo. L. Rev. 677 (1984); *Marcus*, note 54, *supra*, at 449-50.

[67] *Rotolo v. Borough of Charleroi*, 532 F.2d 920, 922 (3d Cir. 1976) (*quoting Valley v. Maule*, 297 F. Supp. 958 (D. Conn. 1968)).

[68] *Marcus*, note 54, *supra*, at 447-449.

[69] *Id.* (noting use of special "fact" pleading rules to resolve questions of standing in such challenges). *See, e.g., Lujan v. Nat'l Wildlife Fed'n*, 497 U.S. 871 (1990) (finding that individualized injury was not pled with sufficient specificity to establish standing to challenge government action).

[70] *See* § 8.03[3], *supra*, discussing *Gillespie v. Goodyear Serv. Stores*, 128 S.E.2d 762 (N.C. 1963).

requirements on disfavored actions introduces the same ad hoc differences of degree in pleading that created such uncertainty under the codes,[71] and thus invites a sufficiency attack on the complaint in every disfavored action. Selective application of heightened pleading requirements also may reflect hidden judicial value preferences about the rights being asserted.[72] Not only are such preferences often contrary to those reflected by the congressional grant of federal jurisdiction to hear the judicially disfavored actions, but they may also be based on erroneous assumptions about the number of claims that are frivolous.[73] It is arguably for the legislature and the rulemakers to articulate and implement such preferences, not the courts.[74] Furthermore, more affluent (hence well-counseled) litigants can almost always meet a special pleading requirement whereas, the pro se litigant often cannot. The difference will not necessarily reflect differences between the merits of their claims.

The Supreme Court's decision in *Leatherman v. Tarrant County Narcotics Intelligence and Coordination Unit*[75] may halt this trend. There the district court had applied the Fifth Circuit's heightened pleading standard to dismiss two civil rights complaints alleging municipal liability. In a brief opinion, the Court unanimously found it "impossible to square the 'heightened pleading standard' . . . with the liberal system of 'notice pleading' set up by the Federal Rules."[76] Rule 9(b) *does* impose specific pleading requirements in certain cases, but its very existence precludes applying them to unenumerated cases. This reasoning applies with equal force to other applications of the heightened pleading standard and therefore may indicate its demise.

This is not to conclude that bare notice should always be sufficient under modern pleading rules. Scholars have, in fact, remarked on "the puzzling persistence of pleading practice" into the next millenium, concluding that, in a small but significant number of cases, heightened pleading and its enforcement by Rule 12 motion practice help to implement substantive law and dispose of unsupportable claims.[77] The federal form complaints suggest that the complaint should state the circumstances, occurrences, and events

---

[71] *See Rotolo*, 532 F.2d at 924-925 (Gibbons, J., dissenting) (faulting majority for introducing "puzzling" standard of pleading sufficiency that evidently contemplates the pleading of evidence "beyond any prior holding of this court").

[72] *Id.* at 927 ("The explanation . . . for the imposition of a fact pleading requirement in . . . [civil rights] cases must be found in the attitude of the court toward the rights being asserted.")

[73] *Id. See, e.g.*, Eisenstadt, *§ 1983: Doctrinal Foundations and An Empirical Study*, 67 Cornell L. Rev. 482, 537 (1982) ("The vast majority of non-prisoner section 1983 civil rights cases involve classic rights of obvious importance; the trivial claims are a sideshow.").

[74] The federal rulemakers have already set out a few special pleading requirements in Rule 9. *See* § 8.04[4], *infra*. Arguably the omission of other special pleading requirements was intentional and should be cured by the rulemakers, subject to congressional disapproval, *see* § 1.02 (the rulemaking process), *supra*, rather than by the courts.

[75] 507 U.S. 163 (1993).

[76] *Id.* at 168.

[77] Marcus, *The Puzzling Persistence of Pleading Practice*, 76 Tex. L. Rev. 1749 (1998).

that give rise to the claim, even though they can be stated quite generally.[78] Although a plaintiff is not required to plead facts "in support of every arcane element of his claim," he should not omit those facts that "would clearly dominate the case," or else the court may fairly assume that they do not exist.[79] It may even be fair to require that a sufficient pleading allege facts establishing a civil analogue to probable cause in criminal proceedings — probable cause to believe in the existence of a claim entitling plaintiff to relief.[80] This intermediate view of notice pleading leaves most of the work of discovery, guidance and merits dispositions to other procedural devices under the rules, but still affords appropriately limited scope for merits dispositions on the pleadings in appropriate cases.

[2] Consistency and the Theory of the Pleadings in Modern Pleading

Whatever view is taken of the basic requirement of notice pleading, the de-emphasis of pleading under modern notice pleading has substantially eliminated the theory-of-the-pleadings approach[81] and the related concepts of variance and election of remedies. "It is not necessary to set out the legal theory on which the claim is based,"[82] so long as there exists some theory that would entitle the claimant to relief. The test for the sufficiency of a pleading is whether the pleader has stated a claim under *any* legal theory, not just under *his* asserted theory of the pleadings. Rule 8(e)(2) expressly permits the pleading of alternative or hypothetical claims and defenses and as many claims or defenses as a party has "regardless of consistency," and Rule 8(a) permits demands for alternative types of relief. The rulemakers recognized that a party often does not know enough to elect a legal theory at the start of the litigation and that a compelled election by the pleadings would either encourage needlessly verbose pleading, defeating the objective of short and plain statements, or entrap the uninformed.

If the pleadings are of reduced significance before trial, after trial they "lose such little significance as they had before, and judgment is to be in accordance with the evidence."[83] Rule 15(b) permits amendment of the pleadings to conform to the evidence at trial, and indeed provides for constructive amendment when the parties have consented to any variance from the pleadings.[84] As discussed in more detail below,[85] the focus of the rule on amendment is properly now on possible prejudice to the opposing parties, rather than on the initial intent of the pleader in electing his legal

---

[78] *Wright* § 68 (citations omitted).

[79] *O'Brien v. Di Grazia*, 544 F.2d 543, 544 n.3 (1st Cir. 1976). *See also Daves v. Hawaiian Dredging Co.*, 114 F. Supp. 643, 645 (D. Haw. 1953); *Wright & Miller* § 1216. This proposition is reinforced by the care and candor requirements of Rule 11. *See* § 8.05[2] (certification), *infra*.

[80] *See James, Hazard & Leubsdorf* § 3.6.

[81] *See* § 8.03[2] (cause of action and theory of pleadings in code pleading), *supra*.

[82] *Siegelman v. Cunard White Star, Ltd.*, 221 F.2d 189, 196 (2d Cir. 1955) (Harlan, J.).

[83] *Wright* § 68.

[84] *See* § 8.10[2] (amendment during and after trial), *infra*.

[85] *See* § 8.10, *infra*.

theory. Moreover, Rule 54(c) provides that "every final judgment shall grant the relief to which the party in whose favor it is rendered is entitled, even if the party has not demanded such relief in the party's pleadings."[86]

For several reasons, however, the theory of the pleadings doctrine is not wholly dead. First, the substantive law may require a party to elect his remedies. Thus a party that started by seeking one remedy or asserting one theory may be estopped from switching in mid-stream to another when defendant has reasonably relied in some fashion on the initial election.[87] But the election is not compelled as a matter of pleading form in such a case; it is rooted in the substantive law of estoppel.[88]

Second, the theory of the pleadings may determine which statute of limitations is applicable to the action[89] and whether the pleader is entitled to a jury trial as a matter of right.[90] Limitations periods vary by type of action, and constitutional and some statutory guarantees of jury trial are often tied to historical forms of action or other particular kinds of suit.[91]

Third, federal judges are authorized by Rule 16 to frame pretrial orders that may require the parties to exchange pretrial briefs in which they commit to particular legal theories.[92] Such orders are binding unless modified, and the last pretrial order "shall be modified only to prevent manifest injustice."[93]

Fourth, obligations of candor and care may also restrict a pleader's freedom to plead inconsistently, change his legal theory, or introduce new lines of proof. "[A]lternative pleading is not permitted when in the nature of things the pleader must know which of the inconsistent averments is true and which is false."[94]

[3] The Form of Notice Pleading

Modern notice pleading requires no "technical forms of pleading."[95] While sufficient under the rules, the form pleadings that accompany the federal

---

[86] *See, e.g., Webb v. Arresting Officers*, 749 F.2d 500 (8th Cir. 1984) (plaintiff was entitled to judgment on his post-trial theory that defendants had a duty to intervene for his protection, as long as it was tried and proven, even though this theory was never alleged in the pleadings and his pleaded theory of unnecessary force was not proven).

[87] *See generally* Clark, *Handbook of the Law of Code Pleading* § 77 (2d ed. 1947).

[88] *Id.*

[89] *See generally* § 8.08[2][b] (the statute of limitations), *infra*.

[90] *See* § 12.07[1] (right to jury trial), *infra*.

[91] For example, the Seventh Amendment provides that "[i]n suits at common law, where the value in controversy shall exceed twenty dollars, the right of trial by jury shall be preserved." U.S. Const. amend. VII. It thus ties the right to a jury trial to actions that originated in the common law or are analogous to common law actions and is inapplicable to equitable actions. *See* § 12.07[1] (right to jury trial), *infra*.

[92] *See* § 12.03[3] (pretrial orders), *infra*.

[93] Rule 16(e).

[94] *Church v. Adler*, 113 N.E.2d 327, 332 (Ill. App. Ct. 1953). *See* § 8.05[2] (certification), *infra*.

[95] Rule 8(e)(1).

rules are only examples.[96] A pleading need only include a caption, numbered paragraphs containing averments "limited as far as practicable to a statement of a single set of circumstances," and separate counts for different claims or defenses ("whenever a separation facilitates the clear presentation of the matters set forth").[97] Averments may be incorporated by reference and by attachment to the pleading.[98] None of these requirements is strictly enforced because "[a]ll pleadings shall be so construed as to do substantial justice."[99]

[4] Special Pleading Rules in Modern Pleading

Notice pleading is the norm. Yet most modern pleading jurisdictions retain a few idiosyncratic special pleading rules, in addition to judge-made special pleading requirements for disfavored litigation. Special pleading rules are adopted for practical reasons which are reflected in Rule 9. They may be enforced by motions to strike or dismiss or for more definite statements.[100]

Some special pleading rules were adopted to discourage disfavored litigation. Fraud suits, for example, are disfavored because of the injury they may do to reputations and their potential to intimidate.[101] Claims of mistake are also disfavored because they upset the normal business expectations underlying contract law. As a result, Rule 9(b) requires that "circumstances constituting fraud or mistake shall be stated with particularity." It must be harmonized, however, with the general pleading directives of Rule 8; Rule 9(b) "does not require nor make legitimate the pleading of detailed evidentiary matter."[102] The Supreme Court has also reminded us to harmonize Rule 9(b) with "the flexibility provided by Rule 11(b)(3),"[103] which allows anticipatory pleading: pleading of contentions "likely to have evidentiary support after a reasonable opportunity for futher investigation or discovery."[104] What this kind of specific pleading requirement really achieves is only a marginal increase in the trial court's discretion to use the pleadings to screen disfavored litigation, usually without much lasting effect.[105]

---

[96] Rule 84.

[97] Rule 10(a) & (b).

[98] Rule 10(c).

[99] Rule 8(f).

[100] *See* § 8.07[2][a] (challenging defects of form), *infra.*

[101] *See, e.g., Ross v. A.H. Robins Co.,* 607 F.2d 545 (2d Cir. 1979), *cert. denied,* 446 U.S. 946 (1980) (citing importance of fair notice, of protecting defendants from harm to reputation and goodwill, and of reducing possibility that plaintiffs will pursue largely groundless fraud claims for their *in terrorem* settlement value).

[102] *Id.* at 557 n.20.

[103] *Rotella v. Wood,* 528 U.S. 549 (2000).

[104] *See* § 8.05[2][b], *infra.*

[105] *See generally* Richman, et al., *The Pleading of Fraud: Rhymes Without Reason,* 60 S. Cal. L. Rev. 959 (1987); Baskin, Note, *Using Rule 9(b) to Reduce Nuisance Securities Litigation,* 99 Yale L.J. 1591 (1990).

Legislatures are free, of course, to impose special pleading requirements by statute to discourage disfavored litigation. An example is the 1995 Private Securities Litigation Reform Act,[106] which was passed to curb alleged abuses in federal securities litigation. The Act requires the plaintiff to "state with particularity facts giving rise to a strong inference that the defendant acted with the requisite state of mind" for liability.[107] It also requires specific pleading for alleging false or misleading statements. The Act appears not to have had a dramatic effect on pleading practice, but it certainly encourages courts to take a closer look at securities fraud complaints.[108]

Other special pleading rules promote pleading efficiency and convenience. Under the law of contract, the plaintiff usually must have performed all conditions precedent to defendant's contractual obligations before he may complain of a breach. But in the typical case in which defendant does not dispute performance of such conditions precedent, it would be wasteful to require plaintiff to plead them compendiously. Rule 9(c) therefore permits plaintiff to aver generally the performance of all conditions precedent and requires defendant to deny performance "specifically and with particularity."[109] The same rationale accounts for the requirement in Rule 9(a) that defendant specifically challenge the legal existence or capacity of a party to sue.

Special pleading is sometimes required to avoid surprise. The averment of injury or breach of contract puts defendant fairly on notice that the kinds of damages usually associated with injury (pain and suffering) or with breach (lost profits on the contract) will be claimed. No special pleading of such *general damages* is required. But general pleading is insufficient to put defendant on notice of unusual or unanticipated damages of a sort not ordinarily associated with the alleged injury or breach. Rule 9(g) therefore requires that items of *special damage* "be specifically stated." For example, the failure specifically to plead damages for higher blood pressure said to have been caused by an automobile collision prevented their recovery in *Ziervogel v. Royal Packing Co.*,[110] because this kind of damage, unlike damages for back or neck injuries, is not a normal and expected consequence of such an accident.

Finally, special pleading may reflect the requirements of the substantive law.[111] The usual rule of contract law, for example, is that plaintiff may only recover those damages within the contemplation of the parties at the

---

[106] Pub. L. 104-52, 109 Stat. 737 (codified in scattered sections of 15 U.S.C. (Supp. I 1995)).

[107] *Id.*

[108] *Marcus*, note 77, *supra*, at 1765-1767.

[109] *See generally* § 8.06[2], *infra*, for discussion of the allocation of pleading burdens.

[110] 225 S.W.2d 798 (Mo. Ct. App.1949). Other special damages include medical expenses, unusual injuries such as induced abortion, epilepsy and insanity, expenses incurred in mitigation, and losses of use and income. *See Restatement (Second) of Torts* § 904, cmt. b (1979).

[111] *See* Parness et al., *The Substantive Elements in the New Special Pleading Laws*, 78 Neb. L. Rev. 412 (1999).

time that the contract was made.[112] The pleading of "specials" in a contract case is therefore required to state the plaintiff's prima facie case. Similarly, the law's solicitude for free expression and competition, and its suspicion of intangible injuries to reputation, are reflected in the common substantive requirement that a plaintiff suing for defamation, slander, libel or disparagement show special damages and their proximate causation by the tort.[113] A pleading that omits such specific allegations not only offends special pleading rules, but fails to state a claim for relief.

§ 8.05   Candor and Care Requirements in Modern Pleading

The simplicity and flexibility of modern notice pleading has expanded opportunity for the careless or sharp practitioner to abuse pleading to bluff, bargain, delay, or harass. Motion practice[114] has been the most effective tool for coping with such abuses. However, most jurisdictions have also imposed candor or care standards on litigants and/or their attorneys, requiring *verification* or *certification* of pleadings.[115]

[1]   Verification

Verification of a pleading attests under oath to the truth of its contents, effectively transforming it into an affidavit usable as evidence at trial when the averments are made on the pleader's personal knowledge. Jurisdictions that still require verification reserve it for pleadings in actions that turn uniquely on allegations whose truth or falsity are known only to the parties, such as domestic relations actions. Verification is not generally required of federal pleadings[116] because it would defeat the intentions of the federal rulemakers by either preventing the unsure plaintiff from filing at all or forcing her into a premature election of facts. Moreover, the requirement that *parties* verify their pleadings is ineffective to encourage good faith and reasonable inquiry by their *attorneys*, whom many regard as the principal source of procedural abuse in modern litigation.

[2]   Certification and Rule 11

A certification requirement suffers neither of these defects. Instead of verifying the allegations of the pleading, the signatory — usually the attorney of record or pro se litigant — certifies only to proper purpose and

---

[112] *See, e.g., Hadley v. Baxendale*, 156 Eng. Rep. 145 (1854).

[113] *See, e.g., Fairyland Amusement Co. v. Metromedia, Inc.*, 413 F. Supp. 1290 (W.D. Mo. 1976) (defamation, slander and libel complaint dismissed for plaintiff's failure to plead specifically its loss of patronage as a result of the false publication).

[114] *See* § 8.07 (motion practice), *infra*.

[115] In addition, federal courts have both statutory and inherent power to punish attorney and litigant misconduct. *See* § 8.05[2][d] (sanctions), *infra*.

[116] *But see* Rule 23.1; *cf.* Rules 27, 65 & 68. *See Surowitz v. Hilton Hotels Corp.*, 383 U.S. 363 (1966) (purpose of verification for shareholder derivative suits under Rule 23.1 is to discourage "strike suits," filed to coerce settlement regardless of their truth).

reasonable care in filing the pleading. Rule 11 is an example of a particularly strong certification requirement. Many states have modelled their own certification requirements on some version of the federal rule.[117]

[a] Rule 11 in General[118]

Prior to 1983, Rule 11 provided that by signing a pleading, motion or other paper, an attorney or party certified that he had read the pleading, that "to the best of his knowledge, information, and belief" there was "good ground to support it," and that it was "not interposed for delay." The rule authorized but did not mandate unspecified "disciplinary action" for *"willful* violation[s]."[119] The implied prerequisite of subjective intent and the absence of any required sanctions, however, rendered the pre-1983 rule of little use in federal courts. Only 19 cases involving Rule 11 motions were reported between 1938 and 1983.[120]

Concluding that "[e]xperience shows that in practice Rule 11 has not been effective in deterring abuses,"[121] the Advisory Committee on Civil Rules completely revised the rule in 1983. The 1983 revision provided that by signing a pleading or other paper, the attorney or party certified that, "to the best of his knowledge, information, and belief formed after reasonable inquiry it is well-grounded in fact and warranted by existing law or a good faith argument for the extension, modification, or reversal of existing law, and that it is not interposed for any improper purpose." Under the 1983 rule, it was not only what an attorney actually believed (subjective good faith) that mattered, but what he should have believed as a competent

---

[117] Hess, *Rule 11 Practice in Federal and State Court: An Empirical, Comparative Study,* 75 Marq. L. Rev. 313, 315 n.8, 316 n.9 (1992); *Report of the Special Committee to Consider Sanctions for Frivolous Litigation in New York State Courts,* 18 Fordham Urb. L.J. 3, 32-33 (1990) (comparing state approaches to abusive litigation).

[118] Probably more has been written about Rule 11 since 1983 than about any other civil procedure topic. *See generally* Vairo, *Rule 11 Sanctions: Case Law Perspectives and Preventive Measures* App. F (2d ed. 1995 Supp.) (listing law review articles). The rule has spawned its own looseleaf service, *id.,* its own newsletter, *see Attorney Sanctions Newsletter* (Shepard's), several book-length analyses, *see, e.g.,* Section of Litig., American Bar Ass'n, *Sanctions: Rule 11 & Other Powers* (M. Nelken, ed.) (3d ed. 1992); Joseph, *Sanctions: The Federal Law of Litigation Abuse* (1989), and a host of empirical studies. *See, e.g.,* Marshall, *et al., The Use and Impact of Rule 11,* 86 Nw. U. L. Rev. 943 (1992); Federal Judicial Center, *Rule 11: Final Report to the Advisory Comm. on Civil Rules of the Jud. Conf. of the U.S.* (undated), *summarized in* Wiggins, et al., *The Federal Judicial Center's Study of Rule 11,* 2 FJC Directions (1991); Burbank, American Judicature Soc'y, *Rule 11 in Transition: The Report of the Third Circuit Task Force on Federal Rule of Civil Procedure 11* (1989).

[119] *Wright & Miller* § 1331 (emphasis added).

[120] Risinger, *Honesty in Pleading and Its Enforcement: Some "Striking" Problems With Federal Rule of Civil Procedure 11,* 61 Minn. L. Rev. 1, 35-37 (1976). Of course, one would expect that most Rule 11 motions are unreported. *See Wiggins,* note 118, *supra,* at 7 (finding that only 6.6% of district court cases involving Rule 11 activity were reported, and that reporting practices were highly variable); *Burbank,* note 118, *supra,* at 59 (only 9% of dispositions involving Rule 11 were reported in Third Circuit sample; only 33% were available on Lexis). But even if ten times as many cases were decided as were reported prior to 1983, the reported case data would indicate fewer than 200 Rule 11 cases over forty-five years.

[121] Rule 11 advisory committee's notes (1983).

attorney after reasonable prefiling inquiry (objective reasonableness).[122] The substitution of an objective for a subjective standard made it easier for courts to find violations, and the mandatory sanction provision of the 1983 rule appeared to require them to punish such violations.

Practice under the 1983 rule, however, suggested to some that the pendulum had swung too far. Between 1983 and 1993, there were 6000 reported Rule 11 cases.[123] Eighty-one% of the federal judges surveyed in one study thought that the 1983 rule had a positive effect,[124] and the actual percentage of cases in which Rule 11 activity occurred was reported at only 2-3%.[125] Yet critics charged that enforcement was inconsistent and unpredictable; that the rule was enforced disproportionately against plaintiffs in general (and civil rights plaintiffs in particular) with chilling effects on novel plaintiffs' litigation; that courts relied almost exclusively on fee-shifting and compensation as sanctions, effectively and perhaps unlawfully modifying the American rule against fee-shifting; that sanctions were often imposed without fair procedure; and that Rule 11 motion practice had generated a Kafkaesque nightmare of satellite litigation (including Rule 11 motions against Rule 11 motions).[126] These criticisms were not always supported by the empirical data, and some may have been premature (reflecting transitional problems in judicial applications of the 1983 rule revisions), but enough persisted to prompt another rule revision in 1993.

As discussed in subsections b and c below, the 1993 rule equalized the burdens imposed by the rule on plaintiffs and defendants. As discussed in subsection d below, it abolished mandatory sanctions in favor of discretionary non-monetary sanctions. It also made several other significant changes, several of which are noted in the remainder of this subsection.

First, Rule 11(b) expanded the scope of certification from a pleading or other paper to individual "claims, defenses, and other legal contentions" and

---

[122] *See* Rule 11 advisory committee's notes (1983). Although the text of the 1983 rule contained both objective and subjective components, the rulemakers clearly intended to eliminate the necessity for a finding of subjective bad faith as a predicate for sanctions, in a deliberate departure from prior case law. *See, e.g., Eastway Constr. Co. v. City of New York*, 762 F.2d 243, 253 (2d Cir. 1985). The no-improper-purpose requirement also prohibited, for example, the filing of tactical pleadings or motions to upset settlement negotiations in order to obtain fee-related concessions from defendant in other litigation, *In Re Itel Securities Litigation*, 596 F. Supp. 226 (N.D. Cal. 1984), *aff'd*, 791 F.2d 672 (9th Cir. 1986); motions to disqualify opposing counsel for the purpose of harassing the other side and increasing the costs of litigation, *Wold v. Minerals Eng'g Co.*, 575 F. Supp. 166 (D. Colo. 1983) (imposing attorneys fees on party who made the motion for these purposes); or attempts to continue the "economic and political warfare" of labor negotiations by using litigation to intimidate. *W.S.B. Elec. Co. v. Rank and File Comm. to Stop 2-Gate Sys.*, 103 F.R.D. 417 (N.D. Cal. 1984).

[123] Spiegel, *The Rule 11 Studies and Civil Rights Cases: An Inquiry into the Neutrality of Procedural Rules*, 32 Conn. L. Rev. 155, 157 (1999). This number of *reported* cases indicates that there may have been as many as 17,000 Rule 11 cases altogether in this decade. *See id. supra.*

[124] *Wiggins*, note 118, *supra*, at 34.

[125] *Id.* at 6.

[126] *See, e.g., Wright & Miller* § 1332; *Burbank*, note 118, *supra*, at 57, 65; Nelken, *Has the Chancellor Shot Himself in the Foot? Looking for a Middle Ground on Rule 11 Sanctions*, 41 Hastings L.J. 383 (1990); Schwarzer, *Rule 11 Revisited*, 101 Harv. L. Rev. 1013 (1988).

"allegations and other factual contentions." It thus rejected the pleading-as-a-whole approach to Rule 11 taken by some courts, by which they found a violation only when the pleading as a whole (and not just some part of it) violated the good grounds and proper purposes requirements.[127] Still, the 1983 Advisory Committee cautioned that Rule 11 motions "should not be made or threatened for minor, inconsequential violations." Inclusion of a minor ungrounded allegation or argument in an otherwise well-grounded paper thus should not be treated as a violation. Furthermore, the relative importance in the paper of the offending section may still be considered in deciding the severity of any sanction, as we discuss below in section d.

Second, the 1993 rule amendments compromised on the issue whether litigants have a continuing duty to correct or even withdraw papers in light of post-filing events. Most courts under the 1983 rule had rejected the concept of continuing duty in favor of a "snapshot rule." This focused only on whether a paper complied with the rule in "the instant when a picture is taken — when the signature is placed on the document."[128] These courts rejected the concept of continuing duty both because of the phrasing of the 1983 rule and the updating burden that such a duty would impose. In contrast, a few courts had imposed such a duty to effectuate the purpose of the rule.[129] The 1993 amendments provided that the rule is violated by "signing, filing, submitting, *or later advocating*" a paper when the litigant knows that it is no longer well-grounded.[130] Thus a lawyer who during a pretrial conference presses a claim or defense would be subject to the rule's obligations "measured as of that time" — not only as of the time she signed the paper containing the claim or defense.[131] On the other hand, the 1993 rule amendments did not saddle a litigant with the burden of curing pleadings by formal amendments to correct or withdraw such claims or defenses.[132]

Nevertheless, a litigant may formally withdraw such a claim or defense to bring itself into the rule's "safe harbor." Rule 11(c)(1)(A) grants a litigant 21 days between service and filing of a Rule 11 motion[133] to correct or

---

[127] *See, e.g.*, Tobias, *Civil Rights Plaintiffs and the Proposed Revision of Rule 11*, 77 Iowa L. Rev. 1775, 1780 (1992). The majority of courts that had considered the issue had rejected the pleadings-as-a-whole approach. *See Section of Litig.*, note 118, *supra*, at 3.

[128] *See, e.g.*, *Thomas v. Capital Sec. Serv., Inc.*, 836 F.2d 866, 874 (5th Cir. 1988).

[129] *See cases cited in* Klausner, Note, *The Dynamics of Rule 11: Preventing Frivolous Litigation By Demanding Professional Responsibility*, 61 N.Y.U. L. Rev. 300, 325-326 n.195 (1986).

[130] Rule 11(b) (emphasis added).

[131] Rule 11(b) advisory committee's notes (1993). The 1993 amendments thus make it clear that Rule 11 applies to the complaint in a case that has been removed from state to federal court once the plaintiff "advocates" the claims in that complaint in federal court.

[132] *See* Simpson, Note, *Why Change Rule 11? Ramifications of the 1992 Amendment Proposal*, 29 Cal. W. L. Rev. 495, 508 (1993).

[133] The safe harbor is available only against Rule 11 motions and does not apply to show cause orders issued at the court's own initiative. Rule 11(c)(1)(B). The 1993 Advisory Committee reasoned that show cause orders will ordinarily only be issued in extreme situations akin to contempt of court, which do not deserve any safe harbor. Rule 11 advisory committee's notes (1993).

withdraw the offending paper. This provision is intended to reduce the amount of satellite litigation under the rule by letting rule offenders moot Rule 11 motions before they are filed in court. It may only codify what some lawyers are doing already. On the other hand, some critics view this informal practice of "threat and retreat" as "problematic," concluding that its codification will accentuate "one of [the former] Rule's worst features. . . ."[134] Justice Scalia also objected to the safe-harbor provision on the ground that it will encourage abusers, because they "will be able to file thoughtless, reckless, and harassing pleadings, secure in the knowledge that they have nothing to lose. . . ."[135]

[b] Evidentiary Support

Rule 11(b)(3) and (4) require litigants to certify that their factual allegations or denials of factual allegations "have evidentiary support or, if specifically so identified, are likely to have evidentiary support after a reasonable opportunity for further investigation or discovery." This provision clarifies and expands the 1983 rule in several respects.

Because it extends to *denials* of factual allegations, the 1993 rule has helped equalize the burden imposed on plaintiffs and defendants. By insisting just on *evidentiary support*, the rule makes clear that the litigant is not required to certify that its factual contentions will prevail.[136] Moreover, by authorizing certification of allegations that "likely" will have such support, the rule gives plaintiffs the same option of "information-and-belief" pleading now afforded defendants by Rule 8(c). This also lessens the rule's previously disproportionate impact on plaintiffs. The provision slightly relaxes the former rule's ban on "file now, check later" practice, by affording "a reasonable [post-filing] opportunity for further investigation" of specifically identified information-and-belief contentions, so long as the litigant has done its best before filing.[137] If that investigation turns up no evidentiary support for such contentions, then the litigant may not continue to advocate them.

At the same time, tolerance of anticipatory, "likely-to-have-support" pleading poses a dilemma for the pleader. On one hand, the pleader is not expressly required to have that support at the time of the pleading, provided he specifically identifies the "likely-to-have-support" contentions as such. On the other hand, the Advisory Committee warned that this tolerance "is not a license to join parties, make claims, or present defenses without any factual basis or justification."[138] What must the pleader do to engage in such anticipatory pleading without running afoul of the rule? The Advisory Committee's notes, coupled with the rule, suggest an answer.[139] First, he

---

[134] Tobias, *Reconsidering Rule 11*, 46 U. Miami L. Rev. 855, 877 (1992).

[135] Dissenting statement of Justice Scalia on Amendments to the Federal Rules of Civil Procedure, 113 S. Ct. CCCVI, CCCVII (1993).

[136] Rule 11(b) & (c) advisory committee's notes (1993).

[137] *Id.*

[138] *Id.*

[139] *See* Pondrom, Comment, *Predicting the Unpredictable Under Rule 11(b)(3): When Are Allegations "Likely" to Have Evidentiary Support*, 43 UCLA L. Rev. 1393 (1996) (suggesting the answer in the text).

must still conduct a prefiling inquiry which is reasonable in the circumstances. Second, he must have some "factual basis" for his contentions, even if it is not yet in evidentiary form. Third, he must, if challenged, be able to demonstrate that there was a need and reasonable opportunity for further discovery, by showing that circumstances beyond his control—such as time constraints or his adversary's or a third party's control of the information—prevented him from obtaining evidentiary support before filing.

Reasonableness of the required inquiry both before and after filing takes into account the litigant's access to necessary factual information and time available in which to make inquiry. Since the litigant's state of mind is not controlling, reasonableness is open to empirical verification. The focus is upon the facts of the prefiling investigation, although the 1983 Advisory Committee expressly cautioned the courts against using hindsight in making that examination.[140]

The cases suggest that the requisite prefiling factual investigation must at least include a thorough interview with the client and the key witnesses, if they are available.[141]

> To decide if the attorney may rely solely on his client, he should determine if his knowledge is direct or hearsay and check closely the plausibility of the client's account. When an attorney must rely on his client, he should question him thoroughly, not accepting the client's version on faith alone. However, "if all the attorney has is his client's assurance that facts exist or do not exist, when a reasonable inquiry would reveal otherwise, he has not satisfied his obligation."[142]

It follows that when an attorney can obtain factual information from public sources, he must do so and cannot rely solely on his client.[143] On the other hand, if the necessary information is primarily within the control of the prospective defendants, reliance on the client is reasonable under the rule.[144]

[c] Legal Support

Reasonable inquiry into the law is what any competent attorney would make into the standard legal research sources. She must determine that any legal position asserted in a filing is warranted by existing law. Alternatively, in order not to chill advocacy for change in the law, the rule shelters "nonfrivolous argument for the extension, modification, or reversal

---

[140] Rule 11 advisory committee's notes (1983).

[141] See Wold v. Minerals Eng'g Co., 575 F. Supp. 166, 167 (D. Colo. 1983); Rhinehart v. Stauffer, 638 F.2d 1169, 1171 (9th Cir. 1979) (decision under pre-1983 Rule 11).

[142] Nassau-Suffolk Ice Cream, Inc. v. Integrated Resources, Inc., 114 F.R.D. 684, 689 (S.D.N.Y. 1987) (quoting Coburn Optical Indus., Inc. v. Cilco, Inc., 610 F. Supp. 656, 659 (M.D.N.C. 1985); other citations omitted). See generally Ward, Note, Rule 11 and Factually Frivolous Claims — The Goal of Cost Minimization and the Client's Duty to Investigate, 44 Vanderbilt L. Rev. 1165 (1991).

[143] Kendrick v. Zanides, 609 F. Supp. 1162, 1172-1173 (N.D. Cal. 1985); Mohammed v. Union Carbide Corp., 606 F. Supp. 252 (E.D. Mich. 1985).

[144] See, e.g., Kamen v. American Telephone & Telegraph Co., 791 F.2d 1006 (2d Cir. 1986).

of existing law. . . ."[145] Critics argued that this shelter was insufficient for civil rights plaintiffs, who often advocate the recognition of new rights.[146] The 1993 amendments to the rule therefore added "[arguments for the] . . . establishment of new law" to the shelter.

Must such plaintiffs flag such claims as novel to alert the court and the opposing parties? Some courts concluded that they must, but the 1993 Advisory Committee said that "arguments for a change of law are not required to be specifically so identified, [although] a contention that is so identified should be viewed with greater tolerance under the rule."[147]

Does the duty of legally-warranted argument imposed by Rule 11(b)(2) carry with it a corollary duty of candor, for example, to disclose contrary legal authority in the papers? Assuming *arguendo* that the uncited authority was directly contrary, the Ninth Circuit Court of Appeals nevertheless concluded that

> neither Rule 11 nor any other rule imposes a requirement that the lawyer, in addition to advocating the cause of his client, step first into the shoes of opposing counsel to find all potentially contrary authority, and finally into the robes of the judge to decide whether the authority is indeed contrary or whether it is distinguishable.[148]

The court acknowledged that the ethical rules proposed by the American Bar Association prohibit an attorney from knowingly failing to disclose "legal authority in the controlling jurisdiction known to the lawyer to be directly adverse to the position of the client and not disclosed by opposing counsel."[149] But it concluded that Rule 11 should not be used for broad-spectrum enforcement of ethical obligations.[150]

Arguably, the court of appeals ignored both the language and the history of the Rule.[151] Focusing only on the requirement that a filing be warranted by existing law, the court disregarded the independent requirement that it not be interposed for *any* improper purpose.[152] A knowing omission of

---

[145] For examples of frivolous legal claims, *see, e.g., Heimbaugh v. City and County of San Francisco*, 591 F. Supp. 1573 (N.D. Cal. 1984) (complaint alleged that city's ban on playing softball on field reserved for hardball violated First Amendment right to advocate democracy in sports); *Blair v. Shenandoah Women's Center, Inc.*, 757 F.2d 1435 (4th Cir. 1985) (attorney for a man who filed suit against a women's shelter in which his wife sought refuge from his abuse was properly assessed attorney's fees in view of the complaint's scandalous accusations and frivolous legal positions).

[146] See critics cited and analyzed in Spiegel, *The Rule 11 Studies and Civil Rights Cases: An Inquiry in the Neutrality of Procedural Rules*, 32 Conn. L. Rev. 155, 158 n.12 (1999).

[147] Rule 11(b) & (c) advisory committee's notes (1993).

[148] *Golden Eagle Distributing Corp. v. Burroughs Corp.*, 801 F.2d 1531, 1542 (9th Cir. 1987).

[149] 801 F.2d at 1539, *citing* American Bar Ass'n, *Model Rules of Professional Conduct* R. 3.3(a)(3) (1983).

[150] 801 F.2d at 1539, 1542. *But see* Floyd, *Candor Versus Advocacy: Court's Use of Sanctions to Enforce the Duty of Candor Toward the Tribunal*, 29 Ga. L. Rev. 1035 (1995) (endorsing such use of Rule 11).

[151] *See Golden Eagle*, 809 F.2d 584, 586 (9th Cir. 1987) (Noonan, Sneed, Anderson, & Kozinski, JJ., dissenting from denial of *reh'g en banc*).

[152] *See* § 8.05[d], *infra*.

directly contrary authority within the controlling jurisdiction evidences an intent to mislead the court. Filing with that intent is surely filing with an improper purpose. Moreover, a filing would appear to be unwarranted when it is directly contrary to the legal authority within the controlling jurisdiction. Courts have therefore divided over the duty of candor that was rejected by the Ninth Circuit.[153]

Does a court's eventual rejection of a legal argument necessarily suggest that its proponent violated Rule 11? The rule's express embrace of "nonfrivolous" suggests the contrary; nonfrivolous is not the same as correct. On the other hand, the same phrase focuses more judicial attention under the rule on the quality of a litigant's legal argument than on its prefiling inquiry. Indeed, one judge has suggested that "the submissions of the parties are to be marked on a scale of 'A' through 'F.' Anything falling on the far side of 'C' merits not only the loss of one's case but loss of one's shirt as well."[154] This kind of standard invites rulings that are based on product rather than on conduct, and rulings that risk conflating the merits of claims and defenses with the care with which they are asserted.[155] The Advisory Committee acknowledges this risk, and tries to guard against it by directing a court to take into account a litigant's prefiling conduct: "the extent to which a litigant has researched the issues and found some support for its theories even in minority opinions, in law review articles, or through consultation with other lawyers. . . ."[156]

[c] Improper Purpose

The converse question has divided the courts—whether a court's acceptance of a legal argument or, more broadly, finding that a paper is well-founded, necessarily suggests that Rule 11 was *not* violated. The Seventh Circuit may have rejected this proposition by asserting that it may be necessary to explore the filer's subjective intent even if the paper was objectively well-founded.[157] Several other appellate courts have taken the opposite view, holding that the filing of a well-founded complaint is not ordinarily sanctionable under the improper purpose standard (at least absent unusual circumstances, such as multiple filings amounting to harassment).[158]

---

[153] *See, e.g.,* cases cited in *Klausner,* note 129, *supra,* at 321 n.164; *DeSisto College, Inc. v. Line,* 888 F.2d 755, 766 (11th Cir. 1989) (rule imposes duty of candor); *Cousin v. D.C.,* 142 F.R.D. 574, 577 (D.D.C. 1992) (imposing sanctions for failing to disclose and discuss adverse authority).

[154] *Szabo Food Serv., Inc. v. Canteen Corp.,* 823 F.2d 1073, 1085 (7th Cir. 1987) (Cudahy, J., concurring in part and dissenting in part). *See* Levine, *Seeking a Common Language for the Application of Rule 11 Sanctions: What Is "Frivolous"?,* 78 Neb. L. Rev. 677, 679-685 (1999) (criticizing inconsistency of courts' interpretation of frivolous legal arguments and urging a graduated standard instead).

[155] *See generally* Burbank, note 5, *supra,* at 10-13; Burbank, *The Transformation of American Civil Procedure: The Example of Rule 11,* 137 U. Pa. L. Rev. 1925, 1933-1934 (1989).

[156] Rule 11(b) & (c) advisory committiee's notes (1993).

[157] *Szabo Food Serv., Inc. v. Canteen Corp.,* 823 F.2d 1073, 1083 (7th Cir. 1987), *cert. dismissed,* 485 U.S. 901 (1988).

[158] *Moore* § 11.11[8][d] (citing 2d, 5th and 9th Circuits).

The latter holdings reflect several problems in finding a violation of Rule 11's improper purpose provision. The first is that the rule generally tests papers by objective, reasonable lawyer standards, rather than by the filer's subjective intent. The Ninth Circuit has concluded that "because of the objective standard applicable to Rule 11 analysis, a complaint that is found well-grounded in fact or law cannot be sanctioned as harassing regardless of the attorney's subjective intent."[159] Second, even if subjective intent may be appropriately considered in deciding whether a filing has an improper purpose, its proof is circumstantial and problematic. It must necessarily be inferred from the paper itself, as well as from the consequences of filing. When the paper is well-founded, the circumstantial evidence is in conflict even if the consequences are delay or expense to opponents. Finally, sanctioning colorable claims may raise constitutional questions by deterring the presentation of grievances to the courts.[160] The Second Circuit has also suggested that filing to generate adverse publicity for the defendants may be constitutionally protected under the First Amendment; "[i]t is not the role of Rule 11 to safeguard a defendant from public criticism that may result from the assertion of nonfrivolous claims."[161] On the other hand, assertion of an *unfounded* claim to use the judicial forum for a public protest has been held sanctionable by the D.C. Circuit.[162] Clearly, it is easier to infer improper purpose from an unfounded paper.

But if improper purpose can only be inferred from unfounded filings, the improper purpose provision of the rule would be superfluous. Such papers already violate the warranted-by-law and evidentiary-support provisions of the rule. For the improper purpose standard to play any independent role, it must be applicable to even well-founded papers in unusual circumstances which circumstantially prove an improper intent. The most common circumstances involve multiple filings and a pattern of harassment. Courts have also inferred improper purposes from the timing of filing when it results in strategic delays.[163]

[e] Sanctions

Rule 11 formerly provided that, after finding a violation, a court "shall impose appropriate sanctions," including reasonable attorneys fees. Although it also authorized nonmonetary sanctions, 95% of all sanctions imposed under the rule were monetary, including some very substantial fee awards.[164] Courts under the former sanctions regime appeared to have

---

[159] *Hudson v. Moore Business Forms, Inc.*, 836 F.2d 1156, 1159 (9th Cir. 1987).

[160] *Moore* § 11.11[8][d].

[161] *Sussman v. Bank of Israel*, 56 F.3d 450, 459 (2d Cir.), *cert. denied sub nom. Bank of Israel v. Lewin*, 516 U.S. 916 (1995).

[162] *Saltany v. Reagan*, 886 F.2d 438 (D.C. Cir. 1989).

[163] *See, e.g., Aetna Life Ins. Co. v. Alla Med. Servs., Inc.*, 855 F.2d 1470, 1476 (9th Cir. 1988) (emphasizing pattern of abusive litigation and successive papers in approving sanctions, even when papers were nonfrivolous); cases cited at *Moore* § 11.11[8][a] n.64.

[164] *See, e.g., Avirgan v. Hull*, 932 F.2d 1572 (11th Cir. 1991) (over $1 million); *Brandt v. Schal Assocs., Inc.*, 131 F.R.D. 485 (N.D. Ill. 1990) (over $350,000).

lost sight of the fact that Rule 11's purpose is deterrence rather than compensation.[165] Rule 11(c)(2) attempts to correct this by making sanctions discretionary and by expressly reminding the court of the availability of nonmonetary sanctions, including orders to pay penalties into court. The 1993 Advisory Committee presented examples of orders striking the offending paper; admonishing, reprimanding, or censuring the offender; requiring the offender to participate in educational programs; or referring the matter to disciplinary authorities. Moreover, when the court on motion does impose a monetary sanction, the sanction is limited to the reasonable attorneys' fees and other expenses "incurred as a direct result of the violation" and may not be awarded against a represented party for violations of Rule 11(b)(2) — the warranted-by-the-law certification requirement.

The court's discretion in awarding sanctions is limited. Although the 1993 Advisory Committee apparently rejected a least-severe sanction standard,[166] it did provide in Rule 11(c)(2) that sanctions "shall be limited to what is sufficient to deter repetition of [the violative conduct] or comparable conduct by others similarly situated." It suggested that the factors that should inform discretion include

> [w]hether the improper conduct was willful, or negligent; whether it was part of a pattern of activity, or an isolated event; whether it infected the entire pleading, or only one particular count or defense; whether the person has engaged in similar conduct in other litigation; whether it was intended to injure; what effect it had on the litigation process in time or expense; whether the responsible person is trained in the law; what amount, given the financial resources of the responsible person, is needed to deter that person from repetition in the same case; [and] what amount is needed to deter similar activity by other litigants. . . .[167]

The 1993 amendment also assures a minimum of procedural fairness in the sanctioning process. All motions for sanctions may be made only "after notice and a reasonable opportunity to respond," and a court may impose sanctions on its own initiative only after issuing an order directing a party to show cause why the party has not violated the rule.[168] In addition, Rule 11(c) requires a sanctions order to describe the offending conduct and "to explain the basis for the sanction imposed." This provision assures an adequate basis for appellate review, which was not always provided under the former Rule 11 practice.[169]

Finally, the advisory committee's notes to the 1993 amendment reaffirm that Rule 11 is not the exclusive source of sanctioning authority in federal

---

[165] Rule 11 advisory committee's notes (1983) (noting that "the word 'sanctions' in the [rule] caption . . . stresses a deterrent orientation in dealing with improper pleadings, motions or other papers").

[166] See Tobias, note 134, supra, at 881.

[167] Rule 11(c) advisory committee's notes (1993).

[168] Rule 11(c)(1)(B). Previously, courts had not always afforded fair notice and an opportunity to be heard when they imposed sanctions sua sponte. See Wiggins, note 118, supra, at 17.

[169] See, e.g., Brown v. Fed'n of State Med. Bd., 830 F.2d 1429, 1438-1440 (7th Cir. 1987).

court. Congress has by statute authorized courts to assess costs, including attorneys' fees, against an attorney who "multiplies the proceedings in any case unreasonably and vexatiously."[170] This statute differs significantly from Rule 11. It is broader because it applies to the whole course of counsel's litigation conduct (not just filing papers) and imposes a continuing duty to avoid dilatory tactics. But it is also narrower because it requires subjective bad faith by counsel and does not apply to clients.[171] The Supreme Court has also held that federal courts retain inherent power to discipline attorneys and parties who appear before them.[172] Although Rule 11's procedures ordinarily supersede the courts' inherent powers in cases to which the rule applies, these powers may be used to punish in-court conduct and inappropriate oral remarks beyond the reach of the rule.

[f] Assessment

In the first edition of this book, we suggested that vigorous enforcement of Rule 11 could make kitchen-sink pleadings and mechanical Rule 12 motions[173] endangered species, while over-zealous enforcement of Rule 11 risked a return to the problems of unfairness and inefficiency that plagued code pleading. In the second edition, we predicted that the 1993 amendments made both outcomes less likely, because, first, the de-emphasis of monetary sanctions would diminish incentives to file Rule 11 motions, and, second, the authorization of information-and-belief pleading, coupled with the safe harbor provision, would give litigants more leeway in pleading.

Early assessments of the amendment's effect appear to be consistent with these predictions. Commentators have noted a "marked decline in formal Rule 11 activity" and in corresponding satellite litigation, as well as an amelioration of the rule's chilling effect on novel claims and arguments.[174] A 1995 survey of judges and lawyers provided lukewarm support for these assessments.[175] While most thought "groundless litigation" a "small" problem which had not changed much since the amendments, 14% of the judges and 11-13% of the lawyers thought it had declined. Substantial majorities supported the safe harbor provision and more than one-third of the judges thought it had reduced rule activity on their dockets, a conclusion which individual courts have stated in their reported opinions.[176] These

---

[170] 28 U.S.C. § 1927.

[171] *See United States v. Teamsters,* 948 F.2d 1338, 1334 (2d Cir. 1991). The statute also lacks Rule 11's safe harbor and separate motion provisions.

[172] *See Chambers v. NASCO,* 501 U.S. 32 (1991).

[173] *See* § 8.07 (motions practice), *infra.*

[174] *See, e.g.,* Vairo, *Rule 11 and the Profession,* 67 Ford. L. Rev. 589, 626, 643 (1998); *cf.* Hirt, *A Second Look at Amended Rule 11,* 48 Am. U. L. Rev. 1007 (1999) (noting "anecdotal evidence" of these effects but concluding that it may be premature to declare complete success).

[175] Shapard *et al.* (Federal Judicial Center), *Report of a Survey Concerning Rule 11, Federal Rules of Civil Procedure* (1995).

[176] *See* cases cited by *Hirt,* note 174 *supra,* at 1030-1031. Whether the safe harbor also has revived professional collegiality and civility by making lawyers talk to each other, as some had hoped, is more doubtful. *See id.* at 1031, 1041 (citing judicial opinions expressing this hope); Vairo, note 174 *supra,* at 643-647), (raising doubts).

assessments shows that Justice Scalia's fear that the 1993 amendments would "gut" the rule[177] has not materialized.

On the other hand, a majority of judges and lawyers in the 1995 survey supported changing the rule to make compensation, as well as deterrence, a purpose of sanctions. Perhaps, the more rigorous pre-filing inquiry is intercepting *negligently* filed papers, or the safe harbor is being used to correct or withdraw them, with the result that the unsupported papers that remain may more often be pressed intentionally. If so, they are papers for which non-monetary sanctions seem inadequate to lawyers who incur uncompensated expenses in opposing them. This conclusion is consistent with the claim that other, less circumscribed sanctions, such as those afforded by 28 U.S.C. § 1927 or the courts' inherent power,[178] are being used with increasing frequency since the 1993 amendments.[179]

Finally, the 1993 amendments do not fully address a serious problem of certification: its tendency to focus judicial sanctioning attention on a litigant's product rather than her conduct. It has proven impossible to draw a bright line between unsuccessful or merely inept papers and factually unwarranted or frivolous papers. But, as one critic puts it, Rule 11 was never intended as "an open-ended charter for upgrading the legal profession."[180] The proper focus of a certification rule is on a litigant's conduct in investigating the facts and researching the law before filing; other motions are available to test the merits and other devices (such as continuing legal education) to improve the bar's competency.

§ 8.06   The Complaint

In most modern pleading systems, the complaint (and any other pleading that sets out a claim for relief) should contain a statement of jurisdiction when necessary, a statement of the claim, and a demand for relief.[181] The federal complaint is illustrative.

[1]   Statement of Jurisdiction

Rule 8(a) requires the claimant to include a statement of the "grounds upon which the court's jurisdiction depends" unless the court already has jurisdiction and the claim needs no independent grounds. This requirement reflects the limited jurisdiction of the federal courts,[182] and similar requirements apply to state courts of limited jurisdiction as well. Because the chief workhorses of state judicial systems are usually courts of general jurisdiction, no such jurisdictional statement is required for claims filed there, unless a jurisdictional requirement is built into the substantive claim itself.

---

[177] Dissenting statement of Justice Scalia on amendments to the Federal Rules of Civil Procedure, 113 S. Ct. CCCVI, CCCVIX (1993).

[178] *See* § 8.05[2][e], *supra.*

[179] *Vairo*, note 174 *supra*, at 643.

[180] *Burbank*, note 118, *supra*, at 13.

[181] *See* Rule 8(a).

[182] *See* § 5.01[2] (federal subject matter jurisdiction), *supra.*

The content of the jurisdictional statement depends upon how the court's subject matter jurisdiction is defined.[183] In federal courts, jurisdictional allegations that track the language of Form 2 are sufficient. Technical forms of pleading are no more necessary to plead jurisdiction than to plead a claim. Even with respect to jurisdictional allegations, pleadings should be construed liberally to do substantial justice. The court should search not just the pleading, but the whole record, to see if it will support subject matter jurisdiction.[184] By statute, defects in the pleading of jurisdiction can also be cured through amendment in the trial court or on appeal.[185] Note, however, that these rules apply only to the cure of defects in the *allegation* of jurisdiction; they cannot be invoked to supply jurisdiction that was not present at the commencement of the action.[186]

[2] Statement of Claim and the Burden of Pleading

Matters of form and detail in modern claim pleading were discussed in section 8.04. Here we will consider what elements must be pleaded and by whom. The substantive law from which the claim arises provides an answer to the first question. Special pleading rules like Rules 8(c) and 9 or precedent generally supply an answer to the second question. "Precedent as such," however, "does nothing for the inquiring mind."[187] Thus it is useful to consider the logic of allocating burdens in pleading. We start with the burden of producing evidence at trial, which the burden of pleading usually follows.

A plaintiff has the burden of producing evidence at trial that would enable a rational trier of fact to find for him (1) *if* he also carries his burden of persuasion, *i.e.*, persuades the trier of fact that it is more probable than not that he is correct, and (2) *unless* defendant in turn carries *her* burden of producing evidence that would enable the trier of fact to find that she has a defense.[188] When the plaintiff does not carry his initial burden of production, the court will dismiss the action and enter judgment as a matter of law for the defendant.[189]

To the plaintiff typically (though not invariably) goes the burden of pleading matters for which he has the initial burden of production at trial: the prima facie case.[190] One reason is that the plaintiff is challenging the status quo and may fairly be asked to demonstrate why. Another is the assumption that if he is unable with due candor and care to plead such

---

[183] *See* §§ 5.03 (federal question jurisdiction) & 5.04-5.06 (diversity), *supra*.

[184] *Wright* § 69 (citations omitted).

[185] 28 U.S.C. § 1653.

[186] *See* § 5.01[1] (subject matter jurisdiction generally), *supra*.

[187] Cleary, *Presuming and Pleading: An Essay on Juristic Immaturity*, 12 Stan. L. Rev. 5, 10 (1959).

[188] *Id.* at 15-16. "Burden of proof" is often used as a shorthand reference for the burdens of production and persuasion together. *See generally* § 12.01 (burdens and standards of proof), *infra*.

[189] *See* Rules 41(b) & 50(a), and §§ 11.04[2] & 12.09[1], *infra* respectively.

[190] *See* § 8.04[1] (notice pleading), *supra*.

matters, he will probably also be unable to satisfy his burden of production at trial. If his case would be dismissed at trial, it would be wasteful to let it get that far. Requiring the plaintiff to plead those elements as to which he would have the burden of production at trial forces him to expose any basic infirmity in the case at the pleading stage, permitting its dismissal at the front of the litigation.

The defendant has the burden of pleading the elements as to which she carries the burden of production at trial. This allocation is efficient because it relieves the plaintiff of the task of pleading the negative of every possible defense, including many on which the defendant might never rely. It also forces the defendant to identify the specific defenses on which she will rely, information that would be withheld from plaintiff and the court until trial were the burden of pleading the nonexistence of all possible defenses placed on plaintiff.

Whether a jurisdiction classifies a particular element as part of the plaintiff's prima facie case or as part of a defense depends upon a highly variable mix of policy, fairness, convenience and probability considerations, as well as history and accident.[191] *Gomez v. Toledo*[192] illustrates the interplay of some of these. Gomez sued a public official for violating his civil rights. The Supreme Court had held that such officials are entitled to a qualified immunity from liability for acts performed in the reasonable belief that they were lawful. *Gomez* posed the question whether a civil rights plaintiff has the burden of pleading the defendant's bad faith and unreasonable belief as part of his *prima facie* case, or whether the defendant has the burden of pleading good faith and reasonable belief as part of his defense. The Court placed the burden on the defendant, reasoning in part that "whether such immunity has been established depends on facts peculiarly within the knowledge and control of the defendant."[193] Not only would it therefore be more convenient for defendant to assume the burden, but it would be unfair to ask the plaintiff to plead a state of mind that turns on factors "which [he] cannot reasonably be expected to know."[194]

[c] Demand for Relief

The demand for relief has lost much of the significance it held at common law because most modern pleading systems frequently authorize the court to "grant the relief to which the [prevailing party] is entitled, even if the party has not demanded such relief in the party's pleadings."[195] Any other rule would be a reversion to the discarded doctrines of the theory of the pleadings and election of remedies.[196]

---

[191] *See generally Cleary*, note 187, *supra*. Some of these we have already considered in analyzing special pleading rules. *See* § 8.04[4], *supra*.

[192] 446 U.S. 635 (1980).

[193] *Id.* at 641.

[194] *Id.*

[195] Rule 54(c). *See, e.g., Bail v. Cunningham Bros., Inc.*, 452 F.2d 182 (7th Cir. 1971).

[196] *See* § 8.04[2] (consistency and the theory of the pleadings in modern pleading), *supra*.

Nevertheless, the demand for relief is useful even in a modern notice pleading jurisdiction. When the court's jurisdiction is limited by an amount in controversy,[197] the demand for monetary relief, or *ad damnum*, may determine the grounds for jurisdiction. The type of relief demanded also has jurisdictional significance in those systems that have maintained the division between law and equity. It can bear on the availability of a jury trial, which is often tied to particular kinds of actions.[198]

Finally, the prayer for relief may set a ceiling on the plaintiff's recovery in the event of default — judgment resulting from defendant's failure to appear or otherwise defend.[199] Default, after all, is sometimes strategic, reflecting defendant's cost-benefit analysis of defending an action. To perform that analysis, defendant must know the maximum cost of not defending, information that is conveyed by the demand for judgment contained in the complaint. If, after defendant's default, the judgment could exceed the demand in the complaint, this cost-benefit analysis would be impossible, and default would cease to be a viable strategic option. Rule 54(c) therefore provides that "[a] judgment by default shall not be different in kind from or exceed in amount that prayed for in the demand for judgment."

§ 8.07 Challenging Pleadings: Motion Practice

[1] Motion Practice in General

One of the principal reforms carried forward from code pleading to the federal rules was the reduction of the many responsive pleadings at common law[200] to just three responses: motion, answer[201] and (when permitted) reply.[202] A *motion* is an application to the court for an order. It must state with particularity the grounds upon which it relies. A supporting memorandum of authorities and a proposed form of order often accompany a motion.[203] Like pleadings, motions are subject to the candor and care requirements of Rule 11 and do not require any technical forms.[204]

The federal rules and many state rules in notice pleading jurisdictions permit the defendant to file a motion attacking the complaint in lieu of an answer. Federal Rule 12(g) requires the movant to join in any pre-answer

---

[197] *See* § 5.06 (amount in controversy), *supra*.

[198] *See* § 12.07[1] (right to a jury), *infra*.

[199] *See* § 11.02 (default), *infra*

[200] *See* § 8.02[1](common law pleading), *supra*.

[201] *See* Rule 7(c).

[202] *See* § 8.09 (the reply), *infra*.

[203] *See* Rule 7(b)(1) & Form 19. Motions are usually written, but can be made orally in the course of a recorded hearing. Rule 7(b)(1) is often implemented by more detailed local rules, promulgated by authority of Rule 83. *See, e.g.*, Local Civil Rule 7 of the United States District Court for the District of Columbia (establishing page limits and requirements for included matter).

[204] *See* Rules 7(b)(3) & 8(e)(1).

motion all the Rule 12(b) defenses and Rule 12 motions "then available to him." This rule eliminates the undesirable practice of successive pre-answer motions in favor of a single, omnibus pre-answer motion in federal courts.

The pre-answer motion may be used to present what the common law called dilatory defenses, including matters in abatement and challenges to jurisdiction.[205] In some jurisdictions, some of these defenses can only be presented by motion; in federal court, all the Rule 12(b) defenses can be asserted by motion or in a responsive pleading. Such attacks do not go to the merits, or, ordinarily, to the sufficiency of the pleading alone. Therefore, a motion presenting them may be decided on the basis of materials submitted by the parties, as well as on the pleadings.

In contrast, a pre-answer motion that presents the defense of failure to state a claim (Rule 12(b)(6)) or defense (Rule 12(f)) attacks the substantive content of a pleading and must usually be decided upon the face of the pleading alone. However, the court may take judicial notice of the law, other pleadings, its own records and universally undisputed facts.[206] Moreover, in federal courts, the submission of materials outside the pleadings in support of or opposition to a Rule 12(b)(6) motion is not forbidden. It simply converts the Rule 12(b)(6) motion into a motion for summary judgment subject to the usual procedural safeguards of Rule 56.[207] Thus, the common law rule against speaking demurrers[208] has been discarded by the federal rules.

After the pleadings have closed in federal court, either side may seek judgment on the pleadings under Rule 12(c). This motion goes to the merits insofar as they appear from the pleadings. Whereas the scope of a Rule 12(b)(6) motion is confined to the face of the complaint, a Rule 12(c) motion takes in all the pleadings on file. Submission of materials outside the pleadings converts the Rule 12(c) motion to a motion for summary judgment. In fact, Rule 12(c) motions have been largely superseded by motions for summary judgment and are today "little more than . . . relic[s] of the common law and code eras."[209]

Some have suggested that the de-emphasis of pleading in modern civil practice has made Rule 12(b)(6) motions relics as well, infrequently made

---

[205] *See* § 8.02[1] (common law practice), *supra.*

[206] This is an over-simplification of the nuances of judicial notice. *See* Fed. R. Evid. 201.

[207] *See* § 11.03[2] (procedure for summary judgment), *infra.* Submission of such materials in support of a Rule 12 motion asserting defenses 12(b)(1)-(5) or (7) does not convert it into a summary judgment motion. The latter is used to test the merits of a claim, while these defenses "only challenge the propriety of the court adjudicating the claim before it and do not reach the validity of the claim itself." *Wright & Miller* § 1366. *See. e.g., Weidner Comm., Inc. v. H.R.H. Prince Bandar Al Faisal*, 859 F.2d 1302, 1306 n.6 (7th Cir. 1988) (noting that Rule 12(b)(2) motion cannot be converted into summary judgment motion); *Haase v. Sessions*, 835 F.2d 902, 905-907 (D.C. Cir. 1987) (holding that Rule 12(b)(1) motion cannot be converted to summary judgment motion, although defendant may challenge standing by formally moving for summary judgment).

[208] *See* § 8.02[1] (common law practice), *supra.*

[209] *Wright & Miller* § 1369.

and rarely dispositive.[210] Data from selected district courts in 1975 and 1988 indicate that Rule 12(b)(6) motions were made in 13-15% of the sampled cases, granted in 8-12% of the sampled cases (*e.g.*, 52-65% of the time), and dispositive in 3-6% of the sampled cases (*e.g.*, 51-72% of the granted cases).[211] These data support the assertion that Rule 12(b)(6) motions are rarely completely dispositive, although they apparently dispose of approximately as many cases as does trial. But it does not follow that they are useless relics. Even if a motion does not finally dispose of a case, it may eliminate some marginal claims and parties, or at the very least signal the defendant's determination to litigate with immeasurable but real effect on settlement dynamics. A Rule 12(b)(6) motion "that whittles a complaint with twenty claims down to two viable claims has not been a failure in terms of merits dispositions."[212] Moreover, if heightened pleading requirements survive the Supreme Court's decision in *Leatherman v. Tarrant County Narcotics Intelligence and Coordination Unit*,[213] Rule 12(b)(6) motions may be effective in the sub-set of cases to which such standards are applied.

[2] Bases for Motions

[a] Defects of Form

Because modern notice pleading does not require technical forms of pleading, attacks on pleadings for defects of form are virtually extinct in modern pleading jurisdictions. Under the federal rules, the only defects of form that can be challenged are that the complaint is unintelligible or that it contains "redundant, immaterial, impertinent, or scandalous matter."[214]

A complaint that is too vague, ambiguous or confused to enable the defendant to respond may be attacked by a Rule 12(e) motion for more definite statement in the federal courts, or by a special demurrer in states that retain this nomenclature.[215] In a notice pleading jurisdiction, however, discovery, and not pleading, is the device intended to obtain information about an adversary's case. Accordingly, a Rule 12(e) motion should not be granted just because the movant wants to know more than enough to prepare some response. In light of the leeway afforded by the rules to formulate responses,[216] few litigants are able to make the necessary showing.[217]

---

[210] *Wright* § 66; A. Miller, *The August 1983 Amendments to the Federal Rules of Civil Procedure: Promoting Effective Case Management and Lawyer Responsibility* 7-8 (1984).

[211] T. Willging, *Use of Rule 12(b)(6) in Two Federal District Courts* 6-8 (Federal Judicial Center 1989). These data are inflated by the inclusion of prisoners' cases, which are probably more vulnerable to 12(b)(6) dismissal than other cases. *Id.* at 7 & Table 2, 8 n.19.

[212] Marcus, *The Puzzling Persistence of Pleading Practice*, 76 Tex. L. Rev. 1749, 1756 (1998). Such a whittling effort may also encourage settlement.

[213] 507 U.S. 163 (1993). *See* § 8.04[1] (specificity of modern pleadings), *supra*.

[214] Rule 12(f).

[215] *See, e.g.*, Cal. Civ. Proc. Code § 430.10(f) (West 1992).

[216] *See, e.g.*, *Hodgson v. Virginia Baptist Hosp., Inc.*, 482 F.2d 821 (4th Cir. 1973) (denying Rule 12(e) motion because Rule 8(b) permitted the response that defendant lacks knowledge

Rule 12(f) motions to strike (delete) any of the various kinds of improper matter from a pleading are even less likely to be granted than Rule 12(e) motions. As long as pleadings are not shown to the jury, quibbling about how immaterial, nasty or gratuitous they are is a waste of everyone's time unless their availability in the public record is likely to prejudice the movant. Rule 12(f) motions to strike improper matter are therefore universally disfavored. Usually the allegations that have been stricken were obviously prejudicial: describing a car as a "death trap," or plaintiff's co-conspirators as "strong arm men" and "racketeers."[218]

[b] Waivable Preliminary Defenses

Lack of personal jurisdiction,[219] improper venue,[220] insufficiency of process (the papers served on the parties),[221] and insufficiency of service[222] are typical defenses that can or must be asserted by pre-answer motion. They are personal to the defendants, and their availability is usually clear from the outset of litigation. In almost all jurisdictions, therefore, defendants are required, on penalty of waiver,[223] to raise them preliminarily, before the court and the parties invest much time in the litigation or reach the merits. Federal Rules 12(g) and 12(h)(1) provide that these defenses are waived unless they are asserted in a single pre-answer motion, or, if none is filed, in an answer or reply or any amendment thereto permitted as a matter of course.

Rule 12's treatment of waivable defenses suggests a simple rule of thumb in federal court: a party should assert them in her first defensive paper. The same applies in many state courts as well.

In many states, all of these defenses except improper venue are or can be asserted by *motions to quash* service. In a few, the assertion of defenses to the complaint constitutes a general appearance, submitting to the jurisdiction of the court. It is therefore necessary to *appear specially* to

---

or information sufficient to form a belief as to the truth of an averment in complaint); *see generally* § 8.08[1] (denials), *infra*.

[217] Rule 12(e) motions have been used in two other limited settings. They have been invoked to enforce Rule 9(b) requirements for special pleading of fraud and mistake. *See Moore* § 12.36; *Wright & Miller* § 1300; *see generally* § 8.04[4], *supra*. This use of the motion makes a reasonable accommodation between these requirements and Rule 8(a)'s requirement for a "short and plain statement," without requiring dismissal of a complaint. Rule 12(e) motions are also sometimes used to uncover threshold defenses such as the statute of limitations or fraud. *See Wright & Miller* § 1376.

[218] *See* S. Yeazell, *Civil Procedure* 453 n.7 (4th ed. 1996) (citing cases). *Cf. Theriault v. Silber*, 574 F.2d 197 (5th Cir. 1978) (striking "vile and insulting" references to trial judge in appellant's notice of appeal). Rule 12(f) may also be used to attack the substantive sufficiency of a pleading, *see* § 8.07[2][c] (failure to state defense), *infra*, and, in a few courts, to strike averments of fraud or mistake that violate Rule 9(b). *See Wright & Miller* § 1300.

[219] Rule 12(b)(2). *See* Chapter 3, *supra*.

[220] Rule 12(b)(3). *See* Chapter 6, *supra*.

[221] Rule 12(b)(4). *See* § 4.03, *supra*.

[222] Rule 12(b)(5). *See* § 4.03, *supra*.

[223] *See* § 3.03[2] (waiver of personal jurisdiction defense), *supra*.

assert the defense of lack of personal jurisdiction.[224] Rule 12(b) effectively eliminates the need for special appearances in federal court by expressly providing that "[n]o defense or objection is waived by being joined" with any other in a responsive pleading or motion.

[c] Failure to State a Claim (or Defense), and Other Nonwaivable Defenses

The defenses of failure to state a claim or defense, lack of subject matter jurisdiction, and, in federal courts, failure to join a party under Rule 19[225] are not waived by their omission from a pre-answer motion.[226] Rule 12(h)(3), in fact, provides that the defense of lack of subject matter jurisdiction may be raised at any time, while Rule 12(h)(2) states that the other nonwaivable defenses may be asserted in any pleading, by motion for judgment on the pleadings, or even "at the trial on the merits."[227] Were the rule otherwise, judgments could be recovered on claims or defenses unrecognized by the law, and courts would be unable to protect absent parties whose indispensability to the litigation first becomes evident as it progresses.

The most common nonwaivable defense is the failure to state a claim. It is asserted by a Rule 12(b)(6) motion in federal court and by general demurrer in many state courts. The test for disposition of the motion depends on the jurisdiction's requirement for stating a claim or cause of action.[228] All well-pleaded facts (e.g., not legal conclusions, rank opinion or speculation) in the challenged pleading are taken as true for purposes of the motion or demurrer, and all reasonable inferences are drawn in favor of the pleader.[229] The province of Rule 12(b)(6) motions and demurrers is to question the availability of a legal formula justifying relief on the alleged facts, not to test or determine the facts themselves. On the other hand, "courts are not . . . required to speculate that factual propositions unmentioned, or evidentiary links unrevealed, are among the facts plaintiff intends to prove at trial."[230]

---

[224] For more extensive discussion of opportunities in state and federal court to question personal jurisdiction, *see* § 3.03[2][b] (special and general appearances), *supra*.

[225] *See* § 9.05[2] compulsory joinder, *infra*.

[226] Rule 12(h)(2) & (3).

[227] A failure to state a claim is usually raised at trial by a motion for dismissal (or judgment as a matter of law in federal courts) in a trial to the court, Rule 52(c), *see* §§ 11.04[2] & 12.10, *infra*; and by a motion for a directed verdict (or for judgment as a matter of law in federal courts) in a trial to a jury. Rule 50(a). *See* § 12.09[1] (directed verdicts), *infra*. The phrasing of Rule 12(h)(2) suggests that a post-answer 12(b)(6) motion is not a proper vehicle for asserting the defense.

[228] *See generally* Yoichiro, *Function of Rule 12(b)(6) in the Federal Rules of Civil Procedure: A Categorization Approach*, 15 Campbell L. Rev. 119 (1993); §§ 8.03 (code pleading), 8.04[1] (modern notice pleading), & 8.06[2] (statement of claim), *supra*.

[229] *See Moore* § 12.34. The same standards are applied in the determination of Rule 12(c) motions for judgment on the pleadings. *Id.*, § 12.38. *Cf.* § 12.09[3][c] (comparing these with motions for directed verdict), *infra*.

[230] *ACLU Found. S. Cal. v. Barr*, 952 F.2d 457, 472 (D.C. Cir. 1991) (stating also that "[a] court must take care not to put words into counsel's mouth by reading into a complaint factual allegations not fairly comprehended within what is actually asserted.").

In some code pleading states, a demurrer was overruled unless the entire pleading was defective.[231] This is no longer true in most jurisdictions, and a litigant can attack part of the complaint, usually a count, for failure to state a claim. Technically, perhaps, a Rule 12(f) motion to strike the defective count or claim is the correct vehicle under the federal rules.[232] However, since Rule 8(e)(1) abolished technical forms of motions, a Rule 12(b)(6) motion should be equally effective.

The phrasing of the latter ("failure to state a *claim* upon which relief can be granted"), suggests its unsuitability for attacking the legal insufficiency of a *defense*. Instead, a Rule 12(f) motion to strike is used for this purpose. The test for striking a defense for insufficiency is analogous to that used in deciding a Rule 12(b)(6) motion for failure to state a claim.[233]

[3] Consequences of Challenging a Pleading

[a] Successful Challenge

One reason why Rule 12(b)(6) motions appear so ineffective is that a plaintiff will often moot a strong pre-answer motion by amending his defective complaint. Rule 15(a) allows a party to amend his pleading once "as a matter of course" at any time before a responsive pleading is filed, and a pre-answer motion is not a responsive pleading.[234] Depending upon the federal circuit, amendment as of right or by permission is available even *after* a motion to dismiss has been granted, unless the court indicates that no curative amendment is possible.[235]

If plaintiff opts to amend, he runs the risk of waiving his argument that the original complaint was sufficient. Both state and federal courts are divided on this question of waiver. The better federal rule appears to be that such a plaintiff waives his objection to the court's dismissal order only insofar as it applies to technical defects in the original complaint. He may still argue, on appeal of an unfavorable final judgment after trial of the amended complaint, that the erroneous grant of the Rule 12(b)(6) motion against his original complaint "struck a vital blow" to a substantial portion of his case.[236]

---

[231] *See* C. Clark, *Handbook of the Law of Code Pleading* § 79 (2d ed. 1947).

[232] *See, e.g., Mills v. Fox*, 421 F. Supp. 519 (E.D.N.Y. 1976) (striking punitive damages not recoverable under state law); *Fry v. Lamb Rental Tools, Inc.*, 275 F. Supp. 283 (W.D. La. 1967) (striking demand for damages for losses not recoverable under state law).

[233] *See, e.g., Donovan v. Robbins*, 99 F.R.D. 593 (N.D. Ill. 1983). *But see generally* Loomis, *Motion to Strike Affirmative Defenses — The Equivalent of Partial Summary Judgment*, 13 Am. J. Trial Advocacy 645 (1989) (asserting that the no-genuine-issue standard for summary judgment (*see* § 11.03[3], *infra*) is different, but used by some courts to decide Rule 12(f) motions to strike affirmative defenses, even though the rule does not provide for converting such motions to summary judgment).

[234] Rule 7(a). *See generally* § 8.10[1] (amendment before trial), *infra*.

[235] *See* § 8.10[1] (amendment before trial), *infra*, noting split in the circuits.

[236] *See, e.g., Wilson v. First Houston Inv. Corp.*, 566 F.2d 1235, 1238 (5th Cir. 1978), *vacated on other grounds*, 444 U.S. 959 (1979); *Blazer v. Black*, 196 F.2d 139, 143-144 (10th Cir. 1952) (dictum).

If the plaintiff stands on his original complaint and takes a successful appeal from its dismissal, the complaint will be reinstated and the defendant will have to file a responsive pleading. If the appellate court affirms the dismissal, however, the plaintiff will have forfeited his opportunity to amend[237] unless the appellate mandate preserves it.[238]

[b] Unsuccessful Challenge

The options posed by denial of defendant's motion to dismiss are simpler. She may, of course, file an answer, although in federal court she cannot include the waivable defenses if they were omitted from her motion.[239] By answering, she forgoes the opportunity to obtain immediate appellate review of the denial of her motion, unless the jurisdiction permits interlocutory appeals, because there is no final judgment from which to take an appeal.[240]

Depending upon the jurisdiction, she may also waive her preliminary defenses by going forward. But she can preserve the defense that the complaint fails to state a claim by nurturing it throughout the litigation with motions at trial for dismissal, directed verdict, or, in federal courts, for judgment as a matter of law, and after trial, for judgment notwithstanding the verdict, and by appropriate evidentiary objections at trial. It will thereby be preserved on appeal of an eventual final judgment. In federal courts, it is preserved by the original Rule 12 motion.[241]

Alternatively, the defendant may elect to stand on her motion and refuse to answer. This course will result in the entry of a default judgment[242] against her, from which she can appeal. If the appellate court agrees with her, it should remand with leave for plaintiff to amend. But if the court affirms, defendant may lose the opportunity to defend on the merits.

§ 8.08 The Answer

The answer may contain three kinds of responses: denials controverting the pleader's allegations, defenses, and claims by the defendant.[243]

[1] Denials

In all jurisdictions, the defendant must in her answer admit or deny all the well-pleaded allegations of the complaint. An admission presumptively

---

[237] Some appellate courts have taken the view that the plaintiff-appellant also waives the right to argue any alternative legal theories that might have formed the basis of an amended complaint. *See Mitchell v. Archibald & Kendall, Inc.*, 573 F.2d 429, 433 (7th Cir. 1978) ("By appealing, the plaintiffs-appellants elected to stand on their original complaint and thereby relinquished the legal theory they now assert.").

[238] Federal appellate courts have broad remedial powers. 28 U.S.C. § 2106.

[239] *See* § 8.07[2][b] (waivable preliminary defenses), *supra*.

[240] *See* § 13.03 (final judgment rule), *infra*.

[241] Rule 46

[242] *See* § 11.02 (default), *infra*.

[243] *See* Form 20.

takes the issue from the fact-finder and is conclusive at trial. The old common law plea of the general issue theoretically survives as a *general denial* of each and every allegation of the complaint,[244] but it will almost always be impossible to square with candor and care requirements like those of Rule 11.[245] Instead, most defendants *specifically deny* particular paragraphs or sentences of the complaint. In fact, Rule 8(b) commands that "denials shall fairly meet the substance of the averments denied. When a pleader intends in good faith to deny only a part or a qualification of an averment, he shall specify so much of it as is true and material and shall deny only the remainder." Failure to deny an allegation in a required responsive pleading, other than an allegation of the amount of damages, is deemed an admission.[246] But answers do not require technical forms and are construed, like all pleadings, to do substantial justice.

A well-known case, *Zielinski v. Philadelphia Piers, Inc.*,[247] illustrates some of these principles. In a personal injury suit, defendant generally denied a paragraph in the complaint that alleged that a forklift "owned, operated and controlled" by it and its employees was negligently driven so that it hit and injured the plaintiff. In fact, unknown to plaintiff, defendant had sold its business and transferred its employees to a third party prior to the accident, retaining only ownership of the forklift. By the time that plaintiff learned of these facts, it was too late under the applicable statute of limitations to sue the third party. Plaintiff therefore argued that the defendant's denial was ineffective and should be treated as an admission for purposes of the action.

The court ruled that defendant's failure to deny specifically the "operated and controlled" allegations in the quoted paragraph deprived plaintiff of warning that he had sued the wrong defendant. Although defendant's denial was literally true,[248] it did not "fairly meet the substance of the averments denied."[249] Moreover, not only should defendant have admitted ownership, but it should also have admitted that the forklift hit and injured the plaintiff, which was known to it from an accident report. Although a defective denial should not automatically be deemed an admission under the federal rules, the circumstances, compounded by a misleading and inaccurate answer to interrogatories during discovery, justified finding the defendant equitably estopped from denying ownership and agency for purposes of the action.

---

[244] *See* Rule 8(b) (expressly authorizing general denial).

[245] *See, e.g., Williamson v. Clapper*, 199 P.2d 337, 339 (Cal. Ct. App. 1948) ("loose practice of pleading [general denial] which results in the incorporation in the answer of known false denials is to be condemned"). Rule 8(b) takes some pains to warn counsel of the danger of such "known false denials" by reminding him that a general denial controverts even routine jurisdictional allegations in the complaint.

[246] Rule 8(d). *See Lipton Indus., Inc. v. Ralston Purina Co.*, 670 F.2d 1024, 1030 (C.C.P.A. 1982).

[247] 139 F. Supp. 408 (E.D. Pa. 1956).

[248] Because plaintiff used conjunctions to connect different averments, the entire paragraph was true literally only if all of its conjoined averments were true.

[249] Rule 8(b).

When a defendant neither knows nor can learn whether an averment in the complaint is true or false, most jurisdictions permit him to say so in the answer with the effect of a denial.[250] But he cannot blind himself to what he should know, and facts presumptively within the control or knowledge of the defendant may be deemed admitted if he responds with an empty-headed denial of knowledge or information.[251] Moreover, Rule 11(b)(4) imposes a duty of reasonable inquiry on defendant by which he may obtain the necessary knowledge or information and explicitly applies to "denials of factual contentions."

[2] Other Defenses

[a] Preliminary, Nonwaivable and Affirmative Defenses

Besides denials, an answer should contain "in short and plain terms" other defenses to each claim in the complaint. Unless they have been waived by their omission from a pre-answer motion, some or all of the preliminary defenses may be asserted by an answer or, when permitted, a reply.[252] The nonwaivable defenses may also be asserted.

A defendant should also plead his *affirmative defenses*, if any. An affirmative defense is the lineal descendant of the common law plea in confession and avoidance[253] — in effect, an excuse or justification for his action that would avoid plaintiff's claim, even if that claim is proven at trial. It differs from its ancestor in that confession is no longer a predicate for avoidance, because a defendant may combine denials and affirmative defenses in his answer under modern pleading rules.[254] It differs from a counterclaim in that an affirmative defense makes no claim against any party and seeks no relief other than the defeat of plaintiff's claim.[255] Finally, it differs from a denial in that it does not tend to controvert the plaintiff's *prima facie* case, but instead affirmatively asserts new matter outside that case and beyond the plaintiff's claim.

Because such matter is new, it is not put in issue by a defendant's general or specific denials of the plaintiff's allegations. Affirmative defenses must be pleaded "as a condition to the admissibility of such evidence at the trial."[256] When defendant has failed to plead an affirmative defense, the

---

[250] *Id.* (defendant "is without knowledge or information sufficient to form a belief as to the truth").

[251] *See, e.g., Mesirow v. Duggan*, 240 F.2d 751, 756 (8th Cir. 1957); *Oliver v. Swiss Club Tell*, 35 Cal. Rptr. 324 (Cal. Ct. App. 1963).

[252] Rule 12(b); Form 20.

[253] *See* § 8.02[1] (common law pleading), *supra.*

[254] *See, e.g.*, Rule 8(e)(2).

[255] In any event, the federal rules are merciful to the defendant who confuses an affirmative defense and a counterclaim in his pleading, requiring the court to treat the pleading "as if there had been a proper designation." Rule 8(c).

[256] *Layman v. Southwestern Bell Tel. Co.*, 554 S.W.2d 477, 479 (Mo. Ct. App. 1977).

admissibility of some tendered evidence will depend upon whether it goes to the plaintiff's *prima facie* case or whether it is truly new matter. If the latter, it may not come in unless the opposing party fails to object or the court permits amendment of the pleadings during trial.[257] One traditional test for deciding this question — and thus for identifying affirmative defenses — is whether the tendered evidence "tend[s] to *destroy* rather than *avoid* the cause of action as alleged by the complaint."[258] Another formulation is whether it arises by logical inference from the allegations of plaintiff's complaint.[259]

For example, when the complaint is for trespass and alleges plaintiff's ownership of the property and defendant's entry, evidence of defendant's title by adverse possession is logically related to ownership and tends to destroy an essential allegation of plaintiff's complaint. It is therefore admissible under a general denial, and the defendant need not plead an affirmative defense of adverse possession.[260] On the other hand, evidence of an easement is not admissible in defense of a trespass action unless defendant has pleaded an easement as an affirmative defense. Such evidence does not controvert ownership, but only goes to show justification for disturbing it.[261]

The distinction between evidence supporting defendant's denials and evidence that is admissible only in support of a pled affirmative defense, however, is not always easy to follow. This only reflects the fact that the underlying question is simply one of allocating pleading burdens. It is therefore decided less often by logic or formula than by precedent, itself based upon idiosyncratic considerations that vary from jurisdiction to jurisdiction.[262] For this same reason, however, the problem is today more theoretical than real. Most state jurisdictions have identified affirmative defenses by precedent, rule or statute. The picture is not as clear in federal court. Rule 8(c) lists many of the affirmative defenses available there. But federal courts also borrow from the forum state's laws or rules to identify affirmative defenses not listed in Rule 8(c).[263]

The risk that the evidence will be excluded or that amendment will be denied dictates pleading an issue as an affirmative defense when in doubt.[264] In a few jurisdictions, the danger of this strategy is that by

---

[257] *See* § 8.10[2], *infra.*

[258] *Denham v. Cuddenback*, 311 P.2d 1014, 1016 (Or. 1957) (emphasis in original).

[259] C. Clark, *Handbook of the Law of Code Pleading* § 96 (2d ed. 1947).

[260] *Denham*, 311 P.2d at 1017.

[261] *Layman*, 554 S.W.2d 477.

[262] *See* § 8.06[2] (statement of claim and burden of pleading), *supra.*

[263] Such local law is not binding because, under the *Erie* doctrine, the allocation of the burden of pleading is a procedural matter to be decided as a matter of federal law. *See Palmer v. Hoffman*, 318 U.S. 109, 117 (1943) (implying that burden of pleading is controlled by Rule 8(c), though burden of proof is a question of local law in diversity cases) (dictum); *see generally Wright & Miller* § 1272; § 7.04, *supra.* On the nature and effect of the *Erie* doctrine generally, *see* Chapter 7, *supra.*

[264] *See Wright & Miller* § 1278 (footnote omitted).

pleading an issue as an affirmative defense, defendant may be considered to have assumed the burden of proof, even if it would otherwise rest on the plaintiff.[265] This result is unsound because it elevates the form of pleading over the often substantive policy underlying the allocation of the burden of proof.[266] It will often be wise even in such jurisdictions for defendant to plead the matter as an affirmative defense. Otherwise, he risks exclusion of the relevant evidence altogether.[267]

Most modern pleading jurisdictions do not permit a reply to defenses asserted by answer unless the court orders one.[268] Absent a reply, allegations supporting a defense are simply taken as denied by plaintiff.[269] Challenges to the legal sufficiency of defenses are made by a Rule 12(f) motion to strike in federal courts or by demurrer in states that retain the device.[270]

[b] A Note on the Affirmative Defense of the Statute of Limitations

This common affirmative defense merits further discussion because of its significance to procedure. Statutes of limitation require claimants to file their claims within a given time period or lose them. They reflect a conviction that, after the passage of the limitations period, realization of the substantive goals underpinning the claim is less important than protecting opposing parties from the frustrations of coping with stale claims. Chief among these frustrations are the loss from delay of evidence that might have defeated the claim and the emotional stress and financial uncertainty generated by the specter of future litigation.[271] The availability of statutes of limitations defenses depends upon three factors.

The first factor is when the claim *accrued* or came into existence. In most jurisdictions, tort actions accrue at the time of the injury[272] and contract actions accrue at the time of the breach,[273] but there are many nuances in the law governing accrual of actions.

The second factor is the *period of limitation*. This also varies enormously from jurisdiction to jurisdiction, although short (one year) periods are commonly associated with intentional torts and disfavored actions like

---

[265] *See James, Hazard & Leubsdorf* § 4.7.

[266] *See Moore* § 8.07.

[267] There will usually be no reason why defendant cannot raise the matter in his answer *both* by specific denial and by affirmative defense.

[268] *See, e.g.,* Rule 7(a).

[269] Rule 8(d).

[270] *See* § 8.07[2][c], *supra.*

[271] *See, e.g., Elkins v. Derby,* 525 P.2d 81 (Cal. 1974). *See generally* 51 Am. Jur. 2d *Limitation of Actions* §§ 17-18 (1970 & Supp. 1999).

[272] *See, e.g., Roberts v. Richard & Sons, Inc.,* 304 A.2d 364 (N.H. 1973); 51 Am. Jur. 2d *Limitation of Actions* § 135 (1970 & Supp. 1999).

[273] *See, e.g., Struthers Wells-Gulfort, Inc. v. Bradford,* 304 So. 2d 645 (Miss. 1974); 51 Am. Jur. 2d *Limitation of Actions* § 126 (1970 & Supp. 1999).

defamation,[274] intermediate (two or three year) periods with negligence and oral contract claims,[275] and longer periods (five or six years) with actions involving written contracts and instruments.[276] The longest periods are associated with claims to enforce previously awarded judgments.[277]

The last factor is when the period *tolls* or stops running. In most statutes, the period is tolled by the commencement of an action in court, but the rules defining commencement vary. Some statutes define commencement as filing plus service on the defendant. Others state that the period is tolled by filing, if service on defendant is accomplished within some additional short period — "service tail" — after filing.[278] Because of the potentially harsh application of a statute of limitations, many jurisdictions have statutory exceptions[279] or *equitable tolling* doctrines, whereby defendant's fraudulent concealment of his wrongdoing or other good reason is said to toll the period until plaintiff knew or should have known of her injury or that she had an action against defendant.[280] By statute, periods are often tolled during the legal incapacity of plaintiff to sue as a result of her minority or incompetency.[281]

State statutes of limitations are regarded as substantive law for *Erie* purposes, and therefore control in federal diversity actions.[282] Because there is no federal statute of limitations for many federal claims, courts often borrow state statutes of limitations in federal question cases,[283] if they are not inconsistent with the purpose of the federal law.[284] Federal equitable tolling doctrines are still applied to borrowed periods, creating an often confusing hybrid law of limitations in federal courts.[285]

When the ground for a limitations defense is obvious from the face of the complaint, it can be raised by a Rule 12(b)(6) motion, or in some state courts, by demurrer.[286] This procedure is disfavored by many courts, however, because it complicates plaintiff's offer of factual matter in avoidance of the defense, such as fraudulent concealment under the doctrine of equitable

---

[274] *See, e.g.,* Md. Cts. & Jud. Proc. Code Ann. § 5-105 (1984) (assault, slander, libel).

[275] *E.g., id.,* at § 5-101 (contracts).

[276] *E.g., id.* at § 5-102(a) (1) (twelve years for instruments under seal).

[277] *See, e.g.,* N.Y. Civ. Prac. L. & R. 211 (McKinney 2000) (twenty years).

[278] *See, e.g.,* Okla. Stat. tit. 12, § 97 (repealed 1984), analyzed in *Walker v. Armco Steel Corp.*, 446 U.S. 740, 751-52 (1980) and § 7.04[2], *supra.*

[279] *See, e.g.,* N.Y. Civ. Prac. L. & R. 213(8) (McKinney 2000).

[280] 51 Am. Jur. 2d *Limitation of Actions* §§ 146-169 (1970 & Supp. 1999).

[281] *See, e.g.,* N. Y. Civ. Prac. L. & R. 208 (McKinney 2000) (infancy and insanity toll the statute).

[282] *See* § 7.03[1] (analyzing the *York* decision), *supra.*

[283] *See* § 5.03 (statutory scope of federal question jurisdiction), *supra.*

[284] *See, e.g., Banks v. Chesapeake & Potomac Tel. Co.*, 802 F.2d 1416 (D.C. Cir. 1986). *See generally* Note, *Limitation Borrowing in Federal Courts*, 77 Mich. L. Rev. 1127 (1979); § 7.07 (federal common law), *supra.*

[285] *See Banks*, 802 F.2d at 1420. *See also Holmberg v. Ambrecht*, 327 U.S. 392 (1946) (fraudulent concealment tolls borrowed state statute of limitations).

[286] *See* Comment, *Raising Defense of Statute of Limitations by Demurrer, Equivalent Motion to Dismiss, or by Motion for Judgment on Pleadings*, 61 A.L.R.2d 300 (1999).

tolling.[287] Even when the defense appears on the face of the complaint, therefore, these courts have urged that it be raised by answer, which presents plaintiff the opportunity to seek leave to reply, and that it be presented for decision by motion for summary judgment.[288]

[3] Claims by Way of Answer

A defendant may also respond to the complaint by asserting claims against the plaintiff, other defendants or third parties.[289] Claims against existing parties are usually asserted in the answer.[290]

§ 8.09 The Reply and Other Pleadings

Under the federal rules, further pleading is necessary after an answer only if the latter introduces a claim. Such a claim is tantamount to a complaint. Rule 7(a) therefore requires a reply to a counterclaim[291] denominated as such and answers to all other claims[292] included in the original answer. No other pleadings are allowed as of right, and all averments in the last required pleading are deemed denied or avoided.[293] The abandonment of issue-identification as the primary function of pleading accounts for this early cut-off; the complaint, answer and reply suffice to give fair notice.

On rare occasions, the defendant may want the plaintiff to respond to an answer in order to ascertain what issues plaintiff will contest at trial. More rarely, the plaintiff herself may wish to respond affirmatively to new matter pleaded as an affirmative defense in the answer, by, for example, pleading facts showing fraud in response to the affirmative defense of release. Replies in these circumstances are not required or permitted as of right. Rule 7(a) does, however, give courts discretion to allow a reply, and on rare occasions they do so.[294] Although some states once mandated a reply to affirmative defenses,[295] today the pleading rules in most modern pleading jurisdictions do not require replies.

---

[287] See Marcus, *Fraudulent Concealment in Federal Court: Toward a More Disparate Standard?*, 71 Geo. L.J. 829, 902-904 (1983).

[288] See, e.g., *Richards v. Mileski*, 662 F.2d 65, 73 (D.C. Cir. 1981). See generally Hurd, *The Propriety of Permitting Affirmative Defenses to Be Raised by Motions to Dismiss*, 20 Memphis St. U. L. Rev. 411 (1990).

[289] See generally §§ 9.04 (cross-claims), 9.05 (permissive and compulsory party joinder), & 9.06 (impleader), *infra*.

[290] See, e.g., Rules 13 (counterclaims and cross-claims) and 22 (interpleader); Form 20.

[291] See § 9.03, *infra*.

[292] See §§ 9.04, 9.05[1] & 9.06, (cross-claims, permissive party joinder, and impleader, respectively), *infra*.

[293] Rule 8(d).

[294] "[O]ccasions when this power should be or has been exercised are extremely rare." *Wright* § 66. "The theory is that by the complaint and the answer each of the parties will have indicated the general position he is taking in the litigation, and that further pleading is not worth the trouble." *Id.*

[295] See *id.*

The only other pleading contemplated under federal and many state rules is a supplemental pleading "setting forth transactions or occurrences or events which have happened since the date of the pleading sought to be supplemented."[296] Such pleadings are most commonly used to allege new damages,[297] or affirmative defenses that have accrued since filing of the complaint, such as discharge in bankruptcy, release or *res judicata*. Before a supplemental pleading may be filed the court must grant leave and may set conditions designed to minimize its complicating or prejudicial impact on the pending litigation.[298] To the same ends, no responsive pleading is required or permitted to a supplemental pleading unless the court so orders.[299]

§ 8.10   Amendment of Pleadings

One key to the de-emphasis of the pleadings in modern procedure is liberal amendment. Accordingly, many modern pleading jurisdictions allow amendment without permission early in litigation, and almost all provide liberal opportunities for amendment by permission later. The remaining constraints on amendment are functional rather than formalistic, imposed by concerns for efficient judicial administration, prejudice to opposing parties, and, where applicable, the policy of the statute of limitations. Widely copied in the states, Rule 15 accommodates these concerns and is therefore the focus of this section.

[1]   Amendment Before Trial

The earlier an amendment is made, the less likely it is to disrupt judicial administration or prejudice opposing parties. Rule 15(a) therefore provides that a party may amend "once as a matter of course" (without permission from the court or consent of other parties) before a responsive pleading is served, or within twenty days of service if no responsive pleading is required. Because a Rule 12(b) motion to dismiss is not a responsive pleading within the definition of Rule 7, Rule 15(a)'s language permits one amendment as of right to cure defects raised by such a motion, without the necessity of any hearing or ruling on the motion. Such an amendment promotes efficient judicial administration and ordinarily works no prejudice against other parties who have not yet invested resources in responsive

---

[296] Rule 15(d). Amendment, in contrast, deals with events that occurred prior to the date of the pleading sought to be amended. *See generally* § 8.10 (amendment), *infra*.

[297] *See, e.g., Fritz v. Standard Sec. Life Ins. Co. of N.Y.*, 676 F.2d 1356, 1358 & nn.3 & 4 (11th Cir. 1982) (supplemental complaint for insurance payments that accrued after filing of complaint); *McHenry v. Ford Motor Co.*, 269 F.2d 18 (6th Cir. 1959) (complaint to enjoin flooding of plaintiff's land; supplemental pleading to recover for new damage to plaintiff's house).

[298] The relevant factors are comparable to those considered in granting leave to amend. *See* § 8.10[1] (amendment before trial), *infra*.

[299] Rule 15(d).

pleadings and who are typically given ample time to respond[300] to the amended pleading.[301]

Once issues have been joined by the filing of a responsive pleading, amendment would usually moot that pleading and necessitate preparation and filing of a new responsive pleading. In light of this inefficiency and the possible prejudice to the adverse parties, leave of court is required to amend.[302] Rule 15(a) provides, however, that it "shall be freely granted when justice so requires." Provided that amendment will promote disposition of the action on the merits, there is virtually a presumption favoring it. This presumption is only rebutted by a showing that the amendment is unreasonably dilatory, futile or in bad faith, or that the opposing party will be unduly prejudiced.[303]

Beeck v. Aquaslide'N' Dive Corp.[304] illustrates this standard. In its answer to a complaint for personal injury, the defendant admitted design and manufacture of the water slide alleged to have caused the injury. Subsequently, after the statute of limitations on plaintiff's personal injury claim had expired, defendant sought to amend its answer because it belatedly discovered that it had not manufactured the defective slide. The trial court granted defendant leave to amend its answer in order to deny design and manufacture. Plaintiff appealed from a judgment on an eventual verdict for defendant, asserting that the grant of leave to amend was error. The appellate court affirmed.

The amendment was not futile, for it presented what proved to be a winning defense, and it permitted the parties to litigate a material factual issue on the merits. In addition, there was no evidence of bad faith or unreasonable delay. Defendant had relied on the conclusions of three different insurance companies in preparing its initial answer and had

---

[300] Rule 15(a) provides that a response shall be made within the original time remaining for response or ten days after service of the amended pleading, whichever is longer.

[301] After a motion to dismiss has been granted, some of this efficiency is lost because the court has already ruled. The Second Circuit therefore holds that the right to amend without permission terminates unless the court, in ruling on the motion, explicitly grants leave to amend. *See Elfenbein v. Gulf & Western Indus., Inc.*, 590 F.2d 445, 448 & n.1 (2d Cir. 1978). In contrast, other circuits distinguish dismissal of the complaint from dismissal of the action, and read Rule 15(a) literally to allow a plaintiff to amend once as of right after dismissal of the complaint pursuant to a pre-answer motion. *See Ruby v. Secretary of Navy*, 365 F.2d 385, 387 (9th Cir. 1966), *cert. denied*, 386 U.S. 1011 (1967); *222 East Chestnut Street Corp. v. Lakefront Realty Corp.*, 256 F.2d 513 (7th Cir. 1958), *cert. denied*, 358 U.S. 907 (1958). Most of the remaining circuits have taken the intermediate position that plaintiff may amend with leave of court after dismissal, unless the court either holds that no amendment is possible or that dismissal of the complaint also constitutes dismissal of the action. *See Czeremcha v. Int'l Ass'n of Machinists and Aerospace Workers, AFL-CIO*, 724 F.2d 1552 (11th Cir. 1984).

[302] Leave is requested by filing a motion to amend with the proposed amendment. *Wright & Miller* § 1485.

[303] *See Foman v. Davis*, 371 U.S. 178, 182 (1962); *Espey v. Wainwright*, 734 F.2d 748, 750 (11th Cir. 1984) ("This policy of Rule 15(a) in liberally permitting amendments to facilitate determination of claims on the merits circumscribes the exercise of the trial court's discretion; thus, 'unless there is a substantial reason to deny leave to amend, the discretion of the trial court is not broad enough to permit denial.' ") (citations omitted).

[304] 562 F.2d 537 (8th Cir. 1977).

promptly sought amendment upon discovering their error in identifying the slide's manufacturer.

Plaintiffs were unable to show undue prejudice sufficient to overcome these justifications for the amendment. They were, of course, disadvantaged on the merits by the amendment, which interjected a new and difficult fact issue into the litigation. But this kind of prejudice cannot be undue because it is inherent in every amendment, otherwise the movant would not seek amendment. Instead, undue prejudice ordinarily consists of "preparation prejudice" flowing from delay in offering the amendment — a substantial litigation disadvantage that the party opposing the amendment would not have faced had the amended pleading been filed originally. In *Beeck*, plaintiffs might well have made this showing by persuading the court that the amendment came too late for them to sue other parties under the applicable statute of limitations. But the trial court found that causes of action in fraud or contract might still be available against other parties, and that such parties might be equitably estopped [305] from asserting a limitations defense. [306] On this record, the appellate court saw no abuse of discretion and affirmed the judgment for defendants.

Even when a proposed amendment may prejudice opposing parties, the court may impose conditions upon the amendment that alleviate the prejudice. For example, allowance of the amendment may be accompanied by a grant to the party opposing it of additional discovery, continuances or time extensions. Financial prejudice may be controlled by conditioning amendment upon payment of costs. [307]

[2] Amendment During and After Trial

At common law, evidence offered outside the issues framed by the pleadings was inadmissible because *variance* from the pleadings was forbidden. [308] Rule 15(b), in deliberate contrast, anticipates such variance and authorizes curing amendments by consent and over objection, during trial and even after judgment, "to conform to the evidence." [309]

[a] Conforming Amendment By Consent

The parties may always expressly consent to the trial of issues outside the pleadings. Rule 15(b) provides that the issues will then be treated as if they had been raised in the pleadings. Unpleaded issues may also be tried by implied consent of the parties. In either case, a party may move at any time, even after judgment, to amend the pleadings to conform to the evidence, although amendment is not necessary.

---

[305] *See* § 8.08[2][b] (the statute of limitations defense), *supra*.

[306] 67 F.R.D. 411, 415 (S.D. Iowa 1975).

[307] *See Wright & Miller* § 1486.

[308] *See* § 8.02[1] (common law practice), *supra*.

[309] A more functional version of the doctrines of variance and of the theory of the pleadings, *see* § 8.04[2], *supra*, is now embodied in the provision for binding pretrial orders. *See* Rule 16(e); § 12.03[3] (binding effect of pretrial orders), *infra*.

Implied consent presupposes both knowledge that an unpleaded issue has been injected into the litigation and a meaningful opportunity to litigate the issue.[310] Usually the offer of evidence bearing upon an unpleaded issue gives the requisite notice, and a failure to object signifies implied consent. This basis for inferring consent fails, however, when the evidence is also applicable to pleaded issues.

In *Moore v. Moore*,[311] for example, after trial of a husband's complaint for child custody, the trial court granted the wife's motion to amend her answer to include counterclaims for custody, child support, separate maintenance and attorney's fees. On appeal, the appellate court reasoned that the complaint for custody necessarily raised the issues of which parent was entitled to custody and of support for that custody, putting the husband on notice of these claims. The court also concluded that the husband had impliedly consented to trial of these issues by introducing evidence on them and failing to object to the wife's offer of evidence of the child's financial needs. However, the issue of separate maintenance, involving the marital relationship, is not normally litigated in a suit focused on child custody.

> While evidence of [the wife's] financial needs was admitted without objection relatively late in the proceedings, we cannot conclude that this evidence was so uniquely pertinent to her support alone, in contrast with the custody or the child support issues, that it justifies our concluding that appellant had adequate, timely notice of, and an opportunity to contest, a claim by his wife for her own support.[312]

The appellate court therefore ruled that the trial court abused its discretion in granting the amendment to add the separate maintenance claim.

A failure to object to evidence that is apposite to both pleaded and unpleaded issues may evidence consent when combined with other indicia. The test for implied consent searches the entire record and considers a party's conduct in all the circumstances. In *Nielson v. Armstrong Rubber Co.*,[313] the plaintiff moved at the close of the evidence to amend his simple negligence complaint to include a claim of strict products liability. While the defendant had not objected at trial to evidence of dangerousness and of failure to include a warning, he argued that this evidence applied to the negligence claim as well as the unpleaded claim of strict products liability. Yet the defendant had received plaintiff's pretrial memorandum citing the law of products liability, introduced evidence to rebut a strict liability claim, and been present when the trial court said, "it seems to me that we have now amended our pleadings."[314] On the whole record, defendant clearly had

---

[310] *See Moore v. Moore*, 391 A.2d 762, 768 (D.C. 1978).

[311] *Id.*

[312] *Id.* at 770. *See also DCPB, Inc. v. City of Lebanon*, 957 F.2d 913, 917 (1st Cir. 1992) ("The introduction of evidence directly relevant to a pleaded issue cannot be the basis for a founded claim that the opposing party should have realized that a new issue was infiltrating the case.").

[313] 570 F.2d 272 (8th Cir. 1978).

[314] *Id.* at 275.

notice and an opportunity to litigate the unpleaded issue, and the amendment to conform to the evidence was proper.

[b] Conforming Amendment Over Objection

The functional approach to amendment is most dramatically reflected by the provision for conforming amendment over the objection that evidence is outside the issues framed by the pleadings. Rule 15(b) encourages the federal courts to grant such amendments "freely when the presentation of the merits of the action will be subserved thereby" and the objecting party fails to make a showing of prejudice "in maintaining his action or defense upon the merits." This provision offers further proof of the sympathetic climate for permissive amendment generally.[315]

Nevertheless, the presumption favoring amendment is slightly weakened once trial has begun, given the lateness of the amendment and its effect on the on-going trial.[316] To the extent that the objecting party complains that he needs more preparation time to litigate the unpleaded issue, Rule 15(b) expressly authorizes continuances. In jury cases, however, a mid-trial continuance may not be a realistic option.

[c] The Objecting Party's Tactical Dilemma

When evidence apposite to an unpleaded issue is introduced at trial, the adverse party may feel, under Rule 15(b), that he is damned if he objects and damned if he does not. By objection, he invites a motion for a conforming amendment, which the court will often grant under the liberal standard embodied in the rule. The most an objecting party usually stands to gain is a continuance to prepare to meet the new evidence and/or conditions on amendment, such as the payment of costs.

On the other hand, if he fails to object, he runs a substantial risk that his muteness will be taken as implied consent to the interjection of the new issue. Moreover, by this tactic, he waives his opportunity to litigate the merits of the new issue, since the introduction of rebuttal evidence and other defensive conduct might be taken as further indicia of consent.

The safe course in these circumstances is to object and defend. This is also the course most in keeping with the purposes of modern pleading, because it subserves presentation and decision on the merits and rejects sandbagging and pretense as litigation tactics.

[3] Amendment and the Statute of Limitations

[a] Relation Back of Amendments Amending Claims

When the applicable statute of limitations expires between the date of an original pleading and the date of a proposed amendment to it, is the

---

[315] See § 8.10[1] (amendment before trial), *supra*.

[316] These same considerations account for the restrictive "only-to-prevent-manifest-injustice" test for amending final pretrial orders. See Rule 16(1), discussed in § 12.03[3], *infra*.

amendment time-barred or does it take (*relate back* to) the date of the original pleading? In federal and most state courts, the answer to this question depends on the nature of the amendment. In federal court, an amendment amending claims relates back if relation back is permitted by the state or federal law that provides the applicable statute of limitations, or if it is allowed by Rule 15(c)(2).

When the amendment presents a claim that is completely new and factually unrelated to the original claims, it operates, in effect, as an independent original action brought after the applicable limitations period has expired. Allowing it to relate back would offend the policy of limitations — to protect against stale claims and assure repose [317] — no less than would an original action brought beyond the limitations period.

But when the amendment presents a matter that is closely related to a timely-filed original pleading, allowing it to relate back would not offend the policy of limitations. In that case, the filing of the original pleading gives defendant notice to start gathering evidence before it grows stale and to plan for the possibility of liability under any closely related pleading. Almost all jurisdictions therefore today permit relation back in these circumstances. This policy, which is implicit in Rule 15(c)(2) and (3) is made explicit by the corresponding North Carolina rule: a claimed added by amendment "is deemed to have been interposed at the time the claim in the original pleading was interposed, unless the original pleading does not give notice of the transaction, occurrence, or series of transactions or occurrences, to be proved pursuant to the amended pleading." [318]

The problem is to identify how close the relationship between the original pleading and its amendment must be before the jurisdiction will allow relation back of the latter. In code pleading jurisdictions, the solution was to allow relation back of amendments as long as they did not change the cause of action originally pleaded. [319] When cause of action is defined narrowly in terms of legal right or a particular legal theory, this approach to relation back is correspondingly restrictive. For example, some courts deny relation back to an amendment in a malpractice action adding a claim of failure to obtain informed consent to an original complaint sounding only in negligence. [320]

Rule 15(c)(2) rejects the cause of action concept [321] and instead premises relation back on a transactional relationship between the original pleading and the amendment. [322] In a modern notice pleading jurisdiction, a

---

[317] *See* § 8.08[2][b] (the affirmative defense of limitations), *supra*.

[318] N.C. R. Civ. P. 15(c).

[319] *See* § 8.03[2] (the cause of action in code pleading), *supra*.

[320] *See, e.g., Keenan v. Yale-New Haven Hosp.*, 355 A.2d 253 (Conn. 1974).

[321] *See* § 8.04[2] (theory of pleadings in modern pleadings), *supra*.

[322] It allows relation back, *inter alia*, when "the claim or defense asserted in the amended pleading arose out of the conduct, transaction, or occurrence set forth or attempted to be set forth in the original pleading. Rule 15(c)(2). Transactional relationship is also the nexus for many joinder provisions of the federal rules, *see* §§ 9.03-9.08[1], *infra*, one possible test for identifying a constitutional "case or controversy" for purposes of supplemental jurisdiction,

complaint gives the defendant notice "that the whole transaction described in it will be fully sifted, by amendment if need be,"[323] and that liability for claims arising out of the transaction may be premised not only on the legal theory articulated in the complaint, but also on any other legal theory that the transaction might support.[324] The wise defendant therefore gathers evidence concerning and prepares to defend the transaction and not just the theory of recovery articulated in the complaint.

The transactional relationship test clearly permits relation back of amendments that merely change the legal theory on which plaintiff seeks relief for the identical transaction. An example is an amendment adding a strict products liability claim to a complaint that originally asserted a simple negligence claim arising out of injuries received in the use of a product, or an amendment adding a claim for failure to obtain informed consent to a negligent malpractice claim.[325]

On the other hand, Rule 15(c)'s concern with fairness and notice to the party opposing the pleading informs the liberality with which courts should apply the transactional standard. *McGregor v. Louisiana State University Board of Supervisors*,[326] supplies a good illustration. A handicapped law student sued the school and its officials for violating the Rehabilitation Act of 1973 by denying him advancement to his second year. His original, timely complaint asserted that the school discriminated against him by insisting that he take a full-time schedule, have in-class exams, and attain a certain GPA before he advanced. After the statute of limitations had run, he sought to amend his complaint by adding due process claims on the ground that the school had provided no written procedure concerning his right to appeal denial of his petitions to the school. Although an expansive reading of Rule 15(c) might view this claim as arising from the same transaction as his original claim (his failure to advance), the appellate court agreed with the district court that the original complaint had not put defendant on notice of the due process claim. That complaint made no mention whatever of any appeals procedures or policy, and therefore, the court concluded, the amendment "set forth new and distinct conduct, transactions, or occurrences not found in the original complaint."[327] The court clearly applied the transaction standard "with an eye toward what legitimately should have been known or recognized within the scope of the litigation as a result of the initial pleadings."[328]

---

see §§ 5.08 & 5.11, *supra*, and the modern test for the scope of claim preclusion. *See* § 16.03[2], *infra. But see* Kane, *Original Sin and the Transaction in Federal Civil Procedure*, 76 Tex. L. Rev. 1723 (1998) (arguing that different purposes of these provisions and doctrines call for different interpretations of "same transaction").

[323] *Barthel v. Stamm*, 145 F.2d 487, 490-491 (5th Cir. 1944), *cert. denied*, 324 U.S. 878 (1945).

[324] *See* §§ 8.04[1] & [2] (modern notice pleading), *supra.*

[325] *See, e.g., Neeriemer v. Superior Court*, 477 P.2d 746 (Ariz. Ct. App. 1970). *See also De Malherbe v. Int'l U. of Elevator Constructors*, 449 F. Supp. 1335 (N.D. Cal. 1978) (adding constitutional claim to statutory discrimination claim).

[326] 3 F.3d 850, 863-864 (5th Cir. 1993).

[327] *Id.* at 864.

[328] *Kane*, note 323, *supra*, 76 Tex. L. Rev. at 1728.

[b]   Relation Back of Amendments Amending Parties

Amendments seeking to change parties beyond the applicable period of limitations are more problematic because the original pleading did not formally put the new party on notice. When the new party is a defendant, relation back is far more likely to be prejudicial than relation back of a new claim against an original defendant.[329] As a general rule, then, such amendments are disallowed in most jurisdictions. Exceptions are made to the general rule when the amendment arises out of the same transaction as the original pleading and the new party had timely notice of the original pleading. In federal court, again, an amendment amending parties relates back if relation back is permitted by the state or federal law that provides the applicable statute of limitations, or if it is permitted by Rule 15(c)(3).[330] Thus, relation back is determined under the most forgiving of the applicable laws.

Many jurisdictions permit relation back of an amendment which simply corrects a *misnomer* — a reasonable mistake in the name of the party intended to be sued.[331] In such a case, the party intended to be sued received notice of the action from the original complaint. No real change in parties is made and no offense is done the policy of limitations by what is in effect a typographical correction to the pleadings.

Relation back is also permitted in some jurisdictions when there is sufficient *identity of interests* between the party originally sued and the new party that notice to the former can be imputed to the latter. In *Stauffer v. Isaly Dairy Co.*,[332] for example, the plaintiff timely sued the Isaly Dairy Company of Pittsburgh, a corporation maintaining the same address as the proper defendant, the Isaly Dairy Company, and served a common officer of both corporations. The court held that an amendment to name the proper defendant related back because the intermingling of the corporations gave

---

[329] Relation back of amendments substituting new plaintiffs may not present comparable problems because a substitution will often cause no prejudice to the defendant. *See e.g.*, *Staggers v. Otto Gerdau Co.*, 359 F.2d 292, 297 (2d Cir. 1966). The relation back of additional plaintiffs, however, may in some cases allow tardy plaintiffs to increase geometrically defendant's potential liability and the tactical complexity of their defenses long after the statute of limitations has run. *See Leachman v. Beech Aircraft Corp.*, 694 F.2d 1301, 1309 (D.C. Cir. 1982). In these cases, the courts have imposed requirements for relation back approximating those of Rule 15(c)(3). *See, e.g., Andujar v. Rugowski*, 113 F.R.D. 151 (S.D.N.Y. 1986).

[330] *But see Arroyo v. Pleasant Garden Apartments*, 14 F. Supp. 2d 696 (D.N.J. 1998) (finding that state law forbidding relation back of amendment adding parties is controlling under Erie (*see* § 7.04, *supra*), despite Rule 15(c)(3). Because Rule 15(c)(3) is "arguably procedural," commentators have argued that it should prevail over inconsistent state law and most courts have so ruled. *See Moore* 15.20[2] (citing cases). On the other hand, its effect on the state's substantive law of limitations might be thought sufficient to raise a question whether it runs afoul of the Rules Enabling Act.

[331] *See, e.g., Grooms v. Greyhound Corp.*, 287 F.2d 95 (6th Cir. 1961) (amendment to change name from "Pennsylvania Greyhound Lines, Inc." to "The Greyhound Corporation"); *Clark v. Southern Ry. Co.*, 87 F.R.D. 356 (N.D. Ill. 1980) (amendment to change name from "Southern Railway Systems" to "Southern Railway Company").

[332] 211 N.E.2d 72 (Ohio Ct. App. 1965).

the impression that they were one and the same. The rationale is both imputed notice and equitable estoppel.[333]

Rule 15(c)(3) takes an approach in some respects broader and in some respects narrower than that suggested by these exceptions. Under the rule, an amendment amending the parties relates back if (1) it asserts a claim arising out of the same conduct, transaction, or occurrence set out in the original pleading, and (2) within the 120-day period provided by Rule 4(m) for service of process,[334] the party added by amendment (3) received such notice of the institution of the action that he would not be prejudiced in defending on the merits and (4) knew or should have known that the action would originally have been brought against him, but for a mistake in identity of the proper party.

The first requirement is the core transactional relationship requirement for any relation back, and the third and fourth requirements encompass most misnomer and identity of interests cases, although they are not confined to them.

The second requirement was revised in 1991 to change the result reached by the Supreme Court in *Schiavone v. Fortune.*[335] Under the prior version of Rule 15(c), the party added by amendment had to receive the requisite notice "within the period provided by law." *Schiavone* posed the question whether the "period provided by law" referred literally only to the applicable limitations period or whether it included any reasonable period tacked on for service of the complaint as well.[336] The Court ruled that it referred only to the limitations period, even though the original complaint was filed within the limitations period and the amended party had received the notice of the filing within the 120-day period provided by Rule 4 for service of process.

The 1991 amendment to Rule 15(c) clearly changes this result by expressly making that 120-day period the period within which the amended party must receive the requisite notice of the institution of the original action.[337] In other respects, however, *Schiavone* may still do mischief. For example, the *Schiavone* dissenters argued in part that Rule 15(c)'s test for amending parties is "utterly irrelevant" to a simple misnomer case because a "technical correction" of name of the party does not change the party.[338]

---

[333] The estoppel theory extends beyond the identity of interests case to any case in which the proper defendant has lulled plaintiff into suing the wrong defendant. *See Zielinski v. Philadelphia Piers, Inc.*, 139 F. Supp. 408 (E.D. Pa. 1956), *discussed in* § 8.08[1] (denials) *supra. See generally Wright & Miller* § 1500.

[334] *See* § 4.03[2], *supra.*

[335] 477 U.S. 21 (1986).

[336] *See* § 8.08[2][b] (statute of limitations), *supra.* The question arose under statutes that provide that the limitations period is tolled by filing of the complaint, provided that service is perfected within some additional number of days or "tail period" after filing. *See Ingram v. Kumar*, 585 F.2d 566 (2d Cir. 1978), *cert. denied*, 440 U.S. 940 (1979) (relation back permitted when service is accomplished within a reasonable time allowed under the federal rules for service of process but after the statute has run).

[337] *See, e.g., Worthington v. Wilson*, 790 F. Supp. 829 (C.D. Ill. 1992).

[338] 477 U.S. at 35 (Stevens, Burger, & White, JJ., dissenting).

By affirming dismissal of the complaint, the majority rigidly, but perhaps properly under the rule,[339] rejected the misnomer exception. The rule's test thus may have superseded this common law exception.

Whether it has also superseded the identity-of-interest exception, is not yet known.[340] This exception is related to the more general question of how much "notice" is required to satisfy the rule. The Advisory Committee's notes to the rule state that notice "need not be formal."[341] Yet more may be needed than notice of the litigation-provoking transaction because Rule 15(c)(3) itself speaks of "notice of the institution of the action."[342] A mere demand letter threatening to sue has also been held insufficient.[343] In contrast, a letter from the mistakenly named defendant to the proper one advising of the pendency of the lawsuit, and warning of the possibility that the latter might be drawn into the lawsuit, was held sufficient.[344]

[c] Responding to Amendment

The Supreme Court has reminded us that the propriety of amendment depends not only on "the state of affairs prior to amendment"—presumably including the reasons for and timing of the amendment—"but also on what happens afterwards."[345] Because amendment may change the claims or defenses asserted against a party, the rule directs that she be given an opportunity of at least ten days to respond.[346] This can apply even to amendments after trial. In *Nelson v. Adams*,[347] the district court amended a judgment to add a new (though closely affiliated) party without giving him an opportunity to respond and the court of appeals affirmed, finding no prejudice. The Supreme Court reversed, holding that the new party was entitled to be served with the amendment and to respond, unless he had consented to the amendment. In dictum, it added that the same is true for amendments which relate back.

---

[339] The Advisory Committee Note to the 1966 amendments stated that Rule 15(c) had been changed to state more clearly when amendments "changing the party against whom a claim is asserted (*including an amendment to correct a misnomer or misdescription of a defendant*) [emphasis added] shall 'relate back'." *But see Dandrea v. Malsbary Mfg. Co.*, 839 F.2d 163 (3d Cir. 1988) (holding, despite *Schiavone*, that mere correction of misnomer is not a change of party to which Rule 15(c)'s amendment-of-party provision applies); *Wright & Miller* § 1498 (correcting a misnomer is not "changing the party" and therefore not subject to the amendment-of-party provision of Rule 15(c)).

[340] *See also Williams v. Army & Air Force Exch. Serv.*, 830 F.2d 27, 30 (3d Cir. 1987) (finding "with some discomfiture" that *Schiavone* "inexorably" requires rejection of identity of interests exception on facts similar to *Schiavone*).

[341] Rule 15(c) advisory committee's notes (1966).

[342] *But see* Wright & Miller § 1498.

[343] *See Schrader v. Royal Caribbean Cruise Line, Inc.*, 952 F.2d 1008, 1012-1013 (8th Cir. 1991).

[344] *Loveall v. Employer Health Serv., Inc.*, 196 F.R.D. 399 (D. Kan. 2000).

[345] *Nelson v. Adams*, 529 U.S. 460, 466 (2000).

[346] Rule 15(a).

[347] 529 U.S. 460 (2000).

§ 8.11 A Concluding Note on Common Sense in Pleading

Professor Moore once said that "what was a good pleading before [the federal rules] continues to be good pleading" today. [348] By this assertion, he was stating more than the uninteresting truism that the federal rules are no more demanding than code pleading or the common law. He was also emphasizing that good pleading, as distinguished from technically sufficient pleading, obeys the rules of common sense and good practice, as well as the formal procedural rules of the jurisdiction.

For example, despite the rejection of the doctrine of the theory of the pleadings in modern jurisdictions, no competent attorney files a pleading without having formulated a primary legal theory of recovery or defense. [349] Ordinarily, the attorney formulates that theory after preliminary factual investigation of her client's story and initial legal research into alternative legal theories available in the jurisdiction. She then drafts her pleadings to reflect at least the primary theory of recovery or defense. She may also include alternative theories as well, as a precaution against dismissal and factual surprises during discovery.

Moreover, she ordinarily will plead each and every element of her legal theories. Less might suffice, but the complaint is intended not only to give minimal notice that would survive motions to dismiss, but also to create impressions in the minds of the defendant and the judge. A full complaint helps educate the defendant about his potential exposure in the litigation and to prepare him for settlement negotiations. It also helps justify the judge's investment of time in the action. Furthermore, a full complaint can provide the plaintiff's first discovery; "a plaintiff who includes rifle-shot allegations may be rewarded with precise admissions and denials that advance the case." [350]

Common sense also cautions against pleading or motion practice aimed at trapping, surprising or delaying your opponent. The pleader who seeks to divert the parties and the court from the merits more often than not succeeds only in alienating them, and in encouraging satellite litigation culminating in sanctions under amended Rule 11 or its state counterpart. The pay-off from deploying modern pleading rules in service of functions for which they were not intended is rarely worth the effort. Real pay-offs lie in marrying the persuasive power of careful pleading with effective discovery, well-researched and analyzed legal theories and a thorough practical understanding of the parties' willingness and ability to litigate the merits. The rules of pleading — like all rules of procedure — are never a substitute for common sense; they are only a framework within which it must be applied.

---

[348] J. Moore *Moore's Federal Practice* § 8.02. (2d ed.)

[349] *See Wright & Miller* § 1219.

[350] Marcus, *The Puzzling Persistence of Pleading Practice*, 76 Tex. L. Rev. 1749, 1768 (1998).

Chapter 9

COMPLEX PLEADING AND PRACTICE

§ 9.01 Overview

[1] Definitions of Complex Litigation

The simplest case consists of one claim brought by a single plaintiff against a single defendant. Any expansion of the number of claims (and possibly the number of parties) beyond this minimal configuration represents a form of complex litigation.

It is most useful to approach complex litigation by focusing on claims rather than parties. It is possible to increase the number of claims adjudicated in a case without necessarily increasing the number of parties.[1] The case is complicated by expansion of a claim *and* a party whenever the added claim requires for its binding adjudication the presence of an additional party before the court.[2]

Most of this chapter treats complex litigation in this traditional sense. Recently, the term has taken on a second meaning: to describe litigation scattered over many states (often in both state and federal courts) that arises from a common event or wrong. The wrong might stem from an air crash or from disease attributed to a substance like asbestos. We conclude the chapter with a review of recent developments in this area.

[2] Reasons for Complex Litigation

Complicating civil litigation with multiple claims, multiple claimants, or multiple parties claimed against, carries inevitable risks. Possibilities for delay and confusion arise when multiple claims compete for attention. This is even more likely to be true when multiple plaintiffs or defendants separately exercise their litigation prerogatives through discovery, pretrial motions and trial of the case.[3] Complex litigation thus bears a burden of justification. It satisfies the burden in two ways.

---

[1] Claim joinder, counterclaim and cross-claim rules perform this function and are the subject of Part A of this chapter, *infra.*

[2] Claim expansion which also requires party expansion occurs through permissive and compulsory joinder, impleader, interpleader, intervention, and class actions — treated in Part B of this chapter, *infra.*

[3] "Additional parties always take additional time. Even if they have no witnesses of their own, they are the source of additional questions, objections, briefs, arguments, motions and the like which tend to make the proceeding a Donnybrook Fair." *Crosby Steam Gage & Valve Co. v. Manning, Maxwell & Moore Inc.,* 51 F. Supp. 972, 973 (D. Mass. 1943).

[a] Judicial Efficiency

Delayed and laborious as complex litigation may be in the short run, a multiple-claim or multiple-party lawsuit is usually preferable to multiple lawsuits. When it averts multiple lawsuits, complex litigation becomes the lesser of two evils, expediting resolution of the entire controversy and avoiding the drain on party and judicial resources caused by inefficient, often redundant litigation.[4]

The wisdom of this objective is most evident when the lawsuit averted would have gone over much of the same ground. Many procedural devices for joining additional claims or parties thus require a nexus between the subject matter of successive claims.[5] Even where claims are unrelated, however, litigating both in one case may promote more efficient use of judicial resources.[6]

[b] Avoiding Prejudice to a Party or Absentee

The substantive rights of either an absentee or a party may be prejudiced if the absentee is not made an additional party in the case. Prejudice in this sense is different from the prejudice of added expense and delay of protracted litigation. For example, substantive prejudice is a concern when an absentee runs the risk of being adversely affected by the outcome in a case without an opportunity to influence that outcome as only parties can.[7] Another example occurs when an existing party suffers from the court's failure to have before it all those involved in the controversy, creating for that party the prospect of conflicting judgments and multiple liability.[8] In both examples, justifications for adding a party go beyond mere judicial efficiency.

[3] How the Federal Rules of Civil Procedure Facilitate Expansion of Claims and Parties

Like other aspects of civil procedure, the law of claim and party joinder has undergone substantial change. The courts of the United States, the fifty states, and the District of Columbia each administer their own law in the field. For our primary model when discussing complex litigation, we will use the Federal Rules of Civil Procedure.

---

[4] Courts are motivated by the same concerns in giving preclusive effect to their judgments. The trend is toward giving judgments greater preclusive effect, penalizing piecemeal litigation and delay. *See generally* Chapter 15, *infra.*

[5] *See* for example, discussion of compulsory counterclaims, cross-claims, and necessary and indispensable parties in §§ 9.03, 9.04 & 9.05[2], *infra.*

[6] This is the assumption underlying claim joinder and permissive counterclaims. *See* §§ 9.08[1], 9.02 & 9.03, *infra.*

[7] This problem is addressed by Rule 24(a), governing intervention of right. *See* § 62[A], *infra.*

[8] A problem addressed, for example, by Rule 19(a), governing joinder of necessary parties. *See* § 9.05[2], *infra.*

The approach of the federal rules is typical of approaches taken elsewhere.[9] The objective is to combine received traditions[10] with an appreciation of the practical necessities of modern civil litigation into a more or less cohesive body of rules. These rules seek to sort, authorize and limit structural devices which enlarge litigation from the minimum configuration of one plaintiff, one defendant and one claim. However, the rules alone cannot alter the jurisdiction of federal courts or venue of federal actions.[11]

In this chapter, we will examine claim and party expansion situations usually taken up by rules.[12] We will consider the functional effect of each rule, justification for its use and limitation, and special problems or issues.

PART A
Adding Claims Without Adding Parties

In this Part we will consider multiclaim procedure: rules governing claim joinder, counterclaims, and cross-claims. These procedural devices add claims to the litigation, but do not, by themselves, authorize the addition of parties.[13] Each of the multiclaim rules we will consider has the purpose of reducing delay, needless repetition, and expense in civil litigation by reducing the possibility of multiple lawsuits. The function of multiclaim rules, then, is to promote the adjudication of as many claims as possible in the first instance.

---

[9] Most state procedural systems use the approach and often a good deal of the language of the Federal Rules of Civil Procedure. *See generally* Oakley & Coon, *The Federal Rules in State Court: A Survey of State Court Systems of Civil Procedure,* 61 Wash. L. Rev. 1367 (1986); § 2 n.13 and accompanying text, *supra.*

[10] Multiclaim and multiparty rules have their antecedents in English law, often in equity practice. For one example, see Hazard, *Indispensable Party: The Historical Origin of a Procedural Phantom,* 61 Colum. L. Rev. 1254 (1961).

[11] Rule 82. Until recently, the federal courts extended the reach of federal subject matter jurisdiction and venue through common law. *See* §§ 9.03, 9.04 & 9.05[2], *supra.* Much of that law has now been codified. *See generally* § 5.08, *supra.*

[12] Beyond the federal rules of civil procedure, statutes governing interpleader and multidistrict consolidation of pretrial proceedings are of sufficient general importance to be covered in this chapter. *See* §§ 9.07 & 9.10[2], *infra.*

[13] Thus, while Rule 13(h) indicates that one may join a party in order to make a counterclaim or cross-claim, the provision makes clear that such expansion must separately satisfy rules pertaining to party joinder (one of the multiparty rules discussed in Part B, *infra*). Of course, once an additional party has been brought into the litigation on the authority of one of the multiparty rules, the extent to which he may thereafter claim or be claimed against is usually governed by the multiclaim rules discussed in this Part. *Cf. Wright & Miller* § 1655 ("If the requirements for joinder of parties [under Rule 20] have been satisfied . . . Rule 18 [claim joinder] may be invoked independently to permit plaintiff to join as many other claims as he has against the multiple defendants. . . .").

§ 9.02   Claim Joinder[14]

Rule 18 governs claim joinder, the process by which one who has made a claim may join further claims with it against the same opponent.[15] Rules of civil procedure treating aspects of complex litigation are usually two-sided in their effect. They authorize, but also limit, claim or party expansion.[16] Rule 18 is an exception. It authorizes claim joinder without limitation.[17] Rule 18(a) states that "[a] party asserting a claim to relief" of any kind "may join, either as independent or as alternate claims, as many claims . . . as the party has against an opposing party."[18] A claimant wishing to assert entirely unrelated claims against the same party finds no obstacle in Rule 18. For two reasons, however, possibilities for multiple claim adjudication in federal court are not as great as the bare language of Rule 18 might suggest.

First, Rule 18 does not insulate claims from difficulties unrelated to the joinder rules. A federal rule of civil procedure cannot "extend or limit the jurisdiction of the United States district courts or the venue of actions therein."[19] Consider the following example. Federal plaintiff A wishes to make two unrelated claims against defendant B. The first falls within the court's general federal question jurisdiction.[20] The second is based on state law. Absent either diversity of citizenship between A and B or the requisite jurisdictional amount,[21] there is no original federal subject matter jurisdiction over the second claim. Supplemental jurisdiction requires a close relationship between the subject matter of the two claims.[22] Rule 18 may

---

[14] *See generally Moore* §§ 18.01-18.23; *Wright & Miller* §§ 1581-1594; Kaplan, *Continuing Work of the Civil Committee: 1966 Amendments of the Federal Rules of Civil Procedure (II)*, 81 Harv. L. Rev. 591, 591-598 (1968); Blume, *A Rational Theory for Joinder of Causes of Action and Defences, and for the Use of Counterclaims*, 26 Mich. L. Rev. 1 (1927).

[15] Rule 18 authorizes claim but not party joinder. Rule 20 governs the latter, and permits party joinder only when at least one claim arising out of the same transaction or occurrence is applicable to the joined parties and a question of law or fact is common. For further discussion of the requirements of Rule 20, *see* § 9.05[1], *infra*.

[16] See for example, limitations placed on party joinder discussed in the preceding note or on the availability of crossclaims discussed in § 9.04, *infra*.

[17] *Cf.* Greenbaum, *Jacks or Better to Open: Procedural Limitations on Co-Party and Third-Party Claims*, 74 Minn. L. Rev. 507, 532 (1990) (noting acceptance of the view that Rule 18 enables one to "raise any claim against another party after raising a qualifying claim."). Rule 13 similarly permits counterclaims without limitation. *See* § 9.03, *infra*.

[18] Elements of a "claim" are defined in Rule 8(a). For discussion of claim pleading under the federal rules, *see* §§ 8.04 & 8.06[2], *supra*. Most state procedural systems employ the same approach and much of the same language as federal Rule 18. *E.g.,* Ala. Code R. Civ. P. 18; Del. Code Ann. R. Civ. P. 18; Ky. Rev. Stat. Ann. R. Civ. P. 18.01.

[19] Rule 82. The reference is to federal subject matter jurisdiction. *Cf. Snyder v. Harris,* 394 U.S. 332, 337 (1969) (even if expansion of federal diversity jurisdiction might otherwise be implied from an amendment making class actions more available under Rule 23, such expansion was prohibited under Rule 82).

[20] 28 U.S.C. § 1331, *discussed in* § 5.03, *supra*.

[21] The prerequisites for general diversity jurisdiction under 28 U.S.C. § 1332, discussed in §§ 5.04-5.06, *supra*.

[22] 28 U.S.C. § 1367, *discussed in* § 5.11, *supra*.

appear to authorize both claims, but it will not save the second from dismissal for lack of subject matter jurisdiction.

Second, Rule 18 merely allows parties to *plead* claim joinder. It does not guarantee that the claims will be tried together. "The rule addresses pleadings, not trials. The district judge may order separate trials of claims or issues."[23]

The availability of other means for regulating the entry and trial of multiple claims explains in part why Rule 18 contains no limitation on claim joinder. A further reason can be found in the fact that prior attempts to distinguish between permissibly and impermissibly joined claims proved unsatisfactory. Common law and code distinctions were often difficult to administer,[24] generating unproductive litigation. The original Rule 18 attacked the problem by largely eliminating the possibility of impermissible claims. The process was completed with amendment of paragraph (a) of the rule in 1966.[25]

§ 9.03   Compulsory and Permissive Counterclaims[26]

When a party claims against one who previously claimed against him, the claim back is called a *counterclaim*.[27] Rule 13 divides these into *compulsory counterclaims* under paragraph (a) and *permissive counterclaims* under paragraph (b).[28]

Important consequences can turn on this distinction, as we shall see. However, the status of a counterclaim as compulsory or permissive has nothing to do with its availability to a party under the joinder rules. The

---

[23] *Moore* § 18.02[6]. "The district court has broad authority to proceed with separate trials for a variety of reasons, including the prevention of embarrassment, delay, prejudice or expense." *Id.*

[24] *Wright & Miller* § 1581.

[25] Prior to the amendment, the language of the rule "led some courts to conclude that the rules regulating joinder of parties were intended to be superimposed on Rule 18(a) and encouraged them to apply special restrictions to the joinder of claims in multiparty situations." *Id.* § 1583.

[26] *See generally Moore* §§ 13.01-13.50; *Wright & Miller* §§ 1401-1430; Comment, *Narrowing the Scope of Rule 13(a)*, 60 U. Chi. L. Rev. 141, 141-142 (1993); Kennedy, *Counterclaims Under Federal Rule 13*, 11 Hous. L. Rev. 255 (1974); Wright, *Estoppel By Rule: The Compulsory Counterclaim Under Modern Pleading*, 38 Minn. L. Rev. 423 (1954).

[27] Counterclaims evolved from the common law claims of *recoupment* and *set-off*. C. Clark, *Handbook of the Law of Code Pleading* 633-636 (2d ed. 1947). By recoupment, defendant was entitled to defeat or reduce the plaintiff's recovery by pleading a claim against him arising out of the same transaction as the plaintiff's claim. By set-off, defendant was permitted to plead a transactionally unrelated claim against the plaintiff, provided that it was a claim for a liquidated sum. *See generally* J. Koffler & A. Reppy, *Handbook of Common Law Pleading* § 278 (1969); B. Shipman, *Handbook of Common-Law Pleading* §§ 209-210 (3d ed. 1923).

[28] Many state procedural systems also maintain the distinction (*e.g.*, Fla. R. Civ. P. 1.170(a) & (b); Ind. Code Ann. Ct. R. Trial 13(A) & (B); N.M. Stat. Ann. R. Civ. P. Dist. Ct. 1-013(A) & (B)), but some do not. New York is an example of the latter. *See* D. Siegel, *Practice Commentary to N.Y. CPLR 3019*, McKinney's Consolidated Laws of New York, vol. 7B (1991) ("Every counterclaim in New York is permissive, even if its subject matter relates to [plaintiff's] claim.").

scope for counterclaims under Rule 13 is unlimited,[29] like that for claim joinder under Rule 18.[30] But Rule 13 is also like Rule 18 in that satisfaction of the rule offers no guarantee that the counterclaim will be adjudicated at the same time as the preceding claim, or at all. The counterclaim must conform to the requirements of venue and federal subject matter jurisdiction,[31] and the court presented with the counterclaim is free "to order separate trial of a particular issue if this is in fact more convenient or desirable."[32]

The difference between compulsory and permissive counterclaims is important. The status of a claim as permissive may confer an advantage in the realm of preclusion law. Compulsory counterclaims take their name from the fact that parties having them must either plead or forfeit them.[33] In contrast, one may plead a permissive counterclaim or reserve it for future litigation.[34] At the same time, permissive counterclaims are more likely to encounter jurisdictional obstacles. A counterclaim beyond original federal court jurisdiction cannot be brought within the language of the supplemental jurisdiction statute[35] unless it is so related in subject matter to plaintiff's claim that it would also meet the test for compulsory counterclaims.[36] Merely permissive counterclaims thus are often ineligible for supplemental jurisdiction.

Counterclaims are permissive unless they meet the compulsory-counterclaim test of Rule 13(a). The test involves several prerequisites.[37] However, just one, "that the claim arise out of the transaction or occurrence

---

[29] "It is immaterial whether the counterclaim is legal or equitable, in contract or in tort, or even whether it has any connection with plaintiff's claim." *Wright* § 79, at 564.

[30] *See* § 9.02, *supra.*

[31] Compulsory counterclaims fare better here. *See* note 57, *infra.*

[32] *Wright* § 79.

[33] This is sometimes called preclusion by rule and is discussed in § 15.03[3], *infra.*

[34] "The defendant or party who did not choose the forum or control the litigation, although bound on those matters actually litigated, should not be bound on those claims that, under the law of the first forum, he was not compelled to litigate." Scoles, *Interstate Preclusion by Prior Litigation,* 74 Nw. U. L. Rev. 742, 754 (1979).

[35] 28 U.S.C. § 1367, discussed in § 5.11, *supra.*

[36] Prior to enactment of the statute in 1990, the same distinction limited the availability of ancillary jurisdiction. The doctrine of ancillary jurisdiction tracked compulsory counterclaim, cross-claim and impleader definitions found in the Federal Rules of Civil Procedure. *Owen Equip. & Erection Co. v. Kroger,* 437 U.S. 365, 375 & n.18 (1978). It appears that these applications of ancillary jurisdiction have been preserved and codified under § 1367. See §§ 5.08-5.11, *supra.*

[37]

In an action in personam, a claim defendant has against plaintiff is a compulsory counterclaim if it meets four conditions. It must: (1) arise "out of the transaction or occurrence that is the subject matter of the opposing party's claim;" (2) be matured and owned by the pleader at the time he serves his pleading; (3) not require for its adjudication the presence of third parties of whom the court cannot acquire personal jurisdiction; and (4) not have been, at the time the original action was commenced, the subject matter of another pending action.

Wright § 79 (footnotes omitted).

that is the subject of the opposing party's claim," has posed problems. [38] At least four different definitions of the required transactional nexus have been suggested in the cases. [39] The "same issue" test suffers a timing problem, since it is hard to know what the issues of law and fact are before the plaintiff has replied to the counterclaim. The *"res judicata"* test asks whether a judgment in the case would bar a subsequent suit on a reserved counterclaim. But "[t]his is no test at all," Professor Wright notes, because, absent a compulsory counterclaim rule, counterclaims can be sued upon independently. [40] The "same evidence" test is more useful because it assures that compulsory joinder of the counterclaim will produce real economies by preventing duplicative discovery and trial of the same evidence in successive lawsuits. Yet it fails to reach counterclaims which are logically part of the existing controversy between the parties, but which require different proof. In addition, both the same-issue and same-evidence tests are ambiguous because they do not indicate how close to identical the issues or evidence need be.

Most federal courts therefore have adopted a fourth, more generous transactional test: whether the counterclaim is logically related to the existing claim against the prospective counterclaimant. [41] For example, plaintiff debtor sued her lender on a truth-in-lending cause of action in *Plant v. Blazer Financial Services, Inc.* [42] The lender counterclaimed with a state law cause of action on the debt. Because the parties were not diverse, the counterclaim could only be heard if it was compulsory and therefore within the court's supplemental (then termed, ancillary) jurisdiction. Although a truth-in-lending claim and a debt counterclaim pose different issues of law and fact and involve substantially different evidence, [43] the court of appeals applied the logical relationship test to affirm the judgment on the counterclaim. "Applying the logical relationship test literally to the counterclaim in this case clearly suggests its compulsory character," reasoned the court, "because a single aggregate of operative facts, the loan transaction, gave rise to both plaintiff's and defendant's claim." [44]

"The hallmark of [the logical relationship] approach is its flexibility." [45] In this respect and in its ultimate reach, the logical relationship test for

---

[38] *Id. Cf.* Comment, *Narrowing the Scope of Rule 13(a)*, 60 U. Chi. L. Rev. 141, 141-142 (1993) (different interpretations of the requirement persist).

[39] *See Wright* § 79.

[40] *Id. See generally* § 15.03[3] (preclusion by rule), *infra.*

[41] *Wright & Miller* § 1410.

[42] 598 F.2d 1357 (5th Cir. 1979).

[43] *See, e.g., Whigham v. Beneficial Fin. Co.*, 599 F.2d 1322, 1323-1324 (4th Cir. 1979) (noting these differences in holding the debt counterclaim not compulsory).

[44] *Plant*, 598 F.2d at 1361. *Cf. Moore v. New York Cotton Exchange*, 270 U.S. 593, 610 (1926) ("[The transaction] is the one circumstance without which neither party would have found it necessary to seek relief."). The *Plant* court noted a split in the courts on the issue whether a counterclaim on the debt is compulsory in truth-in-lending suits, but also attributed it primarily to judicial concern about the chilling effect of such counterclaims on private enforcement of federal truth-in-lending policy. *But see Peterson v. United Accounts, Inc.*, 638 F.2d 1134 (8th Cir. 1981) (despite some overlap of issues, there is no logical relationship between collection claim and truth-in-lending counterclaim).

[45] *Wright & Miller* § 1410.

compulsory counterclaims is very similar to the "transactional relationship" test for modern claim preclusion.[46] This is not surprising. The ultimate concern of both compulsory counterclaim rules and the law of claim preclusion is the appropriate scope of a lawsuit.

§ 9.04   Cross-Claims[47]

When a party claims against a co-party (rather than an opposing party) the claim is called a cross-claim. Cross-claims in federal court are governed by Rule 13(g), which states:

> A pleading may state as a cross-claim any claim by one party against a co-party arising out of the transaction or occurrence that is the subject matter either of the original action or of a counterclaim therein or relating to any property that is the subject matter of the original action.[48]

Most federal courts have interpreted the "transaction-or-occurrence" requirement to mean that there must be a logical relationship[49] between the cross-claim and either the original action or a counterclaim.[50]

The scope for cross-claims is less than the scope for permissive counterclaims in Rule 13(b),[51] and slightly larger than that created for compulsory counterclaims under 13(a).[52] Like compulsory counterclaims, cross-claims are generally within federal courts' supplemental jurisdiction.[53] They differ, however, in an important respect. While the holder of a compulsory counterclaim must plead or forfeit it, one may either plead a cross-claim or reserve it for further litigation; cross-claims are never compulsory under Rule 13(g).[54]

A cross-claim arguably makes co-parties opposing parties. This means that, should the target of a cross-claim wish to direct a claim back against the cross-claimant, this claim back would be a counterclaim.[55] For Rule

---

[46] See § 15.03[2] (discussing the emergence of § 24 of the *Restatement (Second) of Judgments*), *infra.*

[47] See generally Moore §§ 13.60 -13.80; *Wright & Miller* §§ 1431-3143; Note, *Defining "Co-Party" Within Federal Rule of Civil Procedure 13(g): Are Cross-Claims Between Original Defendants and Third-Party Defendants Allowable?*, 66 Ind. L.J. 549 (1991).

[48] Many state systems have adopted this approach. *E.g.,* Ala. Code R. Civ. P. 13(g); Minn. Stat. Ann. R. Civ. P. Dist. Ct. 13.07; N.C. Gen. Stat. § 1A-1, R. 13(g).

[49] See the discussion of the role of the logical relationship test in determining compulsory counterclaims at § 9.03, notes 13-22 and accompanying text, *supra.*

[50] *Wright & Miller* § 1431.

[51] "It is immaterial whether the [permissive] counterclaim is legal or equitable, in contract or in tort, or even whether it has any connection with plaintiff's claim." *Wright* § 79.

[52] That the scope of cross-claims is somewhat greater than that of compulsory counterclaims may be suggested from Rule 13(g)'s inclusion of contingent as well as ripened claims. *See Wright & Miller* § 1431. Nonetheless, "most courts have held that the standards developed for dealing with compulsory counterclaims also apply to cross-claims under Rule 13(g)." *Id.* § 1432.

[53] See § 5.11, *supra.*

[54] *Moore* § 13.70[1]. Cross-claims are in this sense like permissive counterclaims. *See* § 59.03 *supra.*

[55] *See Moore* § 13.71[1]. The shift follows the language of Rule 13. Both paragraph (a) (com-

13 to treat this last claim as a counterclaim rather than as a cross-claim may mean that the claimant will lose it if it is compulsory and he fails to plead it.

Consider the following illustration. A, B, C and D enter into various construction and material supply contracts related to a large public works project. A sues B, C and D for breach of one of the contracts.[56] B counterclaims against A for breach of the same contract and pleads a claim against C for breach of a different but related contract. So long as it is sufficiently related to the subject matter of the original claim or counter-claim, B's claim against C is a good cross-claim.[57] If C has a claim against B sufficiently related to B's cross-claim, C must plead it back against B as a compulsory counterclaim. If C has any other claim against B, he has the option of pleading it as a permissive counterclaim.

Rule 13(g) also permits cross-claims against a party on the theory that he "is or may be liable to the cross-claimant for all or part of a claim asserted in the action against the cross-claimant." The rule thus provides a joinder mechanism for contingent or derivative claims described in § 60.[58]

---

pulsory counterclaims) and (b) (permissive counterclaims) describe the claimant's target as the "opposing party." *Cf.* Greenbaum, *Jacks or Better to Open: Procedural Limitations on Co-Party and Third-Party Claims*, 74 Minn. L. Rev. 507, 520-521 (1990) ("[M]ost courts and commentators read the Rules to incorporate a shifting status based on the actual posture of the parties. Thus, if B brings a cross-claim against C, B then becomes an opposing party to C because they now are formally opposing each other on a claim.").

[56] The procedure permitting A to join B, C and D as multiple defendants is discussed in § 9.05, *infra.*

[57] In a well-known case, the Sixth Circuit ruled on facts like these that the two contracts were sufficiently related to the same construction project to bring the cross-claim within the "transaction or occurrence" test of Rule 13(g). *Lasa Per L'Industria Del. Marmo Societa Per Azioni of Lasa, Italy v. Alexander,* 414 F.2d 143 (6th Cir. 1969).

[58] The comparable joinder device for such claims against outsiders is impleader. *See* § 9.06, *infra.*

PART B
Adding Claims by Adding Parties

§ 9.05 Permissive and Compulsory Joinder[59]

[1] Permissive Joinder

Federal Rule 20 authorizes the permissive[60] joinder of claims by multiple plaintiffs or against multiple defendants. In either case, the rule permits the assertion of "any right to relief" held "jointly, severally or in the alternative," so long as claims joined to bring multiple parties into the lawsuit are "in respect of or arising out of the same transaction, occurrence, or series of transactions or occurrences and if any question of law or fact common to all will arise in the action." The object of Rule 20 "is to promote trial convenience and expedite the final determination of disputes, thereby preventing multiple lawsuits."[61] To achieve this purpose, it authorizes party joinder to a substantially greater extent than was possible under common law or code systems.[62]

Common law and code systems generally permitted parties plaintiff to join their claims only with reference to rights held in common (jointly). The distinction between rights held jointly and rights held individually (severally) was often difficult for courts to draw. This restricted and complicated joinder practice.[63] Rule 20 clarified matters and increased judicial efficiency by extending party joinder to both categories of claims.[64] It expanded

---

[59] *See generally, Moore* §§ 19.01-19.09, 20.01-20.09; *Wright & Miller* §§ 1601-6160; Steinman, *Postremoval Changes in the Party Structure of Diversity Cases: The Old Law, the New Law, and Rule 19*, 38 Kan. L. Rev. 863, 908-927 (1990); Tobias, *Rule 19 and the Public Rights Exception to Party Joinder*, 65 N.C. L. Rev. 745 (1987); Freer, *Rethinking Compulsory Joinder: A Proposal to Restructure Federal Rule 19*, 60 N.Y.U. L. Rev. 1061 (1985); McCoid, *A Single Package for Multiparty Disputes*, 28 Stan. L. Rev. 707 (1976); Kaplan, *Continuing Work of the Civil Committee: 1966 Amendments of the Federal Rules of Civil Procedure (I)*, 81 Harv. L. Rev. 356, 358-375 (1967); *Developments in the Law — Multiparty Litigation in the Federal Courts*, 71 Harv. L. Rev. 874, 879-897 (1958); Reed, *Compulsory Joinder of Parties in Civil Actions*, 55 Mich. L. Rev. 327 (1957).

[60] Rule 20 permits but does not require party joinder. In contrast, Rule 19 mandates party joinder whenever feasible. *See* § 9.05[2], *infra.* The distinction created between federal Rules 19 and 20 has its counterpart in many state procedural systems. *E.g.,* Del. Code Ann. R. Civ. P. 19-20; Ky. Rev. Stat. Ann. R. Civ. P. 19.01-20.01; Minn. Stat. Ann. R. Civ. P. Dist. Ct. 19.01-20.01.

[61] *Wright & Miller* § 1652. *Accord, Moore* § 20.02[1][a].

[62] *Friedenthal, Kane & Miller* § 6.4. The scheme set out in Rule 20 corresponds more closely to English practice. *See Moore* § 20.03.

[63] *Ryder v. Jefferson Hotel Co.,* 113 S.E. 474 (S.C. 1922), is as an example frequently cited. Plaintiffs, who were husband and wife, alleged that they suffered humiliation and financial loss when ousted from their hotel room by defendant. South Carolina procedure permitted plaintiffs to join their claims only with reference to jointly held interests. A majority of the South Carolina Supreme Court concluded that the Ryder's interests were several, likening them to those of two railroad passengers suing for injuries from a train wreck. The dissent argued that the injury alleged in the case was to a jointly held interest, likening plaintiffs to a partnership.

[64] "Illustratively, suppose a bus collides with an automobile. All of the bus passengers who

joinder of parties defendant by permitting joinder of multiple defendants claimed against alternatively.[65]

The test for party joinder under Rule 20 is two-fold. The claims supporting party joinder must (1) arise from the same transaction or occurrence and (2) have in common a question of law or fact. The common question requirement is easier to satisfy, since only one common question of law or fact need exist to connect the claims.[66] The transaction or occurrence requirement of Rule 20(a) also appears in paragraphs (a) and (g) of Rule 13, governing compulsory counterclaims and cross-claims respectively.[67] The prevailing interpretation of the requirement in all three settings appears to be the same: a logical relationship between claims.[68] This flexible interpretation of the requirement[69] facilitates joinder.[70]

Should the prerequisites for permissive joinder of parties be as accommodating as those for compulsory counterclaims and cross-claims? While all have the common purpose of promoting judicial efficiency, it is at least arguable that Rule 20 should have more limited application because it encumbers the suit with an additional party as well as an additional claim.[71]

On the other hand, Rule 20 only operates at the pleading level. It does not guarantee that multiparty claims joined will be tried at the same time, or that all will be tried in federal court. The limitations of subject matter jurisdiction and venue may pose problems.[72] The burdensome presence of an added party can be avoided, moreover, even when proper jurisdiction and venue exist. "[T]he convenience of the parties and the court can be fully

---

suffered personal injuries or property damage may join as plaintiffs in a single action against defendant under Rule 20(a), even though their respective claims are several rather than joint." *Wright & Miller* § 1654.

[65] "The need for alternative joinder of defendants typically arises when the substance of plaintiff's claim indicates that he is entitled to relief from someone, but he does not know which of two or more defendants is liable under the circumstances set forth in the complaint." *Id.*

[66] *Wright & Miller* § 1653.

[67] *See* §§ 9.03 & 9.04, *supra.*

[68] "Usually, a court applies the transaction or occurrence requirement in a particular case by asking whether there is a logical relationship between the claim involving the party to be joined and the rest of the case." *Friedenthal, Kane & Miller* § 6.4. This is also how the requirement is read concerning compulsory counterclaims and cross-claims. *See* §§ 9.03 & 9.04, *supra.* For discussions of alternative tests for transaction or occurrence, *see* § 9.03, notes 13-21, *supra.*

[69] At the same time, the language of the transaction or occurrence requirement in Rule 20 should at least prevent joinder of claims evolving from entirely different facts, even if identical in type. Most federal courts have so read the rule. *See, e.g., Saval v. BL Ltd.,* 710 F.2d 1027 (4th Cir. 1983); *Abraham v. Volkswagen of America, Inc.,* 103 F.R.D. 358 (W.D.N.Y. 1984); *Walker v. City of Houston,* 341 F. Supp. 1124 (S.D. Tex. 1971).

[70] Professor Wright notes approvingly that "it seems practically desirable to give the broadest possible reading to the permissive language of Rule 20(a)." *Wright* § 71.

[71] *See* § 9.01, *supra.*

[72] *Moore* §§ 20.07-20.08. In contrast, compulsory counterclaims and cross-claims are sheltered by the supplemental jurisdiction statue, *see* § 9.03, *supra,* and pose no serious venue problems.

protected, though joinder is allowed, by separate trials, pursuant to Rules 20(b) and 42(b). . . ."[73]

[2] Compulsory Joinder

Compulsory joinder has its origin in equity practice. Rule 19 governs compulsory joinder in federal court. We have seen that Rule 20 is not compulsory, that it merely determines how much freedom exists under the rules for joinder of parties plaintiff or defendant. In contrast, Rule 19 treats situations where the quality of the adjudication will suffer without the absentee. Rule 19(a) provides a framework for determining whether the absentee is a necessary party: one whose relation to the case is such that he must be joined if he can be. When joinder of a person falling under Rule 19(a) is not feasible, Rule 19(b) provides a framework for determining whether the person's absence is so problematic to the case that it cannot go on without him. Cases under this rule may be subject to as many as three inquiries: (1) *necessity* of joinder of the absentee, (2) *feasibility* of joinder; and (3) *indispensability* when necessary joinder is not feasible.

[a] Necessary Parties Under Rule 19(a) — When Must Joinable Persons Be Brought In?

The object of rules facilitating expansion of claims and parties in civil litigation is either to reduce delay, needless repetition and expense in civil litigation, or to avoid prejudice to a party or absentee.[74] The multiclaim rules considered earlier share the first objective with Rule 20. Compulsory joinder under Rule 19 also fosters judicial efficiency, but it is most concerned with the second objective. Absentees falling within Rule 19(a) are sometimes called *necessary parties*.[75] Paragraph (a) sets up three separate categories of necessary parties, requiring that each "shall be joined as a party in the action" when joinder is feasible. The three categories are couched in flexible, pragmatic terms.

One is necessary according to Rule 19(a)(1) if "in his absence complete relief cannot be accorded among those already parties." Emphasis here is on "the desirability of joining those persons in whose absence the court would be obliged to grant partial or hollow rather than complete relief to the parties before the court."[76]

In close cases, it may be necessary to determine whether the absence of a person makes likely further lawsuits among those already parties or, whether, instead, "meaningful relief can be granted without the absentee."[77]

---

[73] *Wright* § 71.

[74] *See* § 7.04, *supra.*

[75] Frequently used, the term is misleading in one respect. Since inability to join such persons described in Rule 19(a) does not invariably lead to dismissal of the suit, *see* § 9.05[2][c], *infra,* they may not be necessary in an absolute sense. A more accurate (if unwieldy) term would be "conditionally necessary parties." *James, Hazard & Leubsdorf* § 10.11; *Moore* § 19.04[1].

[76] Rule 19, advisory committee's notes (1966).

[77] *Moore* § 19.03[2][d].

One is also a necessary party when, according to Rule 19(a)(2)(i), "he claims an interest relating to the subject of the action and is so situated that the disposition of the action in his absence may . . . as a practical matter impair or impede his ability to protect that interest. . . ." Here the rule "recognizes the importance of protecting the person whose joinder is in question against the practical prejudice to him which may arise through a disposition of the action in his absence."[78] Emphasis on practical impairment means that it is not necessary for the absentee to risk the possibility of being bound by the case in a formal sense.[79] What is necessary is a prospect of detriment to the absentee from the case serious enough to entitle him to an opportunity to influence the outcome in ways only a litigant can.[80] At the same time, one whose interests may be thus impaired by the litigation probably has a right to intervene in the case.[81] An absentee's opportunity to intervene thus may be taken into account in determining prejudice to the absentee in the absence of joinder.[82]

Finally, one who "claims an interest relating to the subject of the action" is a necessary party according to Rule 19(a)(2)(ii) when "disposition of the action in his absence may . . . leave any of the persons already parties subject to a substantial risk of incurring double, multiple, or otherwise inconsistent obligations by reason of his claimed interest."[83] The strongest case for Rule 19(a)(2)(ii) joinder is where a party, usually a defendant, risks either double liability or inconsistent judgments.

Consider occasions for Rule 19(a)(2)(ii) joinder through the following illustration. Plaintiff A sues a bank to recover funds. An adjudication that A is entitled to the funds will bind the bank defendant to A but will not bind absentee B, who intends to bring suit against the Bank claiming the same funds. The bank thus runs the risk of having to pay two judgments, or twice the value of the obligation. If, instead, B was joined with A in the initial suit, the court would determine which of the two was entitled to recover. That single adjudication would bind the bank in favor of the winning claimant, but it would also bind the losing claimant in favor of

---

[78] Rule 19, advisory committee's notes (1966).

[79] Indeed, the constitutional law of due process will usually prevent that from happening. See § 15.08[1], infra.

[80] Party prerogatives include setting boundaries of materiality through pleadings, developing the facts by discovery, creating parts of the factual record, and appeal.

[81] Intervention of right is usually governed by Rule 24(a)(2), discussed more fully in § 9.08[1], infra. The language used in Rules 19(a)(2)(i) and 24(a)(2) to describe practical impairment to interests of the absentee is almost identical. The opportunity of absentees described in Rule 19(a)(2)(i) for timely intervention under Rule 24(a)(2) is limited only when their interests are adequately represented by one already a party, or when their joinder would have defeated diversity jurisdiction.

[82] It would be difficult to reach any other conclusion. When the absentee could intervene but chooses not to, any practical impairment from the litigation seems almost self-inflicted. Unfortunately, the availability of intervention makes it harder to identify a discrete role for Rule 19(a)(2)(i).

[83] A party prejudiced in the manner described in Rule 19(a)(2)(ii) will sometimes be able to resort to interpleader to force all competing claimants to make their claims against him in one proceeding. On interpleader, see generally § 9.07, infra.

the bank. A single lawsuit would remove the risk to the bank of double liability.[84]

The bank in our illustration may urge B's joinder by also arguing that, even if successive suits do not lead to double liability, they may produce inconsistent judgments. Suppose the bank prevails in A's suit through favorable determination of an issue broad enough to defeat B's claim as well. If B is not made a party to the initial case, B will be entitled to relitigate the issue, resulting in the possibility of inconsistent judgments.[85] In addition, the bank can argue that B's joinder should be required simply to spare the bank the vexation and expense of litigating in two lawsuits rather than one. On the other hand, plaintiff can counter that he should be allowed to pick his defendants.[86]

So long as joinder is feasible, a person necessary according to Rule 19(a) must be joined in order for the lawsuit to continue.[87] If the person will not enter the lawsuit voluntarily, he will in most cases be brought in under the rule as a defendant.[88] This is true whether the person joined is a claimant or one claimed against.[89] If the absentee is a claimant, however, the court may realign an involuntarily joined claimant to determine jurisdiction in diversity cases.[90] In addition, Rule 19(a) provides that an absentee claimant may be made "in a proper case, an involuntary plaintiff."

---

[84] In a case corresponding to this illustration, the court invoked Rule 19. *See Rapoport v. Banco Mexicano Somex, S.A.,* 668 F.2d 667 (2d Cir. 1982).

[85] This is not double liability, since the bank will be liable only to B. Yet it seems no more than fair for the bank to have an opportunity to bind both A and B to a determination favorable to the bank in the initial suit. This is especially true since B might have been able subsequently to use offensive non-mutual issue preclusion had the issue in an initial suit between the bank and A alone come out in B's favor. *See* § 15.08[2], *infra.* The prospect of inconsistent judgments has been used to require joinder. *E.g., Lopez v. Martin Luther King, Jr. Hosp.,* 97 F.R.D. 24 (C.D. Cal. 1983).

[86] Every application of joinder under Rule 19(a)(2)(ii) would by definition seem to avert multiplicity of litigation. This feature has been stressed in some cases. *E.g., Walsh v. Centeio,* 692 F.2d 1239 (9th Cir. 1982). It is uncertain, however, how much play this factor will or should have in cases where defendant cannot persuasively argue risk of multiple liability or inconsistent judgments. At some point, what has been called the " 'plaintiff autonomy' premise," *James, Hazard & Leubsdorf* § 10.12, becomes a potent counterforce to claimant joinder. There is considerable tradition and sentiment behind the notion that plaintiffs are entitled to sue whomever they want. This notion explains why, under federal procedure and that of many states, joint tortfeasors are not considered necessary parties by reason of their tortfeasor relationship alone. *E.g., Temple v. Sythes Corp.,* 498 U.S. 5, 7 (1990) ("It has long been the rule that it is not necessary for all joint tortfeasors to be named as defendants in a single lawsuit.").

[87] The court "will usually give the plaintiff an opportunity to add the absentee. If the plaintiff fails to do so, the court may dismiss the action because of plaintiff's noncompliance." *Moore* § 19.04[4][a].

[88] *Id.* § 19.06.

[89] Rule 19(a) states that if an absentee "should join as a plaintiff but refuses to do so, he may be made a defendant."

[90] *See, e.g., Keith v. Volpe,* 858 F.2d 467, 476 (9th Cir. 1988). *See generally* § 5.04[2] (diversity between whom?), *supra.*

Relatively few absentees, however, are subject to involuntary plaintiff treatment. [91]

[b] Rule 19(a) — When is Joinder of a Necessary Party Feasible?

However necessary a person might be to the lawsuit, his joinder may be infeasible for one of three reasons. Rule 19(a) makes clear that the person can only be joined when "subject to service of process" (personal jurisdiction) and when his joinder "will not deprive the court of jurisdiction over the subject matter of the action. . . ." Moreover, it also excuses an involuntarily joined party from the case if he "objects to venue and [his] joinder . . . would render the venue of the action improper. . . ."

Insurmountable difficulties may arise when it is necessary to serve process beyond the borders of the state where the federal court is sitting. We saw earlier that Congress has limited the service-of-process authority of federal courts in most cases to that enjoyed by local state courts. [92] Rule 4 relaxes this constraint to a degree regarding joinder of parties necessary under Rule 19, authorizing process against them (and therefore personal jurisdiction) up to a distance of 100 miles from the federal courthouse. Although useful "in major metropolitan areas that span more than one state," the so-called 100-mile bulge "is of limited importance given the general expansion in availability of extraterritorial service under state long-arm statutes." [93]

Even if Rule 19 had made no reference to the topics, it would have been clear that the rule alone could not create subject matter jurisdiction or venue. A federal rule of civil procedure cannot "extend or limit the jurisdiction of the United States district courts or the venue of actions therein." [94] What is more, express requirements in Rule 19 for subject matter jurisdiction and venue forestalled applications of ancillary jurisdiction and ancillary venue [95] that were possible in certain other multiclaim and multiparty settings before the enactment of supplemental jurisdiction. [96] Problems

---

[91] There must be "a relationship between the plaintiff and the absentee such that the absentee must allow the use of its name as plaintiff to enable the extant plaintiff to secure relief. Courts have sound such relationships in cases involving exclusive licensees of patents and beneficial owners of copyrights." *Moore* § 19.04[4][b](footnote omitted).

[92] *See* § 3.01[2][b], *supra*.

[93] *Moore* § 19.04[2].

[94] Rule 82. The reference is to federal subject matter jurisdiction. *Cf. Snyder v. Harris*, 394 U.S. 332, 337 (1969) (even if expansion of federal diversity jurisdiction might otherwise be implied from an amendment making class actions more available under Rule 23, the same was prohibited under Rule 82).

[95] *But see* Fraser, *Ancillary Jurisdiction of Federal Courts of Persons Whose Interest May Be Impaired If Not Joined*, 62 F.R.D. 483 (1967) (arguing that the objectives of ancillary jurisdiction would be well served by giving play to the doctrine in Rule 19 joinder situations). Now, under the recently enacted supplemental jurisdiction statute, federal subject matter jurisdiction is unavailable for most applications of Rule 19. For discussion of the statute, *see* §§ 5.08-5.11, *supra*.

[96] For an explanation of prior doctrines of ancillary jurisdiction in complex litigation, *see* § 9.03, *supra*.

therefore arise from attempts to join one who would destroy diversity jurisdiction[97] or who properly objects to venue.[98]

[c] Rule 19(b) — When Are Persons Who Cannot Be Joined Indispensable?

Rule 19(b) states that when one necessary under paragraph (a) "cannot be made a party,[99] the court shall determine whether in equity and good conscience the action should proceed among the parties before it, or should be dismissed,[100] the absent person being thus regarded as indispensable." Rule 19(b) then sets out four factors to be weighed in each case before the court decides whether the case should go on without the absentee. In presenting these considerations, the approach taken in the rule is somewhat unusual. Criteria listed in the rules may be serial[101] or cumulative,[102] but they usually line up in support of a common conclusion. Rule 19(b) instead lists factors supporting opposite results.

The first factor is "to what extent a judgment rendered in the person's absence might be prejudicial to him or those already parties. . . ." This is the same concern expressed earlier in subclauses (i) and (ii) of Rule 19(a)(2).[103] Tempering the effect of the first factor is the second factor, "the extent to which, by protective provisions in the judgment, by the shaping of relief, or other measures, the prejudice can be lessened or avoided. . . ." The third factor, "whether a judgment rendered in the person's absence will be adequate," is the same concern expressed earlier in Rule 19(a)(1).[104] It is counterbalanced by the fourth factor, "whether the plaintiff will have an adequate remedy if the action is dismissed for nonjoinder."

This list of factors offers no reasons for concern about the absence of a party beyond those previously raised in Rule 19(a). It is evident from the manner in which the factors are juxtaposed, however, that reasons for treating an absentee as a necessary party under Rule 19(a) will not invariably support a decision to dismiss the case when joinder is infeasible. The Supreme Court's decision in *Provident Tradesmen's Bank v. Patterson*[105] bears this out.

---

[97] *Provident Tradesmen's Bank v. Patterson*, 390 U.S. 102 (1968).

[98] *See Wright & Miller* § 1610.

[99] Technically, the venue hurdle created in Rule 19(a) comes after the absentee has been joined. Joinder in such cases (although temporary and unavailing) is feasible in a narrow sense. Yet it is better to read Rule 19(b) to apply to joinder problems including "limitations on service of process, subject matter jurisdiction, *and venue.*" Rule 19, advisory committee's notes (1966) (emphasis added). On feasibility of joinder, see generally § 9.05[2][b], *supra.*

[100] A 19(b) motion to dismiss may be made at the outset of the case under Rule 12(b)(7), or it may be made later in accordance with Rule 12(h)(2).

[101] For example, satisfaction of any of the three categories in Rule 19(a) makes an absentee a necessary party. *See* § 9.05[2][a], *supra.*

[102] For example, satisfaction of all of the four categories of Rule 23(a) is necessary for a class action. *See* § 9.09, *infra.*

[103] For discussion of this concern as manifested in Rules 19(a)(1)(i) & (ii), see § 9.05[2][a], *supra.*

[104] For discussion of this concern as manifested in Rule 19(a)(1), see § 9.05[2][a], *supra.*

[105] 390 U.S. 102 (1968).

The *Provident* case resulted from a motor vehicle accident which caused multiple deaths and serious injury. Various tort claimants sued the indigent estate of one driver (Cionci) and an insurance company for a declaratory judgment that Cionci was driving the car of one Dutcher with Dutcher's permission. If the car was driven with Dutcher's permission, then Cionci's estate shared with Dutcher coverage on Dutcher's liability insurance policy. That policy had been issued by the insurance company defendant.

The Court concluded that Dutcher's relationship to the lawsuit was such that Rule 19(a) required him to be joined, if joinder was feasible. It was not. Dutcher's citizenship would have destroyed diversity of the parties upon which the lower court's jurisdiction depended. That brought the Court to Rule 19(b). The Court concluded that suit should go on without Dutcher. The case suggests some of the circumstances in which it is possible to preserve suit in the absence of one deemed necessary under Rule 19(a).

First, plaintiffs had fully litigated their case at the trial level without Dutcher (defendants having made no Rule 19 challenge there). Stressing the fourth factor in Rule 19(b), the Court noted the unfairness of forcing plaintiffs to start from scratch in state court. The Court declined to speculate whether a Rule 19 dismissal of plaintiffs' case before trial would have afforded them an "adequate remedy" in state court. "After trial, however, the adequacy of this hypothetical alternative, from the plaintiffs' point of view, was obviously greatly diminished."[106]

Second, plaintiffs undercut perhaps the strongest argument in favor of a Rule 19(b) dismissal by agreeing to limit all of their claims to the amount of the insurance policy issued by the defendant insurance company.[107] The insurer otherwise would have faced the risk of paying twice on the same policy,[108] a form of prejudice from proceeding without Dutcher which would be entitled to considerable weight under the first factor in Rule 19(b).[109]

It is impossible to lay down hard and fast rules about the application of the four factors of Rule 19(b). "[T]o a substantial degree the effective operation of the rule depends on the careful exercise of discretion by the district court."[110]

---

[106] 390 U.S. at 112. Continuing, the Court observed: "Their interest in preserving a fully litigated judgment should be overborne only by rather greater opposing considerations than would be required at an earlier stage when the plaintiffs' only concern was for a federal rather than a state forum." *Id.* It is conceivable that the Supreme Court would have been presented with a fully litigated judgment, even if defendants had sought dismissal of the suit on Rule 19(b) grounds prior to trial. This is because denial of the motion to dismiss probably would not have been reviewable prior to trial. *See* § 13.04 (limited authority of federal appellate courts to hear interlocutory appeals), *infra*. It is unclear whether plaintiff's "interest in preserving a fully litigated judgment" would be as strong under this scenario.

[107] 390 U.S. at 116.

[108] Had plaintiffs preserved the option of suing Dutcher in a subsequent lawsuit, Dutcher would have claimed sole protection under the policy and probably would have been able to relitigate the permission issue. *Id.* at 115. If successful, Dutcher would prevent the insurer from subtracting from its liability coverage amounts paid out to cover Cionci.

[109] This corresponds to risk to a party of double liability, identified in Rule 19(a)(2)(ii) and discussed in § 9.05[2][a], *supra*.

[110] *Wright & Miller* § 1608. A survey of cases interpreting the factors appears, *id.*, and in *Moore* § 19.05.

§ 9.06 Impleader[111]

Impleader reduces the possibility of duplicative litigation. It addresses situations where one outside the litigation may either share or be legally responsible for defendant's liability to plaintiff.[112] Defendant under such circumstances is often able to bring in (implead) the outsider and thereby settle all legal questions in the initial case.

Consider the following situation — first, without impleader. Customer sues retailer on a product liability claim. The facts of the case are that, if retailer is held liable, he will have a strong argument that the manufacturer should *indemnify* or reimburse him for all or part of that liability.[113] However, the consumer does not join the manufacturer as a co-defendant,[114] nor does the manufacturer seek to intervene.[115]

If the consumer obtains a judgment against the retailer, retailer must thereafter bring a separate lawsuit against the manufacturer for indemnification. Moreover, because the manufacturer was not a party to the consumer's lawsuit, the manufacturer is free to relitigate issues determined there which underlie the consumer's judgment against the retailer.[116]

On the other hand, impleader would permit the retailer to join the manufacturer in the initial suit. As a party to the case, the manufacturer will then be bound along with the retailer to an adjudication of issues establishing the consumer's right to recover against the retailer. In addition, the retailer may obtain an adjudication of its indemnification claim in the same lawsuit. Permitting impleader in such cases "will avoid circuity of action and eliminate duplication of suits based on closely related matters."[117]

Impleader enjoys widespread use in federal and many state courts.[118] Rule 14 authorizes it in the former. Within ten days after service of the defendant's answer, Rule 14 permits defendant to serve a *third-party*

---

[111] *See generally Moore* §§ 14.01-14.42; *Wright & Miller* §§ 1441-1465; Greenbaum, *Jacks or Better to Open: Procedural Limitations on Co-Party and Third-Party Claims*, 74 Minn. L. Rev. 507, 525-531 (1990); Feirich, *Third Party Practice,* 1967 Ill. L.F. 236; *Developments in the Law — Multiparty Litigation in the Federal Courts,* 71 Harv. L. Rev. 874, 906-913 (1958).

[112] When a co-defendant is in this position, the proper device for asserting this legal responsibility in federal court is a cross-claim. *See* § 9.04 (discussing Rule 13(g)), *supra.*

[113] *See generally* Symposium, *Products Liability: Economic Analysis and the Law,* 38 U. Chi. L. Rev. 1 (1970).

[114] For discussion of joinder under Rule 20, see § 9.05[1], *supra.*

[115] For discussion of intervention under Rule 24, see § 9.08, *infra.*

[116] The manufacturer would be a stranger to the first suit and therefore could not be bound by issue preclusion. *See* § 15.08, *infra.*

[117] *Wright & Miller* § 1443. *Friedenthal, Kane & Miller* § 6.9, note that

[t]he availability of impleader saves the time and cost of duplicating evidence in two proceedings, avoids inconsistent results on related claims based on identical or similar evidence, and eliminates the serious prejudice to the original defendant that might result from a time lag between the plaintiff's judgment against him and a judgment in the defendant's favor against the third-party defendant.

[118] *Friedenthal, Kane & Miller* § 6.9.

complaint on the outsider.[119] In this capacity, defendant becomes a *third-party plaintiff,* the outsider a *third-party defendant.* The third-party defendant or any other party to the suit may move to strike defendant's impleader, either by arguing that it is beyond the scope of Rule 14, or that the court should use its discretion to refuse impleader even if the rule appears satisfied.[120]

The rule requires that the nature of the third-party claim be such that the third-party defendant "is or may be liable" to the third-party plaintiff "for all or part of the plaintiff's claim against him." For impleader to work, it is often necessary to bring in the third-party defendant before the third-party plaintiff's liability to plaintiff can be established. Rule 14 thus authorizes impleader against one who "*may be* liable."[121] An eventual judgment for the original plaintiff binds not only the defendant/third-party plaintiff, but also precludes the third party defendant from relitigating issues underlying the third-party plaintiff's liability to the original plaintiff.[122]

The heart of impleader is the requirement that the claim supporting it be based on secondary or derivative liability. That is, the third-party plaintiff must seek reimbursement from the third-party defendant for all or part of the former's liability to plaintiff.[123] It is not enough that the impleader claim arose out of the same transaction or occurrence as the original plaintiff's claim; the impleader must, in addition, be contingent or derivative.[124]

While the third-party plaintiff's liability is established by a judgment for plaintiff against the third-party plaintiff, the existence of the contingent or derivative liability is a separate question. The answer to it is not supplied by Rule 14, which merely provides the procedure by which such a duty is asserted as an impleader claim.[125] Instead, the answer must be found in

---

[119] Rule 14(a) requires court approval for service of the third-party complaint after the ten-day period.

[120] *See* text accompanying notes 131-135, *infra.*

[121] Emphasis added. This language in the rule has long been interpreted to permit impleader even when the claim against the third-party defendant is not yet ripe for suit under applicable substantive law because the third-party plaintiff's liability has yet to be determined. *See, e.g.,* the well-known case, *Jeub v. B/G Foods, Inc.,* 2 F.R.D. 238 (D. Minn. 1942).

[122] Rule 14(a) confers litigant status on the third-party defendant in the case, thereby creating an opportunity for the third-party defendant to join with the third-party plaintiff in attempting to defeat plaintiff's claim. The rule states that "[t]he third-party defendant may assert against the plaintiff any defenses which the third-party plaintiff has to the plaintiff's claim."

[123] "The secondary or derivative liability notion is central and it is irrelevant whether the basis of the third-party claim is indemnity, subrogation, contribution, express or implied warranty, or some other theory." *Wright & Miller* § 1446 (citing illustrative cases). Thus, except for admiralty and maritime claims treated separately in Rule 14(c), the rule does not permit defendant to implead an outsider on the theory that the outsider should be liable to plaintiff *instead* of the defendant. *Wright & Miller* § 1444; *Friedenthal, Kane & Miller* § 6.9.

[124] *See, e.g., National Bank of Canada v. Artex Indus., Inc.,* 627 F. Supp. 610, 613 (S.D.N.Y. 1986). *See generally Wright & Miller* § 1446.

[125] *See, e.g., Assicurazioni Generali S.p.A. v. Terranova,* 40 Fed. R. Serv. 2d (Callaghan) 850, 852 (S.D.N.Y. 1984) ("Rule 14 provides only a procedural means of adding a [third-party] defendant; it does not confer any substantive rights on the [third-party] plaintiff.").

the applicable substantive law. Four common theories of contingent or derivative liability are indemnity, subrogation, contribution and warranty. Their precise elements vary somewhat from jurisdiction to jurisdiction.

A right to *indemnification* either arises out of an express contractual provision whereby one party agrees to indemnify (or "hold harmless") another for certain liabilities, or by implication.[126] A right to indemnification will be implied when a person without fault is held legally liable for damages caused by the fault of another.[127]

Subrogation is the succession of one person to the rights of another.[128] "Subrogees are generally joint tortfeasors or innocent insurers who have compensated the insured for an injury resulting from the negligence of a third-party."[129] An insurer sued by its insured on an insurance policy may therefore implead the negligent third party on a subrogation theory to the extent that the insurer is or may be liable to its insured on the policy.

The right of *contribution* typically arises among joint tortfeasors, two or more persons who are jointly or severally liable in tort for the same injury.[130]

Finally, a *warranty,* in the impleader context, is an express or implied statement or representation typically made by a seller to a buyer or others in the chain of product distribution regarding the character of or title to the product.

Thus, in our hypothetical product liability suit, the retailer may in most jurisdictions implead the manufacturer either on the basis of an express indemnification clause in a sales contract or on the implied indemnity theory that the retailer is or may be liable to the consumer for defects in the product which are the fault of the manufacturer. Alternately, he may base his impleader on a theory of contribution, if he and the manufacturer are jointly or severally liable for causing the consumer's injury. Finally, he may invoke warranty, on the theory that the manufacturer expressly or impliedly warranted the product to be free of defects and should therefore reimburse the retailer for any liability arising from a product defect.

Since Rule 14 focuses on an easily defined and demonstrable source of judicial inefficiency, it is not surprising that federal courts have usually given it a sympathetic reading. At the same time, the rule is permissive rather than compulsory. Parties claimed against are not obliged to implead

---

[126] *See, e.g., Terranova,* 40 Fed. R. Serv. 2d at 852 (*construing* New York law); *Anderson v. Dreibelbis,* 104 F.R.D. 415 (E.D. Pa. 1984) (*construing* Pennsylvania law), *aff'd,* 787 F.2d 580 (3d Cir. 1986).

[127] *Terranova,* 40 Fed. R. Serv. 2d at 852; *Anderson,* 104 F.R.D. at 416-417.

[128] *See, e.g., Terranova,* 40 Fed. R. Serv.2d at 853. "[S]ubrogation is of two kinds, 'legal' and 'conventional.' The former is grounded in equity and arises by operation of law, which gives to a third person who has been compelled to pay a remedy against one who, in justice, ought to pay. 'Conventional' subrogation is grounded upon contract, express or implied." *Insurance Co. of North America v. Medical Protective Co.,* 768 F.2d 315, 320 (10th Cir. 1985).

[129] *Terranova,* 40 Fed. R. Serv. 2d at 853 (*construing* New York law).

[130] *Id.* at 852-853 (*construing* New York law); *Anderson,* 104 F.R.D. at 416 (*construing* Pennsylvania law).

an outsider, and whether particular applications of the rule should be permitted when impleader is sought is a matter best left to the sound discretion of the court.[131] In exercising its discretion, a federal court will balance potential savings of time and resources through impleader[132] against any problems posed by addition of the third-party defendant. In some cases these problems will be sufficient to defeat impleader.

For example, the court should not permit impleader when it seems reasonably clear that defendant will defeat plaintiff, with or without the added presence of a third-party defendant. From the court's case-management perspective, impleader would simply burden the case with a gratuitous party. In addition, subjecting the third-party defendant to the angst and expense of participation under these circumstances seems unfair.

There are also circumstances where the federal court should use its discretion to refuse impleader even though plaintiff may prevail and thus prompt a further lawsuit between defendant and the outsider. For example, the added presence of a third-party defendant may unduly delay trial for plaintiff.[133] Or the employer-defendant to a *respondeat superior* claim of negligence could prejudice the plaintiff by impleading a shallow-pocket employee whose presence might prompt a sympathetic jury to return a smaller verdict on the underlying claim against the deep-pocket employer.[134] There may also be "a lack of similarity between the issues and evidence required to prove the main and third-party claims. . . ."[135] Many of these problems, however, can be cured without disallowing the impleader by ordering separate trials under Rule 42, should the prejudice be a factor come trial.[136]

Rule 14 authorizes inclusion of third-party defendants without confronting extrinsic difficulties of personal jurisdiction, subject matter jurisdiction

---

[131] *Wright & Miller* § 1443.

[132] Prejudice to the defendant from proceeding in the absence of the outsider does not seem to play a very large role in justifying impleader. Yet the possibility of prejudice can be quite real. Recall the possibility for the retailer of conflicting judgments in the hypothetical opening this section. However, the appropriate response in such cases may be for defendant to argue compulsory joinder of the outsider under Rule 19(a), or dismissal of the case under 19(b) if joinder is not feasible. *See* § 9.05[2], *supra.*

[133] For discussion of this point and illustrative cases, see *Wright & Miller* § 1443.

[134] *See, e.g., Goodhart v. United States Lines Co.,* 26 F.R.D. 163 (S.D.N.Y. 1960) (impleader of employee is denied when it could serve only to suggest to the jury that the employee will pay the judgment or to threaten the employee with bankruptcy unless he testifies favorably to the employer). For further discussion of this point and illustrative cases, see *Wright & Miller* § 1443.

[135] *Wright & Miller* § 1443.

[136]

[T]he court always must remain flexible in its approach to an attempted impleader and should bear in mind that means other than dismissal may be available to prevent prejudice or confusion. Thus, if it appears that the action may become unduly complex because unrelated issues or evidence are present, or if knowledge of the identity or existence of a third party may cause prejudice to any litigant, the proper remedy is for the court to permit impleader and then to order separate trials pursuant to Rule 42 if any of these concerns becomes a reality.

Id.

and venue which could actually prevent the third-party defendants from entering the suit. A federal court usually enjoys only as much personal jurisdiction as the courts of the forum state.[137] Rule 4(k)(1)(b) supplements this for process under Rules 14 and 19 with the so-called 100-mile bulge — an added reach of 100 miles from the federal courthouse[138] — which may be inadequate to reach a prospective third-party defendant. The picture is brighter for federal subject matter jurisdiction and venue, however. Impleader claims that would not be within the original subject matter jurisdiction of federal courts now appear covered by the supplemental jurisdiction statute.[139] Similarly, venue does not appear to pose much of a problem in the impleader setting.[140]

§ 9.07   Interpleader[141]

"Interpleader is a form of joinder open to one who does not know to which of several claimants he or she is liable, if liable at all."[142] Interpleader resembles impleader[143] in that it protects one claimed against from multiple and possibly inconsistent lawsuits,[144] and it resembles permissive joinder[145] in that it permits a party to sort out its legal relationships with a number of opposing parties simultaneously.[146]

Absent interpleader, the party claimed against might have to defend against competing claimants in different courts, perhaps in different parts of the country. This might lead to multiple liability, inconsistent judgments,[147] or (at the very least) the vexation of multiple lawsuits.[148]

---

[137] See § 3.01[2][b], supra.

[138] A more detailed explanation appears at § 9.05[2][b], supra.

[139] See § 9.03, supra.

[140] "The prevailing interpretation of the federal venue rule is that if venue is properly established for the original action, the third-party defendant cannot object that venue would have been improper if the action had originally included him as a defendant." James, Hazard & Leubsdorf § 10.18. Recent statutory developments in federal venue have, if anything, made the possibility of venue for impleader claims more secure. See § 6.01, supra.

[141] See generally Moore §§ 22.01-22.04; Wright & Miller §§ 1701-21; Comment, Can Statutory Interpleader Be Used As a Remedy By the Tortfeasor in Mass Tort Litigation?, 90 Dick. L. Rev. 439 (1985); Comment, Deference to State Courts in Federal Interpleader Actions, 47 U. Chi. L. Rev. 824 (1980); Hazard & Moskovitz, An Historical and Critical Analysis of Interpleader, 52 Cal. L. Rev. 706 (1964); Developments in the Law — Multiparty Litigation in the Federal Courts, 71 Harv. L. Rev. 874, 913-928 (1958).

[142] Wright § 74. It "is a procedural device which enables a person holding money or property, in the typical case conceded to belong in whole or in part to another, to join in a single suit two or more persons asserting mutually exclusive claims to the fund." Moore § 22.02[1].

[143] See § 9.06 (Rule 14), supra.

[144] James, Hazard & Leubsdorf § 10.19.

[145] See § 9.05[1] (Rule 20(a)), supra.

[146] Interpleader is most like the part of Rule 20(a) "allowing the joinder of plaintiffs in the alternative when they are uncertain which of them has the right to relief and the joinder of defendants in the alternative when it is uncertain which of them is liable." Wright & Miller § 1702.

[147] Multiple liability and inconsistent judgments, the most troublesome byproducts of an excessive number of lawsuits, are described at § 9.05[2][a], supra.

Interpleader permits one (called a stakeholder) to avoid this by forcing all claimants to proceed against him in one lawsuit.[149]

Although many states authorize interpleader, interpleader in federal court is often preferable, at least in cases where the party claimed against faces the prospect of litigation spread across more than one state. This is not because of any advantage offered by the Federal Rules of Civil Procedure. Federal Rule 22, covering interpleader, provides little not already afforded by the rules of a majority of state courts.[150] Rather, it is because Rule 22 is usually overshadowed by an additional procedural remedy available only in federal court: statutory interpleader.[151] Congress created a special enclave of subject matter jurisdiction within the interpleader statute,[152] complemented the arrangement with a statute creating special venue possibilities,[153] and (most significant in creating an advantage over interpleader actions in state court) liberalized service of process and, therefore, personal jurisdiction.[154]

Whether proceeding by statute or Rule 22, the stakeholder deposits with the court the stake (fund) — property or money[155] — which is the target of the competing claims against the stakeholder. The stakeholder may then seek interlocutory relief, enjoining maintenance of other suits against him with respect to the fund during the federal interpleader action.[156] There are two stages to federal interpleader adjudications.

---

[148] Professor Wright has suggested that the possibility of vexatious multiple lawsuits can alone be sufficient to justify interpleader. *Wright* § 74. *Treinies v. Sunshine Mining Co.*, 308 U.S. 66 (1939), is a famous example of interpleader as a response to the concerns listed in the text. Two factions claimed right of ownership to the same block of mining company stock. One claimed on the strength of a Washington court judgment, the other on an Idaho judgment. Uncertain which judgment to honor, the mining company cleared the air by interpleading both claimants in a single action in federal court.

[149] Interpleader is most frequently used as a basis for commencing suit, but it can be initiated in ongoing litigation through a counterclaim, cross-claim or third party claim. *See generally Wright & Miller* § 1708.

[150] The language of the state rules is often nearly identical. *E.g.*, Fla. R. Civ. P. 1.240; N.M. Stat. Ann. R. Civ. P. Dist. Ct. 1-022; Wis. Stat. Ann. § 803.07.

[151] *See* 28 U.S.C. § 1335.

[152] Section 1335 requires diversity of citizenship between only two or more of the adverse claimants (called *minimal diversity) see* § 5.04[2], *supra* and, at least $500 in controversy, measured by the value of the stake. In contrast, a federal interpleader action brought solely under Rule 22 would have to qualify either under the general diversity statute, 28 U.S.C. § 1332, requiring complete diversity of citizenship between the stakeholder and all of the claimants, and more than $75,000 in controversy, or under some federal question jurisdictional grant. *See Wright* § 74.

[153] Statutory interpleader has its own venue statute, 28 U.S.C. § 1397, permitting suit in any district where a claimant resides.

[154] 28 U.S.C. § 2361 authorizes service of process on all competing claimants in any judicial district of the United States. "Thus, in statutory interpleader actions, only those claimants who cannot be found or who reside outside of the United States are beyond the reach of the statute." *Friedenthal, Kane & Miller* § 16.12.

[155] The stakeholder will usually be permitted to give a bond in lieu of money. *Moore* § 22.03[1][b].

[156] Injunctive authority in statutory interpleader cases is explicit in 28 U.S.C. § 2361. *Wright & Miller* § 1717.

In the "first stage," the court determines whether interpleader is appropriate on the facts of the case. If so, in the "second stage," the court adjudicates the adverse claims and distributes the stake.[157]

The stakeholder may be either disinterested or interested. If disinterested, he takes the position that one of the claimants is entitled to the fund — stage two of the interpleader action will determine which. A disinterested stakeholder participates only in stage one. After a hearing, the court decides if the stakeholder is entitled to an interpleader remedy. If he is, he is excused from further involvement in the case, leaving the fund with the court to be fought over by rival claimants.[158] However, the stakeholder's lack of interest in the stake is no longer a prerequisite for interpleader. An interested stakeholder may remain to participate in stage two of the interpleader action, claiming that he is obligated to no one and, in effect, competing with the rival claimants for the fund.

State Farm Fire & Casualty Company v. Tashire[159] offers a good illustration of the scope of federal interpleader. Stakeholder State Farm filed an interpleader action in Oregon federal court based on both the statute and Rule 22, in response to claims made on a $20,000 insurance policy. Its insured had been operating a truck when he collided with a bus in California. The accident resulted in two deaths, injuries to many people, and lawsuits seeking more than $1,000,000 in damages from the insured and the bus company, among others. The federal district court directed claimants to make all of their claims against the stakeholder, its insured, the bus company, and the bus driver in the interpleader action. Reversing, the federal court of appeals viewed the case as altogether inappropriate for interpleader. The Supreme Court reversed in turn, holding that statutory interpleader was available to State Farm to confine to one lawsuit all claims made on the $20,000 policy. The Court refused, however, to resurrect interpleader on the scale attempted by the district court. It noted that "State Farm's interest in this case, which is the fulcrum of the interpleader procedure, is confined to its $20,000 fund."[160] The insurer

> should not be allowed to determine that dozens of tort plaintiffs must be compelled to press their claims — even those claims which are not against the insured and which in no event could be satisfied out of the meager insurance fund — in a single forum of the insurance company's choosing. There is nothing in the statutory scheme, and very little in the judicial and academic commentary upon that scheme, which requires that the tail be allowed to wag the dog in this fashion.[161]

---

[157] *Moore* § 22.03[1][a] (footnote omitted).

[158] *See Moore* § 22.03[2][a].

[159] 386 U.S. 523 (1967).

[160] 386 U.S. at 535.

[161] *Id.* "We recognize," added the *Tashire* Court, "that our view of interpleader means that it cannot be used to solve all the vexing problems of multiparty litigation arising out of a mass tort. But interpleader was never intended to perform such a function, to be an all-purpose bill of peace." *Id.*

§ 9.08 Intervention [162]

The party joinder devices we have examined so far are available only to one already a party in the case. Intervention differs in that it provides a means for outsiders to make themselves parties. Federal court interventions usually are governed by Rule 24, which has its counterpart in most state procedural systems. [163] The rule contemplates both intervention of right under 24(a) and permissive intervention under 24(b).

[1] Intervention of Right

Rule 24(a) states that an outsider who makes

timely application shall be permitted to intervene in an action: (1) when a statute of the United States confers an unconditional right to intervene; or (2) when the applicant claims an interest relating to the property or transaction which is the subject of the action and he is so situated that the disposition of the action may as a practical matter impair or impede his ability to protect that interest, unless the applicant's interest is adequately represented by existing parties.

Most applications for intervention of right are made under Rule 24(a)(2). [164] To qualify, the applicant must satisfy three requirements.

First, the applicant must demonstrate that the lawsuit carries a possibility of detriment to him serious enough to entitle him to an opportunity to influence the outcome in ways that only a litigant can. [165] It is no longer necessary for the applicant to demonstrate that the lawsuit is capable of binding him in a formal sense. [166] Rule 24(a)(2) contemplates merely

---

[162] *See generally Moore* §§ 24.01-24.24; *Wright & Miller* §§ 1901-1923; Appel, *Intervention in Public Law Litigation: The Environmental Paradigm*, 78 Wash. L. Q. 215 (2000); Tobias, *Standing to Intervene*, 1991 Wis. L. Rev. 415; Tobias, *Intervention After Webster*, 38 Kan. L. Rev. 731 (1990); Greenbaum, *Government Participation in Private Litigation*, 21 Ariz. St. L. Rev. 853, 900-970 (1989); Shreve, *Questioning Intervention of Right—Toward a New Methodology of Decisionmaking,* 74 Nw. U. L. Rev. 894 (1980); Symposium, *Problems of Intervention in Public Law Litigation*, 13 U.C. Davis L. Rev. 211 (1980); Brunet, *A Study in the Allocation of Scarce Judicial Resources: The Efficiency of Federal Intervention Criteria,* 12 Ga. L. Rev. 701 (1978); Shapiro, *Some Thoughts on Intervention Before Courts, Agencies, and Arbitrators,* 81 Harv. L. Rev. 721 (1968).

[163] *E.g.,* Ind. Code Ann. Ct. R. Trial 24; N.C. Gen. Stat. § 1A-1 T. 24; Minn. Stat. Ann. R. Civ. P. Dist. Ct. 24.

[164] The function of subdivision (1) of Rule 24(a) is to note provisions for intervention of right appearing elsewhere in federal statutes. For examples, *see Moore* § 24.02. Absent acknowledgement in Rule 24 of the existence of prior federal statutes governing intervention, the latter might have been extinguished by the rule because the Rules Enabling Act, 28 U.S.C. § 2072, states that "[a]ll laws in conflict" with the federal rules "shall be of no further force or effect after such rules have taken effect."

[165] Party prerogatives include setting boundaries of relevancy through pleadings, developing facts by discovery and creating parts of the factual record, and appealing adverse judgments.

[166] The Supreme Court had given this narrow reading to an earlier version of Rule 24 in *Sam Fox Publishing Co. v. United States,* 366 U.S. 683 (1961), prompting amendment of the rule in 1966.

"practical" impairment. The Supreme Court has noted that the applicant need only have a "significantly protectable interest."[167] However, the scope of absentee interests protected through intervention of right has proven difficult to define precisely.[168]

Second, the applicant must demonstrate a substantial possibility that none of the present parties will adequately represent his interest. A successful applicant will thereafter make or defend against a claim,[169] generally aligning himself with one already a party. The adequacy question thus boils down to whether the existing party can be expected to represent the applicant's interests adequately in the course of representing his own. If so, the applicant has no right to intervene under Rule 24(a)(2). When the applicant's stake in the outcome is no greater than that of an existing party with whom the applicant would be aligned, and when that existing party is not in collusion with an opposing party, incompetent, or hostile toward the applicant, representation by the existing party often will be deemed adequate and intervention of right will be denied.[170]

Third, the application must be timely. Rule 24 sets no deadline for interventions. Absentees may move to intervene after trial of the case and even on appeal. Since, however, the intervener takes the case as he finds it,[171] the later he intervenes the fewer opportunities he will have to influence the outcome. Moreover, it is generally true that interventions become increasingly difficult to justify as the case unfolds.[172] Two questions recur when the timeliness of the application is an issue: whether the court and those already parties will suffer from the fact the application did not come

---

[167] *Diamond v. Charles*, 476 U.S. 54, 68 (1986).

[168] Professor Shapiro noted that "[t]he range of possible interests may defy adequate classification, spreading over a spectrum that is extremely hard to chart." Note 162, *supra*, at 740. Examples include the possible *stare decisis* impact of the case on the applicant, *e.g.*, *Atlantis Dev. Corp. v. United States*, 379 F.2d 818, 822 (5th Cir. 1967), and possible frustration of the applicant's opportunity to obtain future injunctive relief. *E.g.*, *Stallworth v. Monsanto Co.*, 558 F.2d 257, 268 (5th Cir. 1977).

[169] Rule 24(c) requires the applicant's motion to intervene to "be accompanied by a pleading setting forth the claim or defense for which intervention is sought."

[170] *See, e.g., Delaware Valley Citizens' Council for Clean Air v. Commonwealth of Pa.*, 674 F.2d 970 (3d Cir. 1982). In some cases, the argument for inadequate representation will be that the interest of the applicant in the outcome is, upon careful examination, more focused or more intense than that of the existing party with whom the applicant would be aligned. Consider, for example, the facts of a well-known intervention case, *Ford Motor Co. v. Bisanz Bros.*, 249 F.2d 22 (8th Cir. 1957). Plaintiffs sued to shut down a railroad spur as a private nuisance. Ford sought to intervene on the side of the railroad defendant on the ground that it could not continue to operate one of its plants if it could not use the spur. The court ruled that Ford was entitled to intervention as of right. Ford had far more to lose from elimination of the spur than did the railroad. Therefore, while there was no suggestion that the railroad would be less than diligent in protecting *its* interests, the railroad's stake in the outcome did not give it the same incentive that Ford had to litigate vigorously.

[171] *Cf. Arizona v. California*, 460 U.S. 605, 615 (1983) ("Of course, permission to intervene does not carry with it the right to relitigate matters already determined in the case, unless those matters would otherwise be subject to reconsideration.").

[172] Thus, "[t]here is considerable reluctance on the part of the courts to allow intervention after the action has gone to judgment and a strong showing will be required of the applicant." *Wright & Miller* § 1916.

earlier,[173] and whether the applicant can be faulted for applying as late as he did.[174] The latter point can be resolved in favor of intervention when, for example, applicant's earlier motion would have failed because representation by an existing party then seemed adequate.[175]

[2] Permissive Intervention

Rule 24(b) states in part that an outsider who makes "timely application . . . may be permitted to intervene in an action: . . . (2) when an applicant's claim or defense and the main action have a question of law or fact in common."[176] The present-day function of Rule 24(b)(2) seems confined to promoting judicial economy. Therefore, permissive intervention is warranted only when savings of party and judicial resources from avoiding an extra lawsuit outweigh costs from the added presence of the intervener.[177] Concern over the latter is clear from the last sentence in Rule 24(b)(2): "In exercising its discretion the court shall consider whether the intervention will unduly delay or prejudice the adjudication of rights of the original parties."[178]

Rule 24 does not require applicants to confine their motion to intervene to either paragraph (a) or (b). Applicants frequently seek both in the alternative. Since intervention of right is narrower in scope, adding a

---

[173] For a survey of federal decisions on this point, see *Wright & Miller, id.*

[174] For a survey of federal decisions on this point, see *Wright & Miller, id.*

[175] *Smuck v. Hobson,* 408 F.2d 175 (D.C. Cir. 1969), is a noted example. Applicants' interests were at least arguably represented by the defendant until defendant decided not to appeal an adverse ruling by the federal district court. The court of appeals granted intervention, thus avoiding a Catch-22 interplay of the adequacy-of-representation and timeliness concerns which would have shut off the possibility of intervention altogether.

[176] Subdivision (1) of Rule 24(b) recognizes the possibility of a statutory "conditional right to intervene." The functional relationship between (b)(1) and (b)(2) is thus the same as that between (a)(1) and (a)(2) described at note 164, *supra.*

[177] *See Shreve,* note 162, *supra,* at 908-909:

A grant of intervention may adversely affect the original parties in a number of ways. Intervention forces the nominal co-party to relinquish partial management of the case. Moreover, the intervener may complicate the original parties' preparation and litigation of the case by maintaining a separate position on existing issues or by adding new claims, parties, or witnesses. Thus, the existing parties' expectations of an expeditious adjudication and an orderly resolution of their claims . . . may be defeated by the delays and complications accompanying intervention. In addition, the complications resulting from intervention may so strain the resources of the original parties that their continued ability to participate is jeopardized, and the forum becomes correspondingly less accessible.

In times of crowded dockets, the court may also have a concern in keeping the case from becoming too burdensome and, in the interests of justice, seeing that the reasonable concerns of existing parties are protected. Related are the interests of the original parties and the court in settling cases, and the concern that an intervener might effectively block settlement.

Reprinted by special permission of the Northwestern University Law Review, © 1980 by Northwestern University School of Law, volume 74.

[178] Quoting this passage, the Supreme Court observed: "Particularly in a complex case . . ., a district judge's decision on how best to balance the rights of the parties against the need to keep the litigation from becoming unmanageable is entitled to great deference." *Stringfellow v. Concerned Neighbors in Action,* 480 U.S. 370, 380 (1987).

request for permissive intervention provides the applicant with a fall-back position.

[3] Comparing Intervention of Right and Permissive Intervention

If an application for intervention falls within Rule 24(a), the paragraph provides that it "shall" be granted. If the applicant merely satisfies 24(b), intervention "may" (or may not) be granted. The reason for different treatment can be found in the interests of the applicant in intervening that are reflected in each paragraph. Intervention of right under Rule 24 (a) secures participation in the case for one whose substantive interests may be compromised.[179] Permissive intervention under Rule 24(b) rarely does more than advance the interest of the applicant and possibly the court in more cost-efficient litigation.[180]

The impact of the distinction on an applicant's chances for successful intervention is two-fold. First, the greater premium Rule 24(a) places on interventions is likely to influence the federal district court as initial decisionmaker. Second, while a decision denying permissive intervention is insulated from review by the trial court's discretion,[181] the decision that the applicant is not entitled to intervene of right is open to a considerable measure of appellate redecision.[182]

The distinction may in addition affect the court's willingness to attach conditions when it grants a motion to intervene. Limitations on the nature and degree of the applicant's participation are not uncommon in permissive

---

[179] Minus reference to the possibility of inadequate representation, the relationship of the absentee to the lawsuit is the same as that described in Rule 19(a)(2)(i) of one who must be joined if feasible. *See* § 9.05[2][a], *supra.*

[180] It is thus comparable to permissive party joinder under Rule 20. *See* § 9.05[1], *supra.*

[181] *E.g., County of Orange v. Air California,* 799 F.2d 535 (9th Cir. 1986) ("If there is no right to intervene under Rule 24(a), it is wholly discretionary with the court whether to allow intervention under Rule 24(b) and even though there is a common question of law or fact, or the requirements of Rule 24(b) are otherwise satisfied, the court may refuse to allow intervention."). *See Wright & Miller* § 1913 (citing numerous examples).

[182] Most federal courts of appeal have regarded the Rule 24(a)(2) questions of whether the applicant risks practical impairment from the outcome of the case and whether applicant's interests are adequately represented by an existing party to be open to reexamination on appeal. "[T]he appellate court can substitute its judgment for that of the trial court if it regards the urgency as great enough to warrant a determination that intervention should be of right." *James, Hazard & Leubsdorf* § 10.17. *But see United States v. Hooker Chemicals & Plastics,* 749 F.2d 968, 990 (2nd Cir. 1984) (noting the traditional distinction between reviewing standards for (a) and (b) intervention denials but stating, "it is now the rule in this circuit that denials of motions to intervene as of right under Rule 24(a)(2) also are to be reviewed under an abuse of discretion standard.").

Refusals to grant intervention based on untimeliness are regarded as discretionary, whether the application is grounded on (a) or (b) of Rule 24. Therefore, a finding that an application to intervene of right is untimely "will be reviewed only for an abuse of discretion." *Wright & Miller* § 1916.

interventions under Rule 24(b), but the propriety of similarly limiting 24(a) interveners of right is open to question. [183]

§ 9.09 Class Actions[184]

Parties brought in through the joinder devices we have considered so far share active participation with all other parties in the case. Modern rules of procedure, consolidated litigation, [185] even specially constructed courtrooms, [186] may enable courts to accommodate many active participants in a single case.

There are limits, however. Exercise of the prerogatives of party participation [187] is time-consuming. A distinguished federal trial judge once observed: "Additional parties always take additional time. Even if they have no witnesses of their own, they are the source of additional questions, objections, briefs, arguments, motions and the like which tend to make the proceeding a Donnybrook Fair." [188] Procedural safeguards offered for dividing cases or trials that have grown too large [189] or for staggering the adjudication of claims within a case [190] provide only limited protection. Courts must draw the line somewhere, [191] protecting those already parties and themselves from congestion which would overwhelm the case.

---

[183] See *Kennedy,* note 162, *supra,* at 366; *Shapiro,* note 162, *supra,* at 759. Courts refused to limit Rule 24(a) interventions in *Spangler v. United States,* 415 F.2d 1242 (9th Cir. 1969), and *Exchange Nat'l Bank of Chicago v. Abramson,* 45 F.R.D. 97 (D. Minn. 1964). *But see Harris v. General Coach Works,* 37 F.R.D. 343 (E. D. Mich. 1968) (appearing to limit a Rule 24(a) intervener).

[184] The literature on class actions is voluminous. *See, e.g., Moore* §§ 23.01-23.87; *Wright & Miller* §§ 1751-1805; H. Newberg, *Newberg on Class Actions* (3d ed. 1992); Coffee, *Class Action Accountability: Reconciling Exit, Voice, and Loyalty in Representative Litigation,* 100 Colum. L. Rev. 370 (2000); Hazard, *The Futures Problem,* 148 U. Pa. L. Rev. 1901 (2000); Wasserman, *Dueling Class Actions,* 80 B.U. L. Rev. 461 (2000); Silberman, *The Vicissitudes of the American Class Action—With a Comparative Eye,* 7 Tulane J. of Int'l & Comp. L. 201 (1999); Hazard, Gedud & Sowle, *An Historical Analysis of the Binding Effect of Class Suits,* 146 U. Pa. L. Rev. 1849 (1998); Shapiro, *Class Actions: The Class as Party and Client,* 73 Notre Dame L. Rev. 913 (1998); Symposium, *The Institute of Judicial Administration Research Conference on Class Actions,* 71 N.Y.U. L. Rev. 1 (1996); Coffee, *Class Wars: The Dilemma of the Mass Tort Class Action,* 95 Colum. L. Rev. 1343 (1995); *Manual for Complex Litigation (Third)* §§ 30.1-30.4 (1995).

[185] See § 9.10, *infra.*

[186] See "Megacourtroom," *Time,* March 18, 1985 at 67 (discussing the construction of a "megacourtroom" for Manville Corp. asbestos litigation).

[187] See § 9.08, *supra.*

[188] *Crosby Steam Gage & Valve Co. v. Manning, Maxwell & Moore,* 51 F. Supp. 972, 973 (D. Mass. 1943) (Wyzanski, J.).

[189] See § 9.02, *supra.*

[190] Federal Rule 54(b) provides, "[w]hen more than one claim for relief is presented in an action . . ., or when multiple parties are involved, the court may direct the entry of a final judgment as to one or more but fewer than all of the claims or parties." *See* § 13.03[2] (finality in multi-party and multi-claim cases), *infra.* Many state procedural systems have similar provisions allowing piecemeal adjudication. *E.g.,* Ind. Code Ann. Ct. R. Trial 54(B); Ky. Rev. Stat. Ann. R. Civ. P. 54.02; Minn. Stat. Ann. R. Civ. P. Dist. Ct. 54.02.

[191] See for example, discussion of concerns weighing against permissive intervention at § 9.08, *supra.*

The special contribution of the class action device is to facilitate adjudication of additional claims without enlarging the number of active parties. This usually works by designating a party (or parties)[192] to litigate not only for himself but also as a representative for a group (the class). Class members will be bound by the outcome of the case. That is, they will fare on issues common to the class as does their class representative. However, only their class representative will be an active litigant. They will remain passive, unless they exclude themselves from the lawsuit (*opt out*)[193] or appear in the litigation to litigate actively along with the class representative.[194]

[1] Class Actions Under Rule 23

[a] Prerequisites

Most federal court class actions are governed by Rule 23.[195] Plaintiff usually is the class representative. He pleads an individual claim, but also pleads the existence of a class and a claim or claims on their behalf.[196] Rule 23(c)(2) provides for certification of the case as a class action, stating that, "[a]s soon as practicable after the commencement of an action brought as a class action, the court shall determine by order whether it is to be so maintained." Filing a complaint alleging the existence of the class and

---

[192] There can be and often is more than one class representative. For convenience, however, we will use the singular form.

[193] Federal Rule 23 and the class action provisions of most states have a mechanism for class members with discrete claims to exclude themselves from class actions, avoiding preclusive effects of a judgment later in the case. The process is often called "opting out." Furthermore, "[c]ourts have the discretionary power under Rule 23(d) to extend the exclusion option to Rule 23(b)(1) and (b)(2) suits." *Newberg*, note 184, *supra*, § 16.14. For a critique of current practice, *see* Note, *Class Actions in the Asbestos Context: Balancing the Due Process Considerations Implicated by the Right to Opt Out*, 70 Tex. L. Rev. 211 (1991); Note, *Constrained Individualism in Group Litigation: Requiring Class Members to Make a Good Cause Showing Before Opting Out of a Federal Class Action*, 100 Yale L.J. 745 (1990).

A class member who opts out probably will be unable to exploit through nonmutual offensive issue preclusion a judgment thereafter rendered in favor of the class. *Wright & Miller* § 1789. This is because, by opting out of the class, the party knowingly foregoes an earlier opportunity to litigate the issue. *See* § 15.08[2][b], *infra*.

[194] Federal Rule 23 raises possibilities that class members might either appear or intervene in the action. The rule does not explain how the two differ. *See* Newberg, note 184, *supra*, at § 16.6. Professors Wright and Miller suggest that courts may be reluctant to complicate class actions by permitting extensive use of either device. *Wright & Miller* § 1799.

[195] Prior to its 1966 amendment, Rule 23 also governed actions now treated by Rules 23.1 and 23.2. Rule 23.1 deals with shareholder derivative actions. Rule 23.2 "enables a representative suit to be brought by or against the associaion itself." *Moore* § 23.2.02.

[196] Much less frequently, plaintiff sues against rather than on behalf of a class. *See* Taylor, *Defendant Class Actions Under Rule 23(b)(2): Resolving the Language Dilemma*, 40 Kan. L. Rev. 77 (1991); Comment, *Mandatory Notice and Defendant Class Actions: Resolving the Paradox of Identity Between Plaintiffs and Defendants*, 40 Emory L.J. 611 (1991); Comment, *Defendant Class Actions and Federal Civil Rights Litigation*, 33 UCLA L. Rev. 283 (1985).

pleading class claims will usually toll the applicable statute of limitations against members of the putative class.[197]

The burden is on plaintiff to demonstrate that the requirements of Rule 23 have been met. To succeed under the rule, a case must (1) conform to the four requirements of paragraph (a); (2) satisfy two further requirements not expressly stated in the rule;[198] and (3) fit into one of the categories in Rule 23(b).

Rule 23(a) states:

> One or more members of a class may sue or be sued as representative parties on behalf of all only if (1) the class is so numerous that joinder of all members is impracticable, (2) there are questions of law or fact common to the class, (3) the claims or defenses of the representative parties are typical of the claims or defenses of the class, and (4) the representative parties will fairly and adequately protect the interests of the class.

Subdivisions (1) and (2) pose rudimentary questions about the appropriateness of the case as a class action. The first is sometimes called the "numerosity" requirement.[199] If the group offered as a class is so small that active participation of each member is feasible, there is no need for the class action device.[200] The second is sometimes called the "commonality" requirement.[201] If the group does not share issues in common, there is no material in the case for a class-wide adjudication.[202]

The purpose of subdivision (3) (the "typicality" requirement) and subdivision (4) of Rule 23(a) is to assure that representation of the passive class members' interests will be good enough[203] to make it fair to bind them by

---

[197] Usually, the statute of limitations will either resume running or begin running anew if certification is eventually denied, depending on the statute. *See, e.g., Chardon v. Fumero Soto,* 462 U.S. 650 (1983) (the statute of limitations began running anew after class certification was denied).

[198] The class must be capable of definition. It must describe a group that genuinely exists, and it must do so with sufficient clarity to inform the court and the party opposing the class of the stakes in the litigation. *See Manual,* note 184, *supra,* § 30.14. The representative must also be a member of the class. *Wright & Miller* § 1761. *Cf. General Tel. Co. of the Southwest v. Falcon,* 457 U.S. 147, 156 (1982) ("We have repeatedly held that a class representative must be part of the class.") (quoting *East Texas Motor Freight System v. Rodriguez,* 431 U.S. 395, 403 (1977)). This also satisfies the requirement under Article III of the United States Constitution that the class representative have standing. *Ortiz v. Fiberboard Corp.,* 527 U.S. 815 (1999).

[199] *E.g., General Tel. Co. of the Southwest v. Falcon,* 457 U.S. 147, 156 (1982).

[200] "The question of what constitutes impracticability . . . depends on the particular facts of each case and no arbitrary rules regarding the size of classes have been established by the courts." *Wright & Miller* § 1762.

[201] *E.g., General Tel. Co. of the Southwest v. Falcon,* 457 U.S. 147, 156 (1982).

[202] "It is important to note that this provision does not require that all the questions of law and fact raised by the dispute be common . . . . All that can be divined from the rule itself is that the use of the plural 'questions' suggests that more than one issue of law or fact must be common to members of the class." *Wright & Miller* § 1763.

[203] "Quality of representation embraces both the competence of the legal counsel of the representatives and the stature and interest of the named parties themselves." *Wright & Miller* § 1766.

the result in the case.[204] If subdivisions (3) and (4) had been omitted from Rule 23(a), the constitutional law of due process doubtless would have required federal courts to supplement the rule with these requirements.[205] As it is, Rule 23(a)(3) and (4) not only reflect due process requirements, but probably secure a greater measure of protection for class members by advancing nonconstitutional policies of procedural fairness.[206]

A class action brought under Rule 23 must also fall within one of the four categories contained in paragraph (b) of the rule. The first two categories exist in Rule 23(b)(1) which "permits a class action where this is necessary to avoid possible adverse effects on the opponents of the class or on absent members of the class."[207] The justification for class actions under (b)(1) is generally understood to be narrower than that of merely promoting judicial economy. Thus, "subdivision (b)(1)(A) is applicable when practical necessity forces the opposing party to act in the same manner toward the individual class members and thereby makes inconsistent adjudications in separate actions unworkable or intolerable."[208]

The third category is in Rule 23(b)(2), authorizing a class action when "the party opposing the class has acted or refused to act on grounds generally applicable to the class, thereby making appropriate final injunctive relief or corresponding declaratory relief with respect to the class as a whole. . . ." Rule 23(b)(2) has figured prominently in federal suits directed against state or local officials, where relief sought often is declaratory or injunctive. While (b)(2) was created "essentially as a tool for facilitating civil rights actions,"[209] it is not limited to such cases.[210]

---

[204] Of the two, subsection (4) reflects this purpose most clearly. Subsection (3) does not appear to add much, although it "assures that the claims of the representative party are similar enough to the claims of the class so that he will adequately represent them." *Wright & Miller* § 1764.

[205] This is evident from the Supreme Court's opinions in *Hansberry* and *Mullane,* discussed in § 9.09[2][c], *infra. Cf. Wright & Miller* § 1765 ("The binding effect of all class action decrees raises substantial due process questions that are directly relevant to Rule 23(a)(4).").

[206] It is difficult and (from the standpoint of administering Rule 23) unnecessary to determine precisely where constitutional requirements end and prudential, rule-based requirements begin. For discussion of the adequate representation requirement in class actions, *see* Degnan, *Forward: Adequacy of Representation in Class Actions,* 60 Cal. L. Rev. 705 (1972); Note, *Class Actions: Defining the Typical and Representative Plaintiff Under Subsections (a)(3) and (4) of Federal Rule 23,* 53 B.U. L. Rev. 406 (1973).

[207] *Wright* § 72. Class actions under Rule 23(b)(1)(A) are designed to avert prejudice to the party opposing the class "if inconsistent results in individual adjudications establish incompatible standards of conduct to which he must adhere, as in a suit by taxpayers to invalidate municipal action or in a suit involving the rights and duties of riparian owners." *Id.* Class actions under Rule 23(b)(1)(B) protect absent class members from the relative disadvantage of pursuing their interests in individual lawsuits, "as in a suit to compel reorganization of a fraternal association or a suit by stockholders to compel declaration of a dividend." *Id.* The latter category also includes actions presenting multiple claims against a common limited pool of assets.

[208] *Wright & Miller* § 1773. For recent discussion of the scope and application of Rule 23(b)(1), see *Ortiz v. Fiberboard Corp.,* 527 U.S. 815 (1999).

[209] *Moore* § 23.43[1][a].

[210] *See* The Advisory Committe Note to the 1966 amendment to Rule 23.

The accepted reading of Rule 23(b)(2) is that "[t]he subdivision does not extend to cases in which the appropriate final relief relates exclusively or predominantly to money damages."[211] Note that this standard does not necessarily exclude from (b)(2) cases seeking damages as well as declaratory or injunctive relief.[212] The question is whether the damages portion of the remedial package predominates. One study concluded that "cases involving claims for both money damages and injunctive or declaratory relief present significant difficulties of classification" under Rule 23.[213]

Rule 23(b)(3) creates a final, significant category of class actions.[214] It authorizes the device when, in the language of (b)(3), "the court finds that the questions of law or fact common to the members of the class predominate over any questions affecting only individual members, and that a class action is superior to other available methods for the fair and efficient adjudication of the controversy."[215]

Subdivision (b)(3) has greater scope than (b)(1) or (2) in one respect and less in another. While (b)(1) and (2) demand a closer relationship among class interests than the requirement in Rule 23(a)(3) that there be predominant common questions of law or fact,[216] predominance is enough for (b)(3). On the other hand, the court may certify (b)(1) and (2) classes without findings required under (b)(3) that class issues predominate and that the class action is superior to other forms of adjudication.

Despite these differences in description, the categories created in Rule 23(b) are not mutually exclusive. Some class actions appropriate to (b)(1) or (2) also appear to fit within (b)(3).[217] In such cases, certification under (b)(1) or (b)(2) can offer advantages over certification under (b)(3). This is because Rule 23(c)(2) requires notice to be sent to members of a (b)(3) class

---

[211] Rule 23 advisory committee's notes (1966). On distinctions between damages, injunctions and declaratory judgments, see Chapter 14, *infra*.

[212] Thus, "several courts have allowed Rule 23(b)(2) actions involving damages or back payments when the primary relief sought was an injunction." *Wright & Miller* § 1775 (citing examples).

[213] *Report and Recommendations of the Special Committee on Class Action Improvements,* note 184, *supra* at 197. The Committee went on to note that "an artful pleader can endeavor to make the declaratory or injunctive relief appear to 'predominate'." *Id.*

[214] "The great bulk of reported cases in which class actions have been allowed under the revised rule have been (b)(3) actions." *Wright* § 72.

[215] To aid in resolving these issues, Rule 23(b)(3) identifies four considerations:

> (A) the interest of members of the class in individually controlling the prosecution or defense of separate actions; (B) the extent and nature of any litigation concerning the controversy already commenced by or against members of the class; (C) the desirability or undesirability of concentrating the litigation of the claims in the particular forum; (D) the difficulties likely to be encountered in the management of a class action.

[216] Members of a 23(b)(2) class must be united in their request for an injunction or declaratory judgment. Satisfaction of (b)(1) will only be possible when the interests of individual class members, although discrete, resemble one another to a large degree. For examples, see note 207, *supra.*

[217] *See, e.g., Wright & Miller* § 1772 (raising the possibility of "an action . . . under both Rule 23(b)(1) and Rule 23(b)(3).").

and gives them the opportunity to request exclusion from ("opt out of") the class.[218]

It is now clear that the requirements posed by subdivisions (a) and (b) of Rule 23 apply also to classes certified solely for purposes of settlement.[219]

[b] Reconciling Judicial Economy and Public Law Enforcement in (b)(3) Class Actions

A major goal in drafting Rule 23(b)(3) was one we have encountered previously in this chapter — judicial economy.[220] If only judicial economy was involved, the arguments for and against Rule 23(b)(3) certifications would follow a familiar pattern. The argument for certification would be that efficiency would result from simultaneous adjudication of elements of individual claims common to the class, while the counter-argument would be that maintenance of a class action would confuse and delay the case in ways counterproductive to judicial economy and prejudicial to interests of those opposing the class.[221]

The picture for (b)(3) class actions is complicated, however, by the recurrent suggestion that they perform a function apart from promoting judicial economy — that of providing a means for private citizens to sue in the public interest. Thus viewed, Rule 23(b)(3) should be given maximum play when class representatives can, as private attorneys general, protect members of the public who are unable to protect themselves.[222] But it is possible to argue that, since the private attorney-general theory has greatest application when class members' damage claims are too small to be viable as individual lawsuits,[223] use of the idea to justify (b)(3) class

---

[218] See Wright & Miller § 1772. On notice in (b)(3) actions, see § 9.09[2][c], infra. On opt-out procedure, see note 193, supra.

[219] Ortiz v.Fiberboard, 527 U.S. 815 (1999); Amchem Products v. Windsor, 521 U.S. 591 (1997).

[220] "Subdivision (b)(3) encompasses those cases in which a class action would achieve economies of time, effort, and expense, and promote uniformity of decision as to persons similarly situated, without sacrificing procedural fairness or bringing about other undesirable results." Rule 23, advisory committee's notes (1966).

[221] The same pattern would be followed, for example, in arguments for and against permissive intervention. See § 9.08[2], supra.

[222] Government lawyers litigate to protect the public, but they labor with limited resources and limited authority to obtain compensation for those who have been wronged by violation of federal law. Seeking damages for himself and a group of people similarly wronged, the class representative supplements the role of government lawyers. He becomes a kind of private attorney general, blurring the line between public and private litigation. See Garth, Nagel & Plager, The Institution of the Private Attorney General: Perspectives from an Empirical Study of Class Action Litigation, 61 S. Cal. L. Rev. 353 (1988); For theories underpinning the private attorney general concept, see Meltzer, Deterring Constitutional Violations by Law Enforcement Officials: Plaintiffs and Defendants as Private Attorneys General, 88 Colum. L. Rev. 247 (1988); Cheng, Important Rights and the Private Attorney General Doctrine, 73 Cal. L. Rev. 1929 (1985).

[223] Rule 23(b)(3) class actions in federal court "have been especially popular in antitrust and securities fraud cases, where individual persons allegedly injured are in a poor position to seek redress, either because they do not know enough or because the cost of suit is disproportionate to each individual claim." Wright § 72. See also Duval, note 184, supra. It

actions stands the rule on its head. That is, assuming that (b)(3) was intended to promote judicial economy,[224] it would seem to have the opposite effect when used to facilitate litigation which could not exist otherwise.[225]

One way to resolve the conflict between judicial economy and public law enforcement would be to place in Rule 23(b)(3) a provision expressly recognizing the latter.[226] Meanwhile, Supreme Court rulings on Rule 23 and on other aspects of federal procedure have impeded implementation of the private attorney-general theory of class actions in federal court.[227] However, the concept has fared better in class action practice in some state courts.[228]

[2]   Class Actions in Federal and State Court

[a]   Comparative Availability of Federal and State Class Actions

Procedural opportunities for one filing suit in state court often are about the same as they would be in federal court. A federal forum offers a clear advantage in a few situations.[229] However, a suit brought on behalf of a nationwide class — especially when individual class claims are small —

---

is certainly true that many claims of class members or even class representatives in such cases would not support the cost of a separate lawsuit. For example, the individual damage claim of Mort Eisen, class representative in the multimillion dollar case, *Eisen v. Carlisle & Jacquelin,* 417 U.S. 156 (1974), was for $70. Used in this manner Rule 23(b)(3)

> can break the connection between access to courts and financial wherewithal. In damage class actions, attorneys' fees are paid not by the named plaintiffs, but by the class as a whole, in the form of a pro rata deduction from the class recovery. Since the fee is contingent upon victory, no class member loses anything from class suit; since the fee is shared, no single class member pays more than a small part of the costs of an attorney.

Developments in the Law — Class Actions, note 184, *supra,* at 1354.

[224] *See* Rule 23(b)(3) advisory committee's notes (1966).

[225] One commentator wrote of the private-attorney-general argument, "this purpose is enunciated nowhere in Rule 23. Furthermore, in practice such a principle — if embodied within (b)(3) — would produce a direct conflict with the professed purpose of economy of time, expense and effort." Weithers, *Amended Rule 23: A Defendant's Point of View,* 10 B.C. Ind. & Com. L. Rev. 515, 518 (1969); *cf. Eisen v. Carlisle & Jacquelin,* 391 F.2d 555, 572 (2d Cir. 1968) (Lumbard, C.J., dissenting) ("The appropriate action for this Court is to affirm the district court and put an end to this Frankenstein monster posing as a class action."). *But see* Ford, *Federal Rule 23: A Device for Aiding the Small Claimant,* 10 B.C. Ind. & Com. L. Rev. 501, 504 (1969) (one of the purposes of revised Rule 23 is "taking care of the smaller guy") (quoting Professor Kaplan, Reporter for the Advisory Committee).

[226] This was proposed by the *Report and Recommendations of the Special Committee on Class Action Improvements,* note 184, *supra,* and by the Office for Improvements in the Administration of Justice (OIAJ) of the United States Department of Justice. The OIAJ proposal is discussed in Berry, *Ending Substance's Indenture to Procedure: The Imperative for Comprehensive Revision of the Class Damage Action,* 80 Colum. L. Rev. 299 (1980); Note, *Reforming Federal Class Action Procedure: An Analysis of the Justice Department Proposal,* 16 Harv. J. Legis. 543 (1979).

[227] *See* § 9.09[2], *infra.*

[228] *Id.*

[229] See for example, the discussion of statutory interpleader in § 9.07, *supra.*

is likely to fare better in the courts of some states today than in federal court.[230]

We will examine two reasons. First, states are somewhat less inclined to follow the federal rules model when treating class actions,[231] and several have promulgated class rules more accommodating than Federal Rule 23.[232] Second, even state courts presented with language in their class action rules identical to Rule 23 are not bound by federal court interpretations of the latter,[233] and are in any event free from the constraints of subject matter jurisdiction which further limit federal class actions.

[b]   Problems Small-Claim, Large-Class Actions Pose in Federal Court

The Supreme Court's decision in *Eisen v. Carlisle & Jacquelin*[234] sharply curtailed Rule 23(b)(3) litigation involving small claims in federal court. The

---

[230] At the same time, class actions can succeed under Federal Rule 23(b)(3), particularly when a governmental entity is willing to litigate on behalf of the class, or when the size of individual class claims increases. Multistate class actions are at times easier to maintain in federal court because the courts of some states are still reluctant to take them on. Moreover, antitrust and certain other federal claims can be heard only in federal court. *See* § 5.01[2], *supra*. States, however, may take jurisdiction over class actions based on *state* antitrust law. *See generally* Hovenkamp, *State Antitrust in the Federal Scheme*, 58 Ind. L.J. 375 (1983).

[231] According to a leading study, "only a minority of states have embraced the system and philosophy of the Federal Rules wholeheartedly enough to permit classification as true federal replicas." Oakley & Coon, *The Federal Rules in State Courts: A Survey of State Court Systems of Civil Procedure,* 61 Wash. L. Rev. 1367, 1369 (1986). A number of states pick and choose models among the federal rules, adopting some (perhaps most), but not all. In this regard, Rule 23 appears to be among those most frequently passed over. For example North Carolina and Wisconsin modelled their intervention rules closely upon Federal Rule 24, but ignored Federal Rule 23. For more on how states approach the subject, see Skirnick & Avery, *The State Court Class Action — A Potpourri of Differences*, 20 Forum 750 (1985); and the state-by-state survey of state class action law appearing in *Newberg*, note 184, at Appendix 13-2.

[232] Florida amended its class action law "to eliminate problems in the federal rule through court decisions." Fla. R. Civ. P. 1.240 committee's note (1980). Like Florida, New York also rejected the federal approach and adopted more liberal class action law. N.Y. Civ. Prac. L. & R. Art. 9. Comparable departures from the federal approach await approval in Oregon. Comment, *Oregon Class Actions: The Continuing Need for Legislative Reform*, 72 Or. L. Rev. 205 (1993).

[233] The meaning of even identical language in a state rule raises a question of state rather than federal law. Under such circumstances, federal court interpretations of the federal rules (even those by the United States Supreme Court) are no more than persuasive precedent. The best and final authority on the meaning of all state law is the highest state court. *See* § 7.06[1], *supra*. At the same time, federal rule decisions can be quite persuasive when a state court is looking at the same language in its own rule. The following response of an Indiana court may be typical.

Indiana . . . Rule 23 is the general rule governing class actions. With two exceptions it follows the federal rule, F.R.C.P. 23, verbatim. In addition, our civil code study commission comments direct the bar, with approval, to the note of the Advisory Committee to the federal rule.

For these reasons, and because this is an area of complex litigation where the bench and bar are greatly benefited by a broad body of interpretative law, we will, as far as possible, adopt the federal interpretation of the language of the rule.

Bowen v. Sonnenburg, 411 N.E.2d 390, 396-397 (Ind. 3d Dist. Ct. App. 1980).

[234] 417 U.S. 156 (1974).

Court read Rule 23(c)(2) to require individual notice of the action at the representative's expense to each member of a (b)(3) class whose name and address was available to the class representative. Later, in *Oppenheimer Fund, Inc. v. Sanders*,[235] the Supreme Court ruled that the class representative was also required to pay the party opposing the class the latter's expenses in compiling the names and addresses of the class for the representative. Resulting expense dampened the private-attorney-general movement in federal court.[236] However, since *Eisen* and *Oppenheimer* were not constitutional law decisions, they do not control class actions in state courts. States are free to adopt class rules philosophically opposed to *Eisen.*[237]

The availability of class actions under Federal Rule 23(b)(3) is also limited by the reluctance of many federal courts to certify class actions if the process of distributing damages to individual class members seems too complicated or the prospect of actual reimbursement to class members uncertain. Federal courts must take these factors into account,[238] and obstacles to class certification increase when classes become larger and the size of individual claims smaller. Yet certification may be warranted even in such cases, when it is possible to determine (without examining individual class claims) both the liability of the opposing party to the entire class[239] and the total amount of damages inflicted upon the class.[240] Certification in this setting may turn on the legitimacy of so-called *fluid recovery.*

---

[235] 437 U.S. 340 (1978).

[236] Costs generated by *Eisen* and *Oppenheimer* will be beyond the means of most class representatives and are in any event greatly disproportionate to the value of the representative's personal claim.

[237] *See e.g.,* N.Y. Civ. Prac. L. & R., Art. 9.

[238] The interests of members of Rule 23(b)(1) and (2) classes tend to be closely tied. "But in an action under Rule 23(b)(3) the members are loosely bound together by common questions of law or fact and considerations of convenience. Even the damages they seek generally are individual in character and disparate in amount." *Wright & Miller* § 1784. The requirement in Rule 23(b)(3) that class issues predominate in the case and concern in (b)(3)(D) over "difficulties likely to be encountered in the management of a class action" make the rule sensitive to possible difficulties in distributing damage awards to individual members of the class. *Id.*

[239] The feasibility of proving defendants wrong class-wide will depend on the facts and plaintiff's theory of liability. Antitrust cases are frequently susceptible to such proof. *See* note 240, *infra.* On the other hand, proof of class-wide fraud under § 10(b) of the Securities Exchange Act of 1934 may be more problematic. *See generally* Note, *The Impact of Class Actions on Rule 10b-5,* 38 U. Chi. L. Rev. 337 (1971).

[240] For example, consider the antitrust case where plaintiff's class is the public with whom the defendants transacted business during a given period. Whether plaintiff's class has been wronged as a matter of antitrust law, and, if so, in what amount, are not simple questions. At the procedural level, however, these issues are often quite susceptible to class-wide resolution, *e.g.,* resolution without the necessity of examining a single individual class claim. Common issues would include whether defendants engaged in price-fixing and, if so, the amount of their total charges to the class during the relevant period, and the differential between those charges and the charges defendants would have made in the absence of price-fixing.

Fluid recovery is a means of disposing of the portion of class-wide damages which goes unclaimed by class members by directing that it be spent in the public interest in a way at least generally responsive to concerns raised in the case.[241] Small-claim, large-class actions may proceed from adjudication of defendant's liability to the class to class-wide assessment of damages and the creation of a fund.[242] After attorney's fees and expenses for litigation and for administering the fund are deducted, the balance of the fund theoretically goes to class members in proportion to the value of their individual claims. But most small-claim, large-class actions offer the likelihood that a substantial portion of the class fund will go unclaimed. This may be because many members of the class are unknown and may not learn of the existence of a class award or because the sum involved may be so small that some class members will not bother to apply for their individual recoveries. Most lower federal courts have refused to administer class actions offering the prospect of substantial unclaimed recovery, "unless it is part of a distribution arising out of a settlement."[243] In contrast, some state courts have been more willing to employ fluid recovery.[244]

Supreme Court rulings on federal subject matter jurisdiction have also limited availability of small-claim, large-class actions in federal court. They have done so in two respects. First, in *Snyder v. Harris*[245] and *Zahn v. International Paper Co.*,[246] the Court limited the availability of general diversity jurisdiction[247] for class actions by ruling that class members with

---

[241] On the topic of fluid recovery, see *Developments*, note 184, *supra* at 1516-1523; *Newberg*, note 184, *supra*, §§ 13.46-13.51; Malina, *Fluid Class Recovery as a Consumer Remedy in Antitrust Cases*, 47 N.Y.U. L. Rev. 477 (1972). Cases utilizing the device include *Gordon v. Boden*, 586 N.E.2d 461 (Ill. App. Ct. 1991) (damages from sale of adulterated orange juice products available either to fund a charitable project to benefit class or to reduce the price of future product sales); *Bruno v. Superior Court*, 179 Cal. Rptr. 342 (Cal. Ct. App. 1981) (profits from illegal milk prices applied to lower the price of milk in the future); *Market Street Railway v. Railroad Comm.*, 171 P.2d 875 (Cal. 1946) (profits from illegal train fares directed to upgrade train facilities). These cases share features common to most fluid recovery cases: (1) the fund is fluidly distributed only after an attempt is made to reach and compensate class members directly for their actual harm; and (2) the means chosen to dispose of the fund is calculated to provide some advantage to members of the class who were not individually compensated. That is, those wronged through past purchase of milk or train tickets are among those most likely to share in the advantage of reduced prices in the future. Of course, the process is inexact. Reduced prices in the future will be a windfall for those members of the class who did make individual claims against the fund and for members of the public not wronged in the past. Iowa, North Dakota and New Jersey have codified their law of fluid recovery. *See Newberg*, note 184, *supra*, § 13.49.

[242] "Utilizing procedures to distribute a lump sum recovery is judicially economical since it eliminates the need for separate trials on damage issues. In a case involving an extremely large plaintiff class whose members only have small individual claims, the savings in time and expense for all will be considerable." *Wright & Miller* § 1784.

[243] *Id.* A well-known example of the latter is *West Virginia v. Chas. Pfizer & Co*, 440 F.2d 1079 (2d Cir. 1971), *cert. denied*, 404 U.S. 871 (1971), an antitrust case in which the court administered a settlement fund of $100,000,000.

[244] See the discussion of state decisions in note 241, *supra*.

[245] 394 U.S. 332 (1969).

[246] 414 U.S. 291 (1973).

[247] Created under 28 U.S.C. § 1332. For discussion of the federal courts' general diversity jurisdiction, see §§ 5.04-5.06, *supra*.

"separate and distinct claims" had individually to satisfy the amount-in-controversy requirement.[248] This problem may now be solved by extending supplemental jurisdiction to hear below-amount claims, but the courts are divided about the permissibility of this reading of the supplemental jurisdiction statute.[249] Second, the Court ruled in *Coopers & Lybrand v. Livesay*[250] that the federal district court's refusal to certify a class action was not appealable by right as a final order.[251] The Court was unmoved by the argument that such a refusal (technically interlocutory) often ends small-claim class actions as effectively as a final order.[252] Since law limiting the subject matter jurisdiction of federal courts has no effect on state courts, the Court's rulings in *Snyder, Zahn* and *Coopers & Lybrand* suggest further circumstances where class actions may fare better in the latter.[253]

The actual notice requirement of Rule 23(c)(2), the reluctance of federal judges to employ fluid recovery, and constraints on federal subject matter jurisdiction combine to restrict the availability of small-claim, large-class actions in federal court. This has led to more careful consideration of possible advantages from filing a class action in state rather than federal court.[254] Several state courts have willingly provided a sanctuary for nation-wide class actions that are difficult or impossible to bring in federal court.[255] The reservations that courts of other states have about

---

[248] *Snyder*, 394 U.S. at 335. Interestingly, the other condition of § 1332, that the citizenship of the parties be diverse, does not require investigation of the citizenship of passive class members. Requisite diversity exists when all class representatives have state citizenship different from that of the party or parties opposing the class. *Supreme Tribe of Ben Hur v. Cauble*, 255 U.S. 356 (1921).

[249] *See* § 5.11[2][b], *supra* (discussing the disagreement).

[250] 437 U.S. 463 (1978), *discussed in* § 13.03[1], *infra*.

[251] 28 U.S.C. § 1291 confers a right of appeal to the appropriate federal court of appeals from "all final decisions of the district courts of the United States." On the subject matter jurisdiction of federal courts of appeals, see generally §§ 13.03-13.05, *infra*.

[252] In the abstract, an order denying class certification is interlocutory rather than final because the individual claim of the unsuccessful class representative remains for adjudication. In small-claim class actions, however, the representative's individual claim *alone* is usually incapable of justifying the continued costs of litigation. The refusal to certify the class in such actions is tantamount to a final order dismissing the case. Some federal courts took cognizance of these practical implications, reading 28 U.S.C. § 1291 broadly enough to reach certification denials that sounded the "death-knell" for the litigation. *E.g., Eisen v. Carlisle & Jacquelin*, 370 F.2d 119 (2d Cir. 1966), *cert. denied*, 386 U.S. 1035 (1967). *Coopers & Lybrand* expressly repudiated the death-knell doctrine. For further discussion of this case, see § 13.03[1], *infra*. Discussions about appellate review in this area appear in Solimine & Hines, *Deciding to Decide: Class Action Certification and Interlocutory Review by United States Courts of Appeals Under Rule 23(f)*, 41 Wm. & Mary L. Rev. 1531 (2000); Kruse, *Appealability of Class Certification Orders: The "Mandamus Appeal" and a Proposal to Amend Rule 23*, 91 Nw. U. L. Rev. 704 (1997).

[253] States are free to impose similar constraints under local law, but may choose not to. Thus, many states do permit aggregation of claims without reference to jurisdictional amount. *Newberg*, note 184, *supra*, § 13.24. Fewer states permit interlocutory appeal of denial of class certification. "There does appear to be a slight trend, however, toward a more liberal approach." *Id.*, § 13.19.

[254] For a survey of possible advantages from filing in state court, see *Newberg*, note 184, *supra*, at § 13.03. *Id.* § 13.45, at 87.

[255] "[R]ecent United States Supreme Court cases restricting access to the federal courts in

entertaining these cases may lessen over time, particularly in light of the Supreme Court's decision in *Phillips Petroleum Company v. Shutts.* [256]

Prior to *Shutts,* it was unclear whether a state court could exercise personal jurisdiction over passive members [257] of a plaintiff class when their contact with the forum was so tenuous that the constitutional law of due process would have prevented jurisdiction over the same persons as defendants. [258] Some state courts refused to entertain nationwide class actions because of what they perceived to be the lack of minimum contacts [259] between the forum and nonresident members of the plaintiff class. [260] *Shutts* gave state courts the green light by ruling that the relationship between the forum and members of the plaintiff class did not have to meet the stringent due process requirements applied to the relationship between a forum and defendants. The minimum contacts test did not apply. [261]

---

class actions suits have made it necessary for state courts to hear nation-wide class actions." *Shutts v. Phillips Petroleum Co.,* 679 P.2d 1159, 1169 (Kan. 1984), *rev'd on other grounds, Phillips Petroleum Co. v. Shutts,* 472 U.S. 797 (1985). *See also Miner v. Gillette Co.,* 428 N.E.2d 478 (Ill. 1981); *Schlosser v. Allis-Chalmers Corp.,* 271 N.W.2d 879 (Wis. 1978); *Anthony v. General Motors Corp.,* 109 Cal. Rptr. 254 (Cal. Ct. App. 1973); *Paley v. Coca Cola Co.,* 209 N.W.2d 232 (Mich. 1973). *Cf.* G. Tarr & M. Porter, *State Supreme Courts in State and Nation* 45 (1988) (noting that a number of states, "either through legislation or court decisions, have developed guidelines on class actions that are considerably more liberal than those prevailing in the federal courts."). At the same time, care must be taken not to overstate the receptiveness of state courts per se. *Cf. Newberg,* note 184, *supra,* at § 1346 (a 1992 observation that, "[s]tate courts are not known for their eagerness to certify large plaintiff classes, though such cases have been certified and tried successfully.").

[256] 472 U.S. 797 (1985).

[257] Passive members are those remaining in the class who neither serve as class representatives nor surface by appearance or intervention. *See* notes 193-194 and accompanying text (the distinction between active and passive class members), *supra.*

[258] *See* Note, *Jurisdiction Over Unnamed Plaintiffs in Multistate Class Actions,* 73 Cal. L. Rev. 181 (1985); Comment, *Jurisdiction and Notice in Class Actions: "Playing Fair" with National Classes,* 132 U. Pa. L. Rev. 1487 (1984).

[259] On the function of the minimum contacts test in regulating personal jurisdiction, see § 3.09[1], *supra.*

[260] *E.g., Feldman v. Bates Mfg. Co.,* 362 A.2d 1177 (N.J. Sup. Ct. 1976); *Klemow v. Time,* 352 A.2d 12 (Pa.), *cert. denied,* 429 U.S. 828 (1976).

[261] The Court stated that "[b]ecause States place fewer burdens upon absent class plaintiffs than they do upon absent defendants in nonclass suits, the Due Process Clause need not and does not afford the former as much protection from state-court jurisdiction as it does the latter." 472 U.S. at 811. All that due process required of plaintiffs' class actions was adequate representation by the class representative accompanied by notice to class members that was reasonable under the circumstances of the case. *See* note 271 & accompanying text, *infra.* On the significance of *Shutts* state class actions, see Note, *Due Process and Equitable Relief in State Multistate Class Actions After Phillips Petroleum Co. v. Shutts,* 68 Tex. L. Rev. 415 (1989); Wood, *Adjudicatory Jurisdiction and Class Actions,* 62 Ind. L.J. 597 (1987); Miller & Crump, *Jurisdiction and Choice of Law in Multistate Class Actions After Phillips Petroleum Co. v. Shutts,* 96 Yale L.J. 1 (1986); Kennedy, *The Supreme Court Meets the Bride of Frankenstein: Phillips Petroleum Co. v. Shutts and the Multistate Class Action,* 34 Kan. L. Rev. 255 (1985). The Supreme Court recently questioned whether its *Shutts* ruling should apply in class actions where members did not receive notice or a clear opportunity to opt out of the class. *Ortiz v. Fiberboard Corp.,* 527 U.S. 815, 847-848 (1999). The minimum contacts requirement may reappear in such cases.

[c] Due Process Requirements Common to Federal and State Class Actions

One source of law limits federal and state class actions alike: the constitutional law of due process. The function of the modern class action in federal and most state courts is to bind the class members by the outcome as though they were active parties in the case.[262] This raises due process considerations, since one cannot be bound without participating in a judicial proceeding unless his interests are adequately represented.

Hansberry v. Lee[263] continues to be of central importance in elaborating the constitutional standard. *Hansberry* established a principle essential for true class actions, that (under the right circumstances) class action judgments could bind passive class members.[264] Yet the due process ruling in *Hansberry* also imposed important limits on class actions. The Court stated that it was "justified in saying that there has been a failure of due process only in those cases where it cannot be said that the procedure adopted, fairly insures the protection of the interests of absent parties who are to be bound by it."[265] Thus, "members of a class not present as parties to the litigation may be bound by the judgment where they are in fact adequately represented by parties who are present. . . ."[266]

When is an absent class member "adequately represented?" In answering this question, due process doctrine places greatest reliance on the opinion held prior to the proceeding by the person to be bound. A passive class member may be thought to express his own favorable opinion on adequacy of representation when he knowingly permits the class representative to act for him. He likely will be bound by the class judgment in such cases — even if the representation of the class representative turns out to be lackluster.[267] But, even if the work of the class representative will be superlative, the class member is entitled whenever possible to decide before the fact whether he wants to entrust his interests to that person. Naturally, the class member is only able to control how his interests will be represented if made aware of the case prior to adjudication. That is why in due process doctrine the concept of adequate representation is closely tied to that of notice.

---

[262] "Class actions rest on a relatively simple proposition: self-selected class representatives and their lawyers, properly supervised by the court, can represent class members as a group sufficiently well to overcome members' individual rights to be heard." Garth, *Studying Civil Litigation Through the Class Action,* 62 Ind. L.J. 497, 497 (1987). "The fascination of foreign scholars with class actions is fairly easy to explain: this principle of representation remains unacceptable to almost the entire legal world outside of the United States." *Id.*

[263] 311 U.S. 32 (1940).

[264] "[T]here is scope within the framework of the Constitution for holding in appropriate cases that a judgment rendered in a class suit is *res judicata* as to members of the class who are not formal parties to the suit." 311 U.S. at 42.

[265] *Id.*

[266] *Id.* at 42-43.

[267] *Id.* at 43 (class members are bound "where they actually participate in the conduct of the litigation in which members of the class are present as parties.").

The classic statement on the extent of notice required for binding adjudications appears in *Mullane v. Central Hanover Bank & Trust Co.*[268]

An elementary and fundamental requirement of due process in any proceeding which is to be accorded finality is notice reasonably calculated, under all the circumstances, to apprise interested parties of the pendency of the action and afford them an opportunity to present their objections. The notice must be of such nature as reasonably to convey the required information, and it must afford a reasonable time for those interested to make their appearance. But if with due regard for the practicalities and peculiarities of the case these conditions are reasonably met, the constitutional requirements are satisfied.[269]

This is a pragmatic approach to notice. *Mullane* holds that actual notice to those to be bound by the litigation is always required where practicable.[270] Furthermore, *Mullane* indicates that those for whom individual notice is impracticable may only be bound under special circumstances. That is, notice to them must be attempted by the best alternative means (possibly publication), and there must be a strong showing that they will be adequately represented by one before the court.[271]

The interplay of due process and rule requirements for class actions varies within federal Rule 23. Subdivision (c)(2) of Rule 23 governs (b)(3) actions. The first part of Rule 23(c)(2)[272] appears to have been written under *Mullane*'s influence. Unfortunately, (c)(2) thereafter loses much of its *Mullane*-like flexibility, mandating individual notice to all class members whose names and addresses are known — without reference to practicability.[273] Once it read (c)(2) to require notice in the manner indicated above,[274] the Supreme Court found it unnecessary to reach the

---

[268] 339 U.S. 306 (1950). On *Mullane* and this topic generally, see § 4.02[1] (special due process concerns arising from class actions), *supra*.

[269] *Id.* at 314-315 (citations omitted).

[270] *Id.* at 318.

[271] Because the Court required mail notice to trust beneficiaries whose addresses were known, it was comfortable excusing such personal notice for beneficiaries whose addresses were not known or were ascertainable only at considerable expense. It reasoned that

[t]his type of trust presupposes a large number of small interests. The individual interest does not stand alone but is identical with that of a class. The rights of each in the integrity of the fund and the fidelity of the trustee are shared by many other beneficiaries. Therefore notice reasonably certain to reach most of those interested in objecting is likely to safeguard the interest of all since any objection sustained would inure to the benefit of all. We think that under such circumstances reasonable risks that notice might not actually reach every beneficiary are justifiable.

Id. at 319.

[272] "In any class action maintained under subdivision (b)(3), the court shall direct to the members of the class the best notice practicable under the circumstances."

[273] At the same time, Rule 23(c)(2) does not reduce notice flexibility under *Mullane* for (b)(3) class members whose names and addresses cannot be ascertained. Concerning this group, "it should be remembered that Rule 23(c)(2) only directs the court to give 'the best notice practicable under the circumstances.'" *Wright & Miller* § 1786. When some class members are individually notified, notice by publication to those whose whereabouts are unknown will often suffice. *Id.*

[274] *Eisen v. Carlisle & Jacquelin*, 417 U.S. 156 (1974), discussed at note 234 and accompanying text, *supra*.

question whether due process required such notice as well.[275] Federal class actions under Rule 23(b)(1) and (2) are not subject to (c)(2), but only to the general limitations of due process,[276] as are state class actions.[277]

[d] Recent Developments in Complex Litigation — Will the Importance of Class Actions Diminish?

Rule 23 and its state counterparts do not operate in isolation from broader developments in complex litigation. Particularly in tort cases, the trend toward multiparty, multiforum civil litigation has tested (and at times over-taxed) the class action device. The problem has been that, "just as the courts were broadening access to the judicial system through class actions, the overall number and complexity of cases exploded."[278] Mass disaster litigation has been a factor. But the main contributors to the problem have been various types of toxic tort cases, where injuries tend to be numerous and widely dispersed.[279] Proposals for managing these newest and most perplexing forms of complex litigation[280] dwell less on class actions and more on broad-spectrum, interrelated changes throughout the entire law of civil procedure. Should these proposals become law, the lustre and relative importance of class actions would fade.

Even if procedural reforms bypassing class actions do not occur, the nearly thirty years since Rule 23 was rewritten have taken their toll. Restrictions pertaining to notice to the class, damage distribution, and federal subject matter jurisdiction have impaired the operation of the federal rule. State courts have often been conservative in the use of class actions as well. Yet, if the current importance of class actions is not as sweeping as some might have wished, it is still great.[281]

---

[275] See Homburger, *State Class Actions and the Federal Rule,* 71 Colum. L. Rev. 609, 646 (1971) (arguing "there is nothing in *Hansberry* or *Mullane* to suggest a constitutional prohibition against dispensation with notice in any kind of class suit if procedural fairness and adequacy of representation are safeguarded in other ways.").

[276] *Newberg,* note 184, *supra,* § 8.05.

[277] See *Phillips Petroleum Co. v. Shutts,* 472 U.S. 797, 811-812 (1985).

[278] Note, *Merit-Based Class Action Certification: Old Wine in a New Bottle,* 78 Va. L. Rev. 1101, 1101 (1992).

[279] See, e.g., Coffee, *Class Wars,* note 1, *supra;* Symposium, note 1, *supra;* Mullinex, *Resolving Aggregate Mass Tort Litigation: The New Private Law Dispute Resolution Paradigm,* 33 Valparaiso U. L. Rev. 413 (1999); Carrington & Apanovich, *The Constitutional Limits of Judicial Rulemaking: The Illegitimacy of Mass Tort Settlements Negotiated Under Federal Rule 23,* 39 Ariz. L. Rev. 461 (1997); Marcus, *Reexamining the Bendectin Litigation Story,* 83 Iowa L. Rev. 231 (1997).

[280] See § 9.10[2], *infra* (recent trends in complex litigation).

[281] Shapiro, note 184, *supra,* at 913. *Cf.* Morawetz, *Bargaining, Class Representation, and Fairness,* 54 Ohio St. L.J. 1, 1 (1993) ("Millions of people are represented through class actions.").

§ 9.10   Consolidating Cases — Current Law and Possibilities for the Future

[1]   Current Law

[a]   Intradistrict Consolidation — Rule 42(a)[282]

Federal Rule 42(a) authorizes "joint hearing or trial" for cases pending within the same judicial district "involving a common question of law or fact." A number of states have essentially the same rule.[283]

The object of Rule 42(a) is to promote judicial economy.[284] Judicial economy has been a recurrent theme in this chapter. Yet Rule 42(a) functions in relative isolation. It does not appear in the pleading or parties sections of the federal rules, as do the other rules we have considered. It has also been suggested that "it would be a mistake to interpret this rule in the light of presuppositions springing from the joinder rules."[285]

Therefore, one cannot simply assume that Rule 42(a) provides a means of reconstructing litigation along lines possible under federal joinder rules before the cases were filed. The availability of consolidation is in one respect more restricted than joinder, since "in a suit between a single plaintiff and a single defendant, plaintiff may join all of his claims, no matter how unrelated, against the defendant. If he brings separate actions, however, only those actions having a common question of law or fact may be consolidated."[286] In another respect, consolidation is less restricted.

> [M]ore than one party can be joined on a side only if there is asserted for or against all of them one or more claims for relief arising out of the same transaction or occurrence or series of transactions or occurrences. This is in addition to the requirement of some question of law or fact common to all the parties. But the common question by itself is enough to permit consolidation, even if the claims arise out of independent transactions.[287]

---

[282] *See generally Moore* §§ 42.10-42.14; Steinman, *The Effects of Case Consolidation on the Procedural Rights of Litigants: What They Are, They Might Be Part I: Justiciability and Jurisdiction (Original and Appellate)*, 42 UCLA L. Rev. 717 (1995); Steinman, . . . *Part II: Non-Jurisdictional Matters*, 42 UCLA L. Rev. 967 (1995); Marcus, *Confronting the Consolidation Conundrum*, 1995 BYU L. Rev. 879; *Wright & Miller* §§ 2382-86; *Manual for Complex Litigation (Third)* § 31.11 (1995); Virden, *Consolidation Under Rule 42 of the Federal Rules of Civil Procedure*, 141 F.R.D. 169 (1992). *Cf.* Goldberg & Brett, *Consolidation of Individual Plaintiff Personal Injury-Toxic Tort Actions*, 11 J. L. & Com. 59 (1991) (discussing applications of Rule 42(a) in asbestos injury litigation); Silver, *Comparing Class Actions and Consolidations*, 10 Rev. of Litig. 495 (1991) (comparing Rules 23 and 42(a)).

[283] *E.g.*, Del. Code Ann. R. Civ. P. 42; Minn. Stat. Ann. R. Civ. P. Dist. Ct. R. 42.01; N.M. Stat. Ann. R. Civ. P. Dist. Ct. 1-042.

[284] "The obvious virtue of consolidation is that it increases the productivity of the judicial system by arranging for simultaneous resolution of issues or entire actions." *Friedenthal, Kane & Miller* § 6.2.

[285] *Wright & Miller* § 2382.

[286] *Id.*

[287] *Id.*

Orders granting or denying Rule 42(a) motions to consolidate are interlocutory and hence difficult to appeal.[288] The federal court's authority to consolidate exists only when two or more cases present a common issue of law or fact. Presence of a common issue empowers the court to order consolidation but does not require it to do so. This is an area where considerable discretion should and does exist. "It is for the court to weigh the saving of time and effort that consolidation would produce against any inconvenience, delay or expense that it would cause."[289]

A federal trial judge has authority under Rule 42(a) to consolidate only cases pending within her judicial district. She may not use the rule to consolidate cases pending in more than one district.[290] The Judicial Panel on Multidistrict Litigation may order consolidation of such cases for pretrial purposes,[291] however, and a trial judge may weigh the possibility of consolidation in deciding whether to transfer a case to another district.[292]

[b] Federal Multidistrict Litigation Under Section 1407[293]

Section 1407(a) of Title 28 reads in part: "When civil actions involving one or more common questions of fact are pending in different districts, such actions may be transferred to any district for coordinated or consolidated pretrial proceedings." By authorizing multidistrict consolidation, Section 1407 exceeds Rule 42(a) in scope. However, it is more narrow than Rule 42(a) in two respects. Section 1407 applies literally only to pretrial proceedings[294] and only to cases having common questions of fact.[295] Moreover, it authorizes transfers only when they "will be for the convenience of the parties and witnesses and will promote the just and efficient conduct of such actions."[296]

---

[288] *Moore* § 42.12. *See generally* § 13.03 (final judgment rule), *infra*.

[289] *Wright & Miller* § 2383. Weighing against consolidation are possibilities of juror confusion, delay, administrative difficulties and prejudice to a party. *Moore* § 42.10[5].

[290] *Moore* § 42.11[1]. *See In re Penn Central Commercial Paper Litigation*, 62 F.R.D. 341 (S.D.N.Y. 1974), *aff'd*, 515 F.2d 505 (2d Cir. 1975).

[291] 28 U.S.C. § 1407. *See* § 9.10[2], *infra*.

[292] 28 U.S.C. § 1404. *See generally* § 6.02[2] (venue transfer), *supra*.

[293] *See generally Wright & Miller* §§ 3861-3867; *Manual*, note 282, *supra*, § 31.13; Comment, *The Judicial Panel on Multidistrict Litigation: Time for Rethinking*, 140 U. Pa. L. Rev. 711 (1991); Howard, *A Guide to Multidistrict Litigation*, 124 F.R.D. 479 (1989).

[294] Rule 42(a) contemplates "joint hearing or trial" and has been read to cover pretrial as well as trial proceedings. "If one of the purposes of consolidation for trial be to expedite the proceedings and avoid needless time and expense to the litigants and to the court, such objectives are as desirable and as attainable in the period utilized in preparing for trial." *Manual*, note 282, *supra*, § 31.11 (*quoting MacAlister v. Guterma*, 263 F.2d 65, 68 (2d Cir. 1958)).

[295] Rule 42(a) encompasses "actions involving a common question of *law or* fact" (emphasis added).

[296] 28 U.S.C. § 1407(a). For additional discussion comparing Rule 42(a) with § 1407, see Murphy, *Unified and Consolidated Complaints in Multidistrict Litigation*, 132 F.R.D. 597 (1991); Note, *Consolidation and Transfer in the Federal Courts: 28 U.S.C. Section 1407 Viewed in Light of Rule 42(a) and 28 U.S.C. Section 1404(a)*, 22 Hastings L.J. 1289 (1971).

Congress enacted Section 1407 in response to the confusion and repetition generated by multiple antitrust suits in the electronics industry in the 1960s.[297] Section 1407 creates a "judicial panel on multidistrict litigation"[298] which decides when cases should be consolidated for pretrial proceedings and to which judge they should be transferred. The section has been invoked most frequently in antitrust cases and "common disaster (air crash) actions, patent and trademark suits, products liability actions and securities law violation actions."[299] Section 1407 has been quite useful in expediting and reducing the expense of discovery. The section also permits judges to whom cases have been transferred (*transferee* courts) to consider a variety of pretrial motions, including motions capable of terminating all or part of the consolidated litigation.[300] Section 1407(a) requires return to the courts of origin (*transferor* courts) of transferred cases which are still alive when multidistrict proceedings are over.[301] In practice, however, transferee courts had frequently retained the cases for consolidated trial. "Federal courts had achieved this result either by securing the consent of the parties or by invoking Section 1404(a), the general transfer provision"[302] to effect a "self-assignment" of the case for trial. In *Lexecon v. Milberg Weiss*,[303] however, the Supreme Court put an end to the practice, holding that self-assignment by a § 1407 transferee court is prohibited by the plain language of § 1407.[304]

[2] Possibilities for Sweeping Consolidation — The Complex Litigation Proposals

We have used in this chapter a rudimentary idea of complex litigation — any enlargement of the minimum model of one plaintiff, one defendant, and one claim. Some commentators, however, are inclined to reserve the term for greatly complicated controversies. Thus a report of the American

---

[297] *The Judicial Panel*, note 293, *supra*, at 1001.

[298] The panel "shall consist of seven circuit and district judges . . . no two of whom shall be from the same circuit." 28 U.S.C. § 1407(d).

[299] *Wright & Miller* § 3862 (*quoting* from the legislative history of § 1407). *See also* Atkins, *An Apologia for Transfer of Aviation Disaster Cases Under Section 1407* 38 J. Air L. & Com. 205 (1972).

[300] "Although the transferee judge has no jurisdiction to conduct a trial in the transferred cases, the judge may terminate actions by ruling on motions to dismiss or for summary judgment or pursuant to settlement and may enter consent decrees." *Manual*, note 282, *supra*, § 31.132.

[301] "Each action so transferred shall be remanded by the panel at or before the conclusion of such pretrial proceedings to the district from which it was transferred unless it shall have been previously terminated. . . ." 28 U.S.C. § 1407(a).

[302] *Wright & Miller* § 3862. On § 1404 transfer, see § 6.02[2], *supra*. On the whole, "the great majority of cases transferred by the Panel under section 1407 have been disposed of by transferee courts and not remanded to their original districts." *The Judicial Panel*, note 293, *supra*, at 1001-02. The Federal Courts Study Committee has recommended that § 1407 be amended to expressly authorize "consolidated trial as well as pretrial proceedings. . . ." *Report of the Federal Courts Study Committee* 45 (1990).

[303] 523 U.S. 26 (1998).

[304] *See* text quoted in note 301, *supra* (which uses the mandatory "shall").

Law Institute defines complex litigation as "multiparty, multiforum litigation . . . characterized by related claims dispersed in several forums and often involving events that occurred over long periods of time."[305]

This situation, observes the study, "presents one of the greatest problems our courts currently confront."[306] Many feel that reforms are badly needed, particularly for tort controversies having interstate or national impact.[307] In response, Congress,[308] the American Law Institute,[309] and other groups[310] have studied initiatives to streamline civil procedure in toxic tort or mass disaster cases.

The reforms contemplated in these studies vary in approach and ambition. Yet all reflect a common concern about the litigation of highly related claims that now must be spread over many states (often in both state and federal courts). "Repeated relitigation of the common issues in a complex case unduly expends the resources of attorney and client, clogs already overcrowded dockets, delays recompense for those in need, and brings our legal system into general disrepute."[311]

Reinforced by the criticisms of many commentators, these initiatives will likely cause some measure of reform. Changes that occur may not be limited to the federal law of intradistrict and multidistrict consolidation. Simultaneous and uniform treatment of a significantly larger mass of claims will require revision of current law in many procedural areas. These include federal subject matter jurisdiction and venue, personal jurisdiction, intervention, *res judicata*, state-federal and state-to-state consolidation, and choice of law.[312]

---

[305] American Law Institute, *Complex Litigation: Statutory Recommendations and Analysis* Ch. 2, comment (a) (1993).

[306] *Id.* In far-flung asbestos litigation against Johns-Manville, the number of damage claims has probably passed 100,000 and is still rising. *Id.* at Reporter's Notes to comment (a).

[307] *E.g.*, Mullenix, *Beyond Consolidation: Post-Aggregative Procedure in Asbestos Mass Tort Litigation*, 32 Wm. & Mary L. Rev. 475 (1991); Rowe, *Jurisdictional and Transfer Proposals for Complex Litigation*, 10 Rev. Litig. 325 (1991); Zimand, *National Asbestos Litigation: Procedural Problems Must Be Solved*, 69 Wash. U. L.Q. 899 (1991). *Cf.* Sanders, *The Bendectin Litigation: A Case Study in the Life Cycle of Mass Torts*, 43 Hastings L. J. 301 (1992).

[308] *See* Geyh, *Complex Litigation Reform and the Legislative Process*, 10 Rev. Litig. 401 (1991).

[309] *See* note 305, *supra*. For a review of the ALI study, see Shreve, *Reform Aspirations of the Complex Litigation Project*, 54 La. L. Rev. 1139 (1994).

[310] *See* National Conference of Commissioners on Uniform State Laws, Uniform Transfer of Litigation Act (1991); ABA Commission on Mass Torts, Report to the House of Delegates (Nov. 1989).

[311] *Complex Litigation*, note 305, *supra*.

[312] An excellent discussion of how the reform proposals target particular areas of procedural law appears in *Rowe*, note 307, *supra*.

Chapter 10

DISCOVERY

§ 10.01 Overview

Before filing a complaint, most plaintiffs and their lawyers make some effort to gather facts about the events that gave rise to suit. The lawyer ordinarily will interview the client and obtain information from the client's agents. He may also interview witnesses. But this kind of self-help can only advance the fact-gathering so far for several reasons. Many of the most important facts are often within the knowledge and control of the prospective defendant. A wary prospective defendant may stonewall the lawyer who tries to interview him. Ex parte interviews also require the lawyer to walk a tight ethical line. Ethical rules in many jurisdictions prohibit the lawyer from stating or implying that he is disinterested, misstating the facts, engaging in conduct to embarrass, delay or burden a third person, or, in a few jurisdictions, giving advice or secretly taping the interview.[1] After the complaint has been filed, these rules prohibit him from communicating at all about the subject of suit with a party represented by a lawyer without that lawyer's consent (unless authorized by law).[2] This prohibition poses especially difficult problems of interpretation when the party is an organization and the witness is a present or former employee.[3]

Formal discovery of facts under court rules picks up where self-help leaves off and avoids most of these problems. Liberalization of such discovery was the most dramatic procedural reform brought by the Federal Rules of Civil Procedure in 1938.

No longer can the time-honored cry of "fishing expedition" serve to preclude a party from inquiring into the facts underlying his opponent's case. Mutual knowledge of all relevant facts gathered by both parties is essential to proper litigation. To that end, either party may compel the other to disgorge whatever facts he has in his possession.[4]

Liberal discovery permitted the deemphasis of pleading and more liberal amendment. It made trial preparation more effective. Along with liberal

---

[1] *See generally* Center for Professional Responsibility (American Bar Ass'n), *Annotated Model Rules of Professional Conduct* Rule 4.1, Rule 4.3, Rule 4.4 (1999); Farage, *Ex Parte Interrogation: Invasive Self-Help Discovery*, 94 Dick. L. Rev. 1 (1989).

[2] *Annot. Model Rules*, note 1, *supra*, Rule 4.2.

[3] *See, e.g.,* Iole & Gotz, *Ethics or Procedure? A Discovery-Based Approach to Ex Parte Contacts with Former Employees of a Corporate Adversary*, 68 Notre Dame L. Rev. 81 (1992); Becker, *Conducting Informal Discovery of a Party's Former Employees: Legal and Ethical Concerns and Constraints*, 51 Md. L. Rev. 239 (1992); Gurr, *Ethics of Conducting Ex Parte Interviews*, 3 St. John's J. Legal Comment. 234 (1988).

[4] *Hickman v. Taylor*, 329 U.S. 495, 507 (1947) (citation omitted).

joinder and broadened preclusion, liberal discovery promoted judicial efficiency by making it easier to dispose of the entire controversy in one lawsuit.[5] The federal discovery rules proved so useful that a majority of states adopted them,[6] including some that have otherwise retained their own procedural rules.[7]

We therefore use the federal discovery rules as a model for the discussion of formal discovery. Part A explores *what* information can be discovered under the federal rules (the scope of discovery). Part B considers *how* such information can be discovered and used at trial (the mechanics of discovery). After discussing required disclosures, we survey the principal discovery methods, including depositions (oral or written examinations of live witnesses), interrogatories (written questions answered in writing), requests for production of documents and things or for entry upon land, and physical or mental examinations.[8] Finally, Part C considers the judicial *control* of discovery and discovery abuse.

The reported, visible law of discovery is relatively straightforward. Problems arise almost exclusively in its application, usually out of sight of the national reporters and law services.[9] Discovery rulings are often by magistrates rather than judges and rarely generate extensive trial (much less appellate) opinions.[10] As a result, lower court decisions should often be viewed as fact-bound rulings rather than as legal precedents. Moreover, litigants often negotiate discovery disputes outside the court, as they are encouraged and authorized to do by Rule 29. "The very existence of the rules encourages lawyers to use more efficient and economical means to exchange information [including] [b]ilateral trading of documents, cooperative bartering of information, mutual alteration of procedures . . . ."[11]

Litigants use discovery for overlapping purposes. The most significant is to prepare for trial and to avert surprise. Discovery permits a plaintiff who has commenced suit on the barest of facts to flesh out and, with liberal amendment, even alter his case for trial.[12] It also affords parties opposing

---

[5] On the interrelation of pleading, complex litigation, discovery and preclusion in modern civil procedure, see *James, Hazard & Leubsdorf* § 11.16; Shreve, *Preclusion and Federal Choice of Law*, 64 Tex. L. Rev. 1209, 1215 (1986).

[6] *See Friedenthal, Kane, & Miller* § 7.1.

[7] *See, e.g.*, Va. Rules Ann. 4:1-4:12 (2000) (adopting federal discovery rules almost verbatim, while otherwise retaining vestiges of code and common law pleading); Fla. R. Civ. P. 1.280-1.380 (patterned on federal discovery provisions as amended in 1970).

[8] Requests for admission are an additional discovery method, but are primarily used at the close of discovery as a pretrial device. They are therefore discussed as such in § 12.02, *infra*.

[9] "Thankfully, most of the mountainous volume of the District Courts' pre-trial activity never reaches the pages of a report or the files of a computer." *Union City Barge Line, Inc. v. Union Carbide Corp.*, 823 F.2d 129, 134 n.10 (5th Cir. 1987).

[10] This is in part because of the general federal rule against interlocutory appellate review. *See* §§ 13.02 & 13.03, *infra*.

[11] R. Haydock & D. Herr, *Discovery Practice* § 1.1 (3d ed. 1996).

[12] At the same time, liberal discovery, pleading and amendment rules can combine to invite frivolous litigation by making it easier for plaintiff's counsel to file first and closely examine the claim later. Attorney certification requirements and sanctions for improper certification offer some protection against this. *See* Rule 11 (certification for pleadings and motion papers) discussed in § 8.05[2], *supra*, and Rule 26(g) (certification of discovery requests, responses and objections), discussed in § 10.13[1], *infra*.

claims the same opportunity to prepare for trial. In addition, discovery helps to streamline the trial itself by permitting pretrial authentication of documents, "nailing down" the likely testimony of witnesses, and creating a storehouse of recollection-refreshing and impeaching material.[13]

On the other hand, the removal of all surprise at trial is not necessarily beneficial. Judge Aldrich observed:

> Not merely may too many rehearsals, in the form of too much discovery, take the bloom off the opening night, but this absence of freshness may make the performance sterile. A certain amount of surprise is often the catalyst which precipitates the truth. Alternatively it may serve as a medium by which the court or jury may gauge the accuracy of the account.[14]

Realizing this, the experienced litigator seeks both to prepare as thoroughly as possible for trial and to preserve as much surprise as possible in her case. These dual purposes coexist uneasily and often strain the discovery rules.

A second purpose of discovery is to preserve evidence for trial. When witnesses are likely to be unavailable for trial, due to age, illness or location beyond the reach of the trial court, their testimony can be preserved by deposition. The discoverer with this purpose cannot simply fish for information. She must be concerned about the content and admissibility of the elicited testimony at trial because she has no second chance at the witness.[15]

Third, discovery can be used to narrow or eliminate issues. By ascertaining whether and which issues are genuinely disputed, discovery can set up Rule 12(b) dismissals, summary judgment and issue-narrowing or eliminating pretrial orders that can substantially simplify trial.[16] Perhaps even more important in light of litigation statistics, this use of discovery may even encourage settlement.[17] The discoverer with this objective may, contrary to the usual practice, *invite* discovery of the strengths of her case.

But the sheer burden of discovery can also extort settlement, particularly when the resources of the parties are unequal.[18] Discovery thus can have a fourth (and illicit) purpose: harassment, delay and attrition.[19] The Supreme Court has noted that

> to the extent that . . . [discovery] permits a plaintiff with a largely groundless claim to simply take up the time of a number of other people,

---

[13] *See, e.g.,* Haydock & Herr, note 11, *supra,* § 1.1; *James, Hazard & Leubsdorf* § 5.2.

[14] *Margeson v. Boston & Maine R.R.,* 16 F.R.D. 200, 201 (D. Mass. 1954).

[15] *See Haydock & Herr,* note 11, *supra,* § 3.4.2.

[16] *Id.* § 1.1.

[17] *But cf. Moore* § 26.02[2] (noting that discovery may discourage settlement and that settlement pressures may encourage withholding of unfavorable matter in discovery).

[18] *See id.,* § 26.02.

[19] *See Herbert v. Lando,* 441 U.S. 153, 202 (1979) (Marshall, J., dissenting) (libel case in which defendant's editor was deposed intermittently for one year, yielding 3000 pages of testimony and 240 exhibits in 26 volumes of transcript).

with the right to do so representing an *in terrorem* increment of settlement value, rather than a reasonably founded hope that the process will
reveal relevant evidence, it is a social cost rather than a benefit.[20]

Considerable uncertainty remains over the prevalence of the problem and
the most effective cure.[21]

The discoverer's mix of purposes determines the scope, frequency, and
methods of the discovery she will pursue. We shall see that most discovery
goes on without court involvement. When a party does ask for judicial
intervention (either to block or coerce discovery), a comparison of the
benefits of proper discovery with the costs of improper or excessive discovery
suggests how much and what kind of control a court should impose. Read
the remaining sections of this chapter with this comparison in mind.

PART A
Scope of Discovery

§ 10.02 In General

Rule 26(b) describes what may be discovered under the federal rules[22]
and effectively erects a presumption of discoverability.[23] A party may
discover any matter that is (1) "relevant to the claim or defense of any party"
and reasonably calculated to lead to discovery of admissible evidence, and
neither (2) privileged nor (3) prepared or acquired in anticipation of
litigation or for trial, unless (4) discovery has been otherwise limited by
a protective order of the court. A special showing is required for discovery
of *work product* prepared or acquired in anticipation of litigation or for trial.
Sections 10.03 to 10.06 successively treat each of these aspects of the scope
of discovery, except that the discussion of protective orders has been
deferred to § 10.13[3] in Part C on the control of discovery.

§ 10.03 The Fading Federal Presumption of
Discoverability

[1] Relevant to the Claim or Defense of Any Party

Rule 26(b)(1) originally fixed the scope of discovery as "relevant to the
subject matter." One appellate court paraphrased it as "any matter that
bears on, or reasonably could lead to other matter that could bear on, any

---

[20] *Blue Chip Stamps v. Manor Drug Stores*, 421 U.S. 723, 741 (1975).

[21] *See* § 10.12 (abuse of discovery), *infra*.

[22] What *must* be discovered (required disclosures) is discussed in Part B, section 10.07,
together with other general aspects of the mechanics of discovery. Limitations on the
permissible scope of discovery apply to required disclosures.

[23] Disputes concerning the scope of discovery are usually resolved in favor of allowing discovery. This outcome reflects in part judges' and magistrates' awareness that orders allowing
discovery are far less likely to be reversed on an eventual appeal than orders limiting or
prohibiting it. R. Haydock & D. Herr, *Discovery Practice* § 1.4 (3d ed. 1996).

issue that is or may be in the case, . . . not limited to issues raised by the pleadings . . . [or] to the merits of the case. . . ."[24] In antitrust or business tort litigation, for example, virtually any matter involving the industry of which the parties are part arguably satisfied that standard. In securities fraud litigation, theoretically any factor that may affect the market for the stock at issue would satisfy that standard. In light of the generality with which discovery requests can be framed under the rules, some questioned whether the original relevant-to-the subject matter standard imposed any practical limit on federal discovery.

Heeding these doubts, the rulemakers changed the relevancy standard in 2000 by differentiating party-controlled discovery from court-ordered discovery. For the former, the standard was changed to "relevant to the claim or defense of any party."[25] This standard is narrower than the original standard because it is tied to the pleadings (which assert the claims or defenses of the parties), but also arguably broader than the alternative standard "relevant to the issues," which had initially been adopted by some states[26] and urged by some critics of the original rule. At the same time, the rulemakers authorized the court, on good cause shown, to allow discovery under the original "relevant-to-the subject-matter discovery" standard.[27]

Whether the change in the relevancy standard for party-controlled discovery would make much difference, standing alone, is questionable. The Advisory Committee itself admitted that the dividing line between the standards "cannot be defined with precision," and then proceeded to suggest, for example, that in a negligence or product liability suit arising from an incident, "incidents of the same type, or involving the same product, could be properly discovered under the revised standard."[28] Ironically, it was precisely in products liability suits, however, that some defense lawyers said that the old standard was abused to dragnet burdensome but remotely relevant information about similar products. The Advisory Committee's own explanations, therefore, lend some credence to the prediction that this "semantic change is unlikely to have much salutary effect on the conduct of discovery in the hurly-burly world of litigation."[29]

On the other hand, the change in the relevancy standard for party-controlled discovery should not be viewed in isolation from the authorization for court-controlled discovery under the old relevancy standard. Responding to the common complaint of litigators that courts have failed to intervene in discovery disputes early or often enough, the Advisory

---

[24] *Oppenheimer Fund, Inc. v. Sanders*, 437 U.S. 340, 351 & n.12 (1978) (citations omitted). *Compare Kelly v. Nationwide Mut. Ins. Co.*, 188 N.E.2d 445 (Ohio C.P. 1963) (applying relevancy-to-the-issues standard under former Ohio rules).

[25] Rule 26(b)(1).

[26] *E.g.*, Ohio. *See Kelly*, 188 N.E.2d 445 (discussing old and new Ohio rules).

[27] Rule 26(b)(1).

[28] Rule 26(b)(1) advisory committee's note (2000).

[29] Beckerman, *Confronting Civil Discovery's Fatal Flaws*, 84 Minn. L. Rev. 505, 510-511 (2000).

Committee explained that the latter part of the amendment "is designed to involve the court more actively in regulating the breadth of sweeping or contentious discovery."[30] Courts are likely both to enforce the "claim or defense" standard more often, given the fallback of court-ordered "subject matter" discovery for good cause shown, and to play a more active role in managing more sweeping discovery. Considering both of these effects of the rule amendment, at least one commentator has concluded that it reverses the presumption of discoverability:

> Instead of assuming that any matter relevant to the subject matter is discoverable, with the burden on the party opposing discovery to show non-relevance, burden, or privilege, the presumption is that information beyond "claims or defenses" is *not* discoverable. The burden is newly placed on the party seeking discovery either to convince the judge that the information sought falls within the core definition of relevance or to make an undefined and "flexible" showing that there is good cause to allow further discovery.[31]

Finally, as a corollary of the amendment's effect on discovery, some commentators have predicted that it will impact pleading. They speculate that the "claim or defense" standard will cause plaintiffs to draft more particularized allegations in order to obtain needed discovery, threatening abandonment of notice pleading and a return to "fact pleading"[32] with all of its problems[33] and attendant motion practice.[34] Whether this amendment will have this result depends on how grudgingly the courts construe "claim or defense" and "good cause" for invoking broader "subject matter" discovery.

Skepticism about the semantic precision of the amendment may be besides the point. The change is really intended as a signal to the parties to try to confine discovery to the pleadings and to the court to watch closely if more is sought. Even the change fails to supply a bright line for changing the scope of discovery in individual cases, it will succeed on the Advisory Committee's terms if it gradually causes a change in the mind set of litigators and the courts which reduces the breadth of discovery at the margins.

A better answer may be to limit directly the amount of discovery, or to emphasize and expand the courts' discretionary powers to control discovery

---

[30] Rule 26(b)(1) advisory committee's notes (2000).

[31] Thornburg, *Giving the "Haves" a Little More: Considering the 1998 Discovery Proposals*, 52 SMU L. Rev. 229, 251 (1999) (emphasis in original) (commenting on relevancy standard in 1998 proposal identical to that adopted in 2000). *See also* Stempel, *Politics and Sociology in Civil Rulemaking: Errors of Scope*, 52 Ala. L. Rev. 529, 584-586 (2001) (agreeing that rule change shifts "burden of uncertainty" from those opposing discovery to those seeking it, and finding change "misguided" for this and other reasons).

[32] *See, e.g., Beckerman*, note 29, *supra*, at 541; Tobias, *Congress and the 2000 Federal Civil Rules Amendments*, 22 Cardozo L. Rev. 75, 83 (2000).

[33] *See* § 8.03[3] (discussing the specificity of fact pleading).

[34] Joseph, *Civil Rules II*, Natl. L.J., April 24, 2000, A17 ("It would be reasonable to anticipate more Rule 12 motion practice, including Rule 12(f) motions to strike . . . which now may have a discernible impact on the scope of discovery.").

on an ad hoc basis. The rulemakers have done both. In 1993 and again in 2000, they amended the discovery rules to impose quantitative limits on depositions and interrogatories, as we discuss in Part B. They also authorized courts to limit discovery pursuant to Rule 26(b)(2) when "the burden or expense of the proposed discovery outweighs its likely benefit." The rule had previously been amended in 1983 to give the courts the power to control "the frequency or extent of use" of discovery. [35]

[2] Reasonably Calculated to Lead to the Discovery of Admissible Evidence

Rule 26(b)(1) provides that "[r]elevant information need not be admissible at the trial if the discovery appears reasonably calculated to lead to the discovery of admissible evidence." What a witness has heard about the issues in the case, for example, is usually hearsay which may be inadmissible at trial unless it falls within an exception to the evidentiary rule against hearsay or constitutes an admission by a party. It is still discoverable, however, because it may lead to the discovery of the identity of fact witnesses [36] or other facts that might themselves be admissible. Similarly, information about a subsequent repair may be inadmissible at trial to prove negligence because of the public policy to encourage such repairs. [37] Nevertheless, it is discoverable as relevant to a claim in a negligence action. [38]

[3] Examples and Problem Areas

[a] Information Already in the Discoverer's Possession

Even when the discoverer already knows or possesses certain information, he is entitled to discover it from his adversary. A party is entitled to discover what the other parties know and contend, in order to facilitate his own preparation and possible settlement. Moreover, knowledge is not the same thing as proof, which is what will be required at trial. A party is entitled to whatever jury impact he can get from proving the facts through evidence produced by his adversary. A court always retains the power, however, to intervene in particular cases when discovery becomes "*unreasonably* cumulative or duplicative . . . [or] the party seeking discovery has had ample opportunity by discovery in the action to obtain the information

---

[35] *See* § 10.13[2] (managerial orders), *infra.*

[36] Rule 26(a)(1) requires initial disclosure of the identity of fact witnesses, and Rule 26(a)(3) requires pretrial disclosure of the identity of trial witnesses (persons who *will* be called to testify). Prior to the 1993 amendment mandating such disclosures, some courts ruled that a party is not entitled to discover the identity of trial witnesses. *Moore* § 26.57[4]. They reasoned that the discoveree often does not know her trial witnesses until the eve of trial, or that the identity of such witnesses should be protected as work product under Rule 26(b)(3). Some state courts still follow this reasoning, although many require the mutual identification of trial witnesses in connection with a final pretrial conference. *See, e.g., Ladner v. Ladner*, 436 So.2d 1366, 1372 (Miss. 1983) (construing state discovery rule modeled on Rule 26(b)). *See generally* § 12.03 (pretrial conference), *infra.*

[37] Fed. R. Evid. 407 advisory committee's note.

[38] *See, e.g., Culligan v. Yamaha Motor Corp., U.S.A.*, 110 F.R.D. 122, 124 (S.D.N.Y. 1986).

sought. . . ."[39] If the opposing party has already admitted a fact, for example, a court might conclude that discovery of the fact is "unreasonably cumulative," or that the burden or expense of such discovery outweighs its likely benefit.[40]

[b] Impeachment Material

Except for required disclosures under Rule 26(b)(1)-(3)[41] discovery is not limited to direct substantive evidence, but includes material that may impeach an opponent's witnesses. Discovery of material that may impeach the discoverer's own witnesses has been more troublesome to the courts. Some have held that discovery is ordinarily not proper "where the only purpose . . . is to prevent effective cross-examination."[42]

Discovery of surveillance evidence, often movies made by defendant's representatives of plaintiff at work or play after the accident in a personal injury case, furnishes a good example. Many courts reason that surveillance movies, created after commencement of the litigation, have nothing to do with the merits, contain information already intimately and better known to the discoverer, and serve as a possible check on a "fertile field for fraud and magnification."[43] Moreover, impeachment material is gathered or developed in preparation for trial, and thus may fall within the spirit, if not always the letter, of Rule 26(b)(3)'s protection for work product.[44]

The trend in the modern cases, however, is to require discovery of even impeachment material. One important reason is that the assumption that matter useful for impeachment has nothing to do with the merits is not always reliable. The same matter can be used to advance a party's substantive position and to impeach.[45]

A second and more commonly articulated reason is that impeachment material poses its own risk of fraud and magnification. In *Boldt v. Sanders*,[46] for example, one of the plaintiffs in a personal injury action denied having suffered any prior accidents or personal injuries and sought discovery from defendant of any information that would contradict that denial. Defendant's objection rested on "the premise that defendant's evidence which plaintiffs seek to elicit constitutes the unblemished truth which, if prematurely disclosed, will prevent defendant from revealing to the jury

---

[39] Rule 26(b)(1)(i) & (ii) (emphasis supplied). *See* § 10.13[2] (managerial orders), *infra*.

[40] *See* Rule 26(b)(2)(i) & (iii). *But see Cornet Stores v. Superior Court*, 492 P.2d 1191 (Ariz. 1972) (stipulation that plaintiff was highest paid manager will not foreclose discovery of pay of other managers in wrongful discharge action).

[41] *See* § 10.07, *infra*.

[42] *Stone v. Marine Trans. Lines, Inc.*, 23 F.R.D. 222, 226 (D. Md. 1959).

[43] *Zimmerman v. Superior Court*, 402 P.2d 212, 219 (Ariz. 1965) (Struckmeyer, J., dissenting).

[44] *See DiMichel v. South Buffalo Ry. Co.*, 604 N.E.2d 63 (N.Y. 1992), *cert. denied*, 510 U.S. 816 (1993). *See generally* § 10.05 (work product), *infra*.

[45] *See Wright* § 81.

[46] 111 N.W.2d 225 (Minn. 1961).

the sham and perjury inherent in plaintiffs' claims."[47] The court rejected this premise, posing the equally plausible hypothetical of the defendant who "has resorted to fraud and perjury in fabricating pictures of what purport to be plaintiff's physical activities subsequent to the accident, and has manufactured evidence to prove that plaintiff sustained his injuries in prior accidents."[48] Absent a principled basis for choosing between these possibilities, the court fell back on the general rule of mutual discoverability.[49]

[c] Opinions and Contentions

Discovery is not limited to facts, but may also include opinions held by non-experts[50] and contentions regarding the facts or the application of law to the facts. This scope of discovery is expressly set out in Rule 33(b) concerning interrogatories and Rule 36(a) concerning requests for admissions, because they are most often used to probe opinions or contentions. But it is also implicit in Rule 26(b)(1)'s generic statement of the scope of discovery.[51] The only limitation is that the discoveree may defer responding until he has completed discovery of his own and thus had an opportunity to form informed opinions and contentions.[52]

The discoverer, however, may not ask what the law is, because the parties' legal conclusions are considered irrelevant. Only the court can say what the law is.[53] Similarly, the discoverer is not entitled to the discoveree's rank speculation on hypothetical facts, unrelated to the facts or the application of the law to the facts in the case.[54] Relevancy is probably also at the bottom of this restriction because untrammelled speculation by a witness or a party is arguably not relevant to anything.

[d] Insurance and Other Information About Financial Assets

Rule 26(a)(1) expressly requires disclosure of insurance agreements available to satisfy any or all of any eventual judgment, even though they remain inadmissible at trial. Prior to the 1970 amendment to the rule, some federal courts had denied discovery on relevancy grounds, and many states still do.[55] But the existence of insurance can be relevant to the issue of

---

[47] *Id.* at 227.

[48] *Id.*

[49] Many courts have qualified that rule with regard to impeachment material, however, by giving the discoveree the opportunity to depose the discoverer first before having to disclose the impeachment material. *See, e.g., Daniels v. Nat'l R.R. Passenger Corp.*, 110 F.R.D. 160, 161 (S.D.N.Y. 1986).

[50] For discussion of the discovery of opinions held by experts, see section 10.06, *infra.*

[51] *See Moore* §§ 26.41, 26.43.

[52] *See* Rules 33(b) & 36(a).

[53] *See, e.g., O'Brien v. Int'l Bnd. of Elec. Workers*, 443 F. Supp. 1182 (N.D. Ga. 1977) (an interrogatory requesting an explanation as to why provisions of a union constitution are not deprived of effect by a federal statute seeks purely legal conclusions).

[54] *Moore* § 26.41.

[55] *See James, Hazard, & Leubsdorf* § 5.8 (noting arguments against relevancy in an action

ownership. More important, it almost always bears significantly on settlement negotiations. It was chiefly to advance the social policy of encouraging settlement that the 1970 amendment made insurance agreements expressly discoverable.

Other information concerning the discoveree's financial position might also be useful in settlement negotiations, but is far less open to discovery. In support of the 1970 amendment, the Advisory Committee observed that insurance is an asset created specifically to satisfy claims, the insurer often controls the lawsuit, the information is usually available only from the insured or the insurer, and no privacy concerns are implicated by its discoverability.[56] None of these considerations in allowing discovery of insurance agreements applies to routine discovery of other financial assets. A party's general assets are obviously not created for the express purpose of satisfying a legal claim and are usually invested with significant privacy interests.

Accordingly, unless the amount of a party's assets is itself a relevant issue in the case, as it would be in an action to enforce a money judgment or in an action for punitive damages measured by the amount of the assets,[57] discovery of assets other than insurance, and of related information such as tax returns and bank statements, is sometimes denied. Even when assets are relevant and discoverable, privacy concerns may warrant postponing discovery until the discoveree has had an opportunity to contest the claim to which the assets are relevant.[58]

[e] Electronic Information[59]

Rule 26(b)(2) is silent about information stored in electronic form. In fact, the discovery rules generally appear to be document-oriented. Yet "[e]lectronic devices have begun to replace paper as a primary means of storing information, just as the Internet has begun to replace the postal system as the primary means of transmitting information."[60] Discovery will therefore necessarily increasingly focus on computer-stored information, including e-mail, web caches, cookies and other forms of electronic information which do not fall easily under the rubric of "document." In fact, the

---

against the insured); Annotation, *Pretrial Examination or Discovery to Ascertain from Defendant in Action for Injury, Death, or Damages, Existence and Amount of Liability Insurance and Insurer's Identity*, 13 A.L.R.3d 822 (1967 & 2000 Supp).

[56] Rule 26(b)(2) advisory committee's note (1970).

[57] *See, e.g., Renshaw v. Ravert*, 82 F.R.D. 361, 363 (E.D. Pa. 1979) (punitive damages).

[58] *See, e.g., Larriva v. Montiel*, 691 P.2d 735, 737-738 (Ariz. App. 1984) (discoverer must first make *prima facie* showing that he will be entitled to present punitive damages claim to jury).

[59] *See, e.g.,* Scheindlin & Rabkin, *Electronic Discovery in Federal Civil Litigation: Is Rule 34 Up to the Task?*, 41 B.C. L. Rev. 327 (2000); Jessen, *Special Issues Involving Electronic Discovery*, 9 Kan. J.L. & Pub. Pol'y 425 (2000); Meyer & Wraspir, *E-Discovery: Preparing Clients for (and Protecting Them Against) Discovery in the Electronic Information Age*, 26 Wm. Mitchell L. Rev. 939 (2000); Robins, *Computers and the Discovery of Evidence — a New Dimension to Civil Procedure*, 17 J. Marshall J. Computer & Info. L. 411 (1999).

[60] *Scheindlin & Rabkin*, note 59, *supra*, at 331.

Manual for Complex Litigation advises that "[a]ny discovery plan must address relevant issues, such as the search for, location, retrieval, form of production and inspection, preservation, and use at trial of information stored in mainframe or personal computers or accessible 'online.' "[61]

Fortunately for discovery in the electronic age, Rule 34, (which allows requests for production of documents "and things") defines documents to include "other data compilations from which information can be obtained, translated, if necessary, by the respondent through detection devices into reasonably usable form." Even though some forms of automatically computer-generated electronic information — like temporary and backup files or cookies — do not fit even this definition very well (they are not "compiled" consciously by the user), the courts have almost universally interpreted Rule 34 to allow discovery of electronic information if it is relevant and non-privileged.[62] The emerging and still unresolved issues, instead, concern the form in which such information must be produced and the allocation of cost for producing it.[63]

§ 10.04 The Non-Discoverability of Privileged Matter

Discovery in every jurisdiction extends only to unprivileged matters.[64] *Privilege* is a legal term of art. It refers to the protection from disclosure that the common law, statute, or rule[65] affords particular communications in order to promote relationships to which confidential communication is essential. Although their elements vary, most privileges require the communications for which the privilege is sought (1) to have been made with an expectation of confidentiality, that is (2) essential to a socially approved relationship or purpose and (3) has not been waived by disclosure of the contents of the communications to persons outside the relationship.[66] The attorney-client, doctor-patient, priest-penitent, interspousal privilege and the privilege against self-incrimination are commonly recognized privileges.[67] A privilege that will bar evidence at trial will also prevent disclosure of the same evidence in discovery.[68]

Privileges are narrowly construed in order to minimize their effect on liberal disclosure.[69] The proponent of a privilege has the burden of

---

[61] *Manual for Complex Litigation* § 21.446 (3d ed. 1995).

[62] *Id.* at 350 (citing authorities and "the absence of any recent decisional law or commentary taking a contrary position" as of 2000).

[63] *See* § 10.10[1] (procedure for making document production requests), *infra*.

[64] *See, e.g.*, Rule 26(b)(1).

[65] *See, e.g.*, Fed. R. Evid. 501 (incorporating federal common law).

[66] *See, e.g.*, R. Haydock & D. Herr, *Discovery Practice* § 2.1 (23 ed. 1996).

[67] Litigants, and occasionally courts, loosely and inaccurately describe as "privileges" the protection accorded to trial preparation materials, which are discoverable upon the proper special showing, *see* §§ 10.05 & 10.06, *infra*, or to materials like trade secrets or membership lists, which are discoverable but often subject to discovery limitations established by a court order to protect their confidentiality. *See* § 10.13[3], *infra*.

[68] This is because violation of the confidence compromises the relationship in either event.

[69] *Moore* § 26.47[1].

establishing its existence. This ordinarily requires him to lay a foundation for the existence of the privilege by supplying enough information about the circumstances of the communication to show that it is privileged. This foundation requirement is codified in Rule 26(b)(5). The 1993 Advisory Committee cautions that a party's failure to supply this information will not only subject it to sanctions under Rule 37, but may also waive the privilege.

Although detailed discussion of particular privileges belongs to the law of evidence rather than to civil procedure, it is useful to develop the attorney-client privilege as an example. Probably the classic judicial statement of the privilege is found in *United States v. United Shoe Machinery Corp.*:[70]

> The privilege applies only if (1) the asserted holder of the privilege is or sought to become a client; (2) the person to whom the communication was made (a) is a member of the bar of a court, or his subordinate and (b) in connection with this communication is acting as a lawyer; (3) the communication relates to a fact of which the attorney was informed (a) by his client (b) without the presence of strangers (c) for the purpose of securing primarily either (i) an opinion on law or (ii) legal services or (iii) some assistance in some legal proceeding, and not (d) for the purpose of committing a crime or tort; and (4) the privilege has been (a) claimed and (b) not waived by the client.

It is the communication itself, not the underlying facts, that is privileged.[71] Thus a client cannot cloak evidence with the privilege simply by telling it to his lawyer. The privilege is unavailable if third parties were present at the communication, destroying its confidentiality, or if the client has waived it by subsequent disclosure.[72] Finally, the privilege is not available to protect communications made for improper purposes.[73]

§ 10.05 Work Product[74]

Work product can be defined preliminarily as information prepared or obtained in anticipation of litigation or preparation for trial. In the landmark case of *Hickman v. Taylor,*[75] the Supreme Court recognized a common

---

[70] 89 F. Supp. 357, 358 (D. Mass. 1950). *See generally* P. Rice *et al., Attorney-Client Privilege in the United States* (1993); E. Epstein & M. Martin, *The Attorney-Client Privilege and the Work Product Doctrine* (2d ed. 1989); J. Gergacz, *Attorney-Corporate Client Privilege* (1987).

[71] *See, e.g.,* Upjohn Co. v. United States, 449 U.S. 383, 395-396 (1981).

[72] Indeed, one court has even held the privilege waived by the clients' discarding of privileged documents in a trash dumpster from which they were removed by an enterprising if pungent third party. *Suburban Sew'N Sweep, Inc. v. Swiss-Bernina, Inc.,* 91 F.R.D. 254 (N.D. Ill. 1981).

[73] *See generally* Rice, note 70, *supra,* §§ 8.2-8.15.

[74] *See generally* E. Epstein & M. Martin, *The Attorney-Client Privilege and the Work Product Doctrine* (3d ed. 1997); Thornburg, *Rethinking Work Product,* 77 Va. L. Rev. 1515 (1991); Anderson, Candieux, Hays, Hagerty, & Kaplan, *The Work Product Doctrine,* 68 Cornell L. Rev. 760 (1983); Annotation, *Developments, Since Hickman v. Taylor, of Attorney's "Work Product" Doctrine,* 35 A.L.R.3d 412 (1971 & 1993 Supp.).

[75] 329 U.S. 495 (1947).

law qualified immunity of work product from discovery. The rulings in this case were subsequently codified and enlarged by Rule 26(b)(3). Subdivision 1 of this section discusses *Hickman*; Subdivision 2 defines work product more thoroughly in terms of Rule 26(b)(3); Subdivision 3 discusses how the immunity is asserted during discovery; and Subdivision 4 discusses how it is overcome.

[1] *Hickman v. Taylor* and Work Product Immunity

Originally the federal rules of civil procedure contained no provisions regarding discovery of work product. A few lower federal courts recognized a federal common law [76] protection for such materials. In 1947, the Supreme Court endorsed and explained this common law protection in *Hickman v. Taylor*.

Hickman arose out of the accidental sinking of a tugboat and the resulting death of five crew members. Three days after the sinking, the tug owners and their underwriters employed attorney Fortenbaugh and his firm to defend them against potential suits by the decedents' representatives and to sue a third party for damages to the tug. After a public hearing before the United States Steamboat Inspectors at which the surviving crew members testified, Fortenbaugh privately took written statements from the survivors. He also interviewed other fact witnesses and made memoranda of the interviews.

A decedent's representative ultimately sued the tug owners and filed interrogatories directed to them. One interrogatory asked whether statements of the surviving crew members had been taken and required any written statements to be attached to the answers [77] and any oral statements to be set forth in detail. [78] Additional interrogatories sought the identity and content of any other oral or written statements, memoranda or reports made concerning the subject matter of the suit.

The tug owners admitted in answers prepared by Fortenbaugh that statements had been taken, but declined to set forth the answers' contents in part on the ground that they were "privileged matter obtained in preparation for litigation." [79] The district court ruled that the written witness statements taken by Fortenbaugh were not privileged and ordered Fortenbaugh to produce them. [80] When he refused, he was ordered

---

[76] For discussion of specific federal common law, see § 7.07, *supra*.

[77] Technically, this part of the plaintiff's discovery request was improper. Document production from a party is ordinarily obtained by filing a request for production of documents pursuant to Rule 34. *See* § 10.10[1] (procedures for production requests), *infra*.

[78] *Hickman*, 329 U.S. at 498.

[79] *Id.* at 499.

[80] This order was also then improper. Interrogatories and, at the time, requests for production of documents could only be directed at parties, and Fortenbaugh was not a party. The only proper procedure for obtaining documents from a non-party was then to take her deposition and, in that connection, to serve her with a *subpoena duces tecum*. *Id.* The Supreme Court noted this but it did not figure in the Court's holding. 329 U.S. at 503-504.

imprisoned for contempt. The Court of Appeals reversed, ruling that the information was "work product" and as such privileged from discovery. The Supreme Court affirmed on somewhat different reasoning.

The Court first rejected Fortenbaugh's claim of privilege. It noted that the attorney-client privilege extends neither to information obtained from third parties outside the attorney-client relationship nor to all material prepared by counsel for his own use in prosecuting his client's case.[81] The purpose of the attorney-client privilege is to encourage full disclosure of information between an attorney and her client by protecting the confidentiality of their communications.[82] That purpose did not apply to the materials Fortenbaugh had prepared.

This conclusion, however, did not answer the discovery question presented by the case. The Court held that discovery of attorney Fortenbaugh's work product "contravenes the public policy underlying the orderly prosecution and defense of legal claims," absent any showing of necessity beyond mere relevance or any claim that denial of discovery would cause undue prejudice.[83]

> In performing his various duties, it is essential that a lawyer work with a certain degree of privacy, free from unnecessary intrusion by opposing parties and their counsel. Proper preparation of a client's case demands that he assemble information, sift what he considers to be the relevant from the irrelevant facts, prepare his legal theories and plan his strategy without undue and needless interference. This work is reflected, of course, in interviews, statements, memoranda, correspondence, briefs, mental impressions, personal beliefs, and countless other tangible and intangible ways — aptly though roughly termed by the Circuit Court of Appeals in this case as the "work product of the lawyer." Were such materials open to opposing counsel on mere demand, much of what is now put down in writing would remain unwritten.[84]

The Court made clear, however, that the immunity accorded work product is qualified. When the discoverer goes beyond a bare demand, and shows that production is "essential to preparation" of his case and that denial of discovery would cause hardship because "witnesses are no longer available or can be reached only with difficulty," production of "relevant and non-privileged facts . . . in an attorney's file" should be allowed.[85] The plaintiff in *Hickman* had made no such showing. On the contrary, his counsel admitted that he wanted the witness statements "only to help prepare himself to examine witnesses and to make sure that he [had] overlooked

---

[81] *Id.* at 508.

[82] *See* § 10.04 (privilege), *supra. See generally Moore* § 26.70[8] (comparing the attorney-client privilege and the protection of attorney work product).

[83] *Hickman*, 329 U.S. at 509-510.

[84] *Id.* at 510-511. *But see Thornburg*, note 74, *supra*, at 1526-1532 (arguing that the adversary system itself provides sufficient inducement for thorough, written preparation, without the need for work product immunity).

[85] *Hickman*, 329 U.S. at 510.

nothing."[86] He had ready access to the surviving crew members' prior public testimony before the Steamboat Inspectors and apparently to the witnesses themselves. Moreover, the Court emphasized, he could employ interrogatories to the tug owners to obtain any relevant and non-privileged facts known to them, including any facts learned by their attorney.[87]

Finally, the Court implied that although a showing of necessity and hardship would be sufficient to require production of the written witness statements, it might not be enough to require production of oral witness statements taken by Fortenbaugh, "whether presently in the form of his mental impressions or memoranda."[88] It reasoned that in addition to the previously discussed policy arguments for protection, there is special concern about making the attorney a witness, by forcing him to testify to the contents of oral witness statements he has taken. As Justice Jackson noted in his concurring opinion,

> [t]he lawyer who delivers such statements often would find himself branded a deceiver afraid to take the stand to support his own version of the witness's conversation with him, or else he will have to go on the stand to defend his own credibility — perhaps against that of his chief witness or possibly even his client.[89]

Discoverability of such statements could thus transform the attorney from officer of the court into ordinary witness, contrary to the standards of the profession.[90]

Hickman stood as the common law foundation for the qualified immunity of attorney work product for twenty-three years. Finally, the 1970 amendments to the federal rules codified and enlarged much of the common law doctrine.

[2] Defining Work Product

Rule 26(b)(3) enlarges the common law protection from attorney work product to "documents and tangible things . . . prepared in anticipation of litigation or for trial by or for another party or . . . [his] representative." Where the rule applies, it supplants the common law doctrine of *Hickman*. But *Hickman* still controls the discovery of intangible materials that literally fall outside the rule,[91] and its spirit animates the rule.

---

[86] *Id.* at 513.

[87] *Id.*

[88] *Id.* at 512.

[89] *Id.* at 517.

[90] American Bar Ass'n, *Model Rules of Professional Conduct* Rule 3.7 (1999). *But see Thornburg*, note 74, *supra*, at 1540-1544 (arguing that the problem is more imaginary than real because attorneys can have others interview witnesses, tape-record the interview, or simply depose the witnesses).

[91] Such discovery is not expressly anticipated by the rule. *See Moore* § 26.70[2].

[a] Documents and Tangible Things

The Court in *Hickman* emphasized that although the written witness statements and Fortenbaugh's memoranda were not discoverable on a bare demand, the discoverer was free to obtain the facts gleaned by Fortenbaugh by interrogatories to his clients. Rule 26(b)(3) rather crudely reflects this distinction between the documents assembled by the client or his representatives and the same persons as sources of discoverable fact by protecting only "documents and tangible things." The qualified immunity for work product does not protect against discovery of facts contained in the work product, including the identity of fact witnesses or the existence of the protected documents and things, "if a litigant can figure out the right question to ask."[92]

In application, however, the distinction is not so clean. Since the rule could be easily circumvented if a discoverer could require the discoveree to describe in detail the contents of protected documents, courts deny such discovery on the theory that it is "the equivalent to discovery of the documents themselves" and therefore prohibited by the rule,[93] or that it violates the broader common law rule of *Hickman*.[94] The distinction is subtle; you may obtain the facts in the document, but may not require the discoveree to recreate the document for you. It is also logical. By its organization and fact selection, the written presentation of the facts often reflects tactical or strategic emphases and priorities that are at the heart of the immunity, even though the bare facts themselves are not. The same reasoning is sometimes given for the denial of discovery of what questions an attorney privately put to a witness.[95]

A similar concern for circumvention of the rule is leading some courts to restrict discovery of even the facts themselves when that discovery is sought from the parties' attorneys, rather than from their clients or other witnesses. Not only does the deposition of an opposing attorney unnecessarily make a witness of the attorney (contrary to *Hickman*'s admonition), but it inevitably targets the attorney's mental impressions and legal theories by forcing her to reveal what she thought important enough to remember. Accordingly, the Court of Appeals for the Eighth Circuit upheld an attorney's refusal during her deposition to acknowledge even the existence of trial preparation materials.[96] It reasoned that

---

[92] *Thornburg*, note 74, *supra*, at 1520. *See generally Wright* § 82.

[93] *See, e.g., Peterson v. United States*, 52 F.R.D. 317, 322 (S.D. Ill. 1971).

[94] *Cf. Gilhuly v. Johns-Manville Corp.*, 100 F.R.D. 752 (D. Conn. 1983); *Bercow v. Kidder, Peabody & Co.*, 39 F.R.D. 357 (S.D.N.Y. 1965).

[95] *See, e.g., Ford v. Philips Electronics Instruments Co.*, 82 F.R.D. 359 (E.D. Pa. 1979) (discovery denied "insofar as defendant's question attempted to elicit from the witness the specific questions that plaintiff's counsel posed to him, or even the area of the case to which he directed the majority of his questions," but not "insofar as it was directed to the substance of the witness' knowledge of the relevant facts.").

[96] *Shelton v. American Motors Corp.*, 805 F.2d 1323 (8th Cir. 1986). *See generally* Waits, *Opinion Work Product: A Critical Analysis of Current Law and a New Analytical Framework*, 73 Ore. L. Rev. 385 (1994) (criticizing *Shelton*); Note, *Suppose You Want to Depose Opposing Counsel*, 73 Minn. L. Rev. 1116 (1989) (arguing that courts should only limit and not prohibit depositions of opposing counsel).

[i]n cases that involve reams of documents and extensive document discovery, the selection and compilation of documents is often more critical than legal research. We believe [that the attorney's] selective review of [her client's] numerous documents was based on her professional judgment of the issues and defenses involved in this case. Moreover, . . . any recollection [she] may have of the existence of documents in [her client's] possession likely would be limited to those documents she has selected as important to her legal theories concerning this case.[97]

In addition, the court more generally disapproved of the "increasingly popular" device of deposing opposing counsel and emphasized that henceforth it should be limited to cases in which the discoverer can make the kind of showing of substantial need and undue hardship required by Rule 26(b)(3) for discovery of tangible trial work product.[98]

In short, although Rule 26(b)(3) expressly only protects tangible work product, in the form of documents and other tangible things, the common law declared by *Hickman* extends such protection to some intangible work product as well when it would advance the policies articulated in *Hickman*. Some commentators have urged a distinction between "direct" intangible work product, such as a lawyer's testimony about her trial strategy, and "indirect" intangible work product, such as a lawyer's selection of documents to use at a deposition (from which strategy could at best be inferred circumstantially[99]), arguing that only the former ordinarily deserves protection, but the courts have yet to adopt this distinction or any other consistent framework for treating intangible work product.[100]

[b] Prepared in Anticipation of Litigation or for Trial[101]

Because qualified work product immunity is designed to promote "the public policy underlying the orderly prosecution and defense of legal claims,"[102] the immunity is limited by Rule 26(b)(3) to materials "prepared in anticipation of litigation or for trial." Litigation need not be pending, but a mere contingency is insufficient. One court has asserted that "the lawyer must at least have had a subjective belief that litigation was a real possibility, and that belief must have been objectively reasonable."[103] Most courts add that the primary purpose of preparing the documents must have

---

[97] *Id.* at 1329 (citations omitted).

[98] *Id.* at 1330. *See generally* Simmons, Note, *Deposing Opposing Counsel Under the Federal Rules: Time for a Unified Approach*, 38 Wayne L. Rev. 1959 (1992).

[99] *See* Holmes, *The Disruption of Mandatory Disclosure With the Work Product Doctrine: An Analysis of a Potential Problem and a Proposed Solution*, 73 Tex. L. Rev. 177, 188 (1994).

[100] *Waits*, note 96, *supra*. *See* § 10.05[4][c] (discussing opinion work product), *infra*.

[101] *See generally* Cohn, *The Work Product Doctrine: Protection Not Privilege*, 71 Geo. L.J. 917, 925-929 (1985); Oberbilling, *Work Product Discovery: A Multifactor Approach to the Anticipation of Litigation Requirement of Federal Rule of Civil Procedure 26(b)(3)*, 66 Iowa L. Rev. 1277 (1981).

[102] *Hickman*, 329 U.S. at 509.

[103] *In re Sealed Case*, 146 F.3d 881, 884 (D.C. Cir. 1998).

been to assist in such litigation.[104] Thus, documents prepared for ordinary business purposes (*e.g.*, a routine accident report), public regulatory requirements (*e.g.*, statutorily-required report to police of automobile accidents involving injuries), or other nonlitigation purposes (*e.g.*, self-evaluation) are not protected.[105]

Purpose alone, however, is often unhelpful as a test for the applicability of the immunity. For example, because it is the ordinary course of business for an insurer to investigate claims in anticipation of litigation, the purpose test alone is unavailing to classify claims investigation materials. Instead, the court must also consider all the circumstances of preparation, including who prepared the materials and precisely when they were prepared in relation to anticipated litigation.[106] A few courts have therefore rejected the primary purpose standard as too narrow in favor of the formulation "prepared because of" the prospect of litigation, which encompasses some business documents not intended to assist in the litigation.[107] A memorandum prepared to assess the effects of possible litigation on the desirability of a merger would qualify as work product under this standard, for example, even though it was not prepared primarily to assist in litigation.

Carver v. Allstate Insurance Co.[108] is illustrative. In an action to recover proceeds under a fire insurance policy and statutory penalties for the insurer's bad faith refusal to pay, the insured sought discovery of daily investigative reports or "diary sheets" prepared by the insurer's claims adjusters. The court allowed discovery of the diary sheets prepared by the initial claims adjuster during the first two months after the fire. It reasoned that such reports are not primarily prepared for the contingency of litigation but rather for the routine business purpose of deciding whether to pay or resist the claim.

However, the court denied discovery of the diary sheets of a second claims adjuster to whom the claim was assigned after the first claims adjuster determined that the claim would be substantial and that the origins of the fire were suspicious. At that point, all the circumstances indicated that the insurer's activities shifted from "mere claims evaluation to a strong anticipation of litigation."[109] The court acknowledged that although an insurer always works in anticipation of litigation, at some point the probability of litigation becomes substantial and imminent, triggering the qualified immunity for materials prepared thereafter.

---

[104] *See, e.g., Janicker v. George Washington University*, 94 F.R.D. 648 (D.D.C. 1982).

[105] *See generally* Rule 26(b)(3) advisory committee's note (1970); Wilson, Note, *The Work Product Doctrine: Why Have an Ordinary Course of Business Exception?*, 1988 Colum. Bus. L. Rev. 587.

[106] *See* Wright § 82.

[107] *United States v. Adlman*, 134 F.3d 1194 (2d Cir. 1998). *See, e.g.*, McNamar, *Business Planning as It Should Be*, 34 Val. U. L. Rev. 201 (1999); Yablon & Sparling, *United States v. Adlman: Protection for Corporate Work Product?*, 64 Brook. L. Rev. 627 (1998).

[108] 94 F.R.D. 131 (S.D. Ga. 1982).

[109] *Id.* at 135.

[c] By a Party or His Representative

Although *Hickman* dealt just with materials prepared by an attorney, preparation of materials in anticipation of litigation or for trial routinely and necessarily requires the assistance of non-attorneys, as well the parties themselves. Rule 26(b)(3) thus expressly extends the qualified immunity to materials prepared by a party or a party's representative, "including his attorney, consultant, surety, indemnitor, insurer, or agent."[110] This enlargement of the literal original common law rule accounts in part for Rule 26(b)(3)'s abandonment of the phrase "attorney work product" in favor of "trial preparation materials."

[3] Asserting the Qualified Immunity

While the burden rests on the discoverer to overcome a properly asserted qualified immunity for work product,[111] the discoveree must first lay a proper foundation for the immunity. As previously noted in connection with claims of privilege,[112] this requirement is codified in Rule 26(b)(5). Disregarding the requirement risks sanctions as well as waiver of the immunity. The rule does not specify what information must be provided. "Details concerning time, persons, general subject matter, etc., may be appropriate if only a few items are withheld, but may be unduly burdensome when voluminous documents are claimed to be privileged or protected, particularly if the items can be described by categories."[113] This advice of the Advisory Committee must be taken cautiously because the case law is hostile to blanket claims of privilege.[114]

[4] Overcoming the Qualified Immunity

Once qualified work product immunity has been properly asserted, the burden of overcoming it shifts to the discoverer and depends upon whether the work product consists of *witness statements* requested by the witness, other *factual work product*, or *opinion work product*.

[a] Witness Statements Requested by the Witness

Although witness statements qualify as work product, Rule 26(b)(3) expressly provides that a party or witness may on demand obtain a copy of his own substantially verbatim statement[115] concerning the subject

---

[110] Materials prepared by a party's expert are covered by Rule 26(a)(2) (testimonial expert's written report) or Rule 26(b)(4) (other experts). *See* § 10.06, *infra*.

[111] *See* § 10.05[4], *infra*.

[112] *See* § 10.04 (non-discoverability of privileged matters), *supra*.

[113] Rule 26(b)(5) advisory committee's note (1993).

[114] *See, e.g., Eureka Financial Corp. v. Hartford Accident & Indem. Co.*, 136 F.R.D. 179, 182 (E.D. Cal. 1991). A court may also disregard an untimely establishment of foundation for the immunity. *Peat, Marwick, Mitchell & Co. v. West*, 748 F.2d 540, 541-542 (10th Cir. 1984), *cert. dismissed*, 469 U.S. 1199 (1985).

[115] *See* Waits, *Work Product For Witness Statements: Time for Abolition*, 1985 Wis. L. Rev. 305 (criticizing applicability of this provision only to a witness's own statement).

matter of the action. The 1970 Advisory Committee gave a partial explanation of this exception to qualified immunity in terms of the importance of a person's statement, which is admissible against him at trial as an admission. Since a person who gives a statement without insisting on a copy often does so without benefit of counsel, in ignorance of its legal consequences, and "at a time when he functions at a disadvantage," the Committee reasoned that its discoverability would increase fairness.[116]

[b] Factual Work Product

The immunity for factual work product can be overcome only upon showing by the discoverer of "substantial need of the materials in the preparation of his case" and "that he is unable without undue hardship to obtain the substantial equivalent by other means."[117] Although the cases do not always sharply distinguish these requirements, they are logically discrete.

Substantial need refers to the importance of the materials to the discoverer's case. *Hickman* itself demonstrates that substantial need means more than that the materials will help the discoverer make sure that he has overlooked nothing, because the Court rejected that showing. Such need, the "natural desire to learn the details of his adversary's preparations for trial," is present in every case and cannot be the substantial need required to overcome the immunity.[118] Nor, obviously, will mere relevance to a claim or defense suffice, or else substantial need would be redundant with the generic scope of discovery.[119] But the stronger the relevance and importance to the discoverer's claim or defense-in-chief, the more likely a court is to find this requirement satisfied.[120]

Hickman also demonstrates that *undue hardship* from denial of discovery cannot exist when a party has other reasonable access to the information. There the discoverer had access to contemporaneous sworn testimony and to the witnesses themselves. When matter is unavailable to the discoverer because the witnesses have died, moved beyond the reach of compulsory process, lost their memories, deviated from their prior testimony or refused to cooperate, undue hardship can be established.[121] Similarly, the physical disappearance or alteration of evidence reflected in work product, such as

---

[116] Rule 26(b)(3) advisory committee's notes (1970). *See generally* § 10.03[3][b] (discoverability of impeachment material), *supra*.

[117] Rule 26(b)(3).

[118] *Alltmont v. United States*, 177 F.2d 971, 978 (3d Cir. 1949), *cert. denied*, 339 U.S. 967 (1950) (pre-rule decision).

[119] *See* § 10.03[1] (relevancy), *supra*.

[120] *See, e.g., Wheeling-Pittsburgh Steel Corp. v. Underwriters Laboratories, Inc.*, 81 F.R.D. 86 (D.C. Ill. 1978) (statistical data on damages could not be properly analyzed without discovery of work product consisting of methodology used in computing damages). *See generally Wright & Miller* § 2025.

[121] Rule 26(b)(3) advisory committee's note (1970). *See In re International Sys. & Controls Corp. Securities Litig.*, 693 F.2d 1235 (5th Cir. 1982) (noting memory loss and cost of obtaining information elsewhere as appropriate particularized showings to make out undue hardship). *See generally* Atwood, Note, *Rule 166b: The Discovery of Work Product Based on Substantial Need and Hardship*, 42 Baylor L. Rev. 573, 579-587 (1990) (surveying federal cases).

photographs of skid marks or conditions at the scene of an accident, may establish undue hardship — indeed, impossibility — in obtaining the substantial equivalent by other means.[122] More generally, any time that important facts are exclusively in the control of the discoveree, the undue hardship requirement should be satisfied.[123]

[c] Opinion Work Product[124]

Hickman implied that special protection was due an attorney's mental impressions and legal theories — what might be termed *opinion work product*. Rule 26(b)(3) gave expression to this implication by providing that in ordering discovery of work product after the required showing has been made, "the court shall protect against disclosure of the mental impressions, conclusions, opinions, or legal theories of an attorney or other representative of a party concerning the litigation."

Many courts and commentators have read this clause to confer an absolute protection on opinion work product, citing the mandatory verb "shall" in the rule.[125] When factual and opinion work product are intermixed, a court can often protect the latter by inspecting the materials *in camera* (out of the presence of counsel seeking discovery) and ordering disclosure only of segregable factual materials.

Arguably, however, Rule 26(b)(3) does not expressly prohibit disclosure of opinion work product; it only commands the courts to "protect against disclosure." In *Upjohn Co. v. United States*,[126] the Supreme Court suggested that opinion materials merit "special protection" and cited Rule 26(b)(3) and *Hickman* for the proposition that such materials cannot be disclosed "simply" on the usual showing of substantial need and undue hardship.[127] The Court did not reach the question of what further showing might suffice. Lower federal courts have on rare occasions allowed discovery of even opinion work product when attorneys or other representatives are charged with coercion, malpractice, fraud, or crime, or when their opinions and impressions are pivotal to bad faith, limitations, laches or estoppel issues in the lawsuit.[128] The additional showing that these cases apparently have

---

[122] *See, e.g., Rackers v. Siegfried*, 54 F.R.D. 24 (W.D. Mo. 1971) (ordering discovery of insurance adjuster's measurements of skid marks).

[123] *See Moore* § 26.70[5].

[124] Waits, note 96, *supra*; Smith, Comment *The Potential for Discovery of Opinion Work Product Under Rule 26(b) (3)*, 64 Iowa L. Rev. 103 (1978); Note, *Protection of Opinion Work Product Under the Federal Rules of Civil Procedure*, 64 Va. L. Rev. 333 (1978).

[125] *See, e.g., Duplan Corp. v. Moulinage et Retorderie de Chavanoz*, 509 F.2d 730 (4th Cir. 1974), *cert. denied*, 420 U.S. 997 (1975); *United States v. Chatham City Corp.*, 72 F.R.D. 640, 643 n.3 (S.D. Ga. 1976). *See generally Wright* § 82.

[126] 449 U.S. 383 (1981).

[127] *Id.* at 401.

[128] *See, e.g., Holmgren v. State Farm Mut. Auto. Ins. Co.*, 976 F.2d 573 (9th Cir. 1992) (bad faith denial of insurance claim); *In re Sealed Case*, 676 F.2d 793, 807 (D.C. Cir. 1982) (crime/fraud); *Byers v. Burleson*, 100 F.R.D. 436, 439 (D.D.C. 1983) (limitations); *Donovan v. Fitzsimmons*, 90 F.R.D. 583 (N.D. Ill. 1981) (reliance on advice-of-counsel defense); *Bird v. Penn Cent. Co.*, 61 F.R.D. 43, 47 (E.D. Pa. 1973) (laches). *See generally* Halfenger, Comment, *The Attorney Misconduct Exception to the Work Product Doctrine*, 58 U. Chi. L. Rev. 1079 (1991).

in common is that the attorney's or other representative's opinions are themselves an issue in the lawsuit, for which evidence is unavailable by other means.

§ 10.06 Experts[129]

[1] In General

In *Hickman*, Justice Jackson observed that "[d]iscovery was hardly intended to enable a learned profession to perform its functions . . . on wits borrowed from the adversary."[130] Nor was discovery intended to enable attorneys to prepare for trial with experts borrowed from their adversaries. Indeed, the concern about free-loading discovery is especially acute in the case of experts retained in anticipation of litigation because of the substantial fees experts often demand. On the other hand, the complexity and importance of expert testimony at trial also present a very real risk of surprise to opposing parties who have not had discovery of the expert.

The rules balance these concerns by differentiating between, on one hand, experts expected to testify at trial (*testifying experts*) and, on the other hand, those merely retained or specially employed in anticipation of trial who are not, however, expected to testify (*non-testifying experts*). Rule 26(a)(2) requires disclosure of the identity and expected testimony of the testifying experts and Rule 26(b)(4)(A) permits their depositions.[131] Rule 26(b)(4) conditionally protects the non-testifying experts from discovery absent a special showing.

Neither part of the rule, however, protects against discovery of an expert who acquires his information as an actor or viewer in the transactions or occurrences that give rise to the lawsuit.[132] Thus, the police officer who responds to the accident scene, the doctor who attends in the emergency room, and the mechanic who services the car whose brakes failed, are all just ordinary fact witnesses, subject to orthodox discovery under the rules, even though they may also be experts.[133]

---

[129] *See generally* Brennan, *Must the Show Go On? Defining When One Party May Call or Compel an Opposing Party's Consultative Expert to Testify*, 78 Minn. L. Rev. 1191 (1994); Graham, *Expert Witness Testimony and the Federal Rules of Evidence: Insuring Adequate Assurance of Trustworthiness*, 1986 U. Ill. L. Rev. 90; Graham, *Discovery of Experts Under Rule 26(b)(4) of the Federal Rules of Civil Procedure: Parts I & II*, 1976 U. Ill. L.F. 895, 1977 U. Ill. L.F. 169.

[130] 329 U.S. at 516 (Jackson, J., concurring).

[131] Discovery of reports of physical or mental examinations conducted pursuant to Rule 35 is governed separately by its provisions. *See* § 10.11 (procedure for taking physical and mental examinations), *infra*.

[132] Rule 26(b)(4) advisory committee's note (1970).

[133] *See, e.g., Nelco Corp. v. Slater Elec., Inc.*, 80 F.R.D. 411 (E.D.N.Y. 1978) (expert may be deposed as an "actor" in the events that are the subject of the litigation). Of course, the rule shields only the facts and opinions held by the expert. " 'It does not . . . excuse the party from disgorging what facts he may have in his possession' " or allow him to insulate those facts from discovery by giving them to an expert. *Marine Petroleum Co. v. Champlin Petroleum Co.*, 641 F.2d, 984, 994 (D.C. Cir. 1980) (*quoting* J. Moore, *Moore's Federal Practice* ¶ 26.66[2]) (2d ed.).

Rule 26 does not address per se the issue of discovery of experts who have been consulted in anticipation of litigation but not retained or specially employed.[134] The 1970 Advisory Committee's notes suggest that the omission was intentional, and that discovery of such experts, or even of their identity, is precluded.[135] The omission of any provision for discovery of generally employed non-testifying experts arguably creates the same inference. Some courts, however, have rejected that inference for such a "party-expert" on the grounds that he is more partisan than professionally objective.[136] If such an expert learned facts and acquired opinions in anticipation of litigation, however, any materials that he has generated reflecting those facts and opinions would presumably be independently protected from discovery by ordinary work product immunity.[137]

A 1991 amendment to Rule 45 may have modified this law by acknowledging the possibility of discovery of "unretained experts,"[138] subject to motions to quash or modify discovery or trial subpoenas. Prior to the amendment, some courts treated unretained and unconsulted experts as ordinary witnesses who are not exempt from the citizen's duty to give evidence. But the problem of freeloading noted above applies to such experts with special force. "[C]ompulsion to give evidence may threaten the intellectual property of [such] experts denied the opportunity to bargain for the value of their services," noted the 1991 Advisory Committee. Rule 45(c), therefore, now allows for motions to quash or modify any subpoena that "requires disclosure of an unretained expert's opinion or information not describing events or occurrences in dispute and resulting from the expert's study made not at the request of any party" unless the requesting party can show substantial need for such testimony and undue hardship and assures that she will reasonably compensate the expert.

[2] Testifying Experts

The 1970 Advisory Committee concluded that any prohibition of discovery from the testifying expert "produces in acute form the very evils that discovery has been created to prevent." The complexity of expert testimony and frequent prior experience of the testifying expert with the rigors of cross-examination require particularly careful preparation by the

---

[134] See Brennan, note 129, supra.

[135] The 1970 Advisory Committee said that the rule "precludes discovery against experts who were informally consulted in preparation for trial, but not retained or specially employed. As an ancillary procedure, a party may on a proper showing require the other party to name experts retained or specially employed, but not those formally consulted."

[136] See, e.g., Kansas-Nebraska Natural Gas v. Marathon Oil Co., 109 F.R.D. 12, 15-16 (D. Neb. 1985). For an especially thoughtful discussion of the issue, see also Virginia Elec. & Power Co. v. Sun Shipbuilding & Dry Dock Co., 68 F.R.D. 397, 406-410 (E.D. Va. 1975). See generally Pielemeier, Discovery of Non-testifying "In-House" Experts Under Federal Rule of Civil Procedure 26, 58 Ind. L.J. 597, 625 (1983) (arguing that "discovery of in-house experts should be treated in the same manner as discovery of 'retained or specially employed' experts" under Rule 26(b)(4)).

[137] See § 10.05 (work product), supra.

[138] Rule 45(c).

cross-examiner.[139] If a discovery bar handicaps that preparation, the careful lawyer will often compensate by going slow, over-preparing expert rebuttal testimony, or seeking a continuance to prepare in mid-trial, all in derogation of Rule 1's goal of a "just, speedy and inexpensive determination of every action."

Rule 26 originally accommodated these concerns by allowing limited discovery of the testifying expert by interrogatories, with a possibility of discovery by deposition on court order. Because lawyers usually draft the answers to interrogatories, however,[140] this mode of discovery was often insufficient to prepare for the examination of expert witnesses. On the other hand, parties often overcame this problem by agreeing to reciprocal deposition discovery of their expert witnesses.

The 1993 amendment now solves the problem by rule. Rule 26(a)(2) requires parties at least ninety days before trial (or at times directed by the court) to disclose the identity and report the expected testimony of their testifying experts. The required report must include a complete statement of the expert's opinion, as well as the basis and reasons for the opinion, any underlying data and supporting exhibits, the expert's qualifications and publications within the preceding ten years, the expert's compensation, and a listing of other cases in which the expert has testified in the preceding four years. The report, then, is intended to be the functional equivalent of the expert witness's testimony. It also includes precisely the kinds of information needed to cross-examine the witness effectively at trial. Rule 26(b)(4) also allows a party to depose a testifying expert without leave of court after the report is provided. These two discovery devices are expected to work together; a complete report may obviate or at least shorten the deposition of the expert witness.

[3] Retained or Specially Employed Non-Testifying Experts

There is less need for discovering facts known and opinions held by an expert who is not expected to testify at trial, at least when a party can reasonably consult or retain a comparable expert. Rule 26(b)(4) therefore permits discovery by interrogatories or deposition of "retained or specially employed" non-testifying experts only "upon a showing of exceptional circumstances under which it is impracticable for the party seeking discovery to obtain facts or opinions on the same subject by other means." The discoverer can meet this burden by showing that the expert had a unique and irreplicable opportunity to view the scene or to conduct tests relevant to the subject matter,[141] or, more rarely, that the expert is one of a kind.

---

[139] These characteristics of expert testimony are aggravated in federal court by Federal Rule of Evidence 702, which permits an expert to give his opinion without prior disclosure of the underlying facts, contrary to the common law procedure. The opposing party may therefore have to bring out the factual predicate on cross-examination, a procedure with traps for the unprepared.

[140] *See* Rule 26(a)(2) advisory committee's note (1993); § 10.09[2], *infra*.

[141] *See, e.g., Delcastor, Inc. v. Vail Assoc., Inc.*, 108 F.R.D. 405 (D. Colo. 1985) (expert's opinion concerning cause of mudslide is discoverable where he was only expert to have examined mudslide area immediately following the slide).

The mere fact that no other expert will hold precisely the same opinion is insufficient, if comparable experts are practically available to the discoverer.[142] Any court-ordered discovery of such a non-testifying expert is ordinarily conditioned on fee-sharing.[143]

PART B
Mechanics of Discovery

§ 10.07　Required Disclosures and Other General Mechanics

Each of the federal modes of discovery has distinctive characteristics, explored in the succeeding sections. But most discovery also shares several common features, unless exempted by local rule, court order, or party stipulation under Rule 29. The parties [1] must begin the discovery process with a mandatory planning conference, [2] make certain disclosures thereafter without being asked in most cases, and [3] supplement the required disclosures and specified discovery responses at appropriate intervals.

[1]　Mandatory Discovery Conference and Discovery Plans

Rule 29 has long permitted the parties to stipulate to the mechanics of most discovery, partly in the (often forlorn) hope that discovery could proceed cooperatively without a need for judicial intervention. In 1993, Rule 26(f) was amended to require the parties to confer as soon as practicable[144] to discuss the case and possibilities for settlement, to arrange for required disclosures, and to develop a discovery plan incorporating these and other agreements for subsequent discovery. Rule 26(d) forbids them from taking any discovery prior to this conference.[145]

---

[142] *Marine Petroleum Co. v. Champlin Petroleum Co.*, 641 F.2d 984, 996 (D.C. Cir. 1980) (*on pet. for reh'g*) (the rule's reference to the "same subject" is not to the particular expert's testimony itself, but rather to its subject matter).

[143] Rule 26(b)(4)(C).

[144] Tracing the amended rule's circumlocutory statement of timing requirements suggests that parties will ordinarily have to meet within 69 days of the appearance of a defendant or 99 days after the complaint has been served. *See* Rules 16(b) (mandating issuance of discovery scheduling order within ninety days after the appearance of "a" defendant or 120 days after the complaint was served on "a" defendant) and 26(f) (mandating planning conference at least 21 days before a scheduling order is due).

[145] Rule 27, however, permits discovery by deposition even before litigation commences in order to *perpetuate* (preserve) testimony regarding "'any matter that may be cognizable in" (within the subject matter jurisdiction of) a United States court. A person seeking such pre-complaint discovery must establish that the matter would be within the subject matter jurisdiction of a federal court, that he is presently unable for good cause to bring an action in any court, and that there is a substantial danger that the testimony sought would become unavailable before a complaint can be filed. *See, e.g., In re Borland*, 79 F.R.D. 665 (D.D.C. 1978). Generally it is not sufficient reason that he does not know whether a claim exists; pre-action discovery is not intended to be a fishing expedition for a claim. *Id.* at 668 n.3. Rule 27(a) also requires the discoverer to describe the subject matter of the intended action, the facts he seeks to establish and why, and the identities of prospective adverse parties who are entitled to notice of pre-action depositions.

Within fourteen days after the conference, the parties must submit a report of their plan to the court. The rules anticipate that the plan will be incorporated into the scheduling order that the court is required by Rule 16(b) to issue within 120 days after the complaint has been served.

The mandatory conference requirement is clearly intended to require cooperative discovery and thereby reduce the need for subsequent judicial intervention into the discovery process. But in many cases the parties will have to confer while Rule 12 motions to dismiss the complaint are still pending and before any answers have been filed. It is unclear how much a conference in such cases can accomplish towards identifying disputed facts, promoting settlement, or even determining the amount and timing of discovery.

[2] Required Disclosures[146]

The 1993 rule amendments adopted provisions for self-executing discovery of three kinds: initial disclosures of basic information, disclosures of expert testimony (discussed above in section 10.06[2]), and pretrial disclosures of trial evidence. The provisions for required disclosures have teeth: a party who without substantial justification fails to disclose material subject to required disclosure is precluded under Rule 37(c)(1) from using that material as evidence at trial.

[a] Initial Disclosures

Rule 26(a)(1) requires initial disclosure (within fourteen days after the Rule 2b(f) discovery conference) of the basic information needed in most cases to prepare for trial or to assess settlement, except in eight categories of cases which historically involve little or no discovery.[147] This information is usually targeted anyway by discovery requests (if discovery is taken at all). The requirement is intended merely to "accelerate the exchange of basic information" and "eliminate the paper work involved in requesting" it, according to the 1993 Advisory Committee.

Basic information covered by Rule 26(a)(1) includes the identity of possible fact witnesses, and identification of documents in the possession, custody or control of a party, "that the disclosing party may use to support its claim or defenses, unless solely for impeachment." Parties need not actually produce these documents; the purpose of initial disclosure is only

---

[146] *See generally* Huang, *Mandatory Disclosure: A Controversial Device With No Effects*, 21 Pace L. Rev. 203 (2000); Issacharoof & Loewenstein, *Unintended Consequences of Mandatory Disclosure*, 73 Tex. L. Rev. 753 (1995); Bell *et al., Automatic Disclosure in Discovery — the Rush to Reform*, 27 Ga. L. Rev. 1 (1992); Winter, *Forward: In Defense of Discovery Reform*, 58 Brook. L. Rev. 263 (1992); Mengler, *Time for Reform?*, 138 F.R.D. 155 (1991); Mullenix, *Hope Over Experience: Mandatory Informal Discovery and the Politics of Rulemaking*, 69 N.C. L. Rev. 795 (1991); ; Schwarzer, *The Federal Rules, the Adversary Process, and Discovery Reform*, 50 U. Pitt. L. Rev. 703, 721-23 (1989).

[147] Rule 26(a)(1)(E) (including, for example, petitions for habeas corpus, actions to quash administrative subpoenas, and actions by the United States to recover benefit payments or collect student loans).

to identify them to help the parties refine subsequent discovery requests. Moreover, voluminous documents may be identified by category. In short, initial disclosures under Rule 26(a)(1)(A) and (B) are the functional equivalent of responses to interrogatories asking a party to identify witnesses and documents or other tangible things relevant to allegations in the pleadings.[148] Rule 26(a)(1)(C) and (D) require parties also to disclose computations of damages and to produce underlying documents and other evidence, as well as insurance agreements that may be used to satisfy all or part of a judgment which may be entered in the action.

The "use-to-support" relevancy standard for initial disclosures was added by amendment in 2000 to replace the more problematical original standard: "relevant to disputed facts alleged with particularity in the pleadings." The original standard was always somewhat at odds with the liberal "notice pleading" requirements of Rule 8,[149] and also with the usual chronology of litigation, in which it is the answer (often coming after initial disclosures are due) which places pleaded facts in dispute. Moreover, the original standard was also criticized for placing lawyers in an awkward conflict by forcing them to disclose unfavorable information to their adversaries.[150] The new standard alleviates these concerns. The amended rule specifically addresses the timing problem by providing that a party may object that initial disclosures are "inappropriate in the circumstances of the action" and then await the court's ruling before making the disclosures. A party is no longer required to disclose to an adversary unfavorable information that it does not intend to use.[151] This not only reduces any alleged conflict for the disclosing lawyer, it also substantially narrows the scope[152] — and therefore burden — of the initial disclosures.

[b]   Pretrial Disclosures

In addition to the required disclosure of expert witness testimony (discussed in section 10.06[2]), the parties must exchange lists of trial witnesses and trial exhibits at least thirty days before trial. This disclosure includes not only witnesses and exhibits that a party expects to present at trial, but also those that the party may use if the need arises (other than any held in reserve solely for impeachment purposes). Fourteen days after the required exchange, the parties must serve and file any evidentiary objections they have to the materials that have been listed by the opposing parties. Objections not made (other than objections under Federal Rules of Evidence 402 (relevancy) and 403 (prejudice)) are waived.

These exchanges are not really discovery at all; they are more accurately viewed as part of the trial process. Indeed, before the 1993 amendment,

---

[148] Rule 26(a)(1) advisory committee's note (1993).

[149] Rule 9 identifies only a few categories of allegations which must be plead with particularity. *See* § 8.04[4] (discussing special pleading requirements).

[150] *See, e.g., Bell,* note 146, *supra,* at 46 n.175.

[151] Rule 26(a)(1) advisory committee notes (2000). "Use" is not limited to trial; it includes any use at pretrial conferences or to support a motion. *Id.*

[152] Tobias, *Congress and the 2000 Federal Civil Rules Amendments,* 22 Cardozo L. Rev. 75, 79 (2000).

many courts required such exchanges in connection with the final pretrial conference.[153] Such exchanges not only facilitate trial preparation, but also permit *in limine* (at the threshold of trial) rulings on the evidence that help streamline trial.

[c] An Assessment of Required Disclosure

The promulgation in 1993 of provisions for required disclosures of expert witness testimony and of trial witnesses and trial evidence in essence just codified what many federal courts were already doing. These provisions were generally uncontroversial. The requirement for initial disclosures of basic information, however, was new and very controversial. Indeed, Justice Scalia objected to it as "potentially disastrous and certainly premature."[154] Critics argued that it was potentially disastrous for several reasons.

First, they raised the specter of satellite litigation.[155] By tying the disclosure requirement to the specificity of pleading, the rules would "create problems rather than solve them because the attention of lawyers and judges will likely be deflected from the modern use of broad and liberal notice pleading under the federal rules to the archaic and discredited search for the 'supposedly exact pleading' to determine what is discoverable."[156] Justice Scalia therefore concluded that required initial disclosure would

likely *increase* the discovery burdens on district judges, as parties litigate about what is "relevant" to "disputed facts," whether those facts have been alleged with sufficient particularity, whether the opposing side has adequately disclosed the required information, and whether it has fulfilled its continuing obligation to supplement the initial disclosure.[157]

Another critique was that the burden of required disclosure fell unfairly on one side. Some early critics alleged that required disclosure unfairly burdened the plaintiff to the advantage of product liability defendants and other defendants.[158] But many product liability, toxic tort, and securities fraud plaintiffs start litigation on relatively little information beyond the facts of their own injury. The burden of initial disclosure on them may be slight, while "the potential scope of document disclosure that may be required [of a corporate defendant] under such an amorphous standard is virtually unlimited."[159]

---

[153] *See* § 12.03[2] (procedures for pretrial conferences), *infra*.

[154] *Amendments to the Federal Rules of Civil Procedure*, 113 S. Ct. CCC, CCCIX (1993) (dissenting statement of J. Scalia).

[155] *See generally* Sugarman & Perlin, *Proposed Changes to Discovery Rules in Aid of "Tort Reform": Has the Case Been Made?*, 42 Amer. U. L. Rev. 1465 (1993); *Bell*, note 146, *supra*, at 43-45.

[156] *Sugarman & Perlin*, note 155, *supra*, at 1481, *quoting Charbonnier v. Amico*, 324 N.E. 2d 895, 899 (Mass. 1975).

[157] 113 S. Ct. at CCCIX (emphasis in original).

[158] *Sugarman & Perlin*, note 155, *supra*, at 1495; *Mengler*, note 146, *supra*, at 159, 162.

[159] *Bell*, note 146, *supra*, at 39; McMahon & Schwartz, *Analysis of Amendments to the Federal Rules of Civil Procedure As Approved by the Judicial Conference and Forwarded to the Supreme Court* 15 (ALI-ABA 1993).

Third, critics argued that the initial disclosure rule would increase discovery costs, by imposing initial disclosures in cases that would otherwise have little or no discovery, and by adding another costly layer of discovery to cases in which well-heeled parties would pursue specific discovery anyway after such disclosures.[160]

Empirical studies of experience with initial disclosures through 1997 refute the first critique. The rule generated surprisingly little satellite litigation.[161] A majority of defendants' and plaintiffs' lawyers alike also reported that the rule had no perceived effect on the length of cases, fairness of outcome, or prospects for settlement.[162] Their shared perceptions do not support the critique that initial disclosures would favor one side or the other. Moreover, the empirical evidence suggests that initial disclosures had little or no effect on costs or time spent in litigation.[163] On the other hand, one study did report that in 89% of the cases in which initial disclosure was made, further discovery took place — "disclosure infrequently replace[d] discovery entirely."[164] Thus, although initial disclosure apparently did not increase discovery costs, it did not reduce them either or avoid later, discretionary discovery.

If these findings are accurate, they raise the question why the rulemakers did not just drop initial disclosures in 2000, instead of refining them? One commentator has suggested that the Advisory Committee acknowledged the rule's minimal effect, "but . . . evinced reluctance to abandon the mechanism altogether and attempted to maintain a vestige of the notion."[165] A better answer may be that even if only a minority of lawyers (39%) reported that initial disclosures decreased overall expenses,[166] this result was enough to justify retaining the rule, especially if its costs are reduced by categorically exempting certain proceedings which usually lack discovery, and by narrowing the scope of disclosure to materials which will be used to support a claim or defense. Unless the latter change fosters satellite litigation, in short, the amended Rule 26(a)(1) may reduce discovery costs in a minority of cases while doing no harm in most of the rest.

---

[160] See, e.g., id., at 40, 45; 113 S. Ct. at CCCIX (dissenting statement of J. Scalia). Some critics add that the frontloading of discovery costs may actually impede settlement by giving the parties too great an investment in continuing the litigation. See Issacharoff & Loewenstein, note 146, supra, at 786; Cure, Practical Issues Concerning Arizona's New Rules of Civil Procedure: A Defense Perspective, 25 Ariz. St. L.J. 55, 57 (1993).

[161] Kakalik et al., Rand Institute for Civil Justice, Discovery Management: Further Analysis of the Civil Justice Reform Act Evaluation Data, 39 B.C. L. Rev. 613, 658 (1998) (hereinafter "Rand Report"); Willging et al., Federal Judicial Center, An Empirical Study of Discovery and Disclosure Practice Under the 1993 Federal Rule Amendments, 39 B.C. L. Rev. 525, 535 (1998) (hereinafter "FJC Survey").

[162] FJC Survey, note 161, supra, at 563.

[163] Rand Report, note 161, supra, at 658-661; FJC Survey, note 161, supra, at 563; Huang, supra, note 146, at 263. The FJC Survey did find that of the minority of lawyers who reported that initial disclosures had affected litigation, most thought the effects were positive. See FJC Survey, note 161, at 237 (explaining FJC data).

[164] FJC Survey, note 161, supra, at 559.

[165] Tobias, note 152, supra, at 82.

[166] FJC Survey, note 161, supra at 563.

[3] Supplementation of Discovery

The typical litigator has several cases pending at the same time. In each there may be substantial discovery. The burden of continuously reviewing old discovery responses for accuracy and updating them whenever new information becomes available would be great. On the other hand, a failure to supplement an incorrect, misleading or obsolete discovery response may give rise to the very surprise at trial that discovery was intended partly to avoid.

Rule 26(e) originally struck a compromise between these two concerns by imposing a quite limited duty of supplementation on party-discoverees. That compromise was partly undone by the 1993 rule amendments, which require a party to correct or complete its required disclosures (as well as any deposition given by its expert witness), if the additional or corrective information has not already been made known to other parties. This expanded duty to supplement is as broad as the scope of required disclosures. It obligates a lawyer to keep track of all information that might make previous disclosures incomplete or incorrect in any respect.

Rule 26(c) extends the same duty to prior responses to an interrogatory, request for production, or request for admission. The lawyer must therefore also monitor the completeness and correctness of such responses throughout the lawsuit. Only responses given in deposition (except depositions by expert witnesses) are exempted, presumably on the theory that these are often given by non-party witnesses and that monitoring them would be extremely burdensome, if not impossible.

Ordinarily, only incurably prejudicial breaches of the rule will support sanctions or constitute grounds for relief from judgment.[167] A common sanction for breach of the duty to supplement is exclusion at trial of evidence withheld by the discoveree.[168] This sanction is inappropriate, however, if a continuance and opportunity for mid-trial discovery can enable the discoverer to overcome his surprise and prepare effective cross-examination and rebuttal.[169]

---

[167] *See, e.g., Johnson v. H.K. Webster, Inc.*, 775 F.2d 1, 7-8 (1st Cir. 1985). For discussion of the rule of prejudicial error, see § 13.08[1], *infra.*

[168] *See, e.g., Scott & Fetzer Co. v. Dile*, 643 F.2d 670 (9th Cir. 1981) (failure to list 20 of 23 trial witnesses and 26 of 51 exhibits in response to interrogatories prejudicially denied the discoverer the right to prepare effective cross-examination and rebuttal and requires their exclusion, especially where the undisclosed witnesses included an expert witness and were used to support a previously undisclosed theory of the case).

[169] *See, e.g., Moore v. Boating Ind. Assoc.*, 754 F.2d 698 (7th Cir. 1985); *Lewis Refrig. Co. v. Sawyer Fruit, Veg. & Cold Storage Co.*, 709 F.2d 427 (6th Cir. 1983); *Gebhard v. Niedzwiecki*, 122 N.W.2d 110 (Minn. 1963) (suggesting that preclusion is proper when the violation is wilful and the discoveree seeks to benefit from it "at a time when the harm cannot be undone").

§ 10.08   Depositions

[1]   Procedure for Taking

A deposition is the recorded examination of a live witness under oath by oral or written questions before a qualified oath administrator,[170] who is usually a court reporter.[171] The deposition may be recorded by sound, sound-and-visual, or stenographic means at the expense of the taker. In a Rule 30 deposition upon oral questions, an attorney asks the questions and the deponent answers spontaneously, like an examination of a witness at trial. In a Rule 31(a) deposition upon written questions, the discoverer serves his direct questions on the deponent and the other parties in advance, after which any cross, redirect or recross questions[172] are served. The oath administrator reads the written questions to the deponent, who answers them live, if not quite spontaneously (given the prior opportunity to rehearse the answers). Interrogatories differ from the deposition upon written questions partly in that answers to interrogatories are written and often prepared by a party's attorney.[173]

A party does not ordinarily need leave of court to take a deposition unless the deposition would exceed the seven-hour durational limit set by Rule 30(d)(2) or the ten-deposition numerical limit established by Rule 30(a)(2)(A). The procedure for orally deposing a party under Rule 30 is simply to serve the deponent and parties reasonable written notice of the time and place of the deposition and identity of the deponent,[174] as well as a Rule 34 request for production of documents when documents are sought in connection with the deposition.[175] A party must comply with the notice or seek a protective order[176] because, by the initial service of process on her, she has already been subjected to the personal jurisdiction of the court and therefore brought within the reach of properly invoked procedural rules.

This is not true of a non-party witness, however. To compel the attendance at deposition of a non-party witness, the discoverer must first procure

---

[170] *See* Rule 28 (persons before whom depositions may be taken).

[171] Depositions traditionally have been recorded by a court reporter. The 1993 rule amendments liberalized the requirements for taking of depositions by non-stenographic means. *See* Rules 30(b)(2)-(4). The parties no longer need to agree to non-stenographic means or obtain a court order; such means are available *unless* the court orders otherwise. Parties must still stipulate to or obtain a court order for taking depositions by telephone or other remote electronic means. *See* Rule 30(b)(7).

[172] Direct examination is a party's questioning of his own witness. Cross-examination is questioning of a witness called by an opposing party. Redirect is direct examination of a witness after cross-examination. Recross is cross-examination of a witness after redirect. *See generally* *McCormick on Evidence* § 4 (J. Strong, 4th ed. 1992).

[173] See § 10.09 (interrogatories), *infra*.

[174] Rule 30 (b)(1). The notice must be accompanied by the direct questions in the case of a deposition upon written questions. Rule 31(a).

[175] Rule 30(b)(5).

[176] See § 10.13[3] (protective orders), *infra*.

the issuance of a *subpoena*[177] from the court for the district in which the deposition will be taken.[178] The non-party witness may ask the court to quash or modify the subpoena if it allows insufficient time for compliance, necessitates excessive travel, requires disclosure of protected or confidential information, or subjects the witness to undue burden.[179]

Under Rule 30(b)(6), a party may name as a deponent in his notice and subpoena a corporation, agency, partnership or other legal entity and describe the matters on which examination is requested. The entity must then designate one or more officers, directors, managing agents or other persons with relevant knowledge to testify on its behalf. As noted below[180] the deposition of a person so designated may be offered at trial as direct evidence against the designating entity. Rule 30(b)(6)'s legislative history suggests that it was intended simply as a device to facilitate the discovery of appropriate witnesses who could provide further discovery regarding an institutional litigant, in order "to defeat a shield of obfuscation and inefficiency that could be thrown up by . . . [such a] litigant."[181] Instead, it has sometimes been misused to force such litigants to create a witness who can give a "grand synthesis" of evidence to bind the litigant.[182]

The chief difference between the conduct of a deposition upon oral questions and examination of a witness at trial is the absence of the trial judge. Consequently, objections to the competency of the witness or to the competency, relevancy, or materiality of testimony are preserved until trial, when the judge can rule upon them. Rule 32(d)(3)(A) expressly states that they are not waived by a failure to make them at the deposition. In contrast, objections to errors which "might be obviated, removed, or cured if promptly presented" are waived if not seasonably made before or during the deposition.[183] These include objections to the qualifications of the presiding officer, to errors and irregularities in the notice, to the manner of taking the deposition, oath or affirmation, to the conduct of the parties, or to the form of the questions. For example, "when did you stop beating your wife [or husband]?" is objectionable as to form, for it assumes a predicate. But the objection could be obviated by reforming the question as several separate questions: "Did you beat your wife [husband]?; [if yes] did you stop?; [if yes] when?"[184] If the objecting party could defer the objection to this question until the deposition is offered at trial, it could deprive the examiner of an opportunity to reform the question.

---

[177] *See* Rule 45. A *subpoena duces tecum* must be used if document production is sought in connection with the deposition.

[178] Rules 30(a) & 45. Many states provide for the issuance of subpoenas for depositions to be used in proceedings pending in other states. *See e.g.*, Ariz. R. Civ. Proc. 30(h) (WESTLAW 2001); Me. R. Civ. Proc. 30(h) (WESTLAW 2001).

[179] Rule 45(c)(3).

[180] *See* § 10.08[2] (use and value of depositions), *infra*.

[181] Sinclair & Fendrich, *Discovering Corporate Knowledge and Contentions: Rethinking Rule 30(b)(6) and Alternative Mechanisms*, 50 Ala. L. Rev. 651 (1999).

[182] *Id.*

[183] Rules 32(d)(2) & (3)(B).

[184] *See generally McCormick on Evidence*, note 172, *supra*, at §§ 5-7.

Despite the preservation of most objections until the proffer of deposition testimony as evidence at trial, some lawyers make them anyway, not only to create a technically unnecessary record, but sometimes also to educate the witness or obstruct the examination. Indeed, some lawyers instruct the witness not to answer questions that do not call for privileged information, in effect daring the examiner to halt the deposition to seek judicial assistance. The 1993 amendment to Rule 30(d) now discourages both tactics by requiring objections to be made concisely and in a "non-argumentative and non-suggestive manner," and by forbidding instructions not to answer except when necessary to preserve a privilege, comply with a court order, or to present a motion to limit or terminate the deposition.[185] Rule 32(d)(3) authorizes a court to grant such a motion upon a showing that the examination is being conducted oppressively or in bad faith.

The amended rule does not deal directly with a similar deposition tactic: mid-deposition coaching of deponents in private lawyer-client discussions. Some courts, however, are inferring authority from the rules to combat this tactic.[186] Complaining that "[t]he witness comes to the deposition to testify, not to indulge in a parody of Charlie McCarthy, with lawyers coaching or bending the witness's words to mold a convenient record," one court has prohibited private lawyer-client discussions during depositions and deposition recesses, except for the limited purpose of deciding whether to assert a privilege.[187] This court's order, like amended Rule 30(d)(1), reflects the proposition that "[i]n general, counsel should not engage in any conduct during a deposition that would not be allowed in the presence of a judicial officer."[188]

At the completion of the deposition, a transcript of the recorded examination may be prepared by a court reporter or by any party, according to Rule 30(e). On request by the deponent or a party, the transcript is submitted to the deponent for correction and signature. The presiding officer is then responsible for sealing the deposition with her certificate and filing it in the court in which the action is pending or sending it to the lawyer who noticed the deposition, along with the originals or copies of any documents marked for identification during the deposition.[189]

---

[185] Rule 30(d)(1).

[186] On deposition ethics generally, see Darby, *The Law and Ethics of Civil Depositions*, 57 Md. L. Rev. 273 (1998); Kerper & Stuart, *Rambo Bites the Dust: Current Trends in Deposition Ethics*, 22 J. Legal Prof. 103 (1997-1998); Cary, *Rambo Depositions: Controlling an Ethical Cancer in Civil Litigation*, 25 Hofstra L. Rev. 561 (1996). Some jurisdictions have adopted voluntary "civility codes" to deal with this and related problems of "Rambo" tactics in civil litigation, *see, e.g., D.C. Bar Voluntary Standards for Civility in Professional Conduct* (1997), but there is yet little evidence that they have changed the adversarial dynamics which seem to breed such tactics.

[187] *Hall v. Clifton Precision*, 150 F.R.D. 525, 528 (E.D. Pa. 1993).

[188] Rule 26(d) advisory committee's note (1993).

[189] Rule 30(f).

[2]   Use and Value of Depositions

Under Rule 32(a) any or all of a deposition may be used at trial, as if the witness were then present and testifying against any party who had notice of the deposition and a reasonable opportunity to obtain counsel or to move for a protective order. The proponent of the deposition testimony may offer it in stenographic form, or in nonstenographic form if he also provides the court and the parties with a transcript. Indeed, Rule 32(c) allows any party to a jury trial to demand that deposition testimony offered as substantive evidence be presented in nonstenographic form, when it is available. When a party offers only part of a deposition in evidence, she designates the relevant part and submits it to the judge in a bench trial or causes it to be read or played to the jury in a jury trial. Under Rule 32(a)(4), an adverse party may require the proponent to introduce additional parts "which ought in fairness to be considered with the part introduced."

Hearsay is an out-of-court statement offered in evidence to prove the truth of the matter stated.[190] The rule against the admissibility of hearsay would thus appear to prohibit the offer of deposition testimony at trial unless it falls within one of the rule's many exceptions. By providing that the deposition is to be tested for admissibility as if it were given live, however, Rule 32(a) is itself an exception to the rule against hearsay.[191] The rule echoes the Federal Rules of Evidence by permitting the use of deposition testimony to impeach or contradict the deponent as a witness,[192] or as an admission of a adverse party or officer, director, managing agent or designated deponent of an adverse party.[193] In addition, Rule 32(a) permits the use of deposition testimony at trial when the deponent is unavailable because of death, illness, age, imprisonment or is beyond the reach of process.

However, Rule 32 only overcomes the initial hearsay hurdle to the use of a deposition. The rules of evidence still apply to admission of its contents.

Speaking metaphorically, a deposition is like a box that contains certain evidence. The court must make two determinations. The first is a procedural one: whether to admit the box itself into the trial. In making this assessment, the court applies . . . [Rule 32 or its state equivalent]. Once the court has decided that the deposition meets these procedural requirements, the court then must address the ancillary evidentiary issues such as whether the contents of the box qualifies as admissible

---

[190] Fed. R. Evid. 801(c).

[191] *Wright* § 84.

[192] *Compare* Rule 32(a)(1) *with* Fed. R. Evid. 801(d)(1) (prior inconsistent statement is not hearsay).

[193] *Compare* Rule 32(a)(2) *with* Fed. R. Evid. 801(d)(2) (admission by party-opponent is not hearsay). Who is a managing agent for purposes of this provision is decided pragmatically, depending on the scope of the deponent's job responsibilities, assigned discretion and identification with an employer's interests. *See generally* R. Haydock & D. Herr, *Discovery Practice* § 3.10.1 (3d ed. 1996); *cf.* Massey, *Depositions of Corporations: Problems and Solutions — Fed. R. Civ. P. 30(b)(6)*, 1986 Ariz. St. L.J. 81.

evidence. This step is akin to opening the box, assessing its content and then ruling on its admissibility.[194]

The availability of a deposition in lieu of live testimony helps to make it the most valuable method of discovery. So does its flexibility. The contemporaneity of the examination upon oral questions permits the discoverer to frame follow-up questions, pursue new and unanticipated leads, observe demeanor, and pin down witnesses in order to foreclose factual arguments or at least lay a foundation for later impeachment.[195] Finally, the deposition usually is the only method of discovery available against non-party witnesses to elicit testimonial evidence.[196]

On the other hand, the chief drawback of depositions is their expense. Not only do they consume enormous amounts of attorney time in preparation, travel and taking, but court reporter fees and travel expenses can also mount quickly, putting extensive deposition discovery beyond the reach of many litigants. In addition, a deposition can educate the deponent, provide a useful rehearsal of examination at trial for the deponent and opposing parties, and of course, elicit and perpetuate unhelpful testimony.[197] On balance, however, almost all practitioners would agree that these drawbacks of deposition discovery are outweighed by its advantages.

§ 10.09 Interrogatories

[1] Procedure for Asking

Interrogatories are written questions directed to a party, who must answer them in writing and under oath, or (by his attorney) object with particularity. Although the client often supplies all or part of the underlying facts, his attorney usually prepares both the answers and the objections. If the objection is to the entire set of interrogatories on grounds of undue burden, it can also be made by a motion for a protective order under Rule 26(c).[198] The mere burden of preparing answers is not ordinarily a valid objection to interrogatories, however.[199]

Interrogatories target not just what is known by the discoveree, but also what is reasonably obtainable by him — "the collective knowledge" of the recipient.[200] "A party is charged with knowledge of what his agents know, or what is in records available to him, or even, for purposes of Rule 33,

---

[194] *Shives v. Furst*, 521 A.2d 332, 335-336 (Md. Ct. Spec. App. 1987).

[195] *See generally Haydock & Herr*, note 193, *supra*, § 3.1.1; *Hall v. Clifton Precision*, 150 F.R.D. 525, 528 (E.D. Pa. 1993) (noting that depositions serve the purpose of "the memorialization, the freezing of a witness's testimony at an early stage of the proceedings").

[196] A subpoena can be used to require a non-party witness to produce documents for inspection. *See* Rule 45.

[197] *See generally Haydock & Herr*, note 193, *supra*, § 3.1.2.

[198] *Moore* § 33.175.

[199] *Id.* § 33.173[3].

[200] R. Haydock & D. Herr, *Discovery Practice* § 4.6.1 (3d ed. 1996).

what others have told him on which he intends to rely in his suit."[201] Even if a duty of reasonable inquiry was not already implicit in Rule 33, it is now explicit in Rule 26(g)'s certification requirement for discovery responses and objections.[202]

On the other hand, interrogatories do not require the discoveree to do the discoverer's work for him by undertaking elaborate investigations, discovery and data compilation.[203] The standard is reasonableness under the circumstances. Moreover, when the answer to an interrogatory can be ascertained from the discoveree's business records as easily by the discoverer as by the discoveree, the latter has the option under Rule 33(c) of specifying the relevant records and making them available in lieu of answer. The specification requirement precludes the tactic of referring the discoverer to an undifferentiated haystack of records in which the needle may be buried.

There are no special limitations on the form or subject of interrogatories apart from the generic limitations of Rule 26(b). But under Rule 33(b) a court may postpone the time for answering *contention interrogatories*[204] which require the discoveree to apply the law to the facts (e.g., "Do you contend that the plaintiff assumed the risk of the collision?"), because he may not know what his contentions will be until completion of discovery or a late pre-trial conference.[205] Were the rule otherwise, the discoveree might be forced into a premature statement of what his legal contentions *will be*, evoking shades of the now-discarded theory of the pleadings.[206] In contrast, requiring the party after discovery and on the eve of trial to state what his contentions *are* is not only fairer but conducive to issue-narrowing and surprise-avoidance at trial. Indeed, the parties are sometimes required to exchange their contentions in pre-trial briefs anyway,[207] whether or not contention interrogatories are pending.

The 1970 Advisory Committee concluded that interrogatories had generated a greater percentage of objections and motions than any other discovery method. Probably the most common objection is that they are *unduly burdensome*. The reason for the frequency of this objection is obvious. The discoveree is ordinarily inclined to read interrogatories narrowly and against their drafter. Knowing this, and not sure what information is out there, the discoverer drafts numerous and sweeping interrogatories to defeat narrow constructions. As a result, the undue burden often used to

---

[201] *Wright* § 86. *See, e.g., Brunswick Corp. v. Suzuki Motor Co.*, 38 Fed. R. Serv. 2d (Callaghan) 1246, 1248 (E.D. Wis. 1983); *Riley v. United Air Lines, Inc.*, 32 F.R.D. 230, 233 (S.D.N.Y. 1962). Rule 26(b)'s limits on the scope of discovery still apply, including the qualified immunity for work product. *See* § 10.05, *supra*.

[202] *See* § 10.13[1] (certification), *infra*.

[203] *See, e.g., La Chemise Lacoste v. The Alligator Co.*, 60 F.R.D. 164 (D. Del. 1973).

[204] *See In re Convergent Technologies Securities Litig.*, 108 F.R.D. 328, 332 (N.D. Cal. 1985) (defining different kinds of contention interrogatories).

[205] *Id.* at 333-334.

[206] *See* § 8.03[2] (theory of pleadings), *supra*.

[207] *See* § 12.03[1] (pretrial), *infra*.

lie simply in the great number of the interrogatories. The burden may be aggravated by indiscriminate use of *pattern* or *form interrogatories* — standardized, form-book interrogatories for particular kinds of cases [208] — and by multiplication of interrogatories by means of elaborate definitions. Overbreadth is also a common ground for an undue burden objection. Yet a litany of terms like "overly broad, burdensome, oppressive and irrelevant" does not satisfy Rule 33(a)'s requirement that the grounds for the objection be stated with specificity. The discoveree should specify by affidavit his claim of undue burden. [209]

The 1993 amendments to the discovery rules were intended to reduce the need for and abuse of interrogatory practice. "Because Rule 26(a)(1)-(3) requires disclosure of much of the information previously obtained by [interrogatories]," the 1993 Advisory Committee reasoned, "there should be less occasion to use [them]." In addition, a party may now ask no more than twenty-five interrogatories (including all discrete subparts) without leave of court. [210] Finally, Rule 33(b) now requires a party not only to state the grounds for objections with specificity, but to "answer to the extent the interrogatory is not objectionable."

[2]   Use and Value of Interrogatories

Rule 33(b) provides that answers to interrogatories may be used to the extent permitted by the rules of evidence. They can therefore usually be used against the discoveree as a party admission, but not by him as substantive evidence. They do not ordinarily bind or limit proof by the discoveree, who may depart from them, modify them, or attempt to explain them away at trial. [211] But in the exceptional case of the discoverer's reasonable and detrimental reliance on the answers, the courts have used concepts of estoppel or preclusion to give greater effect to interrogatory answers. [212]

---

[208] *See, e.g. Robbins v. Camden City Bd. of Educ.*, 105 F.R.D. 49 (D.N.J. 1985) (259 interrogatories were repetitious and objectionable as a result of discoverer's nonspecific use of several sets of pattern interrogatories); *Blank v. Ronson Corp.*, 97 F.R.D. 774, 745 (S.D.N.Y. 1983) (sanctions may be appropriate when interrogatories have been produced by "some word-processing machine's memory of prior litigation"). There is nothing wrong with the discriminating use of pattern interrogatories as long as they are tailored to the facts of the particular case. *See Haydock & Herr*, note 200, *supra*, §4.4.4.

[209] *See, e.g., Roesberg v. Johns-Manville Corp.*, 28 Fed. R. Serv. 2d (Callaghan) 1170 (E.D. Pa. 1980); *In re Folding Carton Antitrust Litig.*, 83 F.R.D. 260, 264 (N.D. Ill. 1979).

[210] Rule 33(a). How much this numerical limitation will reduce litigation about interrogatories is unclear. In the past such numerical limits have generated arid controversies about how multi-part interrogatories should count towards the limit. The Advisory Committee tried to anticipate this problem by noting that "a question asking about communications of a particular type should be treated as a single interrogatory even though it requests that the time, place, persons present, and contents be stated separately for each such communication."

[211] Rule 33(b) advisory committee's note (1970).

[212] *See generally Moore* § 37.96. *Cf., e.g., Zielinski v. Philadelphia Piers, Inc.*, 139 F. Supp. 408 (E.D. Pa. 1956) (relying on estoppel-type theory to preclude defendant from introducing evidence on an issue as to which plaintiff was misled by defendant's interrogatory answers), discussed in § 8.08[1], *supra*.

The chief appeal of discovery by interrogatories is that they are a cheap way to access the collective knowledge of a party. Some have called them the poor man's deposition. For two reasons, however, this tag is unwarranted. First, their economy is one-sided and therefore often only temporary. It is cheap for the discoverer to prepare a set of interrogatories, but can be time-consuming and thus expensive for the attorney for the discoveree to draft answers to them. Once reciprocal discovery by interrogatories is initiated, these costs are reversed. Second, the attorney will often find some colorable objection to the most difficult interrogatories or draft answers that are as unhelpful as he can make them. Consequently, a federal judge has described interrogatories as "useless because any lawyer who can't answer interrogatories without giving [an] opponent useful information is not worth his salt."[213]

This critique is exaggerated. The attorney's role in drafting answers will usually make interrogatories ineffective to discover subjective and interpretative information, including state of mind, or complex information that will require explanation.[214] On the other hand, well-drafted interrogatories can be effectively used to pinpoint the existence and location of witnesses and evidence not already disclosed pursuant to Rule 26(a), to make more specific the factual basis for pleading allegations, and (towards the end of the discovery period) to narrow the issues.

§ 10.10 Production and Entry Requests

[1] Procedure for Making

Rule 34(a) authorizes the discoverer to request that a party produce and permit the inspection and copying of documents, or the copying, testing or sampling of things, or entry upon land. A request must designate the documents, things or land with reasonable particularity and specify the time, place and manner of production or entry.[215] At the specified time and place, the discoveree must either permit inspection or entry, or object by item, specifying her grounds. A mere "litany of . . . boilerplate objections," however, is insufficient because it fails to show specifically how a discovery request is burdensome or oppressive by affidavit or other evidence substantiating the objections.[216]

A Rule 34 production request embraces not only that which is in the possession of the discoveree but also documents and property within her custody or control.[217] *Control* means that the discoveree has a legal right

---

[213] Quoted in Brazil, *View From the Front Line: Observations By Chicago Lawyers About the System of Civil Discovery*, 1980 A.B. Found. Res. J. 217, 233. *See also In re Convergent Technologies Securities Litig.*, 108 F.R.D. 328, 338 (N.D. Cal. 1985).

[214] *Haydock & Herr*, note 200, *supra*, at § 4.6

[215] *See* Official Form 24.

[216] *See, e.g., St. Paul Reinsurance Co., Ltd. v. Commercial Finan. Corp.*, 198 F.R.D. 508 (N.D. Iowa 2000) (imposing Rule 26(g) sanction for such objections, by requiring objecting lawyer to write and submit for publication an article explaining why they were improper!).

[217] *See, e.g., Weck v. Cross*, 88 F.R.D. 324 (N.D. Ill. 1980). *See generally* Note, *Meaning of "Control" in F.R.C.P. 34*, 107 U. Pa. L. Rev. 103 (1958).

to the document or thing or to enter upon the land.[218] The discoveree cannot avoid production by giving possession of a document or thing to an agent, such as her attorney. The rule thus embraces items in the actual or constructive possession of the discoveree, whether or not she owns them.

The requested documents or things must be described with sufficient clarity for a party of ordinary intelligence to understand what is meant and for the court to determine whether the items have been produced.[219] This task is now made substantially easier by the disclosures required by Rule 26(a).[220] The 1993 Advisory Committee reasoned that these required disclosures will enable parties to "frame their document requests in a manner likely to avoid squabbles resulting from the wording of the requests." Rule 34(b) expressly permits designation of items by category. The practice is to arrange categories by subject matter and to cross-reference all documents identified by required disclosures or in answers to any prior interrogatories. The discoveree should ordinarily produce or object in kind, by item or category, but the practice is often to produce documents *en masse*. The 1980 amendment to Rule 33(b) prohibited the deliberate burial of potentially useful documents among the undifferentiated mass by requiring the discoveree to produce documents "as they are kept in the usual course of business" or by the categories of the request.

Requests for production of electronic information have raised a host of unresolved issues under Rule 34. Electronic data in raw binary form is useless; must the producing party also produce its code for interpreting that data? Rule 34's reference to "translation . . . by the respondent through detection devices into reasonably usable form" suggests an affirmative answer, but production of codes may raise trade secret issues calling for protective orders from the court. Can the producing party simply produce the electronic data in hard copy form, denying the requesting party the ability to manipulate the data without, at least, incurring the burden of manually inputting the hard copy data back into electronic form? The cases are divided,[221] but the answer may enormously impact the expense of discovery. They are also not consistent about the allocation of that expense.[222] These, and other issues emerging from the discovery of electronic information, are beyond the scope of this treatise, but they appear to be sufficiently serious as to call for an overhaul of Rule 34, if not other anachronistically document-oriented discovery rules, in the near future.

---

[218] *See Searock v. Stripling*, 736 F.2d 650, 653-654 (11th Cir. 1984).

[219] *See In re Hunter Prod., Inc.*, 21 Bankr. 188 (Bankr. D. Mass. 1982) (specification inadequate when it requires discoveree to form subjective opinion in order to determine what is requested). *See generally* R. Haydock & D. Herr, *Discovery Practice* § 5.8 (3d ed. 1996).

[220] *See* § 10.07[2], *supra*.

[221] *Compare Anti-Monopoly v. Hasbro, Inc.*, 1995 WL 649934 (S.D.N.Y. 1995) (allowing discovery of data in computerized form even though respondent had already produced hard copy) *with Williams v. Owens-Illinois, Inc.*, 665 F.2d 918 (9th Cir. 1982) (denying discovery of computerized data even though using the hard copy would be more time-consuming and expensive for the requesting party). *See generally* Scheindlin & Rabkin, note 59, *supra* at 352-356 (2000).

[222] *See Scheindlin & Rabkin*, note 221, *supra*, at 356-361.

Production requests and requests for entry upon land may be directed only to parties. But Rule 45 allows the issuance of subpoenas for document production by non-parties. Prior to the amendment of this rule in 1991, the primary method of obtaining documents from non-parties was deposing the custodian of the documents. This cumbersome technique is no longer necessary; a subpoena to compel production of documents by a non-party independent of any deposition is now essentially the equivalent of a Rule 34 request for production of documents by a party. The chief differences lie in the geographic reach of such subpoenas (limited to places within the district of the issuing court, within 100 miles of the place of production or inspection therein, or a place allowed by relevant state or federal statute or state court rule)[223] and in the procedure for objecting to a subpoena (motions to quash or modify).[224]

[2] Use and Value of Production and Entry Requests

The fruits of production and entry requests can be used at trial subject to the rules of evidence. The practice is often to procure the discoveree's agreement at the time of production to the use of copies in lieu of the originals at trial, obviating one evidentiary objection.

The document production request is the most frequently used discovery device, as well as one which generates a high percentage of discovery problems.[225] Production requests are widely used as a step in discovery prior to depositions. They can be highly productive relative to their cost, although, like interrogatories, they generate a large number of undue burden objections. In addition, document production requests frequently provoke objections of attorney-client privilege and work product immunity, leading to motions to compel and attendant hearings with occasional *in camera* inspection of the disputed documents by a judge or magistrate.

§ 10.11 Physical and Mental Examinations

[1] Procedure for Taking

When the physical or mental condition of a party (or person in the custody or legal control of a party) is in controversy, a court may on motion and for good cause shown order her to undergo a physical or mental examination under Rule 35. Together with Rule 27 (prelitigation deposition), discovery that exceeds the numerical limits on depositions or interrogatories, and discovery under matter going beyond claims or defenses, this discovery

---

[223] Rule 45(b) & (c)(3)(B)(iii).

[224] Rule 45(c). Of course, a person responding to a subpoena may withhold a document on a claim of privilege or work product, provided that the claim is made expressly and with sufficient foundation to enable the discoverer to contest the claim. Rule 45(d)(2).

[225] Willging et al., *An Empirical Study of Discovery and Disclosure Practice Under the 1993 Federal Rule Amendments*, 39 B.C. L. Rev. 525, 554 (1998) (reporting that higher percentage of lawyers reported problems in document discovery than in initial disclosures, expert disclosure, or depositions).

method requires a court order and a showing of good cause. These requirements and the limitation of examinations to conditions in controversy
reflect the strong privacy interest counterbalancing this form of discovery.[226] The same privacy interest is reflected in Rule 37(b)(2)(D), which
makes contempt of court available for disobedience of any discovery order
except a Rule 35 order. Similar concerns have created considerable variety
among the states in their rules for discovery by physical or mental examination.[227]

Rule 35(a) limits persons who are subject to discovery by examination
to parties or persons in their *custody or legal control*.[228] In light of the
privacy concern, the legal control limitation of Rule 35(a) has been read
much more narrowly than the roughly comparable provision of Rule 34 for
requests for production and entry. Minor children are in the custody of their
parents for purposes of examination when the parents sue for injuries to
their children.[229] It is less clear whether a wife is within the legal control
of her husband when he sues for injuries to her.[230] But a party's agent,
such as a driver/employee in a personal injury action arising from a traffic
accident, is usually not within the party's legal control.[231]

The showing that the condition is in controversy must establish more
than relevancy. The condition is usually put in controversy by the pleadings. A complaint to recover for personal injuries is the classic illustration,
putting in controversy the related condition of the plaintiff. But the
requisite controversy is also shown when the condition contributes to the
accident, bears on performance of a contract or other obligation, is the
subject of an alleged libel to which truth is asserted as a defense, or is
asserted as a defense of incompetency.[232]

The Supreme Court decision in *Schlagenhauf v. Holder*[233] illustrates the
in-controversy requirement and how it is satisfied. In a complicated
personal injury litigation arising out of a bus and truck collision, the
defendant truck owners cross-claimed against the defendant bus company

---

[226] The Supreme Court has ruled that these interests do not make Rule 35 "substantive"
for purposes of compliance with the Rules Enabling Act. *Sibbach v. Wilson & Co.*, 312 U.S.
1 (1941). *See* § 7.04[2] (state law and federal rules of civil procedure), *supra*.

[227] *See, e.g.*, Cal. Civ. Proc. Code § 2032 (WESTLAW 2001) (expressly includes agents of
a party, unlike Rule 35); Md. R. Civ. Proc. R. 2-423 (1993) (providing that court order may
regulate filing and distribution of examination findings and examiner's testimony at trial
instead of federal rule of reciprocity discussed *infra*).

[228] When the examinee is a non-party in the custody or legal control of a party, the order
actually issues to the party, who is merely obligated to use good faith efforts to produce the
attendance of the examinee at the examination. Rule 35(a) advisory committee's note (1970).

[229] *See Wright & Miller* § 2233.

[230] *Id.* (concluding that she is).

[231] Although some commentators have argued the contrary, see R. Haydock & D. Herr,
Discovery Practice § 6.2.1 (3d ed. 1996), the legislative history of Rule 35 suggests that agents
are not within its scope. *See Schlagenhauf v. Holder*, 379 U.S. 104, 115 n.12 (1964). In many
cases involving agents, however, the discoverer can avail himself of the rule by naming the
agent as a defendant.

[232] *See, e.g.*, cases cited in *Moore* § 35.03; *Wright & Miller* § 2232.

[233] 379 U.S. 104 (1964).

and its driver. The truck owner alleged that the bus company knew that its driver's eyes and vision were impaired. The truck owner's attorney filed an affidavit stating that the bus driver had seen red lights for ten to fifteen seconds before the accident and had been involved in a prior accident. On these allegations, the district court ordered a battery of physical, visual and mental examinations. The court of appeals denied a petition for a writ of mandamus[234] against the trial judge.

On *certiorari*, the Supreme Court emphasized that the requirements of Rule 35(a) "are not met by mere conclusory allegations of the pleadings . . . but require an affirmative showing by the movant."[235] Applying this principle, the Court found that nothing in the pleadings or the affidavit showed that the bus driver's general physical or mental condition was in controversy.[236] The Court suggested that the allegation in the cross-claim that the bus driver's eyes and vision were impaired, in conjunction with the affidavit, might have supported the eye examination had one been ordered alone. But it nevertheless vacated the eye examination order, too, in light of the necessity for remanding the case anyway for reconsideration of the other orders.

Weighing the in-controversy and good cause requirements, the Court noted that "the ability of the movant to obtain the desired information by other means is also relevant."[237] Accordingly, courts have analogized *good cause* to the undue hardship requirement for overcoming the qualified immunity of work product under Rule 26(b)(3), and thus measured it by the reasonable availability of the information from other sources.[238] In *Crider v. Sneider*,[239] for example, a defendant's loss of recollection due to traumatic amnesia did not establish good cause for a physical examination under a state discovery rule like Rule 35 because information about the accident could be discovered from other sources.

An order to submit to examination should specify the conditions and scope of the examination. One of the reasons for vacating the orders for multiple examinations in *Schlagenhauf* was that they were framed too generally, possibly leaving the internal medicine examination open to blood tests, cardiograms, or X-ray examinations — some of which were irrelevant under any theory of the case.[240] In specifying the condition and scope of the examination, a court must balance the discoverer's needs against the privacy interest and safety of the examinee.[241]

---

[234] *See* § 13.04[3] (mandamus), *infra*.

[235] 379 U.S. at 118.

[236] Justice Black dissented with a characteristically pithy argument that when a bus driver has had a prior accident, it is fair to ask, "What's the matter with the driver? Is he blind or crazy?" *Id.* at 123 (Black, J., concurring in part and dissenting in part).

[237] *Id.* at 110.

[238] *Compare Anson v. Fickel*, 110 F.R.D. 184 (N.D. Ind. 1986) (good cause found where discoverer had already tried to obtain information by other means), *with Marroni v. Matey*, 82 F.R.D. 371 (E.D. Pa. 1971) (good cause lacking where no such showing made).

[239] 256 S.E.2d 335 (Ga. 1979).

[240] *Schlagenhauf*, 379 U.S. at 121 n.16.

[241] *Wright* § 88.

Rule 35(b) establishes a rule of reciprocity for the exchange of examination reports. The examinee is entitled to the report of the examination upon request. In exchange, she must produce any prior reports of examinations of the same condition, and she waives any privilege she has regarding the testimony of anyone who has or will examine her concerning that condition.

The actual practice under Rule 35 and comparable state provisions is less formal. Usually the parties stipulate to physical and mental examinations and the exchange of relevant examination reports without seeking any court order.[242]

[2]　Use and Value of Physical and Mental Examinations

Examination results may be used at trial subject to the rules of evidence. In most cases, the physician-patient privilege is waived voluntarily by a party-examinee's proffer of evidence, or, in some states, by statute. The examining doctor typically qualifies as an expert, and other experts may also testify on the basis of the examination when it is the kind upon which experts in the field reasonably rely.[243]

A physical or mental examination is an expensive form of discovery because the discoverer must pay the fees of the examining doctor. Yet it is often essential. No one has raised doubts of the value of Rule 35, although some have argued for its extension to non-parties, such as agents and spouses, in particular cases.[244]

PART C
Control of Discovery

§ 10.12　The Abuse of Discovery[245]

Discovery abuse is a chronic complaint of litigators. It is also the rallying cry of rule reformers and a major justification for periodic amendments to the discovery rules. Yet there is no corresponding consensus about what discovery abuse is or how often it occurs, let alone what should be done about it. Litigators are likely to describe it, "quite simply, [as] what your opponent is doing to you."[246] The 1983 Advisory Committee identified the problems as over-discovery and evasion.[247]

---

[242] *Id.*

[243] *See generally* Fed. R. Evid. 702-705. Use of such trial experts is subject to the required disclosure requirements of Rule 26(a)(2). *See* § 10.07[2], *supra.*

[244] *See James, Hazard & Leubsdorf* § 5.6.

[245] *See generally* Beckerman, *Confronting Civil Discovery's Fatal Flaws*, 84 Minn. L. Rev. 505 (2000); Brazil, *Civil Discovery: How Bad Are the Problems?*, 67 A.B.A.J. 450 (1981); Levine, *"Abuse" of Discovery: or Hard Work Makes Good Law*, 67 A.B.A.J. 565 (1981); Connolly, Holleman & Kuhlman, *Judicial Controls and the Civil Litigative Process: Discovery* (Federal Judicial Center 1978); Agnew, Note, *Recent Changes in the Federal Rules of Civil Procedure: Prescriptions to Ease the Pain?*, 15 Tex. Tech. L. Rev. 887 (1984) (hereinafter *Recent Changes*).

[246] A. Miller, *The August 1983 Amendments to the Federal Rules of Civil Procedure: Promoting Effective Case Management and Lawyer Responsibility* 31 (1984).

[247] Rule 26(b) advisory committee's note (1983).

Over-discovery (or runaway discovery) can be redundant discovery. It can also be discovery that is disproportionate to the individual lawsuit as measured by its nature and complexity, the amount in controversy, the social significance of the issues, and the relative resources of the parties.[248] *Evasion* consists of conduct calculated to prevent, distort or stall disclosure of information legitimately sought through discovery.[249]

The 1983 Advisory Committee did not address the prevalence of these problems. However, other studies have suggested that, while they are common in large and complex cases, they do not permeate the majority of federal filings.[250] A 1997 survey of lawyers by the Federal Judicial Center indicated that 61% of the lawyers in complex cases reported discovery problems, compared to 50% of lawyers in "somewhat complex cases" and 33% in non-complex cases.[251] It also found that lawyers in high-stakes cases were twice as likely to report multiple discovery problems as lawyers in low-stakes cases.[252] Lawyers hired for complex high-stakes cases probably view discovery as simply another tool for conflict.

The line separating over-discovery and evasion from vigorous advocacy is therefore difficult to draw. Some of what may be portrayed as the former may be inherent in an open-ended and party-regulated discovery scheme. Judge Easterbrook has observed that

> [l]awyers cannot limit their search for information in discovery, because they do not know what they are looking for. They do not know when to stop, because they never know when they have enough. . . . When the stakes are high — and often the stakes for corporations are many times the ad damnum of the complaint — it is worthwhile to invest the legal resources needed to produce even a small change in the probable outcome. Lawyers practicing in good faith, therefore, engage in extensive discovery; anything less is foolish.[253]

If the client can afford it, a lawyer may heed the ethical admonition to represent clients with "zeal in advocacy"[254] by pursuing discovery with a vengeance. The adversary process also encourages the aggressive lawyer to pursue remote but possible discovery targets or to assert every colorable

---

[248] *See* text accompanying § 10.03[1] n.5 (noting that over-discovery involves both discovery breadth and depth), *supra*.

[249] *See Brazil*, note 1, *supra*, at 451; *Recent Changes*, note 1, *supra*, at 909.

[250] *See, e.g., Brazil*, note 245, *supra*, at 452; *Connolly*, et al, note 245, *supra*, at xi; *Levine*, note 1, *supra*, at 567 (ascribing perception of widespread abuse to anecdotal evidence from large and complex cases).

[251] Willging et al., *An Empirical Study of Discovery and Disclosure Practice Under the 1993 Federal Rule Amendments*, 39 B.C. L. Rev. 525, 554-555 (1998). *See also* Nelson, *The Discovery Process as a Circle of Blame: Institutional, Professional, and Socio-Economic Factors That Contribute to Unreasonable, Inefficient, and Amoral Behavior in Corporate Litigation*, 67 Fordham L. Rev. 773 (1998) (explaining discovery abuse in high-stakes corporate litigation).

[252] *Id.* at 555.

[253] Easterbrook, *Discovery as Abuse*, 69 B.U. L. Rev. 635, 641 (1989) (footnote omitted).

[254] American Bar Ass'n, *Model Rules of Professional Conduct* Rule 1.3 comment (1999) (hereinafter *ABA Model Rules*).

ambiguity or objection in response to discovery requests. Reciprocity and cooperation are, after all, not hallmarks of the hotly contested lawsuit; the litigation process has been described as "inherently partisan and contentious," which makes the expectation of cooperation in discovery "a striking anomaly."[255] And, regrettably, there is a greater tendency for over-discovery and evasion when lawyers are compensated by the hour.[256]

On the other hand, over-discovery and evasion may also result from premeditated abuse. *Predatory discovery*[257] is intended less to uncover information than to delay, harass, embarrass or financially burden the discoveree. Evasion for the same purposes becomes *obstruction* of discovery. Predatory discovery and obstruction are correctly viewed as the abuse of discovery, often characterized by rule violations and by unethical conduct.[258]

While there is no bright line separating systemically caused over-discovery and evasion from improperly motivated predatory discovery and obstruction, the distinction may still be worth drawing because these problems suggest somewhat different solutions. The systemic origins of over-discovery and evasion suggest systemic solutions: changes in attitudes and economic incentives of the bar, generic limitations on discovery, and managerial controls by the courts, at least in large and complex cases. Most of these limitations and controls would be applied at start of and during discovery to avoid over-discovery and evasion. This was the approach of the 1993 discovery rule reforms although they were not limited to large and complex cases. In contrast, predatory discovery and obstruction are less open to cure from front-end limitations and controls. Given their improper purposes and bad faith, they may require more and tougher sanctions for discovery rule violations.

§ 10.13   Front-End Controls: Preventing the Abuse of Discovery

The federal rules take three approaches to preventing discovery abuse. First, they require parties or their attorneys to certify to the reasonable basis, proper purpose and proportionality of discovery requests and responses. Second, they permit and encourage judicial management of discovery by pretrial conferences and managerial orders regulating discovery. Finally, they authorize the issuance of protective orders against specific hardships from discovery.

---

[255] *Beckerman*, note 245, *supra*, at 521.

[256] *See generally Recent Changes*, note 245, *supra*, at 909-911.

[257] The phrase is from *Marrese v. American Academy of Orthopedic Surgeons*, 726 F.2d 1150, 1164 (7th Cir. 1984).

[258] *Cf. ABA Model Rules*, note 245, *supra*, Rules 3.2-3.4. *See generally* Sarazen, Note, *An Ethical Approach to Discovery Abuse*, 4 Geo. J. Legal Ethics 459 (1990).

[1] Certification Requirements

Rule 26(g) imposes two different kinds of certification requirements on discovery initiatives. It requires an attorney or unrepresented party to certify to knowledge, information or belief, formed after reasonable inquiry, that a disclosure under Rule 26(a)(1) or (3) is "complete and correct as of the time it is made." The 1993 Advisory Committee cautioned, however, that the rule does not require exhaustive inquiry so early in the case. Instead, the type of investigation that is required in connection with Rule 26(a) disclosures will depend upon

> the number and complexity of the issues; the location, nature, number, and availability of potentially relevant witnesses and documents; the extent of past working relationships between the attorney and the client, particularly in handling related or similar litigation [e.g., is client a re-peat player?]; and of course how long the party has to conduct an investigation, either before or after the filing of the case.[259]

In addition, Rule 26(g) imposes a certification requirement for discovery requests, responses and objections parallelling that of Rule 11. The purpose of this certification requirement is to deter over-discovery and evasion by making "each attorney stop and think about the legitimacy of a discovery request, a response thereto, or an objection."[260] By signing such a request or response, the attorney certifies that "he has read . . . [it] and that to the best of his knowledge, information and belief formed after reasonable inquiry it is . . . consistent with these rules and warranted" by law, "not interposed for any improper purpose," and not disproportionate to the needs of the case.

The reasonable basis-in-law and proper-purpose certifications generally track those required by Rule 11.[261] An attorney is not required, however, to certify to the truthfulness of her client's factual responses to a discovery request.[262]

It is doubtful whether these certification requirements had really added much to the deterrence of predatory discovery or obstruction of discovery,[263] since the discovery rules have always implicitly prohibited such conduct. But the additional certification that discovery is not disproportionate to "the needs of the case, the discovery already had . . ., the amount in controversy, and the importance of the issues . . . .," may awaken some attorneys to the impropriety of over-discovery. According to one authority,

> [i]t is no longer sufficient, as a precondition for conducting discovery, to show that the information sought "appears reasonably calculated to lead to the discovery of admissible evidence." After satisfying this threshold requirement counsel *also must* make a common sense determination, taking into account all the circumstances, that the information sought

---

[259] Rule 26(g) advisory committee's note (1993).

[260] Rule 26(g) advisory committee's note (1983).

[261] *See* § 8.05[2] (certification), *supra.*

[262] Rule 26(g) advisory committee's note (1983).

[263] *See* § 10.12 (discovery abuse), *supra.*

is of sufficient potential significance to justify the burden the discovery probe would impose, that the discovery tool selected is the most efficacious of the means that might be used to acquire the desired information (taking into account cost effectiveness and the nature of the information being sought), and that the timing of the probe is sensible, *i.e.*, that there is no other juncture in the pretrial period when there would be a clearly happier balance between the benefit derived from and the burdens imposed by the particular discovery effort.[264]

This certification requirement incorporates this common sense determination into discovery even in the absence of appropriate managerial orders by the court under Rule 26(b)(1).[265]

Rule 26(g) mandates appropriate sanctions against the person who certifies in violation of the rule, the party on whose behalf the corresponding disclosure, request or response was made, or both.[266] In practice, violations of Rule 26(g) will usually be accompanied by violations of other discovery rules subject to sanction under Rule 37, and Rule 26(g) sanctions can be decided simultaneously with Rule 37 sanctions.[267] The 1993 Advisory Committee emphasized, however, that Rule 11 no longer applies to such violations.

[2] Managerial Orders

Section 76 suggests that one reason for over-discovery and evasion is that discovery is an open-ended party-regulated adversarial process. One obvious response is more judicial regulation. The 1980 and 1983 amendments to the rules provided this by authorizing and encouraging early judicial intervention by pretrial conference, and by empowering the court, as educated by such conferences, to issue managerial discovery orders.[268] The 1993 amendments strengthened the courts' managerial powers because the Advisory Committee believed that "there [was] a greater need for early judicial involvement to consider the scope and timing of the disclosure requirements of Rule 26(a) and the presumptive limits on discovery imposed" by the rules. The 2000 amendments reinforced the court's powers, by making it the gatekeeper for discovery of matters beyond the claims or defenses in the case, yet relevant to the subject matter.[269] Some states have

---

[264] *In re Convergent Technologies Securities Litig.*, 108 F.R.D. 328, 331 (N.D. Cal. 1985) (Brazil, Mag.) (emphasis in original).

[265] *See* § 10.13[2](managerial orders), *infra*.

[266] *See, e.g., Appeal of Licht & Semonoff*, 796 F.2d 564 (1st Cir. 1986) (dismissing, for lack of jurisdiction, appeal of unreported decision that Rule 26(g) was violated by use of depositions to harass opponents in proxy contest and to gain information for that contest, rather than to advance the lawsuit).

[267] *See, e.g., Perkinson v. Houlihan's/D.C., Inc.*, 108 F.R.D. 667 (D.D.C. 1985); *Tise v. Kule*, 37 Fed. R. Serv. 2d (Callaghan) 846 (S.D.N.Y. 1983). *See generally* § 10.14[2] (nature and incidence of sanctions), *infra*.

[268] *See Stillman v. Odeon*, 102 F.R.D. 286 (S.D.N.Y. 1984) (the amendments encourage courts to take a "strong supervisory role in discovery and to consider innovative cost-shifting concepts").

[269] *See* § 10.03[1], *supra*.

accomplished the same ends more indirectly by fixing discovery time limits by rule for civil actions, categorized by their complexity or amount in controversy.[270]

The courts have long had the power under Rule 16 to hold pretrial conferences and issue orders which encompass discovery, and Rule 16(b) contemplates that the court may hold a discovery conference after the parties have conferred and submitted a discovery plan.[271] Whether or not a discovery conference is held by the court, it "shall" enter an order identifying issues for discovery purposes, limiting and scheduling discovery (including required disclosures), determining other matters incidental to discovery, such as cost allocation, and limiting the time by which the parties must complete discovery.[272]

Against reduction of over-discovery and evasion that such rules might provide must be balanced the risk that they will prompt over-management, especially in routine and relatively simple litigation. Rule 16(b) thus provides that local rules may exempt categories of inappropriate cases. Whether this will be sufficient to prevent unwarranted application of the rule's requirements remains to be seen.

If Rules 26(g) and 16(b) supply the occasion for managerial intervention by the courts into discovery, Rule 26(b)(1) supplies the tools "to enable the court to keep tighter rein on the extent of discovery," according to the 1993 Advisory Committee. Rules 30 and 33 presumptively limit the number of depositions and interrogatories, and Rule 26(b)(2) allows courts by local rule or order to alter these limits, as well to limit the length of depositions or the number of requests for admissions. Perhaps more important, Rule 26(b)(2) also provides that the frequency and use of discovery "shall be limited if the court determines that" the discovery sought is excessive for any of three overlapping reasons.

Rule 26(b)(2)(i) requires the court to limit discovery which is unreasonably cumulative or duplicative or is obtainable from a less burdensome and expensive source. Under this provision, courts have prohibited discovery by interrogatories when the discoverer has already obtained the same information from the subject by depositions.[273]

Rule 26(b)(2)(ii) requires the court to limit discovery when the discoverer has had ample prior opportunity to discover the information sought. This rule has been used to justify court-imposed time limits on discovery.[274]

---

[270] See, e.g., D.C. Super. Ct. R. 26(d) (fixing 120-day limit on discovery in simple nonjury cases and 180-day limit in simple jury cases; classified as simple or complex at time of filing).

[271] Rule 26(f) formerly required such a conference on motion by a party. The 1993 amendment deleted the requirement, apparently on the assumption that the mandatory planning conference of the parties would substitute for it and generate a discovery plan on which the court can base the still-required discovery scheduling order. See § 10.07[1], supra.

[272] See generally § 12.03 (pretrial conference), infra.

[273] See, e.g., Continental Ill. Nat'l Bank & Trust Co. v. WH Venture, Civ. A. No. 84-5673 (E.D. Pa. March 13, 1986) (magistrate's decision) (stating that ordinarily "a motion to compel answers to subsequent interrogatories seeking to elicit the same information as obtained by way of the earlier depositions should be denied," but allowing interrogatory discovery to enable discoverer to close gaps in deponents' answers).

[274] See, e.g., Slomiak v. Bear Stearns & Co., Inc., 597 F. Supp. 676 (S.D.N.Y. 1985).

Finally, Rule 26(b)(2)(iii) requires the court to limit discovery when "the burden or expense of the proposed discovery outweighs its likely benefit, taking into account the needs of the case, the amount in controversy, the parties' resources, the importance of the issues at stake in the litigation, and the importance of the proposed discovery in resolving the issues." The rule thus gives a federal court the power to "limit unnecessarily expensive discovery."[275] When this limitation should be imposed depends on the facts of the case. In *TIE/Communication, Inc. v. Bumper Products Corp.,*[276] the discoverer sought to re-depose a corporate employee after having failed to inquire into a subject during the first deposition "due to inadvertence." Refusing to block the deposition, the court considered that the subject involved $100,000, 30% of the damages claimed, that the parties would have to get together anyway for other employee depositions, and that the party opposing discovery had shown no special hardship.

The cases reported to date suggest that the courts have not yet made much use of the managerial power that Rule 26(b)(2)(i)–(iii) requires them to exercise. Stressing the difficulty trial courts face balancing discovery benefits against burdens, one appellate judge has predicted that unless the imbalance is dramatic, "past habit is likely to cause the court to permit it."[277] But the 2000 amendment to the rule expressly cross-references the Rule 26(b)(2) managerial power in Rule 26(b)(1) to remind the courts of their authority and obligation, and the Supreme Court has itself emphasized that Rule 26(b)(2)(iii) "vests the trial court with broad discretion to tailor discovery narrowly and to dictate the sequence of discovery."[278] Perhaps such pointed reminders will yet overcome "past habit."

[3] Protective Orders Against Specific Hardship[279]

Upon motion and for good cause shown, almost all jurisdictions authorize the entry of orders protecting against burdensome or oppressive discovery. Rule 26(c), for example, authorizes the federal courts to issue *protective orders* on motion and the movant's certification that she has conferred in good faith with other parties to resolve the dispute. Protective orders are not materially different from what we have termed *managerial orders,*[280] but protective orders have traditionally been issued to protect against specific hardships from discovery[281] rather than to manage and control over-discovery. In deciding a motion for a protective order, the court must

---

[275] *Brock v. Panzarino*, 109 F.R.D. 157, 160 (E.D.N.Y. 1986) (properly rejecting this argument as a way around Rule 26(b)(3)'s protection of witness statements).

[276] 1987 U.S. Dist. LEXIS 10037 (E.D. Pa. Nov. 6, 1987).

[277] Winter, *Forward: In Defense of Discovery Reform*, 58 Brook. L. Rev. 263, 265 (1992).

[278] *Crawford-El v. Britton*, 523 U.S. 574, 598 (1998).

[279] *See generally* Guenego, Note,*Trends in Protective Orders Under Federal Rule of Civil Procedure 26(c): Why Some Cases Fumble While Others Score*, 60 Fordham L. Rev. 541 (1991); Marcus, *Myth and Reality in Protective Order Litigation*, 69 Cornell L. Rev. 1 (1983).

[280] *See* § 10.13[2], *supra.*

[281] *See Cipollone v. Liggett Group, Inc.*, 785 F.2d 1108, 1121 (3d Cir. 1986) (stressing burden on movant to show particular need for protection).

balance hardship to the discoveree if discovery is allowed as sought against the hardship to the discoverer if discovery is denied or restricted.[282] Most commonly, parties seek protective orders against unduly burdensome or invasive discovery.

Discovery can be unduly burdensome because of the location or condition of the discoveree. For example, because there are no geographic limitations on the location of opposing-party depositions, they are sometimes noticed for locations distant from the residence of the party-deponent. A protective order changing the location of the deposition or conditioning it on payment of travel expenses may be appropriate.[283] Or the age or health of a deponent may make a scheduled all-day deposition unduly burdensome and present good cause for shortening it, spacing it, or preventing it in favor of a less burdensome discovery method such as interrogatories.[284]

Discovery may be unduly invasive when it probes matter that, though unprivileged, is confidential. Predatory discovery, in fact, probes such matter more to embarrass and harass the discoveree than to obtain information.[285] As a result, parties often argue confidentiality when they seek a protective order.[286] In commercial litigation, for example, confidentiality is often invoked to protect trade secrets or customer lists from competitors.[287] It has also been invoked to protect against unconditional discovery of financial information, group membership information, peer review information in connection with tenure, promotion and other personnel decisions, and institutional self-critiques.[288] However, the courts have been vigilant in requiring a specific showing of hardship from discovery of confidential matters and have rejected conclusory assertions by the discoveree of embarrassment or unfairness.[289]

---

[282] See Marrese v. American Academy of Orthopaedic Surgeons, 726 F.2d 1150, 1159 (7th Cir. 1984) (en banc).

[283] See, e.g., Haviland & Co. v. Montgomery Ward & Co., 31 F.R.D. 578, 580 (S.D.N.Y. 1962).

[284] Id. See generally Dickerson, Deposition Dilemmas: Vexatious Scheduling and Errata Sheets, 12 Geo. J. Legal Ethics 1 (1998) (discussing protective orders and other responses to vexatious deposition scheduling).

[285] See, e.g., Seattle Times Co. v. Rhinehart, 467 U.S. 20 (1984) (noting that such discovery implicates not only privacy interests but also litigants' interests in unimpeded access to the courts if they are forced to forego pursuit of their claims rather than give up their privacy); Marrese v. American Academy of Orthopaedic Surgeons, 726 F.2d 1150, 1161 (7th Cir. 1984) (en banc) (finding a "hint of predatory discovery" in plaintiff's request for membership information as a basis for deposing members who voted against his application).

[286] See Dore, Secrecy By Consent: The Use and Limits of Confidentiality in the Pursuit of Settlement, 74 Notre Dame L. Rev. 283 (1999).

[287] See McKown, Discovery of Trade Secrets, 10 Santa Clara Computer & High Tech L.J. 35 (1994).

[288] See generally Moore §§ 12.101, 26.104, 26.105 (listing cases). Cf. Granger v. National R. Passenger Corp., 116 F.R.D. 507 (E.D. Pa. 1987) (applying "critical self-analysis doctrine" to protect recommendations in railroad's accident analysis).

[289] See, e.g., Cipollone v. Liggett Group, Inc., 649 F. Supp. 664 (D.N.J. 1986) (rejecting as unspecific cigarette manufacturers' sweeping claims that discovery of information regarding their knowledge of the health risks of smoking might prove embarrassing, detrimental to the market price of their stock, and helpful to their competitors or other plaintiffs).

Prohibition of discovery is just one of eight different types of protective orders that Rule 26(c) describes. This mix reflects the rule's strong preference for orders restricting discovery rather than denying it altogether. A court may impose conditions on the location, method, scope, and sequence of discovery, or on any other incident of discovery as required to give sufficient protection to the movant. When the asserted hardship is invasion of confidentiality, for example, the court may restrict disclosure to particular parties or their attorneys and prohibit dissemination of the discovered information. In commercial litigation, *umbrella protective orders* are commonplace, extending protection against dissemination to any document that the discoveree designates confidential without any individualized review by the court.[290]

In *Seattle Times Co. v. Rhinehart*,[291] the Supreme Court rejected a First Amendment challenge to the entry of a protective order restricting dissemination of information obtained by discovery. There the defendant newspaper in a defamation action sought discovery of the plaintiff religious group's membership and donor lists, candidly acknowledging that such information might be disseminated in newspaper articles. The Court first emphasized that litigants have no First Amendment right of access to information made available only for purposes of trying a suit and that such discovery is not a traditionally public source of information.[292] It then found that "the prevention of abuse that can attend the coerced production of information under a state's discovery rule is sufficient justification for the authorizing of protective orders."[293]

On the other hand, the Supreme Court has long acknowledged the public's common law right of access to judicial proceedings and judicial records.[294] If documents under a protective order are actually filed in court or submitted into evidence, the strong presumption of access must be balanced against competing interests to determine whether disclosure will be made. Moreover, even in *Seattle Times*, the Court emphasized that the particular protective order for discovery materials was limited in nature and did not restrict the dissemination of information gained outside the discovery process. Other courts have noted that First Amendment interests of discoverers and the public can sometimes be accommodated by properly limited protective orders, requiring, for example, *in camera* inspection of the information by the trial judge, *redaction* (deletion) of names or other especially private information prior to disclosure, or postponement of discovery of private matter until the discoveree has had the opportunity to test the discoverer's *prima facie* claims or defenses.[295]

---

[290] *See, e.g., Dore*, note 286, *supra*; Marcus, *The Discovery Confidentiality Controversy*, 1991 U. Ill. L. Rev. 457 (1991); *Marcus*, note 279, *supra*, at 9; Miller, *Confidentiality, Protective Orders, and Public Access to the Courts*, 105 Harv. L. Rev. 427 (1991).

[291] 467 U.S. 20 (1984).

[292] *Id.* at 32.

[293] *Id.* at 35-36.

[294] *Nixon v. Warner Communications, Inc.*, 435 U.S. 589 (1978).

[295] *See, e.g., Marrese*, 726 F.2d at 1160.

§ 10.14 Back-End Controls: Sanctions

[1] The Predicate for Sanctions

All procedural systems authorize sanctions against parties and attorneys who violate the discovery rules or discovery orders. Governing law in federal court includes Rules 37 and 26(g), a statute, [296] and common law. [297] Under Rule 37, no party may move for an order compelling discovery or for sanctions without certifying that it has tried in good faith to resolve the discovery dispute with other parties without court action. Sanctions most commonly result from a party's defiance of a prior discovery order. Accordingly, Rule 37(b) authorizes sanctions for a failure to comply with an order to compel discovery or equivalent discovery order. [298] Rules 26(g), 37(c) and 37(d), however, permit the imposition of sanctions without an intervening discovery order in some circumstances. When a discovery order has been violated, or the facts warrant by-passing the usual predicate of a discovery order, the court may impose sanctions tailored to the offense.

The discoverer may move under Rule 37(a) [299] for an order compelling discovery either when the discoveree objects to discovery or responds evasively or incompletely. In the former circumstances, this motion tests any objections that the discoveree has interposed to the requested discovery. [300] If the motion to compel is granted, Rule 37(a)(4) requires the court to award the movant attorney's fees and other expenses incurred in making the motion unless it finds that opposition to the motion was "substantially justified." [301] If the motion is denied, then the discoveree has a similar opportunity for reimbursement and the court may issue a protective order in his favor. "The great operative principle of Rule 37(a)(4) is that the loser pays." [302]

Violation of an order compelling discovery or of an equivalent discovery order, whether or not wilful, [303] is the predicate for discovery sanctions under Rule 37(b). Evincing a general hesitancy about imposing discovery sanctions, [304] the courts have been strict in rejecting arguments that

---

[296] 28 U.S.C. § 1927.

[297] *See Roadway Express, Inc. v. Piper*, 447 U.S. 752, 764-767 (1980).

[298] Equivalent discovery orders include Rule 35 orders providing for physical or mental examinations and arguably Rule 16(b) scheduling orders, although they are not mentioned in Rule 37(b).

[299] A motion seeking an order against a party must be filed in the court where the action is pending. Motions against non-parties must be filed in the court for the district where the discovery is being, or is to be, taken. Rule 37(a)(1).

[300] *See* Rule 33(a).

[301] "The position of the losing side is nonetheless 'substantially justified' if the motion raised an issue about which reasonable men could genuinely differ on whether a party was bound to comply with a discovery rule." *Wright & Miller* § 2288.

[302] *Id.*

[303] *See Societe Internationale Pour Participations Industrielles et Commerciales, S.A. v. Rogers*, 357 U.S. 197 (1958). The violator's *scienter* — state of mind — does go to the severity of sanctions, however. *See* § 10.14[2] (nature and incidence of sanctions), *infra*.

[304] *See* § 10.14[2] (incidence of sanctions), *infra*.

general managerial or pretrial orders not expressly compelling discovery can satisfy Rule 37(b)'s predicate of a discovery order.[305]

When the discoveree simply refuses to respond — fails to appear at all for her deposition, or to serve any response to interrogatories or production requests — the predicate of a discovery order is eliminated. Rule 37(d) then permits the discoverer to move directly for sanctions short of contempt and for all expenses caused by the failure of discovery, not just those incurred in making the Rule 37(d) motion. Efficiency is the rationale for this shortcut to sanctions. Requiring a court order to compel a response, followed in all likelihood by a second motion to test objections made in the compelled response, would intolerably delay discovery in many cases and invite abuse.[306] Rule 37(d) therefore, provides that a failure to respond is not excused upon the ground that the discovery is objectionable, unless the discoveree has applied for a protective order. The proper way to object to discovery is to apply for such an order under Rule 26(c) or to make the objections in a written response or at the deposition.

An order compelling discovery is not a prerequisite for sanctions in some additional situations. Rule 37(g) provides for the award of expenses against an attorney who fails to participate in good faith in the framing of a discovery plan under Rule 26(f). Rule 37(c) provides a self-executing sanction for a party's prejudicial failure to disclose information required to be disclosed by Rule 26(a), by precluding that party from using the information as evidence at trial. More importantly, Rule 26(g) requires appropriate sanctions against an attorney or party for violation of its certification requirement.[307] Because most violations of the discovery rules can also be construed as violations of the certification requirement, Rule 26(g) may encourage federal courts to impose discovery sanctions more often without an intervening order compelling discovery.[308]

Rule 26(g) also supplies the sole authority under the rules for imposing sanctions for over-discovery. A limiting order under Rule 26(b)(2)(i)–(iii) or 26(c) need not precede these sanctions,[309] although it is likely that some courts will infer the necessity of one due to the novelty of the offense[310] and their accustomed sanctions practice.

---

[305] *See, e.g., Salahuddin v. Harris*, 782 F.2d 1127 (2d Cir. 1986) (neither Rule 30(a) order *allowing* deposition nor "implied orders" provide the predicate for Rule 37(b) sanctions).

[306] *Moore* § 37.90. "Rule 37(d) deals, then, with failure to make the initial response required by the Rules, while subdivisions (a) and (b) provide a method of resolving differences between the parties and enforcing the court's determinations." *Id.*

[307] *See also* § 12.02[1] (requests for admissions), *infra*, discussing sanction of expenses for unjustified refusals to admit under Rule 36.

[308] *See, e.g., St. Paul Reinsurance Co., Ltd. v. Commercial Finan. Corp.*, 198 F.R.D. 508 (N.D. Iowa 2000) (imposing Rule 26(g) sanction *sua sponte*, without prior order compelling discovery, on discovery respondent for making boilerplate and frivolous objections).

[309] *See, e.g., Hayes v. National Gypsum Co.*, 38 Fed. R. Serv. 2d (Callaghan) 645 (E.D. Pa. 1984) (awarding expenses incurred by discoveree because of duplicative discovery, despite the absence of any court-ordered limit on same).

[310] *See* § 10.13[2] (managerial orders), *supra.*

[2]   The Nature and Incidence of Sanctions

Courts have long had discretion to impose discovery sanctions under rules like Rule 37(b) and 37(d).[311] Often, however, they have been reluctant to exercise that discretion. This created a climate conducive to discovery abuse.

The typical pattern of sanctioning that emerges from the reported cases is one in which the delay, obfuscation, contumacy, and lame excuses on the part of litigants and their attorneys are tolerated without any measured remedial action until the court is provoked beyond endurance. At that point the court punishes one side or the other with a swift and final termination of the lawsuit by dismissal or default. This "all or nothing" approach to sanctions results in considerable laxity in the day-to-day application of the rules. Attorneys are well aware that sanctions will be imposed only in the most flagrant situations.[312]

For two reasons, this historical reluctance may be abating. First, the Supreme Court has taken notice of it and reminded the trial courts that the purpose of sanctions is to deter as well as to punish.[313] Second, Rule 26(g) imposes mandatory sanctions for violation of the discovery certification requirements.[314] Since virtually any discovery abuse or discovery rule violation can be construed as a violation of the certification requirement, Rule 26(g)'s mandate may carry well beyond its literal boundaries into Rule 37.

At the same time, courts retain discretion to decide the severity of the sanction even under Rule 26(g). Limited only by the due process requirement that the sanction be proportionate to the offense,[315] or that the same be "just" and "appropriate" in the language of the Rules, federal courts may choose from a range of Rule 37(b) sanctions varying in severity.[316] The court may award discovery expenses against the violator, deem established facts that were the object of discovery,[317] prevent the violator from presenting certain evidence or supporting or opposing certain claims or defenses, strike all or part of the pleadings, hold the violator of a discovery order (other

---

[311] Both of these subprovisions provide that the court ". . . *may* make such orders in regard to the failure [to comply with a discovery order or to respond] as are just. . . ." (emphasis supplied).

[312] R. Rodes, K. Ripple & C. Mooney, *Sanctions Imposable for Violations of the Federal Rules of Civil Procedure* 85 (Fed. Jud. Ctr. 1981). Copyright © 1981 by the Federal Judicial Center. Reprinted with permission. *See also* Brazil, *Civil Discovery: How Bad Are the Problems?*, 67 A.B.A.J. 450, 456 (1981) (noting that attorneys believe that courts fail miserably in imposing sanctions).

[313] *National Hockey League v. Metropolitan Hockey Club, Inc.*, 427 U.S. 639 (1976) (*per curiam*). *See also Roadway Express, Inc. v. Piper*, 447 U.S. 752 (1980).

[314] Rule 26(g) advisory committee's note (1983).

[315] *See Insurance Corp. of Ireland, Ltd. v. Compagnie des Bauxites de Guinea*, 456 U.S. 694 (1982).

[316] *See generally* Slawotsky, *Rule 37 Discovery Sanctions — the Need for Supreme Court Ordered National Uniformity*, 104 Dick. L. Rev. 471 (2000) (surveying sanction practice and finding that relatively unguided discretion has led to disuniformity).

[317] *Id.* (jurisdictional facts).

than one for a physical or mental examination) in contempt,[318] dismiss the action, or render judgment by default.

The latter sanctions of dismissal or default are the most severe,[319] presupposing correspondingly severe abuse of discovery. Accordingly, the courts have suggested that "wilfulness, bad faith, or . . . fault" must be found before dismissal or entry of default is appropriate, even though no such scienter requirement attaches to the underlying finding that a discovery rule or order has been violated.[320]

The question whether these severe sanctions are appropriate is further complicated when they are levied for transgressions by the attorney rather than the party. The courts have always been reluctant to penalize parties on the merits for the acts of their attorneys, at least absent the client's knowledge or complicity.[321] For example, before the drastic sanction of dismissal is imposed for discovery misconduct of an attorney, the Court of Appeals for the Third Circuit has required the trial court to consider whether the party is responsible for the conduct, the degree of the party's responsibility, the resulting prejudice to the opposing party, whether the attorney has had a history of dilatory discovery tactics, whether the conduct was wilful or in bad faith, whether other effective sanctions short of dismissal are viable, and whether the party's claim or defense is "meritorious."[322]

---

[318] See Neibarger, *Chipping Away at the Stone Wall: Allowing Federal Courts to Impose Non-Monetary Sanctions Upon Errant Attorneys Without a Finding of Contempt*, 33 Ind. L. Rev. 1045 (2000) (proposing other non-monetary sanctions in addition to contempt for discovery abuse).

[319] See, e.g., *Trans World Airlines, Inc. v. Hughes*, 449 F.2d 51 (2d Cir. 1971) (default judgment for $145 million against Howard Hughes for his failure to comply with order to appear for deposition), *rev'd on other grounds sub nom., Hughes Tool Co. v. TWA*, 409 U.S. 363 (1973).

[320] *Societe Internationale Pour Participations Industrielles et Commerciales v. Rogers*, 357 U.S. 197, 212 (1958). *See also Cine Forty-Second St. Theatre Corp. v. Allied Artists Pictures Corp.*, 602 F.2d 1062, 1065 (2d Cir. 1979).

[321] *See generally* Renfrew, *Discovery Sanctions: A Judicial Perspective*, 67 Cal. L. Rev. 264, 273-274 (1979). *But see Link v. Wabash R.R. Co.*, 370 U.S. 626, 633 (1962) (a litigant chooses counsel at his peril).

[322] *Poulis v. State Farm & Casualty Co.*, 747 F.2d 863, 868–870 (3d Cir. 1984). *See also Scarborough v. Eubanks*, 747 F.2d 871 (3d Cir. 1984). In these companion cases (ironically involving the same attorney) the court, respectively, affirmed dismissal for a pattern of dilatory conduct which prejudiced the opposing party, but reversed dismissal for a failure to abide court-ordered deadlines, when no prejudice resulted and the opposing party also missed them. *See also Bluitt v. Arco Chemical Co.*, 777 F.2d 188, 190-191 (5th Cir. 1985).

Chapter 11

DISPOSITION WITHOUT TRIAL

§ 11.01 Overview

All procedural systems provide a variety of alternatives for obtaining judgment before trial. If a defendant fails to respond to a pleading within the time designated for response, he is in *default* and subject to entry of a *default judgment,* discussed in section 11.02. If defendant responds by successfully attacking the pleading, it may be dismissed, as previously discussed in section 8.07. When materials outside the pleadings are submitted in support of some motions attacking the pleadings, the motions are converted to motions for *summary judgment,* discussed in section 11.03. Summary judgment is also available to either party whenever it can show that there is no genuinely triable issue of material fact and that it is entitled to judgment as a matter of law. Finally, when the plaintiff elects to withdraw his action before a final judgment on the merits, he may seek a *voluntary dismissal* or *nonsuit.* Alternatively, if he simply abandons the action by failing to prosecute or disobeys court orders or rules, he is subject to *involuntary dismissal* or *compulsory nonsuit.* Dismissals and nonsuits are discussed in Section 11.04.

§ 11.02 Default

Our procedural systems rely principally on the parties to move cases along. A party's complete failure to respond to a pleading exposes an adversary to costly delay and uncertainty. Almost all systems therefore make *default judgments* available as a protection for the rights of the claimant. At the same time, all procedural systems prefer dispositions on the merits to default judgments.[1] Rule 55 is quite typical in reconciling these concerns by assuring that the unresponsive party is aware of the risk of such a judgment. The usual pattern under the rule begins when the default is noticed in some fashion, as by entry on the docket. Only after entry of default may the court, in its discretion and often pursuant to notice and hearing, enter a default judgment.

---

[1] *See, e.g., Varnes v. Glass Bottle Blowers' Ass'n,* 674 F.2d 1365 (11th Cir. 1982); *Ellingsworth v. Chrysler,* 665 F.2d 180 (7th Cir. 1981). Default judgments are common, nevertheless. In the general trial courts of Maine and Delaware, for example, approximately 3% and 15% of civil cases, respectively, ended in default judgments. State of Maine, Administrative Office of the Courts, *1987 Annual Report* 90 (1988) and Administrative Office of the Courts, *1982 Annual Report of the Delaware Judiciary* 79 (1983), cited in Sterling & Schrag, *Default Judgments Against Consumers: Has the System Failed?,* 67 Denver U. L. Rev. 357 (1990).

[1] Default and Its Entry

A party is in default and subject to the rules governing default judgments when he "fails to plead or otherwise defend," as by filing motions to attack the adversary's pleadings.[2] Default is a corollary to the strict time limits most systems impose for responding to pleadings.[3] When a party has responded within the time limit by pleading or attacking the complaint, his subsequent failure to appear for trial does not, without more, place him in default. By pleading, he places the case at issue, obligating his adversary to put on his proof in order to recover a judgment.[4]

Rule 55 authorizes the clerk to enter a default when it appears from the docket or is shown by affidavit of the claimant. *Entry of default* is simply a notation of the fact of default and an interlocutory — interim — step towards the entry of a default judgment. It cuts off the defaulting party's right to further notice, unless he has appeared in the litigation.[5]

Rule 55(c) authorizes the court in its discretion to set aside an entry of default upon good cause shown. The court may consider the defaulting party's wilfulness, prejudice to the adversary should the default be set aside, and the existence of any meritorious defense to the claim.[6] The courts' preference for merits dispositions, however, usually leads to leniency towards the defaulting party on motions to set aside the entry of default where he evinces a desire to correct the default.[7]

[2] Entry of Default Judgment

Judgment may follow entry of default in two ways. Clerks have authority under Rule 55(b)(1) to enter default judgments, but only if the defaulting party is not an unrepresented minor or incompetent, that party has not appeared in the action, and the claimant shows by affidavit that the relief sought is a liquidated (arithmetically ascertainable) sum. Only the court may enter judgment in all other cases. When the defaulting party has appeared, notice and possibly a hearing will be necessary.[8]

An *appearance* is any action that demonstrates sufficient interest by the defaulting party in the litigation to suggest that he might contest the award

---

[2] *See, e.g.,* Rule 55(a). *See generally* Schultz, *Sanctioning Defendants' Non-Willful Delay: The Failure of Rule 55 and a Proposal for Its Reform,* 23 U. Rich. L. Rev. 203, 204 (1989).

[3] *See, e.g.,* Rule 12(a) (requiring a party against whom a claim is pled to answer, reply or move against the pleading under Rule 12 within 20 days after service).

[4] *See, e.g., Coulas v. Smith,* 395 P.2d 527 (Ariz. 1964) (rules governing default judgments are inapplicable to judgment entered against a defendant who answered the complaint and a cross-claim, but then failed to appear at trial). *See generally Bass v. Hoagland,* 172 F.2d 205 (5th Cir. 1949), *cert. denied,* 338 U.S. 816 (1949). Most courts are also empowered by rule, statute or inherent power to enter penalty default judgments against parties who violate rules or orders of the court. *See, e.g.,* federal rules 11, 16, 26(g) and 37.

[5] *Moore* § 55.12[1]. *See* § 11.02[2] (defining appearance), *infra.*

[6] *Id.* § 55.50[1].

[7] *Id.* ; *Wright & Miller* § 2692.

[8] Rule 55(b)(2).

of relief by default judgment and therefore could benefit from notice of application for such a judgment. A party usually appears formally by filing a *praecipe* or notice of appearance by his attorney, or by making other submissions to the court during the lawsuit. In part to encourage settlement efforts by parties, the courts have also found the necessary appearance from participation in protracted settlement negotiations, correspondence, or other communications inconsistent with the complete abandonment of the litigation and disregard for judicial process. [9]

After any required notice, Rule 55(b)(2) authorizes the court to conduct a hearing on the proper measure of relief. The judicial hearing is not a trial in most systems, and there is no right to a jury. Some states, however, entitle the non-defaulting party who previously claimed a jury to a jury trial on damages. [10] The default establishes all well-pleaded facts as true and forecloses any offer of proof by the defaulting party as to liability. However, the defaulting party does not admit conclusions of law and in many jurisdictions may still argue that his adversary's pleading states no claim. [11] Defendant also may offer evidence on the measure of relief. Courts use their discretion to determine whether to enter a default judgment at all, what proof to allow, and how much and what kind of relief they will grant. [12]

Like other final judgments, default judgments are subject to timely post-judgment attack under Rule 60(b). [13] Courts are particularly apt to grant a motion to vacate a default judgment when the defaulting party was served constructively rather than in person, [14] or was denied notice of the application for judgment to which his prior appearance entitled him. Relevant factors are otherwise the same as those considered on a motion to set aside entry of default, with one important difference. The systemic interest in finality of judgments [15] enters into the equation as a counterweight to leniency. Doubts are still resolved in favor of the defaulting party, [16] but

---

[9] *See generally Moore* § 55.21[2]. If, however, during informal communications, the defaulting party was clearly informed of his adversary's intent to seek a default judgment, then the court will usually not find an appearance entitling the defaulting party to notice under Rule 55(b)(2). *Compare Wilson v. Moore & Associates, Inc.*, 564 F.2d 366 (9th Cir. 1977) (plaintiff's counsel warned defendant by letter that failure to answer would place him in default; no appearance), *with Lutomski v. Panther Valley Coin Exchange*, 653 F.2d 270 (6th Cir. 1981) (informal contacts regarding proper amount of damage constituted an appearance).

[10] *See, e.g.*, Va. Sup. Ct. R. 3:17.

[11] *See, e.g., Laruso v. Krieger*, 698 S.W.2d 760 (Tex. Ct. App. 3d Dist. 1985); *Moore* § 55.12[1].

[12] The last is subject to Rule 54(c)'s limitation of the relief to the kind or amount sought in the pleaded demand for relief. *See* § 8.06[3] (demand for relief), *supra*.

[13] *See* § 12.11[2][b] (motions to vacate judgment within one year), *infra*. The Supreme Court has held that due process forbids states from conditioning such relief on the existence of a meritorious defense, if the default was entered without proper notice to defendant. *Peralta v. Heights Medical Center, Inc.*, 485 U.S. 80 (1988).

[14] *See, e.g.*, N.Y. Civ. Prac. L. & R. § 317 (McKinney, WESTLAW through 2000); Va. Code Ann. § 8.01-322 (LEXIS 1999-2000).

[15] *See* § 13.01 (overview of appeal), *infra*.

[16] *Hritz v. Woma Corp.*, 732 F.2d 1178, 1185 (3d Cir. 1984). *See generally Schultz*, note 2, *supra*, at 213-214, 216-220 (finding that courts frequently reject default as an inappropriate sanction for non-willful delay).

the courts are less lenient than they are in finding good cause to set aside interlocutory entries of default.[17]

§ 11.03 Summary Judgment

[1] Purposes

Once pleadings were only open to facial attack.[18] The truth and sufficiency of facts supporting a pleading could be tested only at trial.[19] Summary judgment evolved to intercept before trial factually insufficient claims or defenses — those which would probably suffer a motion for a directed verdict (now termed judgment as a matter of law in federal courts)[20] at trial. The Supreme Court, in fact, has characterized summary judgments as pretrial equivalents of directed verdicts.[21] The summary judgment motion permits a party to go beyond the pleadings to show that there is no genuine dispute of material fact that would necessitate or justify the expense of trial, and to argue that the court should enter judgment for him on some or all claims and defenses as a matter of law. Like the motion for directed verdict, it is consistent with the right to jury trial because it tests whether there is any genuine factual dispute for the jury to resolve.

By forcing the parties to preview their trial evidence and to relate it to their legal theories, summary judgment may result in discovery. The risk of judgment posed by a motion for summary judgment may force the parties to sift the typically undifferentiated mass of evidence produced by normal discovery methods to identify their material evidence. "The very intimation of mortality when summary judgment is at issue assures us that the motion will be rebutted with every factual and legal argument available."[22]

A related (but probably insufficient) purpose of summary judgment is educating the parties and the court about the case. Often a motion for summary judgment presents the first occasion for the parties to pull the case together, set priorities in their claims and defenses, relate the facts unearthed by discovery to their legal theories, and assess overall strengths and weaknesses. Even when existence of a factual dispute causes it to fail,

---

[17] *Wright & Miller* § 2692. *See generally* Kane, *Relief from Federal Judgments: A Morass Unrelieved By a Rule,* 30 Hastings L.J. 41 (1978) (urging amendment to Rule 55(c) to make explicit that the standard for relief from entry of default is more lenient than the standard for relief from default judgment).

[18] *See* § 8.07[1] (motion practice in general), *supra.*

[19] *See* C. Clark, *Code Pleading* § 80 (2d ed. 1947); Bauman, *Evolution of the Summary Judgment Procedure,* 31 Ind. L.J. 329 (1956).

[20] *See* § 12.09[1] (directed verdicts), *infra.*

[21] *See Anderson v. Liberty Lobby, Inc.,* 477 U.S. 242, 250 (1986) (the standard governing summary judgment "mirrors the standard for a directed verdict. . . ."). *Cf.* § 12.09[3][c] (discussing how motions for summary judgment and directed verdict bear a functional resemblance to motions to dismiss for failure to state a claim, for judgment on the pleadings and for judgment notwithstanding the verdict).

[22] *Georgia Southern & Flor. Ry. v. Atlanta Coast Line R.R.,* 373 F.2d 493, 498 (5th Cir.), *cert. denied,* 389 U.S. 851 (1967). *See also Clark,* note 19, *supra,* § 13.02

the motion may promote settlement by alerting the nonmovant and the court to the weakness of the nonmovant's case.[23] Alternatively, the motion may at least simplify eventual trial by illuminating the genuine issues.

On the other hand, until recently at least, the movant often paid a price for such education by having to preview his *own* evidence. Thus, commentators cautioned that

the decision to make a summary judgment motion involves a balancing of the possible damage to the movant's case by educating the opponent through supporting documents against the possible termination of the case through a favorable ruling on the motion and the possible advantage of learning more about the opponent's case through his supporting affidavits.[24]

In addition, an unsuccessful summary judgment motion may evoke a legal ruling that will haunt the movant later in the case.[25]

A trio of decisions by the Supreme Court in 1986, however, changed the price of summary judgment for some movants. Today a movant who would not have the burden of persuasion at trial may be able to move for summary judgment on little more than a bare motion, placing almost the entire cost of summary judgment on the plaintiff. This possibility invites abuse of the motion as a tool for discovery, or worse, harassment. One appellate court has commented that the motion "has often been used improperly: as a discovery device; to educate the trial judge; in the hope, however faint, of quick victory; and in the expectation, frequently realized, of retarding the progress of a suit and making litigation more expensive."[26] Rule 11[27] (or its state procedural equivalent) acts as a control on such abuse in theory, but it is unclear how effective for this purpose it is in practice.

[2] Procedure

[a] Initial Motion

A motion for summary judgment may be filed by any party, although it is in practice primarily a defendant's device.[28] The motion asserts that

---

[23] *See* McLauchlan, *An Empirical Study of the Federal Summary Judgment Rule,* 6 J. Legal Stud. 427, 458 (1977); *cf.* Schwarzer, *The Analysis and Decision of Summary Judgment Motions* 69 (1991).

[24] R. Figg, R. McCullough & J. Underwood, *Civil Trial Manual* 347 (ALI-ABA student ed. 1974). Copyright © 1974 by the American Law Institute. Reprinted with permission of the American Law Institute — American Bar Association Committee on Continuing Professional Education. *See also* Kennedy, *Federal Summary Judgment: Reconciling Celotex v. Catrett with Adickes v. Kress and the Evidentiary Problems Under Rule 56,* 6 Rev. Litig. 227, 253 (1987).

[25] *See* § 15.14 (law of the case), *infra.*

[26] *Professional Managers, Inc. v. Fawer, Brian, Hardy & Zatkis,* 799 F.2d 218, 221-222 (5th Cir. 1986).

[27] *See* § 8.05[2], *supra;* Dyer, *A Genuine Ground in Summary Judgment for Rule 11,* 99 Yale L.J. 411 (1989).

[28] *McLauchlan,* note 23, *supra,* at 441. Defendant may usually move at any time. Plaintiff must wait a period of time after serving the complaint to enable the defendant to obtain counsel and materials beyond the pleadings with which to respond to the motion. *See, e.g.,* Rule 56(a) (20 days unless adverse party has served a motion for summary judgment).

there is no triable or "genuine" issue of material fact and that the moving party is entitled to judgment as a matter of law.[29]

While it is customary for the movant to support the motion with affidavits and other materials, federal Rule 56 expressly authorizes the motion "with or without affidavits."[30] However, many federal courts have adopted local rules requiring the movant to accompany his motion with a statement of undisputed material facts, citing to supporting materials or the record.[31] Some states have also taken this approach.[32]

The movant may support the motion with "the pleadings, depositions, answers to interrogatories, and admissions on file . . .,"[33] and any other materials that present facts that would be admissible at trial.[34] The summary judgment motion looks prospectively to what can be proven at trial;[35] the admissibility limitation ensures that "trial would [not be] futile on account of lack of competent evidence."[36] For example, material grounded in rumor and hearsay will not support summary judgment.[37] Evidentiary defects in supporting materials are waived if not challenged, just as they would be at trial.[38]

While oral evidence has supported the motion in rare cases, and Rule 43(e) authorizes the court to hear such evidence, its routine acceptance would convert summary judgment procedure into a trial.[39] Rule 56 and all

---

[29] See, e.g., Rule 56(c); Cal. Civ. Proc. Code § 437c(c) (West, WESTLAW through 2000). See § 11.03[3] (the standard for summary judgment), infra.

[30] See Celotex Corp. v. Catrett, 477 U.S. 317, 323 (1986).

[31] Note, Court Examination of the Discovery File on a Motion for Summary Judgment, 79 Mich. L. Rev. 321, 325 n.19 (1980) (listing 28 district courts that have adopted such rules) (hereinafter cited as Court Examination). While such local rules are probably consistent with Rule 56 (see § 1.02, supra, and Rule 83), a local "procedure" adopted by individual judges requiring advanced screening of summary judgment motions was found inconsistent and therefore invalid in Brown v. Crawford County, 960 F.2d 1002 (11th Cir. 1992). The Court of Appeals there noted that a survey had identified no less than thirty federal courts with local rules that conflict with Rule 56. Id. at 1009 n.10, citing Local Rules Project 140 (1989).

[32] See, e.g., Cal. Civ. Proc. Code § 437c(b) (West, WESTLAW through 2000).

[33] Rule 56(c). See generally Brunet, Summary Judgment Materials, 147 F.R.D. 647 (1993).

[34] See, e.g., Duplantis v. Shell Offshore, Inc., 948 F.2d 187 (5th Cir. 1991); Canada v. Blain's Helicopters, Inc., 831 F.2d 920, 925 (9th Cir. 1987); Aguilera v. Cook County Police & Corrections Merit Board, 760 F.2d 844, 849 (7th Cir. 1985), cert. denied, 474 U.S. 907 (1985); Brown v. Trans World Airlines, Inc., 746 F.2d 1354, 1358-1359 (8th Cir. 1984). But cf. Kennedy, note 24, supra, at 256 (rule is ambiguous). See generally Brunet, note 33, supra, at 653-655.

[35] See Duane, The Four Greatest Myths About Summary Judgment, 52 Wash. & Lee L. Rev. 1524, 1535-1541 (1995).

[36] Kern v. Tri-State Ins. Co., 386 F.2d 754, 756 (8th Cir. 1967); See Schwarzer, Summary Judgment: A Proposed Revision of Rule 56, 110 F.R.D. 213, 220 (1987).

[37] See, e.g., Schwarzer, note 36, supra.

[38] See, e.g., Catrett v. Johns-Manville Sales Corp., 826 F.2d 33, 37 (D.C. Cir. 1987), cert. denied, Celotex Corp. v. Catrett, 484 U.S. 1066 (1988); McCormick's Handbook of the Law of Evidence § 4, at 140 (J. Strong 4th ed. 1992). But see Schwarzer, note 23, supra, at 51 (criticizing the waiver rule).

[39] See Stewart v. RCA Corp., 790 F.2d 624 (7th Cir. 1986) (asserting that although Rule 43(e) gives judges full menu of methods for gathering evidence to resolve disputes, Rule 56 is not intended to resolve disputes).

but one state therefore permit the use of affidavits (sworn written statements) to support summary judgment motions. Affidavits must be made on personal knowledge by someone competent to testify.[40] Like all supporting materials, they must "set forth facts as would be admissible in evidence."[41] Hearsay, speculation, conclusions of law, conclusory ultimate facts, and promises that the necessary evidence will be offered at trial therefore cannot support a motion for summary judgment, even when presented by an otherwise proper affidavit.[42]

When admissible material is offered in support of a Rule 12(b)(6) motion to dismiss for failure to state a claim or a Rule 12(c) motion for judgment on the pleadings, these federal rules provide that the motions shall be treated as summary judgment motions. In addition, when evidentiary material in the record suggests the availability of summary judgment, a federal court may grant summary judgment *sua sponte* (on its own, without motion).[43] Fair notice to the opposing party and an opportunity to respond are prerequisites for either the conversion of a Rule 12 motion to a summary judgment motion or *sua sponte* action by the court.

[b] Responses to the Motion

Within a reasonable period of time set by rule,[44] the non-movant may respond to summary judgment motion in three ways and may also cross-move for summary judgment.

---

[40] Sinclair & Hanes, *Summary Judgment: A Proposal for Procedural Reform in the Core Motion Context*, 36 Wm. & Mary L. Rev. 1633, app. B (1995).

[41] Rule 56(e). *See, e.g., Sitts v. U.S.,* 811 F.2d 736 (2d Cir. 1987).

[42] *See, e.g., Leonard v. Dixie Well Service & Supply, Inc.,* 828 F.2d 291 (5th Cir. 1987) (bare statement that plaintiff was a "[s]eaman" when that is the issue will not suffice); *Campbell v. Ft. Worth Bk. & Trust Co.,* 705 S.W.2d 400 (Tex. Ct. App. Dist. 2 1986, *writ ref'd n.r.e.*) (averments "to the best of my knowledge" do not represent the required personal knowledge). *See generally Brunet,* note 33, *supra,* at 658-659. On the other hand, as long as the information contained in the affidavit meets the requirements of Rule 56(e), the fact that it is unsigned does not bar its use to oppose summary judgment. The absence of signature goes only to the form of the affidavit, not to the reliability of its contents. *See Curnow v. Ridgecrest Police,* 952 F.2d 321 (9th Cir. 1991), *cert. denied,* 506 U.S. 972 (1992).

[43] *See United States v. Grayson,* 879 F.2d 620 (9th Cir. 1989) (approving *sua sponte* summary judgment, even without notice to losing party, when that party has "full and fair opportunity to ventilate the issues"); *Portsmouth Square v. Shareholders Protective Comm.,* 770 F.2d 866 (9th Cir. 1985) (affirming trial court's *sua sponte* summary judgment based on plaintiff's inability to establish genuine dispute of material fact in pretrial brief and supporting evidentiary materials). *See generally Celotex,* 477 U.S. at 326 ("district courts are widely acknowledged to possess the power to enter summary judgments *sua sponte,* so long as the losing party was on notice. . . .") (dictum). When courts are reluctant to assert this power, they can usually accomplish the same ends by inviting the parties to file for summary judgment.

[44] Rule 56(c) assures a party opposing summary judgment at least ten days before hearing on the motion in which to respond. Many state rules provide an even longer response time in recognition of the time which a party may need to gather materials in opposition to summary judgment. *See, e.g.,* Cal. Civ. Proc. Code § 437c(a) (West, WESTLAW through 2001) (28 days). A court may properly disregard untimely submissions. *See Lujan v. National Wildlife Fed'n,* 497 U.S. 871, 894-897 (1990).

First, he may present an affidavit under Rule 56(f) stating why he cannot now present facts in opposition to summary judgment.[45] Because most jurisdictions permit defendants to file summary judgment motions at any time, a rule like Rule 56(f) is necessary to give the plaintiff time to undertake discovery.[46] When plaintiff files such an affidavit, the court may either deny the motion for summary judgment or grant a continuance so plaintiff can later respond with affidavits in opposition to summary judgment. The reasonableness of plaintiff's request for time is a crucial factor in the exercise of the court's discretion.[47] It is an abuse of discretion for a court to grant summary judgment without affording the opposing party a reasonable opportunity to take discovery pertinent to the motion, even when that party has not filed a Rule 56(f) affidavit.[48] "If the documents or other discovery sought would be relevant to the issues presented by the motion for summary judgment," one appellate court has said, "the opposing party should be allowed the opportunity to utilize the discovery process to gain access to the requested materials."[49]

Second, even when a party could file materials in opposition to the motion, he may do nothing. Rule 56(e) expressly requires a response with supporting materials only "[w]hen a motion for summary judgment is made and supported as provided in this rule." The federal rule therefore casts a burden of production upon the movant to make a *prima facie* showing that there is no genuine dispute of material fact. This must be satisfied before the burden shifts to the opposing party.[50] In *Adickes v. S.H. Kress & Co.*,[51] for example, the Supreme Court reversed a summary judgment in favor of the defendant restaurant in a civil rights action despite plaintiff's failure to oppose the motion with admissible materials. The case arose from the plaintiff's arrest for vagrancy. Although the defendant properly denied

---

[45] *See generally* Brunet, *Summary Judgment: Federal Law & Practice* § 7.02 (2d ed. 2000); Lapham, *Summary Judgment Before the Completion of Discovery: A Proposed Revision of Federal Rule of Civil Procedure 56(f)*, 24 U. Mich. J.L. Ref. 253, 267-281 (1990).

[46] *See, e.g.,* Cal. Civ. Proc. Code § 437c(h) (West, WESTLAW 2001); N.Y. Civ. Prac. L. & R. § 3212(f) (McKinney, WESTLAW 2001).

[47] *Compare Littlejohn v. Shell Oil Co.,* 483 F.2d 1140 (5th Cir.) (*en banc*), *cert. denied,* 414 U.S. 1116 (1973) (abuse of discretion in the district court's refusal of a continuance pursuant to Rule 56(f), when the 56(f) affidavit demonstrated that the evidence was in the control of the movants and there were complicating factors regarding agreements between counsel about the timing of discovery), *with Walters v. City of Ocean Springs,* 626 F.2d 1317 (5th Cir. 1980) (grant of summary judgment affirmed when the opposing party had ample time to discover allegedly essential non-party witnesses).

[48] *See, e.g.,* Snook v. Trust Co. of George Bank, 859 F.2d 865 (11th Cir. 1988).

[49] *Id.* at 870.

[50] *See Celotex,* 477 U.S. at 330-331 (Brennan, J., dissenting). *See generally* § 11.03[3][b] (relation of summary judgment standard to trial burdens), *infra*; Mullenix, *Summary Judgment: Taming the Breast of Burdens,* 10 Am. J. Trial Advoc. 433, 441 (1987). Of course, the nonmoving party will rarely take the risk of not responding. *Id.*

[51] 398 U.S. 144 (1970). *Adickes* also suggested that the moving party had to "foreclose the possibility" that the nonmovant might prevail at trial. 398 U.S. at 157. *See* Issacharoff & Loewenstein, *Second Thoughts About Summary Judgment,* 100 Yale L.J. 73, 80 & n.39 (1990) (citing cases). The Court subsequently rejected this implication. *See Celotex Corp. v. Catrett,* 477 U.S. 317 (1986); § 11.03[3][b], *infra*.

a conspiracy, evidence in the record that the arresting policeman had been in defendant's restaurant permitted the inference that he and the defendant had conspired to deny the plaintiff service, creating a genuine dispute of material fact.

If, on the other hand, the movant meets her burden of production and the opposing party does nothing, then Rule 56(e) expressly provides that summary judgment "shall be entered against him." To thus avoid summary judgment, the opposing party "may not rest upon the mere allegations or denials" of his pleading, but his "response, by affidavits or otherwise as provided in this rule, must set forth *specific facts* showing that there is a genuine issue for trial."[52] The reason for the exclusion of mere pleadings is clear; the very purpose of summary judgment is "to separate what is formal or pretended in denial or averment from what is genuine and substantial, so that only the latter may subject a suitor to the burden of a trial."[53] Thus, the nonmovant — no less than the movant — must present materials that would be admissible in evidence. But the Supreme Court has said in dictum that "[w]e do not mean that the non-moving party must produce evidence in a form that would be admissible at trial in order to avoid summary judgment."[54] A few courts have read this dictum in isolation to permit the nonmoving party to oppose a summary judgment motion with unauthenticated or otherwise inadmissible evidence.[55] A more faithful reading is that the Court merely meant that depositions were not required and that evidence could be presented in any of the forms approved by the rule, not that the evidence itself could be inadmissible.[56]

The Supreme Court has applied the specific-fact requirement rigorously, emphasizing that a court may not infer specific facts from conclusory affidavits. "Rather, the purpose of Rule 56 is to enable a party who believes there is no genuine dispute as to a specific fact essential to the other side's case to demand at least one sworn averment of that fact before the lengthy process of litigation continues."[57] When local rules require the movant to

---

[52] Emphasis supplied.

[53] *Richard v. Credit Suisse,* 152 N.E. 110, 111 (N.Y. 1926) (Cardozo, J.). Verified pleadings, *see* § 8.05[1] (verification), *supra,* however, are sworn statements which may be treated as affidavits, if they are made upon personal knowledge by a competent affiant and present admissible facts. *See, e.g., Forts v. Malcolm,* 426 F.Supp. 464, 466 (S.D.N.Y. 1977).

[54] *Celotex,* 477 U.S. at 324 (emphasis added).

[55] *See, e.g., Offshore Aviation v. Transcon Lines, Inc.,* 831 F.2d 1013, 1015 n.1 (11th Cir. 1987); *Bushman v. Halm,* 798 F.2d 651, 654 n.5 (3d Cir. 1986). *See generally* Nelken, *One Step Forward, Two Steps Back: Summary Judgment After Celotex,* 40 Hastings L.J. 53, 56, 60-62 (1988) (noting that majority's statements in *Celotex* regarding formal requirements for evidence on summary judgment invited lower court confusion).

[56] *See, e.g., Duplantis v. Shell Offshore, Inc.,* 948 F.2d 187 (5th Cir. 1991). *See generally Brunet,* note 33, *supra,* at 656-657; *Schwarzer,* note 23, *supra,* at 50.

[57] *Lujan v. National Wildlife Fed'n,* 474 U.S. 871, 888-889 (1990). *See generally Brunet,* note 33, *supra,* at 661-663. The specific-fact requirement may preclude reliance on an expert's affidavit if the affiant fails to state specifically the factual basis on which it rests. *Compare Mid-State Fertilizer Co. v. Exchange Nat'l Bank,* 877 F.2d 1333, 1339 (7th Cir. 1989) (so ruling) *with Bulthuis v. Rexall Corp.,* 777 F.2d 1353, 1356 (9th Cir. 1985) (allowing consideration of such an affidavit, subject to moving party's right to request disclosure of underlying facts),

file a statement of undisputed material facts, the opposing party is usually required to deny specifically those facts that he contends are genuinely disputed and to file a counter-statement, or the court may accept movant's statement as admitted.[58]

Finally, the opposing party is free to make a cross-motion for summary judgment. He does not concede the absence of genuine issues on the initial motion by doing so. The filing of cross-motions does not require the court to grant either; it may deny both. Each stands on its own bottom.[59]

[c] Disposition and Appeal

To grant summary judgment, a court must conclude that the movant has met its burden of showing that the material facts are undisputed and that it is entitled to judgment as a matter of law.[60] An evidentiary hearing will not usually attend this determination, although the court may hear oral arguments on the motion. Some federal cases suggest that "the court is obliged to take account of the entire setting of the case and must consider all papers of record as well as any materials prepared for the motion."[61]

This obligation may be qualified, however, by local rules requiring submission of statements of undisputed facts and of counter-statements.[62] When a party fails to identify relevant parts of the record and material facts, these rules deem admitted the adverse party's statements. This makes the disposition of summary judgment more efficient.

One commentator has persuasively argued that the dramatic expansion of discovery since the enactment of the federal rules would make a record-searching obligation on the court inconsistent with Rule 1's admonition that the rules be administered to "secure the just, speedy, and inexpensive determination of every action."[63] Reflecting this view, several circuit courts have held that a court ruling on summary judgment is not required to consider what the parties fail to point out.[64]

If the court finds that the movant has met his burden, it may enter judgment on a claim or defense. It may enter judgment on the issue of

---

amended on other grounds, 789 F.2d 1315 (9th Cir. 1985). See generally Schwarzer, note 23, supra, at 52-57; Brunet, The Use and Misuse of Expert Testimony in Summary Judgment, 22 U.C. Davis L. Rev. 93 (1988).

[58] See, e.g., Wienco, Inc. v. Kathan Ass., Inc., 965 F.2d 565 (7th Cir. 1992).

[59] See Schwarzer, note 23, supra, at 73.

[60] See § 11.03[3][b] (relation of standard for summary judgment to trial burdens), infra.

[61] Celotex, 477 U.S. at 331 n.2 (Brennan, J., dissenting) (citing cases).

[62] See note 31, supra. In Stepanischen v. Merchants Dispatch Transp. Corp., 722 F.2d 922, 930-931 (1st Cir. 1983), the court of appeals, acknowledging that the whole-record obligation posed "the specter of district court judges being unfairly sandbagged by unadvertised factual issues," endorsed adoption of such local rules.

[63] Court Examination, note 31, supra, at 322. See also Schwarzer, note 23, supra, at 49 (arguing that record-searching often poses "an unmanageable burden" on the trial judge).

[64] Shotak v. Tenneco Resins, Inc., 953 F.2d 909, 915 n.7 (5th Cir.) ("Rule 56 does not impose upon the district court a duty to sift through the record. . . ."), reh'g en banc denied, op. withdrawn, in part, 1992 U.S. App. LEXIS 5388 (5th Cir. Mar. 26, 1992), cert. denied, 506 U.S. 832 (1992); Downes v. Beach, 587 F.2d 469 (10th Cir. 1980).

liability alone, even though the amount of damages remains for trial.[65] A federal judge need not make findings of fact or conclusions of law in granting summary judgment,[66] but the Supreme Court has pointedly reminded the lower federal courts that such "findings are extremely helpful to a reviewing court."[67]

If the ruling does not obviate trial, Rule 56(d) requires the court "if practicable [to] ascertain what material facts exist without substantial controversy and what material facts are actually and in good faith controverted." The purpose of this provision "is to salvage constructive results of the court's denial of a properly-brought but unsuccessful summary judgment motion."[68] The key words, however, are "if practicable." The salvage operation usually fails because of the trial courts' reluctance to hazard Rule 56(d) orders in cases that will be tried anyway.

While summary judgments address the merits, they may not be immediately appealable. Summary judgment as to liability alone is interlocutory in character and identified as such under Rule 56(c). Therefore it is not ordinarily appealable in the federal system.[69] Similarly, summary judgment with respect to fewer than all the claims or parties is also not (without more) considered final for purposes of federal appeal, although a court may direct entry of a final judgment in such cases in conformity with Rule 54(b).[70] The reviewing court on appeal decides for itself whether the record, when viewed most favorably to the loser,[71] reveals any genuine issue of material fact and whether the prevailing party was entitled to judgment as a matter of law.[72]

[3] The Standard for Summary Judgment

[a] In General

Rule 56(c) codifies the traditional summary judgment standard, stating that judgment shall be rendered if the movant carries his burden of showing "that there is no genuine issue as to any material fact and that . . . [he] is entitled to judgment as a matter of law." Most state rules phrase the

---

[65] Rule 56(a) & (c). See, e.g., Leasing Serv. Corp. v. Graham, 646 F. Supp. 1410 (S.D.N.Y. 1986); see generally Schwarzer, note 23, supra, at 71 (noting possibility that such partial judgments may encourage settlement).

[66] Rule 52(a). See Anderson v. Liberty Lobby, Inc., 477 U.S. 242, 250 (1986).

[67] Id. at 250 n.6.

[68] SFM Corp. v. Sundstrand Corp., 102 F.R.D. 555, 558 (N.D. Ill. 1984). "There is no such thing as a Rule 56(d) motion;" 56(d) orders are the residual of properly-brought summary judgment motions, not proper ends by themselves. Id. at 661, 662 (citing cases). See generally Wright & Miller § 2737. Because a Rule 56(d) order does not dispose of any claims or defenses, it is more appropriately called a partial summary adjudication (see Wright & Miller § 2737) or partial summary determination (see James, Hazard & Leubsdorf § 4.11) than summary judgment.

[69] See § 13.03[1] (the final judgment rule in general), infra.

[70] See § 13.03[2] (finality in multi-claim and multi-party cases), infra.

[71] See, e.g., Walters v. City of Ocean Springs, 626 F.2d 1317, 1322 (5th Cir. 1980).

[72] See Schwarzer, note 23, supra, at 79; § 13.09[2][a] (de novo review standard), infra.

standard similarly or identically.[73] Because the primary purpose of summary judgment is to avoid an unnecessary trial, the court searches for a genuine issue the determination of which at trial might affect the outcome of the lawsuit. If it finds such an issue, its inquiry is at an end and summary judgment must be denied. The court's function is to determine whether there is such an issue, not to resolve it. A party is entitled to *try* the genuinely disputed issues of material fact and cannot be deprived of the protections of the trial process by summary determination of disputed facts.

Issues of material fact are those "that might affect the outcome of the suit under the governing law."[74] A *material* fact is an essential element of claim or defense for purposes of summary judgment.[75] In a creditor's action on a guaranty, for example, whether the debtor has complied with the underlying agreement by submitting timely financial reports is clearly a material fact because the answer to it can decide the lawsuit.[76] In contrast, the issue whether the parties had reached an oral agreement is immaterial to summary judgment when such an agreement would be unenforceable under the statute of frauds. The controversy over the existence of the agreement is superfluous, since it cannot affect the outcome of the lawsuit.[77]

A *genuine dispute* is one which a reasonable jury could resolve against the movant.[78] The Supreme Court has declared that the standard for summary judgment mirrors the standard for directed verdict (now judgment as a matter of law in federal courts), "which is that the trial judge must direct a verdict if, under the governing law, there can be but one reasonable conclusion as to the verdict."[79] Thus, summary judgment should be granted if the evidence is such that it would require a directed verdict (or judgment as a matter of law) for the movant at trial.[80]

Summary judgment decisions regularly repeat the formula that the judge should not herself weigh the evidence and determine the truth of the matter, but should only determine whether there is a genuine issue for trial.[81] After paying lip service to this formula, the Supreme Court in *Anderson v. Liberty Lobby, Inc.*[82] implicitly recognized that some weighing

---

[73] *See, e.g.,* Cal. Civil Proc. Code § 437c(c) (West, WESTLAW 2001) ("there is no triable issue as to any material fact and that the moving party is entitled to judgment as a matter of law").

[74] *Anderson,* 477 U.S. at 248. *Schwarzer,* note 6, *supra,* at 43-44. Whether something is a fact is often a difficult question in itself. *See id.* at 13-37; § 13.09[2][a], *infra.*

[75] Louis, *Federal Summary Judgment Doctrine: A Critical Analysis,* 83 Yale L.J. 745, 747 (1974). *Cf.* § 8.06[2] (the burden of pleading a claim), *supra.*

[76] *United Brands Co. v. Intermediate Credit Corp.,* 426 F. Supp. 856 (S.D.N.Y. 1977).

[77] *Soar v. National Football League Players Ass'n,* 438 F. Supp. 337 (D.R.I. 1975), *aff'd,* 550 F.2d 1287 (1st Cir. 1977).

[78] *Anderson v. Liberty Lobby, Inc.,* 477 U.S. 242, 248 (1986).

[79] *Id.* at 250. *See also* Rule 50(a).

[80] *Id.* (citation omitted). *But see Kennedy,* note 24, *supra,* at 232-234 (arguing differences between the standards); *Mullenix,* note 30, *supra,* at 467-468 (same); § 11.03[3][d], *infra.*

[81] *Id.*

[82] 477 U.S. 242 (1986).

of the evidence is unavoidable because the judge decides whether the dispute is one that a jury could *reasonably* resolve against the movant. The *Anderson* Court restated the inquiry as "whether the evidence presents a sufficient disagreement to require submission to a jury or whether it is so one-sided that one party must prevail as a matter of law."[83] The Court added that the standard for summary judgment "necessarily implicates the standard of proof that would apply at the trial on the merits."[84] In the normal civil case the judge must therefore determine whether a reasonable jury could resolve the issue for the non-movant by a preponderance of the evidence.[85] As one district judge has explained, "a directed verdict analysis necessarily involves a qualitative evaluation of the evidence, and a decision as to whether a rational factfinder could find in the nonmovant's favor. Such an analysis necessarily calls for a decision of fact, and places the judge in the factfinder's shoes."[86] After *Anderson*, this analysis applies not only to directed verdict, but to summary judgment.

Whether *Anderson* did more than restate the old cliches about summary judgment is unclear. Federal courts still pay lip-service to the following laundry list of considerations assembled by the Court of Appeals for the Fourth Circuit:

> [The non-movant] is . . . entitled, as on a motion for a directed verdict, to have the credibility of his evidence as forecast assumed, his version of all that is in dispute accepted, all internal conflicts in it resolved favorably to him, the most favorable of possible alternative inferences from it drawn in his behalf; and finally, to be given the benefit of all favorable legal theories invoked by the evidence so considered.[87]

Anderson did not purport to invalidate these considerations; it only added the valuative component of reasonableness to each of them. The non-movant still benefits from doubts about the material facts, but only from the reasonable, and not just from the "slightest doubts."[88] Yet, in a companion summary judgment decision, *Matsushita Electric Industrial Co. v. Zenith Radio Corp.*,[89] the Court implied that summary judgment is proper even

---

[83] *Id.* at 251-252.

[84] *Id.* at 252.

[85] *See* § 12.04 (burdens of proof), *infra.* Accordingly, *Anderson* ultimately held that when the more rare clear and convincing standard of proof, *id.*, applies to the issue of actual malice in a defamation case, the proper inquiry on a motion for summary judgment is "whether the evidence presented is such that a reasonable jury might find that actual malice had been shown with convincing clarity." *Anderson,* 477 U.S. at 257.

[86] Richey, *Thoughts on Summary Judgment in Employment Discrimination Cases,* 1 Fed. Jurist 4 (1989) (emphasis in original). Judge Richey decided *Celotex* in the trial court.

[87] *Charbonnages de France v. Smith,* 597 F.2d 406 (4th Cir. 1979).

[88] Courts have occasionally embraced the "slightest doubt" test for summary judgment, to the nearly universal opprobrium of academic commentators. *See, e.g., Wright* § 99; *Wright & Miller* § 2727; *Louis,* note 75, *supra,* at 760-762. This gloss on Rule 56(c) should not survive *Anderson. See* Childress, *A New Era for Summary Judgments: Recent Shifts At the Supreme Court,* 6 Rev. Litig. 263, 280 (1987).

[89] 475 U.S. 574, 596-597 (1986). *See generally Schwarzer,* note 23, *supra,* at 64-68; Levine, Comment, *Summary Judgment: The Majority View Undergoes a Complete Reversal in the 1986 Supreme Court,* 37 Emory L.J. 171, 196 (1989); Friedenthal, *Cases on Summary Judgment: Has There Been a Material Change in Standards?,* 63 Notre Dame L. Rev. 770, 784-787 (1988).

when there are equally plausible competing inferences. This may be technically correct. Yet some courts may take it as an invitation to invade the factfinder's province when the court finds one inference more plausible than another.

Once the trial judge determines that there is no genuine issue of material fact, he has still to decide whether the movant is entitled to judgment as a matter of governing law. Modern pleading jurisdictions usually have dispensed with the doctrine that a party is bound by the legal theory presented in his pleadings, [90] and the court will decide the legal question by any available theory —whether or not pleaded. [91] Mere difficulty of the legal question is not grounds for postponing its decision if the record is sufficiently complete. [92] It is not, after all, a genuine dispute about the law that is reserved for trial, but only a genuine dispute about the material facts. Yet novel or constitutionally sensitive questions of law are often best decided upon the fuller record made at trial. Courts thus have discretion to deny summary judgment "where there is reason to believe that the better course would be to proceed to a full trial." [93]

Although we have been using the jury case as our model, the rules of summary judgment theoretically apply to nonjury cases with equal force. A party is entitled to *try* genuinely disputed facts, whether before a judge (bench trial) or a jury (jury trial). Some commentators and courts, however, argue a party can be deprived of a bench trial by summary judgment "when the question for decision concerns drawing inferences from undisputed evidence, or interpreting and evaluating evidence to derive legal conclusions, [because] a trial *may* not add to the judge's ability to decide." [94] They even urge summary judgment in such cases when the judge needs a fuller record, because she can then simply hold "a limited evidentiary hearing" under Rule 43(e) "to develop the record." [95] This argument either assumes that the opportunity to hear all the evidence in context adds nothing to the accuracy of the fact-finding, or that the nonmoving party may be obliged to make the full record in advance of trial. Both assumptions are controversial, [96] and the latter, coupled with a Rule 43(e) evidentiary hearing, converts the summary judgment hearing into trial-before-trial. [97] And the

---

[90] *See* §§ 8.03[2] (theory of pleadings under the codes) & 8.04[2] (under modern pleading), *supra.*

[91] *See Wright & Miller* § 2725.

[92] *Id.*

[93] *Anderson,* 477 U.S. at 255 (*citing Kennedy v. Silas Mason Co.,* 334 U.S. 249 (1948)). *See generally Wright & Miller* § 2725.

[94] *Schwarzer,* note 23, *supra,* at 39 (emphasis added). *Accord, Nunez v. Superior Oil Co.,* 572 F.2d 1119, 1123-1124 (5th Cir. 1974).

[95] *Id. See also Richey,* note 86, *supra,* at 7.

[96] *See* Stempel, *A Distorted Mirror: The Supreme Court's Shimmering View of Summary Judgment, Directed Verdict, and the Adjudication Process,* 49 Ohio St. L.J. 95, 99, 177-178 (1988) (context of full trial improves accuracy of fact-finding); § 13.09[2][b] (suggesting same rationale for deference to trial court fact-finding).

[97] *See Stewart v. RCA Corp.,* 790 F.2d 624, 628 (7th Cir. 1986) ("If [a judge could make a factual finding at a Rule 43(e) hearing], it would be the end of the difference between

argument ignores or at least blurs the Advisory Committee's distinction between a Rule 52(c) judgment on partial findings in bench trials and summary judgment. These judgments are subject to different standards of appellate review. [98]

[b] Relationship to Trial Burdens

The analogy of summary judgment to directed verdict (or judgment as a matter of law at trial) works well when the movant is the party with the burden of persuasion [99] at trial. His burden on summary judgment is then aligned with his trial burden: to show that there is no genuine dispute concerning all the material factual elements of his claim or affirmative defense. [100] This kind of summary judgment motion can be called a *proof-of-the-elements* motion for summary judgment, made by a claimant for judgment on her claim or, probably more often, by defendant for judgment on an affirmative defense (for which a defendant bears the burden of proof at trial).

Lundeen v. Cordner [101] is a well-known example. The suit involved competing claims for proceeds of a life insurance policy. An intervener claimed that the decedent had intended to change the beneficiaries in intervener's favor. Governing law did not require the change to be written into the policy in order to be effective, so long as the insured's intent was proven. The intervener supported her motion for summary judgment with an affidavit of a neutral witness attesting to decedent's stated intent to change the beneficiaries and to the contents of the change, and with other supporting documentation. The opposing party could point to no specific facts in rebuttal. The court granted summary judgment because the movant, on whom the burden of persuasion would fall at trial, established that there was no genuine dispute concerning all of the essential elements of her claim.

The analogy between summary judgment and directed verdict (or judgment as a matter of law at trial) breaks down, however, when the movant would not have the burden of persuasion at trial. Were the case to go to

---

summary judgment and trial. . . ."); *Wright & Miller* § 2416 ("The purpose of summary judgment in giving a speedy adjudication in cases that present no genuine issue is defeated if the hearing on the motion becomes a preliminary trial."); *Brunet*, note 33, *supra*, at 649-652.

[98] Judgment entered under Rule 52(c) differs from a summary judgment under Rule 56 in the nature of the evaluation made by the court. A judgment on partial findings is made after the court has heard *all the evidence bearing on a crucial issue of fact*, and the finding is reversible only if the appellate court finds it to be "clearly erroneous." A summary judgment, in contrast, is made on the basis of facts established on account of the absence of contrary evidence or presumptions; such establishments of fact are rulings on questions of law as provided in Rule 56(a) and are not shielded by the "clear error" standard of review. *See* Rule 52(c) advisory committee's notes (1991) (emphasis added); § 12.10 (bench trials), *infra*. But *see Schwarzer*, note 23, *supra*, at 79-81 (suggesting clearly-erroneous review for finding of "ultimate facts" by summary judgment).

[99] *See* § 12.04 (burdens of proof), *infra*.

[100] *See generally Louis,* note 75, *supra,* at 747; *Shwarzer,* note 23, *supra,* at 45-46.

[101] 354 F.2d 401 (8th Cir. 1966).

trial, the motion for directed verdict would come after the non-movant has put on its case, and the movant could simply argue deficiencies in that case. But before trial, the non-movant attacked by summary judgment has yet to put on a case. How can the movant then satisfy his burden of production?

If the analogy to directed verdict (or judgment as a matter of law at trial) held, the movant in these circumstances could satisfy his burden by a naked motion putting the opposing party to her proof.[102] We might call this a *no-evidence* or *absence-of-evidence* motion for summary judgment. However, this would invite use of summary judgment as a tool of harassment. The movant would be able to force a preview of the opposing party's evidence without paying the price of previewing his own.[103]

An alternative is to require the movant to support the motion with evidence completely negating the existence of an essential element of the opposing party's case. We might call this a *disproof-of-an-element* motion for summary judgment. In the oft-cited case of *Dyer v. MacDougall*,[104] the defendant to a defamation claim won summary judgment by presenting affidavits of all the persons present at the alleged slander, denying that it took place. This alternative, however, shifts the burden of persuasion from the opposing party (who would have it at trial) to the movant. It may thwart the primary purpose of summary judgment by letting a party who has no evidence that would survive a motion for directed verdict or judgment as a matter of law at trial to remain in the shadows, while a summary judgment movant struggles to prove a negative. For this reason, some commentators have proposed that a summary judgment movant who would not have the burden of persuasion at trial need show only enough evidence to permit — not require — the jury to find in his favor.[105]

---

[102] *See* Currie, *Thoughts on Directed Verdicts and Summary Judgments,* 45 U. Chi. L. Rev. 72, 79 (1977) (urging this construction of movant's burden in order to accomplish summary judgment's purpose of determining whether there is sufficient evidence to justify trial). Texas has expressly authorized a no-evidence motion for summary judgment in its summary judgment rule:

> No-Evidence Motion. After adequate time for discovery, a party without presenting summary judgment evidence may move for summary judgment on the ground that there is no evidence of one or more essential elements of a claim or defense on which an adverse party would have the burden of proof at trial. The motion must state the elements as to which there is no evidence. The court must grant the motion unless the respondent produces summary judgment evidence raising a genuine issue of material fact.

Tex. R. Civ. P. 166(a)(i). *See generally* Frazier et al., *Celotex Comes to Texas: No-Evidence Summary Judgment and Other Recent Developments in Summary Judgment Practice,* 32 Tex. Tech. L. Rev. 111 (2000).

[103] *See* § 11.03[1], *supra,* regarding this built-in control on summary judgment. Rule 11's certification requirements might deter some harassment, *cf.* Pollak, *Liberalizing Summary Adjudication: A Proposal,* 36 Hastings L.J. 419, 428-429 (1985) (urging the adoption of certification requirements in California summary judgment practice in order to reduce the likelihood of such harassment), but summary judgment practice might still be substantially unbalanced.

[104] 201 F.2d 265 (2d Cir. 1952).

[105] *See* Louis, note 75, *supra,* at 748, 753-759.

The Supreme Court addressed but did not clearly resolve this issue in *Celotex Corporation v. Catrett*. [106] Celotex was defendant in a products liability suit brought by a survivor of a victim of asbestosis. It moved for summary judgment on the ground that plaintiff had failed to produce any evidence that Celotex's products were the cause of the asbestosis — a no-evidence motion for summary judgment. The trial court granted summary judgment, and the court of appeals reversed on the grounds that the movant had failed to adduce any affirmative evidence in support of its motion. The Supreme Court reversed and remanded.

Eight Justices rejected the first alternative discussed above, agreeing that, even if a party would not have the burden of production at trial, its case for summary judgment must consist of more than the naked no-evidence motion. They agreed that such a movant must at least identify those portions of the discovery record at summary judgment that demonstrate the absence of a genuine issue of material fact. [107] At least seven Justices also appeared to reject the alternative at the other extreme: that such a movant can only satisfy his summary judgment burden by submitting a disproof-of-an-element motion, with affirmative evidence negating an essential element of the non-movant's case. [108]

The Supreme Court exhibited less certainty over application of these principles, disagreeing about whether Celotex had identified portions of the record showing an absence of a genuine issue of material fact on causation. Moreover, the case left unclear how much beyond a naked no-evidence motion for summary judgment was required of a movant who would not have the burden of persuasion at trial. Celotex had supported its motion for summary judgment by noting that the plaintiff had failed in answers to interrogatories to identify any witnesses who could testify about the decedent's exposure to Celotex's asbestos products. Four Justices thought this enough to satisfy Celotex's burden of production on summary judgment and remanded for the Court of Appeals to decide whether plaintiff's opposing evidence was admissible. [109] Three Justices thought that plaintiff's identification elsewhere in the record of a possible witness on the issue of exposure obligated Celotex to attack the adequacy of the witness's evidence, despite the plaintiff's failure to supply it by affidavit or otherwise. [110] Justice White voted to remand for the Court of Appeals to address this point. [111]

---

[106] 477 U.S. 317 (1986).

[107] *Id.* at 324 (Rehnquist, C.J., writing for the Court), 327 (White, J.), 331 (Brennan, Blackmun, and Burger, JJ., dissenting).

[108] *Id.* at 324 (Rehnquist, C.J., writing for the Court), 337 (Brennan, Blackmun, and Burger, JJ., dissenting).

[109] *Id.* at 328.

[110] *Id.* at 336-339.

[111] *Id.* at 328-329. On remand, the Court of Appeals again held that summary judgment was inappropriate. It found that Celotex waived its objections to admissibility of the plaintiff's evidence by failing to make timely objection below, and then concluded that the evidence raised a genuine issue of material fact concerning causation. *Catrett v. Johns-Manville Sales Corp.*, 826 F.2d 33 (D.C. Cir. 1987), *cert. denied*, 484 U.S. 1066 (1988).

One commentator has suggested a means for reconciling the apparently divergent views of the justices in *Celotex* regarding application of the *Celotex* principles. She suggests that if, during discovery prior to a summary judgment motion, the nonmoving party has identified sources of evidence for elements of its case, then the movant is obliged to track down that evidence by its own discovery before seeking summary judgment. Thus, had the plaintiff in *Celotex* identified during discovery the two possible witnesses who could support her case, the defendant would have been obliged to depose them or take other additional discovery prior to making its motion for summary judgment. This solution seeks to avoid the problem of forcing a nonmoving party to depose her own witnesses in order to avoid no-evidence summary judgment, without relaxing the requirement for admissible evidence.[112]

[c] Particular Issues: Credibility and State of Mind

Numerous courts have said that summary judgment is inappropriate in cases involving issues of credibility and state of mind.[113] They offer different reasons for this view, emphasizing that demeanor is crucial in such cases and uniquely for the fact-finder to assess; that the facts are in the control of the movant where his credibility or state of mind is relevant; that self-interest infuses the statements of the parties and alone raises a triable issue of fact; and that parties opposing summary judgment in such cases are entitled to the incentive to truth provided by the formality of trial.[114]

These points may be valid in particular cases. Nonetheless, summary judgment cases are sufficiently varied to elude this kind of treatment by formula.[115] The better approach is to examine credibility and state of mind objections critically on a case-by-case basis. As Professor Moore has said, "Here, on last analysis, a problem of judging is involved."[116]

Lundeen[117] again provides an illustration. Movant there offered two affidavits by an employee of the company for whom the insured had worked before his death, attesting to the insured's stated intent to change the beneficiaries of an insurance policy purchased by the company. In opposition, the adverse party argued that the employee-affiant's story was so vital

---

[112] *See generally Nelken*, note 55, *supra*, at 75-76.

[113] Lockard, *Summary Judgment in Pennsylvania: Time for Another Look at Credibility Issues*, 35 Duq. L. Rev. 625 (1997) (criticizing Pennsylvania rule restricting summary judgment where supporting evidence is testimonial). *See generally* Sonenshein, *State of Mind and Credibility in the Summary Judgment Context: A Better Approach*, 78 Nw. U. L. Rev. 774, 780 (1983) (citing illustrative cases); Collins, Note, *Summary Judgment and Circumstantial Evidence*, 40 Stan. L. Rev. 491 (1988).

[114] For example, in the oft-cited case of *Poller v. Broadcasting System, Inc.*, 368 U.S. 464 (1962), the Supreme Court cautioned that summary judgment "should be used sparingly in complex antitrust litigation where motive and intent play leading roles, the proof is largely in the hands of the alleged conspirators, and hostile witnesses thicken the plot."

[115] *See First National Bank of Arizona v. Cities Service Co.*, 391 U.S. 253 (1968). *See Wright & Miller* § 2725.

[116] J. Moore, *Moore's Federal Practice* ¶ 56.15[1.-0] (2d ed. 1994).

[117] 354 F.2d 401, discussed in text accompanying note 101, *supra*.

that the case should proceed to trial where his demeanor could be observed during his testimony and where he could be cross-examined.

Affirming the grant of summary judgment for the movant, the appellate court reasoned that the same argument could be leveled at any affidavit offered in support of summary judgment. "[I]f plaintiff's position is correct that an affiant's credibility is always an issue for the trial court, then the granting of summary judgment would be virtually impossible when it is based in any way upon an affidavit."[118] The court's reasoning is persuasive. To accept plaintiff's bald argument would negate the role contemplated for affidavits in Rule 56 and unduly restrict the availability of summary judgments.

Instead, credibility should be put at issue by a showing of "specific facts"[119] raising a genuine issue. While the opposing party in *Lundeen* apparently did not attempt such a showing, the appellate court approved summary judgment only after conducting an unsuccessful search of the record for a genuine issue of credibility. It noted that the employee-affiant was competent and in a position to observe the facts related in his affidavits. He appeared to be an unbiased witness without personal or financial interest in the litigation. His affidavits were "positive, internally consistent, unequivocal, and in full accord with documentary evidence."[120] There was therefore not the slightest indication that he might be impeached by cross-examination or might supply useful information for the opposing party. Finally, that party had made no effort to secure his deposition, which suggested that even she believed there was little to gain from cross-examination.[121]

To block summary judgment, matters of credibility and state of mind should be placed specifically at issue by the traditional modes of impeachment: "bias, interest, prejudice, corruption, defects in testimonial capacity, prior bad acts bearing on veracity, prior convictions, poor character for veracity, and prior inconsistent statements."[122] The interest of a party-affiant or deponent does not invariably raise an issue of credibility; nor is the control of relevant information by the movant always a sufficient reason for the inability of the opposing party to specify facts suggesting

---

[118] 354 F.2d at 409.

[119] Rule 56(e).

[120] *Lundeen,* 354 F.2d at 408.

[121] The affiant was overseas and a deposition upon oral questions would have imposed a substantial expense on the opposing party that would otherwise fall on the movant, who would have had to call the affiant as a witness or offer his deposition at trial to meet its burden of persuasion. Such considerations of relative cost and convenience may fairly be considered in ruling on a summary judgment motion in the circumstances, but it is incumbent on the opposing party to make them known by a Rule 56(f) affidavit. In any event, the opposing party in *Lundeen* did not avail itself of even less expensive discovery options, like a deposition upon written questions. *See* § 10.08[1] (procedure for taking depositions), *supra.*

[122] *Sonenshein,* note 113, *supra,* at 798-801. This obligation is, of course, subject to any reasonable explanation by an opposing party for its inability to present the necessary facts to establish a genuine issue. *See* Rule 56(f).

impeachment. Interest and lack of access together may in particular cases establish a genuine issue.[123]

The allocation of the burden of persuasion at trial is also relevant to credibility issues. When the non-movant would have the burden of persuasion at trial, she may not defeat summary judgment simply by raising an issue of the credibility of the movant's denials of material facts. The reason is that she is not by that showing relieved of her own burden of showing evidence from which a reasonable jury could find in her favor.

> It is axiomatic that a party is not permitted to prove a positive proposition by first offering a witness who refutes the proposition, and then impeaching that witness. The jury cannot on this basis *find* that the positive proposition is a proven fact. . . . [A] contrary rule would permit the jury to find a fact . . . despite the absence of any affirmative evidence of that fact in the record.[124]

On the other hand, when the movant would also have the burden of persuasion at trial, specifically established issues of credibility should be enough to defeat summary judgment.[125]

[d] Assessment

To assess summary judgment, we need to consider what the courts do, what they say, and what effect their actions and rhetoric have on the "just, speedy and inexpensive determination of every action."[126]

Prior to the Supreme Court's *Anderson-Celotex-Matsushita* trilogy of summary judgment opinions in 1986, the traditional view was that summary judgment was rarely granted and that grants were often reversed.[127] Open judicial hostility to summary judgment was not uncommon.[128] But in each of the trilogy cases, the Supreme Court ruled in support of summary judgment, and in *Celotex* the Court sang its praises:

> Summary judgment procedure is properly regarded not as a disfavored procedural shortcut, but rather as an integral part of the Federal Rules

---

[123] *See, e.g., Wilmington Trust Co. v. Manufacturers Life Ins. Co.,* 624 F.2d 707 (5th Cir. 1980) (reversing summary judgment for insurer with burden of proof, when it rested on subjective testimony of the insurer's own employee and when the facts were within the insurer's exclusive knowledge).

[124] *Sonenshein,* note 113, *supra,* at 789. Reprinted by special permission of the Northwestern University Law Review, © 1983 by Northwestern University School of Law, vol. 78. *See Anderson v. Liberty Lobby, Inc.,* 477 U.S. 242, 256-257 (1986).

[125] *See, e.g., Wilmington Trust,* 624 F.2d 707.

[126] Rule 1.

[127] *See, e.g., McLauchlan,* note 23, *supra,* at 449, (reporting 49% reversal rate in sample of federal courts); *Sonenshein,* note 113, *supra,* at 775 n.5 (50% in California; 81.2% in Florida; 50% in Fifth Circuit; 70% of cases that reached Texas Supreme court) (citations omitted); *Kennedy,* note 24, *supra,* at 254 n.112.

[128] *See, e.g., Wells v. Openheimer & Co.,* 101 F.R.D. 358, 359 (S.D.N.Y. 1984) (Knapp, J.) ("motions for summary judgment in this Circuit [2d] were usually a waste of time and should be discouraged"), *vacated,* 106 F.R.D. 258 (S.D.N.Y. 1985). One district judge in New Orleans acknowledged the Fifth Circuit's hostility by posting the sign, "No Spitting, No Summary Judgments!" *Childress,* note 68 *supra,* at 264.

as a whole, which are designed "to secure the just, speedy and inexpensive determination of every action." Fed. Rule Civ. Proc. 1. . . . . Rule 56 must be construed with due regard not only for the rights of persons asserting claims and defenses that are adequately based in fact to have those claims and defenses tried to a jury, but also for the rights of persons opposing such claims and defenses to demonstrate in the manner provided by the Rule, prior to trial, that the claims and defenses have no factual basis.[129]

Depending on their affection for trial, commentators heralded or bemoaned the dawn of a new era in summary judgment. They predicted, and some purported to find, a surge in the filing and success of summary judgment motions, especially motions by defendants.[130]

More than a decade later, we are still not certain whether these predictions have come true, partly because the database of reported decisions omits denials of summary judgment which, as interlocutory decisions, go unreported. The *overall* rate at which summary judgment motions were filed had increased *before* the trilogy, but neither it nor the success rate for summary judgments changed much immediately after.[131] On the other hand, the rate of filing for product liability, antitrust, libel, and civil rights (particularly employment discrimination) cases did significantly increase after the trilogy.[132] Moreover, several commentators have noted a very substantial shift in reported federal case dispositions from dispositions by trial to disposition by summary judgment. One found that in 1973, there were an average of 14 summary judgment dispositions per volume of the Federal Reporter compared to an average of 52 trial dispositions, while the comparable numbers for 1997-98 had changed to 47 summary judgment dispositions compared to 20 trial dispositions.[133] Reporting on "summary judgment at 60" in the D.C. Circuit, Judge Wald also noted that 22% of case terminations in that circuit in 1996-97 were by summary judgment compared to about 3% by trial, leading her to speculate that "summary

---

[129] 477 U.S. 317, 327 (1986) (citation omitted).

[130] *See, e.g.,* Gordillo, Note, *Summary Judgment and Problems in Applying the Celotex Trilogy Standard,* 42 Clev. St. L. Rev. 263 (1994); Issacharoff, note 51, *supra,* at 88-89; *Stempel,* note 96, *supra,* at 99 (stating that the trilogy "effected major changes in summary judgment doctrine and practice"); Howley, Note, *Summary Judgment in Federal Court: New Maxims for a Familiar Rule,* 34 N.Y.L. Sch. L. Rev. 201, 203 (1989) (asserting that new doctrine announced in trilogy "has virtually eliminated trial in certain types of cases").

[131] *Sinclair & Hanes,* note 40, *supra,* at 1660 (reporting that proportion of summary judgment motions granted has not increased significantly through 1993); Cecil, *Trends in Summary Judgment Practice: A Summary of Findings,* 1 FJC Directions 11, 13-14 (1991). These figures omit the special category of prisoner cases, in which the rate declined. The data in the text are drawn from this study.

[132] Wald, *Summary Judgment at Sixty,* 76 Tex. L. Rev. 1897, 1938 (1998) (noting that employment discrimination lawyers widely report more frequent grant of summary judgment in employment discrimination cases than in others); *New Maxims,* note 130, *supra,* at 213-214 n.99, 218-219 n.125; McGinley, *Credulous Courts and the Tortured Trilogy: The Improper Use of Summary Judgment in Title VII and ADEA Cases,* 34 B.C. L. Rev. 203 (1993). *See also* Beiner, *The Misuse of Summary Judgment in Hostile Environment Cases,* 34 Wake Forest L. Rev. 71 (1999) (finding excessive use of summary judgment in sexual harassment cases).

[133] Mollica, *Federal Summary Judgment at High Tide,* 84 Marq. L. Rev. 141, 144, 218-219 (2000).

judgment may in fact be the more commonly used mode of disposition on the merits, outnumbering settlement by court-annexed arbitration, mediation, early neutral evaluation, and other settlement techniques," as well as trial.[134] It is not clear, however, whether such statistics reflect significant increases in the rate of summary judgment or just a decline in the trial rate, due as much to settlement (and attendant dismissal) as summary judgment.

Nevertheless, there is little doubt that the trilogy sent a signal of Supreme Court support for summary judgment to judges looking for help in controlling exploding dockets. The Supreme Court's trilogy, Judge Wald skeptically noted, "promoted summary judgment from a housekeeping device for picking up obviously unworthy cases to a major option to be encouraged, or even pushed, in all kinds of disputes, large and small, even in some involving factual controversies."[135] Advocates of summary judgment certainly tout it as an efficiency tool for clearing dockets and avoiding trial costs.[136]

Yet this accounting is incomplete. It omits the cost of preparing and, more significantly, of opposing the summary judgment motion itself, including some costs (especially to plaintiff) that would not be incurred in trial (e.g., deposing your own witnesses). It also omits the costs of denied motions.[137]

Moreover, the costs of the so-called new summary judgment are not evenly distributed. *Celotex* lowered the price of summary judgment for defendant/movants who would not have the burden of proof at trial.

> Something close to a one page form motion by defendant can throw on the plaintiff the responsibility to dredge, structure, collate and cross-reference all materials in the file to make them available to the judge before trial. Because the material must be reduced to a coherently structured written form, this task can sometimes take as long or longer than actually trying the case.[138]

The low cost to defendant/movants of making a "put-up-or-shut-up" motion and high price to plaintiffs may have altered the balance of power, and, some have suggested, discouraged settlement.[139] On the other hand, this

---

[134] *Wald*, note 132, *supra* at 1915. Because of the number of cases to which the federal government is party, and the possibility that statutory issues are more significant in such cases than in private cases, the D.C. Circuit's experience may not be typical.

[135] *Wald*, note 134, *supra*, at 1913.

[136] *Id.* (implying that summary judgment eases docket pressures). *But see McLauchlan*, note 23, *supra*, at 456-458 (finding little time-saving in summary judgment). Federal judges also report that prompt rulings on motions for summary judgment are among the two most effective methods for controlling groundless litigation. Wiggins, et al., *The Federal Judicial Center's Study of Rule 11*, 2 FJC Directions 31 (1991).

[137] Marcus, *Completing Equity's Conquest? Reflections on the Future of Trial Under the Federal Rules of Civil Procedure*, 50 U. Pitt. L. Rev. 725, 774-775 (1989); *Stempel*, note 96, *supra*, at 171, 191 & n.449.

[138] Risinger, *Another Step in the Counter-Revolution: A Summary Judgement on the Supreme Court's New Approach to Summary Judgment*, 54 Brooklyn L. Rev. 35, 41 (1988).

[139] *See, e.g., Issacharoof*, note 51, *supra*, at 75; *Stempel*, note 96, *supra*, at 161-162, 180-181; *Risinger*, note 138, *supra*, at 39.

result may simply have compensated for unfair advantages plaintiffs enjoyed with notice pleading and essentially unlimited discovery.

But the new summary judgment may also intrude seriously on trial by converting once "summary" proceedings into a full dress trial rehearsal. The possible costs of downgrading trial [140] include diminished accuracy from the loss of demeanor evidence, spontaneity, and of whatever comprehensibility oral testimony affords; loss of participant satisfaction; loss of public interest and access; and loss of confidence in the reliability of judgment because of the substitution of unaccountable federal judges for juries of peers. Some commentators also suggest that litigants pay a price in constitutional rights to try their factual disputes. [141]

Finally, the enthusiasm for summary judgment may also infect other aspects of pretrial practice to facilitate summary disposition. Rule 12 motions to dismiss may more often be converted formally or "informally" to summary judgment, and technical requirements may more often be imposed strictly to yield summary dispositions by procedural default. [142]

While the verdict is still out on the new summary judgment, we should not let Supreme Court rhetoric obscure the fact that summary judgment and directed verdict are not, after all, the same. "The crucial difference between summary judgment and the directed verdict, . . . is that before trial *all* the evidence is not available to the judge for consideration. The directed verdict standard requires that the judge assess what a reasonable jury could find on *all* the evidence, which is not the case at summary judgment." [143] Directed verdict rests on a known record; summary judgment on a predicted record. [144] As Judge Wald put it, summary judgment in her circuit has become "something like a gestalt verdict based on an early snapshot of the case," [145] "applying legal principles to incomplete, often anemic, factual scenarios." [146]

The reliability of factfinding, and often even of law-deciding, is greater the larger the data base. [147] One commentator notes that "the largest increase in the data base and its reliability occurs between summary judgment and directed verdict at the close of the plaintiff's case." [148] To the extent that the new summary judgment, by so emphatically equating summary judgment and directed verdict, "permits courts to conclude a case

---

[140] *See generally Marcus*, note 137, *supra*, at 757-783; *Stempel*, note 96, *supra*, at 171-173, 191.

[141] *Mollica*, note 133, *supra* at 181-205 (arguing that many applications of summary judgment "press against tolerable constitutional limits" established by due process as well as the Seventh Amendment).

[142] *Id.* at 177-178; *Wald*, note 132, *supra*, at 1930-1939.

[143] *Mullenix*, note 50, *supra*, at 474.

[144] *Risinger*, note 138, *supra*, at 37-38.

[145] *Wald*, note 134, *supra*, at 1917.

[146] *Id.* at 1944.

[147] *See Stempel*, note 96, *supra*, at 176-177 (analogizing from statistics).

[148] *Id.* at 177.

as though they did so upon a much richer data base than actually possessed," it may be "bad science and probability theory, as well as bad law."[149]

Having created a more permissive climate for summary judgment by its 1986 trilogy of summary judgment opinions, after two decades the Supreme Court may be tempering its enthusiasm.[150] In opinions reviewing trial court rulings on motions for judgment, the Court has again likened the standard for Rule 50 motions to the standard for summary judgment and then emphasized that trial courts should be cautious to avoid making credibility determinations.[151] Reviewing a summary judgment, it has held it error for a trial court "to resolve the disputed fact of motivation at the summary judgment stage" and noted that a proof-of-the-elements summary judgment "is inappropriate when the evidence is susceptible of different interpretations or inferences by the trier of fact."[152] It has also twice rejected judicial constructions of statutes tending to facilitate summary disposition.[153] None of these opinions carves new ground in summary judgment doctrine, but collectively they may suggest that the Supreme Court is starting to "chip[] away at the edges of the prevailing summariness in federal litigation. . . ."[154]

§ 11.04 Dismissal or Nonsuit

[1] Voluntary Dismissal or Nonsuit

There are times when plaintiff would like to withdraw suit. This happens whenever plaintiff's case seems likely to lead to a binding adjudication that will defeat or compromise his claim and when it seems reasonable to expect a more favorable result from suit brought at a different time or place.[155] If such a plaintiff can obtain dismissal *without prejudice* to his opportunity to litigate the same claim later,[156] he will voluntarily dismiss his claim.

The common law treated plaintiff as master of his case and therefore permitted him to dismiss or take a *nonsuit* without prejudice at any time

---

[149] *Id.*

[150] *See Mollica*, note 133, *supra*, at 205-218 (summarizing more recent Supreme Court cases in arguing that Court is belatedly "resisting the trend towards summariness").

[151] *Id.* at 205-207, analyzing cases, including *Reeves v. Sanderson Plumbing Prod., Inc.*, 120 S. Ct. 2097 (2000), in which the Court stressed that on Rule 50 and Rule 56 motions alike, the trial court should review all the evidence in the record as a whole but "must disregard all evidence favorable to the moving party that the jury is not required to believe," that is, any evidence which is contradicted or impeached. *Id.* at 2110.

[152] *Hunt v. Cromartie*, 526 U.S. 541, 553 (1999).

[153] *See Mollica*, note 133, *supra*, at 212-215.

[154] *Id.* at 218.

[155] For example, when a defendant has asserted a limitations defense that appears to be good in the forum, *see generally* Taylor, Note, *Rule 41(a)(2) Dismissals: Forum Shopping for a Statute of Limitations*, 20 Mem. St. U. L. Rev. 629 (1990), or a troublesome party has intervened or been impleaded, or the court or the jury is likely to rule against the plaintiff.

[156] *See* Chapter 15 (respect for final judgments), *infra*.

before verdict.[157] Today plaintiff's right to dismiss is balanced against the investment of resources made by the other parties and by the court in the lawsuit. Consequently, most systems confine plaintiff's unilateral right to break off the case to the early stages of litigation: prior to the substantial investment of resources in trial,[158] or even prior to the point at which issues are joined. Federal Rule 41(a)(1) adopts the latter point of no return, providing that plaintiff may dismiss once without leave of court by filing notice of dismissal before an answer or motion for summary judgment is served upon him. Thus, a Rule 12(b) motion to dismiss the complaint does not cut off plaintiff's right to such *notice dismissal* unless the motion is converted into a summary judgment motion by the offer of supporting materials outside the pleadings.[159]

After an issue is joined by the service of an answer or motion for summary judgment, plaintiff may voluntarily dismiss only by stipulation of the parties or by order of the court upon such terms and conditions as it deems proper.[160] However, trial courts usually allow such dismissals unless doing so would unavoidably inflict plain legal prejudice on other parties.[161] Prejudice to defendant must ordinarily consist of more than "the mere prospect of a second law suit,"[162] since that prospect is generally present when a plaintiff seeks voluntary dismissal. Furthermore, the court can often alleviate or remove prejudice to other parties by conditioning voluntary dismissal on plaintiff's reimbursement of the parties' costs, production

---

[157] *See* B. Shipman, *Common Law Pleading* §§ 328-329 (3d ed. 1923). In some states, the right to dismiss is still essentially absolute until trial. *See* Ferrini & Winter, *Voluntary Dismissals — From Shield to Sword By the Convergence of Improvident Actions*, 21 J. Marshall L. Rev. 549 (1988) (so characterizing Illinois law).

[158] *See generally* Annotation, *Time When Voluntary Nonsuit or Dismissal May Be Taken as of Right Under Statute So Authorizing at Any Time Before "Trial," "Commencement of Trial," "Trial of the Facts," or the Like,* 1 A.L.R.3d 711 (1965) (discussing rules that permit voluntary dismissal as of right prior to trial or "commencement of trial").

[159] *See* Rules 12(b) & (c). *See generally* §§ 8.07[1] discussing conversion of Rule 12(b)(6) and 12(c) motions to Rule 56 motions) & 11.03[2] (procedure for summary judgment), *supra.* Rule 41(a)(1) is usually (but not always) applied strictly. *See, e.g., American Soccer Co. v. Score First Enter.,* 187 F.3d 1108 (9th Cir. 1999) (even when court treats a hearing as one for summary judgment, the "point of no return" is not reached unless formal motion is filed); *Santiago v. Victim Services Agency,* 753 F.2d 219 (2d Cir. 1985) (motion for a preliminary injunction does not cut off plaintiff's right to notice dismissal). The Supreme Court has held, however, that even a voluntary dismissal as of right does not deprive a court of power to impose Rule 11 sanctions on the plaintiff for filing the dismissed action. *Cooter & Gell v. Hartmax Corp.,* 496 U.S. 384 (1990).

[160] Rule 41(a)(2).

[161] *See, e.g., Paulucci v. City of Duluth,* 826 F.2d 780 (8th Cir. 1987) (denying dismissal, citing absence of explanation for it and prejudice from continuing uncertainty over title to land). *See generally* Ments, Note, *Voluntary Dismissal by Order of Court — Federal Rule of Civil Procedure 41(a)(2) and Judicial Discretion,* 48 Notre Dame Law. 446 (1972); *Moore* § 41.40[5].

[162] *See, e.g., Phillips v. Illinois Central Gulf R.R.,* 874 F.2d 984, 987 (5th Cir. 1989); *see generally Moore* § 41.40[5][c]. *Compare* § 8.10[1] (making same observation with respect to amendment), *supra.* Courts are divided, however, about whether the loss of a good limitations defense is clear legal prejudice to defendant. Some balance the equities when this prejudice is present by considering also plaintiff's diligence and conduct in seeking dismissal and defendant's expenditure of time and money. *See generally Forum Shopping,* note 155, *supra,* at 638-654.

of discovery materials, or fulfillment of other terms.[163] The Supreme Court has asserted that the parties could make their compliance with a settlement agreement one of the judicially-enforcible conditions of voluntary dismissal.[164]

Unless the court specifies otherwise, an initial voluntary dismissal is without prejudice to plaintiff's reinstitution of the action. It leaves the parties in the same position they were in prior to suit, but for the passage of time.[165] Federal courts are empowered by Rule 41(d), however, to require a plaintiff who reinstitutes his action to reimburse the parties for the costs of the previously dismissed action.

Most jurisdictions follow a two-dismissal rule, by which a second voluntary dismissal is *with prejudice* to reinstitution.[166] The second thus operates as an adjudication upon the merits with whatever preclusive effect is given judgments by the law of the rendering jurisdiction.[167]

[2] Involuntary Dismissal or Compulsory Nonsuit

We have noted that a default judgment is available in most jurisdictions for the defendant's failure to respond to claims against him or as a penalty for his disobedience of various procedural rules.[168] *Involuntary dismissal* or *compulsory nonsuit* is an analogous remedy for the defendant when the plaintiff fails to prosecute her claims[169] or to obey court rules or orders.[170]

Rule 41(b) does not define a failure to prosecute, but rules locally adopted by federal courts often do.[171] Disobedience that would justify dismissal also often consists of litigation delays, or of failures to appear, respond or take other required action.[172] Because these matters threaten the trial court's

---

[163] *See, e.g., Radiant Technology Corp. v. Electrovert USA Corp.*, 122 F.R.D. 201 (N.D. Tex. 1988) (identifying factors to be considered in allowing conditional dismissal, as well as in denying dismissal); *see generally* Moore § 41.40[10].

[164] *Kokkonen v. Guardian Life Ins. Co.*, 511 U.S. 375, 381 (1994) (dictum).

[165] Of course, the passage of time is sometimes significant because it may raise the bar of limitations to reinstitution of the action. Some jurisdictions therefore provide by statute for the tolling of the statute of limitations during the pendency of the dismissed or nonsuited action, provided that it is reinstituted within a stated period after the dismissal. *See, e.g.,* Va. Code Ann. § 8.01-229(E) (2000).

[166] *See, e.g.,* Rule 41(a)(1).

[167] *See generally* Chapter 15 (respect for final judgments), *infra.*

[168] *See* § 11.02, *supra.*

[169] *See Ad West Marketing, Inc. v. Hayes,* 745 F.2d 980 (5th Cir. 1984) (failure of attorney representing the plaintiff corporation and two of the cross-defendants to appear for trial justified involuntary dismissal of plaintiff's claims and default judgment against cross-defendants). *See generally* Vineyard, Note, *Dismissal With Prejudice for Failure to Prosecute: Visiting the Sins of the Attorney Upon the Client,* 22 Ga. L. Rev. 195 (1987).

[170] The Supreme Court has excepted the disobedience of discovery rules and orders from operation of Rule 41(b), however, on the theory that discovery sanctions are governed by Rule 37. *Societe Internationale v. Rogers,* 357 U.S. 197, 207 (1958).

[171] *See* Moore § 41.51[1] (listing federal cases based on locally adopted rules). State rules or statutes also treat this. *See, e.g.,* D.C. Super. Ct. R. 41(b) (inaction for 6 months); Fla. Stat. Ann. R. 1.420(e) (West 1994) (inaction for one year).

[172] *See generally* Moore § 41.52 (citing examples).

control over its docket, it follows that it may draw on its inherent powers to dismiss plaintiff's action *sua sponte* (its own initiative).[173]

Involuntary dismissal is a harsh sanction. In exercising discretion to dismiss a claim for want of prosecution or for plaintiff's disobedience of a court rule or order, courts should consider the degree of plaintiff's personal responsibility for the inaction or disobedience, the actual prejudice to defendant, and the availability of lesser sanctions.[174] While Rule 41(b) does not require notice and hearing, they are desirable prior to an order of involuntary dismissal.

Rule 41(b) involuntary dismissals also formerly provided a means for federal courts to decide cases midway through bench (nonjury) trials. Now this purpose is served by motions for judgment as a matter of law under Rule 52(c).[175] In states that have not followed this federal rule change, however, a motion to dismiss at the close of plaintiff's case is still used to put the question whether on the facts and the law plaintiff has met his burden of persuasion.[176] This kind of motion differs from its cousin, the motion for directed verdict in jury cases, because the latter only tests whether plaintiff's evidence could reasonably lead to a favorable verdict.[177] The greater demand placed on plaintiff by a motion for involuntary dismissal reflects the added fact-finding power judges assume in bench trials. Judges may resolve close questions of fact (including issues of credibility) against the plaintiff at the close of his case-in-chief that would otherwise go to juries in a jury case.[178] Involuntary dismissals simply save time by permitting judges to cut bench trials short when an outcome adverse to the plaintiff has become clear.

Involuntary dismissals and compulsory nonsuits are with prejudice to reinstitution of the action in the same court, unless otherwise provided or unless grounded on failure of a precondition to suit.[179] Rule 41(b) expressly identifies jurisdiction, proper venue, or joinder of a party under Rule 19, as such preconditions. Dismissals based on plaintiff's failure to satisfy these conditions do not operate as adjudications upon the merits. In this regard, "jurisdiction" is sometimes expansively construed to include dismissals based on the failure of other preconditions, such as posting of security bonds or filing of good cause certificates in certain immigration proceedings.[180]

---

[173] *See, e.g., Link v. Wabash RR. Co.*, 370 U.S. 626, 629 (1962); *Boudwin v. Graystone Ins. Co.*, 756 F.2d 399 (5th Cir. 1985).

[174] *See, e.g., Boudwin*, 756 F.2d 399; *Scarborough v. Eubanks*, 747 F.2d 871 (3d Cir. 1984). *See generally Failure to Prosecute*, note 169, *supra*, at 206-214.

[175] *See* § 12.10 (bench trials), *infra*.

[176] *See* § 12.04[3](trial burdens), *infra*.

[177] *See* § 12.09[1] (directed verdicts), *infra*.

[178] The judge's view of the facts in a jury trial is comparatively insignificant. When the evidence is rationally capable of supporting a verdict for either side, the jury's conclusion is largely immune from court interference. *See* § 91, *infra*.

[179] *See Semtek Int'l Inc. v. Lockheed Martin Corp.*, 531 U.S. 497, 505 (2001) (holding that R. 41(b) dismissal without prejudice bars refiling in same court).

[180] *See generally Moore* § 41.50[7]. *Cf. Saylor v. Lindsley*, 391 F.2d 965 (2d Cir. 1968) (dismissal for failure to post bond for security for costs does not operate as adjudication upon the merits despite Rule 41(b)'s express language).

§ 11.05 Alternative Dispute Resolution

Parties have also obtained disposition of their disputes without trial by resort to alternative dispute resolution. Alternative dispute resolution (ADR) is as old as formal adjudication, since parties to civil litigation have always had the option of agreeing to settle the case. Growing concern, however, about the time and expense of formal adjudication has led to greater interest in dispute resolution by less formal, expedited means. Among the ADR devices now used in addition to traditional settlement negotiation are *mediation, arbitration,* and *summary jury trials.*

Mediation has been defined as "a dispute resolution process in which disputants are assisted by a neutral third person (the mediator) to come to a mutually satisfying, self-determined solution."[181]

In other words, it is settlement negotiation facilitated by an outsider. Mediation is most likely to succeed in settings where opposing parties have good reason to agree but are hostile, alienated or distrustful. The mediator may perform an evaluative function in clarifying for each party their own best interests. She also performs a facilitative function by serving as a buffer and medium of communication for settlement.[182]

Arbitration is closer in form to litigation itself, inasmuch as the neutral third person (the arbitrator) actually considers the case and designates a winner.[183] Whether parties are required to submit to arbitration and, if so, whether the arbitrator's result is binding, usually depends on the nature of the agreement or prior consent of the parties. Thus, if the parties have contracted to submit their disputes to arbitration, they usually must do so before commencing judicial proceedings.[184] Similarly, if the parties have contracted that the arbitrator's decision is binding, it will usually be given preclusive effect in any subsequent case.[185] Commentators have suggested that the modern trend toward enforcement of contractual arbitration clauses is problematic when it effectively denies those in inferior bargaining

---

[181] National Center for State Courts, *Alternative Dispute Resolution (ADR)* (2001). Discussion of recent developments in mediation practice and theory appear in *Symposium,* 2000 J. of Disp. Resol. 245; and *Symposium on the Structure of Court-Connected Mediation Programs,* 14 Ohio St. J. on Disp. Resol. 711 (1999).

[182] For a critique of the evaluative and facilitative functions of mediation, see Stempel, *The Inevitability of the Eclectic: Liberating ADR from Ideology,* 2000 J. on Disp. Resol. 371.

[183] *See* Nolan-Haley, *Alternative Dispute Resolution in a Nutshell,* Ch. 4 (1992).

[184] *See* The Federal Arbitration Act, 9 U.S.C. § 2 (making contractual arbitration agreements "valid, irrevocable, and enforceable, save upon such grounds as exist at law or in equity for the revocation of any contract."). Section 2 is enforceable in state as well as federal court. *Southland Corp. v. Keating,* 465 U.S. 1 (1984). State laws give similar effect to arbitration agreements. *See, e.g.,* Calif. Code of Civ. Proc. § 1281; Article 75, N.Y. Civ. Prac. L. & R. § 7501; Tex. Civ. Prac. & Rem. § 171.001.

[185] American Law Institute, *Restatement (Second) of Judgments* § 84 (1982). "It is well-settled that the doctrines of res judicata and collateral estoppel apply to arbitration awards." *Nolan-Haley,* note 157, *supra* at 162.

positions — like employees,[186] securities investors,[187] or internet consumers[188] — a subsequent judicial remedy.

Summary jury trials[189] provide the parties with a kind of crystal ball, suggesting the outcome of the case if the labor and expense of formal adjudication is actually undertaken. The parties summarize their evidence to a small test jury that then reports a consensus verdict. While nonbinding, the verdict gives the parties a sense of how a real jury will evaluate the case and thereby facilitates settlement.

---

[186] Sternlight, *Rethinking the Constitutionality of the Supreme Court's Preference for Binding Arbitration: A Fresh Assessment of Jury Trial, Separation of Powers, and Due Process Concerns*, 72 Tulane L. Rev. 1, 7 (1997).

[187] *Id.* at 7-8

[188] Thornburg, *Going Private: Technology, Due Process, and Internet Dispute Resolution*, 34 U.C. Davis L. Rev. 151, 184 (2000).

[189] *See* § 12.03[1][b], *supra*, and acompanying note 175 & 180 for authorities.

Chapter 12

TRIAL AND POST-TRIAL MOTIONS

§ 12.01 Overview: The Trial Process

The incidents of civil trial are similar in most jurisdictions,[1] reflecting the common historical origins of the trial process and the influence of un-written custom. While federal and most state courts have rules of evidence regulating facts at trial,[2] rules of civil procedure usually give little attention to the trial process. The Federal Rules of Civil Procedure are typical in their preoccupation with matters before and (to a lesser extent) after trial. The trial process itself is best introduced chronologically.

[1] Setting the Case For Trial

This initial step in the trial process should in theory await completion of the pretrial process, particularly discovery. However, as Samuel Johnson once said of the prospect of hanging, an early trial date "wonderfully concentrates the mind." Because it forces the pace of litigation, it is increasingly common for courts to set the trial date early as a date by which to reckon in setting deadlines, such as the cut-off of discovery and the completion of pretrial motion practice.[3] Some jurisdictions set the trial date as soon as issues in the case are joined by completion of the pleadings.[4]

[2] Final Pretrial Conference[5]

The use of final pretrial conferences has increased for complex litigation in federal and many state courts. Rule 16 establishes procedure for the former. Parties often exchange briefs (memoranda) at the final pretrial conference, identifying their witnesses and other evidence and delineating their factual and legal contentions. These briefs help the court gauge the time required for trial, streamline the trial itself by flushing out potential evidentiary problems for resolution *in limine* (at the threshold of trial), and may facilitate settlement by previewing the real strength of the parties'

---

[1] *See generally* Tanford, *An Introduction to Trial Law*, 51 Mo. L. Rev. 623 (1986).

[2] *See* § 12.08[2], *infra.*

[3] Rule 16(b)(4) permits but does not require the inclusion of the trial date in the initial pretrial scheduling order.

[4] *See, e.g.,* N.J. Civ. Prac. Rule 4:36-2. Commonly the parties advise the court by memorandum that the case is at issue, after which the court places the case on its trial calendar. *See, e.g.,* Iowa Rule Civ. Proc. R. 181.

[5] *See generally* § 12.03 (pretrial conference), *infra.*

trial positions. They may also present an occasion for summary judgment on some or all of the claims.[6]

Information presented in the parties' briefs and further agreements reached during the final pretrial conference provide material for the court's order. Rule 16(e) states that it "shall control the subsequent course of the action." The order functions as a kind of program for trial. Often it shrinks the bounds of relevancy set by the pleadings alone.[7] It may also restrict the availability of even relevant evidence at trial by limiting sources of proof to those identified in the order.[8] Parties thereafter seeking enlargement of the final pretrial order bear a considerable burden of justification. Rule 16(d) permits modification of the order "only to prevent manifest injustice."

[3] Jury Selection[9]

The jury is selected on the first day of trial after motions *in limine* and other housekeeping matters have been resolved. Jury selection is a two-step process. The first — assembling the *venire* from which the jury panel of twelve or less (plus alternates) is selected — is performed by the clerk's office according to statutory criteria and procedures.[10] The second — questioning (*voir dire*) of the potential jurors (*veniremen*) to select the panel — is performed by counsel, or by the judge with the aid of *voir dire* questions suggested by counsel.

The *voir dire* is intended to expose biases or interests of veniremen that would disqualify them for cause. Usually parties are given unlimited challenges for cause and a limited number of *peremptory* challenges. The latter permit counsel to keep persons off the jury without offering a reason, although the Supreme Court has ruled that civil litigants may not use their peremptory challenges to exclude jurors on account of their race or gender.[11]

While twelve is the traditional number, use of juries of six has grown among federal and many state courts for civil jury trials.

---

[6] This may happen when the parties have narrowed the issues by requests for admissions (discussed in § 12.02, *infra*) or the court orders them to admit or deny factual assertions in each other's pretrial briefs at the pretrial conference. *See* § 12.03[3], *infra*.

[7] *See* § 12.03[3] (pretrial order and its effect), *infra; Wright & Miller* § 1527 (noting that the court "might preclude a party from introducing evidence on a claim or defense that is not revealed" at the final pretrial conference).

[8] *See Wright & Miller* § 1527 (noting that "the court may refuse to allow witnesses not named at the pretrial conference to testify at the trial.").

[9] On jury trials, *see* §§ 12.06 (the tactical decision whether to claim a jury), 12.07 (obtaining jury trial), 12.08 (judge-jury interaction), & 12.09 (taking the case from the jury), *infra*.

[10] *See, e.g.,* 28 U.S.C. §§ 1861-1869.

[11] *See Edmonson v. Leesville Concrete Co.*, 500 U.S. 614 (1991) (race); *J.E.B. v. Alabama*, 511 U.S. 127 (1994) (gender). Three peremptory challenges are permitted in federal courts. 28 U.S.C. § 1870.

[4]   Opening Statements

Once the jury has been empaneled, the plaintiff usually gives the first opening statement. Defendant may go first in rare cases where he concedes plaintiff's case-in-chief and has the burden of producing evidence concerning an affirmative defense. In non-jury cases, the judge often dispenses with the formality of opening statements because he or she has already become familiar with the case from presiding over pretrial hearings or from perusing the pleadings.

A well-organized and persuasive opening can go far to influence a fresh and attentive jury.[12] The function of an opening statement is not merely to preview the evidence but to tell the jury the story of a party's case. This is necessary because the presentation of testimony and tangible evidence during the trial is often piecemeal and unchronological. Plaintiff's opening statement thus gives the jury a road map to follow through trial.

For these same reasons, the defendant usually gives her opening statement after the plaintiff. In many jurisdictions, however, the defendant has the option to wait until plaintiff has presented his evidence. A defendant who has waited until then to open can take plaintiff's evidence into account.[13]

[5]   Presentation of Plaintiff's Case-in-Chief

After opening statements, the parties proceed with their proof. Testimonial evidence enters by direct examination of a witness by the plaintiff's counsel, followed by cross-examination by the defendant's counsel, and then re-direct and re-cross as necessary. Documents and other tangible exhibits are first marked for identification. Once counsel establishes (lays) a foundation for such an exhibit with prior evidence or the foundation was conceded by pretrial admission, the exhibit may be offered for admission.

[6]   Mid-Trial Motion for Directed Verdict, Involuntary Dismissal or Judgment as a Matter of Law

After the plaintiff completes the presentation of his case-in-chief, the defendant may test that case by motion. In a jury trial, defendant moves for a directed verdict or, in federal court, for judgment as a matter of law.[14] The motion tests whether plaintiff has met his burden of production by presenting sufficient evidence to enable a reasonable jury to find for him.[15] When plaintiff's failure to satisfy this burden is sufficiently clear, there is no point in submitting the case to the jury because the judge would have to set aside a verdict for plaintiff on a proper motion for judgment notwithstanding the verdict or, in federal court, for judgment as a matter of law.

---

[12] One commentator asserts that opening statements determine the outcome in 50-85% of the cases. Lundquist, *Advocacy in Opening Statements,* 8 Litig. 23 (1982).

[13] *See* Stramondo & Goodspeed, *Defendant's Presentation,* 57 Mass. L.Q. 179 (1972).

[14] *See* § 12.09[1], *infra.*

[15] *Id.*; § 12.04[2], *infra.*

But if plaintiff has met his burden or if the question is a close one, defendant's motion should be denied[16] without prejudice to defendant's case.

In a non-jury trial, the defendant tests plaintiff's case by a motion for involuntary dismissal or, in federal court, for judgment as a matter of law.[17] Because the trial judge sits as the trier of facts in a non-jury case, this motion tests the sufficiency *and* weight of the evidence. The judge thus may determine the facts and enter judgment against the plaintiff. On the other hand, because defendant has not yet had the opportunity to put on her evidence, the judge who denies defendant's mid-trial motion in a non-jury case will not ordinarily enter judgment against her at this stage.

[7] Presentation of Additional Evidence

If defendant's mid-trial motion is denied, she puts on her evidence on the issues assigned her. Following her evidence, plaintiff may present rebuttal evidence. Defendant, in turn, may present her rebuttal evidence.

[8] Motions at the Close of All the Evidence

At the close of all the evidence in jury trial, either party may make a motion for a directed verdict or, in federal court, for judgment as a matter of law. This motion again tests the sufficiency of the opponent's evidence to support a jury verdict.

[9] Closing Argument

Most jurisdictions permit closing arguments in three parts, with the plaintiff going first and last. Closing argument affords each party an opportunity to put evidence admitted in the case in the best possible light. Counsel may and usually do offer the jury conflicting interpretations of the evidence in their closing arguments, but they may not offer conflicting interpretations of law. The court is the only source of guidance on legal standards by which the jury is to weigh the evidence. Therefore, counsels' closing arguments must be entirely consistent with the court's jury instructions,[18] which usually come later. When they do, the best and most widespread practice is for the court to indicate to counsel prior to closing arguments how it will be instructing the jury.[19]

Unfortunately, some attorneys see in closing argument an opportunity to grandstand, emote, go beyond the evidence, or prey on perceived prejudices of the jury.[20] This behavior can backfire, seeding the trial record with reversible error.

---

[16] *See* § 12.09[3][b], (discussing the importance of reserving close questions for treatment by judgment n.o.v.), *infra*

[17] *See* §§ 11.04[2], *supra,* & 12.10, *infra.*

[18] *Cf. Tanford,* note 1, *supra,* at 692 (noting that it is improper in closing argument for counsel "to discuss law that is not part of the instructions. . . .").

[19] Thus Federal Rule 51 states that "[t]he court shall inform counsel" of its rulings on their requests for instructions "prior to their arguments to the jury."

[20] *Tanford,* note 1, *supra,* at 685-693.

In non-jury cases, post-trial briefs often take the place of closing arguments.

[10] Instructions to the Jury

In most jurisdictions, the judge instructs the jury after closing arguments, although federal judges have the option to instruct "the jury before or after the argument, or both."[21] Usually counsel submit proposed jury instructions, sometimes as early as the final pretrial conference, and the judge advises them of which instructions she will give. Almost all jurisdictions require counsel to object to errors in the instructions before the jury retires. This prevents sandbagging and permits cure of flawed instructions before the jury begins deliberations.

[11] Jury Deliberation and Verdict

After the jury is instructed, it is placed in the custody of a bailiff. It then deliberates privately and, infrequently, may be *sequestered* (isolated) until it reaches a verdict. At the jury's request and upon notice to the parties, the judge may reread some or all of the instructions or permit the jury to re-examine record evidence or rehear testimony. Jurisdictions and individual judges differ in their tolerance for jury possession of written instructions or trial transcripts in the jury room.

At common law, a twelve-person jury had to reach a unanimous verdict. While unanimity is still required of federal juries, the Supreme Court has approved the use of less than twelve jurors. States differ widely in both the number of jurors and the degree of required agreement. However, all are subject to the requirements of due process under the Fourteenth Amendment. The Supreme Court has invoked the Due Process Clause to prohibit six-person, non-unanimous juries in criminal cases.[22] It has yet to define the outer limits of due process in civil state jury cases.

The jury's verdict may take several forms, depending upon the judge's instructions and the jurisdiction. In federal courts, the jury may deliver a traditional *general verdict* finding for or against each party, a *special verdict* answering factual interrogatories framed by the judge, or a combination of these verdicts.[23]

[12] Challenges to Verdict and the Entry of Judgment

After the jury delivers its verdict, the judge may direct entry of judgment upon it. Most jurisdictions, however, authorize motions for judgment notwithstanding the verdict (judgment n.o.v.).[24] Parties in federal court

---

[21] Rule 51. *See generally* § 12.08[3] (instructing the jury), *infra.*

[22] *Burch v. Louisiana,* 441 U.S. 130 (1979); *Ballew v. Georgia,* 435 U.S. 223 (1978).

[23] Jury verdicts are discussed in greater detail in § 12.08[4], *infra.*

[24] "N.O.V." is an abbreviation of the Latin phrase *non obstante veredicto,* which means notwithstanding the verdict. See generally § 12.09, *infra,* for extensive discussion of motions for judgment notwithstanding the verdict and their relation to motions for directed verdicts made earlier in the case (now all called motions for judgment as a matter of law in federal court) and to motions for new trial.

have until ten days after the court's entry of judgment on a verdict to move for judgment as a matter of law, or, alternatively, for new trial.

In non-jury trials, the court finds the facts and enters judgment accordingly. There is no analogue to a motion for judgment n.o.v., although the parties usually can move for reconsideration or amendment of the judgment[25] within a fixed period of time.

[13] Other Post-Trial Motions

In addition to the post-verdict and post-judgment motions noted above, courts permit motions for new trial.[26] Historically, new trials have been granted because of prejudicial conduct by jurors or attorneys, judicial errors, or because the verdict was against the weight of the evidence. New trial orders wipe out the jury verdict, but they do not give movant victory on the merits. The trial judge therefore is given greater power to grant new trials than to grant judgments n.o.v.[27]

After time for moving for judgment n.o.v., judgment as a matter of law, new trial, reconsideration or amendment has passed, trial-level attack on the judgment becomes difficult. What remains for the party aggrieved by the judgment is the limited prospect of extraordinary relief. Most jurisdictions permit post-trial motions to set aside judgments. Federal procedure is typical in providing relief because of clerical error[28] or because circumstances suggest that it would be unfair to enforce the judgment.[29] Extraordinary relief provides a fairly reliable means for correcting clerical errors. To a lesser extent, it functions to vacate default judgments. Beyond that, extraordinary relief is usually unavailable, confined as the term suggests to extraordinary cases. This is consistent with society's interest in the finality of judgments.[30]

---

[25] *See* § 12.11[2][c], *infra*.

[26] New trial motions are discussed in § 12.09[2], *infra*.

[27] On the relationship between judgments n.o.v. (and judgments as a matter of law) and orders for new trial, see §§ 12.09[2][b] & 12.09[3][d], *infra*.

[28] Rule 60(a).

[29] Rule 60(b).

[30] For more extended discussion of Rule 60 and extraordinary relief from judgments, see § 12.11[2][b], *infra*.

PART A
Narrowing Issues and Allocating Burdens

§ 12.02 Requests for Admissions[31]

[1] Procedure for Requesting Admissions

Many jurisdictions provide a procedure like Federal Rule 36 by which a party may request his adversary to admit the truth of any matters within the scope of discovery. Unless amended or withdrawn by leave of court, admissions are binding at trial[32] and thus relieve their proponent of the time and expense of proving the admitted matter. Although the request for admissions is usually classified as a discovery procedure,[33] it presupposes that the requesting party already has sufficient information about the case to formulate the requested admissions, and it is usually filed at the close of discovery. It is therefore more accurately regarded as a pretrial, issue-narrowing procedure and so treated here.[34]

The requested admissions must take a declaratory form that is susceptible to the bare response "admit" or "deny." Federal Form 25 offers the following examples: "That each of the following documents, exhibited with this request, is genuine," and "That each of the following statements is true." Under the federal rules, admissions are subject only to the generic limitations of Rule 26(b).[35] They may embrace disputed issues, ultimate issues (negligence, breach, etc.) as well as evidentiary facts, and the application of law to fact, but not pure legal conclusions.[36] A few courts still disapprove of requests concerning ultimate issues in the case. They do so either on the ground that ultimate issues involve legal conclusions or on the ground that probable denial, followed by a request for expenses under Rule 37(c) should the denying party lose at trial, would circumvent the American rule against awarding attorney's fees to the prevailing party.[37] This reasoning is largely specious, since Rule 37(c) itself exempts

---

[31] See generally Kinsler, *Requests for Admission in Wisconsin Procedures: Civil Litigation's Double-Edged Sword*, 78 Marq. L. Rev. 625 (1995); Finman, *The Request for Admissions in Federal Civil Procedure*, 71 Yale L.J. 371 (1962).

[32] *See, e.g.,* Rule 36(b).

[33] Rule 36, for example, appears at Part V of the federal rules, entitled "Depositions and Discovery."

[34] *See James, Hazard & Leubsdorf* § 5.7 ("[i]n some ways, ... a pleading device that narrows the issues to be tried rather than a discovery device to obtain evidence"); *Wright* § 89 (not, strictly speaking, a discovery device at all); R. Haydock & D. Herr, *Discovery: Theory, Practice, and Problems* § 5.2 (1983) ("more of a trial practice rule").

[35] *See* § 10.03 (scope of federal discovery), *supra.*

[36] *Wright* § 89. *See, e.g., Williams v. Krieger,* 61 F.R.D. 142 (S.D.N.Y. 1973) (request for admission of pure legal conclusion is improper). *See also* Annotation, *Permissible Scope, Respecting Nature of Inquiry, of Demand for Admissions Under State Civil Rules of Procedure,* 42 A.L.R.4th 489; § 10.03[3][c] (discoverability of contentions), *supra;* § 10.09[1] (contention interrogatories), *supra.*

[37] *See, e.g., Naxon Telesign Corp. v. GTE Information Systems, Inc.,* 89 F.R.D. 333 (N.D. Ill. 1980). On the American rule generally, see § 14.01[2], *infra.*

a denying party from sanctions for failing to admit when he had "reasonable ground to believe that he might prevail on the matter." There is usually such reasonable ground on the ultimate issues of liability in the ordinary lawsuit. [38]

To ignore requests for admission is unwise, since Rule 36(a) deems failure to reply an admission. If in reasonable doubt of the truth of a requested admission a party may simply deny. Alternatively, he may object on the ground that the request exceeds the permissible scope of discovery, seek a protective order for any of the reasons listed in Rule 26(c), [39] admit part and deny the balance, qualify his admissions and denials as necessary, or state that after reasonable inquiry the information available to him is insufficient to enable him to admit or deny. [40] To be entitled to the last response, a party may not rely just on his immediate personal knowledge. He must make reasonable inquiry. [41]

Prior to the 1970 amendment to Rule 36, it was unclear whether a defective response to a request for admission relieved the requesting party of the burden of proving the matter at trial. [42] The amended rule permits that party to move before trial to test the sufficiency of answers or objections to requests in order to remove this uncertainty.

An admission obtained under Rule 36, like one appearing in a pleading or by stipulation, takes the admitted matter from the fact-finder and "conclusively establishe[s]" it for purposes of the pending action. [43] No evidence need be proffered to establish the matter admitted, and none will be admitted to refute it, although it is still subject to objections to admissibility. [44] In this respect, admissions are different from the product of the discovery procedures such as answers to interrogatories, which are only evidentiary and therefore subject both to proffer and to rebuttal at trial.

Admissions may be withdrawn or amended with leave of court pursuant to Rule 36(b), however, if it will subserve the presentation of the merits and the party who requested the admission is unable to show prejudice from the amendment. [45] "Although an admission should ordinarily be binding on the party who made it," observes one authority, "there must be room in rare cases for a different result, as when an admission no longer is true because

---

[38] *See generally* Shapiro, *Some Problems of Discovery in An Adversary System*, 63 Minn. L. Rev. 1055, 1078–1092 (1979) (arguing that a party may deny if he reasonably doubts, on the basis of all the admissible evidence known to him, that the requester could prevail at trial).

[39] *See* § 10.13[3] (protective orders against specific hardships), *supra*.

[40] *Compare* Rule 36(a) with Rule 8(b). *Cf.* § 8.08[1] (specific denials), *supra*.

[41] *See, e.g., Al-Jundi v. Rockefeller*, 91 F.R.D. 590, 593–594 (W.D.N.Y. 1981) (blanket assertion that the necessary information is in the knowledge of third persons is insufficient without reasonable inquiry of them). The duty of inquiry is underscored by the certification requirement of Rule 26(g). *See* § 10.13[1] (discovery certification requirement), *supra*.

[42] Rule 36 advisory committee's notes (1970).

[43] Rule 36(b). It supersedes the pleadings *pro tanto*. *Friedenthal, Kane & Miller* § 7.10.

[44] *See Wright & Miller* § 2264.

[45] *See, e.g., Reyes v. Vantage S.S. Co., Inc.*, 672 F.2d 556 (5th Cir. 1982) (admission was based on a faulty assumption).

of changed circumstances or through honest error a party has made an improvident admission."[46] Prejudice in this context means more than that the party obtaining the request will now have to convince the fact-finder of the truth. It means preparation prejudice — any difficulty posed for the requesting party in obtaining and making proof beyond that which would have occurred if no admission had been made.[47]

[2] Use and Value of Requests for Admissions

The chief purpose of requests for admissions is not to discover new information, but rather to expedite trial and to reduce the costs of proof.[48] But the leeway afforded by Rule 36 to deny the important issues and the weak sanction provisions of Rule 37(c) have rendered requests for admissions among the least used, most abused, and often disappointing procedural tools.[49] Requests to admit the authenticity of documentary evidence attached to the request are an exception. Because they are easy to frame and hard to evade, these requests are an effective means of avoiding the time and cost of authentication testimony at trial.

§ 12.03 Pretrial Conference[50]

[1] Purposes

In a pretrial conference, lawyers (and sometimes the parties) meet with judge, magistrate[51] or master before trial. Unknown at common law, the pretrial conference was authorized for the federal courts by Rule 16. It is said to be the most popular federal rule and has stimulated widespread adoption of similar rules in the states.[52]

A primary purpose of pretrial conferences has always been to simplify, shorten, and possibly avoid trial.[53] The 1983 amendments to Rule 16 added

---

[46] *Wright & Miller* § 2264.

[47] *See Brooke Village North Assoc. v. General Elec. Co.*, 686 F.2d 66, 70-71 (1st Cir. 1982). *Compare* § 8.10[1] (amendments in general and the prejudice requirement), *supra*.

[48] *Wright* § 89.

[49] *See, e.g., Shapiro*, note 38, *supra*, at 1078; Cutner, *Discovery — Civil Litigation's Fading Light: A Lawyer Looks at the Federal Discovery Rules After Forty Years of Use*, 52 Temp. L.Q. 933, 981 (1979). *But see Wright & Miller* § 2253 (for their purposes, requests are more effective than other discovery).

[50] *See generally* Shapiro, *Federal Rule 16: A Look at the Theory and Practice of Rulemaking*, 137 U. Pa. L. Rev. 1969 (1989); Brazil, *Improving Judicial Controls Over the Pretrial Development of Civil Actions: Model Rules for Case Management and Sanctions*, 1981 Am. B. Found. Res. J. 873; M. Rosenberg, *The Pretrial Conference and Effective Justice* (1964).

[51] *See* 28 U.S.C. §§ 631, 636 (authorizing participation of magistrates in pretrial proceedings), *construed in Mathews v. Weber*, 423 U.S. 261 (1976). *See generally* Burnett, *Practical, Innovative and Progressive Utilization of United States Magistrates to Improve the Administration of Justice in United States District Courts*, 28 How. L.J. 293 (1985).

[52] *Wright* § 91.

[53] *Id.* § 16.03[1].

another managerial purpose: to control, expedite and reduce the waste of pretrial litigation generally.[54] In addition, pretrial conferences continue to have the secondary purpose of facilitating settlement. The 1993 amendments reinforced all of these purposes.

[a] Managerial Purposes

Pretrial conferences alleviate some of the uncertainty inherent in liberalized pleading, joinder, and discovery.

Modern pleading gives notice to the parties of what the case *may* include; pretrial conferences and orders help to define what the issues *are* on the eve of trial.[55] The order emerging from the final pretrial conference supersedes the sketchy descriptions of the case allowed in notice pleading jurisdictions.[56] That conference comes after the pleader has had the opportunity to develop his case by discovery. It provides a useful occasion for informing the parties and the judge more precisely about the case, lessening surprise at trial.

There is a significant relationship between pretrial conferences and the discovery process. The 1993 amendments to Rule 16 emphasize that "a major objective of pretrial conferences should be to consider appropriate controls on the extent and timing of discovery."[57] Moreover, broad discovery is permissible today in part because the undifferentiated mass of admissible and inadmissible evidence that it produces can be culled at the pretrial conference. The court can require the parties to specify their factual contentions[58] and their evidence for trial, and it can rule on its admissibility *in limine* (at the threshold of trial).[59]

The pretrial conference also complements liberal joinder of claims and parties by providing for on-going and anticipatory control of the resulting complexity.[60] It permits courts to schedule or divide cases when necessary, order early presentation of evidence regarding potentially dispositive issues, limit the time allowed for presenting evidence at trial, and address other managerial problems arising in complex litigation.[61]

[b] Facilitating Settlement

Settlement has been a natural by-product of the pretrial conference in many cases because the exchange of contentions, admissions, and evidentiary specifications, and the prospect of an actual trial soon after the

---

[54] *See* Rule 16 advisory committee's notes (1983); *Moore* § 16.03[1].

[55] *Cf. James, Hazard, & Leubsdorf* § 5.19.

[56] *See* §§ 8.01 (history and functions of pleading) & 8.04 (modern notice pleading), *supra*.

[57] Rule 16(c) advisory committee's notes (1993).

[58] *See* Rules 33(b) and 36(a) (permitting postponement until pretrial conference of discovery of contentions regarding application of law to the facts).

[59] *See* Bacharach, *Motions in Limine in Oklahoma State and Federal Courts*, 24 Okla. City U. L. Rev. 113 (1999).

[60] *See generally* § 9.10 (overview of complex pleading and practice), *supra*.

[61] *See generally The Manual for Complex Litigation* (2d ed. 1985) (recommending at least four pretrial conferences in such cases).

conference, make the parties and their lawyers reassess their cases. Some judges have gone further and affirmatively used the pretrial conference to promote settlement. They see judicial initiatives as necessary to compensate for the frequent hesitation of the parties to display weakness by initiating settlement negotiations.[62] On the other hand, outright coercion of settlement is reversible error,[63] and some judges studiously refrain from becoming involved in settlement. The 1993 amendments to Rule 16 apparently endorse the former view by addressing, though not fully resolving, two issues of settlement that have arisen under the rule.

The first is whether a federal judge may order a represented party to attend a settlement conference. Although the former rule only compelled an attorney who will conduct the trial or an unrepresented party to attend the final pretrial conference, a sharply divided Seventh Circuit Court of Appeals sitting *en banc* ruled in *G. Heileman Brewing Co., Inc. v. Joseph Oat Corp.*,[64] that a federal court had inherent authority to compel a represented party to attend a pretrial conference in order to promote settlement. The dissenters argued that the plain language of Rule 16(d) was exclusive,[65] and that compelling parties to attend was tantamount to compelling them to negotiate, which was an abuse of judicial managerial authority.[66] A 1993 amendment to Rule 16 cautiously sides with the *Heileman* majority by explicitly providing that a court may require a party or its representative to be present or reasonably available by telephone to consider possible settlement.[67]

One federal judge, confronted with particularly contentious counsel, is reported to have said, "I cannot order a duel, and thus achieve a salubrious reduction in the number of counsel to put up with. However, a summary jury trial is so ordered."[68] His order presents a second settlement-related issue under Rule 16: whether it authorizes a federal judge to direct a summary jury trial in order to promote settlement. The summary jury trial is an alternative dispute resolution device by which parties summarize their evidence to a small test jury that then reports a consensus verdict.[69] The

---

[62] *See generally* Merhige & Rubin, *The Role of the Judge in the Settlement Process,* 75 F.R.D. 203, 205 (1978); Craig & Christenson, *The Settlement Process,* 59 F.R.D. 252, 253-255 (1973).

[63] *See, e.g., Kothe v. Smith,* 771 F.2d 667 (2d Cir. 1985); Rule 16 advisory committee's note (1983). *See generally* Menkel-Meadow, *For and Against Settlement: Uses and Abuses of the Mandatory Settlement Conference,* 33 UCLA L. Rev. 485 (1985).

[64] 871 F.2d 648 (7th Cir. 1989).

[65] *Id.* at 658 (Coffey, J., dissenting), 666 (Manion, J., dissenting).

[66] *Id.* at 665 (Easterbrook, J., dissenting).

[67] Rule 16(c). The advisory committee's notes add that this explicit authorization "is not intended to limit the reasonable exercise of the court's inherent powers," citing *Heileman. See also* Civil Justice Reform Act of 1990, 28 U.S.C. § 473(b)(5) (providing that locally adopted plans for reduction of expense and delay may include compulsory attendance requirements).

[68] 78 A.B.A.J. 44 (1992).

[69] *See, e.g.,* Woodley, *Strengthening the Summary Jury Trial: A Proposal to Increase Its Effectiveness and Encourage Uniformity in Its Use,* 12 Ohio St. J. on Disp. Resol. 541 (1997); Wiegand, *A New Light Bulb or the Work of the Devil? A Current Assessment of Summary Jury Trials,* 69 Or. L. Rev. 87 (1990); Webber, *Mandatory Summary Jury Trials: Playing by the Rules?,* 56 U. Chi. L. Rev. 1495 (1989); Posner, *Summary Jury Trial and Other Methods of Alternative Dispute Resolution: Some Cautionary Observations,* 53 U. Chi. L. Rev. 366 (1986).

jury verdict, while non-binding, gives the parties a sense of how a real jury will evaluate the case and thereby facilitates settlement. Summary jury trial may also clarify the issues and make the actual trial more efficient, should settlement fail.

Courts that ordered such summary jury trials before the 1993 amendments to Rule 16 relied in part on the rule's inclusion of "the possibility of settlement or the use of extrajudicial procedures to resolve the dispute" among the permissible subjects of conference, as well as the rule's limited compulsory attendance provision.[70] In *Strandell v. Jackson County*,[71] however, the Seventh Circuit Court of Appeals disagreed, ruling that these provisions of old Rule 16 did not authorize *mandatory* summary jury trial. The 1993 amendments to Rule 16 sidestep this issue by explicitly including as a permissible subject of pretrial conference "the use of special procedures to assist in resolving the dispute *when authorized by statute or local rule.*"[72] The underscored qualifier leaves open the issue of a court's inherent authority to mandate summary jury trial.

The foregoing issues, and the rules' caution in approaching them, indicate that there is still no consensus about whether a judge can take the initiative in settlement during pretrial yet display the neutrality and detachment traditional in our judicial systems,[73] and whether court-ordered alternative dispute resolution is consistent with fair[74] and public[75] process. Even if judicial neutrality can be achieved by assigning different judges to accomplish the managerial and settlement-facilitating purposes of pretrial conferences, the process issues remain, assuring that the settlement-related provisions of Rule 16 will themselves continue to generate litigation.

[70] *See, e.g., McKay v. Ashland Oil, Inc.*, 120 F.R.D. 43 (E.D. Ky. 1988); *American Arabian Oil Co. v. Scarfone*, 119 F.R.D. 448 (M.D. Fla. 1988).

[71] 838 F.2d 884 (7th Cir. 1987).

[72] Rule 16(c)(9) (emphasis added). Such other "special procedures" include mini-trials, mediation, neutral evaluation and nonbinding arbitration. *Id.* advisory committee's notes (1993).

[73] *See generally* Moore, Note, *Mandatory Summary Jury Trials: Too Hasty a Solution to the Growing Problem of Judicial Inefficiency?*, 14 Rev. Litig. 495 (1995); Bundy, *The Policy in Favor of Settlement in An Adversary System*, 44 Hastings L.J. 1 (1992); Resnik, *Managerial Judges*, 96 Harv. L. Rev. 374 (1982); Flanders, *Blind Umpires — A Response to Professor Resnik*, 35 Hastings L.J. 505, 507 (1984). For views by federal judges, *see* Clark, *Objectives of Pretrial Procedure*, 17 Ohio St. L.J. 163, 167 (1956) ("Pre-trial used as a club to force settlements will destroy its utility as a stage of the trial process itself."); Wright, *The Pretrial Conference*, 28 F.R.D. 141, 145-147 (1960) ("we try to take the load off . . . the lawyer's back by telling them what we think the case should settle at. . . .").

[74] *See generally* Metzloff, *Reconfiguring the Summary Jury Trial*, 41 Duke L.J. 806 (1992); Note, *Mandatory Mediation and Summary Jury Trial Guidelines for Ensuring Fair and Effective Processes*, 103 Harv. L. Rev. 1086 (1990); O'Hearne, *Compelled Participation in Innovative Pretrial Proceedings*, 84 Nw. U. L. Rev. 290 (1989).

[75] *See Cincinnati Gas & Elec. Co. v. General Elec. Co.*, 854 F.2d 900 (6th Cir. 1988) (affirming order closing summary jury trial to public), *cert. denied*, 489 U.S. 1033 (1989). *See generally* Wade, Note, *Summary Jury Trials: A "Settlement Technique" That Places a Shroud of Secrecy on Our Courtrooms?*, 23 Ind. L. Rev. 949 (1990).

[c] Assessment

Whether pretrial conferences have successfully accomplished the foregoing purposes is unclear. The evidence that pretrial has shortened trial and reduced congestion is weak, but there is stronger evidence that it has improved the quality of trials by facilitating better presentation of cases and reducing surprise.[76] There is some evidence that it has facilitated settlement, although it is unclear how much of this is a by-product of neutral managerial uses of pretrial and how much the result of more aggressive judicial settlement initiatives.[77] What is clear is that Rule 16 may be changing the adversary system. Instead of leaving its control to the parties by their lawyers, "it directs the sharing of power in handling the processing of a lawsuit."[78] Whether this change is for the better, or whether it is "redefining *sub silentio* our standards of what constitutes rational, fair, and impartial adjudication" in favor of an inquisitorial model of dispute resolution,[79] is an open question.

[2] Procedures for Pretrial Conferences[80]

Rule 16(a) and most state rules make the holding of pretrial conferences discretionary with the trial judge. The advisory committee in 1983 found that mandatory rules result in the over-regulation of some cases and under-regulation of others.[81] Some jurisdictions accordingly make the conference mandatory only in particular categories of cases.[82]

When only one pretrial conference is held, it is usually scheduled after the completion of discovery, shortly before trial.[83] At that point it is reasonable to make the parties specify issues and evidence and to amend the pleadings. Most rules, like Rule 16, also authorize multiple pretrial conferences in the judge's discretion.

Rule 16(b) also requires the judge to enter a scheduling order within 90 days after the appearance of a defendant or 120 days after the complaint

---

[76] *See generally* Flanders, *Case Management and Court Management in United States District Courts* 18-19, 35-37 (1977); *Rosenberg,* note 50, *supra,* at 29-42.

[77] *See generally Rosenberg,* note 50, *supra,* at 49-50; Plourde, *Pretrial in Maine Under New Rule 16: Settlement, Sanctions, and Sayonara,* 54 Me. L. Rev. 111, 126 (1980) (suggesting that the dichotomy is false and that settlement is a co-product of management).

[78] Miller & Culp, "The New Rules of Civil Procedure: Managing Cases, Limiting Discovery," *Nat'l L.J.,* Dec. 5, 1983, at 23-25.

[79] *See Resnik,* note 73, *supra,* at 380. *See also* Peterson, "*Restoring Structural Checks on Judicial Power in the Era of Managerial Judging,*" 29 U.C. Davis L. Rev. 41 (1995).

[80] *See generally* Judicial Conf. of United States, *Handbook for Effective Pretrial Procedure* (1964), *reprinted in* 37 F.R.D. 255; Peckham, *The Federal Judge as a Case Manager: The New Role in Guiding a Case From Filing to Disposition,* 69 Calif. L. Rev. 770 (1981); Note, *Pretrial Conference: A Critical Examination of Local Rules Adopted in Federal District Courts,* 64 Va. L. Rev. 467 (1978); Note, *Pretrial Conference Procedures,* 26 S.C. L. Rev. 481 (1974) (discussing state procedures).

[81] Rule 16 advisory committee's notes (1983).

[82] *See, e.g.,* Wis. R. Civ. Pro. 802.11(1).

[83] *See* Rule 16(d) (providing that the final pretrial conference shall be held as close to the time of trial as reasonable under the circumstances).

is served, setting time limits for joinder and amendment, motion practice, and completion of discovery, and (optionally) setting the dates for mandatory discovery, pretrial conferences, and trial, subject to modification for good cause.[84] This initial order helps accomplish the stated purpose of "establishing early and continuing control" of the lawsuit.[85]

In addition to now authorizing a court to require the attendance or availability by phone of a party or its representative, Rule 16 requires attorneys to prepare for and attend every pretrial conference and requires at least one of the attorneys who will conduct the trial to attend the final pretrial conference.[86] Backed by sanctions under Rule 16(f),[87] these provisions are aimed at preventing the sabotage of effective pretrial by indifferent preparation or the dodge that the attorney is unauthorized to stipulate or enter into other agreements that might be made at pretrial.

Rule 16(c) supplies a non-exhaustive list of the subjects that may be considered in pretrial.[88] Usually the parties will be asked to submit pretrial briefs.[89] These may state the undisputed facts, identify the disputed facts (often with citation to the discovery record), summarize legal contentions, and list trial witnesses and exhibits. The parties may also be required to make authenticity objections to proposed trial exhibits and invited to raise other evidentiary objections that could be ruled upon before trial.[90] Now some of these functions of pretrial briefs are fulfilled instead by Rule 26(a)(3), requiring identification at least thirty days before trial of trial witnesses, exhibits, and other evidence, and objections within fourteen days thereafter (at the risk of waiver). Even with this required pretrial disclosure, however, courts may continue to require the parties to propose findings of fact in their pretrial briefs and to admit or deny each other's proposed findings, as a way of clarifying the issues for trial.[91] Furthermore, to expedite the trial, the court may order early presentation of evidence on a potentially dispositive issue, as noted above, and, more controversially, set reasonable limits on the time allowed for presenting evidence.[92]

By their pretrial briefs, or by formal motion under Rule 15(a), parties often amend their pleadings at pretrial. The imminence of trial creates an incentive to drop borderline claims or defenses for which there was little

---

[84] The rule provides that courts may exempt categories of cases from this requirement. Rule 16(b). The Advisory Committee gave social security benefits, *habeas corpus,* and some administrative law cases as examples. Rule 16 advisory committee notes (1983).

[85] Rule 16(a)(2).

[86] Rule 16(c) & (d).

[87] *See also Link v. Wabash R. Co.,* 370 U.S. 626 (1962) (affirming dismissal under court's inherent power to punish failure to attend pretrial conferences and other misconduct). *See generally* § 12.03[3] (the pretrial order and its effect), *infra.*

[88] *See generally Moore* §§ 16.30-16.36; *Wright & Miller* § 1525.

[89] *Wright & Miller* § 1524.

[90] *See* E. Epstein, "Motions in Limine — A Primer," in *The Litigation Manual* 148 (American Bar Ass'n 1983).

[91] *See* Lempert, "AT&T Case May Become Complex Litigation Model," *Legal Times of Washington,* Feb. 4, 1980, at 1.

[92] Rule 16(c)(14) & (15).

support from discovery and to sharpen or add others suggested by discovery, eliminating the need to accomplish the same end through disruptive midtrial amendments. Moreover, it is well-established that the court may itself redefine or even terminate the lawsuit by entering summary judgment on particular claims and defenses, should the pretrial briefs establish the absence of genuine factual dispute.[93]

The pretrial conference, however, is no substitute for discovery or for trial. Although the 1993 amendments authorize inclusion of "the control and scheduling of discovery" as a pretrial conference subject,[94] perhaps impliedly settling the previously unresolved issue of the courts' authority to order discovery pursuant to a pretrial conference,[95] the conference is still not intended as a discovery tool for the parties. It is surely not a device for deciding disputed issues of material fact; it confers no greater power on the court than it already has under the summary judgment rule.[96]

[3] The Pretrial Order and Its Effect

Rule 16(e) requires the court to enter an order after a pretrial conference to preserve the work done there. The order is often prepared by counsel for the approval of the court.[97] Its content varies with the work of the conference. A 1962 study reported that in one-third of federal pretrial conferences, the trial judge failed to file a pretrial order,[98] although that figure has probably declined since the 1983 amendments to Rule 16. In those cases, however, the parties' pretrial memoranda were often given the same effect as a pretrial order.[99]

Rule 16(e) provides that the pretrial order "shall control the subsequent course of action unless modified," and that the final pretrial order shall be modified "only to prevent manifest injustice." The final pretrial order supersedes the pleadings. Objections to the pleadings, claims and defenses, or issues not incorporated in the order are waived.[100]

---

[93] See, e.g., Portsmouth Square v. Shareholders Protective Committee, 770 F.2d 866 (9th Cir. 1985) ("The court need not await a formal motion, . . . [as long as] the party against whom judgment was entered had a full and fair opportunity to develop and present the facts and legal arguments in support of its position." (citation omitted)). See also Rule 16(c) advisory committee's notes (1983).

[94] Rule 16(c)(6).

[95] See Moore § 16.13[2]

[96] See § 11.03[1] (summary judgment at court's initiative), supra.

[97] Wright & Miller § 1526. The Advisory Committee for the 1983 amendments to Rule 16 were content to leave the question of how a pretrial order should be prepared to the discretion of the presiding judges. Rule 16 advisory committee's notes (1983).

[98] See Report of Proceedings of the Judicial Conference of the United States 79–80 (1962).

[99] See Price v. Inland Oil Co., 646 F.2d 90, 96 (2d Cir. 1981).

[100] See, e.g., Simcox v. San Juan Shipyard, Inc., 754 F.2d 430, 440 (1st Cir. 1985) (Rule 9(b) objection that complaint did not plead fraud with particularity was waived by failure to object to incorporation of fraud claim in pretrial order); Syrie v. Knoll Int'l, 748 F.2d 304, 308 (5th cir. 1984) (incorporation of unpleaded claim into pretrial order amends the pleadings pro tanto).

[A] party need offer no proof at trial as to matters agreed to in the order, nor may a party evidence or advance theories at trial that are not included in the order or which contradict its terms. Disregard of these principles would bring back the days of trial by ambush and discourage timely preparation by the parties for trial.[101]

The binding effect given the pretrial order thus affords the parties a measure of certainty concerning the real issues for trial and their evidentiary burden.

This contrast between the pretrial order and modern pleading merits emphasis. Modern federal pleading is intended only to give notice to the adversary of the events giving rise to a claim or defense. The pleader is not held to any single theory of the pleadings.[102] This system is based on the presumption that pleaders at the outset often lack sufficient information to articulate details and all possible claims or defenses. Modern pleading assumes that parties will be able to ascertain that information by discovery. However, the presumption runs the other way as the parties near the end of the lawsuit. Fairness and trial efficiency then require a higher degree of certainty about what is and what is not at issue.[103]

Exclusion is the typical trial sanction for enlargement of the issues or evidence beyond the pretrial order. Rule 16(f) also authorizes the court to punish disobedience of the pretrial order by striking claims or defenses, dismissing the action, entering a default judgment, or holding the disobedient party in contempt. Thus, the court may refuse to admit into evidence documents that the proponent failed to list in the pretrial order or brief,[104] and it may exclude witnesses that were omitted from final witness lists at pretrial.[105] Similarly, the court may bar a party from asserting a new claim or theory of recovery, if it was omitted from the pretrial order or memorandum.[106]

While final pretrial orders are not ironclad, Rule 16(e) authorizes their modification "only to prevent manifest injustice."[107] In making that

---

[101] *United States v. First Nat'l Bank of Circle,* 652 F.2d 882, 886 (9th Cir. 1981).

[102] *See* § 8.04 (modern notice pleading), *supra.*

[103] This is true even though a pretrial order is generally given a liberal construction to include "any of the possible legal or factual theories that might be embraced by its language." *Wright & Miller* § 1527. *See, e.g., Miller v. Safeco Title Ins. Co.,* 758 F.2d 364 (9th Cir. 1985) (pretrial order statement of issue as whether a debt was secured by a trust deed construed to include issue whether deed was in the nature of a performance bond). *But see Flannery v. Carroll,* 676 F.2d 126, 129 (5th Cir. 1976) ("District courts are encouraged to construe pretrial orders narrowly without fear of reversal.").

[104] *See, e.g., Smith v. Rowe,* 761 F.2d 360 (7th Cir. 1985); *United States v. Rayco,* 616 F.2d 462 (10th Cir. 1980).

[105] *See, e.g., Spray-Rite Corp. v. Monsanto Co.,* 684 F.2d 1226 (7th Cir. 1982), *aff'd on other grounds,* 465 U.S. 752 (1984); *Keyes v. Lauga,* 635 F.2d 330 (5th Cir. 1981).

[106] *See, e.g., Allen v. United States Steel Corp.,* 665 F.2d 689 (5th Cir. 1982); *Price v. Inland Oil Co.,* 646 F.2d 90, 96 (2d Cir. 1981).

[107] A court commits reversible error by amending a pretrial order at trial over objection unless it finds that it is necessary to prevent manifest injustice. *See Hale v. Firestone Tire & Rubber Co.,* 756 F.2d 1322 (8th Cir. 1985).

determination, the court should consider the comparative prejudice to the parties from modifying or failing to modify the order, the impact of modification on the orderly and efficient conduct of the litigation, and any degree of wilfulness, bad faith or inexcusable neglect by the proponent of the modification.[108] For example, modification has been allowed to permit evidence of which the opponent had eleven months' notice despite its omission from the pretrial order,[109] when the opponent mitigated any prejudice to it by effective cross-examination of a previously omitted witness,[110] and when the evidence was newly discovered since the entry of the pretrial order.[111] Modification has been denied when the opponent was lulled into withholding a possible defense by the omission from the pretrial order of an alternative theory of recovery.[112] Of course, when there is no objection to the offer of evidence or claims outside the pretrial order, the court should ordinarily allow it.[113]

Matters pursued at trial that are outside the final pretrial order may also be outside the pleadings. The objecting party actually has two grounds in this situation: Rule 16(e) and the evidentiary grounds of irrelevance or immateriality. The latter are not a very significant addition, however, because Rule 16(e) poses a standard more favorable to the objecting party.[114]

Matters outside the final pretrial order may also be objectionable at trial because they are inconsistent with admissions under Rule 36. Again, Rule 16(e) seems to give more weight to the objection than Rule 36.[115]

In short, because of greater risk of inefficiency and prejudice, requests for modification or amendment of final pretrial orders will usually receive a less generous reception than earlier requests to amend pleadings or admissions.

---

[108] *See United States v. First Nat'l Bank of Circle,* 652 F.2d 882, 887 (9th Cir. 1981) (citations omitted).

[109] *See Joubert v. Travelers Indem. Co.,* 736 F.2d 191, 194 (5th Cir. 1984).

[110] *Syvock v. Milwaukee Boiler Mfg. Co.,* 665 F.2d 149 (7th Cir. 1981).

[111] *See Moore* § 16.78[4].

[112] *See Flannery v. Carroll,* 676 F.2d 126 (5th Cir. 1982).

[113] *See, e.g., Gorby v. Schneider Tank Lines, Inc.,* 741 F.2d 1015 (7th Cir. 1984); *MechMetals Corp. v. Telex Computer Prods., Inc.,* 709 F.2d 1287 (9th Cir. 1983). *Compare* § 8.10[2][a] (conforming amendments by consent at trial), *supra.*

[114] Compare the standard for mid-trial amendment of pleadings in Rule 15(b) (amendments need only subserve the merits and inflict no prejudice on the opposing party) with the presumption against modifying final pretrial orders in Rule 16(e) (they can be modified "only to prevent manifest injustice"). On mid-trial amendments generally, see § 8.10[2], *supra.*

[115] Rule 16(e) seems more stringent, although this time the difference is not as great. Compare the provision in Rule 36(b) for relieving a party of the effects of his admissions (it is "conclusively established unless the court on motion permits withdrawal or amendment of the admission") with the presumption against modifying final pretrial orders in Rule 16(e) (they can be modified "only to prevent manifest injustice"). On the effect of Rule 36 admissions generally, see § 12.02, *supra.*

§ 12.04　Burden of Proof

[1]　In General[116]

Plaintiff sues defendant for negligence. If at trial plaintiff fails to produce any evidence of injury, the court should find for defendant. The result is the same whether the issue is tried to the court or the jury; there is nothing for the jury to decide regarding injury. Suppose, however, that the evidence appears to support the positions of plaintiff and defendant to about the same degree. In that event, too, the court in a bench trial should find for defendant. In a jury trial, the issue would be submitted to a jury. But the court could still influence the jury's deliberations by instructing it that if it finds evidence on a critical point evenly balanced, it should return a verdict for defendant.[117]

Loss in either event stems from plaintiff's failure to meet his *burden of proof*. Evidence scholars[118] have modified the term in some settings by substituting more refined (if not always consistent) terminology to describe what is happening in the foregoing hypothetical. The plaintiff who fails to produce evidence on an essential element of his claim has failed the *burden of production* or *burden of going forward*. In a jury case, he has failed to produce sufficient evidence to reach the jury, and the court should grant a directed verdict or, in federal court, judgment as a matter of law against him. The plaintiff who fails to convince the trier of fact to some pre-established degree of certainty or by a pre-established *standard* of proof of the facts necessary to his claim has failed his *burden of persuasion* or assumed the *risk of nonpersuasion*.[119] In most civil cases, the required standard of proof is a *preponderance of the evidence:* that the facts are more likely than not as the plaintiff contends.

Many of the traditional maxims offered to explain how parties acquire burdens of production and persuasion are of little use. It is said that the burden rests on the party who seeks to disturb the status quo or for whom a particular issue is essential. However, these explanations are only "facile form[s] of statement of the result."[120] It is often defendant who disturbed the status quo outside court; affirmatives can be restated as negatives; and to designate issues as essential begs the question. The explanation that the burden of proof follows the burden of pleading[121] is so often contradicted

---

[116] *See generally* Hay, *Allocating the Burden of Proof*, 72 Ind. L.J. 651 (1997); McCormick on Evidence ch. 36 (J. Strong ed., 4th ed. 1992); J. Maguire, *Evidence: Common Sense and Common Law* (1947); McNaughton, *Burden of Production of Evidence: A Function of a Burden of Persuasion*, 68 Harv. L. Rev. 1382 (1955); *Wright & Miller* § 5122.

[117] *Wright & Miller* § 5122.

[118] *See, e.g.,* Thayer, *Preliminary Treatise on Evidence* 355 (1898).

[119] Some state evidence codes have also adopted such terminology. *See, e.g.,* Or. Rev. Stat. §§ 40.105-40.115, rules 305 & 307 (1999). Federal Rule of Evidence 301 uses "burden of going forward" in juxtaposition to "burden of proof in the sense of the risk of nonpersuasion."

[120] Morgan, *Some Observations Concerning Presumptions*, 44 Harv. L. Rev. 906, 910-911 (1931). *See also* Cleary, *Presuming and Pleading: An Essay on Juristic Immaturity*, 12 Stan. L. Rev. 5 (1959).

[121] *See* Allen, *Presumptions in Civil Actions Reconsidered*, 66 Iowa L. Rev. 843, 849 (1981).

by practice[122] as to be unreliable. Yet, at least initially, the same party usually does assume the burdens of pleading, production and persuasion. That is because each burden is shaped by the same factors, called by one treatise "the Three P's: Policy, Probability, and Possession of [access to] Proof."[123] We will consider the burdens of production and persuasion in greater detail in the subsections which follow.[124]

[2]　The Burden of Production

The plaintiff has the initial burden of production regarding at least some issues. Collectively, they may be called plaintiff's *prima facie* case.[125] Plaintiff must produce sufficient evidence on those issues to enable a reasonable jury, or the judge in a nonjury trial, to find for him absent rebuttal evidence by defendant. If plaintiff does in a jury trial, the court must deny defendant's motion for a directed verdict or judgment as a matter of law.[126] On the other hand, even if defendant fails to produce any evidence in rebuttal, plaintiff ordinarily would not be entitled to a directed verdict or judgment as a matter of law in *his* favor. Instead the jury usually will be asked to decide whether to accept or reject plaintiff's evidence, at least where acceptance turns on credibility and inference.

It is possible, however, for plaintiff to produce so much evidence that — on the strength of it alone — no reasonable jury could decide against him. In such a case, the burden of production shifts from plaintiff to defendant. It is then defendant who must produce sufficient evidence to meet plaintiff's evidence, or he will suffer a directed verdict. If defendant, in turn, produces so much evidence that no reasonable jury could find against him, the burden of production shifts once again to plaintiff.

This process is depicted in Figure 12-1, a variation on the well-known diagram originally proposed by Professor Wigmore.[127]

---

[122] *See, e.g., Palmer v. Hoffman,* 318 U.S. 109, 117 (1943) (federal rules control burden of pleading, but state law in diversity case controls burden of proof); *Knowles v. Gilchrist Co.,* 289 N.E.2d 879 (Mass. 1972) (bailor has burden of pleading negligent bailment, but once bailor has produced evidence establishing bailment and loss of or damage to bailed good, bailee has burden of proof of due care).

[123] *Wright & Miller* § 5122. *See generally McCormick,* note 116, *supra,* § 337 (noting natural tendency to place burdens on party desiring change, special policy concerns such as those disfavoring certain defenses, convenience, fairness, and the judicial estimate of the probabilities as illustrative factors); *Cleary,* note 120, *supra,* at 814.

[124] On the burden of pleading, *see* § 8.06[2] (using *Gomez v. Toledo,* 435 U.S. 635 (1980), to illustrate significance of possession of proof to allocation of burden of pleading), *supra;* § 8.08[2][a] (the burden and affirmative defenses), *supra.*

[125] *See Texas Dept. of Comm'y Affairs v. Burdine,* 450 U.S. 248, 250 (1981).

[126] *See* § 12.09[1] (directed verdict and judgment as a matter of law in general), *infra.*

[127] *See* 9 J. Wigmore, *Evidence* § 2487 (3d ed. 1940).

Figure 12-1

If P has the burden of production on an issue, he must produce sufficient evidence to get past X or he will suffer a directed verdict. If he gets past X into the XZ range, the issue will go to the jury. If, however, he produces so much evidence that he passes Z, then the burden of production shifts to D. Unless D now produces enough evidence to pass Z, he will suffer a directed verdict or judgment as a matter of law. Should he produce enough evidence to cross X, then the burden of production shifts back to plaintiff.[128]

The process is essentially similar in a bench (non-jury) trial, as the Supreme Court explained in *Texas Department of Community Affairs v. Burdine*.[129] *Burdine* was a Title VII employment discrimination case.[130] The court of appeals had held that once plaintiff produced evidence establishing a *prima facie* case of discrimination — that plaintiff applied for a position for which she was qualified and was rejected for reasons which gave rise to an inference of discrimination — the defendant had the burden of proving by a preponderance of the evidence the existence of legitimate, non-discriminatory reasons for its employment action. The Supreme Court reversed. It noted that *"prima facie* case . . . may be used by courts to describe the plaintiff's burden of producing enough evidence to permit the trier of fact to infer the fact at issue."[131] Once plaintiff meets her burden, however, it is not the burden of persuasion that shifts to defendant, but only the burden of producing evidence establishing nondiscriminatory reasons for the defendant's employment action.

> The plaintiff retains the burden of persuasion. [If defendant meets its burden, plaintiff] . . . now must have the opportunity to demonstrate that the proffered reason was not the true reason for the employment decision. This burden now merges with the ultimate burden of persuading the court that she had been the victim of intentional discrimination.[132]

---

[128] To visualize the burden of persuasion, see § 12.04[3], *infra*, explaining line Y in Figure 86-1.

[129] 450 U.S. 248 (1981).

[130] *See generally* Belton, *Burdens of Pleading and Proof in Discrimination Cases: Toward a Theory of Procedural Justice,* 34 Vand. L. Rev. 1205 (1981).

[131] *Id.* at 254 n.7 (citation omitted). If the judge believes plaintiff's evidence, and defendant produces none, the judge is required to enter judgment for the plaintiff. *Id.* at 254.

[132] *Id.* at 256.

[3] The Burden of Persuasion

The burden of persuasion is the requirement that a party convince the trier of fact of the truth of an issue to a predetermined level of certainty.[133] The function of that level or standard of proof is to "instruct the fact-finder concerning the degree of confidence our society thinks he [or they] should have in the correctness of factual conclusions for a particular type of adjudication."[134] In most civil cases society is only minimally concerned with outcome, and the level of certainty is usually expressed as a preponderance of the evidence, sometimes also characterized as the *greater weight of the evidence.*[135] The burden of persuasion by a preponderance of the evidence is harder to visualize accurately by diagram, but inserting a Y through the middle of Figure 86-1 may help. To carry his burden of persuasion by a preponderance of the evidence, P must present evidence that will get past Y. If he presents less, or if the evidence is in equipoise at Y, the jury should find against him.

Diagramming the burden in this way can be misleading, however. It suggests a quantitative standard, as does the phrase *greater weight of the evidence.* The preponderance standard refers not to the quantity of evidence — the greater number of witnesses or exhibits — but rather to its convincing force. Weight or movement on the diagrammed scale therefore represents the degree of persuasiveness or certainty in the fact-trier's mind that the evidence will produce.

In criminal cases and some civil cases society's greater concern in the outcome increases the burden of persuasion. Society's interest in avoiding erroneous criminal convictions accounts for the requirement that the prosecution must prove guilt *beyond a reasonable doubt.*[136] The Supreme Court has required plaintiffs to persuade by *clear and convincing evidence* in some civil cases where interests more significant than money are at stake.[137] This standard falls between preponderance of the evidence and proof beyond a reasonable doubt.[138] It is uncertain whether juries can differentiate such standards, or whether they apply any of them instead of simply deciding "who is right."[139]

---

[133] Allen, *Presumptions, Inferences, Burden of Proof in Federal Civil Actions — An Anatomy of an Unnecessary Ambiguity and a Proposal for Reform,* 76 Nw. U. L. Rev. 892, 908 (1982).

[134] *In re Winship,* 397 U.S. 358, 370 (1970) (Harlan, J., concurring).

[135] *See generally* McCormick, note 116, *supra,* § 339; Orloff & Stedinger, *A Framework for Evaluating the Preponderance-of-the-Evidence Standard,* 131 U. Pa. L. Rev. 1159 (1983).

[136] *See Santosky v. Kramer,* 455 U.S. 745, 755 (1982).

[137] *Addington v. Texas,* 441 U.S. 418, 424 (1979) (civil commitment). *See also Santosky,* 455 U.S. at 745 (termination of parental rights); *Woodby v. Immigration & Naturalization Service,* 385 U.S. 276, 285 (1966) (deportation). At common law in many jurisdictions, fraud and mistake must also be proven by clear and convincing evidence. *See, e.g., Hofmann v. Hofmann,* 446 N.E.2d 499, 506 (Ill. 1983).

[138] One scholar suggested that if preponderance means that a proposition is more probably true than false, clear and convincing means only that it is much more probably true than false. Morgan, *Instructing the Jury Upon Presumptions and Burden of Proof,* 47 Harv. L. Rev. 59, 67 (1933).

[139] *See, e.g.,* O'Reilly, *Why Some Juries Fail,* 41 D.C.B.J. 69 (1974); Winter, *The Jury and the Risk of Non-Persuasion,* 5 Law & Soc'y Rev. 335 (1971); *Morgan,* note 138, *supra,* at 66-67.

[4] Presumptions[140]

The subject of presumptions has been aptly described as "one of the most complex topics in the law of evidence" and "a sea of technicality which defies logical analysis."[141] Extended discussion of presumptions is better left to writers of evidence texts. We will confine our attention here to introductory terminology. The term *presumption* is used to describe at least four different concepts.

First, the presumption of innocence is said to apply in criminal trials. This is not really a presumption at all, but a way of saying that the prosecution has the burden of proof and of suggesting that the standard of proof is beyond a reasonable doubt. It would be more accurate to term it an assumption.

Second, presumption is used generally to refer to a logical inference from the evidence. For example, circumstantial evidence was once treated in the evidence books under the heading "presumptive evidence."[142] Triers of fact draw such inferences all the time. The process does not necessarily relate to burdens of proof.

Third, a presumption may reflect the idea in substantive law that proof of one fact establishes beyond argument the truth of another. Many states, for example, presume the legitimacy of children from proof that they were born to a wife cohabiting with her husband. Such a presumption may or may not be logical, but, in any event, it is not subject to rebuttal, even by evidence of the biological impossibility of paternity.[143] Such *conclusive* or *legal presumptions* are best regarded as part of the substantive law, rather than the law of evidence or procedure.

Finally, the term is used to refer to *rebuttable presumptions* that affect the burden of production and sometimes of persuasion. This happens when plaintiff in establishing one fact is deemed to have established a second, unless the defendant offers evidence rebutting the second fact at trial. For example, evidence that a letter has been properly posted creates a rebuttable presumption of delivery to the addressee. The rebuttable presumption thus operates to satisfy the proponent's burden of production, and a court cannot grant a motion for a directed verdict or judgment as a matter of law grounded on non-delivery once posting has been shown, absent rebuttal evidence.[144]

What happens when the opposing party puts on rebuttal evidence is much more controversial. The two leading alternative theories are illustrated by *Legille v. Dann.*[145] To challenge the presumed fact of delivery, defendant

---

[140] *See generally James, Hazard & Leubsdorf* § 7.17; *Allen,* note 121, *supra; Nesson, Rationality, Presumptions and Judicial Comment: A Response to Professor Allen,* 54 Harv. L. Rev. 1574 (1981); *McCormick,* note 116, *supra,* §§ 342-345.

[141] *Wright & Miller* § 5122.

[142] *Id.*

[143] *See, e.g., Estate of Cornelius,* 674 P.2d 245 (Cal. 1984).

[144] *See McCormick,* note 116, *supra,* § 343 (illustrative rebuttable presumptions).

[145] 544 F.2d 1 (D.C. Cir. 1976).

offered proof of its routine mail-handling practices. Calling it the majority view, the court adopted the "bursting bubble theory" whereby the production of rebuttal evidence causes the original presumption to "burst" and be without further effect in the case. Thus limited, the effect of the presumption

> is merely to invoke a rule of law compelling the [trier of fact] to reach a conclusion in the absence of evidence to the contrary from the opponent. If the opponent does offer evidence to the contrary (sufficient to satisfy the judge's requirement of some evidence), the presumption disappears as a rule of law, and the case is in the [factfinder's] hands free from any rule.[146]

In short, the presumption affects the production burden only. The majority in *Legille* therefore reversed a grant of summary judgment for the party invoking the presumption of delivery and remanded for trial.[147]

The dissenting judge argued in contrast that the rebuttal evidence was not sufficient to overcome the "strong presumption" of delivery.[148] He would have given the delivery presumption continuing effect, even after some rebuttal evidence was produced. This is consistent with the theory that proof of the basic fact shifts the burden of proof (*i.e.*, burdens of both production and persuasion) to the party against whom the presumption operates.[149] Proponents of this approach criticized the bursting bubble theory for subverting substantive policies underpinning presumptions, giving them too "slight and evanescent" an effect.[150]

There are other theories as well.[151] Moreover, statutes may define the effect of presumptions and thus displace judicial doctrine. The same factors that determine the allocation of burdens of production and persuasion ultimately determine the availability of presumptions.[152]

---

[146] *Id.* at 56, *quoting* 9 J. Wigmore, *Evidence* § 2491 (3d ed. 1940).

[147] The majority noted that the presumption of delivery and the presumption of procedural regularity

> both . . . have a common origin in regularity of action. We see nothing suggesting that the methodology buttressing the one is any more or less foolproof than that underpinning the other. We are mindful that some presumptions are founded in part upon exceptionally strong and visible policies, which have been said to persist despite proof rebutting the factual basis for the presumption. The answer here is that from aught that appears the policy reflections are in equilibrium.

Id. at 7 n.39.

[148] *Id.* at 11 (Fahey, J., dissenting).

[149] *See Morgan,* note 138, *supra,* at 83 ("in situations where a presumption owes its origin to an important social policy, it should operate to fix the burden of persuasion").

[150] Morgan & MaGuire, *Looking Backward and Forward at Evidence,* 50 Harv. L. Rev. 909, 913 (1937).

[151] *See, e.g.,* E. Morgan, *Basic Problems of State and Federal Evidence* 28-30 (J. Weinstein, 5th ed. 1976) (listing eight).

[152] *See McCormick,* note 116, *supra* at § 343.

PART B
Trial and Judgment

§ 12.05   Overview

Most civil cases filed never come to trial. Usually they are settled, voluntarily withdrawn, or decided on the merits prior to trial.[153] Yet many cases do require trial. As a more basic matter, the idea and prospect of trial strongly influence the shape of procedure for all civil cases. Pleadings and pretrial proceedings set bounds of inquiry for trial; discovery and less formal means of investigation prepare the parties for trial; and trial can be either a specter that facilitates or an enticement that blocks settlement.[154]

The function of the trial is two-fold: (1) to sift from a controverted factual record the true story — or, at least, the story most likely upon the evidence to be true — and (2) to attach legal significance to that story. The first function culminates in a verdict if performed by a jury or in findings of fact if performed by the judge. The judge always performs the second function, but the manner in which she performs it depends on whether the case is tried with or without a jury. In this Part we will consider some of the ways in which civil procedure is complicated by the fact that some cases are tried through judge-jury collaboration while others are tried by judges alone.

§ 12.06   The Tactical Decision Whether to Demand a Jury Trial

The desirability of the jury as a social institution rests on several assumptions: that collective judgment is superior to individual judgment, that an anonymous collective judgment is more easily accepted by the loser than a personalized individual judgment, and that judgment by one's peers is preferable to judgment by non-peers.[155] While these assumptions have come under attack,[156] the public may still have a mild preference for trial by jury.[157]

---

[153] See Chapter 11 (pretrial judgments), supra.

[154] See Gross & Syverud, Don't Try: Civil Jury Verdicts in a System Geared to Settlement, 44 UCLA L. Rev. 1 (1996) (using empirical evidence to conclude that "the main function of trials is not to resolve disputes but to deter other trials").

[155] For more extended discussion of these considerations, see § 12.08[1], infra. The literature on the nature and significance of jury trials is extensive. See, e.g., Symposium, Jury Reform: Making Juries Work, 32 U. Mich. J.L. Reform 213 (1999); Symposium, The American Civil Jury: Illusion and Reality, 48 DePaul L. Rev. 197 (1998); V. Hans & N. Vidmar, Judging the Jury (1986); Wolf, Trial By Jury: A Sociological Analysis, 1966 Wis. L. Rev. 820 (1966); P. Di Perna, Juries on Trial (1984); J. Frank, Courts on Trial (1949).

[156] See, e.g., Frank, note 155, supra; James, Trial By Jury and the New Federal Rules of Civil Procedure, 45 Yale L.J. 1022 (1936).

[157] Wolf, note 155, supra, at 826 n.14. But see Klein, Unpacking the Jury Box, 47 Hastings L. J. 1325 (1996) (noting growing distrust of juries, partly in response to their growing diversity).

However, such concerns are unlikely to figure greatly if at all in a particular decision whether to demand a jury trial. Nor is that decision usually made in the first instance by a client. Instead, lawyers decide based upon their personal experiences, subjective and intuitive assessments of the probabilities of success, and highly pragmatic considerations of calendar, cost and settlement leverage. To place the procedures for obtaining a jury trial in context, it is useful to identify a few of these necessarily ad hoc factors.

One is counsel's assessment of the need for "jury legislation": jury modification (or even nullification) of the letter of the law. While jury research indicates that judges and juries agree in 75% of all cases, much of their disagreement is due not only to differing assessments of the evidence, but also to the jury's recognition of "values which fall outside the official rules."[158] Juries thus have relaxed the letter of the law by substituting their own notions of comparative negligence for the rule of contributory negligence, or by "improperly" taking into account insurance, collateral benefits, mitigation and ability to pay.[159] Similarly, juries have refused to make findings supporting "technical defenses" based on statutes of frauds or limitations, or on releases or waivers obtained in unequal bargaining situations.[160]

Counsel's subjective and intuitive assessment of the role of sentiment and expertise is another crucial factor in the decision whether to demand a jury trial. When the witnesses for one side are credible, expert or likely to provoke sympathy, the fact may dictate a strong preference for trial by jury. On the other hand, counsel will often favor a non-jury trial when the evidence and the theory of recovery are complex and technical.[161]

Another factor is the nature of the evidence at the margin, evidence arguably inadmissible. When such evidence is damaging to a party, he would ordinarily prefer a jury trial from which that evidence will be excluded to a non-jury trial in which the marginal evidence will taken for what it is worth.[162]

Additional factors include calendar and cost. Jury-tried cases take, on average, 40% longer than judge-tried cases.[163] As a result they are harder

---

[158] Erlanger, *Jury Research in America,* 4 Law & Soc. Rev. 345, 349 (1970).

[159] *Id.* at 350-351. *See generally* Scheflin & Dyke, *Merciful Juries: The Resilience of Jury Nullification,* 48 Wash. & Lee L. Rev. 165 (1991).

[160] *See* Bledsoe, *Jury or Non-Jury Trial — A Defense Viewpoint,* 5 Am. Jur. Trials 123, 135 (1966).

[161] *But see* Clermont & Eisenberg, *Trial by Jury or Judge: Transcending Empiricism,* 77 Cornell L. Rev. 1124 (1992) (raising doubts about the conventional intuition).

[162] "This practice is based on the theory that the judge, with his knowledge of the rules of evidence, can separate the wheat from the chaff and pay no attention to evidence otherwise inadmissible. . . ." *Bledsoe,* note 160, *supra,* at 137.

[163] H. Zeisel, H. Kalven & B. Buchholz, *Delay in the Court* 71–81 (1959). Of course, the proper comparison is not just between trial times, but between the time elapsed from commencement of trial to decision. Jury trials have the virtue of rendering a decision at the close of the trial itself; judges will often delay for months after trial before they render their decisions. *Bledsoe,* note 160, *supra,* at 141–142. Moreover, part of this delay may result from extensive, and therefore expensive, post-trial briefing by the parties.

to schedule and more costly than non-jury trials. The party who seeks a quick result, due to financial need or fear that evidence might be lost, will ordinarily prefer a non-jury trial. Because it is often an injured plaintiff who is in this posture, the demand for a jury trial can work to the defendant's benefit in such circumstances. Even the defendant who is not anxious to go before a jury may consider demanding a jury trial in order to obtain bargaining leverage for a pretrial settlement.

Other factors which may also encourage defendants to demand a jury trial include the requirement for unanimous verdicts and the greater likelihood of reversible errors during jury trials. Where unanimity is required, defendant has but to convince one juror to find for him in order to prevail, a task which may often look more promising than convincing the judge.[164] A defendant anticipating tactical advantages from appeal may also prefer the jury trial because of the opportunities for reversible error in the admission of evidence, instruction of the jury and jury deliberations,[165] although such reckoning is tempered by awareness of the universal rule of greater deference on appeal to jury verdicts than to findings of fact by the judge.[166]

§ 12.07   Obtaining Jury Trial

[1]   The Right to Trial by Jury: The Federal Model

Federal courts and all of their state counterparts give litigants the right in some cases to have the facts tried before a jury. The scope of the right varies from system to system. The United States Constitution does not confer a right to jury trial in state civil cases.[167] The courts of each state honor the right to the extent it is created in their constitutions or local statutes.[168] Federal courts rely on the United States Constitution and federal statutes.

Federal litigants enjoy under the Seventh Amendment a right to trial by jury "[i]n suits at common law, where the value in controversy shall exceed twenty dollars. . . ." In one sense, the Amendment does not *create* a right to jury trial.[169] It merely states that "the right to trial by jury shall be preserved. . . ." The significance of this distinction is that the process of determining which issues[170] entitle a litigant to claim a jury has turned

---

[164] *Bledsoe,* note 160, *supra,* at 141.

[165] *Id.* at 133.

[166] *See* §§ 13.09[2][b] & [c] (federal standards of review for findings by the court and by the jury), *infra.*

[167] In contrast, the Supreme Court has read the Sixth and Fourteenth Amendments to confer a right to jury trial in serious state *criminal* cases. *See, e.g., Duncan v. Louisiana,* 391 U.S. 145 (1968); *Blanton v. City of No. Las Vegas,* 489 U.S. 538 (1989).

[168] *Cf. Friedenthal, Kane & Miller* § 11.7 ("almost all states have . . . constitutional guarantees.").

[169] *See Moore* § 38.10 [1].

[170] "[]The basic decisional unit in determining the existence of a right to jury trial is not the case. It is the particular issue within a case on which jury trial is demanded." *Wright & Miller* § 2302.

more on history than logic. The reckoning point is English common law in 1791, the year the Amendment was ratified.[171]

The right to a jury trial had been enjoyed to a greater or lesser extent in the colonies,[172] but the right preserved in the Seventh Amendment was that which existed under English law. In a long line of decisions,[173] the Supreme Court has read "common law" in the Seventh Amendment to refer to the jurisdiction of English common-law courts in 1791. These courts dispensed remedies "at law," including damage awards. Litigants in these courts enjoyed extensive rights to trial by jury. England administered at the same time a separate system of chancery or "equity"[174] courts, dispensing equitable remedies, including injunctions.[175] Juries were unavailable in equity proceedings. The law-equity distinction has been central in determining the scope of the Seventh Amendment.[176]

The distinction was significantly blurred, however, by the merger of law and equity proceedings brought about by the adoption of the Federal Rules of Civil Procedure.[177] The merger posed several serious questions about the right to jury trial in federal court. The Court answered three of them in a series of Seventh Amendment decisions establishing the modern trend favoring jury trials.[178]

The first question was whether there is a right to jury trial when the plaintiff brings an equitable claim, and defendant brings a legal counterclaim, or vice versa. The Court answered this question in *Beacon Theatres,*

---

[171] Not all agree. *See* A. Amar, *The Bill of Rights: Creation and Reconstruction* 89 (1998) (asserting that reckoning point is forum state law); Krauss, *The Original Understanding of the Seventh Amendment Right to Jury Trial,* 33 U. Rich. L. Rev. 407, 479-480 (1999) (arguing that reckoning point is in the discretion of Congress).

[172] "Each of the thirteen colonies, as might be expected, had developed an individual style and emphasis, in part because each had begun borrowing from a slightly different state of the English historical development." Henderson, *The Background of the Seventh Amendment,* 80 Harv. L. Rev. 289, 299 (1966).

[173] *See* the cases cited in *Moore* § 38.10 [2].

[174] *See* § 8.02[2] (equity pleading and practice), *supra.*

[175] On the modern-day significance of damage and injunctive remedies, see Chapter 14, *infra.*

[176] Juries were also unavailable in English admiralty proceedings. In the broadest sense, then, "those actions that are analogous to 18th-century cases tried in courts of equity or admiralty do not require a jury trial." *Tull v. United States,* 418 U.S. 412, 417 (1987). Recent developments in the Supreme Court's Seventh Amendment jurisprudence suggest continued emphasis on the law-equity distinction, but less attention to the particulars of 18th century English practice. *See* note 146, *supra.*

[177] Rule 2 states: "There shall be one form of action to be known as 'civil action.'" The situation prior to adoption of the Federal Rules has been described as follows:

Unlike some state systems, there have never been separate law and equity courts in the federal judicial system. But the first Process Act of 1789 introduced separate procedures for actions at law and suits in equity; and two distinct procedures for these civil actions — one applicable on the law side, the other on the equity side of the same court —continued down to 1938 when the Federal Rules became effective.

Moore, *1999 Rules Pamphlet Part 1,* ¶ 2.3.

[178] *Cf. Wright* § 92 ("The Supreme Court has been zealous to safeguard, perhaps even to enlarge, the function of the jury.").

Inc. v. Westover. [179] Plaintiff in *Beacon* sued for equitable relief. Defendant counterclaimed for damages on antitrust grounds, demanding a jury trial. The Supreme Court held that, because the law and equity claims had issues in common, the trial court could not first try the equity portion without a jury. To permit this would "compel Beacon to split its antitrust case, trying part to a judge and part to a jury."[180] The Court apparently assumed that, because common factual issues resolved in the initial equity phase of the case would not be open to relitigation in the later jury phase, a jury trial on them would be lost to the defendant altogether.[181]

A second question was whether there was a right to jury trial in an action in which the plaintiff joins legal and equitable claims,[182] and the equitable claims predominate. The Court addressed this question in *Dairy Queen, Inc. v. Wood.*[183] Plaintiff sued over defendant's alleged failure to make payments due under a trademark licensing contract, seeking an injunction against defendant's continued use of the trademark and an accounting for the sum defendant owed. The Court looked behind plaintiff's labels and concluded that "insofar as the complaint requests a money judgment it presents a claim which is unquestionably legal."[184] The Seventh Amendment "right to trial by jury", said the Court, "cannot be made to depend upon the choice of words used in the pleadings."[185] Moreover, the right applies "whether the trial judge chooses to characterize the legal issues presented as 'incidental' to the equitable issues or not."[186]

---

[179] 359 U.S. 500 (1959). *See generally* McCoid, *Procedural Reform and the Right to Jury Trial: A Study of Beacon Theatres, Inc. v. Westover,* 116 U. Pa. L. Rev. 1 (1967).

[180] 359 U.S. at 508.

[181] *Id.* at 508 & n.10. This assumption of *Beacon* has been tied to the law of prior adjudications. *Friedenthal, Kane & Miller* § 11.5. *Accord, Lyttle v. Household Mfg., Inc.,* 494 U.S. 545 (1990). Since, however, the effect of the issue determination in the equity phase of the case is felt prior to judgment, it may be more accurate to attribute any prejudicial effect to the law-of-the-case doctrine. *See generally* § 15.14, *infra.* For discussion of relatively rare instances where that doctrine has been applied to settled issues of fact (rather than law), *see Wright & Miller* § 4478.

Since *Beacon,* the Court has ruled that a party may be precluded from relitigating facts before a jury in a legal action that were decided against him in a separate and prior equitable action. *Parklane Hosiery Co. v. Shore,* 439 U.S. 322 (1979).

[182] Rule 18 expressly permits the joinder of legal and equitable claims. *See generally* § 9.02, *supra.*

[183] 369 U.S. 469 (1962).

[184] *Id.* at 476. Viewing the plaintiff's "accounting" demand "[a]s an action on a debt allegedly due under a contract, it would be difficult to conceive of an action of a more traditionally legal character." *Id.* at 477 (footnote omitted). In fact, an accounting does trace its origins to equity, but the range of remedies now available under the federal rules, including the appointment of a special master under Rule 53(b) to assist the jury in complicated monetary computations, must be considered in characterizing a claim for purposes of deciding the Seventh Amendment question. *See McCoid,* note 179, *supra,* at 8-9.

[185] 369 U.S. at 477-478.

[186] *Id.* at 473. *Accord Tull v. United States,* 418 U.S. 412, 424-425 (1987). Thus, *Beacon* and *Dairy Queen* together stand for the proposition that if, disregarding the parties' labels, there is any claim or defense in the case — incidental or otherwise — that would be characterized as legal at English common law, it must be tried first to a jury upon timely demand.

A third question posed by the merger of law and equity was whether jury trial was available for claims asserted by an historically equitable procedure, such as interpleader, a class action, or a derivative action. All these had been adopted by the Federal Rules of Civil Procedure.[187] The Court answered this question in *Ross v. Bernhard.*[188] Plaintiffs brought a shareholder's derivative action under Rule 23.1. The Court of Appeals held that the action was equitable and that none of it could be tried before a jury. Again the Supreme Court reversed. The shareholder derivative device was a creature of equity, and equitable principles still explain why shareholders in such suits can sue on behalf of the corporation. Yet the Court held that "the right to jury trial attaches to those issues in derivative actions as to which the corporation, if it had been suing in its own right, would have been entitled to a jury."[189] The Court added: "[A]s our cases indicate, the 'legal' nature of an issue is determined by considering, first, the pre-merger custom with reference to such questions; second, the remedy sought; and third, the practical abilities and limitations of juries. . . ."[190]

Congress has created many causes of action which were unknown to English jurisprudence in 1791. Nothing limits the authority of Congress to supplement the Seventh Amendment by creating a right to trial by jury in federal court whenever it wishes to.[191] But, in determining whether a *constitutional* right to jury trial exists for a statutory cause of action in which Congress has not expressly created a right to jury trial, federal courts have been required to determine whether the issue at hand most closely resembles something adjudicated on the law side or on the equity side of the line in 1791.[192] The Supreme Court's decision in *Tull v. United States*[193] provides an example.

The United States brought suit in *Tull* against a developer for violation of the Clean Water Act. The district court denied defendant's demand for a jury trial. After a bench trial (trial before the judge), the court found that defendant acted in violation of the Act and imposed numerous fines. The Court of Appeals affirmed. The Supreme Court reversed on Seventh Amendment grounds. "Prior to the enactment of the Seventh Amendment,"

---

[187] *See* Rules 22, 23 & 23.1 respectively.

[188] 396 U.S. 531 (1970). *See generally* Note, *Ross v. Bernhard: The Uncertain Future of the Seventh Amendment*, 81 Yale L. J. 112 (1971); Comment, *From Beacon Theatres to Dairy Queen to Ross: The Seventh Amendment, The Federal Rules, and a Receding Law-Equity Dichotomy*, 48 J. Urban L. 459 (1971).

[189] 396 U.S. at 532-533.

[190] *Id.* at 538 n.10. The Supreme Court recently extended its holding in *Ross* to the general class action rule, Rule 23. *Ortiz v. Fiberboard Corp.*, 527 U.S. 815, 846 (1999).

[191] For examples, *see Moore* § 38.44[3].

[192] *See* notes 172-176 and related text, *supra.* Congress has also created many administrative enforcement schemes and specialized (Article I or legislative) courts in which it has failed to provide for jury trials. In addition to looking for historical analogies to decide the Seventh Amendment question in such cases, the Supreme Court has suggested that "public rights" can constitutionally be enforced in special non-jury proceedings. *See, e.g., Atlas Roofing Co. v. Occupational Safety & Health Review Comm'n*, 430 U.S. 442, 458 (1977). This formulation leaves the question of how one identifies such rights.

[193] 481 U.S. 412 (1987).

it noted, "English courts had held that a civil penalty suit was a particular species of an action in debt that was within the jurisdiction of the courts of law."[194] The case was thus "clearly analogous to the 18th-century action in debt, and federal courts have rightly assumed that the Seventh Amendment required a jury trial."[195]

Many commentators find the historical approach to defining the scope of the Seventh Amendment troublesome. Even if the content of old English law was clear, analogizing new issues to it would at times be perplexing.[196] Matters are worse because the line between law and equity at that time was not terribly clear.[197] Moreover, sorting cases by historical category obscures useful thought about policies which should shape the contemporary roles of judge and jury. In line with these concerns, the Supreme Court in 1990 appeared reluctant to overstate the importance of specific investigations of 18th-century English practice in resolving jury questions under the Seventh Amendment. Rather, they are "only preliminary" to a more functional question whether the remedy sought as legal or equitable.[198]

On another front, the growing controversy over the role of juries in complex litigation has created additional pressure on the Supreme Court to address the right to jury trial problem in a manner which takes the demands of contemporary litigation more directly into account. Juries in complex cases may be required to listen to more than a year of testimony and to consider reams of documentary evidence. Jury suffering aside, the situation offers the disagreeable prospect of jury members so overwhelmed that they are incapable of rational decision. Perhaps the Seventh Amendment should not be read to require a jury in such cases.[199] Supreme Court dicta may leave room for this conclusion.[200] Perhaps jury deliberation

---

[194] 481 U.S. at 418.

[195] *Id.* Using a similar approach later, in *Feltner v. Columbia Pictures Television*, 523 U.S. 340 (1998), the Supreme Court saw a historic jury analog to the determination of statutory damages under the Copyright Act of 1976 and ruled that a right to jury trial existed under the Seventh Amendment.

[196] Declaratory judgments, for example, posed difficulties of classification. For discussion of developments, *see Friedenthal, Kane & Miller* § 11.4.

[197] *James, Hazard & Leubsdorf* § 8.2.

[198] *Local No. 391 v. Terry*, 494 U.S. 558, 569 (1990). Thus, while historical analysis accounting for the law-equity dividing line is likely to remain central to Seventh Amendment decisions, obsession with historical details of 18th century English practice is waning. Writing separately in *Terry*, Justice Brennan urged a complete break. He wrote that "our insistence that the jury trial right hinges in part on a comparison of the substantive right at issue to forms of action used in English courts 200 years ago needlessly convolutes our Seventh Amendment jurisprudence." *Id.* at 575. "I would decide Seventh Amendment questions on the basis of the relief sought. If the relief is legal in nature, *i.e.*, if it is the kind of relief that historically was available from courts of law, I would hold that the parties have a constitutional right to a trial by jury. . . ." *Id.*

[199] *See Cotton v. Witco Chemical Corp.*, 651 F.2d 274, 276 (5th Cir. 1981) (reversing grant of motion to strike jury demand and stating that if "complexity exception" to Seventh Amendment exists it is only for cases so complex that jury could not render rational decision based upon reasonable understanding of evidence), *cert. denied*, 455 U.S. 909 (1982).

[200] The Court held out the possibility in *Beacon* that there might be "imperative circum-

under such circumstances would produce deliberative incoherence raising countervailing constitutional due process concerns.[201]

On the other hand, the language of the Seventh Amendment may not be broad or general enough to accommodate this policy concern. Nor, for that matter, can we assume that judges as factfinders would necessarily be superior in unraveling complications.[202] The Ninth Circuit noted, in rejecting a complexity exception to the Seventh Amendment, that

> [j]urors, if properly instructed and treated with deserved respect, bring collective intelligence, wisdom, and dedication to their tasks, which is rarely equalled in other areas of public service. . . . We do not accept [the view] "that a single judge is brighter than the jurors, collectively functioning together."[203]

As a result, the complexity exception has met a mixed reception in the appellate courts.[204] The Third Circuit has hinted at one,[205] the Ninth has rejected it,[206] and the Second[207] and Fifth Circuits[208] have refused to apply it using language raising doubt whether it exists. The debate rages on,[209] awaiting Supreme Court resolution.

---

stances" that would justify trying common issues in a nonjury trial, 359 U.S. at 510-511, and in *Dairy Queen* that there might be "a rare case" in which matters "are of such a 'complicated nature' that only a court of equity can satisfactorily unravel them." 369 U.S. at 478. Its refined historical test from *Ross* also directs the courts to take into account the "practical abilities and limitations of juries" when deciding the Seventh Amendment question. 396 U.S. at 538 n.10. But in *Terry*, the Court reminded courts that it had "never relied on [consideration of a jury's competency] 'as an independent basis for extending the right to a jury trial under the Seventh Amendment.'" *Terry*, 494 U.S. at 565 (quoting *Tull*, 481 U.S. at 418 n.4).

[201] *But see SRI Int'l v. Matsushita Elec. Corp.*, 775 F.2d 1107, 1128 (Fed. Cir. 1985) (Markey, C.J., stating additional views) (dictum) (the due process argument "confuses the route with the destination, for 'due process' is just that, a process. . . . It is not a result.").

[202] Nor can we even assume that all factual controversies are capable of rational resolution. *See* § 12.08[1] (the institutional role of juries in difficult cases), *infra*.

[203] *In re U.S. Financial Sec. Litig.*, 609 F.2d 411, 430-431 (9th Cir. 1979) (*quoting* Higginbotham, *Continuing The Dialogue: Civil Juries and the Allocation of Judicial Power*, 56 Tex. L. Rev. 47, 53 (1977), *cert. denied*, 446 U.S. 929 (1980).

[204] *See* Chamberlin, Annotation, *Complexity of Civil Action As Affecting Seventh Amendment Right to Trial By Jury*, 54 A.L.R. Fed. 733 (1981 and 1999 Supp.).

[205] *In re Japanese Electronic Prods. Antitrust Litigation*, 631 F.2d 1069 (3d Cir. 1980).

[206] *In re U.S. Financial Sec. Litig.*, 609 F.2d 411 (9th Cir. 1979).

[207] *City of New York v. Pullman, Inc.*, 662 F.2d 910, 919 (2d Cir. 1981).

[208] *Cotton v. Witco Chem. Corp.*, 651 F.2d 274, 276 (5th Cir. 1981), *cert. denied*, 455 U.S. 909 (1982).

[209] "Much has been written on every side of this argument." *Wright* § 92. *See generally* Lilly, *The Decline of the American Jury*, 72 U. Colo. L. Rev. 53 (2001); Sanders, *Scientifically Complex Cases, Trial by Jury, and the Erosion of Adversarial Processes*, 48 DePaul L. Rev. 355 (1998); Friedland, *The Competency and Responsibility of Jurors in Deciding Cases*, 85 Nw. U. L. Rev. 190 (1990); Devlin, *Equity, Due Process and the Seventh Amendment*, 81 Mich. L. Rev. 1571 (1983).

[2]   Claiming a Jury Trial

State and federal court litigants are free to waive their right to jury trials. Most systems find waiver in the failure of a party to demand a jury within a requisite period of time.[210] Federal Rule 38 provides an illustration.

Rule 38(a) recites that rights to jury trial created under the Seventh Amendment or by congressional enactment "shall be preserved to the parties inviolate." Rule 38(b) describes the procedure for demanding a jury:

> Any party may demand a trial by jury of any issue triable of right by a jury by serving upon the other parties a demand therefor in writing at any time after the commencement of the action and not later than 10 days after the service of the last pleading directed to such issue.[211]

Under Rule 38(d), the failure of a party to make an effective jury demand within the time allowed "constitutes a waiver by the party of trial by jury." Waiver occurs whether the right to trial by jury would have been conferred by the Seventh Amendment or by congressional enactment.[212] This contrasts with the traditional reluctance of the Supreme Court to infer waiver of constitutional rights.[213]

There is a ray of hope for a party neglecting to demand a jury trial, in that the trial court has discretion to order one anyway.[214] However, "district judges have been extremely reluctant to exercise this discretion in favor of jury trial."[215] A party may also amend its pleading to inject a legal issue and start the ten-day clock running again under Rule 39(a), but the courts look askance at amendments made just to recover a previously waived jury right.[216]

---

[210] *James, Hazard & Leubsdorf* § 8.5.

[211] Once a party makes an effective jury demand, he may not withdraw it without the consent of the other parties in the case. Rule 38(d).

[212] A party need not claim a jury to protect his right to jury trial if another party in the case has already claimed one. "[A]ll of the parties to the action who are interested in the issues for which jury trial has been demanded may rely on that demand. . . ." *Wright & Miller* § 2318.

[213] Thus, "it is clear that the test of waiver that is applied to other constitutional rights, that there must have been an intentional relinquishment or abandonment of a known right or privilege, is not applicable to the right to trial by jury." *Id.* (*quoting Johnson v. Zerbst*, 304 U.S. 458, 464 (1938)).

[214] Rule 39(b) states: "notwithstanding the failure of a party to demand a jury in an action in which such a demand might have been made of right, the court in its discretion upon motion may order a trial by a jury of any or all issues."

[215] *Wright & Miller* § 2321.

[216] *See, e.g., American House Products Corp. v. Johnson & Johnson, McNeilab, Inc.*, 5 Fed. R. Serv.2d (Callaghan) 581, 584-589 (S.D.N.Y. 1986).

§ 12.08   Judge-Jury Interaction; Verdicts

[1]   Allocating Issues Between Judge and Jury — An Overview

Unsettled questions about the truth, what did or did not happen, place the case within the sacred preserve of the jury. Jury verdicts should and usually do govern cases where a rational response to the evidence could be a verdict for *either* plaintiff or defendant.

There are at least two arguments for giving juries the last word in such cases.[217] The first is that a group of people (the jury) will be better able to reach the right decision than a single person (judge or juror). The Supreme Court observed:

> Twelve men of the average of the community, comprising men of education and men of little education, men of learning and men whose learning consists only in what they have themselves seen and heard, the merchant, the mechanic, the farmer, the laborer; these sit together, consult, apply their separate experience of the affairs of life to the facts proven, and draw a unanimous conclusion. This average judgment thus given it is the great effort of law to obtain. It is assumed that twelve men know more of the common affairs of life than does one man; that they can draw wiser and safer conclusions from admitted facts thus occurring than can a single judge.[218]

The second argument reaches a conclusion of jury autonomy from the opposite direction. When the evidence provides reasonable bases for conflicting results, perhaps there is no right result.[219] Yet the need for decision remains, and what the judicial process in such cases lacks in precision it can try to make up for in pageantry. Trial before and decision by a jury gives the loser his "day in court" in the fullest popular sense. It seasons resolution of controversies which the law is powerless to decide[220] with a measure of public opinion.

However, there is a serious limitation on jury power. Matters of law are the exclusive concern of the judge.[221] The law-fact distinction pervades law

---

[217] See § 12.06, *supra.*

[218] *Sioux City & Pacific Ry. Co. v. Stout,* 84 U.S. 657, 664 (1874). Today, this rationale is least likely to hold up in exceedingly complex cases, where even the Seventh Amendment right to jury trial is under fire. See § 12.07[1], *supra.*

[219] See Michael, *The Basic Rules of Pleading,* 5 Record of N.Y.C.B.A. 175, 199-200 (1950), *quoted in* J. Cound, J. Friedenthal, A. Miller & J. Sexton, *Civil Procedure: Cases and Materials* 1023 (6th ed. 1993).

[220] The fact that none of the motions for deciding the merits (beginning with demurrer/Rule 12(b)(6) and ending with judgment n.o.v. or judgment as a matter of law) works in such cases means that decision as a pure matter of law never materializes. For a survey and comparison of motions deciding the merits, see § 12.09[3][c], *infra.*

[221] The law-fact distinction is not always easy to draw. *See generally* Brodin, *Accuracy, Efficiency, and Accountability in the Litigation Process — The Case for the Fact Verdict,* 59 U. Cinn. L. Rev.15 (1990). And, as is generally true with the technique of characterization in legal analysis, it is open to abuse. *Cf.* Morse, *Characterization: Shadow or Substance,* 49 Colum. L. Rev. 1027 (1949) (noting frailties of characterization associated with conflict of laws). *See* § 13.09[2][a] (fact-law distinction on appeal), *infra.*

delineating the trial roles of judge and jury, often circumscribing the latter. The judge's function as guardian of the law authorizes him to decide what facts are worthy of the jury's consideration,[222] how the jury should consider them[223] and whether, in appropriate cases, the jury's verdict should be erased[224] or even turned around.[225]

[2] Evidentiary Controls

The first opportunity to examine the evidence goes not to jury but to the judge. When called upon to do so by timely objection, the trial court considers whether the evidence should go to the jury (be admitted). The law of evidence is quite extensive and the subject of a major law school course usually taken after civil procedure.

In setting the scope of discovery,[226] civil procedure gives a less stringent meaning to the term *relevance* than does the law of evidence.[227] Yet relevance (materiality) in the law of evidence is rooted in civil procedure. The boundaries of relevance at trial are set by the pleadings. These boundaries may narrow as a result of motion practice prior to trial[228] or pretrial orders.[229] Or they may be enlarged by amendment conforming the pleadings to evidence admitted at trial.[230]

In federal courts, the law of evidence is codified in the Federal Rules of Evidence. Although these were originally proposed in the same manner as the Federal Rules of Civil Procedure, under authority of the Rules Enabling Act,[231] congressional concern about the displacement of state laws of privilege[232] led to the revision and enactment of the rules as statutory law.[233]

---

[222] *See* § 12.08[2] (evidentiary controls), *infra.* He also decides facts underlying preliminary defenses. *See* §§ 8.07[2][b]& [c], *supra.*

[223] *See* § 12.08[3] (jury instructions), *infra.*

[224] *See* § 12.09[2] (new trials), *infra.*

[225] *See* § 12.09[1][b] (judgments notwithstanding the verdict), *infra.*

[226] Rule 26(b)(1), generally limiting discovery, states that "relevant information need not be admissible at the trial if the discovery appears reasonably calculated to lead to the discovery of admissible evidence." *See* § 10.03 (the federal presumption of discoverability), *supra.*

[227] When evidence offered at trial cannot support any rule of law applicable to the case, to admit it would at best clutter the case with inconsequential fact and at worst induce the jury to render a verdict unsupported by law. The court will exclude such evidence as irrelevant or immaterial. The court may also exclude evidence if it is unreliable (if there is a sufficient possibility that it is not what it is offered to be) or if it is prejudicial (it is likely to inflame or prejudice the jury). *See generally McCormick on Evidence* ch. 16 (J. Strong ed., 4th ed. 1992).

[228] For example, from the award of partial summary judgment. On summary judgments, see generally § 11.03, *supra.*

[229] On pretrial orders, *see* § 12.03[3], *supra.*

[230] *See* § 8.10[2], *supra.*

[231] *See* § 1.02 (explaining procedure for creating federal rules of civil procedure), *supra.*

[232] *Cf.* § 7.04 (discussing relation of federal procedural law and state law), *supra.*

[233] After the Supreme Court transmitted the proposed Federal Rules of Evidence to Congress, Congress deferred their effective date until such time as they were enacted into law. Pub. L. No. 93-12; 87 Stat. 9 (March 30, 1973). The proposed rules, as modified by Congress, were subsequently enacted into law. Pub. L. No. 93-595, 88 Stat. 1926 (Jan. 2, 1975).

[3] Instructing the Jury

In nonjury cases, the judge is both the law enforcer and the trier of fact. Since both functions are performed by the same person, fine distinctions separating the two will usually be unnecessary.

Matters are quite different, however, in jury trials. Jurors use the evidence to answer factual questions.[234] But they may not resolve issues about the meaning or application of law. Only the judge does that.[235] Not only is the judge an authority on all legal questions, she must also see to it that the law is enforced. One way in which the judge must maintain legal control is in the way she instructs (charges) the jury.

> Simple, vague instructions allow the jury to decide the case with little guidance. . . . If a judge gives detailed and comprehensive jury instructions relating to the substantive law to be applied by the jury (as opposed to "housekeeping" instructions), the judge is staking out a relatively large perimeter surrounding the "legal" issues that the jury must not cross. Detailed instructions correspondingly diminish the jury's remaining function, finding the "facts" of the case. The more detailed and comprehensive the instructions, the less discretion the jury enjoys to "make law" by applying its own notions as to what the statute really says, or as to what elementary fairness requires.[236]

Consider an illustration. At trial in an automobile accident case, the jury is presented with conflicting evidence on the question whether plaintiff's own carelessness was a contributing cause of the accident. The jury, not the judge, must weigh the evidence and answer the question. However, only the judge can determine what the answer to the question means to the outcome of the case.[237] Thus, the judge must not only decide what tort law principle applies but limit the work of the jury to the confines of that principle. Assume that the judge concludes that the governing principle is that contributory negligence is an absolute bar to recovery. She might impose this on the jury by saying in her instructions: "Members of the jury, if you find that plaintiff's carelessness was a contributing cause of the accident, you *must* return a verdict for defendant."

In many jurisdictions *pattern jury instructions* have been prepared for use in civil cases.[238] The authority of such standardized instructions lies

---

[234] In federal and many state courts, the judge has the right to comment on the evidence as an aid to the jury. *Moore* § 51.10[3]. He may not distort it or add to it, of course, *see Quercia v. United States*, 289 U.S. 466 (1933), and the jury is typically reminded that, as the sole trier of fact, it has the right to disagree. *See, e.g., Trezza v. Dame*, 370 F.2d 1006, 1009 (5th Cir. 1967).

[235] The point is explored at greater length in the discussion of directed verdicts, judgments notwithstanding the verdict, and judgments as a matter of law in § 12.09, *infra*.

[236] Eades, *The Problem of Jury Instructions in Civil Cases*, 27 Cumb. L. Rev. 1017 (1997).

[237] *But cf.* Wright & Miller § 2503 ("Some of the most famous students of the judicial process have argued that one of the purposes of the jury system is to permit the jury to temper strict rules of law by the demands and necessities of substantial justice, thereby adding a much needed element of flexibility."). *See also* § 12.06, *supra*.

[238] *See, e.g.,* E. Devitt & C. Blackmar, *Federal Jury Practice and Instructions* (4th ed. 1987

somewhere between the authority of appendix of forms to the Federal Rules of Civil Procedure[239] and form pleadings and interrogatories,[240] depending upon how they were assembled. But even when they were assembled by a committee appointed by the courts, they must be used with caution.

They may not be swallowed whole. They are intended as an aid to the preparation of appropriate instruction in a particular case. Each case has its own peculiar facts, and formalized instructions must be tailored to the requirements of the facts and the issues.[241]

The parties have the right to propose appropriate jury instructions. Rule 51 treats the manner in which jury instructions are to be prepared and given in federal court. Parties may file written requests for jury instructions and "[t]he court shall inform counsel of its proposed action upon the requests prior to their arguments to the jury." A federal court may instruct the jury before or after argument or both.

Whether or not the parties request instructions, a judge has the duty in most jurisdictions to instruct the jury on the applicable law.[242] However, the failure to request specific instructions may operate as a waiver; the judge is charged only with instructing on "the broad general fundamental rules of law."[243] Moreover, Rule 51 is typical in providing that a party may challenge instructions on appeal only if he earlier "objects thereto before the jury retires to consider its verdict, stating distinctly the matter objected to and the grounds of the objection." Failure to object usually puts an end to the matter, subject only to a narrow common law power in the appellate courts to correct *plain errors* — errors so egregious that the trial courts should have known them when they saw them.[244]

Errors of law in jury instructions are among the most common grounds for new trials.[245] The appellate courts decide the correctness of the instructions *de novo* (anew).[246] But they view the instructions as a whole, including any curative instructions,[247] and reverse only for prejudicial error.[248]

---

and 1992), which is widely used in federal courts. *See generally Eades*, note 236, *supra*, at 1020-1023; R. Nieland, *Pattern Jury Instructions: A Critical Look at a Modern Movement to Improve the Jury System* (1979).

[239] *See* Rule 84 (making them "sufficient under the rules").

[240] *See* §§ 1.02 (sources of civil procedure) & 10.09[2] (interrogatories), *supra*.

[241] *Devitt & Blackmar*, note 238, *supra*, § 8.03. *See generally* Steele & Thornburg, *Jury Instructions: A Persistent Failure to Communicate*, 67 N.C. L. Rev. 77 (1988).

[242] *See, e.g., Turner Const. Co. v. Houlihan*, 240 F.2d 435, 439 (1st Cir. 1957). *But see Ouille v. Saliba*, 145 So. 2d 468, 469 (Miss. 1963) (in absence of request for instructions on counterclaim, judge "cannot instruct the jury on his own motion").

[243] *Turner Const. Co.*, 240 F.2d at 439.

[244] "Actual reversals on the basis of plain error are rare, though they have become more numerous in recent years." *Wright & Miller* § 2558. *See* § 13.08[2] (preservation of error below as predicate for review), *infra*.

[245] *See* § 12.09[2][c] (new trials), *infra*.

[246] *See* § 13.09[2][a] (the *de novo* standard of review), *infra*.

[247] *See, e.g., Ayoub v. Spencer*, 550 F.2d 164, 167 (3d Cir.), *cert. denied*, 432 U.S. 907 (1977) ("Our function is to determine whether the charge, taken as a whole and viewed in light of the evidence, fairly and adequately submits the issues in the case to the jury.").

[248] Rule 61. *See generally* § 13.08[1] (prejudicial effect as predicate for review), *infra*.

[4] Verdicts

In the usual civil jury trial, the jury is charged with returning a *general verdict,* that is, a verdict for one side or another supplying no explanation why the jury decided as it did. Such verdicts are in extensive use and can work well in relatively simple cases. Their weakness is that they fail to illuminate the jurors' decision-making process. It is fairly easy for jurors to ignore constraints and admonitions in the charge when they can hide behind a general verdict. It is also difficult to preserve the work of the jury if problems arise with the case on appeal of a general verdict.[249]

The *special verdict* is an alternative intended to address these shortcomings. Jury instructions designed to elicit a special verdict contain a series of short-answer fact questions.[250] The jurors answer the questions instead of designating a winner. From all the answers, the judge constructs the equivalent of a general verdict. If the answers appear inconsistent, the judge is obliged to "attempt to reconcile the jury's findings, by exegesis if necessary, . . ." before either resubmitting them or ordering a new trial.[251]

Parties to complex cases may prefer a special verdict because of the guidance it gives the jury in fact-finding.[252] However, they have no right to have the jury return a special verdict in federal courts. They can only request one.[253] Many trial judges have been reluctant to use the device. Some reluctance may stem from the fact that judges are unfamiliar with it. Some apparently comes from a fear of encroaching upon the independence of the jury.[254] Compared to general verdicts at least, special verdicts do impose tighter controls and may therefore reflect a more suspicious attitude toward juries.[255] Finally, some hesitation to use special verdicts

---

[249] "For example, if a prevailing plaintiff asserts several possible theories of recovery, and the appellate court finds the evidence for one of those theories to have been admitted erroneously, a new trial on all issues will be required because there is no way of discovering which theory the jury relied on in reaching the verdict." *Friedenthal, Kane & Miller* § 12.1. In summing up the deficiencies of the general verdict, a recent commentator described it as "the ultimate in 'black box decision-making'. . . . This product of jury deliberations comes into court . . . with no indication whether it is based upon particular findings of fact, or particular interpretation of law, or both, or neither." *Brodin, supra* n.221, at 34.

[250] Rule 49(a), governing special verdicts in federal court, refers to "written questions susceptible of categorical or other brief answer. . . ." On the uses and contributions of special verdicts in federal litigation, see *Brodin, id.* at 62-84.

[251] *Gallick v. Baltimore & O.R.R.,* 372 U.S. 108, 119 (1963). *See generally* Olander, Note, *Resolving Inconsistencies in Federal Special Verdicts,* 53 Fordham L. Rev. 1089 (1984).

[252] *See* Faulkner, *Using the Special Verdict to Manage Complex Cases and Avoid Compromise Verdicts,* 21 Ariz. St. L.J. 297 (1989). Another, less common reason for requesting a special verdict may be to isolate particular facts. For example, a public figure who brings a libel action may be as interested in having a jury find that the libel was false as he is in recovering, and more likely to obtain the former, too, given the heavy burden of proving actual malice.

[253] Rule 49(a) "is permissive, not mandatory. Whether a special or general verdict is to be returned (by the jury) rests in the sound discretion of the trial court." *Wright & Miller* § 2505.

[254] *Friedenthal, Kane & Miller* § 12.1.

[255] A special verdict "puts psychological pressure on the jurors to adhere to their legally prescribed functions and to prevent them from deciding cases on grounds they are instructed to ignore." *James, Hazard & Leubsdorf* § 7.23.

stems from concern about the possibility of inconsistent findings.[256]

Some courts seem receptive to a compromise: a general verdict accompanied with answers to written interrogatories. Federal Rule 49(b) provides this option, again, at the discretion of the court. This verdict form permits jurors to declare a winner but requires them to show their work. However, it is even more vulnerable to inconsistencies than the special verdict, since the jury's answers may be inconsistent not only with each other, but also with the general verdict. Subdivision (b) proposes different solutions for this problem, none of them entirely reassuring.

§ 12.09 Taking the Case From the Jury: Motions for Judgment as a Matter of Law and for New Trial

[1] Directed Verdicts and Judgments N.O.V. Rephrased as Judgments as a Matter of Law

After trial has begun, a party may by motion request the court either to render judgment without letting the case go to a jury verdict, or (if a verdict has been entered) to render judgment opposed to that indicated by the verdict. Traditional terminology for the first such order is *directed verdict* and, for the orders of the second type, *judgment n.o.v.* (or judgment notwithstanding the verdict).

A 1991 amendment to Rule 50 of the Federal Rules of Civil Procedure discarded the two terms in favor of the single phrase, *judgment as a matter of law*. This development must be noted. Yet, for several reasons, it may not be terribly important. First, the amendment will work little if any change in decisionmaking,[257] since the test for a judgment as a matter of law appears to be the same as the test previously applied to both directed verdicts and judgments n.o.v. Second, many state courts will continue for the foreseeable future to be governed by procedural law employing the two older terms. Third, even federal courts may continue to employ them, since directed verdict and judgment n.o.v. are useful to differentiate the two subspecies of the topic covered by the more generic term, judgment as a matter of law.

---

[256] *See generally* Martin, *Rationalizing the Irrational: The Treatment of Untenable Federal Civil Jury Verdicts*, 28 Creighton L. Rev. 683 (1995). Of course, general verdicts, too, can be inconsistent. *Id*. Motions for j.n.o.v. (judgment as a matter of law in federal courts) or new trial can be used to control the jury in such cases. *See* § 12.09, *infra*.

[257] The Advisory Committee note to the 1991 amendment makes this clear, stating that the new terminology "effects no change in the existing standard. That existing standard was not expressed in the former rule, but was articulated in long-standing case law." For a dissenting view, that the outcome in some cases may be affected by the amendment, see Waggoner, *New Rule 50 May End Directed Verdicts for Plaintiffs*, 22 Sw. U. L. Rev. 389 (1993).

The Advisory Committee also stated that the change in terminology was merely a technicality. "If a motion is denominated a motion for directed verdict or for judgment notwithstanding the verdict, the party's error is merely formal. Such a motion should be treated as a motion for judgment as a matter of law in accordance with this rule."

By whatever name, separate procedural devices for taking the jury out of the picture before or after a verdict still function in all American courts. It continues to be important to grasp their similarities and differences and, for convenience and clarity of discussion, it will be useful to refer to them by their traditional titles, directed verdict and judgment n.o.v.

Motions for directed verdict and for judgment notwithstanding the verdict have much in common. Each is governed by the same legal standard. They can and often do address the same factual record. Appellate courts freely reexamine decisions on both. For all that, we shall see that each makes a discrete contribution as part of a series of motions screening the merits of the case.

[a] The Theoretical Justification for Court Intervention in Jury Cases

Recall that the function of the jury is to deliberate, to weigh the evidence in choosing between a result favorable to plaintiff or to defendant. Juries derive their autonomy from the character of the evidence in the case. So long as evidence creates a genuine and substantial controversy over who should win, juries should and do have the last word. Judges have the last word, however, when the evidence supports only one side.[258]

The jury's verdict could coincide with the only right result in such cases. Once, however, the jury loses authority to choose between conflicting results, its presence becomes incidental.

The conclusion that the evidence supports only one result in the case can be as evident to the court before the jury deliberates as after. The first opportunity to end the case thus comes by means of a motion for directed verdict, whereby the court can interpose its decision on the evidence and keep the jury from ever considering the case. The second opportunity comes by means of a motion for judgment n.o.v.[259] (judgment notwithstanding the verdict), whereby the court can reverse a jury verdict unsupported by evidence.[260]

---

[258] That is, they have the authority to resolve the merits of the case in favor of the litigant whose position is supported by the evidence. "Whether the evidence presented at trial is sufficient to create an issue of fact for the jury or will permit the court to enter judgment as a matter of law is solely a question of law to be determined by the trial court." *Wright & Miller* § 2524. In other situations, the judge may not have the last word in this sense but does have the authority to undo the work of the jury by ordering a new trial. *See* § 12.09[2], *infra.* New trial decisions based on an evaluation of the evidence are governed by a different legal standard from the one governing directed verdicts and judgments n.o.v. discussed in this subsection. *Id.*

[259] From the Latin phrase *non obstante veredicto.*

[260] Similarly, the motion makes judgment possible in cases where the jury has been unable to reach a verdict. *See Moore* § 50.02[2].

[b] The Legal Standard Governing Directed Verdicts and Judgments N.O.V.

Each system applies a single legal standard to decide both directed verdicts and judgments n.o.v.[261] Systems have varied, however, in how stringent that standard should be. At one extreme, the judge may not interfere if there is any evidence — even just a "scintilla" — supporting a verdict against the moving party.[262] At the other extreme, a party supported by evidence reasonably capable of supporting a jury verdict could fall prey to one of the motions.[263]

Federal and most state courts steer a middle course. "The court should review the record as a whole," the Supreme Court has said, but "it must disregard all evidence favorable to the moving party that the jury is not required to believe. That is, the court should give credence to the evidence favoring the nonmovant as well as that 'evidence supporting the moving party that is uncontradicted and unimpeached, at least to the extent that that evidence comes from disinterested witnesses.' "[264] On the other hand, the existence of *any* favorable evidence (no matter how meager) will not protect federal litigants from directed verdicts or judgments n.o.v. The test federal courts usually administer has often been called the *substantial evidence* test. Evidence is substantial in this sense when it is capable of providing a reasonable basis for a juror to find for the party opposing the directed verdict or judgment n.o.v. motion. Or, as one federal circuit court put it, the test

is whether the evidence is such that, without weighing the credibility of the witnesses or otherwise considering the weight of the evidence, there can be but one conclusion as to the verdict that reasonable men [or women] could have reached.[265]

To call this the substantial evidence test has always been somewhat misleading.[266] It suggests that the motion tests the quality or weight of

---

[261] Thus, in federal court, the "standard . . . is the same whether it arises in the procedural context of a motion for judgment as a matter of law prior to the submission of the case to the jury or in the context of a renewed motion for judgment as a matter of law after the jury has returned a verdict" *Wright & Miller* § 2524. That standard has been express in Rule 50 since the 1991. After technical revisions made by amendment in 1993, Rule 50 (a) states that a judgment as a matter of law may be entered when "during a trial by jury a party has been fully heard on an issue and there is no legally sufficient evidentiary basis for a reasonable jury find for that party on that issue. . . ."

[262] Predictably, this is often called the "scintilla" rule from the Latin term referring to a mere particle. For discussion of the rule and citation of illustrative Alabama state decisions, see *Friedenthal, Kane & Miller* § 12.3.

[263] *Wright & Miller* § 2538.

[264] *Reeves v. Sanderson Plumbing Products, Inc,* 530 U.S. 133, 151 (2000) (quoting *Wright & Miller* § 2529).

[265] *Simblest v. Maynard,* 427 F.2d 1, 4 (2d Cir. 1970). The United States Supreme Court has observed that "the standard for a directed verdict under Federal Rule of Civil Procedure 50(a) . . . is that the trial judge must direct a verdict if, under the governing law, there can be but one reasonable conclusion as to the verdict. . . . If reasonable minds could differ as to the import of the evidence, however, a verdict should not be directed." *Anderson v. Liberty Lobby, Inc.,* 477 U.S. 242, 250 (1986).

[266] *See* note 261, *supra.*

the evidence, when it really tests whether there is *sufficient* evidence from which a reasonable jury could find against the movant. It is more useful to describe it as a "reasonable juror" test, and the 1991 amendment to Rule 50(a) should encourage this shift in thinking by expressly referring to a "reasonable jury" standard.

[2] New Trial Motions

[a] In General

The most widely used form of judicial control of juries is the order granting a new trial on all or some part of the issues. The power to set aside verdicts and grant new trials was well-established in 1791 and is therefore consistent with the constitutional guarantee of jury trial.[267] All jurisdictions permit this control and confer broad (in some circumstances, practically unreviewable) discretion on the trial judge to deploy it. But all also sharply restrict its availability to a short period — ten days in federal courts[268] — after the verdict is returned or judgment is entered.

The grounds for new trial are as numerous as the sources of possible error in the trial. Some states rules list the grounds,[269] but Federal Rule 59(a) and many state rules simply authorize new trial for "any of the reasons for which new trials have heretofore been granted." Most grounds for new trial, however, fall into two categories. The first and most troublesome category consists of errors in the jury's evaluation of the evidence. The second consists of errors in the trial process, including errors in the law applied.[270]

[b] Evaluative Errors: Verdicts That Are Excessive, Inadequate, Or Otherwise Against the Weight of the Evidence

When the trial judge concludes that the verdict is excessive, inadequate, or otherwise against the weight of the evidence, she is second-guessing the jury in its evaluation of the evidence.[271] Yet, unlike directed verdict,

---

[267] *Capital Traction Co. v. Hof,* 174 U.S. 1, 13-14 (1899):

"Trial by jury," in the primary and usual sense of the term at common law and in the American constitutions . . . is a trial by a jury of twelve men in the presence and under the superintendence of a judge empowered to instruct them on law and to advise them on the facts, and . . . to set aside their verdict if, in his opinion, it is against the law or the evidence.

[268] Rule 59(b).

[269] *See, e.g.,* Minn. R. Civ. P. 59.01.

[270] Another, less important category consists of newly discovered evidence that could not, with reasonable diligence, have been discovered and produced at trial. Since such evidence is rarely discovered within the customarily short time periods for seeking new trial, it is probably just as often advanced in support of a motion for relief from judgment. *See* Rule 60(b)(2), discussed at § 12.11[2][b], *infra.*

[271] Of course, the verdict may be excessive because it exceeds statutory limits. The error is then not evaluative, but an error of law.

judgment n.o.v., or judgment as a matter of law, an order for a new trial on the grounds that the verdict is against the weight of the evidence does not deprive the verdict-winner of jury trial. It only forces him to submit his evidence to a new jury.[272]

This explains why the test for granting new trial is less restrictive than the test for directed verdict/judgment n.o.v.[273] On the other hand, for the judge to set aside the verdict and order a new trial just because she would have decided the case differently would undercut the jury as fact-finder.[274]

The test for federal and most state courts lies somewhere in between. We say "somewhere" because the test is necessarily approximate. One of the most frequently quoted formulas was stated in *Aetna Casualty & Surety Co. v. Yeats*[275] :

> On such a motion it is the duty of the judge to set aside the verdict and grant a new trial, if he is of opinion that the verdict is against the clear weight of the evidence, or is based upon evidence which is false, or will result in a miscarriage of justice, even though there may be substantial evidence which would prevent direction of a verdict.

This formulation makes it clear that the court may grant a new trial even if it finds "substantial evidence" to support the verdict, because on new trial, unlike directed verdict or jnov, the court *does* weigh the evidence, not just test it for sufficiency. Another common formula is that the judge must be left with a definite and firm conviction that a mistake has been committed.[276]

In application, this test must take into account the deliberative skill of the jury in the circumstances of the case. The verdict in "a trial that is long and complicated and deals with a subject matter not lying within the ordinary knowledge of jurors . . . should be scrutinized more closely" than the verdict in a simple trial dealing with familiar subject matter.[277] Certainly, the trial judge should be most hesitant to set aside the verdict and order new trial on evidentiary grounds when the key issue in the case was credibility, a matter classically for the jury.

Another kind of evaluative error is that the verdict is excessive or inadequate as a matter of fact.[278] This is logically no different from a weight

---

[272] His problem is that he gets "too much jury trial, not too little." *Friedenthal, Kane & Miller* § 12.4.

[273] Indeed, were it the same, no new trial should be granted because the court could enter judgment as a matter of law. *Wright* § 95. As a result, only a minority of states have adopted a test analogous to the reasonable jury standard usually used for directed verdict/judgment n.o.v. *See James, Hazard, & Leubsdorf* § 7.28.

[274] Although some states have adopted this "thirteenth juror" test for new trial, *see James, Hazard, & Leubsdorf* § 7.28, it is doubtful that their judges actually exercise as much discretion as the test seems to confer.

[275] 122 F.2d 350, 352-353 (4th Cir. 1941).

[276] *See Wright* § 95.

[277] *Lind v. Schenley Indus., Inc.,* 278 F.2d 79, 90-91 (3d Cir. 1960).

[278] As opposed to excessive as a matter of law. *See* note 271, *supra.*

of the evidence claim. Yet the determination of unliquidated and punitive damages is often so speculative to begin with that judicial intervention on a new trial motion may seem especially problematical. The conditional grant of new trial has often provided a way out, however. The trial judge grants the motion unless the opposing party agrees to a reduction (*remittitur*) or increase (*additur*) of the verdict.[279] In federal courts, the court may order a remittitur if the verdict is so excessive that it "shocks the conscience."[280] The party who consents to such a remittitur waives any right to appellate review of it.[281] The Supreme Court has upheld remittitur against Seventh Amendment attack, relying on historical grounds and some dubious logic, but has condemned additur as unconstitutional.[282]

In *Gasperini v. Center for Humanities, Inc.*,[283] the Supreme Court added a further wrinkle to remittitur practice in federal diversity cases. There state law authorized trial courts to set aside as excessive any verdict which "deviates materially from what would be reasonable compensation." This is a broader standard than the federal miscarriage-of-justice or "shocks the conscience" standard.[284] The Supreme Court held that the state standard served substantive purposes and therefore controlled in a federal diversity case.

The grant of partial new trial limited to the issue of damages is another possibility when the amount of the verdict has been attacked. In federal court, partial new trial "may not be resorted to unless it clearly appears that the issue to be retried is so distinct and separate from the others that a trial of it alone may be had without injustice."[285] Such orders must be made cautiously, however. A jury that has evaluated damages improperly may well also have evaluated liability improperly. In particular, an inadequate verdict may be a compromise verdict which cannot fairly be set aside only in part.

New trial determinations differ from directed verdicts and judgments n.o.v. not just in availability. Decisions granting or denying directed verdicts or judgments n.o.v. are open to reconsideration on review.[286] In

---

[279] He must give the opposing party the option, however, and may not simply fix the proper level of damages himself. *McKinnon v. City of Berwyn,* 750 F.2d 1383, 1389 (7th Cir. 1984). Federal courts are divided on what the proper level should be: the highest reasonable amount, a reasonable amount, or the lowest reasonable amount. *See, e.g., Gorsalitz v. Olin Mathieson Chem. Corp.,* 429 F.2d 1033, 1047 (5th Cir. 1970).

[280] *Moore's* § 59.13[2][g][iii][B]

[281] *Donovan v. Penn Shipping Co.,* 429 U.S. 648 (1977).

[282] *Compare Dimick v. Schiedt,* 293 U.S. 474, 486 (1935) ("what remains is included in the verdict along with the unlawful excess — in that sense it has been found by the jury — and the remittitur has the effect of merely lopping off the excess) *with Jehl v. Southern Pacific Co.,* 427 P.2d 788 (Cal. 1967) (allowing additur in state court). *See* Sann, *Remittiturs (and Additurs) in Federal Courts: An Evaluation With Suggested Alternatives,* 38 Case W. Res. L. Rev. 157 (1988) (urging elimination of remittitur in federal courts to eliminate inconsistency and inefficiency).

[283] 518 U.S. 415, 422 (1996).

[284] *Id.* at 424.

[285] *Gasoline Prod. Co. v. Champlin Refining Co.,* 283 U.S. 494, 500 (1931).

[286] *See* § 12.09[3][b], *infra.*

contrast, it is quite difficult to obtain reversal of the court's decision granting or refusing to grant a motion for new trial. In the first place, the denial
of a new trial motion — standing alone — is interlocutory. It is not appealable until a final judgment is rendered after a new trial, assuming that
the judgment is unfavorable to the party who resisted the new trial.[287]
Even then, it is reviewable only for abuse of discretion.[288] The standard
of review for abuse of discretion when the determination is based on
evidentiary grounds is extremely narrow.[289]

[c] Process Errors

There are a variety of errors that may taint the trial process. These
include judicial errors in instructing the jury or admitting or commenting
on the evidence, and misconduct by parties, counsel, witnesses or jurors,
as well as prejudicial happenstance.[290] The judge has discretion to grant
a new trial under these circumstances.[291] This is subject, however, to the
possibility that the error may be deemed harmless.[292] No verdict may be
set aside and new trial granted unless the error adversely affected the
substantial rights of the complaining party. The trial judge's superior
ability to assess the prejudicial effect of errors on the trial process explains
why he generally enjoys such discretion on ruling on motions for new trial.

Of the sundry errors of trial process which may justify a new trial, jury
misconduct merits further discussion. The historic rule at common law was
that a juror may not impeach his own verdict.[293] The rule was intended
partly to protect the candor of secret jury deliberations and perhaps to
protect the institution of jury fact-finding itself from embarrassing disclosure of its imprecision.[294] Since juries typically deliberate in secret, the rule
made it extremely difficult to prove jury misconduct in many cases.

Today, most jurisdictions have struck a compromise between the desire
to protect candid jury deliberation and the need to control jury misconduct.
Almost all jurisdictions use an exclusionary evidentiary rule to protect the
mental processes of jurors from disclosure.[295] But "the permissibility of
juror testimony hinges upon the purpose for which it is offered."[296] Jurors

---

[287] See § 12.09[3][a], infra.

[288] Id. at 436.

[289] For a discussion of the standard and its application to new trial determinations, see
§ 13.09[2][d], infra.

[290] See generally Moore § 59.13.

[291] In theory, there is no discretion in deciding new trial motions based on judicial errors,
since they present questions of law. In practice, the assessment of their prejudicial effect
invokes a discretion which is entitled to substantial respect on appeal. See James, Hazard,
& Leubsdorf § 7.25. Regarding the appellate review of discretionary orders generally, see
§ 13.09[2][d], infra.

[292] See Rule 61.

[293] See Comment, Impeachment of Jury Verdicts, 25 U. Chi. L. Rev. 360 (1958).

[294] See generally James, Hazard, & Leubsdorf § 7.27.

[295] Friedenthal, Kane & Miller § 12.5.

[296] Attridge v. Cencorp Div. of Dover Tech. Int'l Inc., 836 F.2d 113, 117 (2d Cir. 1987).

are often permitted to testify about extraneous information or outside influence that may have tainted the jury's deliberations.[297]

In re Beverly Hills Fire Litigation[298] supplies a good illustration of the modern rule and suggests one test for jury misconduct. There one of the jurors reported to the jury the results of his home experiment with electrical wiring, in contradiction of expert testimony during the trial. On appeal, the court considered the jurors' testimony about this extraneous information and rejected the verdict winners' arguments that the experimenting juror was only relying on his own general knowledge and common experience. Instead, it found that the juror's actions "went beyond mere general knowledge and was instead a response to the case at hand," prejudicially supplementing the record. It reversed and remanded for a new trial.

In contrast, a closely divided Supreme Court in *United States v. Tanner*[299] held that what the dissenters characterized as "profoundly disturbing" evidence of extensive juror drug and alcohol intoxication *during* deliberations went to the mental processes of the jury and was therefore inadmissible to impeach the verdict. The majority thus aggressively enforced the federal version of the exclusionary evidentiary rule, notwithstanding a strong argument that drug and alcohol consumption are extraneous and antecedent to the jury's deliberative process.

[3] The Interplay of Directed Verdicts and Judgments N.O.V. With Other Procedural Law

[a] The Consistency of Directed Verdicts and Judgments N.O.V. With the Right to Jury Trial

There is no logical difficulty in squaring directed verdicts and judgments n.o.v. with the right in federal court to trial by jury.[300] Such dispositions are unavailable unless the jury could reasonably find only for the moving party. The only function for the jury to perform in such cases would be the ceremonial one of announcing the sole possible result.[301] Since, however, the Seventh Amendment right to jury trial at times represents a triumph of history over logic,[302] the matter requires further discussion.

Directed verdicts have not posed much of a problem. Early on, the United States Supreme Court appeared to regard the authority of courts to direct verdicts as well-established in common law.[303] By 1943, the Supreme Court

---

[297] *See, e.g.,* Fed. R. Evid. 606(b). *See generally Moore* § 59.13[2][e][iii][D].

[298] 695 F.2d 207, 214 (6th Cir. 1982).

[299] 483 U.S. 107 (1987). For a trenchant criticism of the case and an analysis of Fed. R. Evid. 606, *see* Swaine, Note, *Pre-Deliberations Juror Misconduct, Evidential Incompetence, and Juror Responsibility,* 98 Yale L.J. 187 (1990).

[300] For discussion of the latter, see § 12.07[1], *supra.*

[301] "This internally inconsistent practice" was rendered unnecessary by the 1963 amendment of Rule 50(a). *Moore* § 50 App. 102. The rule now states that "[t]he order of the court granting a motion for a directed verdict is effective without any assent of the jury."

[302] *See* § 12.07[1], *supra.*

[303] In *Parks v. Ross,* 52 U.S. 362, 373 (1850), the Court noted that "[i]t is undoubtedly the

observed that Seventh Amendment challenges to federal directed verdicts were "foreclosed by repeated decisions made here consistently for nearly a century."[304]

The Supreme Court did read the Seventh Amendment to block judgment n.o.v. in one famous prerule decision.[305] However, the Court altered its position in later cases,[306] using the well-accepted rule that directed verdicts were permissible to create something of a legal fiction. A federal judge reserving decision on a motion for directed verdict could later turn around a verdict unsupported by evidence on the theory that he was reviving consideration of the motion for directed verdict.[307]

Rule 50(b) codifies this fiction by making judgments n.o.v. available only to the party who has made "a motion for a directed verdict . . . at the close of all the evidence" specifying the grounds on which the motion is based.[308] The court need not expressly reserve decision on the motion; the rule provides that "the court is deemed to have submitted the action to the jury subject to a later determination of the legal questions raised by the motion." The later determination may also be by an appellate court, reversing the trial court's denial of judgment n.o.v.[309] Indeed, the Supreme Court has held that a court of appeals may even direct entry of judgment as a matter of law (instead of remanding) when, after it has excised evidence which was erroneously admitted by the trial court, there is insufficient evidence left to support the jury verdict.[310]

---

peculiar province of the jury to find all matters of fact, and of the court to decide all questions of law arising thereon. But a jury has no right to assume the truth of any material fact, without some evidence legally sufficient to establish it." That directed verdicts differ "in some major respects" from "the historic jury control devices — the demurrer to the evidence, nonsuit, and a motion for new trial . . .," *Friedenthal, Kane & Miller* § 12.3, has not troubled the Supreme Court.

[304] *Galloway v. United States,* 319 U.S. 372, 389 (1943).

[305] *Slocum v. New York Life Ins. Co.,* 228 U.S. 364 (1913).

[306] *E.g., Baltimore & Carolina Line v. Redman,* 295 U.S. 654 (1935).

[307] *Redman,* 295 U.S. at 658-659.

[308] Federal courts usually apply the limitation strictly, and the specification requirement added in 1991 effectively rejected earlier cases holding that something less than a formal motion for directed verdict was sufficient to preserve a party's right to move for judgment n.o.v. *See Moore* § 50.40[3]; Rule 50(a) advisory committee's note (1991 amendment). Since Seventh Amendment concerns are local to federal courts, states — even those which typically adopt language of the Federal Rules of Civil Procedure — are free to dispense with the directed verdict prerequisite in their judgment n.o.v. rules. *See, e.g.,* Ind. R. of Trial Proc., Trial Rule 50.

[309] *Cf. Neely v. Martin K. Eby Const. Co.,* 386 U.S. 317, 322 (1967) ("there is no greater restriction on the province of the jury when an appellate court enters judgment *n.o.v.* than when a trial court does. . . .").

[310] *Weisgram v. Marley Co.,* 120 S. Ct. 1011 (2000).

[b] How Directed Verdicts and Judgments N.O.V. Complement Each Other

Since the same legal standard governs both directed verdicts and judgments n.o.v.,[311] and since they often address the same factual record, it is natural to ask why both are necessary.

The principal contribution of judgments n.o.v. is that they make it possible for trial judges to conserve court and party resources. They do this by permitting trial courts to defer acting on the conclusion that the evidence permits only one result until the jury has deliberated and returned its verdict. For two reasons, this is one of the few instances in civil procedure where delay ultimately serves judicial efficiency. First, if the jury eventually finds for the movant, the trial court is spared from making a ruling that is more vulnerable on appeal than a judgment on a jury verdict. Second, deferring a ruling until a motion for judgment n.o.v. reduces the necessity for retrial of the case if appeal is successfully taken,[312] by allowing the jury to return a verdict that can be reinstated on remand.

Consider an example. Defendant moves for a directed verdict in a federal case. The judge concludes that plaintiff has fallen just short of submitting enough evidence to meet the substantial evidence standard.[313] However, he denies defendant's motion. By delaying decision until the jury has returned a verdict, the judge creates the strong possibility that the jury will return a verdict in favor of defendant. If this happens, the court will never have to pass on the highly reviewable question (whether a reasonable jury could find for plaintiff) posed earlier by defendant's motion for directed verdict.[314] Defendant will be content with the jury verdict. Since there will be substantial evidence supporting the verdict, plaintiff cannot successfully attack it. The case is over.[315]

Let us change one element of our hypothetical case. Assume that the jury returns a verdict for plaintiff. Now the judge must act upon his conviction that plaintiff's case is unsupported by substantial evidence by granting defendant's motion for judgment n.o.v. The judgment n.o.v. option also conserves time and effort in this setting. The trial judge's decision to grant defendant's motion for judgment n.o.v. may be affirmed on appeal. But a new trial should not be necessary even if he is reversed. The appellate court

---

[311] See § 12.09[1][b], supra.

[312] Cf. Friedenthal, Kane & Miller § 12.3 ("By waiting, the judge avoids disputes about the propriety of a directed verdict, as well as appeals from its grant, and also defers to the jury.").

[313] Or concludes that an unsettled question of law makes the decision whether to grant a directed verdict close, even if the evidence is clear. For example, when the legal definition of a particular claim is unsettled, evidence in the case may clearly support the claim as plaintiff defines it and fail with equal clarity to support the claim as defined by defendant.

[314] Appellate courts freely substitute their judgment for that of trial courts when reviewing directed verdicts. Like trial courts they must draw all reasonable inferences favorable to the party opposed to the motion. Moore § 50.92[1].

[315] Cf. Wright & Miller § 2533 ("If the jury agrees with the court's appraisal of the evidence, and returns a verdict for the party who moved for judgment as a matter of law, the case is at an end.").

can merely reinstate the jury verdict. If, on the other hand, the trial court had granted defendant's motion for a directed verdict, reversal would have required an entirely new trial.[316]

A further justification for the added opportunity for decision provided by judgments n.o.v. may be that the quality of decisions will improve if the court has more time to decide. The court really cannot long delay sending the case to the jury in order to mull over a difficult directed verdict question. The prospect of a motion for judgment n.o.v. permits the court to consider the question for a substantially longer period of time.[317]

Directed verdicts also make a discrete and important contribution. First, judgments n.o.v. would often be impossible if the judicial system did not also recognize the possibility of a directed verdict. A constitutional right to jury trial prevents grant of judgment n.o.v. by either the trial or the appellate court absent an earlier motion for directed verdict in federal courts and in the courts of some states.[318] Second, not all cases profit from delaying decision until after the jury has returned a verdict. Directed verdicts make it possible to terminate trial as soon as it becomes clear that the evidence fails to offer a legally permissible choice to the jury. This may be as soon as all the evidence is submitted, when plaintiff has submitted all of his evidence, or, in rare cases, even immediately after plaintiff gives his opening statement.[319]

[c] The Relationship of Directed Verdicts and Motions for Judgments N.O.V. to Motions for Deciding Cases in Lieu of Trial

Directed verdicts and judgments n.o.v. are the last in a series of five motions used to decide civil cases on the merits and thereby interrupt the ordinary trial process. The first such motion in federal court is a motion to dismiss for failure to state a claim upon which relief can be granted.[320] Motions for judgment on the pleadings[321] and for summary judgment[322] follow.

---

[316] "For this reason the appellate courts have repeatedly said that it is usually desirable to take a verdict, and then pass on the sufficiency of the evidence on a post-verdict motion." *Id.*

[317] The directed verdict motion flags the question for the court. The motion for judgment n.o.v. in federal court may come as late as 10 days after judgment. Rule 50(b). The trial court may not unduly delay decision on a motion for judgment n.o.v., but has more time to consider it than was practically available to consider the motion for a directed verdict.

[318] On how the Seventh Amendment requires directed verdict motions as predicates for judgments n.o.v. in federal court, see § 12.09[3][a], *supra*. There is a constitutional right to jury trial in the courts of most states closely patterned on the Seventh Amendment. *See Friedenthal, Kane & Miller* § 11.7.

[319] In spite of the failure of Rule 50 to contemplate the last option, federal "courts have held that they continue to have power to direct a verdict on the opening statement but that the power should not be exercised if there is any doubt about the facts." *Wright & Miller* § 2533.

[320] Rule 12(b)(6), *discussed in* § 8.07[2][c], *supra.*

[321] Rule 12(c), *discussed in* § 8.07[1], *supra.*

[322] Rule 56, *discussed in* § 11.03, *supra.*

Apart from the recent amendment in Rule 50 consolidating directed verdicts and judgments n.o.v. into the single term, *judgment as a matter of law*, there are only a few attempts in the federal rules to inform the reader of the interrelationship of these motions.[323] Yet decisions, commentary and language in the rules support the conclusion that all pose the same test: *Do the established facts support a legal rule which should be applied to decide all or part of the case?*[324]

This is the same question posed by trial itself. We could thus administer this test without motions by sending every case to trial and treating every jury verdict as settled fact. If that was our system, however, it would have two major drawbacks. The facts in some cases are established long before trial. To require them to be tried would needlessly burden the party who holds what should be the winning cards and waste judicial resources. Therefore, the first three motions available permit termination of the case before trial begins. Second, treating jury verdicts as established fact may sometimes deny parties substantive justice. The last two motions offer protection here.

To better understand when and why it is appropriate to decide cases by motion rather than by the ordinary trial process, it is useful to examine our subject in larger perspective. Civil adjudication has two essential functions. One might be called a *law* function. The law function is to attach the proper legal significance to settled facts. The process of research, argument and deliberation making up the law function is indifferent to how or when facts are settled. Courts conclude civil adjudication by performing the law function and may do so as soon as they deem established those facts supporting a case-ending rule. The other essential in civil adjudication might be called the *fact* function. The fact function is to resolve factual controversies. The fact function often consumes a far larger amount of party and judicial resources than the law function.

The first three motions available to decide the merits (dismissal for failure to state a claim, judgment on the pleadings, and summary judgment) serve to reduce the cost of the fact function of civil adjudication. They do this by creating opportunities for courts to deem facts established as early as possible. The existence of three such motions reflects the realization that

---

[323] For example, Rule 12(b) states that when "matters outside the pleading are presented to and not excluded by the court, the [12(b)(6)] motion shall be treated as one for summary judgment. . . ."

[324] Rule 56(c) governing summary judgments makes explicit reference to the test, stating summary judgment "shall be rendered" when affidavits or other types of materials deemed appropriate "show that there is no genuine issue as to any material fact and that the moving party is entitled to a judgment as a matter of law." After recent amendments, Rule 50 makes what was formerly termed directed verdict and judgment available upon a showing that "no legally sufficient basis exists for a reasonable jury" to resolve the case differently; and that the movant is therefore entitled to "judgment as a matter of law." *See also* Rule 12(b) (consideration of matters outside the complaint converts a 12(b)(6) motion to one for summary judgment) & Rule 12(c) (consideration of matters outside the pleadings converts a motion for judgment on the pleadings to one for summary judgment).

the point of the pretrial phase at which facts are established varies from case to case.[325]

Substantially less time and effort will be saved by granting a directed verdict, none by granting judgment n.o.v.[326] The rationale for these motions derives instead from the need to preserve rights of the parties under substantive law. Jurors do not consider substantive law as such, but it determines the freedom they are given by the court's instructions to weigh the evidence.[327] When the evidence is such that jurors could find for a party only by exceeding that freedom, then a verdict for that party would do violence to the substantive rights of the opposing party.[328] The same concern does not arise in nonjury cases since legal guardian and fact-finder are one. That explains why directed verdicts and judgments n.o.v. have no real counterpart in bench trials.[329]

Motions for deciding cases without (or notwithstanding) trial reflect the procedural judgment that it is not always necessary or desirable to reach the merits through the ordinary process of trial. Trials are indispensable only in those cases where the facts never become established prior to trial, and juries have the last word only where the evidence provides reasonable support for either plaintiff or defendant's conflicting versions of the facts.

[d] The Interrelationship of Post-Trial Motion Practice and Dispositions on Appeal

In most jurisdictions, the party against whom a verdict is returned may seek judgment n.o.v. or a new trial in the alternative.[330] The verdict-winner in federal court also may move for a new trial ten days after judgment n.o.v. (judgment as a matter of law) is granted against him.[331] In handling alternative motions, the trial court has a complete range of options. It may grant judgment n.o.v. and a new trial, deny both motions, or grant either

---

[325] In a Rule 12(b)(6) motion, defendant challenges plaintiff's legal theory by using as established fact plaintiff's own allegations. When completed pleadings create established fact, either party may move for judgment on the pleadings. When established facts necessary to decision can only be presented from sources outside the pleadings, either party may move for summary judgment.

[326] Cf. Gregory, One Two Many Rivers to Cross: Rule 50 Practice in the Modern Era of Summary judgment, 23 Fla. St. U. L. Rev. 689 (1996) (arguing that relaxation of standards for summary judgment should diminish use of Rule 50 procedures).

[327] See § 12.08[3], supra.

[328] Cf. Wright & Miller § 2522 (declaring Rule 50 to be "essential to preservation and proper application of the applicable substantive law.").

[329] A federal litigant may move under Rule 41(b) for involuntary dismissal, but the motion is of relatively minor significance. See § 11.04 (involuntary dismissals), supra, § 912.10 (bench trials), infra.

[330] Rule 50(b). He need not await entry of judgment on the verdict in federal court. Rules 50(b) and 59(b) both require only that the motions be filed no later than ten days after entry of the judgment.

[331] Rule 50(c)(2).

motion while denying the other.[332] Each response carries its own implications for appellate review.[333]

When the district court denies judgment n.o.v., but grants new trial, its order is not immediately appealable in the federal system because there is no final judgment.[334] The party may raise the question of the validity of the new trial order only on appeal from an eventual final judgment after the second trial.[335]

When the district court denies judgment n.o.v. and new trial, both decisions are appealable in the normal course. On appeal, the party who prevailed on the motion may argue grounds for a new trial in the event that the appellate court finds error in the denial of the motion for judgment n.o.v.[336] The appellate court may then enter judgment n.o.v., award a new trial, or remand for the trial court to make the new trial determination.[337]

When the district court grants the motion for judgment n.o.v., Rule 50(c) requires it also to rule conditionally on the new trial motion in anticipation of a possible reversal of the judgment n.o.v. on appeal. On appeal, the appellate court will either affirm judgment n.o.v. and end the matter, or reverse. In the event of reversal, when the district court has denied the motion for new trial, the appellate court may order entry of judgment on the verdict, reverse the denial of the motion for new trial and order a new trial, or remand the case to the trial court for reconsideration of the motion for new trial.[338]

When the district court grants the motion for judgment n.o.v. and conditionally grants new trial as well, there is a final judgment from which to appeal. Although the conditional grant of new trial is still technically nonfinal, it is practical to permit the appellate court to review the new trial order because the case is already before it on appeal of the judgment n.o.v. and it has already become familiar with much of the evidence in the case in ruling on that judgment. Rule 50(c)(1) therefore assumes that the appellate court may reach the new trial order if it reverses the judgment

---

[332] In rare cases, the court may deny judgment n.o.v. and order a new trial, when only a motion for judgment n.o.v. is before the court. The language of Rule 50(b) seems to provide for this. Yet the practice should be limited to cases where grounds for judgment n.o.v. exist but the court "believes that the defect in the proof might be remedied on a second trial, or if needed evidence was ruled out by some error of the court." *Wright & Miller* § 2538.

[333] For a more extended discussion of this process, see *Wright & Miller* § 2540; Note, *Post-Verdict Motions Under 50: Protecting the Verdict-Winner,* 53 Minn. L. Rev. 358 (1968). On the limitation on federal interlocutory review, *see* § 13.04, *infra.*

[334] *See* § 13.03 (the final judgment rule), *infra. Cf. Allied Chem. Corp. v. Daiflon, Inc.,* 449 U.S. 33, 34 (1980) (emphasizing unavailability also of *mandamus* to review grant of new trial). An increasing number of state systems, however, do confer appellate jurisdiction over orders granting new trials. *See Friedenthal, Kane & Miller* § 12.4; Rabinowitz, *Appellate Review of Trial Court Orders Granting New Trials,* 8 Rutgers L. Rev. 465 (1954).

[335] *Allied Chem.,* 449 U.S. at 34.

[336] Rule 50(d). *See Neely v. Martin K. Eby Const. Co.* , 386 U.S. 317 (1967).

[337] Rule 50(d). On the authority of the court of appeals to enter a judgment as a matter of law directly, *see Weisgram v. Marley Co.,* 528 U.S. 440, 447-449 (2000).

[338] *Moore* § 50.94.

n.o.v.[339] In this event, the appellate court may remand the case to the trial court for new trial,[340] reverse the grant of the motion for new trial and order entry of judgment on the verdict, or remand the case to the trial court for reconsideration of the motion for new trial.[341]

§ 12.10   Bench Trials (Non-jury Cases)

Some cases are triable only before judges.[342] Others must be tried before a judge because the parties waive their jury claims.[343] Non-jury (bench) trials make up a significant portion of trial litigation.[344] Not only is the bench trial in extensive use, but "it raises . . . fewer procedural problems than does trial to a jury."[345]

The judge in a bench trial is both law enforcer *and* trier of fact. Since these functions are performed by the same person, distinctions between the two do not matter as they do in jury trials. Consequently, directed verdicts and judgments n.o.v., which protect against lawless jury verdicts, have no real counterpart in bench trials. A defendant in a bench trial may move for dismissal, or, in a federal court, for judgment as a matter of law, at the close of plaintiff's submission of evidence,[346] but unlike the motion for directed verdict, this motion is not to avert mischief by the fact-finder. The person ruling on the motion *is* the fact finder. In fact, under Rule 50(c), either party in a bench trial may move for judgment as a matter of law whenever his opponent has been fully heard with respect to a potentially dispositive issue of fact, and the court may (but need not) enter "judgment on partial findings" at any time it can appropriately make a finding of fact on that issue.[347]

---

[339] However, use of any federal rule of civil or appellate procedure as authority for relaxing the finality requirement arguably exceeds the strictures of Federal Rule of Civil Procedure 82 and Federal Rule of Appellate Procedure 1(b) that the rules not be construed to expand jurisdiction.

[340] *Montgomery Ward & Co. v. Duncan,* 311 U.S. 243, 254 (1940) ("If the judgment were reversed, the case, on remand, would be governed by the trial judge's award of a new trial.").

[341] *Moore* § 50.94[2]. As noted earlier, trial courts enjoy considerable discretion in ordering new trials. *See* § 12.09[2], *supra.* However, perhaps because Rule 50(c)(1) explicitly entertains the possibility of reversal, conditional orders granting new trials appear somewhat more vulnerable. *See, e.g.,* the cases cited in *Wright & Miller* § 2540.

[342] The right to a jury trial is protected by constitutional or statutory law, *see* § 12.04[1], *supra,* and "no similar requirement protects trial by the court. . . ." *Beacon Theatres, Inc. v. Westover,* 359 U.S. 500, 510 (1959).

[343] *See* § 12.07[2], *supra.* At the same time, a "court may, if it wishes, submit an issue to an advisory jury on its own initiative, but the verdict of such a jury is advisory only, and the ultimate responsibility for finding the facts remains with the court." *Wright* § 92. Professor Wright adds: "In an action not triable to a jury as of right, the court may, with the consent of both parties, order a trial with a jury whose verdict has the same effect as if trial by jury had been a matter of right." *Id.*

[344] *Id.* at 644 (reporting that more federal cases are tried before judges than before juries).

[345] *Id.*

[346] *See* Rule 52(c).

[347] Rule 52(c) advisory committee's notes (1991).

Nor do new trial motions in jury trials have precise counterparts in bench trials. Most errors prompting new trial orders [348] occur only in jury trials. [349] When an error does arise in a bench trial, the court often simply rehears part of the case or reconsiders its decision. [350] Yet bench trials are not easier than jury trials in all respects. They can put quite a strain on judges who must rule on the admissibility of evidence and consider its weight if admitted, at roughly the same time. [351]

Federal Rule 52(a) requires the court to make findings of fact in non-jury cases or when the jury is used only in an advisory capacity. Often the trial court will direct the prevailing party to prepare proposed findings of fact and the loser to object, as appropriate, and then craft its own findings from the submissions. The appellate courts have sharply chastised the trial courts which do this uncritically, citing the "potential for overreaching and exaggeration on the part of attorneys preparing findings of fact when they have already been informed that the judge has decided in their favor." [352] When, however, the trial court provides a framework for the proposed findings by its bench ruling, the loser takes the opportunity to respond to them, and the court does not simply adopt the findings verbatim, the Supreme Court has approved the process. [353]

Rule 52 states that, on appeal, "[f]indings of fact, whether based on oral or documentary evidence, shall not be set aside unless clearly erroneous, and due regard shall be given to the opportunity of the trial court to judge of the credibility of the witnesses." Thus, judgment in a bench trial differs from summary judgment in that the judge's fact findings in a bench trial are reversible only if clearly erroneous; summary judgment is not similarly shielded on review by the clearly erroneous standard because it is based on the judge's determination, *as a matter of law*, that the material facts are without genuine dispute. [354] Section 13.09[2][b], *infra,* discusses standards of appellate review.

---

[348] *See* § 12.09[2][a], *supra.*

[349] "Although theoretically new trial motions may be granted in judge as well as jury trials, . . . the type of errors meriting a new trial typically arise only in jury trials. For example, even if the court erroneously receives certain evidence in a nonjury trial, the judge simply may disregard that evidence when rendering judgment, avoiding the need for a new trial." *Friedenthal, Kane & Miller* § 12.4.

[350] Thus, motions for rehearing or for reconsideration are probably more common than motions for new trial in bench trials. Indeed, Rule 59 authorizes new trial in bench trials "for any of the reasons for which rehearings have heretofore been granted in suits in equity. . . ."

[351] For an examination of bench trials from the perspective of the trial judge, see Haydock & Sonsteng, *Court Trial Empirical Survey: Interview Responses From Trial Judges Explaining Their Experiences and Views Regarding the Trial of Non-jury Cases,* 11 Wm. Mitchell L. Rev. 775 (1985).

[352] *Anderson v. Bessemer City,* 470 U.S. 564, 572 (1985); *Ramey Const. Co. v. Apache Tribe,* 616 F.2d 464, 466–468 (10th Cir. 1980) (emphasizing also the effect of judicial origination of findings on the quality of decision-making). *See* Fjeldstad, *Just the Facts, Ma'am — A Review of the Practice of the Verbatim Adoption of Findings of Fact and Conclusions of Law,* 44 St. Louis U. L.J. 197 (2000).

[353] *Anderson,* 470 U.S. at 572.

[354] Rule 50(c) advisory committee's notes (1991 amendment).

§ 12.11 Judgments

[1] The Nature and Force of Judgments

Defining the term in a broad sense, Federal Rule 54(a) states that "Judgment . . . includes a decree and any order from which an appeal lies." The rule thus ties judgments to final orders and a small class of interlocutory orders appealable in federal court.[355]

This definition fails to capture the functional significance judgments have in completing the case. In federal court, judgment follows decision. *Decision* describes determinations of fact made by the judge's findings or by jury verdict. *Judgment* "is the pronouncement of that decision and the act that gives it legal effect."[356] The judgment is filed by delivery to the district court clerk and entered through recording by the clerk.[357] While the act of entry is not performed by the court, it is nonetheless important to the force and effect of the judgment.[358]

The significance of a judgment can be twofold. First, judgment either for damages[359] or an injunction[360] gives the judgment-holder leverage over the person against whom the judgment was rendered. The money-judgment-holder has access to special procedures to expedite payment of the award.[361] One ordered to behave a certain way by an injunction must do so or suffer civil and possibly criminal contempt.[362] Second, judgments final and on the merits preclude parties in the future from relitigating issues and whole claims which might otherwise consume time, money and scarce judicial resources.[363]

[2] Resisting Judgments

Parties disadvantaged by judgments must consider what if anything they can do to improve their lot, short of appeal. Three approaches are considered below. One can prevail upon a subsequent court presented with the judgment to declare it unenforceable because it is defective (collateral attack), one can try to be excused from the judgment (extraordinary relief), or one can try to make the judgment more agreeable (amendment).

---

[355] *See* §§ 13.03-13.05, *supra.*

[356] *Wright & Miller* § 2651.

[357] Rule 58.

[358] "[I]t is crucial to the effectiveness of the judgment and for measuring the time periods for appeal and the filing of various post-trial motions." *Wright & Miller* § 2651.

[359] On damages, see generally § 14.01. *infra.*

[360] On injunctions, see generally § 14.02, *infra.*

[361] On the nature of money-judgment enforcement proceedings, see § 15.02, *infra.*

[362] On the prerequisites for civil and criminal contempt, see § 14.02[2], *infra.*

[363] On the prerequisite to claim preclusion that judgments be final and on the merits, see § 15.05, *infra.*

[a] Collateral Attack [364]

So strong is the need to resolve controversies and such is the force of preclusion doctrine that parties are not free to relitigate a prior judgment just because it was wrong on the merits. [365]

There are only a few paths of escape, known as points of collateral attack. The most important are the guarantee of notice and the constraint on territorial jurisdiction which is part of the law of constitutional due process. The likelihood that these or the few other grounds for collaterally attacking judgments [366] will be available in a given case is remote.

[b] Extraordinary Relief

When the time for direct attack on the judgment by motion for judgment n.o.v. or for new trial or by appeal has expired, many jurisdictions provide limited extraordinary relief from the judgment by further motion in the trial court. Federal Rule 60 is typical. Rule 60 sorts problems into serious and not-so-serious categories.

Subdivision (a) addresses the second category, correction by the district court of "clerical mistakes in judgments, orders or other parts of the record." [367] Subdivision (b) addresses the first category:

(1) mistake, inadvertence, surprise, or excusable neglect; (2) newly discovered evidence which by due diligence could not have been discovered in time to move for a new trial under Rule 59(b); (3) fraud (whether heretofore denominated intrinsic or extrinsic), misrepresentation, or other misconduct of an adverse party; (4) the judgment is void; (5) the judgment has been satisfied, released, or discharged, or a prior judgment upon which it is based has been reversed or otherwise vacated, or it is no longer equitable that the judgment should have prospective application; or (6) any other reason justifying relief from the operation of the judgment.

Subdivision (b) states that grounds (1)-(3) must be offered no later than a year from judgment.

It is not easy to obtain relief from a judgment under this provision, but easier certainly than it is to attack collaterally the legal sufficiency of the judgment offered for enforcement in a later lawsuit. [368] Space permits only a few specific comments on the grounds listed in Rule 60(b). [369]

---

[364] On the meaning of collateral attack and how it differs from direct attack, see § 3.04, *supra.*

[365] *See, e.g., Milliken v. Meyer,* 311 U.S. 457, 462 (1940); *Federated Department Stores, Inc. v. Moitie,* 452 U.S. 394, 398 (1981) (stating that the "*res judicata* consequences of a final, unappealed judgment [are not] altered by the fact that the judgment may have been wrong. . . .").

[366] They are discussed in § 3.04[2], *supra.*

[367] Moore § 60.02. *See generally* Donahue, *A History and Interpretation of Rule 60(a) of the Federal Rules of Civil Procedure,* 42 Drake L. Rev. 461 (1993).

[368] See the discussion of collateral attack, § 12.11[2][a], *supra.*

[369] The United States Supreme Court recently reaffirmed the limitation of Rule 60(b) to extraordinary cases. *United States v. Beggerly,* 524 U.S. 38, 47 (1998) ("under the Rule, an independent action should be available only to prevent a grave miscarriage of justice."). For extended discussion of the grounds, see *Wright & Miller* §§ 2858-2864.

Ground (1) is especially suited to relief from default judgments.[370] Rule 55 treats entry of a default and entry of judgment on the default as separate stages. "For good cause shown the court may set aside an entry of default" unaccompanied by judgment.[371] The void-judgment category of ground (4) is limited to a judgment "void only on grounds of lack of jurisdiction or for some failure of due process in the original proceeding."[372] Finally, despite the open-ended phrasing of ground (6), courts have evinced understandable hesitation in using it. It seems to exist for "unusual cases" and "not for the purpose of relieving a party from free, calculated, and deliberate choices he has made."[373]

[c] Amendment

Rule 59(e) gives parties in federal court a brief opportunity to seek amendment of judgment. Rule 59(e) motions resemble in purpose those filed under Rule 60(a).[374] The purpose of each is to give true effect to the judgment by eliminating unwitting error.[375]

However, the motions differ in several respects. Rule 59(e) motions must be filed within ten days from entry of judgment. Timely filing keeps the judgment from becoming final for purposes of appeal. A Rule 60(a) motion can be made at any time without affecting the time for appeal.[376] Moreover, while the focus of Rule 60(a) is on clerical mistakes, Rule 59(e) contemplates mistakes by the court.[377]

---

[370] *See Friedenthal, Kane & Miller* § 12.6, (noting it "most frequently is invoked successfully in the default setting or when the plaintiff's suit was dismissed for failure to prosecute and judgment was entered by mistake since the party fully intended actively to litigate the dispute."). *See generally* Note, *Relief From Default Judgments Under Rule 60(b) — A Study of Federal Case Law,* 49 Fordham L. Rev. 956 (1981). To succeed in having a default judgment vacated, one may have to demonstrate the existence of a "meritorious defense," *Wright & Miller* § 2862, unless the judgment was procured without notice. *See Peralta v. Heights Medical Center, Inc.,* 485 U.S. 80 (1988).

[371] Rule 55(c). *See generally* § 11.02 (default judgments), *supra.*

[372] *Friedenthal, Kane & Miller* § 12.6.

[373] *Wright & Miller* § 2864. "A party remains under a duty to take legal steps to protect his own interests. In particular, it ordinarily is not permissible to use this motion to remedy a failure to take an appeal." *Id.*

[374] *Discussed in* § 12.11[2][b], *supra.*

[375] Parties cannot use Rule 59(e) or Rule 60(a) to alter the intended effect of a judgment. These motions are confined "to clerical errors or matters of clear oversight, not questions involving the right to additional recovery, or a reduction in an award." *Friedenthal, Kane & Miller* § 12.6. Such substantial changes require a motion for new trial made no later than ten days after entry of judgment, or a motion for relief from the judgment, which may or may not be subject to a one-year time limit depending on the ground for relief used. *See* § 12.11[2][b], *supra.*

[376] *Moore* § 60.12.

[377] *Boaz v. Mutual Life Ins. Co. of New York,* 146 F.2d 321 (8th Cir. 1944), is frequently offered as an illustration. There the trial court corrected its error, granting defendant's motion to amend the judgment from dismissal of plaintiff's case without prejudice to dismissal with prejudice. The present version of Rule 59(e) codifies this authority. *Wright & Miller* § 2810.1.

Chapter 13

APPEAL

§ 13.01 Overview

Appeal is the submission of a lower court's disposition of a matter to the review of a higher court.[1] One purpose of appeal is to *assure the correctness of lower court dispositions.*[2] This purpose is reflected by the availability in most judicial systems of at least one layer of obligatory review — appeal as of right. Another purpose of appeal is *institutional review* to assure uniformity in the application of law and to furnish guidance to the lower courts. In many judicial systems, this systemic purpose is served by the availability of some form of discretionary appeal — appeal by permission — to the system's highest court, which allows it to pick and choose its cases for optimal institutional benefit.[3] Both of these purposes of appeal may be at odds with two other objectives of procedural systems: *efficiency* and *finality.* These objectives call for technical (some would say grudging) application of many procedures for appeal, lest the proceedings of the lower courts be disrupted or their judgments depreciated by too ready appeal. Consequently, the law of appeal can be viewed as a fine balance of concern for correctness and uniformity of disposition on one hand, and efficiency and finality on the other.

---

[1] *Rehearing* serves the same purposes as appeal but submits the disposition to review by the same court, although sometimes a different or fuller panel. *See generally* Louisell & Degnan, *Rehearing in American Appellate Courts,* 44 Cal. L. Rev. 627 (1956). A federal *habeas corpus* action effectively submits the state court system's disposition of a criminal case to the review of a federal district court, but that review is only to test the constitutional validity of state detention after the normal course of state appeals, and not to test accuracy of the state courts' judgments. *See* 28 U.S.C. §§ 2241-2255. *Removal* is a procedure for withdrawing the case from the jurisdiction of one court and lodging it with another before any disposition, and therefore is not a form of appeal. *De novo* review may be and is here considered an appeal, but the appeals court decides the matter anew without regard to the prior disposition by the lower court.

[2] *See generally* Shavell, *The Appeals Process as a Means of Error Correction,* 24 J. Legal Stud. 379 (1995).

[3] No litigant is entitled to more than two chances, namely, to the original trial and to a review, and the intermediate courts of review are provided for that purpose. When a case goes beyond that, it is not primarily to preserve the rights of the litigants. The Supreme Court's function is for the purpose of expounding and stabilizing principles of law for the benefit of the people of the country, passing upon constitutional questions and other important questions of law for the public benefit. It is to preserve the uniformity of decision among the intermediate courts of appeal.
Testimony by Chief Justice Taft regarding the "Judges' Bill," *quoted in Dick v. New York Life Ins. Co.,* 359 U.S. 437, 448 (1959) (Frankfurter, J., dissenting). *See generally,* Bradley, *The Uncertainty Principle in the Supreme Court,* 1986 Duke L.J. 1.

Appeal poses five questions: when, where, how, of what and how much? *When* is the question of appealability, discussed in Part A. *Where* and *how* are questions of perfecting the appeal, discussed in Part B. *Of what* and *how much* are questions of the scope and intensity of review, discussed in Part C.

PART A
When? Appealability

§ 13.02 Appealability In General

Appealability poses a choice between appeal of the final judgment at the end of the litigation and one or more *interlocutory* appeals during its course. These alternatives can be compared according to the following formula:

> The costs of allowing interlocutory appeals are the costs of an unnecessary extra appeal if the trial judge turns out to have been correct. (The appeal is an extra one because an appeal will still be allowed at the end.) The costs of not allowing interlocutory appeals are those of an unnecessary or an unnecessarily long trial if the trial judge turns out to have been wrong. If we assume that the costs of an unnecessary extra appeal are approximately the same as the costs of the unnecessary or unnecessarily long trial, the overall costs are proportional to the number of times the trial judge is right versus the number of times he is wrong. If trial judges are right more often than they are wrong (measured by eventual reversal when appeal finally occurs), then the general policy should disfavor interlocutory appeals.[4]

In fact, most trial court rulings are affirmed,[5] and the general policy in the federal system and in most states disfavors interlocutory appeals. On the other hand, a few states assess the costs and benefits differently and allow routine interlocutory appeal.[6] Section 13.03 uses the federal system to discuss the general policy against interlocutory appeal.

---

[4] S. Yeazell, J. Landers, & J. Martin, *Civil Procedure* 848 (3d Ed. 1992). Copyright © 1981 by Little, Brown & Co. Reprinted with permission. *See also Richardson-Merrell Inc. v. Koller*, 472 U.S. 424, 434 (1985) (performing cost-benefit analysis to deny interlocutory appeal of order disqualifying counsel); *Reise v. Board of Regents of Univ. of Wisconsin*, 957 F.2d 293, 295 (7th Cir. 1992), *cert. denied*, 510 U.S. 892 (1993):

> Because almost all interlocutory appeals from discovery orders would end in affirmance (the district court possesses discretion, and review is deferential), the costs of delay via appeal, and the costs to the judicial system of entertaining these appeals, exceed in the aggregate the costs of the few erroneous discovery orders that might be corrected were appeals available.

[5] *Wright & Miller* § 3907. For the twelve months ended Sept. 30, 1998, only 10.4% of the appeals terminated on the merits in federal appellate courts were reversals; almost 86% were affirmances or dismissals. *1998 Admin. Off. U.S. Courts Ann. Rep. Of the Director*, Table B-5, at 114.

[6] *See, e.g.*, N.Y. Civ. Prac. L. & R. 5701(a)(2)(iv) & (v) (McKinney, WESTLAW through L. 2000) (allowing interlocutory appeal of any order which "involves some part of the merits" or which "affects a substantial right"). *See generally* Korn, *Civil Jurisdiction of the New York Court of Appeals and Appellate Division*, 16 Buffalo L. Rev. 307 (1967).

Even in the majority of jurisdictions that disfavor interlocutory appeals, there are exceptions. These include cases in which the costs of error are particularly large and irreversible, the alleged errors involve unresolved questions of law increasing the likelihood of error by the trial judge, or some issues are presented that, as a practical matter, will be lost to a party before appeal from a final judgment can be taken. Interlocutory appeal can have important benefits, as the Supreme Court has explained.

> In certain cases, it may avoid injustice by quickly correcting a trial court's error. It can simplify, or more appropriately direct, the future course of litigation. And, it can thereby reduce the burdens of future proceedings, perhaps freeing a party from those burdens entirely.[7]

Sections 13.04 and 13.05 use the federal system to illustrate typical statutory and judge-made exceptions to the general policy against interlocutory appeal.

§ 13.03 Final Judgment Rule

[1] In General

In most jurisdictions, statute or decisional law has made an entry of final judgment a jurisdictional prerequisite to appeal.[8] The court of appeals must satisfy itself that a final judgment was entered below or dismiss the appeal, whether or not the parties raise this issue.[9] The final judgment rule, or rule against piecemeal appeals, is that the parties can only appeal from a final judgment on all claims in the action, whether the alleged errors are in that judgment or in the pretrial or trial procedures leading to it. The rule thus does not go to *whether* such errors may be appealed, but only *when*. It serves simply "to combine in one review all stages of the proceeding that effectively may be reviewed and corrected if and when final judgment results."[10]

The cost analysis that underlies all questions of appealability suggests that a primary purpose of the final judgment rule[11] is to avoid extra and unnecessary appeals: interlocutory appeals that might be mooted by the further course of litigation should the trial judge change her interlocutory

---

[7] *Johnson v. Jones*, 515 U.S. 304, 309-310 (1995).

[8] *See, e.g.,* 28 U.S.C. § 1291 (granting federal courts of appeals jurisdiction of appeals "from all final decisions" of the district courts). Congress has given the Supreme Court power to define when a district court ruling is final for purposes of appeal under section 1291. 28 U.S.C. § 2072(c). *See generally* Martineau, *Defining Finality and Appealability by Court Rule: Right Problem, Wrong Solution,* 54 U. Pitt. L. Rev. 717 (1993).

[9] *Brown Shoe Co. v. United States,* 370 U.S. 294, 305 (1962).

[10] *Cohen v. Beneficial Indust. Loan Corp.,* 337 U.S. 541, 546 (1949).

[11] On this and other purposes of the rule, see generally Thornburg, *Interlocutory Review of Discovery Orders: An Idea Whose Time Has Come,* 44 Sw. L.J. 1045, 1047-1049 (1990); Note, *Appealability in the Federal Courts,* 75 Harv. L. Rev. 351, 351-352 (1961); *Wright & Miller* § 3907.

decision or the interlocutory appellant ultimately prevail. The rule also promotes consolidation of alleged errors in a single appeal, permitting appellate review of each of them in the context of the whole and on the fullest trial court record.[12] At the same time, the rule helps to expedite the proceedings in the trial court by protecting them from appellate interruption. This promotes efficiency and also comity — the institutional goal of "maintaining the appropriate relationship" between the trial and appellate courts[13] and respect for trial court decisions. Finally, the rule guards against tactical abuse of appeal to harass and delay.

Federal Rule of Civil Procedure 58 makes it easy to identify when a judgment has been entered by requiring judgments to be set forth on a separate document. But whether the judgment is also final has proven a more elusive question. The Supreme Court has declared that a final judgment "ends the litigation on the merits and leaves nothing for the court to do but execute the judgment."[14] Thus, a trial court decision of liability, but not of all damages, is interlocutory. On the other hand, a decision to grant a permanent injunction is final if no other remedy is sought, even though the court nominally retains jurisdiction to assure compliance. Other applications of the concept are more problematic.[15] Uncertainty exists because the courts have sensibly taken a "pragmatic approach to the question of finality" that precludes the formulation of any precise verbal formula for deciding it.[16]

Federal courts carried pragmatism too far in according finality to refusals to certify suits as class actions. The argument was that such decisions sounded a death knell for the litigation because the plaintiffs found it economically imprudent to pursue their claims individually without the incentive of a possible group recovery.[17] Rejecting this view, the Supreme Court noted in *Coopers & Lybrand v. Livesay*[18] that this logic would apply with equal force to many interlocutory orders in ordinary litigation, from venue to discovery and summary judgment, "that may have such tactical

---

[12] Indeed, one scholar has traced the final judgment rule at common law to the need for a full record below. *See* Crick, *The Final Judgment As A Basis for Appeal,* 41 Yale L.J. 539, 542-543 (1932).

[13] *Coopers & Lybrand v. Livesay,* 437 U.S. 463, 476 (1978), *quoting Parkinsen v. April Industries,* 520 F.2d 650, 654 (2d Cir. 1975).

[14] *Catlin v. United States,* 324 U.S. 229, 233 (1945). Requests for attorney's fees are not part of the merits and their pendency does not affect the finality of a decision on the merits. *Budinich v. Becton Dickinson & Co.,* 486 U.S. 196 (1988).

[15] *Compare Catlin, id.* at 232-233 (decree of title in condemnation case is not final decision, when question of compensation is still open), *with Brown Shoe Co. v. United States,* 370 U.S. 294 (1962) (order of divestiture in antitrust case is final decision, even though question how divestiture is to be accomplished is still open).

[16] *Brown Shoe,* 370 U.S. at 306. Professor Wright suggests that the saving grace of the courts' approach is that "in almost all situations it is entirely clear" from the nature of the order or the decisional law that the order is or is not final. *Wright* § 101.

[17] Typically, the prospective individual recovery was insufficient incentive in light of plaintiffs' liability for their own attorney's fees, which might otherwise come out of a class recovery. *See* § 9.08 (class actions), *supra.*

[18] 437 U.S. 463 (1978).

economic significance that a defeat is tantamount to a "death knell' for the entire case."[19] Moreover, whether such orders did sound the death knell would turn on the courts' perception of their impact on the parties in particular cases. The Court concluded that the death-knell doctrine undermined efficient judicial administration by eroding the final judgment rule, while requiring "individualized jurisdictional inquiry" into the financial stamina of the would-be class representatives from case to case.[20]

The *Coopers & Lybrand* Court therefore held "that the fact that an interlocutory order may induce a party to abandon his claim before final judgment is not a sufficient reason for considering it a 'final decision' within the meaning of 28 U.S.C. § 1291."[21] *Coopers & Lybrand* may well have sounded the death knell for other applications of this kind of pragmatic approach to appellate jurisdiction.[22]

[2] Finality in Multi-Claim and Multi-Party Cases

Literal application of the final judgment rule in cases involving multiple claims or parties would prohibit appeal of decisions on individual claims until all have been decided. The result could often be to delay for years review and execution of early-decided claims. On the other hand, if immediate appeal of such decisions were allowed, they would have to be clearly identified as final or parties would be uncertain when to appeal to protect their rights. Federal Rule of Civil Procedure 54(b) provides the solution in the federal system, authorizing the trial court in multi-claim actions to make "express direction for the entry of judgment" on fewer than all of the claims or parties upon "express determination that there is no just cause for delay."[23] Rule 54(b) is not an exception to the final judgment rule, but only a statutory standard for its application in multi-claim and multi-party cases.[24] It applies to trial court decisions that would have been appealable final judgments standing alone, but for the liberal joinder permitted by the federal rules.

A threshold issue on appeal is whether the trial court has finally disposed of an individual *claim* in a multi-claim or multi-party case or merely one of several legal *theories* or alternative *requests for relief* on a single claim. The trial court's determination is not controlling; the appeals court must decide for itself. In *Liberty Mutual Ins. Co. v. Wetzel*,[25] for example, the

---

[19] *Id.* at 470.

[20] *Id.* at 473.

[21] *Id.* at 477 (footnote omitted).

[22] *But see Wright & Miller* § 3912.

[23] Of course, a party with multiple claims could also "manufacture" a final judgment by voluntarily dismissing (*see* § 11.04[1], *supra*) other claims after a court has ruled on the one it wishes to appeal. *See* Cochran, *Gaining Appellate Review by "Manufacturing" a Final Judgment Through Voluntary Dismissal of Peripheral Claims*, 48 Mercer L. Rev. 979 (1997).

[24] *Sears, Roebuck & Co. v. Mackey*, 351 U.S. 427, 435 (1956). The courts are divided on Rule 54(b)'s application in cases that have been consolidated under Rule 42(a). *See* Gerson, *Note, The Appealability of Partial Judgments in Consolidated Cases*, 57 U. Chi. L. Rev. 169 (1990).

[25] 424 U.S. 737 (1976).

plaintiff alleged employment discrimination and sought injunctive relief, damages and attorney's fees. The trial court granted plaintiffs' motion for partial summary judgment, and then purported to direct entry of final judgment pursuant to Rule 54(b) on the issue of liability. Defendant appealed.

The Supreme Court ruled that, notwithstanding entry of judgment under Rule 54(b), the trial court had not finally adjudicated a separate claim for purposes of appeal. Treatment of the liability determination as a declaratory judgment[26] would not alter this since Rule 54(b) is *claim* rather than relief-focussed. The Court held that a "complaint asserting only one legal right, even if seeking multiple remedies for the alleged violation of that right, states a single claim for relief."[27] Since plaintiffs advanced "but one legal theory" (employment discrimination in violation of federal law) applicable to only one set of facts, and since the ruling on liability left open questions of injunctive relief and damages, Rule 54(b) was inapplicable.[28]

The Court expressly refrained from definitively resolving what constitutes a claim for relief under the rules, but its analysis is reminiscent of the tests for deciding a cause of action for purposes of *res judicata* or claim preclusion.[29] In the same vein, the Second Circuit Court of Appeals has suggested the test whether the action involves theories of recovery that could be separately enforced.[30] The Seventh and D.C. Circuit Courts of Appeals noted the affinity to preclusion, holding that when alleged "claims [are] so closely related that they would fall afoul of the rule against splitting claims [under the law of claim preclusion] if brought separately," they do not qualify as separate claims within the meaning of Rule 54(b).[31]

To understand these tests, consider a suit for personal injuries in which the plaintiff alleges several different bases for relief — simple negligence, gross negligence, breach of implied warranty, and breach of express warranty. Summary judgment on any one such basis would not be appealable as judgment on a separate claim under Rule 54(b) because each is an alternative legal theory applicable to the same basic set of facts, and they all assert but one legal right to freedom from personal injury. If plaintiff pursued an action to judgment on any one of these theories, he would be precluded in most jurisdictions from suing separately upon the rest under the doctrine of claim preclusion; separating the action by theories would be splitting a cause of action. Allowing a litigant, even with the assent of the trial court under Rule 54(b), to define a claim as any one such theory while others remain for decision would permit evasion of the final judgment rule.

---

[26] *See* § 14.03 (declaratory relief), *infra.*

[27] *Wetzel,* 424 U.S. at 743 n.4.

[28] *Id.* at 744.

[29] *See* § 15.03, *infra.*

[30] *Rieser v. Baltimore & Ohio R.R. Co.,* 224 F.2d 198, 199 (2d Cir. 1955) (Clark, J.), *cert. denied,* 350 U.S. 1006 (1956).

[31] *Local P-171, Amalgamated Meat Cutters & Butcher Workmen v. Thompson Farms,* 642 F.2d 1065, 1071 (7th Cir. 1981) (adding as another "rule of thumb" the test whether separate recovery is possible on each claim); *Tolson v. United States,* 732 F.2d 998 (D.C. Cir. 1984).

If Rule 54(b) applies, the trial judge must additionally determine that "there is no just reason for delay" in entering final judgment. In part, this involves consideration whether the claims are so interrelated (though separate) that efficient appeal requires review only as single unit.[32] By this reasoning, for example, there may be just reason for delay when the remaining claims include a possible set-off to the separate claim and therefore ought to be considered together, or when they will inevitably present the same issues on appeal as are presented by the separate claim.[33] Determination of "no just reason for delay" also involves consideration of the equities in the litigation, such as a disparity between the statutory and market rates of interest that would cause a claimant to lose money from any delay in execution on a separate claim.[34]

Since the trial judge can best assess the relevant considerations, both determinations are reviewable only for abuse of discretion.[35] An abuse of discretion occurs, for example, when the trial court finds "no just cause for delay" simply because early appellate review of its ruling on the sufficiency of the evidence might avoid possible retrial of the entire case. The Second Circuit Court of Appeals has held that

> absent any special circumstances indicating that adherence to the normal and federally preferred practice of postponing appeal until after a final judgment has been entered, disposing of all the claims of all the parties, will cause an unusual hardship or work an injustice, the district court's preference to have pretrial appellate review of its assessment of the sufficiency of the evidence to support a given claim is an improper basis for the entry of an immediate partial final judgment.[36]

§ 13.04 Statutory Interlocutory Appeal

[1] Statutory Interlocutory Appeal As of Right

Justification for immediate review of interlocutory orders is greatest when they have immediate and irreparable consequences. Then the cost of possible error outweighs the cost of an extra appeal, and there can be no effective later appeal at final judgment. Many jurisdictions allow interlocutory appeal of such orders by statute. As exceptions to the final judgment rule, such provisions are strictly construed, and the scope of appeal is typically limited to issues involving only the interlocutory order.[37] The federal interlocutory appeal provisions are illustrative.

---

[32] *See Curtiss-Wright Corp. v. General Elec. Co.*, 446 U.S. 1, 10 (1980).

[33] *See id.* at 8.

[34] *Id.* at 11.

[35] *See* § 13.09[2][d], *infra.*

[36] *Hogan v. Consolidated Rail Corp.*, 961 F.2d 1021, 1026 (2d Cir. 1992).

[37] *See, e.g., Wright* § 102 (discussing 28 U.S.C. § 1292(a)(1)). Congress has given the Supreme Court rulemaking power to provide for interlocutory appeals not otherwise provided for by the interlocutory appeal statute. 28 U.S.C. § 1292(e). *See generally* Martineau, n. 8, *supra.*

Section 1292(a)(1) authorizes appeal of interlocutory orders granting, modifying, refusing or otherwise affecting injunctions.[38] Orders granting or denying an interlocutory injunction can be as important to the parties as the court's eventual decision whether to grant a permanent injunction.[39] The court's decision has immediate effect, either requiring a party to take or refrain from action or permitting an allegedly harmful action or condition to continue. Costs of error under the circumstances are sufficiently great to justify immediate appellate review.

Section 1292(a)(1) extends to orders addressing motions for preliminary injunctions. Because of the wording of statute, however, some doubt exists concerning its applicability to temporary restraining orders.[40] Federal Rule of Civil Procedure 65 provides for both types of interlocutory injunction.[41] Once it seemed settled that temporary restraining orders were not appealable under the statute. But "[t]he cases seem to be edging slowly toward a principle that rulings with respect to temporary restraining orders are appealable on a sufficiently strong showing of potential irreparable injury."[42]

Because the justification for immediate appellate review is practical, the federal courts look to the practical effect of trial court rulings and not to whether they expressly address injunctive relief. Yet "a litigant must show more than that the order has the practical effect of refusing [or granting] an injunction;" he must also show that it might have "serious, perhaps, irreparable, consequence," and that it can be " 'effectually challenged' only by immediate appeal."[43] The Supreme Court has thus held that the denial of summary judgment in an action for a permanent injunction did not qualify for immediate appeal, because appellants failed to show that it would cause them irreparable harm during the lawsuit, and because permanent injunctive relief might have been obtained after trial.[44] The Court also concluded that denial of class certification in a sex discrimination suit seeking permanent injunctive relief was not immediately appealable; appellant had not sought preliminary injunctive relief nor made any showing of direct and irreparable consequences from the order.[45] In contrast, one federal circuit court has held that an order refusing to enter a consent decree, though not phrased in terms of injunctive relief, was

---

[38] 28 U.S.C. § 1292(a). Similar provisions are common at state law as well. *See, e.g.,* Va. Code Ann. §§ 8.01-670 (LEXIS 1999-2000); 17-116.05 (1988); Md. Code Ann., Cts. & Jud. Pro. Code Ann. § 12-303 (LEXIS 1978-2000). On injunctions generally, see § 14.02, *infra.*

[39] *See generally* Black, *A New Look at Preliminary Injunctions,* 36 Ala. L. Rev. 1 (1984); Leubsdorf, *The Standard for Preliminary Injunctions,* 91 Harv. L. Rev. 525 (1978).

[40] On distinctions between preliminary injunctions and temporary restraining orders generally, see § 14.02[2], *infra;* Nussbaum, *Temporary Restraining Orders and Preliminary Injunctions — Federal Practice,* 26 Sw. L.J. 265 (1972).

[41] *See* § 14.02[2] (provisional equitable relief), *infra.*

[42] *Wright* § 102.

[43] *Carson v. American Brands, Inc.,* 450 U.S. 79 (1981), *quoting Baltimore Contractors, Inc. v. Bodinger,* 384 U.S. 176, 181 (1955).

[44] *Switzerland Cheese Ass'n v. E. Horne's Market, Inc.,* 385 U.S. 23 (1966).

[45] *Gardner v. Westinghouse Broadcasting Co.,* 437 U.S. 478 (1978).

immediately appealable. The order had the effect of denying an injunction directing defendants to restructure their transfer and promotion policies as provided in the proposed consent order, and it imposed irreparable costs from denying the parties the benefits of their negotiated settlement and exposing them to the burden and uncertainties of litigation.[46]

The federal statute also makes immediately appealable orders appointing receivers, or refusing to wind up receiverships or to direct sales or other disposals of property.[47] The possible immediate and irreversible effect of such orders on property transfers justifies the exception to the final judgment rule. Many states make similar exceptions and expand them to a broader category of judicial orders effecting the transfer or attachment of property and changes in title or custody.[48]

[2] Statutory Interlocutory Appeal By Permission

Many jurisdictions also allow discretionary interlocutory appeal, in part to serve the systemic purposes of uniformity and guidance and in part to accommodate unusual cases in which the likelihood of error is so great that a cost analysis supports immediate appeal. Section 1292(b), the federal provision for discretionary interlocutory appeal, is perhaps more onerous than the typical state provision, but still provides a useful illustration.

Section 1292(b) poses three requirements. First, the trial court must have issued an order from which appeal is taken. Section 1292(b) is not a provision for certifying questions to obtain advisory opinions.[49] Second, the trial court must exercise its discretion to certify that the order (a) "involves a controlling question of law as to which there is substantial ground for difference of opinion" and (b) "that an immediate appeal from the order may materially advance the ultimate termination of the litigation."[50] Finally, the court of appeals must also agree in its discretion to allow the appeal.[51]

A section 1292(b) interlocutory appeal differs from an appeal of a Rule 54(b) judgment in two respects: it does not contemplate or require a final judgment on any separate claim in the trial court, and it vests the courts of appeals with complete discretion to take the appeal of a certified question, not just a power of review of the propriety of the trial court certification.

---

[46] *Carson,* 450 U.S. at 83.

[47] 28 U.S.C. § 1292(a)(2).

[48] *See, e.g.,* Minn. Stat. Ann. R. 103.03(c), (f) (West 1993); Va. Code Ann. § 8.01-670 (LEXIS 1999-2000).

[49] *See, e.g., Nickert v. Puget Sound Tug & Barge Co.,* 480 F.2d 1039, 1041 (9th Cir. 1973). A little-used federal statute authorizes certification of particular questions of law from the courts of appeals to the Supreme Court, 28 U.S.C. § 1254(3), and such provisions are fairly common at the state level.

[50] 28 U.S.C. § 1292(b). If the district court refuses to cooperate, that will usually put an end to the matter. In rare cases, appellant can proceed in the face of the district court's refusal to certify under § 1292(b) by seeking a writ of prohibition or mandamus from the court of appeals. *See* § 13.04[3] (mandamus and prohibition), *infra.*

[51] *Id.*

The requirement that the trial court certify a controlling question of law helps to confine discretionary interlocutory appeal to those cases in which the likelihood of trial court error is greatest. For example, when the trial court changes its mind three times on the sufficiency of a novel and potentially absolute defense, there is self-evidently substantial ground for difference of opinion within the meaning of section 1292(b).[52] In contrast, interlocutory orders that lie in the discretion of a trial judge are usually unsuitable for interlocutory review because they do not as clearly pose questions of law, and because their discretionary component makes likelihood of reversible error much smaller.[53] Thus, several circuit courts of appeals have suggested that challenges to trial court discretion in granting or denying federal venue transfers[54] are unsuitable for interlocutory appeal.[55]

Certification that interlocutory appeal will materially advance the litigation speaks to its effect on trial. This varies from case to case, explaining why determinations are discretionary. Section 1292(b) exists only for exceptional cases. Litigation will rarely be advanced by allowing immediate review of orders regarding the sufficiency of pleadings, in light of the ease of amendment, or of any case which is likely to go to trial regardless of the correctness of the interlocutory ruling.[56]

The narrow construction federal courts have given section 1292(b) has severely limited its availability.[57] But the discretion that district courts enjoy as a result may be preferable to greater use of judge-made interlocutory appeal and has the added virtue of statutory legitimation. There is an argument for revitalizing statutory interlocutory appeal "based primarily on the need to clarify the law on issues which typically do not reach appellate courts, and upon a recognition that the vast majority of cases terminate before appeal via settlements or otherwise."[58] Alternatively, the Supreme Court may use its rulemaking power to the same end.[59]

[3] Extraordinary Statutory Review: Mandamus and Prohibition

A few trial court errors may be so costly, either to the parties or to the integrity of the judicial system, that a cost analysis favors immediate appeal even without irreparable harm. Most jurisdictions historically provided interlocutory appeal in these rare cases by petition for a *writ of mandamus*

---

[52] *See, e.g., SEC v. National Student Mktg. Corp.,* 68 F.R.D. 157 (D.D.C.), *aff'd,* 538 F.2d 404 (D.C. Cir. 1975), *cert. denied,* 429 U.S. 1073 (1977).

[53] *See* § 13.09[2][d] (describing deferential appellate review of exercises of discretion), *infra.*

[54] On venue transfers, see § 6.02[2], *supra.*

[55] *See, e.g., Garner v. Wolfinbarger,* 433 F.2d 117 (5th Cir. 1970).

[56] *Wright* § 102.

[57] *See* Solimine, *Revitalizing Appeals in Federal Courts,* 58 Geo. Wash. L. Rev. 1165, 1171-1174, 1193-1201 (1991).

[58] *Id.*

[59] *See* 28 U.S.C. § 1292(e); *Martineau,* note 37, *supra.*

— ordering the trial judge to issue an order or fulfill a mandatory duty — or a *writ of prohibition* — forbidding the trial judge from acting in excess of her jurisdiction. Historical distinctions between the two have faded over time, and in the federal system mandamus is used for both purposes,[60] serving as an extraordinary allowance of statutory[61] review of the propriety of actions in the trial court. It is extraordinary because it is not a substitute for appeal[62] and is therefore only available when there is "no other adequate means to attain" the desired relief from circumstances amounting to "a judicial 'usurpation of power. . . .' "[63]

What circumstances or errors amount to judicial usurpation is neither clear nor uniform across judicial systems. The historical rule was that mandamus extended to "jurisdictional errors," and, indeed, many states authorize it for interlocutory challenges to assertions of subject matter or personal jurisdiction.[64] Another common generalization is that mandamus is in aid of appellate jurisdiction.[65] This explains the availability of mandamus for an order transferring venue out of one federal circuit to another,[66] but is no more helpful than "jurisdictional error" in most cases.

Cases in which the Supreme Court has approved of mandamus[67] suggest two categories. One is breach by the trial judge of a clear legal duty. The Court has approved mandamus on this basis when a trial court, on the grounds that it was too busy, abdicated its duty to try a case by referring it to a special master,[68] and when a trial court denied a party its constitutional right to a jury trial.[69] In contrast, the grant of a new trial, even if error, does not occasion mandamus, there being no clearcut and mandatory standard for granting new trials.[70]

Errors for which appellate review may carry broad precedential significance for judicial administration make up the second category. Thus, while

---

[60] *See Ex Parte Simons,* 247 U.S. 231, 239 (1918).

[61] 28 U.S.C. § 1651 ("the All Writs Act").

[62] *Roche v. Evaporated Milk Ass'n,* 319 U.S. 21, 26 (1943).

[63] *Kerr v. United States District Court,* 426 U.S. 394, 403 (1976), *citing Roche v. Evaporated Milk Ass'n,* 319 U.S. 21, 26 (1943).

[64] *See, e.g, World-Wide Volkswagen Corp. v. Woodson,* 585 P.2d 351 (Okla. 1978), *rev'd,* 444 U.S. 286 (1980) (writ of prohibition against exercise of personal jurisdiction over foreign defendants); Cal. Civ. Proc. Code § 418.10 (West, WESTLAW 2001).

[65] *United States v. Beatty,* 232 U.S. 463, 467 (1914).

[66] *In re Fireman's Fund Ins. Co. v. Pennington,* 588 F.2d 93 (5th Cir. 1979).

[67] *See generally* Annotation, *Mandamus As An Appropriate Remedy to Control Action of Federal Court in Civil Case — Supreme Court Cases,* 57 L. Ed. 2d 1203 (1979).

[68] *La Buy v. Howes Leather Co.,* 352 U.S. 249 (1957). Rule 53(c) expressly states that appointment of a special master "shall be the exception and not the rule," and nothing in the rule or its history authorizes referrals merely because of calendar congestion.

[69] *Beacon Theaters, Inc. v. Westover,* 359 U.S. 500 (1959). *See* Forrester, Note, *Mandamus as a Remedy for the Denial of Jury Trial,* 58 U. Chi. L. Rev. 769 (1991).

[70] *Allied Chem. Corp. v. Daiflon, Inc.,* 449 U.S. 33 (1980). *See generally* § 12.09[2] (new trial), *supra.* A minority of states expressly authorize interlocutory review of new trial rulings. *See, e.g.,* N.Y. Civ. Prac. L. & R. 5602(b)(2)(iii) (McKinney, WESTLAW 2001); Minn. Stat. Ann. R. 103.03(d) (1993).

routine discovery orders will almost never qualify for review by mandamus,[71] an interlocutory order presenting a question of first impression about the federal discovery rules may justify a kind of *supervisory mandamus,* on the theory that appellate precedent in such a case can generally improve the administration of justice.[72]

Mandamus makes the trial judge a litigant by directing the writ at her in form, but the parties conduct the appeal in substance. Considerations of comity between the trial and appellate courts reinforce the policy against piecemeal appeals and the exacting standards for the issuance of the writ to make it truly extraordinary relief.[73] Courts of appeals often strain to avoid censuring a trial judge by issuing a writ of mandamus. Instead, even when the error below calls for correction, an appellate court will typically deny the writ with an opinion expressing confidence that the trial judge will do what the appellate court describes as the right thing,[74] or, at worst, will delay issuance of the writ to allow her time to do so.

§ 13.06   Judge-Made Exceptions to the Final Judgment Rule

[1]   Collateral Order Doctrine[75]

The most important judge-made exception to the final judgment rule in federal courts is for interlocutory orders that are incidental — *collateral* — to the merits and that cannot be effectively preserved for review on appeal from a final judgment. Since they pose no risk of repetitive appellate review, a cost analysis favors interlocutory review.

The leading federal case is *Cohen v. Beneficial Industrial Loan Corp.*[76] The trial court had denied a corporation's motion that the plaintiff be required, pursuant to state statute, to post security for defendant's reasonable expenses in defending a shareholder's derivative action.[77] Acknowledging

---

[71] *See Kerr v. United States District Court,* 426 U.S. 394 (1976). *But see* Thornburg, *Interlocutory Review of Discovery Orders: An Idea Whose Time Has Come,* 44 Sw. L.J. 1045 (1990) (surveying use of mandamus in Texas to review discovery orders and urging interlocutory review of such orders in other courts).

[72] *See, e.g., Schlagenhauf v. Holder,* 379 U.S. 104 (1964) (the appropriate scope of Rule 35); *Colonial Times, Inc. v. Gasch,* 509 F.2d 577 (D.C. Cir. 1975) (question of first impression concerning scope of Rule 30(b)(4)).

[73] *See Kerr,* 426 U.S. at 403.

[74] *See, e.g., id.* at 406; *Colonial Times, Inc. v. Gasch,* 509 F.2d 577 (D.C. Cir. 1975). As an appellate judge has admitted, "[t]his is but a delicate way of issuing the writ, for the trial court would not lightly ignore this court's 'suggestion.'" *United States v. Harrod,* 428 A.2d 30 (D.C. 1981) (Ferren, J., concurring, in an opinion in which JJ. Kelly and Mack join). *See generally* Berger, *The Mandamus Power of the United States Courts of Appeals: A Complex and Confused Means of Appellate Control,* 31 Buffalo L. Rev. 37, 86-87 (1982).

[75] *See* Anderson, *The Collateral Order Doctrine: A "Serbonian Bog" and Four Proposals for Reform,* 46 Drake L. Rev. 539 (1998).

[76] 337 U.S. 541 (1949).

[77] *See* Rule 23.1.

that the final judgment rule would preclude appeal, the Supreme Court nevertheless reasoned that its purposes would not be served by refusing appeal in the circumstances. The trial court's ruling was final as to the subject it addressed, did not touch on the merits of the case, and would therefore not be merged into the final judgment. The Court noted that final judgment would be too late in any event to review the ruling, because the statutory rights would then have been lost, probably irretrievably.[78] The Court, therefore, held that the

> decision appears to fall in that small class which finally determine claims of right separable from, and collateral to, rights asserted in the action, too important to be denied review and too independent of the cause itself to require that appellate consideration be deferred until the whole case is adjudicated.[79]

The Supreme Court maintains that *Cohen* did not amend the final judgment rule, but only "continued a tradition of giving . . . [it] a 'practical rather than a technical construction.' "[80]

The Court has since refined *Cohen* to impose three strict requirements for invocation of the collateral order doctrine.[81] First, the order must finally and conclusively determine the disputed question. In *Cohen,* the court's denial of defendant's motion conclusively disposed of the question of security; that question could only arise at the front of the case. By contrast, a ruling on class certification is expressly subject under Rule 23(c)(1) to revision before final judgment and therefore "inherently tentative"[82] and unsuitable for interlocutory appeal as a collateral order. An order refusing to disqualify counsel is similarly subject to revision (should conflicts of interest materialize later in the litigation) and is therefore not immediately appealable.[83]

Second, the order must resolve an important issue completely collateral to the merits. It must be collateral, because if enmeshed in the merits, it is likely that it can only be fairly assessed after trial.[84] It must be important in terms of the difficulty of resolution it poses and its effect both upon and

---

[78] 337 U.S. at 546–547. The purpose of the security requirement was to discourage frivolous derivative actions, known as "strike suits," and assure reimbursement to the corporation of the reasonable expenses of a successful defense. Appellate correction of the trial court's error after a final judgment would obviously come too late to accomplish the deterrent effect of the security requirement, and in all likelihood too late to assure the corporation of funds from which to collect its expenses.

[79] *Cohen,* 337 U.S. at 546.

[80] *Firestone Tire & Rubber Co. v. Risjord,* 449 U.S. 368, 375 (1981).

[81] *Coopers & Lybrand v. Livesay,* 437 U.S. 463, 468 (1978). The Supreme Court has disapproved a purported exercise of pendent appellate jurisdiction to hear otherwise non-appealable issues in connection with a collateral order appeal, although it did not rule out such jurisdiction in all cases. *Swint v. Chambers County Comm'n,* 514 U.S. 35 (1995). *See generally* Steinman, *The Scope of Appellate Jurisdiction: Pendent Appellate Jurisdiction Before and After Swint,* 49 Hastings L.J. 1337 (1998).

[82] *Id.* at 469 n.11.

[83] *Firestone,* 449 U.S. at 377.

[84] *Id.* at 377, 378.

beyond the litigation.[85] This requirement prevents appeal of interlocutory decisions that, precisely because they are collateral to the merits, are also insignificant. The order regarding security in *Cohen* met this requirement because it did not touch on the merits and presented a "serious and unsettled question."[86] In contrast, an order refusing to certify a class was not completely collateral, since Rule 23's certification provisions expressly require the court to identify common questions of law or fact and make other determinations that inevitably touch on the merits.[87]

Finally, the order must be effectively unreviewable on appeal from the final judgment, so that the "opportunity for meaningful review will perish unless immediate appeal is permitted."[88] Like the order denying security in *Cohen,* this was true of orders denying summary judgment on the defenses of absolute immunity[89] and double jeopardy,[90] both designed to spare a defendant the rigors of trial, a protection that would obviously be irretrievably lost unless immediate appeal is allowed. On the other hand, the Court has held that an order compelling discovery as against a claim of privilege is not immediately appealable. Its theory was that the party may defy the order and then challenge it on direct appeal of a resulting contempt citation.[91]

From time to time, courts have intimated that the importance requirement is a distinct fourth requirement for collateral order appeals,[92] a view for which Justice Scalia has expressed support.[93] Without deciding whether it is, the Supreme Court has nevertheless emphasized that it is not an alternative or dispensable requirement, whose absence can be overcome if the other requirements are satisfied. "To the contrary," the Court has declared, "a third *Cohen* question, whether a right is 'adequately vindicable' or 'effectively reviewable,' simply cannot be answered without a judgment about the value of the interests that would be lost through rigorous application of a final judgment requirement."[94] In short, the collateral order appellant must satisfy all requirements, including the importance requirement.

---

[85] *See Donlon Industries, Inc. v. Forte,* 402 F.2d 935, 937 (2d Cir. 1968).

[86] *Cohen,* 337 U.S. at 546-547.

[87] *Coopers & Lybrand,* 437 U.S. at 468 & n.12. *See also Cauwenberghe v. Biard,* 486 U.S. 517 (1988) (denying collateral order appeal of *forum non conveniens* dismissal because it is not completely separate from the merits); *Richardson-Merrell, Inc. v. Koller,* 472 U.S. 424 (1985) (denying collateral order appeal of order to disqualify counsel for conflict because it is based on the possibility that a conflict will infect the proceedings and is therefore intertwined with the merits).

[88] *Firestone,* 449 U.S. at 377-378.

[89] *Helstoki v. Meanor,* 442 U.S. 500, 506-508 (1979). *See also Puerto Rico Aqueduct and Sewer Auth'y v. Metcalf & Eddy, Inc.,* 506 U.S. 139 (1993) (authorizing collateral order review of 11th Amendment immunity claims).

[90] *Abney v. United States,* 431 U.S. 651, 660-662 (1977).

[91] *Cobbledick v. United States,* 309 U.S. 323, 327 (1940). *See § 13.05[2], infra.*

[92] *See, e.g., Wright & Miller § 3911.*

[93] *Gulfstream Aerospace Corp. v. Mayacamas Corp.,* 485 U.S. 271, 291-292 (1988) (Scalia, J., concurring).

[94] *Digital Equipment Corp. v. Desktop Direct,* Inc., 511 U.S. 863, 878-879 (1994).

[2]　Other Judge-Made Exceptions

The federal courts have made several other exceptions to the final judgment rule. They have permitted immediate appeal of criminal contempt orders because of their serious consequences and practical finality.[95] Courting criminal contempt, however, is a risky way to obtain interlocutory appeal since a wrong guess leaves the appellant with a fine or imprisonment. The courts have also allowed non-parties to appeal civil contempt orders on the theory that they have no standing to appeal from an eventual final judgment.[96] Parties, in contrast, must await the final judgment in pending cases.

The Supreme Court suggested in *Gillespie v. United States Steel Corp.*[97] that it might allow interlocutory appeal when it would save time in the circumstances and was in the spirit of the federal discretionary appeal statute, although the trial court had never certified the question under it. Taken for all it is worth, this reasoning does violence to the statutory scheme and is inconsistent with the federal policy disfavoring piecemeal review. It is not surprising that it has met with little approval.[98] The Court has since acknowledged that "[i]f *Gillespie* were extended beyond the unique facts of that case, section 1291 would be stripped of all significance."[99] *Gillespie* may not have much continuing force.

Finally, an early Supreme Court decision adopted a hardship test, allowing interlocutory appeal of an order that would cause "irreparable injury" before final judgment.[100] While the Court itself has not consistently applied this test in its subsequent decisions, the practical construction it has given the requirement for finality — to the point of rationalizing the collateral order doctrine as a mere application of the statutory requirement — points in the direction of such a test.[101]

---

[95] *See generally Wright & Miller* § 3917; 19 *Moore* § 202.11[a].

[96] *Id.* 19 *Moore* § 1202.11[a]; *Wright & Miller* § 3917. *See generally Shillitani v. United States,* 384 U.S. 364, 369-370 (1966) (explaining that criminal contempt is intended to punish, while civil contempt is intended merely to coerce).

[97] 379 U.S. 148 (1964).

[98] *But see Wright & Miller* §§ 3905, 3913 (approving "pragmatic approach" of *Gillespie* to allow disposition on the merits of appeals mistakenly taken from non-final decisions).

[99] *Coopers & Lybrand,* 437 U.S. at 477 n.30.

[100] *Forgay v. Conrad,* 47 U.S. (6 How.) 201, 205-206 (1848) (review of an order to transfer property).

[101] *See Wright* § 101, *quoting United States v. Wood,* 295 F.2d 772, 778 (5th Cir. 1961), *cert. denied,* 369 U.S. 850 (1962), to same effect. The irreparable injury test has also been endorsed as part of a balancing approach urged by some commentators. *See* Redish, *The Pragmatic Approach to Appealability in the Federal Courts,* 75 Colum. L. Rev. 89 (1975).

PART B
Where and How? Perfecting Appeal

§ 13.07 Appellate Systems

Where an appellant takes an appeal is typically determined by statute or constitutional provision. Systems vary widely from jurisdiction to jurisdiction. A four-tier court system is common, however.

Appeal from the bottom tier, courts of limited jurisdiction, is usually to courts of general jurisdiction which re-try the matter *de novo* (anew). Little or no deference is paid the lower court decision because of the restrictions on its jurisdiction and, in many cases, on its procedures.[102]

Appeal from a court of general jurisdiction is to a true appellate court. This was traditionally to the highest court in many states, but a growing number have created intermediate appellate courts to ease the workload on the highest courts and free them for review on a discretionary basis. Appeal to an intermediate appellate court is usually as of right,[103] as it is in the federal system to the circuit courts of appeals.[104] In some jurisdictions, the decision of the intermediate appellate court is final for the most fact-bound and routine kinds of cases, such as domestic relations and non-capital criminal cases, subject perhaps to discretionary appeal for constitutional questions.

Appeal from the intermediate appellate court to the highest court is predominantly by permission, with exceptions for a small number of important cases selected by the legislatures, such as administrative law cases involving governmental parties or capital criminal cases.[105] Some systems limit the appellate jurisdiction of the highest court by amounts in controversy or subject; most empower the highest court to select, by *certiorari* or other permission, cases posing serious constitutional issues,

---

[102] In the Virginia system, for example, the jurisdiction of the district court is limited by amount in controversy, and the district court rules do not permit full discovery or jury trials. Va. Code Ann. §§ 16.1-77, 16.1-113 (1999). Some courts of general jurisdiction, however, may give great weight to findings of such inferior courts. *See* 5 Am. Jur.2d *Appeal and Error* § 822 (1962 & 1993 Supp.) (listing cases).

[103] *See, e.g.,* Md. Code Ann., Cts. & Jud. Proc. § 12-301 (1998).

[104] 28 U.S.C. § 1291. The mounting workload of the federal appellate courts has prompted some calls for making appeal to them discretionary. *See* Parker & Chapman, *Accepting Reality: The Time for Adopting Discretionary Review in the Court of Appeals Has Arrived*, 50 SMU L. Rev. 573 (1997). Other options include splitting the workload in some circuits by splitting the circuit, *see* Commission on Structural Alternatives for Federal Courts of Appeals, *Final Report* (1998), *discussed in* Tobias, *The Federal Appeals Courts at Century's End*, 34 U.C. Davis L. Rev. 549 (2000), and truncating appellate procedures (including oral argument) as well as the decisionmaking process itself. *See* Richman & Reynolds, *Elitism, Expediency, and the New Certiorari: Requiem for the Learned Hand Tradition*, 81 Cornell L. Rev. 273 (1996) (criticizing this trend and endorsing increase in number of appellate judges as a remedy); Federal Judicial Center, *Stalking the Increase in the Rate of Federal Civil Appeals* 18 (1995) (noting truncated procedures as response to caseload).

[105] *See, e.g.,* Va. Code Ann. § 8.01-670 (2000).

conflicts in the lower courts, or other special needs for appellate guidance. [106]

The United States Supreme Court's rules, for example, list the following factors as relevant in granting *certiorari:* inter-circuit conflicts, conflicts between the courts of appeals and state courts of last resort, interstate conflicts on federal questions, conflicts with Supreme Court decisions on federal questions, important and unsettled federal questions, and other federal rulings calling for the exercise of the Supreme Court's power of supervision. [107] The Supreme Court's *certiorari* jurisdiction is thus highly discretionary, [108] so discretionary that the Court has repeatedly stressed that its refusal to grant review by *certiorari* connotes little if anything about the correctness of the decision below. [109]

In addition, the Supreme Court exercises mandatory appellate jurisdiction in a few very limited circumstances. [110]

§ 13.08   Procedural Steps in Perfecting Appeal

In most jurisdictions the procedures for perfecting an appeal appear in detail in statutes or rules. [111] Consequently, only the broad general outlines of the typical steps are presented in this section, with illustrative citation to the federal rules of appellate procedure. [112]

The first and (in many jurisdictions) only crucial step in taking an appeal as of right is timely filing of notice of appeal. [113] The appellate court usually has discretion to excuse errors or lateness respecting the taking of all subsequent steps, but not respecting the filing of notice of appeal. This step is therefore said to be *jurisdictional* — a predicate to the exercise of appellate power in most systems. [114] Appellant usually must file notice with the court rendering the judgment, not the higher court, and must state clearly what party is appealing from what parts of the judgment. [115] Appellant usually

---

[106] *See, e.g.,* Md. Code Ann., Cts. & Proc. Code Ann. § 12-301-305 (1998).

[107] Sup. Ct. R. 17(1).

[108] *See generally* R. Stern, E. Gressman & S. Shapiro, *Supreme Court Practice* §§ 4.1-4.26 (6th ed. 1978).

[109] *See, e.g., Maryland v. Baltimore Radio Show,* 338 U.S. 912 (1950) (opinion per Frankfurter, J.). *See generally Stern, Gressman & E. Shapiro,* note 8, *supra,* at §§ 5-7; Linzer, *The Meaning of Certiorari Denials,* 79 Colum. L. Rev. 1227 (1979).

[110] 28 U.S.C. § 1253 (authorizing direct appeal from orders granting or denying interlocutory or permanent injunctions by three-judge courts).

[111] Such rules include local rules of appellate courts, which have been proliferating in the federal system. *See* Sisk, *The Balkanization of Appellate Justice: The Proliferation of Local Rules in Federal Circuits,* 68 U. Colo. L. Rev. 1 (1997).

[112] For more detailed description of appellate procedure generally, see P. Carrington, D. Meador & M. Rosenberg, *Justice on Appeal* (1976); R. Stein, *Appellate Practice in the United States* (1981); of federal appellate procedure in particular, see *Wright* § 104.

[113] When the appeal is discretionary, the appellant must file a petition for permission to appeal with the appellate court, instead of notice of appeal in the trial court.

[114] *But see* Hall, *The Jurisdictional Nature of the Time to Appeal,* 21 Ga. L. Rev. 399 (1986) (arguing that appeal periods should be subject to waiver).

[115] *See* Fed. R. App. P. 3.

must pay a filing fee at that time, post a bond for costs on appeal, and (because the pendency of appeal does not alone automatically stay the enforcement of a judgment) either post a *supersedeas* bond to suspend the enforcement of a money judgment or seek a stay from the lower court of other granted relief.[116] In the federal system, the notice of appeal must be filed within 30 days of the entry of judgment or the date of an order deciding any timely filed post-trial ten-day motion[117] in civil actions between private parties.[118]

Second, other parties must file notices of cross-appeal. Timely filing is necessary to preserve any cross-appeal, but the rule is usually framed to allow filing of defensive cross-appeals within a reasonable time after the initial notice of appeal.[119]

Third, the appellant must prepare and transmit the record. The record may comprise the transcript, exhibits and docket from the trial court,[120] but there is substantial variation in what an appellant actually must transmit to the appellate court. Most jurisdictions allow him to designate and appellee to cross-designate parts of the record. As an alternative procedure, some provide for appellant's preparation of a narrative summary of the record, subject to appellee's objections and trial court certification.[121]

Fourth, the parties brief the issues. Usually the appellant and appellee file briefs in succession, and appellant is permitted a shorter reply.[122] In some jurisdictions, the parties support their briefs with a joint appendix of key excerpts from the record.[123]

Finally, the parties may be heard in oral argument some time after submission of their briefs.[124] Summary disposition, with little (*e.g.*, fifteen minutes) or no argument, is an increasingly common response of appellate courts to burgeoning caseloads. Few jurisdictions grant oral argument as of right.

---

[116] *See id.* 7 & 8.

[117] *See id.* 4(a)(4); § 12.09[1] (directed verdicts, judgments n.o.v., and new trial), *supra*. Rule 60 motions for relief from judgment do not toll the 30-day time period for filing notice of appeal. *See* § 12.11[2][b], *supra*.

[118] *See* Fed. R. App. P. 4(a)(4). An untimely post-trial motion does not postpone the time in which to take appeal, *see, e.g., Hulson v. Atchison, Topeka & Santa Fe Ry. Co.*, 289 F.2d 726 (7th Cir. 1961), although the district court may for "excusable neglect or good cause" grant an extension of time up to thirty days. Fed. R. App. P. 4(a)(5). The circuits are split on the question whether improper district court permission to file a post-trial motion out of time can ever postpone the time for filing notice of appeal. The arguments for and against are discussed in *Bailey v. Sharp*, 782 F.2d 1366 (7th Cir. 1986) (Easterbrook, J., concurring).

[119] *See* Fed. R. App. P. 4(a)(3) (within 14 days of notice of appeal by any other party or time provided for original notice, whichever is longer).

[120] *See* Fed. R. App. P. 10(a).

[121] *See* Va. Sup. Ct. R. 5:11(c) & (d). *See also* Fed. R. App. P. 10(c) (authorizing statement of the evidence in limited circumstances); 10(d) (authorizing agreed statement of facts in lieu of the record).

[122] *See* Fed. R. App. P. 28.

[123] *See id.* 30.

[124] *See id.* 34.

PART C
What and How Much? The Scope and Intensity of Review

The appealability of a judgment or interlocutory order does not determine whether or how intensively a particular claim of error will be reviewed. Section 13.08 treats whether an error is within the scope of review (reviewability). Section 13.09 discusses the intensity (standard) of review.

§ 13.09 Scope of Review — Reviewability

Whether a particular claim of error is reviewable on appeal turns on its *prejudicial effect, preservation below* and *presentation above.* Questions of uniformity and systemic guidance aside, appeal is primarily intended to correct improper dispositions by the lower courts when necessary to protect adversely affected parties. The scope of review is therefore restricted to prejudicial errors appealed by aggrieved parties. The systemic goal of efficiency dictates giving the trial court opportunity to correct its own errors and to create a clear record for appeal. The scope of review is therefore further restricted ordinarily to errors that are preserved in the record below. Last, efficiency also requires that the appellant present the error to the appellate court, in order to relieve it of the tedious and wasteful task of searching the record.

[1] Prejudicial Effect

The term *prejudicial effect* is used here to embrace two principles of reviewability. First, the appeal must be taken by an aggrieved party.[125] An aggrieved party is one who did not receive the full disposition he requested. Appeal is to correct an improper disposition below, not to make trials error-free, nor to make clearer the grounds for initial disposition. Appeal will not usually lie to substitute some other ground for a judgment below or to correct findings unnecessary to the judgment,[126] since they are unlikely to be preclusive[127] and so cannot legally aggrieve a party to the judgment. What findings are necessary to a judgment depends on the substantive law.[128]

---

[125] *Deposit Guaranty Nat'l Bank v. Roper,* 445 U.S. 326, 333 (1980). *See generally* 19 *Moore* § 205.04; *Wright & Miller* § 3902. The party is ordinarily party to the judgment, but proper interveners may also appeal if they are aggrieved. *See, e.g., Smuck v. Hobson,* 408 F.2d 175 (D.C. Cir. 1969). Non-parties may argue on appeal by permission, as *amicus curiae. See generally* Note, *The Amicus Curiae,* 55 Nw. U. L. Rev. 469 (1960).

[126] *Electrical Fittings Corp. v. Thomas & Betts Co.,* 307 U.S. 241, 242 (1939) ("A party may not appeal from a judgment or decree in his favor, for the purpose of obtaining a review of findings he deems erroneous which are not necessary to support the decree.").

[127] *See* § 15.07[3] (adjudication of the issue must have been necessary to judgment), *infra.*

[128] The same question of necessity to the judgment is treated under the law of collateral estoppel or issue preclusion. *See* § 15.07[3], *infra.*

These principles are not always easy to apply. Even in damage cases, "amount is not the sole measure of relief to which a party may be entitled."[129] Thus one court has held that a party who recovers a judgment in the amount prayed, but on a theory of indemnification rather than of fraud, may appeal the court's ruling on the fraud theory when that ruling may have collateral effects in subsequent proceedings.[130] The Supreme Court has also allowed an alleged patent infringer to appeal a decree in his favor, when the decree literally incorporated an otherwise immaterial finding that the patent was valid.[131] What these decisions may have in common is a concern for the judgment's possible preclusive effects against the appellant.[132]

Second, errors alleged must have been harmful to the appellant in the sense that they may have materially contributed to the adverse part of the judgment. Congress has given expression to this concept by providing that appellate courts should disregard any errors that "do not affect the substantial rights of the parties."[133] Errors in the exclusion or admission of evidence are frequently rendered harmless by the cumulative weight of other, properly admitted evidence; error at one stage of an action can often be neutralized by curative action at a later stage.

Yet some errors are so central to the integrity of the fact-finding process, or so unsusceptible to proof of actual prejudice, that harm must be presumed. For example, many cases hold that the taint of the jury by exposure to extraneous evidence outside the record falls into this category.[134] Although the proper standard of harmlessness remains an open question, some courts have suggested that a "more probable than not" standard is

---

[129] *Aetna Casualty & Sur. Co. v. Cunningham,* 224 F.2d 478, 480 (5th Cir. 1955). *Cf.* Rule 54(c) (". . . every final judgment shall grant the relief to which the party in whose favor it is rendered is entitled, even if the party has not demanded such relief in his pleadings").

[130] *Aetna Casualty,* 224 F.2d 478.

[131] *Electrical Fittings,* 307 U.S. 241.

[132] The concern in *Aetna* would have been that the finding of no fraud might preclude use of that theory to avoid a later bankruptcy discharge by the judgment debtor, and in *Electrical Fittings* that the finding of patent validity might preclude the judgment winner from asserting a defense to future suits by the patent holder. However, these concerns may be redundant with protections already built into the law of preclusion, which does not usually permit preclusion by judgments that are unreviewable on appeal or by findings that are unnecessary to the judgment. *See* § 15.07[3], *infra.* Commentators have accordingly noted the circularity between the "aggrieved by the judgment" rule and preclusion law. *See, e.g., Wright & Miller* § 3902. Perhaps the Court believed in *Electrical Fittings* that incorporation of the finding in the decree would dignify it sufficiently to give it issue-preclusive effect, and therefore justified appellate reformation of the decree.

[133] 28 U.S.C. § 2111. *See also* Fed. R. Civ. P. 61.

[134] *See, e.g., In re Beverly Hills Fire Litigation,* 695 F.2d 207 (6th Cir. 1982) (juror told jury the results of his own, unsupervised experiment); *Gertz v. Bass,* 208 N.E.2d 113 (Ill. App. Ct. 1965) (bailiff gave jurors a dictionary that defined key terms differently from jury instructions). However, the Supreme Court has held that a juror's mistaken answer to *voir dire* questions, *see generally* § 12.01[3] (selecting a jury), *supra,* is not presumptively harmful absent a showing that the juror answered dishonestly and that an honest answer would have provided a valid basis for a challenge for cause. *McDonough Power Equipment, Inc. v. Greenwood,* 464 U.S. 548, 556 (1984).

most appropriate to civil cases in line with the usual preponderance burden of proof.[135]

[2] Preservation Below[136]

Ordinarily, only errors appearing in the record made below are reviewable. Failure to make timely objection is tantamount to a waiver for purposes of reviewability on appeal. This limitation is necessary to give the trial court the opportunity to correct its own errors and thereby moot an appeal; to guard against sandbagging by the parties below (holding claims of error in reserve in case they lose); and to develop and clarify the record on appeal, which may include the trial court's analysis of the point.[137] In the federal system objection need not take the form of formal exception. It is sufficient that a party makes known to the trial court what action he desires the court to take or the general grounds for his objection.[138] However, creation of a strong record for appeal frequently requires more than cursory objection. In this as in other matters of procedure, a lawyer must be guided by tactical common sense and not just the minimum required by the rules.

Some courts have relaxed their rules for so-called *plain errors*.[139] They reason that "[a] litigant surely has the right to assume that a . . . trial judge knows the elementary substantive legal rules, long established by the precedents and . . . will act accordingly, without prompting by the litigant's lawyer."[140] Although the lay litigant may reasonably make the same

---

[135] *See, e.g., Haddad v. Lockheed California Corp.,* 720 F.2d 1454, 1459 (9th Cir. 1983). Professors Wright and Miller endorse the discussion by the Supreme Court in *Kotteakos v. United States,* 328 U.S. 750, 765 (1946) (". . . if one cannot say, with fair assurance, after pondering all that happened without stripping the erroneous action from the whole, that the judgment was not substantially swayed by the error, it is impossible to conclude that substantial rights were not affected."). *Wright & Miller* § 2883. *See generally* R. Traynor, *The Riddle of Harmless Error* (1970).

[136] *See generally* Martineau, *Considering New Issues on Appeal: The General Rule and the Gorilla Rule,* 40 Vand. L. Rev. 1023 (1987); Dennerline, Note, *Pushing Aside the General Rule in Order to Raise New Issues on Appeal,* 64 Ind. L.J. 985 (1989).

[137] *See Pfeifer v. Jones & Laughlin Steel Corp.,* 678 F.2d 453, 456 (3d Cir. 1982), *vacated and remanded,* 462 U.S. 523 (1983). *See generally* Stone, *Scope of Review and Record on Appeal,* 2 F.R.D. 317 (1943).

[138] Fed. R. Civ. P. 46. *But see* Young, Note, *Should a Motion in Limine or Similar Preliminary Motion Made in the Federal Court System Preserve Error on Appeal Without a Contemporaneous Objection,* 79 Ky. L.J. 177 (1990-1991) (noting that at least three federal circuits require contemporaneous objection at trial to evidence that objector unsuccessfully sought to exclude by motion *in limine*). The requirement for objection to proposed jury instructions may be slightly more exacting, because the rule is stated separately from the general rule regarding objection and requires objections to be stated "distinctly." *Id.* 51. Of course, the lack of objection is excused when there is no opportunity to make one. *Id.* 46.

[139] *See* Fed. R. Evid. 103(d) (nothing in rule requiring objection to evidence precludes "taking notice of plain errors affecting substantial rights although they were not brought to the attention of the court").

[140] *Troupe v. Chicago, Duluth & Georgian Bay Transit Co.,* 234 F.2d 253, 261 (2d Cir. 1956) (Frank, J., concurring).

assumption of his own attorney, concerns for the appearance of justice and the integrity of the legal system make ignorance in the trial judge less tolerable than ignorance in counsel. Yet what errors are plain enough to overcome the normal requirement for objection, not to mention the explicit requirement of Federal Rule of Civil Procedure 51 for objection to jury instructions, is unclear.[141] For example, the Ninth Circuit Court of Appeals has declined to invoke plain error to reach errors in jury instructions in the absence of objection below.[142]

The preservation-below requirement usually applies also to any legal arguments made to *challenge* a judgment. One federal court has explained:

> By requiring parties to present all their legal issues to the district court as well, we preserve the hierarchial nature of the federal courts and encourage ultimate settlement before appeal. It also prevents surprise on appeal and gives the appellate court the benefit of the legal analysis of the trial court.[143]

The same rule is not strictly applied to arguments for *affirmance* of a judgment, even though they may also attack the reasoning of the lower court. Instead, any legal argument that is fairly supported by the record may be made in support of the judgment.[144]

For example, after an appellate court rejected the fraud theory of recovery that plaintiff advanced below to recover a money judgment, it permitted plaintiff/appellee to argue for the first time on appeal a theory of quasi-contract in support of the judgment. It was enough that the new theory "did not contemplate any factual situation different from that established by the evidence in the trial court."[145]

The different treatment on appeal of arguments attacking and supporting the judgment stems from considerations of economy and finality. Entertaining new arguments to attack the judgment detracts from finality by increasing the likelihood of reversal, while entertaining new arguments to support it contributes to finality and avoids an inefficient remand for the trial court to re-enter the same judgment on an alternative ground.[146]

---

[141] As a result, one commentator has criticized the plain error rule as an unpredictable and *ad hoc* "Gorilla Rule." *See Martineau*, note 136, *supra*. He proposes a standard for new issue review on appeal that would be analogous to the standard for Rule 60 motions. *See* § 12.11[2][b], *supra*.

[142] *Moore v. Telfon Communications Corp.*, 589 F.2d 959, 966 (9th Cir. 1978).

[143] *Patterson v. Cuyler*, 729 F.2d 925, 929 (3d Cir. 1984). Some courts have drawn an exception when the legal argument first becomes available on appeal as a result of an unanticipated change in the law and is supported by the record. *See, e.g., Carson Prod. Co. v. Califano*, 594 F.2d 453 (5th Cir. 1979).

[144] *Schweiker v. Hogan*, 457 U.S. 569, 585 n.24 (1982); *United States v. American Ry. Express Co.*, 265 U.S. 425, 435 (1924). "Fairly supported in the record" means not just that the record is sufficient, but that it is in "the same basic posture as it would have been" had the argument been made below. *Friedenthal, Kane, & Miller* § 13.4.

[145] *Ward v. Taggart*, 336 P.2d 534, 537-538 (Cal. 1959).

[146] *See, e.g., Southard v. Southard*, 305 F.2d 730, 732 (2d Cir. 1962) (justifying hearing new argument on appeal by inevitability of trial court judgment on that argument and desirability of expediting termination of litigation).

Arguments in support of the judgment, however, must be distinguished from arguments to enlarge or diminish it. [147] The latter place their proponent in the position of appellant and subject him to the usual requirement of presentation below, as well as the procedural necessity for taking a timely cross-appeal. [148] In *Standard Accident Ins. Co. v. Roberts*, [149] for example, the plaintiffs recovered a judgment against an insurer on an estoppel theory, although the trial court also found no coverage under the insurance contract. On appeal by the insurer, the plaintiffs/appellees argued that the insurer was estopped, that they were covered under the policy, that the contract should have been reformed to cover them, and that they were entitled to reasonable attorneys fees and a statutory penalty. Only the first two arguments were properly made without cross-appeal. Both had been presented below and were, in any event, merely alternative grounds to support the judgment, while the latter two arguments would have modified and expanded the judgment.

[3] Presentation Above

Without more, preservation of the objection or argument in the record below is not sufficient to make it reviewable. Apart from questions of subject matter jurisdiction, which an appellate court must raise at its own initiative, [150] the court will not search the record for error. Instead, the appellant must identify and present the issue in his brief. This requirement obviously promotes efficiency on appeal by sparing the appellate court the rigors of a complete search and by encouraging well-prepared briefs. [151] It also minimizes the likelihood of surprise. In interlocutory appeals it serves the additional purpose of discouraging a party from injecting "a sham issue as the vehicle to . . . [appeal] at the interlocutory stage for a declaration on an order not otherwise reviewable." [152] When review is restricted to just that issue, there is little to be gained by this tactic except delay.

In the Supreme Court, the presentation-above rule is codified as Rule 14.1(a). It provides that "[o]nly the questions set forth in the petition [for certiorari], or fairly included therein, will be considered by the Court." This rule serves two purposes, the Court has explained. It provides respondent with notice of the grounds upon which a petitioner seeks certiorari and thus enables the respondent "to sharpen the arguments as to why certiorari

---

[147] *See, e.g., United States v. American Ry. Express Co.*, 265 U.S. 425, 435 (1924).

[148] *See* § 13.07 (procedural steps in appeal), *supra. See generally* Baughman, *Federal Cross-Appeals — A Guide and a Proposal*, 42 Ohio St. L.J. 505 (1981); Stern, *When to Cross-Appeal or Cross-Petition — Certainty or Confusion*, 87 Harv. L. Rev. 763 (1974); Annotation, *Effect of Party's Failure to Cross-Appeal on Scope of Appellate Review as to Contentions of Party Relating to Judgment Below —-Supreme Court Cases*, 63 L. Ed. 2d 911 (1981).

[149] 132 F.2d 794 (8th Cir. 1942).

[150] This is a particular concern of federal appellate courts. *See* § 5.01[2] (federal subject matter jurisdiction in general), *supra.*

[151] *Cf. Hospital Corp. of America v. FTC*, 807 F.2d 1385, 1392 (3d Cir. 1986) (3 out of 85 pages in a brief is insufficient to present constitutional argument; "[b]revity may be the soul of wit, but seismic constitutional change is no laughing matter").

[152] *See Garner v. Wolfinbarger*, 433 F.2d 117, 120 (5th Cir. 1970).

should not be granted."[153] It also, of course, helps the Court select the cases in which certiorari will be granted, an important consideration for a court that faces over 5000 petitions for certiorari each term.

Like its companions in the law of reviewability, the presentation-above rule is flexible. Many appellate courts assert the power to reach any issue that is sufficiently illuminated to permit decision without further development below — what a disapproving court has described as "a sort of ad hoc pendent jurisdiction."[154] The Tenth Circuit Court of Appeals, for example, has set out criteria for what it unabashedly calls "pendent appellate jurisdiction." These are the sufficiency of the legal and factual development of the pendent issue for review, the overlap between the appealable and the pendent issues, and "whether judicial economy will be better served by resolving the otherwise nonappealable issue, notwithstanding the federal policy against piecemeal appeals."[155] While pendent appellate jurisdiction may promote efficiency in otherwise proper appeals from final judgments, it is more problematic on interlocutory appeals that are justified on issue-specific grounds.[156] Finally, another exception is for a limited category of plain errors that the appellate courts uncover at their own initiative.[157]

§ 13.10 Intensity of Review

[1] In General

Intensity of review means how much an appellate court should defer to or substitute judgment for a decision made below. Intensity of review is issue-specific. It is sometimes said that it depends on whether the issue is fact or law, but this is an oversimplification. Fact-law distinctions merely reflect the subtle interaction of the objectives of correctness, finality and efficiency in shaping intensity of review.

Correctness is best served by adjusting the intensity of review to relative competency. The trial court has all the advantages of being there; it hears all evidence as it comes in, observes the demeanor of witnesses, and experiences nuance and context that are at best imperfectly conveyed by the record considered by the appellate court.[158] Hence the trial court, and the

---

[153] *Yee v. City of Escondido*, 503 U.S. 519 (1992).

[154] *Garner*, 433 F.2d at 120. *See generally Steinman*, note 81, *supra*.

[155] *Colorado v. Idarado Mining Co.*, 916 F.2d 1486, 1491 (10th Cir. 1990), *cert. denied*, 499 U.S. 960 (1991).

[156] *Compare e.g., Energy Action Educ. Found. v. Andrus*, 654 F.2d 735, 745 n.54 (D.C. Cir. 1980) (promotes efficiency) *with* Kanji, Note, *The Proper Scope of Appellate Jurisdiction in the Collateral Order Context*, 100 Yale L.J. 511 (1990) (urging narrow scope of pendent appellate jurisdiction in collateral order appeals).

[157] *See generally* Vestal, *Sua Sponte Consideration in Appellate Review*, 27 Fordham L. Rev. 477 (1959) (also describing other exceptions, including questions of the interpretation of written instruments, important public policy issues, and when justice otherwise demands appellate consideration of an issue in the record).

[158] *See* Rosenberg, *Judicial Discretion of the Trial Court—Viewed From Above*, 22 Syracuse L. Rev. 635, 660-665 (1971).

jury when it is the fact finder, have a comparative advantage in fact finding that justifies substantial appellate deference to findings of fact made below. In addition, the trial court is experienced in making managerial decisions regarding scheduling, managerial limitations on discovery, continuances, and new trial that are not susceptible to precise rules of decision. Best left to the discretion of the trial judge, such decisions should also be reviewed deferentially. In contrast, the appellate court may be superior to the trial court in researching, interpreting and applying the law, due to its specialization in deciding law questions, its customarily greater library and law clerk resources, and its habit of collegial decision-making. Along with the need for uniformity, these considerations justify appellate substitution of judgment for conclusions of law and, arguably, of mixed law and fact.

But these observations are tempered by consideration of the systemic procedural objectives of finality and efficiency. At least when the trial and appellate courts are equally competent, these objectives support limiting review, in order to increase respect for lower court judgments and to discourage the number and individual burden of appeals.

> The judicial process is at best a less than scientific method of determining the facts. All that can be expected is the opportunity to present to a neutral factfinder the parties' respective versions, under rules designed to assure a measure of fairness, and to let that factfinder draw inferences. Since certainty is impossible no matter how often the process is repeated, society's interest emphasizes finality at that point.[159]

Unfortunately many courts have approached the problem of intensity of review with conclusory labels or *standards of review* ("*de novo*," "clearly erroneous," "abuse of discretion"). Students of appellate opinions thus may begin to distrust the standards of review and to conclude that the intensity of review is wholly result-oriented. Indeed, some courts themselves are expressing skepticism. Thus, one circuit reports a split in its ranks

> over whether we must or even can establish fine gradations of judicial review. One school of thought holds that the verbal differences in standards of judicial review (arbitrary and capricious, clearly erroneous, substantial evidence, abuse of discretion, substantial basis, etc.) mark real differences in the degree of deference that the reviewing court should give the findings and rulings of the tribunal being reviewed. The other school holds that the verbal differences are for the most part merely semantic, that there are really only two standards of review — plenary and deferential — and that differences in deference in a particular case depend on factors specific to the case, such as the nature of the issue, and the evidence, rather than on differences in the stated standard of review.[160]

---

[159] *Davis v. United States Steel Supply,* 32 Fed. R. Serv.2d (Callaghan) 727, 740 (3d Cir., 1981) (Gibbons, J. dissenting), *vacated en banc,* 688 F.2d 166 (3d Cir. 1982), *cert. denied,* 460 U.S. 1014 (1983).

[160] *Morales v. Yeutter,* 952 F.2d 954, 957 (7th Cir. 1991) (construing standards of review of administrative decisions) (citations omitted).

But perhaps the schools are not so far apart, if it is recognized that "the verbal differences" are just shorthand ways of describing approximately where on a continuum ranging from 100% substitution of judgment to total deference the intensity of review lies for a particular issue.[161] Figure 13-1 presents the resulting spectrum of review[162] in federal courts, showing traditional standards of review above and types of issues below the horizontal line.

Figure 13-1

Standards of Review

Types of Issues

Location on the spectrum is assigned in accordance with the above-described objectives of appeal and of the procedural system. Of course, jurisdictions will use different labels and make different assignments, depending on their objectives. The next subsection uses the federal system illustratively.

---

[161] Childress and Davis remind us that

[s]tandards of review, though slippery, cannot be dismissed as sheer politics, especially as the court-watcher begins to look at the practical meaning below the surface catchphrase. The ubiquitous standard, either in basic form or as defined and refined, is presented as a meaningful guidepost to frame both the arguments to the appellate court and the court's analytical response. Even when the slogans have no real internal meaning, in many cases it is clear that the issue framing or assignment of power *behind* the words is the turning point of the decision."

1 S. Childress & M. Davis, *Federal Standards of Review* § 1.01 (3d 1999) (footnote omitted).

[162] *Cf.* Sward, *Appellate Review of Judicial Fact-Finding,* 40 Kan. L. Rev. 1, 5 (1991); Schotland, *Scope of Review of Administrative Action — Remarks Before the D.C. Circuit Judicial Conference,* 34 Fed. B.J. 54, 59 (1959).

[2]   The Principal Federal Standards of Review[163]

[a]   De Novo — Questions of Law

Considerations of comparative institutional competency, described in section 13.09[1], coupled with systemic needs for uniformity and guidance in the application of law, dictate plenary or *de novo* review of questions of law. That is, the appellate court decides whether decision of a question of law was right or wrong, freely substituting its judgment for that of the lower court. For all other issues, the lower court receives some measure of deference, and appellate review is correspondingly less intensive.

Characterization of an issue on appeal as law or fact thus directly affects the likelihood of reversal. But no one has yet formulated a rule or principle that will unerringly make the distinction between law and fact. One useful test is whether consistency among decisions on the issue is necessary. The question is more likely to be one of law if it requires a fixed standard that applies to the whole community impartially, because then consistency of decision is necessary which a court can best supply. Questions of statutory intent, sufficiency of a defense, adequacy of jury instructions, admission of evidence, and choice of law are typical questions of law. In addition, trial court grants of motions to dismiss for failure to state a claim, summary judgment, directed verdict, judgment as a matter of law, and judgment n.o.v. are reviewed *de novo*, since these motions are granted "as a matter of law."[164]

In contrast, ad hoc historical questions do not require or permit consistent decisions. These are also questions to which a jury could bring a wealth of ordinary experience.[165] What, when, where, and how something happened, and whether witnesses are telling the truth are thus questions of fact. For example, the Supreme Court held in *Pullman-Standard v. Swint*[166] that the question of discriminatory intent or actual motive is a question of fact, even when characterized as an ultimate fact,[167] and therefore not subject to *de novo* appellate review.

The problem of characterization is complicated by mixed questions of fact and law: "questions in which the historical facts are admitted or established, the rule of law is undisputed, and the issue is whether the facts satisfy the statutory standard, or to put it another way, whether the rule of law as applied to the established facts is or is not violated."[168] Supreme

---

[163] *See generally 1 Childress & Davis*, note 3, *supra*. Kunsch, *Standard of Review (State and Federal): A Primer*, 18 Seattle U. L. Rev. 11 (1994).

[164] *See* § 12.09[3][c], *supra*.

[165] *See Nunez v. Superior Oil Co.*, 572 F.2d 1119, 1126 (5th Cir. 1978) (if an inference "requires 'experience with the mainsprings of human conduct' and reference to 'the data of practical human experience' " it is for the jury, *quoting Commissioner v. Duberstein*, 363 U.S. 278, 289 (1960)).

[166] 456 U.S. 273, 289-290 (1982).

[167] *See* § 8.03[3] (specificity of code pleading), *supra*.

[168] *Pullman-Standard*, 456 U.S. at 289–290 n.19. *See, e.g.*, *Bogardus v. Commissioner*, 302 U.S. 34, 38–39 (1937) (whether monetary awards given taxpayer were taxable compensation or tax-free gifts is a mixed question of fact and law).

Court decisions lend some support to *de novo* review of such questions, but the circuit courts are divided and the Court has not yet ruled definitively.[169] Some commentators have urged deferential review under the clearly-erroneous standard discussed in the next subsection, because the application of law to facts will normally generate little of precedential value. Thus it "does not implicate the central function of an appellate court — to exercise control over the development of law."[170] Others have urged bifurcated review, with de novo review of legal conclusions and effects and deferential review of determinations of underlying facts and factual inferences.[171]

A comparable problem is presented by a fact that is "inseparable from the principles through which it was deduced."[172]

At some point, the reasoning by which a fact is "found" crosses the line between application of those ordinary principles of logic and common experience which are ordinarily entrusted to the finder of fact into the realm of a legal rule upon which the reviewing court must exercise its own independent judgment. Where the line is drawn varies according to the nature of the substantive law at issue. Regarding certain largely factual questions in some areas of the law, the stakes — in terms of impact on future cases and future conduct — are too great to entrust them finally to the judgment of the trier of fact.[173]

They therefore receive *de novo* review on appeal.

The Court has held that the finding of actual malice necessary to establish liability in a libel action by a public figure against a media defendant falls into this category, because of the courts' special responsibility for preserving First Amendment rights and the close relationship between the finding of such constitutional facts and the scope of the right.[174] "The simple fact is that First Amendment questions of 'constitutional fact' compel this Court's *de novo* review," as Justice Brennan put it.[175]

Some of the same considerations counsel *de novo* appellate review of whether a jury award of punitive damages is constitutionally excessive.[176] Unlike jury determinations of compensatory damages, which are essentially factual, the imposition of punitive damages is not factual, but instead an expression of moral condemnation which is subject to substantive limits

---

[169] *Pullman-Standard,* 456 U.S. at 289-290 n.19., citing cases. *See generally* Lee, *Principled Decision Making and the Proper Role of Federal Appellate Courts: The Mixed Questions Conflict,* 64 S. Cal. L. Rev. 235 (1991) (finding a four-way split in the circuits on the issue).

[170] *Lee,* note 169, *supra,* at 236-237 [footnote omitted].

[171] 1 *Childress & Davis,* note 161, *supra,* § 2.18.

[172] *Bose Corp. v. Consumers Union of United States, Inc.,* 466 U.S. 485, 501 n.17 (1984).

[173] *Id.*

[174] *Id.* at 501. *Cf. Baumgartner v. United States,* 322 U.S. 665 (1944) (whether there is clear, unequivocal and convincing proof of conduct that justifies denaturalization is a question that "cannot escape broad social judgments" justifying independent appellate consideration).

[175] *Rosenbloom v. Metromedia,* 403 U.S. 29, 54 (1971) (Brennan, J., joined by Burger, C.J., and Blackmun, J.). *See Roth v. United States,* 354 U.S. 476, 497-498 (1957), for a particularly forceful statement by Justice Harlan of the rationale for this rule.

[176] *Cooper Industries, Inc. v. Leatherman Tool Group, Inc.,* 121 S. Ct. 1678, 1683 (2001).

imposed by the Due Process Clause. The Due Process standard of "gross excessiveness" is a fluid one which takes its meaning from context and case-by-case application. "Independent review" by appeals courts is therefore necessary to control, clarify, and unify the applicable constitutional legal principles, according to the Supreme Court.[177]

One commentator takes issue with the "mixed question," "application of law-to-facts," and "constitutional fact" rubrics federal courts offer to justify *de novo* review of (at least partially) factual matters. He argues that the intensity of review of such matters should reflect "the intellectual processes" by which the particular determination in question has been made: by observation (warranting substantial deference) or by reflection on record evidence (warranting less).[178]

[b] Clearly Erroneous — Findings by the Court

Historically, the law judge was viewed as a surrogate for the jury, while the equity judge was viewed as the equivalent of a master. Factual findings by the former thus received the same deference on review as findings by a jury, while findings by the latter received no special weight except insofar as they rested on determinations of credibility which only the trial judge could make.[179] With the merger of law and equity in the federal courts, these historical practices have also been merged into Federal Rule of Civil Procedure 52, which provides that judge-made "[f]indings of fact, whether based on oral or documentary evidence, shall not be set aside unless clearly erroneous, and due regard shall be given to the opportunity of the trial court to judge of the credibility of witnesses."

The Supreme Court has stated that a finding is clearly erroneous "when although there is evidence to support it, the reviewing court on the entire evidence is left with a definite and firm conviction that a mistake has been committed."[180] It is not enough for the appellate court to conclude that it would have decided the issue differently. The test is not right or wrong, or review would be *de novo*.[181]

How much more is necessary depends not on whether the fact is ultimate or subsidiary,[182] but "on the nature of the materials on which the finding is based"[183] and any other factors that affect the relative competency of trial and appellate courts. Because of the trial judge's unique opportunity

---

[177] *Id.* at 1685.

[178] Christie, *Judicial Review of Findings of Fact*, 87 Nw. U. L. Rev. 14, 56 (1992). See § 13.09[2][b] (explaining variability in clearly erroneous standard), *infra*.

[179] *James, Hazard & Leubsdorf* § 12.9; *Sward*, note 162, *supra*, at 18-20.

[180] *United States v. United States Gypsum Co.,* 333 U.S. 364, 395 (1948).

[181] *See Anderson v. City of Bessemer,* 470 U.S. 564, 573 (1985). On the scope of *de novo* review, see § 13.09[1], *supra*.

[182] *Pullman-Standard,* 456 U.S. at 287 (Rule 52 "does not divide findings into categories"). Categorization of a fact as ordinary fact, mixed question of fact and law, or constitutional fact, on the other hand, can determine whether Rule 52 applies at all. *See* § 13.09[2][a] (*de novo* review), *supra*.

[183] *Baumgartner v. United States,* 322 U.S. 665, 671 (1944).

to observe the demeanor of witnesses, the presumption of correctness is stronger when the finding is based on oral evidence than when it is based on documentary evidence. [184] Rule 52 expressly reminds the appellate court of this by urging "due regard" for that opportunity. The presumption of correctness becomes stronger as trials become longer and more complex, on the theory that the trial court acquires greater intimacy with the evidence from living with it for weeks or months instead of just a few days or hours. [185] In contrast, the trial court's comparative fact-finding advantage diminishes when the evidence is entirely documentary and the trial short and simple. Then the court of appeals has nearly the same opportunity to acquaint itself with the evidence that the trial court had in making the record. The location of the clearly erroneous standard on the spectrum of review in Figure 13-1 (section 13.09[1], *supra*) then shifts slightly to the left.

Prior to 1985, some federal courts went a step further and reasoned that the presumption in such circumstances was not just weakened but eliminated. They declined to apply the clearly erroneous standard of review to judge-made findings based solely on documentary evidence, instead reviewing them *de novo*. [186] These courts arguably disregarded the conjunctive "due regard" phrase in Federal Rule of Civil Procedure 52. Moreover, they were wrong by their own reasoning, because they ignored the superiority in fact finding that a trial judge acquires even in documentary cases from his experience in general and his unavoidable exposure to the whole case in particular. [187] They also ignored the systemic interest in finality, which counsels against *de novo* appellate review of findings even when the trial and appellate courts have the same competency.

In 1985, the Supreme Court put an end to this practice in *Anderson v. City of Bessemer*. [188] There it emphasized that the clearly erroneous standard applies to all judge-made findings, although the strength of the presumption of correctness that it embodies may vary. [189] Rule 52(a) was amended thereafter to make clearer its applicability to all "[f]indings of fact, whether based on oral or documentary evidence."

---

[184] *See Bose Corp.*, 466 U.S. at 497.

[185] *Id. See* Stempel, *A Distorted Mirror: the Supreme Court's Shimmering View of Summary Judgment, Directed Verdict, and the Adjudication Process*, 49 Ohio St. L.J. 95, 177-178 (1993).

[186] *See, e.g., Davis v. United States Steel Supply*, 32 Fed. R. Serv.2d (Callaghan) 727, 733 (3d Cir. 1981) ("the Rule 52(a) 'clearly erroneous' standard does not apply to wholly documentary cases where the record discloses no oral testimony"), *vacated en banc on other grounds*, 688 F.2d 166 (3d Cir. 1982), *cert. denied*, 460 U.S. 1014 (1983); *Orvis v. Higgins*, 180 F.2d 537 (2d Cir.), *cert. denied*, 340 U.S. 810 (1950).

[187] "The trial judge's major role is the determination of fact, and with experience in fulfilling that role comes expertise." *Anderson v. City of Bessemer*, 470 U.S. 564, 574 (1985).

[188] *Id.*

[189] *Id.*

[c] Reasonableness — Findings by the Jury and Some Administrative Agencies

The command of the Seventh Amendment[190] reinforces considerations noted above and requires more deferential appellate review of jury findings than of judge findings. Logically, too, the jury's greater numbers should enhance its fact-finding ability and dilute its biases, entitling its findings to greater weight on appeal. The standard of review is the same as that employed by the trial judge to decide motions for directed verdict, judgment as a matter of law, or judgment notwithstanding the verdict: whether a reasonable jury could have reached the verdict.[191]

Notwithstanding this deferential standard of review, however, there is significant empirical evidence that federal appellate courts are more aggressive in review of jury verdicts for sufficiency of the evidence. They overturned fully half the verdicts appealed in the one-year period from 1984-1985, for example.[192] A large number of these decisions are aimed at so-called excessive jury verdicts.[193]

Statutes subject many administrative agency findings to a reasonableness standard like the standard for deciding motions attacking the jury's verdict.[194] Just as a jury's findings are given deference in part because of its fact-finding abilities, many administrative agency findings receive special weight because of the agencies' expertise in finding particular kinds of facts.

[d] Abuse of Discretion — Discretionary Orders

Hardest to place on the spectrum of review is the *abuse of discretion* standard for reviewing discretionary orders by the trial court. Certain matters are within the discretion of the trial judge because they are largely ad hoc and situation-specific, closely related to calendar and trial management.[195] Decisions regarding scheduling, amendment by permission, complex joinder, consolidation and separation of claims for trial, order of discovery, order of proof and Rules 11 and 37 sanctions are illustrative. A

---

[190] "[N]o fact tried by a jury shall be otherwise re-examined in any Court of the United States, than according to the rules of common law."

[191] *See, e.g., Hersch v. United States,* 719 F.2d 873, 877 (6th Cir. 1983); *Williams v. City of Valdosta,* 689 F.2d 964, 970 (11th Cir. 1982) (*citing Boeing v. Shipman,* 411 F.2d 365, 374-375 (5th Cir. 1969) (*en banc*)). *See* § 12.09[1] (taking the case from the jury), *supra.* The standard of review is nominally the same when the trial judge has denied such motions as when he has granted them, but his decision to let the verdict stand may, as a practical matter, add weight to the verdict.

[192] Schnapper, *Judges Against Juries — Appellate Review of Federal Civil Verdicts,* 1989 Wis. L. Rev. 237, 238.

[193] *Id.* at 313.

[194] The statutory term of art is "supported by substantial evidence," *see* 5 U.S.C. § 706(2)(E), which has been interpreted to mean rational or reasonable. *See generally* B. Schwartz, *Administrative Law* §§ 10.7-10.11 (3d ed. 1991).

[195] *See* Rosenberg, *Judicial Discretion Viewed From Above,* 22 Syracuse L. Rev. 635, 643-653 (1971) (noting that thirty of the Federal Rules of Civil Procedure involve some area of trial court discretion).

right-or-wrong *de novo* standard of review would be difficult (perhaps impossible) to administer in such cases. Instead, the federal courts apply the abuse of discretion standard, which is tolerant of mistakes in exercise of acknowledged discretion.

The difficulty in locating this standard on the spectrum of review is well-illustrated by the review of new trial decisions in jury cases. To grant or deny a new trial is in the discretion of the trial judge, who is best positioned to appreciate whether improper influences or argument tainted a jury verdict or whether the verdict is against the weight of the evidence.[196] When a new trial has been denied for any reason, the deference owed the trial court is reinforced by the deference owed a jury verdict. On the other hand, when a new trial is granted, and the issue is preserved for review on appeal from an eventual final judgment,[197] the trial judge receives less deference.

> This is because when the jury verdict is set aside usual deference to the trial judge conflicts with deference to the jury on questions of fact. When a new trial is granted on the basis that the verdict is against the weight of the evidence . . . [appellate] review is particularly stringent to protect the litigant's right to a jury trial.[198]

In fact, when the trial is simple, the facts highly disputed, and there is no taint from pernicious circumstances, review should be even more intense because of the correspondingly greater likelihood that the jury verdict was sound.[199]

This is only to suggest that the abuse of discretion standard varies in intensity with the breadth of discretion. Accordingly, abuse of discretion really occupies a band in the middle of the spectrum of intensity of review, its precise locus in any particular case depending upon the nature of the discretionary order under review.[200]

[e] No Review — Selective Findings by Administrative Agencies

Placing a "standard of review" at the far left hand point of the spectrum of review seemingly poses an anomaly in that zero substitution of judgment — complete deference — is tantamount to no review. But because the intensity of review is issue-specific, the point is not just hypothetical. It is possible to allow review of a decision and still foreclose review of particular issues within it.

This in fact is what Congress has done with respect to certain fact-bound administrative decisions, typically mass justice benefit determinations by

---

[196] *See* § 12.09 (new trial), *supra.*

[197] *See* § 13.03[1] (final judgment rule), *supra.*

[198] *Hewitt v. B.F. Goodrich Co.,* 732 F.2d 1554, 1556 (11th Cir. 1984).

[199] *See, e.g., Williams v. City of Valdosta,* 689 F.2d 964, 974-975 (11th Cir. 1982).

[200] *Cf. Heat & Control, Inc. v. Hester Industries, Inc.,* 785 F.2d 1017, 1022 (Fed. Cir. 1986). *See generally Childress & Davis,* note 3, *supra,* § 4-154 (asserting that "no single level of deference or scrutiny is intended for the phrase *abuse of discretion*" and that it has a "sliding contextual meaning").

social service agencies.[201] Because of the large number of such decisions, their lack of precedential importance, and the arguably reliable adjudicative process by which they are made in the agencies, Congress has made some of the agencies' substantive decisions final and not subject to review outside the agencies. On the other hand, review-denying statutory provisions usually have not been read to foreclose review of associated issues of procedure, regulatory authority, and constitutional law,[202] which are less likely to flood the federal courts and which may carry precedential value.[203]

---

[201] *See, e.g.,* 38 U.S.C. § 211(a) (providing that "The Administrator shall decide all questions of law and fact necessary to a decision by the Administrator under a law that affects the provision of benefits by the Administrator to veterans. . . . [T]he decision of the Administrator as to any such question shall be final and conclusive and may not be reviewed by any other official or by any court, whether by an action in the nature of mandamus or otherwise.").

[202] The denial of federal court review of bona fide constitutional claims would also raise serious questions of due process. *See* B. Schwartz, note 194, *supra* § 8.40.

[203] *See, e.g., Johnson v. Robison,* 415 U.S. 361 (1974) (statutory review-denying provision does not bar review of constitutional claim); *Carter v. Cleland,* 643 F.2d 1, 3, 5 (D.C. Cir. 1974) (statutory review-denying provisions construed narrowly to allow review of issues of regulatory authority for and constitutionality of agency action).

Chapter 14

REMEDIES

§ 14.01   Damages; Scope of Monetary Recovery[1]

[1]   Compensatory, Punitive, and Nominal Damages

The objective of most civil actions is recovery of damages, a financial award payable from the defendant to the plaintiff. The most common kind of damage formula attaches a monetary value to the difference between what the plaintiff's situation is and what it would have been if the defendant had performed a legal duty owed to the plaintiff — for example, if defendant had not breached its contract with plaintiff, or had not carelessly caused plaintiff physical injury. When defendant has wronged plaintiff, the measure of the wrong is plaintiff's *actual* or *compensatory* damages.[2]

This formula requires the fact-finder to resolve two points in plaintiff's favor before awarding damages. First, plaintiff must have suffered harm capable of monetary quantification.[3] Second, the harm must have been caused by defendant's failure to act as he had a legal duty to act toward plaintiff.[4] It is not necessary that harm suffered by plaintiff be susceptible to precise monetary valuation. At the same time, some wrongs are so difficult to appraise monetarily that courts deny them damage treatment, or permit damages in insignificant amount.[5] When such wrongs can be

---

[1] *See generally* D. Dobbs, *Handbook on the Law of Remedies* §§ 3.1-3.12 (2nd ed. 1993); C. McCormick, *Handbook on the Law of Damages* (1935); Walker & Monahan, *Sampling Damages*, 83 Iowa L. Rev. 545 (1998); Cooter & Eisenberg, *Damages for Breach of Contract*, 73 Cal. L. Rev. 1432 (1985). *See also* § 4.02[2] (prejudgment attachments), *supra,* and § 15.02 (enforcement of money judgments), *infra.*

[2] *Cf.* D. Laycock, *Modern American Remedies — Cases and Materials* 14 (1985) (describing "the essence of compensatory damages" to be "the fundamental principle . . . to restore the injured party as nearly as possible to the position he would have been in but for the wrong.").

[3] Thus, valuation of damage to property is "usually based on the idea that the plaintiff's balance sheet shows a loss of net worth as a result of the defendant's tort or breach of contract." *Dobbs,* note 1, *supra,* § 3.2.

[4] To consider the points in this order probably makes the formula easier to grasp. In litigation, however, the sequence is usually reversed. This is because issues going to whether defendant owed a duty to plaintiff are much more susceptible to pretrial disposition. For example, plaintiff may have a strong case to make at trial that plaintiff suffered harm from defendant's failure to perform under a contract. But plaintiff will never get to make that case if defendant obtains summary judgment because the contract did not comply with the statute of frauds. Defendant would have established thereby that he owed plaintiff no contractual duty. For discussion of how summary judgments and other procedural devices screen out such cases before trial, see § 12.09[3][c], *supra.*

[5] "A plaintiff who loses her pet cat may suffer something that cannot be measured by the market value of the cat." *Dobbs,* note 1, *supra,* § 3.2.

foreseen, they are often better suited for treatment by preventative (injunctive)[6] relief.

In some cases plaintiff will obtain as a substantial element of his total damage recovery a sum unrelated to any actual harm done by defendant. These are *punitive* or *exemplary* damages.[7] The object of this form of damages is to deter defendant and others from similar acts in the future. Only exceptional facts will support punitive damages. Usually they must establish either serious and calculated wrong by the defendant or conduct reflecting rank indifference to public safety or welfare.

It is more difficult to generalize a formula for punitive damages than for compensatory damages. As noted above, courts or juries set compensatory damages through a somewhat empirical approach, measuring the difference in plaintiff's situation with and without defendant's wrong. In contrast, punitive damages are more like ad hoc criminal fines. Moreover, while exaction of compensatory damages is more or less mandatory upon proof of harm from defendant's wrong, plaintiff has no right to punitive damages.

The fact finder's discretion to fix the level of punitive damages in an appropriate case is not unfettered.[8] The constitutional requirement for due process[9] requires that a jury be given some measure of guidance in determining punitive damages, that an award of such damages be reasonable and not grossly excessive, and that there be opportunity for meaningful appellate review.[10] The Court has also said that on appeal of a jury award of punitive damages, an appellate court should independently decide whether the award is reasonable in order to control, clarify, and unify application of the due process standards.[11]

These standards were explored by the Court in *BMW of North America, Inc. v. Gore*.[12] Gore sued his auto dealer for failing to disclose to him that his car had been repainted after being damaged prior to delivery. Awarding

---

[6] *See* § 14.02[1], *infra.*

[7] *See generally* Murphy, *Judgment as a Matter of Law on Punitive Damages*, 75 Tulane L. Rev. 459 (2000); Comment, *Taking the Punitive Damage Windfall Away from the Plaintiff: An Analysis*, 86 Nw. U. L. Rev. 1130 (1992); Daniels & Martin, *Myth and Reality in Punitive Damages*, 75 Minn. L. Rev. 1 (1990); Ellis, *Fairness and Efficiency in the Law of Punitive Damages*, 56 S. Cal. L. Rev. 1 (1982).

Related are statutory provisions for multiple damages — usually a doubling or trebling of compensatory damages. *See generally* Dobbs, note 1, *supra*, § 3.12.

[8] *See generally* Kagan, *Toward a Uniform Application of Punishment: Using the Federal Sentencing Guidelines as a Model for Punitive Damage Reform*, 40 UCLA L Rev. 753 (1993) (urging the imposition of restraints on jury discretion); *Dobbs*, note 1, *supra*, § 3.11(2).

[9] The Eighth Amendment has not had the same bite on punitive damage awards. *See Browning-Ferris Indus. of Vt., Inc. v. Kelko*, 492 U.S. 257 (1989).

[10] *See TXO Prod. Co. v. Alliance Resources Corp.*, 509 U.S. 443 (1993); *Pacific Mutual Life Ins. Co. v. Haslip*, 499 U.S. 1 (1991). The Supreme Court has reaffirmed the role of juries in determining statutory damages in excess of actual harm. *See Fettner v. Columbia Pictures Television*, 523 U.S. 340 (1998).

[11] *Cooper Indus., Inc. v. Leatherman Tool Group, Inc.*, 121 S. Ct. 1678 (2001), discussed in § 13.09[2][a], *supra.*

[12] 517 U.S. 559 (1996).

him compensatory damages of $4000, a jury tacked on $4 million in punitive damages. The Supreme Court reversed. It held that the reasonableness of a jury's award of punitive damages depends upon the reprehensibility of defendant's conduct, the disparity between the actual or potential harm suffered by plaintiff and the award, and the difference between an award and the civil penalties authorized or imposed in similar cases. The dealer's failure to disclose the repainting was not notably reprehensible: there was no evidence that it had acted in bad faith or that its nondisclosure had affected the car's performance, safety, or even (initially) its appearance. The punitive damages award was 500 times the amount of Gore's actual harm, which the Court said must "raise a suspicious judicial eyebrow,"[13] even though there is no constitutionally set maximum ratio of punitive to compensatory damages. Finally, the Court noted that the maximum civil penalty set by state legislatures for deceptive trade practices ranged from $2000 to $10,000, giving the dealer no reason to anticipate the $4 million penalty which the jury had imposed.

Statutes and rules of civil procedure may also limit punitive damage claims. Statutes may place caps on punitive damages or prohibit them altogether for certain claims. Rules may restrict the discovery of evidence needed to argue punitive damages, the evidence permitted to establish them, or the standard used to supervise them both at the trial court and the appellate levels. Indeed, in *Gore*, three concurring justices emphasized that Alabama's failure to supply either legal or quantitative standards that might "significantly cabine the fairly unbounded discretion" given the jury to decide punitive damages which helped to persuade them that the $4 million award was unconstitutionally excessive.[14]

Like punitive damages, *nominal* damages do not reflect real harm, but in contrast they are quite small.[15] When permitted, nominal damages can make possible litigation in which plaintiff either suffered no actual harm or the harm is impossible to prove. They may also play a role when plaintiff seeks but fails to obtain substantial damage recovery, since award of nominal damages often makes the defendant liable for the court costs.[16]

[2] Added Elements in Financial Awards — Costs, Expenses, and Attorney's Fees

Complaints in damage cases seek compensatory, punitive or nominal damages (or some combination thereof) in specific amounts. Most such complaints also request court costs. Expenses awarded as court costs to the winning party (plaintiff or defendant) usually are relatively insignificant.[17]

---

[13] *TXO*, 509 U.S. at 481 (O'Connor, J., dissenting), quoted in *Gore*, 517 U.S. at 583.

[14] *Gore*, 517 U.S. at 595-596.

[15] "Nominal damages are damages in name only, trivial sums such as six cents or $1." *Dobbs*, note 1, *supra*, § 3.3(2). A useful discussion of nominal damages appears in D. Schoenbrod, A. McBeth, D. Levine & D. Jung, *Remedies Public and Private* 482-483 (1990).

[16] *Id.*, § 3.8, at 193. *See, e.g.*, Rule 54(d), *discussed in* § 14.01[2] *infra*.

[17] For example, federal Rule 54(d) authorizes courts to allow "costs . . . as of course to the prevailing party . . .," yet "costs" in this context has been read to cover considerably less than the litigation expenses of the prevailing party.

While English courts usually require the losing party to pay the victor's attorney's fees,[18] there is still a strong tradition against that practice in this country.[19] There are, however, two types of exceptions.

First, certain forms of litigation (although brought by private parties) are considered sufficiently within the public interest to warrant shifting of attorney's fees from the prevailing to the losing party as an incentive to suit.[20] Second, the growing expense of legal services and a general apprehension about indiscriminate civil litigation in this country has led to creation of expense-shifting mechanisms in certain procedural rules. These are intended to compensate parties suffering from opponents' litigation abuses and to provide a corresponding incentive for careful and restrained use of civil procedure. Expense-shifting provisions in federal rules treat the signing of pleadings, motions, and other court papers,[21] discovery abuses,[22] and offers of judgment made prior to trial.[23]

[3] Enforcing Money Judgments

[This topic is discussed in § 15.02, *infra.*]

§ 14.02 Equitable Relief; Injunctions[24]

Injunctions are available in all state and federal courts. They are one of three types of equitable remedies which can be traced to English practice.[25]

---

[18] *Cf. Wright & Miller* § 2665 ("The cardinal principle of the English system has been and continues to be one of total reimbursement.").

[19] Rowe, *Indemnity or Compensation? The Contract with America, Loser Pays Fee Shifting*, 37 Washburn L.J. 317 (1998); *Symposium on Fee Shifting* 71 Chi-Kent L. Rev. 415 (1995); *Fogerty v. Fantasy, Inc.*, 510 U.S. 517 (1994); *Key Tronic Corp. v. U.S.*, 511 U.S. 809 (1994).

[20] Since the Supreme Court's decision in *Alyeska Pipeline Serv. Co. v. Wilderness Society*, 421 U.S. 240 (1975), federal court authority to award attorney fees on this basis has largely been confined to statute. However, the list of such statutes is quite extensive. *Id.* at 260 n.33.

[21] *See, e.g.,* §§ 8.05[2] (federal Rule 11) & 10.13[1] (federal Rule 26(g)), *supra.*

[22] *See, e.g.,* § 10.14[2] (federal Rule 37), *supra.*

[23] For example, federal Rule 68 states that, at any time more than 10 days before trial, "a party defending against a claim may serve upon the adverse party an offer to allow judgment" in a certain amount "to be taken against the defending party. . . ." If the offer is refused and "the judgment finally obtained by the offeree is not more favorable than the offer, the offeree must pay the costs incurred after the making of the offer." On the scope and application of Rule 68, see *Marek v. Chesny*, 473 U.S. 1 (1985); *Delta Air Lines, Inc. v. August*, 450 U.S. 346 (1981). *See generally Wright & Miller* §§ 3001-3005; Rowe & Anderson, *One-Way Fee Shifting Statutes and Offer of Judgment Rules: An Experiment*, 36 Jurimetrics J. 255 (1996). What "costs" Rule 68 takes in is unclear, although the Court in *Marek* gave the term broader application than it usually has in Rule 54(d). *See* § 14.01, note 17, *supra.* Initiatives to amend Rule 68 have failed so far. The rule remains a source of controversy. *See* Margulies, *After Marek, the Deluge: Harmonizing the Interaction Under Rule 68 of Statutes That Do and Do Not Classify Attorney's Fees as "Costs,"* 73 Iowa L. Rev. 413 (1988); Burbank, *Proposals to Amend Rule 68 — Time to Abandon Ship*, 19 Mich. J.L. Reform 425 (1986).

[24] *See generally* D. Laycock, *The Death of the Irreparable Injury Rule* (1991); Shreve, *Federal Injunctions and the Public Interest*, 51 Geo. Wash. L. Rev. 382 (1983); D. Dobbs, *Handbook on the Law of Remedies* §§ 2.1-2.11 (2d ed. 1993); *Developments in the Law — Injunctions*, 78 Harv. L. Rev. 994 (1965); W. de Funiak, *Handbook of Modern Equity* (1956).

[25] The other two are specific performance and judicial administration of estates. F. Maitland, *Equity* 22 (2d rev. ed. 1936).

Injunctions are court decrees which control the behavior of the defendant by ordering him either to act or to refrain from acting in a certain way. While factual elements of damage actions concern the past (what defendant did and what it cost the plaintiff), factual elements in injunction cases concern the future (what the defendant will do to the plaintiff, absent an injunction).

[1] The Shape of Equitable Discretion

Equitable remedies evolved to supplement legal remedies.[26] They were a response to appeals for fairness and justice in what were thought to be especially deserving cases. It continues to be true that equitable remedies rarely exist as a matter of right. The discretion of courts to refuse injunctions is well-established. That discretion takes shape from a set of injunctive prerequisites, often called *equitable jurisdiction,* and from a number of maxims, or *equitable defenses,* further limiting the availability of relief.

The concept of equitable jurisdiction takes in as many as three requirements. Two are keyed on the character of harm plaintiff will suffer without an injunction. First, harm must be immediate and substantial. If the prospect of substantial harm to plaintiff is remote, plaintiff's request for an injunction will usually be denied.[27] Second, harm must be irreparable.[28] This requirement is sometimes stated another way: that plaintiff have no adequate remedy at law.[29] Third and finally, the controversy must provide a manageable setting for injunctive relief. That is, it must be possible for the court to describe the conduct it intends to regulate with sufficient clarity in the decree that it and the parties will not thereafter become ensnared in difficult issues of interpretation and compliance.[30]

Since courts use fairness and justice to support equitable remedies, additional facts showing that plaintiff has been less than fair in his

---

[26] Writing on English practice in the sixteenth century, a distinguished commentator wrote that it was the "intent [of] equity . . . to temper and mitigate the rigour of the law." C. St. Germain, *Dialogues Between a Doctor of Divinity and a Student in the Laws of England* 45 (W. Muchall 18th ed. 1792); *cf.* 4 W. Holdsworth, *A History of English Law* 281 (1924) (equity is necessary in order that the law can do complete justice); P. Hoffer, *The Law's Conscience* 8 (1990) (discussing Aristotle's view of the necessity of equity to lessen the severity of law). *See generally* § 8.02[2] (equity pleading and practice), *supra.*

[27] The classic case illustrating this point is *Fletcher v. Bealy,* 28 Ch. D. 688 (1885) (injunction denied because plaintiff failed to establish that the likelihood of harm to its downstream paper processing operation was both substantial and immediate).

[28] *See generally* Laycock, *Injunctions and the Irreparable Injury Rule,* 57 Tex. L. Rev. 1065 (1979). Whether the irreparable injury still has much life in contemporary injunction cases is a matter of debate. *Compare* Laycock, *Death of the Irreparable Injury Rule,* note 24, *supra,* (arguing that the rule has little remaining significance) *with* Shreve, *The Premature Burial of the Irreparable Injury Rule,* 70 Tex. L. Rev. 1063 (1992) (maintaining that the rule is alive and influential in modern cases).

[29] O. Fiss, *The Civil Rights Injunction* 38 (1978). *See generally* Rendleman, *The Inadequate Remedy at Law Prerequisite for an Injunction,* 33 U. Fla. L. Rev. 346 (1981).

[30] *See* Shreve, *Federal Injunctions and the Public Interest,* note 24, *supra,* at 394. *Cf. de Funiak,* n.24, *supra,* at 24 ("Where the court has the theoretical power to grant an injunction but enforcement is impracticable or impossible, the court will not grant the injunction. It would be derogatory of the dignity of the court to enter orders it could not enforce.").

treatment of defendant may render plaintiff ineligible for an injunction. Maxims like "plaintiff must come to the court with clean hands" and "equity aids only the vigilant"[31] thus function as equitable defenses. Courts have also used the technique of "balancing the equities" to deny plaintiffs injunctions, concluding that it would be much harder for defendant to live with the injunction than for plaintiff to live without it.[32]

[2] Procedure for Obtaining and Enforcing Injunctions

The procedure for obtaining a final (permanent) injunction is a trial on the merits of the case much like that for a damages remedy. It takes time, however, to reach judgment on plaintiff's prayer for a final injunction. During the interim defendant may inflict considerable damage on plaintiff or act to moot the case. All procedural systems thus have provision for provisional (interlocutory) injunctive relief.[33] Federal Rule 65 authorizes both temporary restraining orders and preliminary injunctions.[34] Plaintiff may appeal the denial of a final injunction, and, sometimes, denial of an interlocutory injunction.

What gives interlocutory and final injunctions their force is the prospect that defendants who violate them may be liable for either civil or criminal

---

[31] *See generally* H. McClintock, *Handbook of the Principles of Equity* §§ 26 & 28 (2d ed. 1948) (discussing the development of the clean hands doctrine and the maxim that equity aids only the vigilant). Not all equitable defenses key on plaintiff's conduct. See for example, discussion of the maxim, "Equity Will Not Enjoin a Crime," in *Developments*, note 24, *supra*, at 1013-1018.

[32] *See generally* Thornberg, *Litigating the Zero Sum Game: The Effect of Institutional Reform Litigation on Absent Parties*, 66 Or. L. Rev. 843 (1987); Keeton & Morris, *Notes on "Balancing the Equities"*, 18 Tex. L. Rev. 412 (1940); Mechem, *The Peasant in His Cottage: Some Comments on the Relative Hardship Doctrine in Equity*, 28 S. Cal. L. Rev. 139 (1955). *Cf.* Schoenbrod, *The Measure of an Injunction: A Principle to Replace Balancing the Equities and Tailoring the Remedy*, 72 Minn. L. Rev. 627 (1988) (proposing changes in the approach).

[33] A leading work on provisional injunctive relief is Leubsdorf, *The Standard for Preliminary Injunctions*, 91 Harv. L. Rev. 525 (1978). In addition, *see* Silberman, *Injunctions by the Numbers: Less Than the Sum of Its Parts*, 63 Chi.-Kent L. Rev. 279 (1987); Note, *Formulating a Theory for Preliminary Injunctions*, 72 Iowa L. Rev. 1157 (1987).

[34] Many courts look to the following factors in determining whether to grant preliminary injunctions:

(1) the significance of the threat of irreparable harm to plaintiff if the injunction is not granted; (2) the balance between this harm and the injury that granting the injunction would inflict on defendant; (3) the probability that plaintiff will succeed on the merits; and (4) and the public interest.

Wright & Miller § 2948. The same factors undoubtedly influence decisions whether to issue temporary restraining orders. However, proceedings leading to decision on plaintiff's application for a temporary restraining order tend to be more summary in nature and may, under extraordinary circumstances, be conducted *ex parte*. At the same time, neither Rule 65 nor practice under the rule clearly delineate the two. The Supreme Court has in fact, recently downplayed the importance of Rule 65 as a means of defining federal equity practice. *Grupo Mexicano de Desarrollo, S.A. v. Alliance Bond Fund, Inc.*, 527 U.S. 308 (1999). The distinction between a temporary restraining order and a preliminary injunction may affect the appealability of an order denying relief. *See* § 13.04[1] (statutory appeal as of right), *supra*. On temporary injunctive relief in federal court generally, see *Wright & Miller* §§ 2947-2954.

contempt.[35] Civil contempt adjudications may be either compensatory (producing a sum payable to plaintiff for the violation) or coercive (threatening defendant with damages or incarceration if the violations continue). Criminal contempt sanctions are penal (setting fines payable to the sovereign or fixed jail sentences). Two ways in which this difference manifests itself are in the nature of the proceeding necessary to support a determination of contempt[36] and in the gravamen of the wrong.[37]

Choices presented to the addressee of a provisional or permanent injunction[38] are not limited to compliance or contempt. The party may also seek dissolution or modification of the injunction through appeal, or through rehearing before the court that issued it.[39] This factor can either help or hurt addressees of injunctions. On one hand, the concerns of equity and fairness that support issuance of injunctions[40] also support the idea that addressees should have broad court access to argue why injunctions running against them should be dissolved or at least narrowed. Even courts who issued the injunctions will often reconsider that decision, particularly in light of new evidence or changed circumstances. In doing so, courts are more willing than they usually are to revisit matters already decided.[41] On the other hand, the willingness of courts to entertain challenges against the continued operation of injunctions bolsters their authority to impose

---

[35] Useful general discussions of civil and criminal contempt and how they differ can be found in Bares, *Games Civil Contemnors Play*, 18 Harv. J.L. & Pub. Policy 795 (1995); Dudley, *Getting Beyond the Civil/Criminal Distinction: A New Approach to the Regulation of Indirect Contempts*, 79 Va. L. Rev. 1025 (1993); Rendleman, *Disobedience and Coercive Contempt Confinement: The Terminally Stubborn Contemnor*, 48 Wash. & Lee L. Rev. 185 (1991); Dobbs, *Contempt of Court: A Survey,* 56 Cornell L. Rev. 183 (1971); Comment, *Developments,* note 24, *supra,* at 1086-90.

[36] Civil contempt is an adjunct of the main case. It "[i]s prosecuted in the name of the plaintiff, and largely controlled by the plaintiff. He initiates it with a motion, and up to a point he can abandon it or settle it." D. Laycock, *Modern American Remedies — Cases and Materials* 637 (1985). "Criminal contempt," in contrast, "is prosecuted in the name of the sovereign." There are more opportunities for reversible error, since "defendant gets substantially all the protections of criminal procedure." *Id.* at 636.

[37] Criminal contempts represent a kind of defiant disobedience. They are willful in the sense crimes are usually thought of as willful. In contrast, adjudications of civil contempt proceed from the bare fact of noncompliance. *Cf.* R. Thompson & J. Sebert, *Remedies: Damages, Equity and Restitution* § 3.10 (1983) ("Criminal contempts are those which flout the court's authority; civil contempts are those designed to compel enforcement of court orders.").

[38] Here, the "word 'permanent' signifies not the injunction's duration but rather that it is not contingent upon some further finding on the merits." D. Schoenbrod et al., *Remedies Public and Private* 166 (1990). "A permanent injunction continues to apply unless it expires by its own terms or is later modified or dissolved by a court of competent jurisdiction." *Id.*

[39] For discussion of processes for clarifying, restricting and dissolving injunctions, see Jost, *From Swift to Stotts and Beyond: Modifications of Injunctions in the Federal Courts*, 64 Tex. L. Rev. 1101 (1986); Note, *The Modification of Consent Decrees in Institutional Reform Litigation*, 99 Harv. L. Rev. 1020 (1986); *Developments in the Law*, note 24, *supra* at 1078-1091. The same procedure is available to enlarge injunctions.

[40] *See* note 26, *supra.*

[41] This idea finds support in *Miller v. French*, 530 U.S. 327 (2000), and *Agostini v. Felton*, 521 U.S. 203 (1997). The contrasting reluctance of courts, as a general matter, to return to matters they have already ruled upon is clear from the "law of the case" doctrine, discussed at § 15.14, *infra.*

contempt sanctions against addressees who bypass opportunities for modification or appeal. [42]

§ 14.03 Declaratory Relief[43]

[1] Nature of Declaratory Relief

All judicial remedies proceed from a determination of the rights and obligations of the parties. Courts would otherwise lack the authority to dispense damage awards and injunctions. What sets declaratory judgments apart is that they *only* determine rights and obligations. That may not seem like a lot, but declaratory judgments actually can accomplish a great deal. For example, the fruits of victory for a party threatened with liability are precisely the same in a declaratory proceeding as in a suit for damages — a favorable judgment precluding further litigation.

Requests for declaratory judgments are sometimes made in tandem with requests for damages or injunctive relief. The real significance of the remedy, however, lies in situations where only declaratory relief is available. Frequently the plaintiff in such cases is one who expects eventually to be the target of a claim for damages or an injunction. Plaintiff brings the prospective claimant in as defendant and seeks a favorable adjudication of an issue underlying defendant's prospective claim. [44] Plaintiff's incentive for bringing the declaratory proceeding is to clear the air. The preclusive effect given federal declaratory judgments is typical. "Any such declaration shall have the force and effect of a final judgment or decree and shall be reviewable as such." [45]

[2] The Federal Model

Federal courts were slower to dispense declaratory judgments than many state courts. The problem was uncertainty whether suit for declaratory

---

[42] A graphic illustration of the point can be found in *Walker v. City of Birmingham*, 388 U.S. 307 (1967). The Supreme Court denied defendants an opportunity to raise as a defense to contempt proceedings the unconstitutionality of the state anti-parading law upon which the injunction had been based. The Court noted: "This case would arise in quite a different constitutional posture if the petitioners, before disobeying the injunction, had challenged it in the Alabama courts, and had been met with delay or frustration of their constitutional claims." *Id.* at 318. For examination of the issues raised in *Walker, see* Labunski, *The "Collateral Bar" Rule and the First Amendment: The Constitutionality of Enforcing Unconstitutional Orders*, 37 Am. U. L. Rev. 323 (1988); Redish, *The Proper Role of the Prior Restraint Doctrine in First Amendment Theory*, 70 Va. L. Rev. 53 (1984).

[43] *See generally Wright & Miller* §§ 2751-71; *Developments in the Law — Declaratory Judgments,* 62 Harv. L. Rev. 787 (1949).

[44] In this case, the declaratory judgment action is anticipatory, a kind of preemptive strike. Thus the labels of plaintiff and defendant are the reverse of what they would be if the claimant had been permitted eventually to file suit. *See, e.g., Aetna Life Ins. Co. v. Haworth*, 300 U.S. 227 (1937) (declaratory judgment action filed by insurer against the insured). This reversal may have significant consequences for federal question jurisdiction. *See* § 5.03, *supra.*

[45] 28 U.S.C. § 2201.

relief alone satisfied the case and controversy requirement of Article III of the Constitution. The Supreme Court finally ruled that such suits were ·missible, "so long as the case retains the essentials of an adversary proceeding, involving a real, not a hypothetical controversy. . . ."[46] Congress soon responded by enacting the Federal Declaratory Judgment Act, conferring authority to render declaratory judgments in cases "of actual controversy."[47]

The line between a potential and an actual controversy is not always clear. The best approach is to examine the facts of each case. The Supreme Court's observations in *Aetna Life Insurance Co. v. Haworth* remain a useful guide:

> The controversy must be definite and concrete, touching the legal relations of parties having adverse legal interests. It must be a real and substantial controversy admitting of specific relief through a decree of a conclusive character, as distinguished from an opinion advising what the law would be upon a hypothetical state of facts. Where there is such a concrete case admitting of an immediate and definitive determination of the legal rights of the parties in an adversary proceeding upon the facts alleged, the judicial function may be appropriately exercised. . . .[48]

Even when the prerequisites for a declaratory judgment are satisfied, federal and many state courts have considerable discretion to withhold the remedy. Reasons for doing so include inability of the declaratory judgment to end the controversy, the public interest in delaying suit, and existence of a pending and related action.[49]

Rule 57 extends coverage of the Federal Rules of Civil Procedure to cases under the Declaratory Judgment Act. "The incidents of pleading, process, discovery, trial, and judgment are the same."[50] The parties to a declaratory judgment action have a right to a jury trial, if that right would have existed in the "kind of action in which the issue involved would have been decided if there were no declaratory judgment procedure."[51] In the usual reversed parties case,[52] this inquiry would require application of the modified historical test for the right to jury trial[53] to the action that the declaratory judgment defendant would have brought had not the declaratory judgment plaintiff filed first.

---

[46] *Nashville, Chattanooga, & St. Louis Ry. v. Wallace,* 288 U.S. 249, 264 (1933).

[47] 28 U.S.C. § 2201.

[48] 300 U.S. 227, 240-241 (1937) (citations omitted).

[49] *See Developments — Declaratory Judgments,* note 43, *supra,* at 805-817.

[50] *Wright & Miller* § 2768.

[51] *Wright* § 100.

[52] *See note 44, supra.*

[53] *See* § 12.07[1], *supra.*

Chapter 15

RESPECT FOR FINAL JUDGMENTS

§ 15.01 Overview

[1] Policies That Define and Limit Preclusion

This chapter will examine the manner in which prior adjudications can bind or preclude parties in subsequent lawsuits. The body of law which sets the effect of prior adjudications (judgments) is called *res judicata* or, in modern parlance, *preclusion* doctrine. American courts initially borrowed their law of *res judicata* from English jurisprudence, where the term appears in judicial decisions as early as the thirteenth century.[1] In this country, *res judicata* has always been primarily a creature of judicial doctrine.

The content of preclusion doctrine varies within our system of federal and state courts. The Supremacy Clause of the United States Constitution requires all courts to respect federal law guaranteeing due process to litigants[2] and full faith and credit to the judgments of other states.[3] But these constraints leave each state judicial system a good deal of freedom to fashion its own rules of preclusion. It is clear, for example, that cases decided by the Supreme Court which determine the content of federal court preclusion doctrine are not binding on state preclusion doctrine.[4]

Each system determines how much preclusive effect to give its judgments by weighing policies favoring preclusion against concern that the succeeding case be correctly decided. Commonly accepted policies supporting preclusion derive from the fact that repetitive litigation takes its toll on courts, other litigants and the public. The objectives of *res judicata* are "to save judicial energy, to prevent harassment of the defendant, to further societal interests in the orderly and expeditious resolution of controversies, and to give repose."[5] The concept of repose is especially important.

The deepest interests underlying the conclusive effect of prior adjudication draw from the purpose to provide a means of finally ending private

---

[1] A. Vestal, *Res Judicata/Preclusion* 28-30 (1969).

[2] *See* § 15.06, *infra.*

[3] *See* § 15.10, *infra.*

[4] Within constitutional limits, the courts of each state determine how preclusive their judgments will be. Yet Supreme Court cases can be influential by example. *See, e.g.,* the discussion of *Parklane Hosiery Co. v. Shore,* 439 U.S. 322 (1979), at § 15.08[2][b], *infra.*

[5] A. von Mehren & D. Trautman, *The Law of Multistate Problems: Cases and Materials on Conflict of Laws* 1459 (1965). For further discussion of the policies of *res judicata*, see Vestal, *Rationale of Preclusion,* 9 St. Louis U. L.J. 29, 31-43 (1964).

disputes. The central role of adversary litigation in our society is to provide binding answers. We want to free people from the uncertain prospect of litigation, with all its costs to emotional peace and the ordering of future affairs. Repose is the most important product of *res judicata*. [6]

Concern for correctness of judicial decision is the prudential counterforce to preclusion in all systems. Judge Learned Hand observed that *res judicata* "must be treated as a compromise between two conflicting interests: the convenience of avoiding a multiplicity of suits and the adequacy of the remedies afforded for conceded wrongs." [7] Granted, courts often say that the incorrectness of a judgment does not diminish its preclusive effect. [8] This maxim is likely to be followed when the second suit is merely a replication of the first. The more dissimilar the first and second suits are, however, the more the point loses force. Every system seems to recognize some point where preclusion — although constitutional — is inappropriate because the judgment does not carry a sufficient assurance of correctness to govern the different case as well.

[2] Contemporary Developments [9]

Three contemporary developments in the law of *res judicata* should be noted.

[a] The Restatement (Second) of Judgments

In 1982, the American Law Institute published the *Restatement (Second) of Judgments*. It is difficult to overstate its influence. Even in draft form, the work's treatment of the law of *res judicata* shaped many judicial decisions. Like the Restatements generally, [10] it is a combination of what the law currently seems to be and what the writers would like the law to be. Some of its provisions are more controversial than others, yet there is no question that it is the most authoritative and influential writing on *res judicata* in the legal literature. [11]

[b] Changes in *Res Judicata* Terminology

Res judicata law has long consisted of two subdoctrines. The first concerns how a judgment can foreclose subsequent opportunities to bring a claim or cause of action. This used to be referred to as *merger and bar*

---

[6] *Wright & Miller* § 4403.

[7] *Lyons v. Westinghouse Elec. Corp.* , 222 F.2d 184, 189 (2nd Cir. 1955).

[8] *See, e.g., Federated Department Stores, Inc. v. Moitie*, 452 U.S. 394, 398-39 (1981).

[9] For an excellent and comprehensive treatment of the subject, see D. Shapiro, *Civil Procedure: Preclusion in Civil Actions* (2001).

[10] *See* Wechsler, *Restatements and Legal Change: Problems of Policy in the Restatement Work of the American Law Institute,* 13 St. Louis U. L.J. 185 (1968).

[11] The *Restatement (Second)* received mostly high marks in *Symposium on the Restatement (Second) of Judgments,* 66 Cornell L. Rev. 401 (1981), and criticism in Note, *For One Litigant's Sole Relief: Unforeseeable Preclusion and the Second Restatement,* 77 Cornell L. Rev. 905 (1992).

or simply *res judicata*. While these terms are still employed, the subdoctrine is increasingly described in modern usage as *claim preclusion*. The second subdoctrine concerns how a judgment can prevent relitigation of an issue of fact or law. This used to be referred to as *collateral estoppel by judgment*. That label is in the process of being replaced by the term *issue preclusion*. [12] This chapter will usually refer to the two subdoctrines as claim and issue preclusion.

[c] The Trend of Increased Preclusion

The third modern development in the law of *res judicata* is the tendency of many courts to give greater preclusive effect to judgments. [13] This change is a response to developments elsewhere in modern procedure. First, it has become easier for courts to adjudicate multiple claims and the interests of multiple parties in a single lawsuit. [14] A primary reason for expansion of the permissible scope and complexity of civil lawsuits is to promote more efficient use of judicial resources. By penalizing piecemeal litigation and delay, broadened preclusion pressures litigants to avail themselves of the full range of adjudication opportunities initially provided. [15] Second, many courts and commentators are alarmed that increases in the number of cases filed in federal and state courts [16] will mean that those courts will not be able to handle their cases with the prompt and full attention minimally required in our judicial process. Broadened preclusion may promote conservation of severely-taxed judicial resources. [17]

---

[12] The modern terminology of claim and issue preclusion has been used by the Supreme Court in several cases. *E.g., Migra v. Warren City School District Board of Education,* 465 U.S. 75, 77 n.1 (1984). It was adopted by the American Law Institute in *Restatement (Second) of Judgments* 1 (1982). These changes were brought about primarily through the extensive writing of the late Professor Alan Vestal. *E.g., Res Judicata/Preclusion,* note 1, *supra; Rationale of Preclusion,* note 5, *supra.*

[13] "[T]he trend in the United States is toward increased finality." R. Cramton, D. Currie & H. Kay, *Conflict of Laws: Comments-Cases-Questions* 583 (4th ed. 1987). *See, e.g., White v. Allstate Ins. Co.,* 605 N.E.2d 141 (Ind. Sup. Ct. 1992) (discussing the enlargement of state preclusion doctrine).

[14] *See generally* Chapter 9 (complex pleading and practice), *supra.* The Federal Rules of Civil Procedure and rules governing procedure in many state courts contain liberal provisions for claim and party joinder, pleading amendment and discovery.

[15] Other developments in modern civil procedure also make preclusion easier to justify. For example, broad opportunities for claim pleading, discovery and amendment "enlarge the scope of what might have been litigated by the plaintiff in the first action and should correspondingly enlarge the scope of claim preclusion." *James, Hazard & Leubsdorf* § 11.15.

[16] For some time now, civil case filings in federal and many state courts have been increasing significantly. *See Report of the Federal Courts Study Committee* 4-10 (1990); *The Role of Courts in American Society — The Final Report of the Council on the Role of Courts* 3 (1984); P. Carrington, D. Meador & M. Rosenberg, *Justice on Appeal* 45 (1976).

[17] While some have questioned the relationship between preclusion and judicial economy, *e.g.,* Hay, *Some Settlement Effects of Preclusion,* 1993 Ill. L. Rev. 21 (1993); Cleary, *Res Judicata Reexamined,* 57 Yale L.J. 339, 348-349 (1948); *Wright & Miller* § 4403, it is clear that courts' growing aversion to relitigation is tied to concern over the preservation and effective use of judicial resources. *Vestal,* note 5, *supra,* at 35. *Cf.* Resnik, *Precluding Appeals,* 70 Cornell L. Rev. 603, 611 (1985) ("Resource conservation is a familiar and persistent motif in the literature of courts. Of late, as courts appear both overused and underproductive, interest in economy has increased.").

[3] Litigation Perspectives — Offensive and Defensive Preclusion

The tactical advantages litigants see from preclusion are twofold. First, it is quicker and cheaper to cover ground in the case by incorporating by reference a development that occurred in an earlier case. Second, (and more important) it is better to win by extending a prior judicial victory to your case than to risk the possibility of losing by litigating afresh.

Either plaintiff or defendant may be in a position to argue preclusion. It simply depends on who profits from the prior adjudication.[18] When a litigant argues claim or issue preclusion in order to advance a claim, that is *offensive* preclusion. When a litigant argues preclusion to defeat a claim, it is *defensive* preclusion.[19] Preclusion arguments must be raised in a timely fashion, or they will be waived.[20]

[4] Preclusion Essentials

[a] Claim Preclusion

The basic rule of claim preclusion is that a final judgment on the merits precludes the same parties (and those closely related to them) from litigating the same (or a sufficiently similar) claim in a subsequent lawsuit. Section 15.02 of this chapter examines how identical claims are precluded. Section 15.03 treats the preclusion of similar though nonidentical claims and defenses. Section 15.04 discusses the identity-of-parties requirement, while § 15.05 treats the requirement that judgments be final and on the merits.

[b] Issue Preclusion

The doctrine of issue preclusion supplements claim preclusion by giving a final adjudication preclusive effect in a subsequent case which cannot be said, even in the broadest sense, to share the same claim. The basic rule of issue preclusion is that a final judgment precludes relitigation of the same issue of fact or law, so long as (1) the issue was actually litigated, determined and necessary to the judgment in the prior adjudication, and (2) the circumstances of the particular case do not suggest any reason why it would be unfair to invoke the doctrine. Today's issue preclusion usually does not carry the identity-of-parties requirement found in claim preclusion.

---

[18] It is even possible for *both* plaintiff and defendant to make preclusion arguments in the same case. *See* § 15.06, *infra.*

[19] *Cf. United States v. Mendoza,* 464 U.S. 154, 159 n.4 (1984):

Offensive use of collateral estoppel [issue preclusion] occurs when a plaintiff seeks to foreclose a defendant from relitigating an issue the defendant has previously litigated unsuccessfully in another action against the same or a different party. Defensive use of collateral estoppel occurs when a defendant seeks to prevent a plaintiff from relitigating an issue the plaintiff has previously litigated unsuccessfully in another action against the same or a different party.

[20] *See Arizona v. California,* 530 U.S. 392 (2000).

But due process protects genuine strangers to the original litigation from being bound by issue preclusion. A minority of jurisdictions also still deny strangers use of issue preclusion against original parties by invoking the *mutuality doctrine* — a rule that only one capable of being bound by a prior adjudication may use it to bind another.

The final-judgment requirement of issue preclusion receives no separate attention in this chapter, since it is about the same as the final-judgment requirement for claim preclusion discussed in § 15.05.[21] Section 15.06 of this chapter discusses how issue preclusion differs from claim preclusion. Section 15.07 treats the basic requirements for issue preclusion: that the same issue be litigated and, determined necessary to a prior judgment and that application of the doctrine be fair under the circumstances of the particular case. Section 15.08 considers the possible uses of issue preclusion by and against those not parties to the prior case.

Sections 15.09 through 15.12 explore special preclusion problems arising when the judgment of a court system is presented elsewhere for enforcement. Finally, §§ 15.13 through 15.15 examine legal rules similar in function and purpose to preclusion doctrines.

PART A
Claim Preclusion

§ 15.02 Preclusion When Original And Successive Claims (or Defenses) Are Identical; Dynamics of Judgment Enforcement

The most rudimentary application of the principle of claim preclusion prevents parties from pressing a claim or cause of action[22] identical to one presented in a prior adjudication. If the prior case ends with a judgment which is final and on the merits,[23] parties to it[24] are foreclosed from litigating the same claim in any subsequent proceeding. It does not matter whether judgment in the prior suit was for or against the claimant. The function of the judgment is to make the claim disappear.

When a damage claim is successful, the cause of action represented by the claim becomes a cause of action on the money judgment.[25] The

---

[21] *Cf. Restatement (Second) of Judgments,* note 11, *supra,* § 13 comment g ("Usually there is no occasion to interpret finality less strictly when the question is one of issue preclusion. . . .").

[22] Courts sometimes use the term, "cause of action" in place of the term "claim." *E.g., Nevada v. United States,* 463 U.S. 110, 130 (1983).

[23] The requirement that judgments be final and on the merits is discussed at § 15.05, *infra.*

[24] The identity-of-parties requirement for claim preclusion is discussed at § 15.04, *infra.*

[25] *See* Burbank, *Federal Judgments Law: Sources of Authority and Sources of Rules,* 70 Tex. L. Rev. 1551 (1992); Haig & Kahn, *Representing the Judgment Creditor,* 16 Am. J. Tr. Advoc. 1 (1992); Brown, *Collecting a Judgment,* 13 Litig. 31 (Fall 1986).

Judgments granting injunctive relief (rather than damages) are enforced differently. *See* § 14.02[2], *supra.*

successful claimant becomes a *judgment creditor* and the party who unsuccessfully opposed the judgment becomes a *judgment debtor*. If the judgment debtor fails to satisfy the judgment, the judgment creditor may have to sue again — this time in a supplementary proceeding to satisfy the judgment, or as much of it as possible.

Thanks to claim preclusion, the plaintiff-judgment creditor holds most of the cards in the second proceeding. Procedures to enforce money-judgments vary.[26] However, most are summary in nature and are limited to the same questions: is the defendant in fact the judgment debtor (the person named in the judgment); how much can the judgment debtor pay toward satisfaction of the judgment; and how soon?[27] Judgment enforcement proceedings usually present no opportunity to examine the factual and legal underpinnings of the claim leading to judgment (matters the judgment debtor was free by denials and affirmative defenses to question prior to final judgment).[28] Claim preclusion confines the judgment debtor to a short list of challenges to the validity of the judgment, and it is unlikely that she will be able to raise even these unless the judgment was obtained by default.[29] In short, judgment precludes defendant from improving her position by relitigating the merits.

---

[26] Rule 69(a) generally requires the supplementary procedure for the enforcement of judgments in federal court to "be in accordance with the practice and procedure of the state in which the district court is held. . . ." For comparison of procedures in this country with those abroad, see Juenger, *The Recognition of Money Judgments in Civil and Commercial Matters,* 36 Am. J. Comp. L. 1 (1988).

Even if the judgment debtor has not been sued on the judgment, he may feel pressure to honor it. For example, mere entry of the judgment may act as a lien on real estate held by the judgment debtor in that judicial district. *See, e.g.,* Ind. Code Ann. §§ 34-1-45-2.

[27] Courts often have authority to compel the judgment debtor to disclose her financial worth and to order that judgment debtor's assets be liquidated or placed in receivership to facilitate payment.

[28] It is in this manner that claim preclusion precludes affirmative defenses. *Cf. Restatement (Second) of Judgments* § 18(2), at 152 (1982) ("[T]he defendant cannot avail himself of defenses he might have interposed, or did interpose, in the first action."). *See* § 15.03[3], *infra.*

[29] The judgment debtor may attack a default judgment on grounds that she failed to receive adequate notice of the initial proceeding or that the court rendering the default judgment lacked personal jurisdiction to do so. *Restatement (Second) of Judgments,* note 28, *supra,* § 1 at 30. For discussion of the requirement of adequate notice, *see generally* Chapter 4, *supra;* of personal jurisdiction, *see* Chapter 3, *supra.*

If the defendant participated in the original proceeding instead of taking a default, she may not use these grounds to attack collaterally a judgment otherwise entitled to claim-preclusive effect. For example, if the defendant elects to question personal jurisdiction initially and is unsuccessful, that decision will preclude reexamination of the question when the judgment is presented for enforcement. *See Baldwin v. Iowa State Traveling Men's Ass.,* 283 U.S. 522, 525-526 (1931); *Stoll v. Gottlieb,* 305 U.S. 165, 172 (1938). Also, *see* § 10[B][2], *supra.* Theoretically, broadened principles of preclusion, *see* § 15.03, *infra,* should also prevent collateral attack if the defendant omitted her jurisdictional challenge when participating in the initial proceeding. The tendency in such cases, however, is for courts to reach the same result simply by noting that defendant's participation in the initial proceeding operated as a consent to jurisdiction. *Cf. Insurance Corp. of Ireland Ltd. v. Compagnie des Bauxites de Guinee,* 456 U.S. 694, 703-704 (1982) (explaining how defendant can waive her due process challenge by participating in the initial case).

In rare cases, resistance may be permitted when the court rendering the judgment lacked subject matter jurisdiction, or when the judgment is (under the local law of the place rendering it) unenforceable for some reason. *See* § 3.04[2], *supra.*

The claimant may be disadvantaged by claim preclusion in two ways. First, the initial case may end with a judgment on the merits against her. This will preclude the claimant from relitigating the claim.[30] Less obviously, claim preclusion may also bring adverse consequences to the claimant if she *wins* in the initial case. The damages awarded her in the proceeding may be less than she sought and than she believes she could establish if given another chance to litigate the claim. Yet she will be unable to sue again because her claim *merged* into her judgment.[31] In addition, a final judgment on the merits —whether or not in claimant's favor — may preclude her from presenting claims grounded differently in fact or law from the claim which was the subject of the judgment. The following section discusses how and to what extent judgments preclude such nonidentical claims.

§ 15.03　Preclusion When Original and Successive Claims (or Defenses) Are Not Identical

[1]　How and Why Non-identical Claims are Precluded

Perhaps the most significant feature of claim preclusion is the availability of the doctrine to preclude claims[32] that did not actually appear in the prior adjudication. It has long been accepted that claim preclusion cannot be confined to precluding identical claims.[33] For example, it would be indefensible to permit an automobile accident plaintiff to bring one suit against the other driver for damage to the right fender of plaintiff's car and follow with a second suit for damage to the left fender. All jurisdictions would regard this succeeding property damage claim to be extinguished by judgment in the first suit. This is because the two claims are so related that the doctrine of claim preclusion regards them as parts of what is, in a larger sense, a single claim.

Under modern preclusion law, this expanded concept of a "claim" encompasses all of the alternative legal theories and the full scope of damages or other remedies generated by the facts of the original controversy.[34] Whether all of this broadly conceived claim was actually put forward in

---

[30] "A valid and final personal judgment rendered in favor of the defendant bars another action by the plaintiff on the same claim." *Restatement (Second) of Judgments,* note 28, *supra,* § 19, at 161. The same is true with reference to a judgment rendered in favor of the plaintiff on defendant's counterclaim. *See* § 15.03[3], *infra.*

[31] "The plaintiff cannot thereafter maintain an action on the original claim or any part thereof, although he may be able to maintain an action upon the judgment. . . ." *Restatement (Second) of Judgments,* note 28, *supra,* § 18(1), at 151-52. The same is true with reference to a judgment rendered in favor of defendant on defendant's counterclaim. *See* § 15.02, *infra.*

[32] The term "cause of action" is sometimes used in place of the term "claim." *See* § 15.02, *supra.*

[33] *E.g., Commissioner v. Sunnen,* 333 U.S. 591, 597 (1948); *Cromwell v. County of Sac,* 94 U.S. 351, 352-353 (1877).

[34] *See* Vestal, *Res Judicata/Claim Preclusion: Judgment for the Claimant,* 62 Nw. U. L. Rev. 357, 359-361 (1967); Cleary, *Res Judicata Reexamined,* 57 Yale L.J. 339, 343-344 (1948).

the prior case is immaterial. What matters for claim preclusion is whether it *could* have been put forward.[35] If the new material could have been included in a more complete presentation of the initial claim, the succeeding claim is "swallowed by the judgment in the prior suit. . . ."[36]

Jones v. Morris Plan Bank of Portsmouth[37] is a familiar example. In the first suit, the bank sued Jones and recovered two delinquent car-installment payments. In the second suit, the court held that the prior adjudication extinguished the bank's further rights under the contract, even though Jones had since missed additional payments. The court read the installment contract as creating a right in bank to sue for the entire unpaid balance as soon as Jones missed a payment. For purposes of claim preclusion, the scope of bank's "claim" adjudicated in the first case was what it could have sued for (the entire unpaid balance). Thus defined, that claim (or any part of it) disappeared by merging into the first judgment for the two missed installments.[38]

By holding claimants to the most complete presentation of the claim possible in the initial adjudication, claim preclusion also forecloses alternative legal theories in subsequent litigation. *Roach v. Teamsters Local Union No. 688*[39] illustrates the point. The plaintiffs sued their union local upon the legal theory that the local breached a duty of fair representation imposed by federal statute. After receiving a disappointing recovery, two of the same plaintiffs brought a second suit against the local, this time under a different federal statute which guaranteed them certain rights as union members. The court held that the first suit precluded the second. "We are convinced," stated the court, "that plaintiffs are attempting to recover for a wrong for which they sought recovery" in the prior case.[40] "A party may not litigate a claim and then, upon unsuccessful disposition, revive the same cause of action with a new theory."[41]

[2] The Emergence of § 24 of the Restatement (Second) of Judgments

Courts once limited the preclusive effect of judgments on nonidentical claims by using several different theories. The first *Restatement of Judgments* embraced the *same evidence* test by which claims are deemed the same "if the evidence needed to sustain the second action would have sustained the first action."[42] Still narrower was the *same right* test, which

---

[35] "Claim preclusion refers to the effect of a judgment in foreclosing litigation of a matter that never has been litigated, because of a determination that it should have been advanced in an earlier suit." *Migra v. Warren City School Dist. Bd. of Education,* 465 U.S. 75, 77 n.1 (1984).

[36] *Commissioner of Internal Revenue v. Sunnen,* 333 U.S. 591, 598 (1948).

[37] 191 S.E. 608 (Va. 1937).

[38] *See* § 15.02 (merger generally), *supra.*

[39] 595 F.2d 446 (8th Cir. 1979).

[40] *Id.* at 449.

[41] *Id.* at 450.

[42] *Restatement of Judgments* § 61 (1942). A few modern decisions refer to the test. *See, e.g., Church of New Song v. Establishment of Religion,* 620 F.2d 648, 652 (7th Cir. 1980).

asked whether the two actions asserted infringement of the same right or sought redress for the same legal injury.[43] This test proved imprecise and difficult to apply[44] and has been justly criticized as question-begging.[45]

Many courts have now adopted more expansive and pragmatic definitions. Section 24 of the American Law Institute's *Restatement (Second) of Judgments* exemplifies this modern approach and has been quite influential. Section 24 advances a *transaction* test. It defines the claim precluded by the judgment to include "all rights of the plaintiff to remedies against the defendant with respect to all or any part of the transaction, or series of connected transactions, out of which the [original] action arose." According to the section, "transaction" and "series" of transactions

> are to be determined pragmatically, giving weight to such considerations as whether the facts are related in time, space, origin, or motivation, whether they form a convenient trial unit, and whether their treatment as a unit conforms to the parties' expectations or business understanding or usage.

The transaction test for claim definition set out in Section 24 is only one contemporary approach for articulating the idea that different yet sufficiently related claims should be precluded.[46] Section 24 is, however, the most influential contemporary claim preclusion test. A number of state jurisdictions have adopted it.[47] Many lower federal courts have incorporated Section 24 into federal preclusion doctrine,[48] and the Supreme Court has discussed the section with apparent approval.[49]

---

[43] *E.g., Baltimore S.S. Co. v. Phillips,* 274 U.S. 316, 321 (1927) (referring to "single primary right" and to "cause of action" to decide the scope of the judgment).

[44] *See* C. Clark, *Code Pleading* 134 (2d ed. 1947).

[45] *See James, Hazard & Leubsdorf* § 11.8.

[46] For example, while a number of lower federal courts have utilized § 24, *see* note 48, *infra,* "[o]thers measure the claim by reference to a single transaction or occurrence, all grounds for relief arising out of the conduct complained of, operative facts, or even a 'factual clone.' Two courts of appeals have explained that more traditional tests require search for a common nucleus of operative facts." *Wright & Miller* § 4407. For a survey of earlier approaches, see *Developments in the Law—Res Judicata,* 65 Harv. L. Rev. 818, 824-825 (1952); *Vestal,* note 34, *supra.*

Contemporary tests for claim preclusion are thus similar in approach to those for some forms of joinder, *see* §§ 9.03 (compulsory counterclaims), 9.04 (cross-claims), 9.05[2] (compulsory party joinder); 9.08[1] (intervention of right), *supra.*

[47] *See, e.g., Hadley v. Cowas,* 804 P.2d 1271, 1276 (Wash. App. 1991); *Post v. Schwall,* 460 N.W.2d 794, 797 (Wis. App. 1990); *Kauhane v. Acutron Co. Inc.,* 795 P.2d 276, 279 (Hawaii 1990). Professor Friedenthal earlier found that a majority of states had already embraced a "same operative facts" test indistinguishable in most respects from the transaction test of the *Restatement (Second) of Judgments.* Friedenthal, *Joinder of Claims, Counterclaims, and Cross-Complaints: Suggested Revision of the California Provisions,* 23 Stan. L. Rev. 1, 1213 (1970).

[48] *E.g., Kale v. Combined Ins. Co. of America,* 924 F.2d 1161, 1166 (1st Cir. 1991), *cert. denied,* 502 U.S. 816 (1991); *Aliff v. Joy Mfg. Co.,* 914 F.2d 39, 43 (4th Cir. 1990); *Smith v. Safeco Ins. Co.,* 863 F.2d 403, 404 (5th Cir. 1989).

[49] *Nevada v. United States,* 463 U.S. 110, 130 (1983).

[3] Defendant's Preclusion and Preclusion By Rule

Recall that a final judgment on the merits can preclude not only subsequent claims but also all defenses that were or could have been interposed in the original adjudication.[50] Similarly, a final judgment on the merits of any counterclaim (or cross-claim or third-party claim) asserted by the defendant carries the same claim-preclusive effect as a judgment on plaintiff's claim.[51] Treatment of counterclaims that were available but were not asserted in the prior adjudication is a different and more complicated matter. Under what circumstances is defendant forced to present his claim as a counterclaim or lose it through preclusion?

When a defendant who has been claimed against intends to make a claim in return which is based on the same subject matter, it is more efficient for the defendant to add the second claim to the original suit than to bring a new suit upon it later. The time and expense taken up in trying the two claims will be significantly reduced if they can be tried together.

These concerns are reminiscent of those supporting claim preclusion. If the same party held two claims so related, the doctrine of claim preclusion would in most jurisdictions keep him from splitting the claims and withholding one for later suit. A few commentators[52] and courts[53] have also treated a counterclaim sufficiently related to the original claim as within the doctrine of claim preclusion. Because, however, these situations are often expressly covered by rules of civil procedure, it may be more useful to describe the process as preclusion by rule.[54]

For example, Federal Rule 13(a) states:

A pleading shall state as a counterclaim any claim which at the time of serving the pleading the pleader has against any opposing party, if it arises out of the transaction or occurrence that is the subject matter of the opposing party's claim. . . .[55]

A majority of states have adopted Rule 13(a) as part of their local rules of procedure.[56] The relationship between two claims described in Rule 13(a)

---

[50] See § 15.02, supra. To this extent, it can be said that the res judicata rule applied to the defendant is the "mirror image" of that applied to plaintiff. Friedenthal, Kane & Miller § 14.6.

[51] "A defendant who interposes a counterclaim is, in substance, a plaintiff, as far as the counterclaim is concerned, and the plaintiff is, in substance, a defendant." Restatement (Second) of Judgments § 23 comment a (1982).

[52] E.g., Developments in the Law — Res Judicata, 65 Harv. L. Rev, 818, 831-832 (1952).

[53] See Great Lakes Rubber Corp. v. Herbert Cooper Co. , 286 F.2d 631 (3d Cir. 1961), and the decisions cited in Wright & Miller § 1417.

[54] See generally A. Vestal, Res Judicata/Preclusion 150-163 (1969). "In many ways this analysis provides a more apposite and useful approach to the problem of omitted counterclaims than does the doctrine of claim preclusion. " Wright & Miller § 1417.

[55] "Although Rule 13(a) does not explain the consequences of failure to plead a compulsory counterclaim, virtually all courts agree that a party who fails to plead a compulsory counterclaim cannot raise that claim in subsequent litigation." Comment, Narrowing the Scope of Rule 13(a), 60 U. Chi. L. Rev. 141, 141 (1993).

[56] See Oakley & Coon, The Federal Rules in State Courts: A Survey of State Court Systems

is much like that required for claim preclusion.[57] Claim preclusion and compulsory counterclaim rules also share common goals. Each is "designed to settle the entire dispute between the parties in one proceeding as fairly as that may be done" and to "conserve judicial resources."[58] At the same time, the claim preclusion and compulsory counterclaim rules do not entirely overlap. It is therefore important to consider how the two sources of law interact in counterclaim cases.

Claim preclusion may supplement the effects of preclusion by rule. A counterclaim insufficiently related to the original claim to meet the test of Rule 13(a) is treated as permissive under Rule 13(b). Omitted permissive counterclaims are not subject to preclusion by rule.[59] They may nonetheless be subject to the doctrine of claim preclusion. For example, defendant may have two claims against plaintiff, neither of which is sufficiently related to plaintiff's claim to be compulsory. Because the counterclaims would be only permissive, defendant could withhold one of them without running afoul of preclusion by rule. If, however, defendant's two claims were sufficiently related to each other and defendant presents only one, he might lose the other by operation of claim preclusion.[60]

On the other hand, at least one of the exceptions built into the compulsory counterclaim rule[61] may limit not only preclusion by rule but also the doctrine of claim preclusion. By this exception, a defendant is not required to replead as a counterclaim a claim he made in earlier, pending litigation. Since the federal rules operate (as statutes typically do) to override judicial doctrine, this exception suspends not only preclusion by rule but also the federal doctrine of claim preclusion.[62]

---

of Civil Procedure, 61 Wash. L. Rev. 1367 (1986). *But see* Siegel, N.Y. Civ. Prac. L. & R. § 3019 commentary (McKinney 1991). ("Every counterclaim in New York is permissive, even if its subject matter relates to [plaintiff's] claim.").

[57] *See, e.g.,* the claim comparison required under § 24 of the *Restatement (Second) of Judgments,* discussed at § 115.03[2], *supra.*

[58] Scoles, *Interstate Preclusion by Prior Litigation,* 74 Nw. U. L. Rev. 742, 753 (1979).

[59] Nor, as a general matter, should they be. "The defendant or party who did not choose the forum or control the litigation, although bound on those matters actually litigated, should not be bound on those claims that, under the law of the first forum, he was not compelled to litigate." *Id.* at 754.

[60] *Cf. Restatement (Second) of Judgments,* note 51, *supra,* § 23 (judgment against the defendant on his counterclaim has preclusive effect).

[61] The rule does not apply when the counterclaim needs "for its adjudication the presence of third parties of whom the court cannot acquire jurisdiction." This provision contemplates territorial jurisdiction and not federal subject matter jurisdiction. Rule 13(a) also protects defendant's refusal to plead the counterclaim when, "at the time the action was commenced the claim was the subject of another pending action," or when "the opposing party brought suit upon the claim by attachment or other process by which the court did not acquire jurisdiction to render a personal judgment on that claim and the pleader is not stating any counterclaim under this Rule 13." *See generally* § 9.03 (counterclaims), *supra.*

[62] The exception "provides defendant with the option of continuing the prior action rather than advancing it as a counterclaim in the second action without fear of it being barred if the second action results in a judgment before the claim has been adjudicated in the first action." *Wright & Miller* § 1411.

Some jurisdictions without a compulsory counterclaim rule have declined to preclude unasserted counterclaims as a matter of common law, even when they are transactionally related to plaintiff's claim. For several reasons, however, this generosity may be more apparent than real. First, the common law of preclusion gives preclusive effect to defenses which could have been raised in the first suit,[63] and the facts pertaining to some defenses may also present a potential counterclaim. In such circumstances, defendant cannot always safely predict whether he will be barred from suing on the same facts for an affirmative recovery in a later action.[64] Second, even when claim preclusion poses no bar, issue preclusion may defeat the later action.[65] Finally, some jurisdictions that allow defendants to withhold counterclaims for subsequent suit nevertheless bar subsequent suits which are so closely related to the prior suit that they pose a serious risk of logically irreconcilable judgments.[66] The last problem can even occur for federal court defendants who escape rule preclusion.[67]

[4] Variations from the Norm — Theories of Lesser and Greater Claim Preclusion

Courts share an understanding of the general shape and function of claim preclusion. They do not, however, entirely agree on the limits of the doctrine.

[a] Lesser Preclusion — Claim-Splitting in Accident Cases

As noted above,[68] a variety of narrower approaches to claim definition once dominated. The narrow approach is perhaps most in evidence today in the minority of jurisdictions permitting claim-splitting in accident cases. There accident plaintiffs can split what would elsewhere be thought of as a single claim into separate suits for property damage and personal injury.[69] Courts in such cases reason that injuries to plaintiff's person and her property give rise to separate and distinct claims or causes of action.

---

[63] *See* § 15.02 *supra.*

[64] *Compare, e.g., Mitchell v. Federal Intermediate Credit Bank,* 164 S.E. 136 (S.C. 1932) (judgment on debtor's payment defense to suit on a note precluded debtor's independent action to recover excess payment from creditor), *with Virginia-Carolina Chemical Co. v. Kirven,* 215 U.S. 252 (1909) (judgment in seller's action for payment did not preclude purchaser's subsequent action for damages caused by goods sold). *But see generally Restatement (Second) of Judgments,* note 51, *supra,* § 22 comment d (1982) (mere defensive assertion of facts should not preclude subsequent use of same facts by defendant in suit for affirmative recovery).

[65] *See* § 15.06 (comparing claim and issue preclusion), *infra.*

[66] *See, e.g., University of New Hampshire v. April,* 347 A.2d 446, 450-451 (N.H. 1975); *Chicot County Drainage District v. Baxter State Bank,* 308 U.S. 371 (1940).

[67] The problem comes when plaintiff's original suit is dismissed before defendant was obligated to assert an otherwise compulsory counterclaim. *See Martino v. McDonald's System, Inc.,* 598 F.2d 1079 (7th Cir. 1979) ("counterclaim exception to the *res judicata* rule" does not permit prosecution of a claim that "would nullify rights established by the prior action").

[68] Notes 42-46 and accompanying text, *supra.*

[69] For an excellent discussion of claim-splitting in accident cases, *see* F. James, et al., *Civil Procedure* § 11.10 (5th ed. 2001). (1965).

This view is at odds with the modern trend of giving a broader, more functional definition of a claim for purposes of claim preclusion, and jurisdictions still permitting claim-splitting in accident cases [70] may eventually overrule their precedents and adopt the modern approach.

This is what the Ohio Supreme Court did in one well-known case, *Rush v. City of Maple Heights.* [71] Plaintiff suffered a motorcycle accident. She first sued the city for property damage to her motorcycle, alleging that the accident was caused because the city negligently maintained the street. She obtained a final judgment for $100. Thereafter, she sued the city for personal injuries from the same accident and obtained judgment on a verdict for $12,000. The Ohio Supreme Court reversed on the ground that the judgment in the prior case precluded plaintiffs personal-injury claim. In so doing, the court abandoned its previous position favoring claim-splitting in accident cases. [72] Claim-splitting, it said, "is in conflict with the great weight of authority in this country and has caused vexatious litigation." [73]

[b] Greater Preclusion — Claim Preclusion Unlimited by the Nature of the Claim Presented in the First Case, Or by Concerns of Foreseeability

As noted earlier, the generally accepted test for determining preclusion of nonidentical claims involves a comparison between the claim *actually* presented in the prior adjudication and the new claim. [74] Some courts and commentators have taken the position that this requirement of a nexus between the original and succeeding claims is too confining. They would broaden the scope of claim preclusion by also considering whether a nexus exists between the claim to be precluded and a claim which a party had the *opportunity* to bring in the first case.

The Seventh Circuit took this approach in *Marrese v. American Academy of Orthopaedic Surgeons.* [75] The plaintiffs first sued the Academy in state court, alleging that the Academy had breached a state-law duty to consider fairly their applications for membership. After losing the case, plaintiffs sued the Academy in federal court, alleging violations of federal antitrust

---

[70] Surveys of state jurisdictions permitting claim splitting under these circumstances include Erichson, *Interjurisdictional Preclusion*, 96 Mich. L. Rev. 945, 974 n.141 (1998); and Annotation, *Simultaneous injury to person and property as giving rise to single cause of action,* 24 A.L.R.4th 646, 685-86 (1983).

[71] 147 N.E.2d 599 (Ohio 1958).

[72] *Vasu v. Kohlers, Inc.,* 61 N.E.2d 707, 712 (Ohio 1945), illustrates the prior position. The Ohio Supreme Court said there: "injuries to both person and property suffered by the same person as a result of the same wrongful act are infringements of different rights, and give rise to distinct causes of action, with the result that the recovery or denial of recovery of compensation for damage to property is no bar to an action subsequently prosecuted for the personal injury."

[73] 147 N.E.2d at 604.

[74] *See, e.g.,* the discussion of Section 24 of the *Restatement (Second) of Judgments* at Section 15.03[2], *supra.*

[75] 726 F.2d 1150 (7th Cir. 1984), *rev'd on other grounds,* 470 U.S. 373 (1985). *See* § 15.11[1], *infra.*

law. The Seventh Circuit eventually held that the state case precluded plaintiffs from pressing their federal antitrust claims. The court reasoned that (1) plaintiffs had an opportunity to present state antitrust claims against the Academy in the original state proceeding;[76] (2) had plaintiffs done so, the relation between those state antitrust claims and the federal antitrust claims plaintiffs asserted in the subsequent federal case would have been such that the latter would have been precluded by a judgment in the state case; and (3) the result should not change simply because plaintiffs chose not to present state antitrust claims in their state case. Thus, the Seventh Circuit focused on the nexus between federal antitrust claims presented in the federal case and the claims under state antitrust law which plaintiffs could have raised in the prior state case.[77]

Given the general trend in *res judicata* developments toward greater preclusion,[78] and the urging of many commentators that expansion continue,[79] other courts probably will be tempted in some cases to dispense with a required nexus between a claim actually presented in the prior adjudication and the claim sought to be precluded. It can be argued that such expansion achieves added judicial economy and evokes a familiar theme in claim preclusion doctrine by focusing on what the claimant could have done in the first case.[80]

On balance, however, it may be unwise to so extend claim preclusion. Such an expansion would sometimes force a claimant to join dissimilar claims in the original proceeding, and benefits to litigants and the courts from forced joinder of dissimilar claims are doubtful.

Where . . . claims are factually quite distinct so that there will be no overlap in presenting evidence to support them, much less is to be saved by trying them together, or including them in a single lawsuit to be tried separately. Indeed, trying them together may cause confusion and prejudice.[81]

---

[76] It would have been impossible for the plaintiffs to have presented their *federal* antitrust claims in the original state case. Plaintiffs based their federal claims on Section 1 of the Sherman Act and jurisdiction to hear such claims rests exclusively with the federal courts. *E.g., General Investment Co. v. Lake Shore & Michigan Southern Ry. Co.*, 260 U.S. 261, 287 (1922).

[77] 726 F.2d at 1153, 1154-1155.

[78] *See* § 15.01[2][c], *supra.*

[79] *See, e.g.*, for arguments expanding the scope of claim preclusion, Waggoner, *Fifty Years of Bernhard v. Bank of America is Enough: Collateral Estoppel Should Require Mutuality But Res Judicata Should Not*, 12 Rev. Litig. 391 (1993); Bone, *Rethinking the "Day in Court" Ideal and Nonparty Preclusion*, 67 N.Y.U. L. Rev. 193 (1992).

[80] *Cf.* Note, *For One Litigant's Sole Relief: Unforeseeable Preclusion and the Second Restatement*, 77 Cornell L. Rev. 905, 922 (1992) ("Because the benefits of res judicata depend on the expectation of preclusion shaping litigants' behavior, res judicata only makes sense if it is foreseeable.").

[81] *James*, note 69, *supra*, at 555. Professor James suggested that fear of claim waiver generated by a rule requiring claimant to join dissimilar claims in the first case might defeat judicial economy by forcing parties to introduce claims that would not otherwise have been litigated. At the same time, consequences from the omission of insufficiently related claims would be too severe: "Hardship from oversight would be greatly multiplied if the parties were bound to think of all the aspects of all possible claims against their adversaries." *Id.* at 556.

Another enlarged form of claim preclusion occurs when a court uses the doctrine to block a claim related to one presented by the same plaintiff in earlier litigation although the subsequent claim was unforeseeable at the time of the original case. This has occurred in latent disease litigation. Harm from asbestos exposure provides an example. "Typically, victims first suffer asbestosis; many years later, some of the same victims also develop cancer."[82]

Statutes of limitation in such cases evince a fair and sensible trend. The statute is tolled until plaintiff has been able to discover the subsequent and more serious consequence of asbestos exposure. Yet plaintiff's second case often fares no better than if it had been time barred, because courts invoke claim preclusion to block plaintiff's second case.[83]

It is true that, in this setting, the claim making up plaintiff's successive case is often so closely related as to satisfy that requirement for claim preclusion. But to apply claim preclusion disregards another requirement that should be understood as fundamental to the operation of the doctrine — that it was foreseeable to plaintiff when he omitted the claim from the first case that the omitted claim could be the subject of future litigation.[84] Claim preclusion stops making sense and becomes quite unfair when it is used to punish plaintiff's failure to do the impossible.

§ 15.04 The Identity-of-Parties Requirement

[1] The Relation Between the Identity-of-Parties Requirement and Limitation of Claim Preclusion to the Same Claim

The general rule has long been that strangers[85] to a prior adjudication can neither bind nor be bound by claim preclusion.[86] The technical reason for this is that different parties cannot be involved in literally the same claim or cause of action.[87] This narrow reading of a claim for purposes of claim preclusion does not seem entirely consistent with the rule that non-identical yet similar claims between the same parties are subject to claim

---

[82] Note, *Claim Preclusion in Modern Latent Disease Cases: A Proposal for Allowing Second Suits*, 103 Harv. L. Rev. 1989, 1989 (1990).

[83] *Id.* at 1990-1998.

[84] *See* note 80, *supra.*

[85] In the jargon of *res judicata*/preclusion, those neither parties to nor involved with the prior adjudication are called "strangers" to it.

[86] *See, e.g.,* A. Vestal, *Res Judicata / Preclusion* 50-51 (1969) (stating American, Canadian and English law to be in accord on the principle that "a judgment against one tortfeasor is not a bar to an action against another.") Notwithstanding this rule, it is possible to bind passive members of a plaintiff class without their active involvement in the case. For discussion of how class actions work and of the special treatment they receive under the Constitution, *see* §§ 4.02[1] (constitutional concerns) & 9.09 (class actions generally), *supra.*

[87] *See, e.g., Developments in the Law — Res Judicata,* 65 Harv. L. Rev. 818, 861-862 (1952) ("since a different party is involved in the second action, the cause of action must be different."). *Montana v. United States,* 440 U.S. 147, 154 (1979), makes the same point.

preclusion,[88] and it stands in contrast to the widespread use of issue preclusion *by* strangers to the original proceeding.[89]

Perhaps a better contemporary justification of the identity-of-parties limitation on claim preclusion rests on concerns of party fairness. While issue preclusion usually applies only to fully litigated matters,[90] claim preclusion attaches even to default judgments.[91] It may be only fair to confine the effects of such broad-spectrum preclusion to parties in the first case or those in close relation to them.

[2] The Claim-Preclusive Effect of Judgments Upon Those in Close Relation to Parties

Parties not actually named in the original case may be subject to claim preclusion if they are sufficiently related to original parties. Courts often describe the relationship as *privity.*[92]

Privity is a label for situations where courts have been willing to stretch the identity-of-parties requirement in order to find claim preclusion. Professor Vestal wrote: "Involved seems to be the idea that the precluded party's interests were represented in the first suit, or that the precluded party should have no greater interest than did the losing party in the first suit."[93] A classic example of privity is a party's sale or assignment of his interests to a non-party after commencement of the litigation. The transferee of the interest is then considered bound by a judgment affecting the interest.[94] Courts have used the concept of privity to extend preclusion in many other settings.[95] It is possible to express the principle represented by privity without using the term itself.[96] But, in all cases, it is necessary

---

[88] *See* § 15.03, *supra.*

[89] *See* § 15.08[2], *infra.*

[90] *See* § 15.07[2], *infra.*

[91] *See* § 15.05 and related text, *infra.*

[92] *E.g., Federated Department Stores, Inc. v. Moitie,* 452 U.S. 394, 398 (1981) ("A final judgment on the merits of an action precludes the parties or their privies from relitigating issues that were or could have been raised in that action.").

[93] *Vestal,* note 86, *supra,* at 121.

[94] *Id.*

[95]

This same concept is applied in the case of lessor and lessee and mortgagor and mortgagee where the transfer is made after the start of the litigation in Suit I. This same closeness sufficient to ground preclusion is found in the case of various governmental agencies, guardian and ward, corporation and stockholders, and bankrupt and trustees. In community property states, husband and wife may be held to be in privity. Finally, in the case of a decedent and his successors in interest, the courts have found the closeness so that the label of "privity" may be applied.

Id. at 122-123. Copyright © 1969 by Matthew Bender & Co., Inc. Reprinted with permission.

[96] For example, without using the term privity, the American Law Institute's *Restatement (Second) of Judgments* § 48 (1982) describes circumstances under which one member of the family may be precluded by a prior case brought by another family member for damage to a familial relationship. For additional discussion of parties within the reach of mainstream claim preclusion, see Waggoner, n.79, *supra,* at 395-396; Bone, n.79, *supra,* at 197.

that the closeness of the relationship bear on the claim which was the subject of the first case.

§ 15.05 The Judgment Must Be Final and On the Merits

A lawsuit cannot have preclusive effect until it has been reduced to final judgment.[97]

The law governing finality of a judgment is that of the judicial system where the judgment was rendered. Court systems take different views about what must happen before their judgments become final. Federal courts regard their judgments to be final even if the case is under appeal.[98] In contrast, some state systems do not give finality to their judgments as long as there is a possibility that the outcome will be changed through appeal.[99]

Only judgments on the merits are entitled to claim-preclusive effect. Judgments in favor of the plaintiff are considered to be on the merits. This is true even if the judgment was rendered by default, stipulation between the parties, or summary judgment.[100]

Judgments on the merits for defendants have the same preclusive effect. However, many ways of concluding cases are open to defendants which do not require the court to reach the merits. For example, the defendant may successfully argue that the court lacks personal jurisdiction over him[101] or that an absentee indispensable to the case cannot be brought before the court.[102] Similarly, a defendant in federal court may successfully question the court's subject matter jurisdiction[103] or venue.[104] In such instances, the case is terminated without prejudice to plaintiff's right to refile in a court where the defect which led to initial dismissal can be avoided. Orders dismissing such cases are not judgments on the merits and, hence, do not have claim-preclusive effect.

---

[97] *Restatement (Second) of Judgments* § 13 (1982). For claim preclusion, the significant event is when judgment becomes final, not when the case begins. *Id.* § 14. This means that a suit filed earlier in time may be subject to the preclusive effects of a subsequent suit when the latter is the first to reach final judgment.

[98] "Should the judgment be vacated by the trial court or reversed on appeal, however, *res judicata* falls with the judgment." *Wright & Miller* § 4427.

[99] *See, e.g.,* the discussion of Utah state law in *Chavez v. Morris,* 566 F. Supp. 359 (D. Utah 1983).

[100] *Cf. Restatement (Second) of Judgments,* note 97, *supra,* § 18 comment a ("It is immaterial whether the judgment was rendered upon a verdict or upon a motion to dismiss or upon consent, confession, or default."). Courts are divided concerning the preclusive effect of dismissals based on the legal insufficiency of pleadings. Federal decisions generally regard such dismissals under Rule 12(b)(6) to be preclusive. *See, e.g., Federated Dept. Stores, Inc. v. Moitie,* 452 U.S. 394, 399 n.3 (1981). Many state decisions (either styling their motions in the manner of the federal rule or in the earlier form of demurrer) take the same view. But some do not. *See, e.g., In re Estate of Cochrane,* 391 N.E.2d 35 (Ill. App. Ct. 1979).

[101] *See* Chapter 3 (territorial jurisdiction), *supra.*

[102] *See* § 9.05[2] (compulsory party joinder), *supra.*

[103] *See* Chapter 5, *supra.*

[104] *See* Chapter 6, *supra.*

In other situations, the circumstances of the dismissal may not as clearly suggest whether plaintiff's case has been terminated on the merits. Federal and many state courts usually resolve these ambiguities against plaintiff. Thus, Rule 41(b) of the Federal Rules of Civil Procedure states: "Unless the court in its order for dismissal otherwise specifies, a dismissal other than a dismissal for lack of jurisdiction, for improper venue, or for failure to join a party under Rule 19, operates as an adjudication upon the merits."[105]

PART B
Issue Preclusion

§ 15.06 Issue and Claim Preclusion Compared

[1] How Issue Preclusion Supplements Claim Preclusion

The function of issue preclusion (collateral estoppel) is to advance the objectives of *res judicata*[106] beyond the confines of claim preclusion. Thus, it gives a final adjudication preclusive effect in a subsequent case which cannot be said, even in the broadest sense, to share the same claim.

In some cases, issue preclusion operates where claim preclusion obviously could not apply. For example, a criminal proceeding may be capable of generating issue-preclusive effects on a subsequent civil proceeding.[107]

In other cases the distinction between issue and claim preclusion is more subtle. The situation where plaintiff brings successive property damage and personal injury lawsuits arising out of the same automobile accident provides an example. A majority of jurisdictions would apply claim preclusion to conclude that a final judgment on the merits in the property case

---

[105] However, the federal rule has not always been applied literally to other dismissals "in which the merits could not be reached for failure of the plaintiff to satisfy a precondition." *Costello v. United States,* 365 U.S. 265, 286 (1961). For example, in *Saylor v. Lindsley,* 391 F.2d 965 (2d Cir. 1968), the court declined to give claim-preclusive effect to a dismissal "with prejudice" for failure to post a bond for costs, reasoning that the defendant had not been put to the burden of preparing a defense to the first litigation and would therefore not be unduly inconvenienced by having to defend the second.

[106] *See* § 15.01[1], *supra.*

[107] *E.g., Allen v. McCurry,* 449 U.S. 90 (1980); *White Earth Band of Chippewa Indians v. Alexander,* 683 F.2d 1129 (8th Cir.), *cert. denied,* 459 U.S. 1070 (1982). However, different burdens of proof for civil and criminal proceedings limit the range of issues which are identical in the sense required by claim preclusion. *See generally Restatement (Second) of Judgments* § 85 (1982); Brenner, *"Crossing Over": The Issue Preclusive Effects of a Civil/Criminal Adjudication Upon a Proceeding of the Opposite Character,* 7 N. Ill. U. L. Rev. 141 (1987); Shapiro, *Should a Guilty Plea Have Preclusive Effect?,* 70 Iowa L. Rev. 27 (1984).

Another example of how issue preclusion operates in a sphere separate from claim preclusion may occur in civil litigation, when a prior court decides the identical issue without addressing the merits of plaintiff's claim. *E.g., Deckert v. Wachovia Student Financial Services, Inc.,* 963 F.2d 816 (5th Cir. 1992) (preclusive effect given by a Texas federal court to a prior Texas state court ruling that personal jurisdiction for plaintiff's case was lacking in Texas).

swallows up plaintiff's subsequent lawsuit for personal injury.[108] But the minority of jurisdictions that permit the second suit[109] create opportunities for issue preclusion. Thus, if plaintiff lost the first property damage suit upon a finding of contributory negligence, issue preclusion may deny him the opportunity to relitigate the contributory negligence issue in his subsequent personal injury action. On the other hand, if plaintiff established negligence and recovered in the property damage suit, then plaintiff might argue issue preclusion to advance his personal injury claim.[110]

[2] How Guarantees of Procedural Fairness Limit Each Doctrine

A fundamental guarantee of our judicial process is that no one may have his rights extinguished by a judgment unless he has first received a full and fair opportunity for a hearing. This idea provides an important check on both claim and issue preclusion.[111] It means that the preclusive weight of a final judgment must be commensurate with the opportunities for litigation which preceded it.

Claim and issue preclusion both prevent parties from raising issues,[112] but they reflect differently the constraints of procedural fairness. Claim preclusion prevents a litigant from raising new issues,[113] but usually only upon a demonstration that the party to be bound could have raised the new matters if she had more fully litigated for or against a claim which was presented in the first case.[114] Issue preclusion extinguishes issues that

---

[108] See § 15.03, supra.

[109] See § 15.03, supra.

[110] In that event, defendant might argue claim preclusion, hoping to change the res judicata law of the jurisdiction. This is what happened in Rush v. City of Maple Heights, 147 N.E.2d 599 (Ohio 1958), discussed in § 15.03[4][a], supra. Ohio state trial and intermediate courts ruled in favor of plaintiff on issue preclusion grounds. Given the fairness concerns that should temper applications of issue preclusion, see § 15.08[4], infra, application of the doctrine against the defendant in Rush is open to criticism. The matter became academic when the Ohio Supreme Court reversed and ordered dismissal of the case by invoking claim preclusion.

[111] To preclude parties without affording such fairness protections raises serious questions under the due process clauses of the Fifth and Fourteenth Amendments to the United States Constitution. See Ratliff, Offensive Collateral Estoppel and the Option Effect, 67 Tex. L. Rev. 63, 64 (1988); Pielemeier, Due Process Limitations on the Application of Collateral Estoppel Against Nonparties to Prior Litigation, 63 B.U. L. Rev. 383 (1983); Casad, Intersystem Issue Preclusion and the Restatement (Second) of Judgments, 66 Cornell L. Rev. 510, 517 (1981); Atwood, State Court Judgments in Federal Litigation: Mapping the Contours of Full Faith and Credit, 58 Ind. L. J. 59, 69-70 n.54 (1982). See, in addition, the Supreme Court decisions discussed in § 15.08, infra.

[112] While this is literally the province of issue preclusion, claim preclusion also effectively precludes issues. In fact, it operates on a larger scale than issue preclusion. See, e.g., Federated Dept. Stores v. Moitie, 452 U.S. 394, 398 (1981) (emphasis added):

> There is little to be added to the doctrine of res judicata [claim preclusion] as developed in the case law of this Court. A final judgment on the merits of an action precludes the parties or their privies from relitigating issues that were or could have been raised in that action.

[113] Id.

[114] See § 15.03, supra.

claim preclusion cannot reach,[115] but only those that were litigated in a prior adjudication and necessary to judgment.

§ 15.07   The Same Issue Must Have Been Litigated, Determined and Necessary to the Judgment in the Prior Case

[1]   The Identity-of-Issues Requirement

Issue preclusion (collateral estoppel) can operate only if the issues in the original and succeeding proceeding are identical. Generally, issues of either law or fact qualify.[116] This is true even though courts have occasionally suggested that issue preclusion is not available for issues of law[117] and might be available only as to issues of "ultimate" fact.[118]

Only issues which reappear in subsequent litigation are subject to issue preclusion. Courts have stressed that the identity-of-issue requirement should be taken literally. For example, in *Commissioner of Internal Revenue v. Sunnen*[119] the Supreme Court refused to give preclusive effect to a prior Tax Court determination that a wife's income was not taxable to her husband, even though the original and succeeding cases both involved the husband's practice of transferring rights under patent contracts to his wife. The Court observed that collateral estoppel (issue preclusion) "must be confined to situations where the matter raised in the second suit is identical in all respects with that decided in the first proceeding and where the controlling facts and applicable legal rules remain unchanged."[120]

At the same time, litigants may not escape issue preclusion by dressing up previously litigated issues to make them appear new. This is true even

---

[115] *See* note 107 and related text, *supra.*

[116] *Restatement (Second) of Judgments* § 27 (1982).

[117] *E.g., United States v. Moser,* 266 U.S. 236 (1924). For a critique of this proposition, *see Friedenthal, Kane & Miller* § 14.10. The authors note that the principle that issues of pure law should not be subject to issue preclusion has been hard to articulate and to apply consistently, particularly because it is often difficult to distinguish among issues of law, fact, and mixed law and fact. On preclusion of issues of law generally, see *Restatement (Second) of Judgments,* note 116, *supra,* § 28(2); Buckley, *Issue Preclusion and Issues of Law: A Doctrinal Framework Based on Rules of Recognition, Jurisdiction and Legal History,* 24 Houston L. Rev. 875 (1987); Hazard, *Preclusion as to Issues of Law: The Legal System's Interest,* 70 Iowa L. Rev. 81, 86-87 (1984).

[118] The leading case for the latter proposition is *The Evergreens v. Nunan,* 141 F.2d 927 (2d Cir. 1944), *cert. denied,* 323 U.S. 720 (1944). The case attaches importance to the difference between ultimate facts (which support conclusions of law) and factual determinations leading up to ultimate facts (which are only conclusions of "evidentiary" or "mediate" fact). This has not been a very effective tool for limiting issue preclusion, since "[t]he line between ultimate and evidentiary facts is often impossible to draw." *Restatement (Second) of Judgments,* note 116, *supra,* § 27 comment j. For the same reason, the distinction caused problems in code pleading and was abandoned in the federal pleading rules. *See* §§ 8.03[3] (specificity of fact pleading under the codes) & 8.04[1] (specificity of notice pleading), *supra.*

[119] 333 U.S. 591 (1948).

[120] *Id.* at 599-600.

though a litigant can demonstrate that differences in factual support or legal argument might cause the issue to be resolved differently in the succeeding case.

Thus, for example, if the party against whom preclusion is sought did in fact litigate an issue of ultimate fact and suffered an adverse determination, new evidentiary facts may not be brought forward to obtain a different determination of that ultimate fact. . . . And similarly if the issue was one of law, new arguments may not be presented to obtain a different determination of that issue.[121]

In this way, issue preclusion is like claim preclusion[122] in pressuring litigants to be complete in their initial presentations.

[2] The Issue Must Have Been Litigated and Determined in the Prior Case

One feature setting issue preclusion apart from claim preclusion is that the former only precludes matters which were actually litigated and determined in the prior case.[123] Trials provide a frequent but not exclusive means for determining issues. "An issue may be submitted and determined on a motion to dismiss for failure to state a claim, a motion for judgment on the pleadings, a motion for summary judgment . . ., a motion for directed verdict or their equivalents, as well as on a judgment entered on a verdict."[124] On the other hand, there is considerable support for the rule that default judgments, consent judgments and judgments based on stipulations of fact or admissions should not generate issue-preclusive effects because by them the issues have not been litigated.[125]

There are important reasons why issue preclusion should operate only on issues actually litigated and determined in the prior proceeding. These reasons become clear if, for example, we take a closer look at default judgments. The position under federal doctrine appears to be that default judgments carry no issue-preclusive effects.[126] The rule is well-settled in most state systems.[127] However, New York state courts took the opposite view. Their position was that default judgments could support issue

---

[121] *Restatement (Second) of Judgments*, note 116, *supra*, Section 27 comment c.

[122] *See* § 15.03[1], *supra*.

[123] The parties usually will have raised the issues in their pleadings. However, this will not always be the case. Many systems permit their courts to determine upon the evidence at trial issues which go beyond the pleadings. For example, Rule 15(b) authorizes federal trial courts to grant motions to amend pleadings to conform to the evidence at trial but notes that "failure so to amend does not affect the result of the trial of these issues." *See* § 8.10[2], *supra*.

[124] *Restatement (Second) of Judgments*, note 116, *supra*, § 27 comment d.

[125] *See Arizona v. California*, 530 U.S. 392 (2000) (judgments entered by confession, consent or default should not be entitled to issue-preclusion effect.)

[126] *See Nevada v. United States*, 463 U.S. 110, 130 n.11 (1983); *Parklane Hosiery Co. v. Shore*, 439 U.S. 322, 326 n.5 (1979).

[127] *See, e.g., Gwynn v. Wilhelm*, 360 P.2d 312 (Or. 1961); *Watts v. Watts*, 36 N.E. 479 (Mass. 1894); *Ressequie v. Byers*, 9 N.W. 779 (Wis. 1881).

preclusion with reference to issues which might have been raised if the lawsuit had proceeded.[128]

This position has been justly criticized.[129] A party's decision to take a default in the initial case is not necessarily a reflection of the strength of his opponent's case. Reasons why a party may default may include "the smallness of the amount or the value of the property in controversy, the difficulty of obtaining the necessary evidence, the expense of the litigation, and his own situation at the time."[130] It is also questionable whether endowing default judgments with issue-preclusive effect even achieves *res judicata's* goal of minimizing controversies.

> It is unfair and unwise to go as far as the New York decisions do in enforcing [issue preclusion] on the basis of earlier defaults. The consequence is to make a default so perilous that a well-advised defendant will be driven to litigate any petty claim asserted against him if there is the slightest prospect that a buried issue may be foreclosed in a subsequent suit. In the end this could frustrate the very purpose of *res judicata,* to reduce contention and dispute. Instead of more litigation later, there will be more litigating now.[131]

[3] Determination of the Issue Must Have Been Necessary to Judgment

[a] The Function and Purpose of the Rule

Not only must the same issue have been litigated and determined in the prior proceeding, but the determination must have been necessary to support the judgment there. This added requirement functions with the others to assure that only those who have had a full and fair prior opportunity to litigate issues will be subject to issue preclusion. Insistence that the adjudication be necessary to the judgment "is a protection, for it means that the issue will be really disputed and that the loser will have put out his best efforts."[132]

It also means that the party to be bound will usually have an opportunity to appeal the initial adjudication. In contrast, determinations which are not necessary to support the judgment are usually not appealable. "Such determinations have the characteristics of dicta, and may not ordinarily be the subject of an appeal by the party against whom they were made."[133] Issue preclusion is and should be limited to determinations necessary to support the judgment because "the interest in providing an opportunity for

---

[128] For discussion of these decisions, see Rosenberg, *Collateral Estoppel in New York,* 44 St. John's L. Rev. 165, 174 (1969).

[129] *Id.* at 171-177.

[130] *Cromwell v. County of Sac,* 94 U.S. 351, 356 (1876).

[131] *Rosenberg,* note 128, *supra,* at 177.

[132] *The Evergreens v. Nunan,* 141 F.2d 927, 929 (2d Cir. 1944).

[133] *Restatement (Second) of Judgments,* note 116, *supra,* § 27 comment h.

a considered determination, which if adverse may be the subject of an appeal, outweighs the interest in avoiding the burden of relitigation."[134]

Rios v. Davis[135] is a well-known example. Davis sued Rios for negligence in an automobile collision. The jury found Rios negligent, but also found Davis contributorily negligent, requiring judgment to be entered for Rios. Rios then sued Davis for injuries Rios had received in the same collision. Davis defended on the grounds that the jury's finding in the first case established Rios' contributory negligence and precluded him from relitigating it in the second. The court refused to give the earlier judgment issue-preclusive effect. It said of the first case:

> The finding that Rios was negligent was not essential or material to the judgment and the judgment was not based thereon. . . . Since the judgment was in favor of Rios he had no right or opportunity to complain of or to appeal from the finding that he was guilty of such negligence even if such finding had been without any support whatever in the evidence. The right of appeal is from a judgment and not from a finding.[136]

A test useful to determine whether an issue was necessary to support the judgment is to ask whether, if the issue had been decided the opposite way, the same judgment would have been entered. If so, then judgment did not depend on the way the issue actually was resolved. Applying this test to the *Rios* case, we find that, once the jury found Davis to be contributorily negligent, Rios had to win. Thus, the same judgment would have been entered in the case no matter what conclusion the jury reached concerning Rios's own negligence.

[b] Alternative Determinations

A special problem arises when alternative issue determinations support the judgment. If each is independently capable of supporting the judgment, then neither is necessary to the judgment in a strict sense. Applying the test above, if either issue had been resolved differently, the judgment would have been unchanged.

The weakest case for issue preclusion is when it is unclear which of two grounds supports the judgment. Preclusion is unwarranted in such cases.[137] The problem is that it is impossible to determine whether a given issue was determined at all.

A classroom case, *Illinois Central Gulf R.R. v. Parks*,[138] illustrates this difficulty. A husband and wife were injured when their car collided with one of defendant's trains. In the first suit, the wife sued for her injuries and the husband sued for loss of the services and companionship of his wife.

---

[134] *Id.*

[135] 373 S.W.2d 386 (Tex. Civ. App. 1963).

[136] *Id.* at 387-88. On the last point, see § 13.08[1] (prejudicial effect as requirement for reviewability), *supra.*

[137] *See Restatement (Second) of Judgments* § 27, Comment (i).

[138] 390 N.E.2d 1078 (Ind. Ct. App. 1979).

The wife recovered against the railroad, but the jury returned a general verdict against the husband. In a subsequent lawsuit, the husband sued defendant railroad for his own injuries. The railroad urged claim and issue preclusion. The court rejected both arguments.[139] The railroad based its case for issue preclusion on the possibility that the first jury returned a verdict against the husband because he had been contributorily negligent as driver of the car. The court noted, however, that it was equally possible that the first jury returned a verdict against the husband because the husband proved no damages for loss of his wife's services and companionship. Under this possibility, the contributory negligence issue would not have been determined in the first case at all.[140]

One influential decision denying preclusive effect to a prior adjudication expressly based on alternative grounds is *Halpern v. Schwartz*.[141] *Halpern* rejected the assumption that alternative grounds were as likely as non-alternative grounds to be thoroughly litigated prior to judgment.

> First, if the court in the prior case were sure as to one of the alternative grounds and this ground by itself was sufficient to support the judgment, then it may not feel as constrained to give rigorous consideration to the alternative grounds. Second, since there are alternative grounds which could independently support the prior judgment, vigorous review of an asserted error as to one ground probably would not occur. The losing litigant would have little motivation to appeal from an alleged erroneous finding in connection with one of several independent alternative grounds, since even if his claim of error were sustained, the judgment would be affirmed on one of the other grounds.[142]

Some courts continued to adhere to the older rule.[143] But the *Restatement (Second) of Judgments* endorsed the *Halpern* principle, stating that "[i]f a judgment of a court of first instance is based on determinations of two issues, either of which standing independently would be sufficient to support the result, the judgment is not conclusive with respect to either issue standing alone."[144] At the same time, the *Restatement* regards such determinations as preclusive if both grounds are affirmed on appeal. At this point, "the losing party . . . has obtained an appellate decision on the issue, and thus the balance weighs in favor of preclusion."[145]

---

[139] Whether the husband engaged in a kind of claim-splitting which should have been barred by claim preclusion is an interesting question. Indiana courts appear to be more indulgent on this point than most other jurisdictions. *See* § 15.03, *supra.*

[140] On the issue-preclusion requirement that the issue actually be determined in the prior proceeding, see § 15.07[2], *supra.*

[141] 426 F.2d 102 (2d Cir. 1970).

[142] *Id.* at 105-106

[143] *Compare, e.g., Halpern, id., with In re Westgate-California Corp.*, 642 F.2d 1174 (9th Cir. 1981) (giving preclusive effect to an alternate ground supporting a judgment).

[144] *Restatement (Second) of Judgments*, note 116, *supra*, § 27 comment i (citing *Halpern* with approval).

[145] *Id.*, § 27 comment o.

[4] Application of Issue Preclusion Must Be Fair in the Given Case

The essential prerequisites for issue preclusion discussed in this section all grow out of a concern of procedural fairness —-that litigants have a sufficient opportunity to litigate before they are bound.[146] But issue preclusion's requirement that the same issue be previously determined and necessary to judgment is not always enough to assure procedural fairness.

For example, notwithstanding satisfaction of the above criteria, there should be no issue preclusion if

> [T]here is a clear and convincing need for a new determination of the issue . . . because it was not sufficiently foreseeable at the time of the initial action that the issue would arise in the context of a subsequent action, or . . . because the party sought to be precluded, as a result of the conduct of his adversary or other special circumstances, did not have an adequate opportunity or incentive to obtain a full and fair adjudication in the initial action.[147]

Moreover, the trend, explored in the next section, of relaxing the identity-of-parties requirement for issue preclusion has created a greater need for courts to inquire whether invocation of issue preclusion will be fair under the circumstances of the particular case.[148]

§ 15.08   Who Can Bind and Be Bound by Issue Preclusion?

In most jurisdictions, issue preclusion (collateral estoppel) has no counterpart to the identity-of-parties requirement which limits claim preclusion.[149] It is clear, of course, that issue preclusion can operate when the parties in the succeeding case are the same. Under the right circumstances, however, it may also operate *in favor of* one who was neither a party nor in privity with a party in the earlier case. But issue preclusion is unlikely to operate *against* one who was a complete stranger to the first case.[150]

[1] The General Rule Against Binding Those Who Were Strangers to the Prior Adjudication

The general rule is that strangers to the prior case cannot be bound by it.[151] After entertaining the possibility of change,[152] the Supreme Court

---

[146] On the importance of procedural fairness to preclusion law, see § 15.06[2], *supra.*

[147] *Restatement (Second) of Judgments,* note 116, *supra,* § 28(5).

[148] *See* § 15.08[2], *infra.*

[149] *See* § 15.09, *supra.*

[150] In the jargon of *res judicata*/preclusion, those who had no formal or informal involvement with the prior case are called "strangers" to it.

[151] *See* § 15.06, *supra,* and the authorities surveyed in Ratliff, *Offensive Collateral Estoppel and the Option Effect,* 67 Tex. L. Rev. 63, 64 n.8 (1988).

[152] In *Provident Tradesmen's Bank & Trust Co. v. Patterson,* 390 U.S. 102, 114 (1968), the Court wondered whether a person "should be bound by the previous decision because, although technically a nonparty, he had purposely bypassed an adequate opportunity to intervene." For

reaffirmed the rule in *Parklane Hosiery Co. v. Shore*, noting that it would be "a violation of due process for a judgment to be binding on a litigant who was not a party or a privy and therefore has never had an opportunity to be heard."[153]

Nonparties are occasionally subject to issue preclusion. But this usually occurs only when they chose to involve themselves significantly in the prior case — whether by becoming unusually active amicus curiae,[154] or by furnishing behind-the-scenes assistance to one of the actual parties. For example, in *Montana v. United States*,[155] the Supreme Court held that the United States was bound by issue preclusion even though it was not a party to the prior adjudication. The Court reached this conclusion by noting that the United States subsidized and controlled the actions of one who was a party there. The United States directed decisions to file and to appeal, paid litigation costs, and reviewed and approved papers filed in that case.

For issue preclusion to apply to nonparties, due process probably requires the nonparty to have participated at least informally in the prior adjudication. In contrast, those who did not participate (strangers) probably cannot be bound by issue preclusion. This is true even if a stranger forgoes a clear opportunity to participate in the prior adjudication,[156] and even if the quality of the initial adjudication was so high as to suggest that the stranger will not put on a better case when permitted to relitigate the issue.[157] In this context, due process is not satisfied by adequate or even exemplary representation by another litigant in another case. The sentiment — if not the logic — of due process guarantees strangers some kind of day in court before they can be bound, if for no other reason than to cauterize the wounds of defeat.

---

the argument that issue preclusion should attach under such circumstances, see ALI, *Complex Litigation Project* § 5.05 (1993); Note, *Preclusion of Absent Disputants to Compel Intervention*, 79 Colum. L. Rev. 1551 (1979); Berch, *A Proposal to Permit Collateral Estoppel of Nonparties Seeking Affirmative Relief*, 1979 Ariz. St. L.J. 511 (1979).

[153] 439 U.S. 322, 327 n.7 (1979). On how the Due Process Clause of the United States Constitution functions to prevent applications of preclusion which compromise a party's right to a hearing, see § 15.06[2], *supra*. For subsequent applications of the rule that strangers to a civil lawsuit may not be precluded by it, see Georgia v. South Carolina, 497 U.S. 376, 392 (1990); *Martin v. Wilks*, 490 U.S. 755 (1989). "A judgment or decree among parties to a lawsuit resolves issues as among them, but it does not conclude the rights of stranger to those proceedings." 490 U.S. at 762.

Notwithstanding this rule, it is possible to bind passive members of a plaintiff class without their active involvement in the case. For discussion of how class actions work and of the special treatment they receive under the Constitution, see §§ 4.02[1] (constitutional concerns) & 9.09 (class actions generally), *supra*.

[154] This rarely occurs. "Because the amicus curiae generally lacks party status, or the ability to control the course of the litigation, the private amici can, in most instances, participate in the suit free of the effects of res judicata." Comment, *The Litigating Amicus Curiae: When Does the Party Begin After the Friends Leave?*, 41 Am. U. L. Rev. 1243, 1260-1261 (1992).

[155] 440 U.S. 147 (1979).

[156] *Ratliff*, note 151, *supra*, at 65. Probably the worst that will happen to a party who deliberately forgoes prior participation will be that he may later be denied use of nonmutual issue preclusion. *See* note 33 and accompanying text, *infra*.

[157] *See, e.g., Humphreys v. Tann*, 487 F.2d 666 (6th Cir. 1973).

[2] When Strangers to the Prior Adjudication May Bind Those Who Were Parties

One question has dominated modern-day developments in issue preclusion. When, if ever, can strangers to the prior adjudication invoke the doctrine? Once the rule was never. Applying the *mutuality doctrine,* courts held, that since strangers were safe from the adverse effects of a prior adjudication, they could not use it to their advantage.[158] In time, however, courts began to attach importance to the difference between binding total strangers to the prior litigation and binding those subject to a prior adjudication of the issue, albeit against a different party. While a minority of jurisdictions continue to adhere to the mutuality doctrine,[159] most courts have now dispensed with it in favor of nonmutual preclusion. They permit strangers to the prior case to invoke issue preclusion against those who were parties, whenever it appears from the circumstances that it is fair to do so.

[a] The Decline of the Mutuality Doctrine

The mutuality doctrine rests upon two separate propositions. *First,* strangers to a prior adjudication will not be bound by it. *Second,* it is unfair to permit anyone who cannot be bound by a prior adjudication to use it to bind another. That is, one-way preclusion is unfair; the risk of preclusion from the initial case must be mutual.

The first of these two propositions is still true — federal due process law still seems to protect strangers to a prior adjudication from being bound by it.[160] The widespread collapse of the mutuality doctrine occurred because most jurisdictions no longer accept the second proposition. Swelling dockets and a greater appreciation of the benefits of judicial economy led courts to reexamine the assumption that one-way preclusion was invariably unfair. This resulted in a series of significant state and federal decisions repudiating the mutuality doctrine.

The most significant state case was *Bernhard v. Bank of America.*[161] In the first lawsuit, plaintiff, an estate administratrix, sued her predecessor for failing to include certain funds in his accounting of the assets of the estate. She lost. She then sued the bank in the second lawsuit, claiming that it was indebted to the estate for releasing these same funds without proper authorization. The bank argued that the issue of its authorization had been determined adversely to the plaintiff in the first lawsuit.

The bank was a stranger to the first lawsuit. Thus it could not have been bound[162] had the authorization issue in that case been resolved differently.

---

[158] *E.g., Bigelow v. Old Dominion Copper Mining & Smelting Co.,* 225 U.S. 111, 127 (1912); *Buckeye Powder Co. v. E. I. DuPont de Nemours Powder Co.,* 248 U.S. 55, 63 (1918).

[159] There now appears to be eight states that retain the mutuality doctrine: Alabama, Florida, Georgia, Kansas, Louisiana, Mississippi, North Dakota, and Virginia. Erichson, *Interjurisdictional Preclusion,* 96 Mich. L. Rev. 945, 966-967 (1998) (citing cases).

[160] *See* § 15.08[2], *supra.*

[161] 122 P.2d 892 (Cal. 1942).

[162] *See* § 15.08[2], *supra.*

That is, if the first case determined that the bank released the funds without proper authority, the bank could nonetheless litigate the issue in the second case and attempt to prove that it had been authorized to release the funds. The only way, then, that the California Supreme Court could give preclusive effect to the judgment rendered in the first lawsuit was to dispense with the doctrine of mutuality. It did so, stating that "[N]o satisfactory rationalization has been advanced for the requirement of mutuality."[163]

Two federal cases are also of special importance. In *Blonder-Tongue Laboratories, Inc. v. University of Illinois Foundation*[164] the Supreme Court extensively criticized the mutuality doctrine.[165] The Court refused to invoke the mutuality requirement in *Blonder-Tongue,* but the breadth of its ruling was uncertain. However, in a subsequent case, *Parklane Hosiery Co. v. Shore,*[166] the Court categorically repudiated the mutuality doctrine and thus ended its use in federal courts.[167]

Parklane faulted the mutuality doctrine for "failing to recognize the obvious difference in position between a party who has never litigated an issue and one who has fully litigated and lost."[168] *Parklane* completes the process, begun by *Blonder-Tongue,* of replacing one fairness test with another. The mutuality doctrine rested on the idea that it was invariably unfair to create risk-free opportunities for preclusion, and that benefits of preclusion were spoils of victory earned through the risk of equally adverse consequences had matters in the original suit turned out differently. Rejecting these ideas, *Parklane* declared that henceforth it would be necessary to adduce some particular reason why it would be unfair to bind a party by nonmutual issue preclusion. Attention under this new approach thus shifted from the position of the party wishing to use the doctrine to the position of the party against whom it was invoked.

[b] Limits on Courts' Discretion to Invoke Nonmutual Issue Preclusion

Nonmutual issue preclusion has not been without its critics. Observers were particularly concerned that, when invoked offensively,[169] the doctrine

---

[163] 122 P.2d at 895.

[164] 402 U.S. 313 (1971). For additional discussion of this case, see Corr, *Supreme Court Doctrine in the Trenches: The Case of Collateral Estoppel,* 27 Wm. & Mary L. Rev. 35, 37-39 (1985).

[165] 402 U.S. at 322-327.

[166] 439 U.S. 322 (1979). For an extended discussion of the case, see Holland, *Modernizing Res Judicata: Reflections on the Parklane Doctrine,* 55 Ind. L.J. 615 (1980).

[167] Resnik, *Tiers,* 57 S. Cal. L. Rev. 837, 968 (1984).

[168] 439 U.S. at 327.

[169] Terminology is important here. Effects from a judgment that operate to plaintiff's advantage in the subsequent case are described as "offensive" preclusion, while those operating to defendant's subsequent advantage are described as "defensive" preclusion. For more on the distinction, *see* § 15.01[3], *supra.*

Offensive and defensive classifications apply in the same way to both mutual and nonmutual issue preclusion. Mutual issue preclusion is possible under the mutuality doctrine; nonmutual preclusion is not.

might give a new claimant an unfair advantage over one who was a defendant in a prior adjudication.[170]

For example, Professor Brainerd Currie put forth what he called the "multiple claimant anomaly."[171] In his hypothetical case, fifty injured passengers bring successive suits against a railroad arising from the same train accident. In the first case, the railroad wins by establishing that it was not negligent. When the second passenger brings suit, the court will deny the railroad issue-preclusive effect from the prior determination of no negligence, since the second passenger was a stranger to the first suit.[172] The plaintiff in the second suit is thus free to relitigate the question of the railroad's negligence. In Currie's example, twenty-five passenger plaintiffs bring twenty-five successive lawsuits. Each plaintiff is free to relitigate the negligence issue, but each loses. Then, in the twenty-sixth case, a passenger prevails on the negligence issue and recovers. Currie then poses the question:

> Are we to understand that the remaining twenty-four passengers can plead the judgment in the case of No. 26 as conclusively establishing that the railroad was guilty of negligence, while the railroad can make no reference to the first twenty-five cases which it won?[173]

Abuses of nonmutual offensive preclusion might also lead to proliferation of litigation contrary to one purpose of preclusion.[174] For example, passenger B in Currie's hypothetical might forego an opportunity to join with passenger A in the initial case, taking a "wait and see" attitude. If A wins, B can invoke nonmutual issue preclusion. If A loses, B (a stranger to the first case) is free to relitigate all issues.

The Supreme Court acknowledged all of these concerns in *Parklane.* While it approved offensive nonmutual preclusion for that case, it made clear that the doctrine should not always be available. Federal courts have "broad discretion to determine when it should be applied."[175] They must use their discretion to refuse nonmutual preclusion when circumstances suggest that use of the doctrine against a party to the prior case would be unfair. The

---

Of the cases discussed in this section, *Bernhard* and *Blonder-Tongue* are examples of defensive nonmutual issue preclusion, while *Parklane* is an example of offensive nonmutual issue preclusion.

[170] *See Ratliff,* note 151, *supra;* Currie, *Mutuality of Collateral Estoppel: Limits of the Bernhard Doctrine,* 9 Stan. L. Rev. 281 (1957); Greenebaum, *In Defense of the Doctrine of Mutuality of Estoppel,* 45 Ind. L.J. 1 (1969); Overton, *The Restatement of Judgments, Collateral Estoppel, and Conflict of Laws,* 44 Tenn. L. Rev. 927 (1977). *Cf.* Waggoner, note .79, *supra* (rejecting nonmutual issue preclusion but advocating nonmutual claim preclusion); Note, *Exposing the Extortion Gap: An Economic Analysis of the Rules of Collateral Estoppel,* 105 Harv. L. Rev. 1940 (1992) (criticizing nonmutual preclusion by contending that it is unfair to subsequent plaintiffs).

[171] *Currie,* note 170, *supra,* at 285-89.

[172] *See* § 15.08[1], *supra.*

[173] *Currie,* note 170, *supra,* at 286.

[174] Promotion of judicial economy is a primary purpose of preclusion doctrine. *See* § 15.01[1], *supra.*

[175] 439 U.S. at 331.

Court stated that nonmutual preclusion should be denied when sought by one who deliberately bypassed an opportunity to participate in the original proceeding; when the stake of the party against whom preclusion would be invoked was deceptively small in the original proceeding; when the subsequent proceeding affords significantly more advantageous procedural opportunities for that party; or when there were inconsistent prior judgments.[176]

Of course, *Parklane* is not controlling on state courts.[177] But a large number of state jurisdictions rejecting mutuality have defined and limited nonmutual preclusion in ways similar to Supreme Court's opinion. Since *Parklane* relied in part on a draft provision of the *Restatement (Second) of Judgments,* this consensus is not surprising.

That provision, which became Section 29 of the *Restatement (Second),* expressly rejects the doctrine of mutuality by making issue preclusion available to strangers to the prior adjudication. But Section 29 makes clear that issue preclusion is unavailable if the party who would be bound "lacked full and fair opportunity to litigate the issue in the first action or other circumstances justify affording him an opportunity to relitigate the issue."

Problems of procedural fairness can arise even if the parties in the successive suits are identical.[178] However, Section 29 notes additional problems which may arise when strangers to the first suit attempt to invoke issue preclusion. These include:

(2) The forum in the second action affords the party against whom preclusion is asserted procedural opportunities in the presentation and determination of the issue that were not available in the first action and could likely result in the issue being differently determined;

(3) The person seeking to invoke favorable preclusion, or to avoid unfavorable preclusion, could have effected joinder in the first action between himself and his present adversary;

(4) The determination relied on as preclusive was itself inconsistent with another determination of the same issue. . . .

Clear acknowledgment in *Parklane* and in Section 29 of situations to which nonmutual issue preclusion should not apply has done much to ease apprehensions over rejection of the mutuality doctrine. For example, both *Parklane*[179] and Section 29[180] seem to offer an answer to the so-called

---

[176] *Id.*

[177] Subject only to the due process and full faith and credit constraints of federal law, state courts are free to devise their own answers to preclusion questions. *See* § 15.01[1], *supra.*

[178] *Restatement (Second) of Judgments* Section 28 addresses this. For discussion of Section 28 and how concerns of procedural fairness can prevent application of issue preclusion even when the parties are the same, see § 15.07[4], *supra.* Incorporating Section 28 by reference, Section 29 makes clear that the same factors can be important in ascertaining nonmutual issue preclusion.

[179] *See* § 15.08[2][a], *supra.*

[180] *See Restatement (Second) of Judgments,* note 150, *supra,* §§ 29(3) & (4), quoted in the text of this subsection, *supra.*

multiple claimant anomaly posed earlier in this discussion. It would clearly be unfair to permit a claimant to exploit one judgment that was inconsistent with twenty-five others, and a court faced with such a case is directed to refuse nonmutual preclusion.[181] Courts are similarly directed to deny nonmutual preclusion to claimants who have adopted a "wait-and-see" attitude toward the initial case.[182]

PART C
Inter-System Preclusion

§ 15.09 Intramural and Inter-System Preclusion Compared

Preclusion law is largely common law. Within limits,[183] each judicial court system is free to fashion doctrine determining how much force its judgments should have. When courts of a system are presented with their own judgments, questions concerning the effect of the judgment arise in an *intramural*[184] context. The intramural law that courts apply is their local preclusion law.

Increasingly, courts must also consider the effect of judgments which were rendered outside their system. Then, questions concerning the effect of the judgment arise in an *inter-system* context.[185] For inter-system cases, which body of preclusion law should determine the force and effect of the judgment? Is it measured by the intramural law of the system rendering

---

[181] In addition, *see Restatement (Second) of Judgments,* note 150, *supra,* § 29 comment f:

Giving a prior determination of an issue conclusive effect in subsequent litigation is justified not merely by avoiding further costs of litigation but also by underlying confidence that the result reached is substantially correct. Where a determination relied on as preclusive is itself inconsistent with some other adjudication of the same issue, that confidence is generally unwarranted.

[182] In addition, *see Restatement (Second) of Judgments,* note 150, *supra,* § 29 comment e:

A person in such a position that he might ordinarily have been expected to join as plaintiff in the first action, but who did not do so, may be refused the benefits of "offensive" issue preclusion where the circumstances suggest that he wished to avail himself of the benefits of a favorable outcome without incurring the risk of an unfavorable one.

[183] The Due Process Clause of the United States Constitution limits the preclusive effect a court can give to one of its judgments. *See* § 15.06 note 154 and related text, *supra.*

[184] *See* Casad, *Intersystem Issue Preclusion and the Restatement (Second) of Judgments,* 66 Cornell L. Rev. 510, 511 (1981); *Restatement (Second) of Judgments,* 2 (introduction) (1982).

[185] An elaboration of many of the points under this heading appears in Shreve, *Preclusion and Federal Choice of Law,* 64 Tex. L. Rev. 1209 (1986). On the subject generally, see Erichson, *Interjurisdictional Preclusion,* 96 Mich. L. Rev. 945 (1998); Lilly, *The Symmetry of Preclusion,* 54 Ohio St. L. J. 289 (1993); Shreve, *Judgments from a Choice-of-Law Perspective,* 40 Am. J. Comp. L. 985 (1992); Caust-Ellenbogen, *False Conflicts and Interstate Preclusion: Moving Beyond a Wooden Reading of the Full Faith and Credit Statute,* 63 Ford. L. Rev. 593 (1990); Mortland, *Interstate Federalism: Effect of Full Faith and Credit to Judgments,* 16 U. Dayton L. Rev. 47 (1990); Burbank, *Interjurisdictional Preclusion and Federal Common Law: Toward a General Approach,* 70 Cornell L. Rev. 625 (1985); Atwood, *State Court Judgments in Federal Litigation: Mapping the Contours of Full Faith and Credit,* 58 Ind. L. J. 59 (1982); Casad, note 150, *supra;* Degnan, *Federalized Res Judicata,* 85 Yale L.J. 741 (1976).

the judgment or by the intramural law of the system where the judgment is offered for enforcement?

So long as applicable preclusion law is the same in both systems, the question is academic. The law will often but not always be the same. As noted earlier, systems disagree over whether to permit claim-splitting in traffic accident cases[186] and over whether to refuse nonmutual issue preclusion by invoking the mutuality doctrine.[187] Other differences also exist.[188] When rules conflict, the court where the judgment is presented might have an understandable preference for its own intramural preclusion law. However, federal full faith and credit law severely restricts the court's freedom to disregard the preclusion law of the place rendering the judgment.[189] This appears to be true whether the effect sought from the judgment is claim or issue preclusion.[190]

A different problem exists when foreign-country judgments are presented in the United States for enforcement. Federal full faith and credit law does not reach such cases. The policy arguments for giving preclusive effect to foreign-country judgments are not as strong. At the same time, it would be unwise simply to ignore foreign-country judgments. American courts generally recognize such judgments, but the content of governing law is relatively indistinct.[191]

§ 15.10   The Federal Full Faith and Credit Obligation that Judgments be Given as Much Effect as They Would Have Where Rendered

To a large extent, federal full faith and credit law determines the enforceability of judgments rendered by a court in the United States and presented elsewhere in this country for enforcement. Full faith and credit obligations appear in the Full Faith and Credit Clause of the United States Constitution[192] and in the full faith and credit statute.[193] The basic requirement of each is that a judgment must be given as much effect where

---

[186] See § 15.03, supra.

[187] See § 15.08, supra.

[188] For example, compare the federal court view that its judgments are final during appeal with the Utah state view that does not attach finality to its judgments under such circumstances. See § 15.05, supra. And compare the United States Supreme Court's refusal to give issue-preclusive effect to federal default judgments with the opposing view New York has taken concerning the effect of its state judgments. See § 15.07, supra.

[189] See §§ 15.10-15.11, infra.

[190] "Although it has been suggested that issue preclusion may operate with less force than does claim preclusion under [the federal full faith and credit statute] the cases do not support such a distinction." Atwood, note 151, supra, at 69. See Migra v. Warren City School District Board of Education, 465 U.S. 75, 83 (1984), and McDonald v. City of West Branch, 466 U.S. 284, 291 (1984), each equating claim and issue preclusion for purposes of federal court enforcement of state judgments.

[191] See § 15.12, infra.

[192] U.S. Const. art. IV, § 1.

[193] 28 U.S.C. § 1738.

presented for enforcement as it would have had where rendered. The Full Faith and Credit Clause imposes the rule on states presented with sister-state judgments. The full faith and credit statute protects state judgments in state or federal courts and has been read to protect federal judgments in state court.

[1] Preserving the Preclusive Effect of State Judgments in Sister-State Courts

The Full Faith and Credit Clause of the Constitution[194] contains the requirement that "[f]ull faith and credit shall be given in each State to the public acts, records, and judicial proceedings of every other State." Congress passed the full faith and credit statute in 1790.[195] The statute's requirement, that all courts in the United States give "such faith and credit" to state "records and judicial proceedings" as they would have in the courts of that state, dates from 1790.[196] Except in child custody cases,[197] the Full Faith and Credit Clause and statute govern the recognition and enforcement of state judgments in other state courts.

Initially, some lower courts read the Full Faith and Credit Clause and statute to require only that judgments be taken as *prima facie* evidence in subsequent proceedings. This view would have left courts free, at the very least, to apply their own preclusion law to determine the effect of judgments rendered elsewhere. However, the Supreme Court rejected the view in *Mills v. Duryee*.[198] Invoking both Clause and statute, the Court held that the obligation of full faith and credit to a New York state judgment required the application of New York preclusion law.[199] Of the full faith and credit statute, Justice Story wrote, "we can perceive no rational interpretation of the act . . . unless it declares a judgment conclusive when a Court of the particular state where it is rendered would pronounce the same decision."[200]

---

[194] For examination of the Clause, see Pearson, *Common Law Preclusion, Full Faith and Credit, and Consent Judgments: The Analytical Challenge*, 48 Cath. U. L. Rev. 419 (1999); Whitten, *The Constitutional Limitations on State-Court Jurisdiction: A Historical-Interpretive Reexamination of the Full Faith and Credit and Due Process Clauses (Part One)*, 14 Creighton L. Rev. 499 (1981); Nadelmann, *Full Faith and Credit to Judgments and Public Acts*, 56 Mich. L. Rev. 33, 60 (1957); Sumner, *Full Faith and Credit for Judicial Proceedings*, 2 UCLA L. Rev. 441 (1955); Radin, *The Authenticated Full Faith and Credit Clause: Its History*, 39 Ill. L. Rev. 1 (1944).

[195] Act of May 26, 1790 (now codified as 28 U.S.C. § 1738).

[196] Amendments to the Act of 1790, *reviewed in* Brilmayer, *Credit Due Judgments and Credit Due Laws: The Respective Roles of Due Process and Full Faith and Credit in the Interstate Context*, 70 Iowa L. Rev. 95, 95 n.2 (1984), have not altered its basic standard.

[197] *See* note 206, *infra*.

[198] 11 U.S. (7 Cranch) 481 (1813).

[199] "[I]t is beyond all doubt that the judgment of the Supreme Court of New York was conclusive upon the parties in that state. It must, therefore, be conclusive here also." *Id.* at 484.

[200] *Id.* at 485.

When courts simultaneously invoke the Full Faith and Credit Clause and statute, it is often difficult to determine which is carrying the main weight in decisions to follow the preclusion law of the judgment-rendering state. But it may not be terribly important to distinguish between the two in this context. Perhaps it is enough to collapse both — as one writer has — into "the full faith and credit requirement."[201] While the area is not free of uncertainty,[202] the basic obligation of federal full faith and credit is firm. State courts must give as much effect to sister-state judgments as they would have where rendered.[203]

[2] Preserving the Preclusive Effect of State Judgments in Federal Court

Congress has always had a variety of legislative options in determining the manner and extent to which it wishes to regulate inter-system preclusion.

At one extreme, Congress could have codified intersystem preclusion law, elaborating a precise, systematic scheme to regulate the inter-system enforcement of state and federal judgments.[204] Commentators have suggested that the idea is worth considering,[205] but Congress has never really acted upon it. Except in child-custody cases,[206] Congress has not used its power to extensively regulate inter-system preclusion.

At the other extreme, Congress could have done nothing. If the Supreme Court had interpreted the Full Faith and Credit Clause as self-applying,[207]

---

[201] Casad, *Intersystem Issue Preclusion and the Restatement (Second) of Judgments,* 66 Cornell L. Rev. 510, 520 (1981).

[202] For example, the Supreme Court has had difficulty developing an intelligible standard for determining the effect of state worker's compensation decrees. *See Thomas v. Washington Gas Light Co.,* 448 U.S. 261 (1980); *Industrial Comm'n of Wisconsin v. McCartin,* 330 U.S. 622 (1947); *Magnolia Petroleum Co. v. Hunt,* 320 U.S. 430 (1943). For a discussion of these cases, see W. Richman & W. Reynolds, *Understanding Conflict of Laws* § 114[c][3] (2d ed. 1993).

[203] *See, e.g., Underwriters National Assurance Co. v. North Carolina Life & Accident & Health Ins. Guar. Ass'n,* 455 U.S. 691 (1982); *Durfee v. Duke,* 375 U.S. 106 (1963); *Fauntleroy v. Lum,* 210 U.S. 230 (1908). *See generally* Reynolds, *The Iron Laws of Full Faith and Credit,* 53 Md. L. Rev. 412 (1994).

[204] The Full Faith and Credit Clause, U.S. Const. art IV, § 1, expressly authorizes Congress to enact laws elaborating the obligation of states to respect sister-state judgments. Congress' power to impose upon federal courts a duty to recognize state judgments derives from U.S. Const. art. III, § 1. The Commerce Clause (U.S. Const. art. I, § 8) and the Privileges and Immunities Clause (U.S. Const. art. IV, § 2), provide additional support for a broad statutory scheme.

[205] *See, e.g.,* Currie, *Full Faith and Credit, Chiefly to Judgments: A Role for Congress,* 1964 Sup. Ct. Rev. 89.

[206] The Parental Kidnaping Prevention Act of 1980, 28 U.S.C. § 1738A, augments § 1738 with reference to state child custody decrees. Discussions of the Act appear in Atwood, *Child Custody Jurisdiction and Territoriality,* 52 Ohio St. L. J. 369 (1991); Coombs, *Interstate Child Custody: Jurisdiction, Recognition, and Enforcement,* 66 Minn. L. Rev. 711 (1982).

[207] After early uncertainty, the Supreme Court adopted the view that the clause is self-applying. Jackson, *Full Faith and Credit — the Lawyer's Clause of the Constitution,* 45 Colum. L. Rev. 1, 11 (1945); Cheatham, *Res Judicata and the Full Faith and Credit Clause: Magnolia Petroleum Co. v. Hunt,* 44 Colum. L. Rev. 330, 333 (1944).

congressional inaction might not have diminished state court obligations to enforce sister-state judgments. But federal courts are beyond the textual reach of the Full Faith and Credit Clause.[208] They are probably under no constitutional compulsion to recognize the effects of state judgments created under state preclusion law.[209] Congressional silence, then, would have left federal courts free to determine how much effect to give to state judgments.

Congress decided to steer a middle course. Although the legislative history of the full faith and credit statute[210] is uncertain, it seems clear that Congress intended to impose upon federal courts an obligation to recognize and enforce the judgments of states equivalent to the obligation imposed on states by the Constitution's Full Faith and Credit Clause to recognize and enforce sister-state judgments.[211]

This is how the Supreme Court has read the statute.[212] The Court has made clear that, in cases where the statute applies, "Congress has specifically required all federal courts to give preclusive effect to state-court judgments whenever the courts of the State from which the judgments emerged would do so. . . ."[213]

At the same time, important differences flow from the fact that federal courts' obligation to give effect to state judgments is only statutory. Just as Congress did not have to enact the full faith and credit statute, it is free either to repeal it or to lighten its obligations by amending it to create exceptions. Section 1738 itself contains no exceptions to the obligation of federal courts to honor state judgments, but other federal statutes can suspend that obligation.

Congress has sometimes expressly suspended Section 1738.[214] More often, however, the question will be whether suspension not expressly required is nonetheless necessary to effectuate exclusive federal subject-matter jurisdiction. In short, should an exception to the mandate of Section 1738 be implied from congressional grants of exclusive federal jurisdiction? This question has divided commentators[215] and federal courts.[216]

---

[208] Art. IV, § 1 of the U.S. Constitution imposes a full faith and credit obligation only upon sister states. The Supreme Court noted that federal courts were "not included within the constitutional provision." *Kremer v. Chemical Constr. Corp.*, 456 U.S. 461, 483-484 n. 24 (1982).

[209] *See* Shreve, *Preclusion and Federal Choice of Law,* 64 Tex. L. Rev. 1209, 1223 n.77 (1986).

[210] 28 U.S.C. § 1738.

[211] Atwood, note 185, *supra,* at 67; degnan, note 185, *supra,* at 743-744.

[212] *E.g., Davis v. Davis,* 305 U.S. 32, 40 (1939) ("The Act extended the rule of the Constitution to all courts, federal as well as state.").

[213] *Allen v. McCurry,* 449 U.S. 90, 96 (1980).

[214] The most prominent example is the federal *habeas corpus* statute. 28 U.S.C. § 2254. *See* Currie, *Res Judicata: The Neglected Defense,* 45 U. Chi. L. Rev. 317, 330, 333 (1978).

[215] *Compare, e.g.,* Vestal, *Res Judicata/Claim Preclusion: Judgment for the Claimant,* 62 Nw. U. L. Rev. 357, 374-375 (1967), and Note, *The Collateral Estoppel Effect of Prior State Court Findings in Cases Within Exclusive Federal Jurisdiction,* 91 Harv. L. Rev. 1281, 1290-1291 (1978) (arguing for preclusion), *with* Burbank, *Afterwords: A Response to Professor Hazard and a Comment on Marrese,* 70 Cornell L. Rev. 659, 664 (1985), and *Atwood,* note 185, *supra,* at 63 (arguing against preclusion because of the insulating effect of exclusive federal jurisdiction).

Marrese v. American Academy of Orthopaedic Surgeons[217] presented the Supreme Court with the issue whether exclusive federal antitrust jurisdiction operates as an exception to Section 1738. The Court declined to answer the question but did suggest that exclusive federal jurisdiction would not invariably create an implied exception.[218] The Court also offered some guidelines for resolving "the more general question . . . whether the concerns underlying a particular grant of exclusive jurisdiction justify a finding of an implied partial repeal of Section 1738."

> Resolution of this question will depend on the particular federal statute as well as the nature of the claim or issue involved in the subsequent federal action. Our previous decisions indicate that the primary consideration must be the intent of Congress.[219]

[3] Preserving the Preclusive Effect of Federal Judgments in Other Federal Courts

The preclusive effect to be given to a federal judgment by the court that rendered it, or by any other federal court, is an intramural question of federal preclusion law. The Supreme Court's decisions elaborating federal preclusion doctrine[220] will largely determine the effect of such judgments. When differences exist among the federal circuits concerning questions which the Supreme Court has not passed upon, one might expect the law of the federal circuit in which the judgment was rendered to control. However, a statute which authorizes federal court registration of a judgment "for the recovery of money or property" rendered in another federal district court[221] suggests a different result. Section 1963 provides that "judgment so registered shall have the same effect" as if it had been

---

[216] *Compare, e.g., RX Data Corp. v. Dept. of Social Serv.,* 684 F.2d 192 (2d Cir. 1982), and *Lektro-Vend Corp. v. Vendo Co.,* 660 F.2d 255 (7th Cir. 1981), *cert. denied,* 455 U.S. 921 (1982) (state court judgment denied preclusive effect when federal court had exclusive jurisdiction), *with Nash County Bd. of Educ. v. Biltmore Co.,* 640 F.2d 484 (4th Cir. 1981), and *Derish v. San Mateo-Burlingame Bd. of Realtors,* 724 F.2d 1347 (9th Cir. 1983) (state judgment given preclusive effect notwithstanding exclusive jurisdiction).

[217] 470 U.S. 373 (1985).

[218] *Id.* at 380-381.

[219] *Id.* at 386. The Court then cited *Kremer v. Chemical Constr. Corp.,* 456 U.S. 461 (1982), and *Brown v. Felsen,* 442 U.S. 127 (1979). In *Kremer,* the Court left open the possibility that jurisdiction over claims under Title VII of the Civil Rights Act of 1964 was exclusive in federal court, but found no support in Title VII or its legislative history for the conclusion that it implied an exception to Section 1738. But the Supreme Court refused in *Brown* to give preclusive effect to a prior state judgment in a subsequent federal bankruptcy proceeding within the federal court's exclusive jurisdiction. The *Brown* Court curiously made no reference to Section 1738, but did declare: "While Congress did not expressly confront the problem created by prebankruptcy state-court adjudications, it would be inconsistent with the philosophy of the [federal statutes] to adopt a policy of *res judicata* which takes these [federal bankruptcy] questions away from bankruptcy courts and forces them back into state courts." 442 U.S. at 136.

[220] *E.g., Parklane Hosiery Co. v. Shore,* 439 U.S. 322 (1979). *Parklane* is discussed at § 15.08[2][a], *supra.*

[221] 28 U.S.C. § 1963.

rendered where registered, suggesting that the law of the federal circuit where the federal judgment is presented for enforcement will control.

[4] Preserving the Preclusive Effect of Federal Judgments in State Courts

The Full Faith and Credit Clause of the Constitution and the full faith and credit statute both address state judgments. Neither makes provision for federal judgments in state court. At the same time, "[i]t would be unthinkable to suggest that state courts should be free to disregard the judgments of federal courts, given the basic requirements that state courts honor the judgments of courts in other states and that federal courts must honor state court judgments."[222]

In a series of decisions, the Supreme Court therefore filled the gap by reading the full faith and credit statute to require state courts to respect federal judgments.[223] Congress undoubtedly has the authority to enact legislation protecting federal judgments,[224] but this seems quite beyond the language of section 1738. The Court has never come up with an entirely satisfactory rationale for grafting this requirement onto the statute. After surveying the case law in this area, Professor Ronan Degnan observed that his study did

> not . . . show that the Court was willfully wrong in doing what it did, but that it was wantonly right. By strength of arm and sleight of hand, it achieved a result that is indispensable to federalism. . . . Were there no such rule, it would be necessary to invent one — so invent it the Supreme Court did.[225]

The content of the federal preclusion to be applied by subsequent state (or federal) courts depends on the type of federal judgment offered for enforcement or recognition. Federal question judgments have effect under federal preclusion doctrine. *Parklane* would be an example. Recently, however, the Supreme Court ruled that, by federal common law rule, the preclusive effect of federal diversity judgments must be determined by the intramural preclusion law of the state where the federal court rendering the judgment was sitting.[226]

§ 15.11   Are Other Courts Free to Give Judgments More Effect Than They Would Have Where Rendered?

Conflicts of preclusion law among state and federal courts[227] lead to situations in which the local preclusion law of a court where a judgment

---

[222] *Wright & Miller* § 4468.

[223] *E.g., Embry v. Palmer,* 107 U.S. 3, 9-10 (1882); *Stoll v. Gottlieb,* 305 U.S. 165, 170 (1938).

[224] That authority derives, *inter alia,* from Congress' power to create lower federal courts under Art. III, § 1 of the Constitution. *Degnan,* note 211, *supra,* at 749.

[225] *Id.* Reprinted by permission of the Yale Law Journal Company and Fred B. Rothman & Co. from *The Yale Law Journal,* vol. 85, p. 749, copyright © 1976.

[226] *Setek Int'l Inc. v. Lockheed Martin Corp.,* 531 U.S. 497 (2001). See § 7.07 (discussing federal common law creation).

[227] *See* § 15.09,*supra.*

is presented would give greater preclusive effect to it than would the law of the court rendering the judgment. For example, a federal court, which permits nonmutual issue preclusion, may be presented with a judgment rendered in a state court which still adheres to the limitations of the mutuality doctrine.[228] Under such circumstances, may the federal court disregard the preclusion law of the rendering forum and apply federal doctrine to give issue-preclusive effect to the judgment? Recent Supreme Court decisions suggest not. Whether sister-state courts can augment the preclusive effect of state judgments seems a more open question.

[1] May Federal Courts Give Greater Effect to State Judgments?

There is considerable support for the proposition that the full faith and credit statute[229] prevents federal courts from giving any more preclusive effect to state judgments than they would have under the law of the rendering state. In *Marrese v. American Academy of Orthopaedic Surgeons,*[230] the Supreme Court stated that Section 1738

> directs a federal court to refer to the preclusion law of the State in which judgment was rendered. "It has long been established that § 1738 does not allow federal courts to employ their own rules of *res judicata* in determining the effect of state judgments. Rather, it goes beyond the common law and commands a federal court to accept the rules chosen by the State from which the judgment was taken."[231]

Later in the opinion, the Court read an earlier case[232] to reject "the view that Section 1738 allows a federal court to give a state court judgment greater preclusive effect than the state courts themselves would give to it."[233] The Supreme Court's decisions have not been entirely consistent.[234] However, in *Marrese* and in one decision since[235] the Court seems

---

[228] For a discussion of these conflicting positions, see § 15.08[2], *supra.*

[229] 28 U.S.C. § 1738.

[230] 470 U.S. 373 (1985).

[231] *Id.* at 380, *quoting Kremer v. Chemical Constr. Corp.,* 456 U.S. 461, 481-482 (1982).

[232] *Migra v. Warren City School Dist. Bd of Educ.,* 465 U.S. 75 (1984).

[233] 470 U.S. at 384.

[234] In *Haring v. Prosise,* 462 U.S. 306 (1983), the Court refused to invoke federal doctrine to give greater preclusive effect to a Virginia judgment, but it discussed the possibility at length. *Id.* at 317-323. *Haring* seemed to make clear that, in a deserving case, a federal court could give greater preclusive effect to a state judgment than the state rendering it would. In other cases, the Supreme Court has treated the effect of state judgments in federal court as a matter of federal rather than state law. *Brown v. Felsen,* 442 U.S. 127 (1979); *Montana v. United States,* 440 U.S. 147 (1979). In one case, the Court invoked federal doctrine to permit relitigation in apparent disregard of Section 1738's requirement that a state judgment be given as much preclusive effect in federal court. *England v. Louisiana State Bd. of Medical Examiners,* 375 U.S. 411 (1964). The Court did not criticize any of these prior cases in its later *Marrese* decision.

[235] *Matsushita Elec. Co. v. Epstein,* 516 U.S. 365, 373 (1996); *Parsons Steel, Inc. v. First Ala. Bank,* 474 U.S. 518, 523-525 (1986).

determined that federal courts give state judgments no greater preclusive effect than they would have in the state courts where they originated.[236]

[2] May State Courts Give Greater Effect to Sister-State Judgments?

It is clear that the federal full faith and credit statute applies to sister-state as well as federal courts.[237] There is little to suggest that the added application of the Constitution's Full Faith and Credit Clause to state courts[238] increases their obligation to respect sister-state judgments. If anything, Section 1738 imposes a more stringent obligation than does the Full Faith and Credit Clause.[239] So the legal obligation should be the same for state and federal enforcement courts.

At the same time, the Supreme Court has confined its strongest statements about the deference due to the preclusion law of the rendering states to cases where their judgments were presented in federal court.[240] A few state courts have flatly refused to honor the confines of the preclusion doctrine of the state where the judgment was rendered.[241] Whether or how the Supreme Court will check the impulse of state courts to give greater preclusive effect to sister-state judgments remains to be seen.

[3] Why the Greater-Preclusion Issue Will Rarely Arise Concerning Federal Judgments

Federal doctrine is in the vanguard of the movement to give judgments greater preclusive effect. This is evident from the Supreme Court's rejection of the mutuality doctrine,[242] and from numerous lower federal court

---

[236] For criticism of this position and for the argument that federal courts should give nonmutual, issue-preclusive effect to judgments rendered by states adhering to the mutuality doctrine, see Shreve, *Preclusion and Federal Choice of Law*, 64 Tex. L. Rev. 1209, 1251-1259 (1986).

[237] *Restatement (Second) of Judgments* § 86 comment c (1982). *See, e.g., Underwriter's Nat'l Assurance Co. v. North Carolina Life & Accident & Health Ins. Guaranty Ass'n*, 455 U.S. 691, 694 (1982).

[238] *See* § 15.10, *supra.*

[239] *Cf. Thomas v. Washington Gas Light Co.*, 448 U.S. 261, 270 (1980) (where the plurality opinion observes that the essential obligation to give the same effect to sister-state judgments as they would have where rendered, "[if] not compelled by the Full Faith and Credit Clause itself, is surely required by 28 U.S.C. § 1738.") (citation omitted).

[240] *See* notes 231-233, 235 and related text, *supra.*

[241] *Finley v. Kesling*, 433 N.E.2d 1112, 1116-1118 (Ill. App. Ct. 1982) (refusing to honor a mutuality limitation under Indiana law); *Hart v. American Airlines, Inc.*, 304 N.Y.S.2d 810 (N.Y. Sup. Ct. 1969) (refusing to honor a mutuality limitation under Texas law). *But see Columbia Casualty Co. v. Playtex, Inc.*, 584 A.2d 1214, 1218 (Del. 1991) (honoring a mutuality limitation under Kansas law). The *Columbia Casualty* court observed that, if Delaware courts were to give "the judgments of a sister state greater preclusive effect than they would have in the rendering jurisdiction," the result would be "at variance with the purpose and spirit of the full faith and credit clause." For further discussion of recent case developments, see Shreve, *Judgments from a Choice-of-Law Perspective*, 40 Am. J. Comp. L. 985 (1992).

[242] *See* § 15.08[2][a], *supra.*

decisions giving a broad definition to the "claim" precluded by the federal doctrine of claim preclusion.[243] Therefore, it will be rare for a state court to find the preclusive effect of a federal judgment to be greater under its law than it would be in federal court.

§ 15.12   The Special Problem of Foreign-Country Judgments in State and Federal Courts

State and federal courts in the United States take a more receptive view of judgments rendered abroad than the courts of most other nations.[244] It has been suggested that "[m]ost states accord foreign-country judgments essentially the same status as sister-state judgments."[245] This receptiveness is in part a reflection of a strong tradition of inter-system preclusion within the United States.[246] But it is important to note that the compulsion behind judgment recognition in the latter context is missing when American courts are presented with foreign country judgments.

Neither the Full Faith and Credit Clause of the United States Constitution[247] nor the full faith and credit statute[248] apply to judgments rendered in foreign countries.[249] This is due in part to the limited textual reach of these provisions and in part to the interlocking character that the judgment-rendering and enforcing forums have when both are courts in the United States. That character is lacking in the international setting. Cautioning against treating foreign country judgments under domestic *res judicata* principles, Professors von Mehren and Trautman have noted some fundamental differences between American and foreign courts:

> [O]ne of the purposes of *res judicata* is to maintain the integrity of the domestic judicial system. The case of recognition of internationally foreign judgments is quite different because it may be proper for different legal systems to come to different results on the same set of facts. [And] there are basic differences in the surrounding circumstances. The economic and cultural relationships within a single jurisdiction tend to be closer, and as a result the practical arguments supporting conclusive

---

[243] *See* § 15.03, *supra.*

[244] Von Mehren & Trautman, *Recognition of Foreign Adjudications: A Survey and a Suggested Approach,* 81 Harv. L. Rev. 1601, 1602-1603 (1969). For commentary and legal materials on the United States enforcement of foreign judgments generally, see Silberman & Lowenfeld, *A Different Challenge for the ALI: Herein of Foreign Country Judgments, an International Treaty and an American Statute,* 75 Ind. L.J. 634 (2000); Note, *Universal Justice: The Role of Federal Courts in International Civil Litigation,* 95 Colum. L. Rev. 2120 (1995); Lutz, *Enforcement of Foreign Judgments, Part I: A Selected Bibliography on United States Enforcement of Judgments Rendered Abroad,* 27 Int'l Lawyer 471 (1993).

[245] E. Scoles & P. Hay, *Conflict of Laws* § 24.6 (2nd ed. 1992).

[246] *See* § 15.10, *supra.*

[247] U.S. Const. art. IV, § 1.

[248] 28 U.S.C. § 1738.

[249] Smit, *International Res Judicata and Collateral Estoppel in the United States,* 9 UCLA L. Rev. 44 (1962); W. Richman & W. Reynolds, *Understanding Conflict of Laws* § 109 (2d ed. 1993).

effects for domestic judgments are stronger. At the same time, shared traditions and experience and the identity of procedures and standards help reduce doubt about the quality of justice represented by a judgment. For these reasons, treating recognition problems as an aspect of *res judicata* tends to lead to a confusion of concepts which should be kept separate.[250]

By the same token, important interests may be served when American courts recognize foreign-country judgments. "[I]f in our highly complex and interrelated world each community exhausted every possibility of insisting on its parochial interests, injustice would result and the normal patterns of life would be disrupted."[251]

Perhaps the "shared tradition" in American courts which may most clearly set their adjudications apart from foreign-country adjudications is that all proceedings must be in accordance with the constitutional requirements of due process.[252] It is therefore not surprising that judgments of common-law countries having a due process tradition close to our own are most open to recognition in American courts. For example, in the well-known case, *Somportex Ltd. v. Philadelphia Chewing Gum Corp.* ,[253] the Third Circuit gave effect to an English default judgment.

The *Somportex* court invoked the principle of *comity,* perhaps the most durable of the doctrines addressing the recognition and enforcement of foreign-country judgments.[254] It described comity as

> not a rule of law, but one of practice, convenience, and expediency. Although more than mere courtesy and accommodation, comity does not achieve the force of an imperative or obligation. Rather, it is a nation's expression of understanding which demonstrates due regard both to international duty and convenience and to the rights of persons protected

---

[250] *Von Mehren & Trautman,* note 244, *supra* at 1605-06. Copyright © 1969 by the Harvard Law Review Association. Reprinted with permission.

[251] *Id.* at 1603. The authors suggest that, "at least when judgments emanate from legal systems with well-established legal institutions and traditions," more precise policies supporting recognition of foreign country judgments could be articulated. Their list includes:

a desire to avoid the duplication of effort and consequent waste involved in reconsidering a matter that has already been litigated; a related concern to protect the successful litigant, whether plaintiff or defendant, from harassing or evasive tactics on the part of his previously unsuccessful opponent; a policy against making the availability of local enforcement the decisive element, as a practical matter, in the plaintiff's choice of forum; an interest in fostering stability and unity in an international order in which many aspects of life are not confined to any single jurisdiction.

Id. at 1603-04. Copyright © 1969 by the Harvard Law Review Association. Reprinted with permission.

[252] For discussion of the effect of due process on personal jurisdiction, notice and *res judicata*, see § 15.02, *supra.*

[253] 453 F.2d 435 (3d Cir. 1971), *cert. denied,* 405 U.S. 1017 (1972). The Court relied in part on *Hilton v. Guyot,* 159 U.S. 113 (1895).

[254] The doctrine of reciprocity, which limits the effect of judgments of countries to the effect United States judgments would have in their courts, has played a more limited and controversial role in this area. For a discussion of comity, reciprocity and other doctrines, see *Smit,* note 249, *supra,* at 48-56.

by its own laws. Comity should be withheld only when its acceptance would be contrary or prejudicial to the interest of the nation called upon to give it effect.[255]

Neither Congress nor the executive has acted to create anything approaching comprehensive law governing the recognition of international judgments. Nor has the Supreme Court refined many standards through the development of federal common law.[256] Despite the efforts of individual states,[257] the law remains fragmented.[258] This condition is special cause for concern, because it can affect how courts abroad enforce judgments from United States courts.[259]

PART D
Beyond Preclusion: Additional Doctrines of Repose

Courts employ doctrines in addition to preclusion to reduce frustration and uncertainty generated by recurrent litigation. None of these focus as much as preclusion on the integrity of prior judgments, but they are sufficiently analogous and complementary to preclusion to merit discussion.

§ 15.13 *Stare Decisis*

[1] The Nature of the Doctrine

When a legal issue arises for the first time, trial and appellate courts have the latitude to choose from among competing rules of law, declaring and applying the one which seems the best. *Stare decisis* denies courts the same flexibility when the legal issue recurs in subsequent cases, binding them instead to the approach of the prior case (precedent). The doctrine has been described by one commentator as fostering a "blind imitation of the past."[260] In stifling a continuing search for the best legal answers, *stare decisis* bears a considerable burden of justification. It is justified by the fact

---

[255] 453 F.2d. at 440.

[256] For discussions of federal common law applicable to the recognition of foreign-country judgments, see Brand, *Enforcement of Foreign Money-Judgments in the United States: In Search of Uniformity and International Acceptance*, 67 Notre Dame L. Rev. 253 (1991); Comment, *Judgments Rendered Abroad—State Law or Federal Law?*, 12 Vill. L. Rev. 618 (1967).

[257] On the experience of states that have adopted uniform judgment-recognition acts, and on guidelines for state court decisions provided by *The Restatement (Third) of Foreign Relations Law, see* Brand, note 256, *supra*, at 265-280.

[258] G. Born & G. Westin, *International Civil Litigation in United States Courts* 564 (3d ed. 1996) ("There is presently no uniform national standard governing the enforcement of judgments rendered by foreign courts in the United States.").

[259] *Scoles & Hay*, note 245, *supra*. On the fate of United States judgments abroad, *see Brand*, note 256, *supra*, at 281-83; Hay, *The Recognition and Enforcement of American Money-Judgments in Germany — The 1992 Decision of the German Supreme Court*, 40 Am. J. Comp. L. 729 (1992).

[260] Holmes, *The Path of the Law*, 10 Harv. L. Rev. 457, 469 (1897).

that our judicial process could not cope with the strains which would be caused if legal re-examination was routinely available.

> [R]outine reconsideration of the correctness or propriety of binding precedents would be enormously destructive. Any one at any time can initiate litigation, and if any litigant on the wrong side of the law could force a full dress reconsideration of settled points simply by filing a complaint, it would not only weaken public reliance on the law, but would require judges to hear endless reargument of the same issues.[261]

Stare decisis thus shares the general aim of preclusion to minimize the assorted costs of relitigation.[262] In particular, *stare decisis* bears a functional resemblance to the preclusion of issues of law.[263] However, *stare decisis* differs from preclusion in that it "relates to the orderly development of law. It does not relate to the finality of judgments."[264] This makes *stare decisis* both broader and narrower in scope than preclusion.

The rule protecting a stranger to the prior adjudication from the effects of preclusion[265] has no counterpart in the doctrine of *stare decisis.* On the contrary, the very purpose of *stare decisis* is to settle future legal controversies. The only way one who expects to be a party in future litigation can avert the possible effects of *stare decisis* is to try to influence the legal decision in the initial case through intervention[266] or *amicus curiae* participation.

On the other hand, the effects of *stare decisis* are often less definite than those of preclusion. There are several reasons for this.

[2] The Scope of *Stare Decisis*

[a] Boundaries Set by Legal Analysis

First, the *stare decisis* effect of a case must derive from a well-articulated statement of law that was necessary to explain the decision there. It may be possible to avoid *stare decisis* either by arguing that the court has not

---

[261] 1B J. Moore, *Moore's Federal Practice* ¶ 0.402[3.-1] (2d ed.). *Accord,* B. Cardozo, *The Nature of the Judicial Process* 149 (1921):

> [T]he labor of judges would be increased almost to the breaking point if every past decision could be reopened in every case, and one could not lay one's own course of bricks on the secure foundation of the courses laid by others who had gone before him.

[262] *See* § 15.01[1] (preclusion policies), *supra.*

[263] *See* § 15.07, *supra.*

[264] 1B J. Moore, *Moore's Federal Practice* ¶ 0.402[2] (2d ed.).

[265] Discussed in § 15.08[1], *supra.*

[266] Some courts have recognized possible prejudice from *stare decisis* as a basis for intervention of right. *See, e.g., Natural Resources Defense Council, Inc. v. United States Nuclear Regulatory Comm'n,* 578 F.2d 1341 (10th Cir. 1978), and the cases cited in Shreve, *Questioning Intervention of Right — Toward a New Methodology of Decisionmaking,* 74 Nw. U. L. Rev. 894, 906 (1980); Note, *Federal Civil Procedure: Prejudicial Effects of Stare Decisis Can Compel Intervention of Right Under Rule 24(a),* 1967 Duke L.J. 1251. On intervention generally, see § 9.08, *supra.*

yet clearly formed a principle and the law is still in a state of flux,[267] or that the principle offered for *stare decisis* effect is not a rule necessary to explain the decision, but is instead only a rule mentioned in passing (*dictum*).

Second, it may be possible to avoid a rule entitled to *stare decisis* effect by challenging the applicability of the rule to the facts of the succeeding case. "[T]he scope of a rule of law, and therefore its meaning, depends upon a determination of what facts will be considered similar to those present when the rule was first announced."[268]

The process of determining whether the facts of two cases are sufficiently similar (apposite) that the first serves as precedent for the second, or sufficiently dissimilar that the first is factually distinguishable and hence without binding effect, is at the heart of legal analysis. One must try to determine what policies supported the rule of the first case and the extent to which those policies are implicated in the facts of the second. Factual differences may take the succeeding case out of the sweep of the prior rule. At the same time, cases are rarely if ever entirely identical. One must be alert to the possibility of extending the prior rule of decision to cover new facts.[269]

[b] Boundaries Set by Judicial Structure

Some courts have little choice but to follow apposite precedent. Others are entirely free to disregard it. Still others reserve the authority occasionally to disregard it. These classifications depend on judicial structure, the institutional relationship between the court making the prior decision and the court considering it as precedent.

Precedent is most coercive on the hierarchial inferiors of the court that decided the prior case. Hierarchy is determined by the tiers in a court system's structure. The federal court system and many state systems consist of a trial tier, an intermediate appellate tier and the highest appellate court.[270] In state systems, the last tier is often (but not always) called the state's *supreme* court.[271] In theory at least, the authority of apposite decisions of hierarchial superiors — sometimes called *controlling* precedent — is nearly absolute.[272] The final authority on the meaning of state law

---

[267] *Cf.* P. Atiyah & R. Summers, *Form and Substance in Anglo-American Law* 120 (1987) ("Whenever the substantive reasoning in a case seems at all dubious, the case must go through a period of evaluative trial before it can be regarded as settled and therefore valid law.").

[268] E. Levi, *An Introduction to Legal Reasoning* 2 (1948).

[269] "Not only do new situations arise, but in addition peoples' wants change. The categories used in the legal process must be left ambiguous in order to permit the infusion of new ideas." *Id.* at 3.

[270] *See* § 13.06 (appellate systems), *supra.*

[271] *See generally id.* and § 2.01 (state and federal judicial systems), *supra.*

[272] The principle is widely but not universally honored. Atiyah & Summers suggest that, while lower courts entirely lack the authority to overrule precedents of their hierarchial superiors, note 267, *supra,* at 123, they will sometimes ignore them, "even though the American theory of precedent does not fully acknowledge the practice in so many words." *Id.* at 120.

is the highest court of that state.[273] Similarly, the United States Supreme Court is the final arbiter of the meaning of federal law. When federal and state courts decide federal law issues, they are treated as one expanded court system. The Supreme Court's federal law decisions bind federal and state courts alike as controlling precedent.

At the other extreme, precedent may be no more than *persuasive*. This occurs when a decision from one judicial system is offered as precedent in another. Courts may follow such precedent if they agree with it, but they are under no compulsion to do so.[274] Thus a New York state court may reject a rule of decision in a factually indistinguishable New Hampshire case. One federal circuit court may similarly reject the precedent of another federal circuit. State courts may even reject the decisions of lower federal courts concerning the meaning of federal law.[275]

The precedential effect that the decision has on the same court that rendered it falls somewhere between controlling and persuasive precedent. Courts do not control themselves by their cases in the way they control their hierarchial underlings. American courts borrowed their essential conception of *stare decisis* from England but are less reluctant than English jurists to overrule their own decisions.[276] On the other hand, courts cannot regard their own decisions as lightly as would the courts of other systems. If courts do not give their decisions considerably more weight than persuasive precedent, they will be afflicted with the problems that *stare decisis* was intended to avoid.[277]

The resulting rule is that courts usually, but not invariably, follow their own precedents. When courts do discard their precedents, they are said to *overrule* them. The time at which precedent will fall is often difficult to predict and the process frequently controversial.[278] It is possible, however, to identify some of the circumstances in which it is most likely that a court will overrule its own prior decision:

1. If it is seriously out of keeping with contemporary views of what is right and just;

2. if it has been passed by in the development of the law and no longer fits the general principles that govern like cases and overruling it will not require costly or disruptive readjustment of relationships created in reliance upon it; or

---

[273] Discussed in § 7.06[1], *supra.*

[274] Under a narrower view of *stare decisis,* the influence of persuasive precedent is so slight as to be outside the doctrine. *Atiyah & Summers,* note 267, *supra,* at 115.

[275] *See* Shapiro, *State Courts and Federal Declaratory Judgments,* 74 Nw. U. L. Rev. 759 (1979).

[276] *Atiyah & Summers,* note 267, *supra,* at 123-124.

[277] *See* note 261 and related text, *supra.*

[278] *See, e.g.,* Chief Justice Bell's vigorous dissent to the Pennsylvania Supreme Court's overruling of its decisions limiting recovery for negligently inflicted emotional distress. *Niederman v. Brodsky,* 261 A.2d 84, 90 (Pa. 1970).

3. if the rule has proved to be unworkable or inconvenient in practice and the court is convinced that a different rule will be substantially better, taking into consideration the dislocation a change may produce.[279]

Courts generally will give greater *stare decisis* effect to their settled interpretations of statutes than to either their constitutional decisions or common law precedents. This view is not universally accepted,[280] but it is defensible. A legislature is presumed to acquiesce in the judicial interpretations of its statutes when it does not overrule them by statutory repeal or amendment. This can be seen as a kind of retrospective legislative intent. Moreover, if courts were more willing to reinterpret statutes, this might sap the legislature's initiative to review and periodically revise statutory law. Therefore, "once a decisive interpretation of legislative intent has been made . . . the court should take that direction as given."[281]

§ 15.14 Law of the Case

The law-of-the-case doctrine prevents relitigation of issues of law in the same case.[282] It shares with preclusion the purpose of making litigation more efficient. Unlike preclusion, it operates in advance of final judgment. Since courts have some discretion to depart from the law-of-the-case doctrine, it is similar in operation to *stare decisis*.[283] However, the long range purpose of the law-of-the-case doctrine is more modest than that of *stare decisis*, since the former settles law only for the case at hand.

The doctrine is important to judicial administration. At trial,

the doctrine of the law of the case is little more than a management practice to permit logical progression toward judgment. Prejudgment orders remain interlocutory and can be reconsidered at any time, but efficient disposition of the case demands that each stage of the litigation build on the last, and not afford an opportunity to reargue every previous ruling.[284]

For the trial judge, the law-of-the-case doctrine is one of self-restraint. It offers no protection to the trial court's legal decisions when they are reviewed by an appellate court. But the converse is not true. This is because the law-of-the-case doctrine gives controlling effect to an appellate court ruling if the case is remanded to an inferior court for further proceedings. The doctrine also imposes self-restraint on the appellate court if the case returns by a further appeal.[285]

---

[279] 1B J. Moore, *Moore's Federal Practice* ¶ 0.402[3.-1] (2d ed.).

[280] *See, e.g.,* criticism of the idea in *Cardozo,* note 261, *supra,* at 148.

[281] *Levi,* note 268, *supra,* at 32. Correspondingly, since Congress cannot overturn the Supreme Court's constitutional decisions, these are entitled to the least *stare decisis* effect. *Agostini v. Felton,* 521 U.S. 203, 235-236 (1997).

[282] *See* Steinman, *Law of the Case: A Judicial Puzzle in Consolidated and Transferred Cases in and Multidistrict Litigation,* 135 U. Pa. L. Rev. 595, 597-613 (1987); Parks, *"The Law of the Case" Doctrine in Arkansas,* 50 Ark. L. Rev. 127 (1997).

[283] Discussed in § 15.13, *supra.*

[284] 1B J. Moore, *Moore's Federal Practice* ¶ 0.404[1] (2d ed.).

[285] *Id.*

As with *stare decisis,* the law-of-the-case doctrine permits some flexibility for courts to reconsider their own prior rulings. One court has suggested that reconsideration would be warranted if "the evidence on a subsequent trial was substantially different, controlling authority has since made a contrary decision of the law applicable to such issues, or the decision was clearly erroneous and would work a manifest injustice."[286] In addition, a court is more likely to reconsider one of its legal rulings if it made the ruling when considering a motion for a temporary restraining order or under other hurried circumstances. Similarly, "[e]arly pretrial rulings . . . may often be subject to reconsideration as a case progresses toward trial."[287]

§ 15.15   Inconsistent Factual Positions — Judicial Estoppel

Some courts have refused to permit a litigant to take inconsistent positions in successive lawsuits. Doctrine supporting this is sometimes called *judicial estoppel.*[288] While federal courts and virtually all state courts permit litigants to take inconsistent positions in their pleadings,

> courts do not relish the prospect that an adept litigant may succeed in proving a proposition in one suit, and then succeed in proving the opposite in a second. At worst, successful assertion of inconsistent positions may impose multiple liability on an adversary or defeat a legitimate right of recovery. At best, the judicial system is left exposed to an explicit demonstration of the frailties that remain in adversary litigation and adjudication.[289]

Scarano v. Central Railroad Company[290] is a well-known example. In the first case, plaintiff obtained a substantial damage recovery against his employer for disability resulting from a job-related injury. In the second case against his employer, this time for reinstatement, plaintiff reversed his factual position and sought to prove he was fit for work. The court found the record in the first case insufficiently clear to support collateral estoppel

---

[286] *White v. Murtha,* 377 F.2d 428, 432 (5th Cir. 1967).

[287] *Wright & Miller* § 4478. "Law of the case principles are therefore best understood as rules of sensible and sound practice that permit logical progression toward judgment, but that do not disable a court from altering prior interlocutory decisions in a case." *Steinman,* note 282, *supra,* at 599.

[288] "Judicial estoppel presently appears under a variety of names, especially in state courts. It is frequently called the doctrine of preclusion against inconsistent positions. . . . Less frequently, courts refer to the doctrine as estoppel by oath." Note, *Judicial Estoppel: The Refurbishing of a Judicial Shield,* 55 Geo. Wash. L. Rev. 409, 410 n.8 (1987). *See generally* Moberly, *If at First You Do Succeed: Judicial Estoppel in New Mexico's State and Federal Courts,* 29 N.M. L. Rev. 201 (1999); O'Brien, *To Tell the Truth: Should Judicial Estoppel Preclude Americans with Disabilities Act Complaints?* 73 St. John's L. Rev. 349 (1999); Note, *Judicial Estoppel — Beating Shields into Swords and Back Again,* 139 U. Pa. L. Rev. 1711 (1991); Baron & Martin, *The Application of Judicial Estoppel in Texas,* 41 Baylor L. Rev. 447 (1989); Comment, *Precluding Inconsistent Statements: The Doctrine of Judicial Estoppel,* 80 Nw. U. L. Rev. 1244 (1986).

[289] *Wright & Miller* § 4477.

[290] 203 F.2d 510 (3d Cir. 1953).

(issue preclusion),[291] but nonetheless refused plaintiff an opportunity to prove a lack of disability in the second case. The court said: "Such use of inconsistent positions would most flagrantly exemplify that playing fast and loose with the courts which has been emphasized as an evil the courts should not tolerate."[292] The court went on to say that plaintiff's maneuver "is more than [an] affront to judicial dignity. For intentional self-contradiction is being used as a means of obtaining unfair advantage in a forum provided for suitors seeking justice."[293]

The boundaries of judicial estoppel are difficult to chart. Litigants should be free to change factual positions in succeeding cases when new evidence has come to light or in other circumstances which suggest good reasons for a change of position and no injustice to the opposing party. As the *Scarano* court noted, "each case must be decided upon its own particular facts and circumstances."[294] Perhaps the most that can be said is that courts have the power to refuse adjudication under the inconsistent position doctrine and may use that power in a sufficiently compelling case.

---

[291] Discussed in § 15.07 (requirements for issue preclusion), *supra*. It usually is and should be a requirement for judicial estoppel that the declarant appears to have profited from the first factual position. That is, the court must have relied upon (or ruled consistantly with) the declarant's position in the first case. *Id. Cf. Pegram v. Herdrich*, 530 U.S. 211, 228 n.8 (2000) ("Judicial estoppel generally prevents a party from prevailing in one phase of a case on an argument and then relying on a contradictory argument to prevail in another phase.").

[292] 203 F.2d at 513.

[293] *Id.*

[294] *Id.*, quoting *Galt v. Phoenix Indemnity Co.*, 120 F.2d 723, 726 (D.C. Cir. 1941).

TABLE OF CASES

[References are to sections]

[References are to sections]

[References are to sections]

[References are to sections]

[References are to sections]

[References are to sections]

[References are to sections]

E

[References are to sections]

[References are to sections]

[References are to sections]

H

[References are to sections]

[References are to sections]

[References are to sections]

K

[References are to sections]

[References are to sections]

M

[References are to sections]

TABLE OF CASES

[References are to sections]

N

[References are to sections]

[References are to sections]

Q

R

S

[References are to sections]

[References are to sections]

[References are to sections]

T

[References are to sections]

[References are to sections]

U

V

W

[References are to sections]

[References are to sections]

TABLE OF AUTHORITIES

[References are to sections]

A

[References are to sections]

[References are to sections]

Baughman, *Federal Cross-Appeals—A Guide and a Proposal,* 42 Ohio St. L.J. 505 (1981), 13.08[2] n24

Bauman, *Evolution of the Summary Judgment Procedure,* 31 Ind. L.J. 329 (1956), 11.03[1] n19

Becker, *Conducting Informal Discovery of a Party's Former Employees: Legal and Ethical Concerns and Constraints,* 51 Md. L. Rev. 239 (1992), 10.01 n3

Beckerman, *Confronting Civil Discovery's Fatal Flaws,* 84 Minn. L. Rev. 505, 510-511, 521, 541 (2000), 10.03[1] nn29, 32; 10.12 nn245, 255

Beiner, *The Misuse of Summary Judgment in Hostile Environment Cases,* 34 Wake Forest L. Rev. 71 (1999), 11.03[3][d] n132

Bell, et al., *Automatic Disclosure in Discovery—the Rush to Reform,* 27 Ga. L. Rev. 1, 39, 40, 43-45, 46 n.175 (1992), 10.07[2] n146; 10.07[2][a] n150; 10.07[2][c] nn155, 159, 160

Belton, *Burdens of Pleading and Proof in Discrimination Cases: Toward a Theory of Procedural Justice,* 34 Vand. L. Rev. 254, 254 n.7, 256, 1205 (1981), 12.04[2] nn130 -132

Bender's Forms of Discovery (Matthew Bender), 1.04 n65

Berch, *A Proposal to Permit Collateral Estoppel of Nonparties Seeking Affirmative Relief,* 1979 Ariz. St. L.J. 511 (1979), 15.08[1] n152

Berger, *The Mandamus Power of the United States Courts of Appeals: A Complex and Confused Means of Appellate Control,* 31 Buffalo L. Rev. 37, 86-87 (1982), 13.03[3] n38

Bergman, *Putting Precedent in Its Place: Stare Decisis and Federal Predictions of State Law,* 96 Colum. L. Rev. 969 (1996), 7.06[2] n141

Berry, *Ending Substance's Indenture to Procedure: The Imperative for Comprehensive Revision of the Class Damage Action,* 80 Colum. L. Rev. 299 (1980), 9.09[1][b] n226

Betten, *Instututional Reform in the Federal Courts,* 52 Ind. L.J. 63, 68 (1976), 2.01 n15

Bies, *Conditioning Forum Non Conveniens,* 67 U. Chi. L. Rev. 489 (2000), 6.02[1] n56

Black, *A New Look at Preliminary Injunctions,* 36 Ala. L. Rev. 1 (1984), 13.03[1] n3

Blaze, *Presumed Frivolous: Application of Stringent Pleading Requirements in Civil Rights Litigation,* 31 Wm. & Mary L. Rev. 935 (1990), 8.04[1] n66

Bledsoe, *Jury or Non-Jury Trial—A Defense Viewpoint,* 5 Am. Jur. Trials 123, 133, 135, 137, 141-142 (1966), 12.06 nn160, 162-165

Blume, *A Rational Theory for Joinder of Causes of Action and Defences, and for the Use of Counterclaims,* 26 Mich. L. Rev. 1 (1927), 9.02 n14

Bone, *Mapping the Boundaries of a Dispute: Conceptions of Ideal Lawsuit Structure From the Field Code to the Federal Rules,* 89 Colum. L. Rev. 1 (1989), 3.05[2] n12; 7.04[1] n61

Bone, *Rethinking the "Day in Court" Ideal and Nonparty Preclusion,* 67 N.Y.U. L. Rev. 193 (1992), 15.03[4][b] n79

Borchers, *Jurisdictional Pragmatism: International Shoe's Half-Buried Legacy,* 28 U. Cal. Davis L. Rev. 561 (1995), 3.05[1] n2

Borchers, *Pennoyer's Limited Legacy: A Reply to Professor Oakley,* 29 U. Cal. Davis L. Rev. 115 (1995), 3.05[1] n2

Borchers, *The Death of the Constitutional Law of Personal Jurisdiction: From Pennoyer to Burnham and Back Again,* 24 U.C. Davis L. Rev. 19 (1990), 3.08[3][b] n42

Borchers, *The Origins of Diversity Jurisdiction, The Rise of Legal Positivism, and a Brave New World for Erie and Klaxon,* 72 Tex. L. Rev. 79 (1993), 7.02[3] n20

Born & Westin, *International Civil Litigation in the United States* 137, 564, 655-669 (1989), 4.03[3] nn59, 62; 15.12 n258

Bourne, *The Demise of Foreign Attachment,* 21 Creighton L. Rev. 141, 151 n.84 (1987), 3.02[2] n9

Bowen, "Progress in the Administration of Justice During the Victorian Period," in 1 *Select Essays in Anglo-American Legal History* 516, 527 (E. Freund, et al. eds. 1907), 8.02[2] n27

Bradley, *The Uncertainty Principle in the Supreme Court,* 1986 Duke L.J. 1, 13.01 n3

Brand, *Enforcement of Foreign Money-Judgments in the United States: In Search of Uniformity and International Acceptance,* 67 Notre Dame L. Rev. 253 (1991), 15.12 n256

Bratton, *Pendent Jurisdiction in Diversity Cases—Some Doubts,* 11 San Diego L. Rev. 296, 322-323 (1974), 5.09[2] n25

Brazil, *Civil Discovery: How Bad Are the Problems?,* 67 A.B.A.J. 450-452, 456 (1981), 10.12 nn245, 249, 250; 10.14[2] n312

[References are to sections]

[References are to sections]

Burbank, *The Rules Enabling Act of 1934*, 130 U. Pa. L. Rev. 1015, 1110, 1122-1123 (1982), 1.02 n41; 7.04[2] n73; 7.04[3][b] n101

Burbank, *The Transformation of American Civil Procedure: The Example of Rule 11*, 137 U. Pa. L. Rev. 1925, 1933-1934 (1989), 8.05[2][c] n156

Burbank, *The United States' Approach to International Civil Litigation: Recent Developments in Forum Selection*, 19 U. Pa. J. Int'l Econ. L. 1, 5-8, 4.03[3] n65

Burk, *Federalism in Cyberspace*, 28 Conn. L. Rv. 1095 (1996), 3.12[3] n43

Burnett, *Practical, Innovative and Progressive Utilization of United States Magistrates to Improve the Administration of Justice in United States District Courts*, 28 How. L.J. 293 (1985), 12.03[1] n51

C

Cantor, *Internet Service of Process: A Constitutionally Adequate Alternative?* 66 U. Chi. L. Rev. 943 (1999), 4.01 n15; 4.03[2] n46

Cardozo, *The Nature of the Judicial Process*, 148-149 (1921), 15.13[1] n261; 15.13[2][b] n280

Cardozo, *The Reach of the Legislature and the Grasp of Jurisdiction*, 43 Cornell L.Q. 210 (195 /), 3.07[3] n41

Caron, *The Role of State Court Decisions in Federal Tax Litigation: Bosch, Erie, and Beyond*, 71 Or. L. Rev. 781 (1992), 7.06[1] n126

Carrington, Meador & Rosenberg, *Justice on Appeal* 45, 209 (1976), 2.01 n15; 13.07 n215.01[2][c] n16

Carrington, *"Substance" and "Procedure in the Rules Enabling Act*, 1989 Duke L.J. 281 (1989), 1.02 n41; 7.04[3][b] n101

Carrington & Apanovich, *The Constitutional Limits of Judicial Rulemaking: The Illegitimacy of Mass Tort Settlements Negotiated Under Federal Rule 23*, 39 Ariz. L. Rev. 461 (1997), 9.09[2][d] n279

Carrington & Martin, *Substantive Interests and the Jurisdiction of State Courts*, 66 Mich. L. Rev. 227, 232, 240-241 (1967), 3.10[1] n9; 3.12[3] n39

Cary, *Rambo Depositions: Controlling an Ethical Cancer in Civil Litigation*, 25 Hofstra L. Rev. 561 (1996), 10.08[1] n186

Casad, *Intersystem Issue Preclusion and the Restatement (Second) of Judgments*, 66 Cornell L. Rev. 510, 511, 517, 520 (1981), 15.06[2] n111; 15.09 n184; 15.10[1] n201

Casad, *Personal Jurisdiction in Federal Question Cases*, 70 Tex. L. Rev. 1589 (1992), 3.01[2][b] n21

Casad, *Shaffer v. Heitner: An End to Ambivalence in Jurisdictional Theory*, 26 Kan. L. Rev. 61, 74 (1977), 3.08[1] n7

Casad & Richman, *Jurisdiction in Civil Actions* §§ 1-1[3], 3-1[5][a], 3-1[5][a][1], 3-1[5][b] (3rd ed. 1998), 3.02[2] n7; 3.03[2][b] nn21, 22; 3.03[2][c] nn31, 32

Casto, *The Erie Doctrine and the Structure of Constitutional Revoluations*, 62 Tul. L. Rev. 907, 914-927 (1988), 7.02[2] n13

Catz & Robinson, *Due Process and Creditor's Remedies: From Sniadach and Fuentes to Mitchell, North Georgia and Beyond*, 28 Rutgers L. Rev. 541 (1975), 4.02[2] n32

Caust-Ellenbogen, *False Conflicts and Interstate Preclusion: Moving Beyond a Wooden Reading of the Full Faith and Credit Statute*, 63 Ford. L. Rev. 593 (1990), 15.09 n185

Cavers, *"Habitual Residence": A Useful Concept?*, 21 Am. U.L. Rev. 475, 480 (1972), 3.03[1] n8

Cavers, *The Changing Choice-of-Law Process and the Federal Courts*, 28 Law & Contemp. Probs. 732 (1963), 7.05[2] n110

Cecil, *Trends in Summary Judgment Practice: A Summary of Findings*, 1 FJC Directions 11, 13-14 (1991), 11.03[3][d] n131

Chamberlin, Annotation, *Complexity of Civil Action As Affecting Seventh Amendment Right to Trial By Jury*, 54 A.L.R. Fed. 733 (1981 and 1999 supp.), 12.07[1] n204

Cheatham, *Res Judicata and the Full Faith and Credit Clause: Magnolia Petroleum Co. v. Hunt*, 44 Colum. L. Rev. 330, 333 (1944), 15.10[2] n207

Chemerinsky, *Federal Jurisdiction* § 5.2 (3d ed. 1999), 5.01[2] n19

[References are to sections]

[References are to sections]

[References are to sections]

D

E

[References are to sections]

F

[References are to sections]

G

[References are to sections]

H

[References are to sections]

[References are to sections]

[References are to sections]

[References are to sections]

M

[References are to sections]

[References are to sections]

[References are to sections]

[References are to sections]

[References are to sections]

O

[References are to sections]

P

R

[References are to sections]

Rabinowitz, *Appellate Review of Trial Court Orders Granting New Trials,* 8 Rutgers L. Rev. 465 (1954), 12.09[3][d] n334

Radin, *The Authenticated Full Faith and Credit Clause: Its History,* 39 Ill. L. Rev. 1 (1944), 15.10[1] n194

Ragazzo, *Reconsidering the Artful Pleading Doctrine,* 44 Hastings L.J. (1993), 5.03[2] nn24, 36; 5.07[1] n15

Rand Inst., *The Costs of Asbestos Litigation* (1983), 1.01[3] n10

Rand Report Kakalik, et al., Rand Institute for Civil Justice, *Discovery Management: Further Analysis of the Civil Justice Reform Act Evaluation Data,* 39 B.C. L. Rev. 613, 658 (1998), 10.07[2][c] nn161, 163

Ratliff, *Offensive Collateral Estoppel and the Option Effect,* 67 Tex. L. Rev. (1988), 15.06[2] n111; 15.08[1] n151

Raven-Hansen, *Newsletter of the Section on Civil Procedure, Association of American Law Schools* at 2 (Fall, 1998), 3.12[3] n41

Reappraisal Symposium: A Reappraisal of the Supplemental Jurisdiction Statute: title 28 U.S.C. § 1367, 74 Ind. L.J. 1-250 (1998), 5.11[2][a] nn23, 24; 5.11[2][c] n40; 5.11 n1

Recent Changes Agnew, Note, *Recent Changes in the Federal Rules of Civil Procedure: Prescriptions to Ease the Pain?,* 15 Tex. Tech. L. Rev. (1984), 10.12 nn245, 249, 256

Redish, *Due Process, Federalism, and Personal Jurisdiction: a Theoretical Evaluation,* 75 Nw. U.L. Rev. 1112 (1981), 3.10[2] n19

Redish, *Federal Judicial Independence: Constitutional and Political Perspectives,* 46 Mercer L. Rev. 697 (1995), 1.02 n44

Redish, *Federal Jurisdiction: Tensions in the Allocation of Judicial Power* 149-156 (2d ed. 1990), 2.01 n18

Redish, *Reassessing the Allocation of Judicial Business Between State and Federal Courts: Federal Jurisdiction and "The Martian Chronicles,"* 78 Va. L. Rev. 1769 (1992), 5.02 n1

Redish, "The Power of the Federal Courts to Fashion Federal Common Law," in *Federal Jurisdiction: Tensions in the Allocation of Judicial Power* (2d ed. 1990), 7.07 nn153, 168, 172, 176, 179

Redish, *The Pragmatic Approach to Appealability in the Federal Courts,* 75 Colum. L. Rev. 89 (1975), 13.05[2] n27

Redish, *The Proper Role of the Prior Restraint Doctrine in First Amendment Theory,* 70 Va. L. Rev. 53 (1984), 14.02[2] n42

Redish & Phillips, *Erie and the Rules of Decision Act: In Search of the Appropriate Dilemma,* 91 Harv. L. Rev. 356 (1977), 7.04[3][b] n100

Redish & Woods, *Congressional Power to Control the Jurisdiction of the Lower Federal Courts: A Critical Review and a New Synthesis,* 124 U. Pa. L. Rev. 45, 52-55 (1975), 5.01[2] n15

Reed, *Compulsory Joinder of Parties in Civil Actions,* 55 Mich. L. Rv. 327 (1957), 9.05 n59

Reese, et al., *Cases and materials on Conflict of Laws* 124 (9th ed. 1990), 3.11[2] n10

Reese & Galston, *Doing an Act or Causing Consequences as Bases of Judicial Jurisdiction,* 44 Iowa L. Rev. (1959), 3.07[1] n10; 3.10[1] n4

Reese & Green, *That Elusive Word, "Residence,"* 6 Vand. L. Rev. 561 (1953), 3.03[1] n7

Rehnquist, *Remarks of the Chief Justice,* 21 St. Mary's L.J. 5, 7-9 (1989), 5.04[1] n4

Rendleman, *Disobedience and Coercive Contempt Confinement: The Terminally Stubborn Contemnor,* 48 Wash. & Lee L. Rev. 185 (1991), 14.02[2] n35

Rendleman, *The Inadequate Remedy at Law Prerequisite for an Injunction,* 33 U. Fla. L. Rev. 346 (1981), 14.02[1] n29

Renfrew, *Discovery Sanctions: A Judicial Perspective,* 67 Cal. L. Rev. 264, 273-274 (1979), 10.14[2] n321

Report of Proceedings of the Judicial Conference of the United States, 79-80 (1962), 12.03[3] n98

Report of the Committee on Federal Courts of the New York State Bar Association on Service of Process by Mail Pursuant to Rule 4(c)(2)(C)(ii) of the Federal Rules of Civil Procedure, 116 F.R.D. 169 (1987), 4.03[2] n51

Report of the Federal Courts Study Committee (1990), 9.10[1][b] n302; 15.01[2][c] n16

Report of the Proceedings of the Judicial Conference of the United States, 136, Table C-2 (1999), 5.04[1] n5

[References are to sections]

[References are to sections]

S

[References are to sections]

[References are to sections]

[References are to sections]

[References are to sections]

Stevens, *Venue Statutes: Diagnosis and Proposed Cure,* 49 Mich. L. Rev. (1951), 6.01[1][B] nn6, 7, 8

Stewart, *A New Litany of Personal Jurisdiction,* 60 Colorado L. Rev. 5 (1989), 3.09[1] n2

Stewart, *Forum Non Conveniens: A Doctrine in Search of a Role,* 74 Cal. L. Rev. 1259 (1986), 6.02[1] n39

Stewart, *Why Suits for Damages Such as Bhopal Claims Are Very Rare in India,* Wall St. J., Jan. 23, 1985, at 1, 6.02[1] n48

Stolz, *Federal Review of State Court Decisions of Federal Questions: The Need for Additional Appellate Capacity,* 64 Calif. L. Rev. (1976), 2.01 n15; 3.04[3][b] n24; 5.03[2] n29

Stone, *Scope of Review and Record on Appeal,* 2 F.R.D. 317 (1943), 13.08[2] n13

Story, *Commentaries on the Conflict of Laws* (1834), 3.05[1] n10

Stramondo & Goodspeed, *Defendant's Presentation,* 57 Mass. L.Q. 179 (1972), 12.01[4] n13

Subrin, *How Equity Conquered Common Law: The Federal Rules of Civil Procedure in Historical Perspective,* 135 U. Pa. L. Rev. 909 (1987), 7.04[1] n61

Sugarman & Perlin, *Proposed Changes to Discovery Rules in Aid of "Tort Reform": Has the Case Been Made,"* 42 Amer. U. L. Rev. (1993), 10.07[2][c] nn155, 156, 158

Summers, *Analysis of Factors That Influence Choice of Forum in Diversity Cases,* 47 Iowa L. Rev. 933 (1962), 2.02 n19

Summers, *Pragmatic Instrumentalism in Twentieth Century American Legal Thought—A Synthesis and Critique of Our Dominant General Theory About Law and its Use,* 66 Cornell L. Rev. 861, 867 n.4 (1981), 3.05[2] n12

Sumner, *Full Faith and Credit for Judicial Proceedings,* 2 U.C.L.A. L. Rev. 441 (1955), 15.10[1] n194

Swaine, Note, *Pre-Deliberations Juror Misconduct, Evidential Incompetence, and Juror Responsibility,* 98 Yale L.J. 187 (1990), 12.09[2][c] n299

Sward, *Appellate Review of Judicial Fact-Finding,* 40 kan. L. Rev. 1, 5 (1991), 13.09[1] n5

Symposium, 2000 J. of Dispute Resolution 245, 11.05 n181

Symposium, *Jury Reform: Making Juries Work,* 32 U. Mich. J.L. Reform 213 (1999), 12.06 n155

Symposium, *Problems of Intervention in Public Law Litigation,* 13 U.C. Davis L. Rev. 211 (1980), 9.08 n162

Symposium, *Products Liability: Economic Analysis and the Law,* 38 U. Chi. L. Rev. 1 (1970), 9.06 n113

Symposium, *The American Civil Jury: Illusion and Reality,* 48 Depaul L. Rev. 197 (1998), 12.06 n155

Symposium, *The Fiftieth Anniversary of the Federal Rules of Civil Procedure,* 63 Notre Dame L. Rev. 597 (1988), 7.04[1] n61

Symposium, *The Future of Personal Jurisdiction: A Symposium on Burnham v. Superior Court,* 22 Rutgers L. J. 559 (1991), 3.08[3][b] n42

Symposium, *The Institute of Judicial Administration Research Conference on Class Actions,* 71 N.Y.U. L. Rev. 1 (1996), 9.09 n184

Symposium, *The 50th Anniversary of the Federal Rules of Civil Procedure, 1938-1988,* 137 U. Pa. L. Rev. 1874 (1989), 7.04[1] n61

Symposium—Fifty Years of International Shoe: The Past and Future of Personal Jurisdiction, 28 U. Cal. Davis L. Rev. 513 (1995), 3.06[1][a] n1

Symposium on Fee Shifting, 71 Chi-kent L. Rev. 415 (1995), 14.01[2] n19

Symposium on the Restatement (Second) of Judgments, Cornell L. Rev. 401 (1981), 15.01[2][a] n11

Symposium on the Structure of Court-Connected Mediation Programs, 14 Ohio St. J. on Disp. Reol. 711 (1999), 11.05 n181

T

Tanford, *An Introduction to Trial Law,* 51 Mo. L. Rev. (1986), 12.01 n1; 12.01[9] nn18, 20

Tarr & Porter, *State Supreme Courts in State and Nation* 45 (1988), 9.09[2][b] n255

Taylor, *Defendant Class Actions Under Rule 23(b)(2): Resolving the Language Dilemma,* 40 Kan. L. Rev. 77 (1991), 9.09[1][a] n196

[References are to sections]

V

[References are to sections]

W

[References are to sections]

Y

Z

[References are to sections]

Zeisel, Kalven & Buchholz, *Delay in the Court,* 71-81 (1959), 12.06 n163

Zimand, *National Asbestos Litigation: Procedural Problems Must Be Solved,* 69 Wash. U. L.Q. 899 (1991), 9.10[1][b][B] n307

TABLE OF STATUTES AND RULES

[References are to sections]

FEDERAL STATUTES AND RULES

FEDERAL RULES OF APPELLATE PROCEDURE

FEDERAL RULES OF CIVIL PROCEDURE

FEDERAL RULES OF CIVIL PROCEDURE—Cont.

[References are to sections]

[References are to sections]

[References are to sections]

[References are to sections]

[References are to sections]

[References are to sections]

[References are to sections]

[References are to sections]

INDEX

[References are to sections.]

A

ACCESS DOCTRINES
Personal jurisdiction (See PERSONAL JURISDICTION)
Venue (See VENUE)

ADMISSIONS, REQUESTS FOR
Procedure for . . . 12.02[1]
Use and value of . . . 12.02[2]

ALTERNATIVE DISPUTE RESOLUTION
Generally . . . 11.05

ANSWER
Affirmative defenses
    Generally . . . 8.08[2][a]
    Statutes of limitation and . . . . 8.08[2][b]
Claims by way of answer . . . 8.08[3]
Defenses . . . 8.08[2][a], [b]
Denials . . . 8.08[1]
Nonwaivable defenses . . . 8.08[2][a]
Preliminary defenses . . . 8.08[2][a]
Statutes of limitation and affirmative defenses . . . 8.08[2][b]

APPEALS
Appealability
    Generally . . . 13.01
    Judgment n.o.v., denial of . . . . 12.09[3][d]
Defined . . . 13.01
Final judgment rule (See FINAL JUDGMENT RULE)
Intensity of review
    Generally . . . 13.09[1]
    Abuse of discretion standard . . . . . . 13.09[2][d]
    Clearly erroneous findings by court . . . 13.09[2][b]
    De novo – questions of law . . . . 13.09[2][a]
    Federal system
        Abuse of discretion standard . . . 13.09[2][d]
        Clearly erroneous findings by court . . . 13.09[2][b]
        De novo – questions of law . . . . 13.09[2][a]
        No review standard . . . . 13.09[2][e]
        Reasonableness standard . . . . . 13.09[2][c]
    No review standard . . . 13.09[2][e]

APPEALS—Cont.
Intensity of review—Cont.
    Reasonableness standard . . . . 13.09[2][c]
Interlocutory appeals
    Generally . . . 13.01
    Statutory interlocutory appeal
        As of right . . . 13.03[1]
        By permission . . . 13.03[2]
        Extraordinary review . . . 13.03[3]
        Writ of mandamus or prohibition . . . 13.03[3]
Judgment n.o.v., appealability of denial of . . . 12.09[3][d]
Multi-claim and multi-party cases; final judgment rule . . . 13.02[2]
Perfecting appeal
    Appellate systems . . . 13.06
    Procedural steps in . . . 13.07
Personal jurisdiction . . . 3.03[2][c]
Purpose of . . . 13.01
Reviewability (See subhead: Scope of review— reviewability)
Scope of review—reviewability
    Generally . . . 13.08
    Prejudicial effect . . . 13.08[1]
    Presentation above . . . 13.08[3]
    Preservation below . . . 13.08[2]
Summary judgment, appeals of . . . . 11.03[2][c]

APPEARANCE
Defined . . . 11.02[2]
Personal jurisdiction
    Limited appearances . . . 3.03[2][b]
    Special appearances . . . 3.03[2][b]
Praecipe defined . . . 11.02[2]

B

BENCH TRIALS
Generally . . . 12.10

BURDEN OF PERSUASION
Defined . . . 12.04[3]

BURDEN OF PRODUCTION
Defined . . . 12.04[2]

BURDEN OF PROOF
Generally . . . 12.04[1]
Burden of persuasion defined . . . 12.04[3]
Burden of production defined . . . 12.04[2]
Presumptions . . . 12.04[4]

[References are to sections.]

C

[References are to sections.]

D

[References are to sections.]

[References are to sections.]

E

[References are to sections.]

[References are to sections.]

[References are to sections.]

[References are to sections.]

[References are to sections.]

[References are to sections.]

[References are to sections.]

W